porn studies

porn studies

Edited by Linda Williams

Duke University Press

Durham and London 2004

© 2004 Duke University Press
All rights reserved
Printed in the United States of
America on acid-free paper ∞
Designed by Amy Ruth Buchanan
Typeset in Scala by Tseng
Information Systems, Inc.
Library of Congress Cataloging-in-
Publication Data and additional
permissions information appear on
the last printed page of this book.

contents

acknowledgments

Thanks to Eric Smoodin for encouraging this book in the first place and to Ken Wissoker and Duke University Press for making it happen. Many students in many classes at uc Irvine and uc Berkeley—and not only those who have contributed to this volume—have helped me to better understand the cultural and historical importance of moving-image pornographies. Special thanks to Heather Butler, whose research and enthusiasm have contributed enormously to all aspects of this volume, including the annotated bibliography. Final thanks to many colleagues in "porn studies": Peter Lehman, who was an insightful reader of the manuscript, and Rich Cante, Angelo Restivo, Constance Penley, Tom Waugh, and Eric Schaefer, all of whom I am honored to include in this volume.

Porn Studies:

Proliferating Pornographies

On/Scene: An Introduction

LINDA WILLIAMS

✳ *Porn Studies* grew out of a graduate seminar on pornography in the Film
Studies Program at the University of California, Berkeley. Many of its chapters were originally seminar papers, now much revised, for courses offered
in 1998 and again in 2001. The volume augments the essays by these
younger scholars, many of them still completing their doctorates, with several more established contributors to the field: Rich Cante, Constance Penley, Angelo Restivo, Eric Schaefer, Tom Waugh, and I. The porn studies of
this volume diverge markedly from the kind of agonizing over sexual politics
that characterized an earlier era of the study of pornography. Where once it
seemed necessary to argue vehemently against pro-censorship, antipornography feminism for the value and importance of studying pornography (see,
for example, the 1990s anthologies *Sex Exposed* and *Dirty Looks*), today porn
studies addresses a veritable explosion of sexually explicit materials that cry
out for better understanding. Feminist debates about whether pornography
should exist at all have paled before the simple fact that still and moving-
image pornographies have become fully recognizable fixtures of popular culture.

To me, the most eye-opening statistic is the following: Hollywood makes
approximately 400 films a year, while the porn industry now makes from
10,000 to 11,000. Seven hundred million porn videos or DVDs are rented
each year. Even allowing for the fact that fewer viewers see any single work

and that these videos repeat themselves even more shamelessly than Hollywood (e.g., *Co-ed Cocksuckers 21*, *Talk Dirty to Me 13*, *Dirty Little Sex Brats 14*), this is a mind-boggling figure. Pornography revenues—which can broadly be construed to include magazines, Internet Web sites, magazines, cable, in-room hotel movies, and sex toys—total between 10 and 14 billion dollars annually. This figure, as *New York Times* critic Frank Rich has noted, is not only bigger than movie revenues; it is bigger than professional football, basketball, and baseball put together. With figures like these, Rich argues, pornography is no longer a "sideshow" but "the main event" (2001, 51).[1]

Who is watching all this pornography? Apparently all of us. As the editor of *Adult Video News* puts it: "Porn doesn't have a demographic—it goes across all demographics." The market is "as diverse as America" (Rich 2001, 52). Porn videos are remarkably diverse as well, ranging from the rarefied (s/m, bondage, amputees, geriatric, fat, ethnic, interracial, etc.) to the mainstream hetero product and the enduringly popular gay videos (whose appeal and numbers far exceed the category of a niche market and which are awash with inventive auteurs like Kristen Bjorn, Wash West, Matt Sterling, and others). Along the way there is the smaller niche of lesbian porn (Shar Rednour and Jackie Strano), the seat-of-the-pants, low-budget gonzo of John Stagliano and Ed Powers, and the woman-friendly "erotica" of Candida Royalle.

Mainstream or margin, pornography is emphatically part of American culture, and it is time for the criticism of it to recognize this fact. If feminist debates about the propriety or danger of pornography marked the 1980s and 1990s, along with larger societal debates about censorship in general, the new millennium, in the wake of a remarkably pornographic tale about a president and an intern (see Maria St. John's essay in this volume), has become increasingly used to, if never fully comfortable with, "speaking sex." This is not to say, as I have noted elsewhere, that sexually explicit talk and representation takes place without controversy or embarrassment.[2] We have certainly not attained the "end of obscenity" once optimistically predicted in the late sixties by Charles Rembar (1969). It is to say, however, that long before it surfaced as news from the oval office, speaking sex had ceased to be a private, bedroom-only matter. Today, the very practice of American politics requires a familiarity with the alleged explicit sex acts of Gary Hart, Clarence Thomas, Bill Clinton, Gary Condit, and a great many priests of the Catholic Church. We are compelled to speak sex, whether to protect ourselves or our children from AIDS or other sexually transmitted diseases, or simply as a result of watching *The Sopranos*, *Sex in the City*, or *Queer as Folk*. If *Deep*

Throat (dir. Gerard Damiano, 1972) and a range of other films discussed by Eric Schaefer in this volume, inaugurated a pornographic speaking sex in the early seventies, today, a wide variety of different media have become the venue for the public representation of sex acts. Recently it was possible to view, for example, rock star Tommy Lee and former *Playboy* model Pam Anderson having sex on their honeymoon as still images in *Penthouse* magazine, as streaming video on the Internet Entertainment Group's Web site, and as a home video, *Pam and Tommy: Uncensored and Hardcore* (see Minnette Hillyer's essay in this volume).

Discussions and representations of sex that were once deemed obscene, in the literal sense of being off (*ob*) the public scene, have today insistently appeared in the new public/private realms of Internet and home video. The term that I have coined to describe this paradoxical state of affairs is on/scenity: the gesture by which a culture brings on to its public arena the very organs, acts, bodies, and pleasures that have heretofore been designated ob/scene and kept literally off-scene. In Latin, the accepted meaning of the term *obscene* is quite literally "off-stage," or that which should be kept "out of public view" (OED). On/scene is one way of signaling not just that pornographies are proliferating but that once off (*ob*) scene sexual scenarios have been brought onto the public sphere. On/scenity marks both the controversy and scandal of the increasingly public representations of diverse forms of sexuality *and* the fact that they have become increasing available to the public at large.

To me, the most eloquent example of the paradox of on/scenity was staged in the spectacle of Jesse Helms, standing in the U.S. Senate in 1989, waving the "dirty" photographs by Robert Mapplethorpe, which had been funded by the National Endowment for the Arts (NEA), for all to see.[3] Helms implored his fellow senators to "look at the pictures!", yet at the same time requested that "all the pages, all the ladies, and maybe all the staff" leave the chamber so that the "senators can see what they are voting on" (de Grazia 1992, 637). This spectacle of bringing *on* the obscenity in order to keep it *off*—of Helms exhorting (male) senators to look, even as he tries to keep others (women and young pages) from looking—exemplifies one side of the paradox of on/scenity. It is the side those in favor of more diverse forms of speaking sex tend to relish because it demonstrates the extreme futility of censorship. Jesse Helms in 1989, like Kenneth Starr in 1998, became an unwitting pornographer, pandering the very material he would censor.

However, there is another side of this on/scenity paradox, one not so easily appreciated by civil libertarians. This occurs when those in favor of free speech and speaking sex nevertheless themselves censor some of its more sensational elements. Consider a recent collection of essays on pornography, the very well-meaning, liberal volume, *Porn 101: Eroticism, Pornography, and the First Amendment*, a compendium of articles originally presented in 1998 at the pro–free speech World Conference on Pornography, whose title suggests, but whose presentation contradicts, the arrival of pornography as a legitimate academic subject. This conference, one of whose keynote speaker's was American Civil Liberties Union (ACLU) president Nadine Strossen, enthusiastically defended pornography's right to exist and championed its study from a wide variety of legal, cultural, sociological, and sexological perspectives. Conference sessions overflowed with videos, slides, photos, and other visual exemplars of its topic, not to mention the amusing, genial spectacle of the porn stars in attendance rubbing elbows in the lobby of the Sheraton Universal Hotel with families setting out on tours of Universal Studios. However, in the proceedings of the conference published by Prometheus, the exuberant visuals disappeared. Except for a few antique lithographs, the volume is shockingly denuded of the very illustration that had made the conference so lively.

For example, the very first article, by Jennifer Yamashiro of the Kinsey Institute, describes a breakthrough 1957 legal ruling, eloquently dubbed *U.S. v. 31 Photographs*, that allowed the Kinsey Institute to build its collections of visual erotica and other sexually explicit materials. The article, however, fails to illustrate even one of the famously censored photographs, censoring them, in effect, all over again. Never mind that the article's very point is the importance of the acceptance of such images "on the scene" of the American academic study of sexuality—the very scene of the conference proceedings themselves—and never mind that the slides of these thirty-one photographs occupied the very center of the talk given at the conference.[4] Here is a mirror reversal of the kind of on/scenity displayed by Helms and Starr: a whole conference invoking the visual artifacts of the history and sociology of pornography, which, either due to the timidity of publishers or to that of the book's editors, are not shown.

If *obscenity* is the term given to those sexually explicit acts that once seemed unspeakable, and were thus permanently kept off-scene, *on/scenity* is the more conflicted term with which we can mark the tension between the speakable and the unspeakable which animates so many of our contemporary discourses of sexuality. In Judith Butler's terms, it is both the regulation that inevitably states what it does not want stated (1997, 130) and the opposition to regulation that nevertheless censors what it wants to say. On/scenity is thus an ongoing negotiation that produces increased awareness of those once-obscene matters that now peek out at us from under every bush.

Porn Studies differs from previous anthologies about pornography—including those that purport to legitimize its academic study—in its effort to take pornography seriously as an increasingly on/scene cultural form that impinges on the lives of a wide variety of Americans and that matters in the evaluation of who we are as a culture. It is serious about installing the critical and historical study of pornography in the academic curriculum. To further that end, authors have included images to illustrate their chapters, and a selected annotated bibliography of readings important to the study of pornography as a cultural form—not just as a legal or sociological issue—has been added, along with information on how to locate hard-core materials. In other words, this volume tries to help the teacher and student of pornography roll up their sleeves to begin work in this field rather than to pose the genre as the limit case of cultural analysis—the thing about which there is really nothing to say. Even Frank Rich, author of the *New York Times Magazine* article quoted above, which makes a major economic and social claim for the importance of pornography as a cultural "main event," dismisses its enactments of sexual performances. To Rich, the sex acts are Kabuki-like rituals that bring narrative to a halt, "like the musical numbers in a 30s Hollywood musical" (2001, 92). Rich's point seems to be that these rituals interrupt the more important narrative mission of film. To my mind, however, his analogy misses its point because there is so very much to say about the ritualistic "musical number" quality of the sexual representations of pornographic film and video. I have argued elsewhere that this comparison actually constitutes the inception of an important insight into how we might begin to understand the choreography of performing and laboring bodies in these works (Williams [1989] 1999).

This tendency to dismiss the textual working of popular pornographies is endemic, and not only to journalists like Frank Rich. Slavoj Žižek (1989), for example, argues that "in a 'normal,' non-pornographic film, a love scene is always built around a certain insurmountable limit; 'all cannot be shown'; at a certain point, the image blurs, the camera moves off, the scene is interrupted, we never see directly 'that' (the penetration of sexual organs, etc.)" (1989, 33). Thus a certain "limit of representability" defines the "'normal' love story or melodrama," while pornography by definition *"goes too far"* and thus misses what remained concealed in the "'normal,' nonpornographic love scene" (33). Žižek effectively dismisses the texts of pornography as abnormal representations doomed perpetually to "go too far." By showing "it," pornography becomes simply a "pretext for introducing acts of copulation," "instead of the sublime Thing, we are stuck with a vulgar groaning and fornication" (33). But as many of the essays in this volume argue, there is a great deal to say about the quality and kind of the generic deployments, including the sublimity (see Franklin Melendez) of precisely these performed acts of copulation. How, in fact, do these performed acts construct the "it" that they purport to reveal? Is it perhaps the critic who has not gone far enough in analyzing this construction?

In yet another example of a respected culture critic using pornography as a limit text, Roland Barthes cites a self-portrait by Robert Mapplethorpe as an instance of "blissful eroticism" that leads Barthes to "distinguish the 'heavy' desire of pornography from the 'light' (good) desire of eroticism" (1981, 59). Here, too, the critic works hard to distinguish the (bad) pornographic from the (good) erotic, as if there were never anything erotic in the pornographic (see my essay in this volume). This anthology does not seek to illustrate the distinction between a "good" eroticism and a "bad" pornography. It is no more interested in these distinctions than it is interested in the related debates about pornography within feminism, in which a "bad," androcentric pornography is often opposed to a "good," gynocentric eroticism. Indeed, there are some forms of pornography which either have no interest whatsoever in women's bodies—for example, the vast arena of gay porn (see essays by Tom Waugh, Hoang Tan Nguyen, and Rich Cante and Angelo Restivo)—or which are so exclusively oriented toward these bodies that questions of objectification by male viewers do not apply—as in the much smaller arena of lesbian or dyke porn (see the essay by Heather Butler). As a cultural form that is "as diverse as America," pornography deserves both a serious and extended analysis that reaches beyond polemics and sensationalism.

Part 1, "Contemporary Pornographies," investigates a wide range of contemporary examples showing how new forms of pornography have become part of the fabric of everyday life. As Maria St. John shows in the opening essay, "How to Do Things with the *Starr Report*: Pornography, Performance, and the President's Penis," the on/scenity of sex in the American public domain came clearly into focus during the highly publicized investigation into President Clinton's "physically intimate" encounters with Monica Lewinsky. These scenes, and the spin that surrounded and replayed them, seriously challenged the distinctions, long-teetering in the American imagination, between high and low, public and private, clean and dirty. The intention of Kenneth Starr's report was to cleanse the White House by exposing Clinton's illicit actions and, by impeaching the president, to exorcise the pornographic element. But the exorcism backfired; instead of ejecting Clinton, American popular culture, as St. John explains, popped the report itself into the VCR and played it as pornography. St. John argues that the *Report* is a polymorphous text that inscribes many different conflicting desires by taking up, then abandoning multiple pornographic conventions. In a related vein, Minette Hillyer looks at another instance of "celebrity porn": the hard-core honeymoon of Pamela Anderson and Tommy Lee, which has become the most-watched home movie in recent memory. In both cases, the codes of pornography are discovered at work in forms not originally intended as pornography but ones that have arguably become it. Hillyer explores the question of the relations between home movie and pornography, identifying what she calls the "porning" of domestic footage. Another essay, "Office Sluts and Rebel Flowers," by Deborah Shamoon, considers the intriguing phenomenon of Japanese hard-core ladies' comics, which merge popular forms of romance with sexually explicit drawn images in which codes of vaginal wetness become the visual expression of female pleasure. Shamoon shows how these comics refute many common perceptions about women as consumers of porn. Finally, Zabet Patterson, in "Going On-line: Consuming Pornography in the Digital Era," investigates the ways in which on-line cyberporn introduces new forms of interaction that are less about the encounter of bodies and more about the physical encounter with an eroticized technological apparatus.

One of the serious limitations of much of the earlier writing on pornography (certainly of much feminist scholarship fighting the "porn wars") was the assumption that pornography expressed the power and the pleasure of heterosexual men. Part 2 of this volume, "Gay, Lesbian, and Homosocial Pornographies," discusses many of the features of gay and lesbian pornography that differ from heterosexual forms presumed as dominant. Tom Waugh begins by questioning the supposed heterosexual pleasures of the classical American stag film. He asks about the significance of the male body in a film form that was officially only interested in the female anatomy. He discovers that the homosocial collective experience of "men getting hard watching images of men getting hard watching or fucking women" constituted a major part of the experience. A second essay, by Rich Cante and Angelo Restivo, "The Cultural-Aesthetic Specificities of All-male Moving-Image Pornography," offers an overview of the aesthetics of contemporary gay pornography, arguing that the fantasies constructed by these works create a very different space than does heterosexual pornography. These authors offer an intriguing twist on the quasi-publicness of contemporary pornographies discussed above, suggesting that gay porn has an extra dimension of on/scenity by virtue of its passage through an "imagined public gaze" that establishes the position of the gay man within the social space he inhabits.

Where gay porn is prolific, lesbian porn made *for* lesbians has remained all but invisible until very recently. Both gay and lesbian porn have histories and aesthetics that differ markedly from heterosexual norms. In her essay, "What Do You Call a Lesbian with Long Fingers? The Development of Lesbian and Dyke Pornography," Heather Butler explores the ways in which hard-core pornography has articulated the figure of the "authentic" lesbian since the 1960s. By asking in what ways lesbian pornography has transgressed heterosexual norms to (re)educate the porn spectator, Butler determines that the figure of the butch proves central to the articulation of "authentic" lesbian desire. A final essay by Jake Gerli, "The Gay Sex Clerk: Chuck Vincent's Straight Pornography," investigates the fascinating phenomenon of a gay man who directed straight porn in the late 1970s and early 1980s. Gerli suggests a variety of ways in which Vincent's sexuality manifested a queer perspective on straight porn.

Part 3, "Pornography, Race, and Class," is a short section that opens up a discussion of an area of porn studies barely broached until now: the role of racial stereotypes in a moving-image genre that fetishizes racial difference. Hoang Tan Nguyen asks about the role of the traditionally "undersexed" stereotype of the Asian man in gay pornography, and I ask about the traditionally "oversexed" stereotype of the African American in heterosexual porn. Nguyen's "The Resurrection of Brandon Lee: The Making of a Gay Asian American Porn Star" looks at the case of Asian American porn star Brandon Lee in order to assess changes in the representation of Asian men within the visual economy of North American gay video porn. By probing the relations between Brandon Lee and martial arts star Bruce Lee, his essay explores the racial "packaging" of Brandon Lee from his early appearance in Asian-niche videos to his crossover into mainstream gay videos. My own essay on interracial lust investigates what happens when racialized bodies become the subject of pornography's unique brand of confessing the "truths" of sex. If pornography is a genre that seeks to confess the discursive truths of sex, then what happens when racialized bodies are asked to reveal their particular "truths"? And what does it mean when the taboos enforcing the racial border are systematically violated and "black cock" penetrates "white pussy"? I argue that in American pornography and exploitation films the depiction of black-and-white interracial sex acts depends on the self-conscious cultivation of an anachronistic fear that enhances desire. Finally,

Constance Penley's essay, "Crackers and Whackers: The White Trashing of Porn," argues for a class-based understanding of the genre as a protest against class privilege and bourgeois social values. Pornography—her prime example is *John Wayne Bobbitt: Uncut*—often deploys a "low-class" form of humor associated with dirty jokes and forms of class-based critique.

Part 4, "Soft Core, Hard Core, and the Pornographic Sublime," considers the variety of historically produced technologies that have engendered recognizable forms of pornography in both soft- and hard-core forms. In an era of hard-core on/scenity, the static pinup can seem comparatively tame. Yet as Despina Kakoudaki argues, considered from the perspective of the work it performed in American culture during World War II, the pinup can be seen as a sublime form of patriotic representation as used in magazine photography, film, popular song, and animated cartoon. As such, it offers an important case study for the more far-flung technological and military uses of pornography, reminding us, as Lynn Hunt (1993) has done in another context, that pornography not only functions to arouse its viewers. Eric Schaefer, on the other hand, examines a much later historical development: the influence of 16 mm film technology on a 35 mm, non–hard-core but "adult" film marketplace beginning in the late 1960s, which resulted, eventually, in the transition to hard-core, aboveground, narrative features. Schaefer demonstrates that these feature-length hard-core narratives must now be considered as a brief entr'acte between the plotless underground stag film and the similarly plotless sex acts of much contemporary porn in the video age. Yet unlike previous historians of porn, Schaefer explains, in rich historical detail, just how the transition from nonexplicit sexploitation to explicit hard-core images took place through the intervention of 16 mm formats. In "Video Pornography, Visual Pleasure, and the Return of the Sublime," Franklin Melendez also investigates the relations between technology and sexuality, in this case the newer phenomenon of video. He argues that hard-core pornography as viewed on the VCR in the postmodern era intertwines the allure of the sexually explicit image with the technology that makes it visible. Examining the construction of sexual numbers in one gay and one straight example of contemporary video porn, Melendez explores the relations between the convulsing body and the convulsing machine. In all the above cases, the "excessive" pleasures of the pornographic image are inextricable from the negotiation of a relation to technology, each in their own way offering a form of the sublime.

A final section, "Pornography and/as Avant-Garde," considers the relations between these two seemingly antithetical yet also related forms. Where pornography is formulaic, commercial, and repetitious, the avant-garde is anticommercial, innovative, and often deeply personal. Yet both pornography and the avant-garde have historically been the one place in moving-image culture where a frank interest in sex, and specific sex acts, is not taboo. Ara Osterweil's study of Andy Warhol's *Blow Job*—a minimalist motion portrait of a young man's face as he supposedly receives fellatio off-screen—argues that this film provides an especially useful way of understanding the confluence of the avant-garde and pornography in the sixties. In "Unbracketing Motion Study: Scott Stark's NOEMA," Michael Sicinski examines another minimalist avant-garde work, in this case a film that transforms porn videos into a kind of experimental motion study concentrating on all the in-between moments in which couples awkwardly shift positions, scratch itches, and push hair out of their eyes. Stark's selection of decidedly "unsexy" moments forcefully returns the viewer of NOEMA to a flat fact the pornographic films themselves tend to elide. We are not simply watching "sex"; we are watching the human labor that contributes to the construction of pleasure.

Part Two: The Porn Classroom

One of the marks of pornography's on/scenity is its recent appearance in the academic curriculum. Because the question of pornography's place in the university has been a source of some controversy,[5] and because I hope that this volume can become a useful tool for those who elect to teach and learn about pornography, I would like to begin by explaining my own personal and professional reasons for bringing it on/scene in the classroom. This short essay makes no attempt at suggesting how one should go about teaching pornography—although I hope that the annotated bibliography and list of sources for purchasing videos and DVDs might prove useful to those organizing their own courses. Rather, I here provide an account of the reason why pornography came to appear as an urgent topic in need of teaching to me, and how I first went about teaching it.

In 1989, I published *Hard Core: Power, Pleasure, and the "Frenzy of the Visible,"* a book that examined the genre of heterosexual film pornography from a feminist, Foucaultian perspective. Although I had experimented with teaching some pornographic film in the past in the context of a literature class, and though it was already clear to me that moving-image pornography was the most enduringly popular of all the film (and now video, DVD, and Internet) genres, it was not immediately apparent to me that it belonged in the classroom. It was especially not apparent that I should teach it to young and impressionable undergraduates. Could one ask students to analyze, historicize, and theorize moving images whose very aim was to put them into the throes of sexual arousal? When I teach other film genres (melodrama or horror), analysis of our responses of pity or fear form part of what we examine. Although I knew that it was possible to transcend the initial embarrassment of talking about sexual representations, I was not convinced that even the most highly motivated undergraduates could handle watching and analyzing moving-image or other forms of visual pornography.

Until 1993, the above had seemed compelling enough reasons *not* to teach pornography. However, in that year, Catherine MacKinnon wrote an article for *Ms.* that entirely changed my mind. She argued that the Serbian rapes of Muslim and Croatian women in Bosnia constituted an unprecedented policy of extermination caused by pornography: "The world has never seen sex used this consciously, this cynically, this elaborately, this openly, this systematically, with this degree of technological and psychological sophistication, as a means of destroying a whole people. . . . With this war, pornography emerges as a tool of genocide" (27). Reports by Muslim women that some of the rapes had been videotaped, transformed ordinary rape, MacKinnon believed, into a historically unprecedented atrocity. The real culprit in these rapes was, for MacKinnon, not the Serbian rapists, but the supposed saturation of Yugoslavia with pornography. Such an argument encourages us to shift attention from the real crime of politically motivated rape to the supposedly more heinous crime of filming it. Instead of concentrating on how Muslim and Croatian women became the targets of sexual crimes, MacKinnon preferred to blame pornography as their cause. We come away from her article with the impression that it is pornography that we must fight, not rape.

The notion that pornography raises the misogynous crime of rape to a new level of technically unprecedented genocide is also the premise of MacKinnon's 1993 book *Only Words*. As in the case of Bosnia, it is the mechanically or electronically reproduced images, not the acts themselves, that are taken to be the most reprehensible. Pornography is conflated with genocidal rape, degradation, and abuse. It is never for an instant taken to be a genre for the production of sexual viewing pleasure. For MacKinnon, pornography *is* sexual abuse, pure and simple.

Now these are the kinds of arguments that can only work if one has little knowledge about moving-image pornography, its history, its conventions, and its various uses among very different kinds of viewers. For example, a look at the history of the representation of rape in hard-core, moving-image pornography, teaches that where rape was once represented from a masculinist "lie back and enjoy it" perspective in the old illegal stag films and in the early features, it has increasingly become taboo as women have become a component of the audience (Williams [1989] 1999, 164–65). Indeed, most forms of violence are now strictly taboo, to the extent that the usual fictional fistfights and gunfights of feature films are rarely seen in pornography.

I had endured the argument of *Only Words* without being moved to teach pornography, but the argument about rape in Bosnia was the last straw. This was not a theoretical argument about the evils of porn, it was an argument that encouraged taking action against pornography as if it were the same thing as taking action against rape. As such, it seemed to me to be thoroughly inimical to the goal of feminism. Though I could take satisfaction in Erika Munk's subsequent, well-informed response to MacKinnon's specious arguments, I knew that what had not been adequately countered was a facile fantasy about the root evil of pornography, one that can only persist in ignorance of the genre's history and its close analysis. As a feminist scholar of moving-image pornography, I realized that I had an obligation to do more than write about, or engage in polemics about, pornography. As one of the relatively few scholars in the United States with some expertise in this area, I needed to do what other scholars have done: integrate my scholarship into my teaching. I did not do this lightly, for I was acutely aware of the aforementioned problem of the status of texts that seek to sexually arouse viewers. I resolved nevertheless to teach a course that would approach the history, theory, and analysis of the genre of moving-image pornographies as a way of understanding the various constructions of sexuality and the history of the representations of sexual pleasure. The goal was never to defend pornography against the sex-negative, sex-scapegoating MacKinnons and Andrea Dworkins of this world, but to promote a more substantive, critical and textually aware critique of the most popular moving-image genre on earth.

I cannot say that that first upper-division undergraduate class, offered in the spring of 1994 at UC Irvine, in the heart of conservative Orange County, California, was all that successful. Nor can I say that my experience was at all typical. Nevertheless, it is the story of that class that I would like to tell, since its partial failures seem to me instructive and to offer some examples of the difficulties of bringing this material on/scene. I defined the class from the beginning as an experiment to determine whether the textual study of moving-image pornography had a place in the university curriculum—a question the class would take up at the end of the ten-week quarter. Aware that they were part of an experiment, students were on especially good behavior.

The course was designed to survey the history of American moving-image pornography from early, underground stag films for all-male audiences to the quasi-legitimate couples films of the seventies to the proliferating varieties of gay male, lesbian, bisexual, straight, sadomasochistic, fetishist pornographies available now that low-budget video shooting and home VCR viewing predominate. Casually curious students were warned away by an unusually heavy workload, the inclusion of feminist concerns about power, as well as the genre's concerns about pleasure, and the cross-listing of the course between film studies and women's studies. Thus after an unusually high initial enrollment of over sixty students for a class with no teaching assistants, the course settled down to a comfortable thirty film studies, women's studies, and a few other students.

I began with the premise that since moving-image pornographies existed, we would not take up the question of whether they should exist before we had considered their form and content. Though I was considerably emboldened by the success of my UC Santa Barbara colleague Constance Penley's strategy of teaching pornography as simply another film genre, my own plan was to return to the feminist arguments against pornography once we had actually learned something about the genre. Thus we read MacKinnon's *Only Words* toward the end of the course and attempted to debate the anticensorship, antipornography positions at that time. We saw a group of hardcore stag films the very first day, and we continued to see at least one work of hard-core feature-length pornography each week, and sometimes twice a week. I always showed the films first, then introduced readings about them. We eventually read all of *Hard Core*, many essays from the anthology *Dirty Looks* (Gibson and Gibson, 1993), parts of Foucault's *The History of Sexuality* (1978), and about twelve photocopied articles. Students wrote book reports on a wide bibliography of works related to pornography, took a midterm, made formal group presentations to the class, and wrote a variety of final projects, including some pornographic screenplays, which grew out of their own dissatisfaction with the quality of the scripts in most contemporary porn. One group also made a video of the class as part of our ongoing self-scrutiny. We had three guest speakers: Constance Penley, who spoke on slash fanzines, a man from the Los Angeles chapter of People against Pornography, and Kelly Dennis, a Ph.D. student completing a dissertation on pornographic painting and photography.

Because they had to do group presentations, students began working together to understand difficult material and quickly overcame any embarrassment discussing sex acts in class. These discussions were some of our best. The first five weeks of the class, in which we read *Hard Core* and screened a collection of stag films, *Deep Throat, Behind the Green Door* (Mitchell Bros., 1972), *The Opening of Misty Beethoven* (Radley Metzger, 1975), *In the Realm of the Senses* (Nagisa Oshima, 1976), and a selection of films by Candida Royalle, including what was then her new feature, *Revelations* (1993), were lively and, to my mind, very successful. The second half of the course was less so. The main reason, I think, was the difficulty of teaching the "controversy" of pornography when I and the rest of the students were already so emphatically on the side of anticensorship. Throughout the class, students had been more than willing to criticize pornography, but they were understandably unwilling to challenge its right to exist since the very course they had signed up for was exercising the kind of tolerance of and even frank interest in sexual representation that the MacKinnon position wanted to revoke. So the debates about pornography turned out not to hold great interest for students—which is not to say that we did not have our own debates of what constituted offensive material!

The course syllabus had contained a fairly conventional, boldface warning that I had intended to warn away the squeamish: "Many of the films, videos, and images we will see in this class are bound to be offensive to some viewers. Please do not take this class unless you are willing to look closely at a wide variety of explicit, hard-core pornographic sexual representations and to discuss and write about them with the same kind of attention you would give to any other popular cultural form." I had considered other ways of dealing with this problem. It is common in some women's studies classes presenting images, though not teaching the genre, of pornography to ask students to sign a consent form saying that they are warned that they may be viewing some possibly horrendous materials, but then to provide for the possibility for students to excuse themselves from screenings or images that offend them too much. This tactic seems to me counterproductive. It assumes that the topic of hard-core pornography is beyond the pale, ob/scene not on/scene. The consent approach tends to make the course all about finding that moment of most extreme offense, when the offensive text does what it is all along expected to do.

I did not want to set myself up for such reactions since our main object was to study the genre closely. However, I did try, in my boldfaced first sentence, to steer away those students able to judge that they might take offense. I knew, of course, that my warning itself constituted an invitation to be on the lookout for what is most offensive and to register it with dramatic means. What I did not anticipate was that it would be the men in the class who would eventually register offense most dramatically. For the most part, however, and certainly in the first half of the class, students tended to use journals effectively as a way of expressing both offense and occasional pleasure in often quite lengthy daily entries. This way of letting off steam seemed to work well for the first half of the class.

The stag films that occupied us first, although often quite misogynist, seemed, because of their distance in time, merely quaint. Students marveled at black-and-white, silent-movie sex. They did not seem to bother too much about the sexual politics of this sex. They were more amazed, I think, at the fact that people back then *had* sex, especially non–missionary position sex. Even pornography from the seventies still had a patina of age—those sideburns, that hair! Although *Deep Throat* and *Behind the Green Door* certainly proved offensive to many of the women in the class, they watched with interest and simply vented their objections to the disregard of female pleasure and autonomy in articulate discussions of plot, motive, and the mise-enscène of sexual positions. They voiced anger at the archaic representation of "ravishment" in *Behind the Green Door*, the ubiquity of "money shots" throughout the feature-length form of the genre, and the frequent lack of convincing female orgasm. But as we moved into the eighties and nineties, and pornography went from relatively high-budget film to low-budget video, and as students began to see reflected in these videos corporeal styles closer to their own, distance became harder to achieve.

As it turned out, however, it was the women in the class who were much better able to handle offense and to keep a critical distance on the material, even as it got closer to home. Many of these women, although heterosexuals, found the woman-oriented porn of Candida Royalle too tame, while they enjoyed the butch/femme roles of *Suburban Dykes* and the fluidities of bisexual porn. Female-to-female sex outside the context of "the male gaze" seemed exhilarating to them, even if it did not appeal to their own propensities. On the other hand, while the men in the class had nodded in agreement with the women's criticism of heterosexual pornography geared to men, they did not express any deeply felt offense themselves. They also nodded in agreement at the greater empowerment of women in lesbian pornography. But as might have been predicted, they were not themselves similarly exhilarated by gay male porn. The sense of offense from these (presumably straight) undergraduate males almost became palpable as we screened William Higgins's

The Young and the Hung (1985) and, later, *Bi and Beyond: The Ultimate Sexual Union* (1986) and a few men made dramatic, door-slamming exits. In the discussion that followed the screening, tensions were exacerbated by the fact that some of the women students took this opportunity to take revenge on the males who had finally been made to squirm by the use of male bodies as sexual objects of desire. For example, here is a journal entry by the woman student who wreaked the most revenge:

> I believe what I liked so much about this movie was the thought that after all these screenings, finally "our guys" would feel a little uncomfortable. This time, *male* bodies were used as masturbation aids. . . . Did it turn them on? If it did, did they spend the rest of the weekend worrying about their "proper heterosexuality"? If yes, would they EVER admit it in class?? What does that say about the way society still constructs "lesbianism" as foreplay and homosexuality as a major taboo? *Finally, what is the role of homoeroticism in a patriarchal, homophobic culture*; i.e., . . . is not any kind of extreme male sexism and phallocentrism merely disguised homo-sexuality? I think my head is gonna explode.

This same student then precipitated the most traumatic of our class discussions by pointedly asking the men in the class how they felt in response to the gay porn. Up until this moment, no one had asked this question. Though there had been ample discussion of the political implications of various sexual acts and positions, no one had been willing to say publicly either "this turns me on" or "this disgusts me" without giving either a safe political or aesthetic reason for such a reaction (nor did I ever ask anyone to say what turned them on, though the issue was lurking in the background throughout the class). Though the question was obvious and important, it thus represented something of a breach of class etiquette, made no less serious by the fact that it was uttered, and was understood to be uttered, in a spirit of revenge. Since almost all the pornography we had seen up to that point had concentrated, at least ostensibly and despite the obsession with money shots, on women being fucked, and on women voicing pleasure at being fucked, the woman who asked the question was saying, by implication, "If you don't like the spectacle of a man being fucked, now you know how we women feel." But she was also saying, somewhat more tauntingly, what if you *do* like seeing a man being fucked? All but one of the men denied feeling anything but a healthy, virile disgust either at the aesthetic crudeness of the film or at what today are judged unsafe sex practices. The exception was a young biology major, new to the kind of media study conducted in this class, who admitted, with disarming honesty, that the film made him uncomfortable because he was afraid that if he liked it, it would mean he was gay.

What is the proper "pedagogy of pornography" at a moment like this? This was a class that had shown quite a bit of respect and honesty up until this point. Yet here was a strong expression of homophobia. Was it my job to "correct" the homophobia of the fearful males, to take the side of the more tolerant women in pouncing on their reactions? I knew that if I simply corrected the male homophobia and continued with our screening of gay and bisexual pornographies as scheduled, we would no longer be able to talk honestly as a class. The offended heterosexual males would simply clam up. Perhaps ironically, I had taken it as a good sign that the male students had felt free to express their homophobia in the midst of so much politically correct position taking. I was actually pleased that at least one male had expressed what seemed to me the root cause of homophobia, not irrational fear of homosexuality, but fear of becoming homosexual. Should I press on with more films and threaten these males more? In the end, I decided to cancel further examination of gay and bisexual pornography.

Looking back on it today, I feel this was a mistake. In effect, I fostered an atmosphere in which a fear of homosexuality could be expressed in order to curtail what seemed to me a worse evil: the sort of pseudosophisticated condemnations of unsafe sex practices or critiques of silly plots that the majority of the straight men voiced, but really only to cover up deeper anxieties. The danger was that feminist political correctness would make it impossible for homophobic males to say what they honestly felt. Here is an example of the kind of reasoning that arose in the face of the women's criticism of overt homophobia:

> Today we covered a tough topic, gay male sex. A lot of people left when the film started. I said earlier I'd sit through it all to learn but this was hard. I did stay and found it very offensive. But not in the way you would think. I found it offensive in the same way I find straight porn offensive. It is how the men talk. "Fuck me up the ass," "harder" all that crap. Even when guys talk to women in films like that it bothers me. The act of anal sex doesn't shock me cause we've seen it with women. It was just the way they talked to each other I disliked. I figure if it doesn't turn you on it may work for someone else. The basic plot was ridiculous and so thats [sic] not a good start. . . . A big offense was also the fact that there were

no condoms in sight. That's bad, especially in these times. You've got to send the right message.

Now, this was a fairly savvy male film studies major who knew it would be uncool to say he was offended by male anal penetration. What he says instead is that he takes offense by a ridiculous plot (hardly the strong feature of any porn) and that he does not like the "dirty talk" (also true of much heterosexual porn) or the lack of condoms (in 1986, condoms were not yet *de rigueur* in gay porn). Notice also how this student rather enigmatically approaches the question of turn-on: "I figure if it doesn't turn you on it may work for someone else." I think this could be translated as saying that he is not turned on, but if someone else is, that may mean that this person is gay. Any vulnerability to or any pleasure taken in these images clearly frightens this student. There is nowhere to go in a class discussion with such a defensive attitude. Although this student is full of a sense of the *offense* of this work, he is not willing to attribute it to a sexuality he personally finds threatening. The feminist ethic of the classroom had made this too unpopular. Only the less sophisticated biology major was willing to confront his own vulnerability.

In response to this kind of stonewalling from most of the males, the female student who had precipitated the crisis wrote:

Today's in-class discussion was *exactly* what I had expected. . . . Don't I sound incredibly smug? [In the margin I noted that another student's journal had accused her of being smug when she asked the question in class, and though I was glad she precipitated our discussion by asking how the men felt in response to the film, that I wished she could ask it non-smugly so as to make them less defensive] . . . I *do* respect the honesty of some of our male fellow students. But here were also some remarks that frightened me: "Anal penetration isn't meant to be," "I found the gay porn offensive . . . but of *course*, I've also found the other screenings offensive!" etc. I am frightened because these remarks are not made by crusading fundamentalists, but by young, bright college students in the 90s. . . . For them *it is okay* to talk about the "abnormal character" of anal penetration. It *is okay* to point out the glorification of promiscuity only in gay porn. It *is okay* to "feel more offended" by this alternative than by any other. And finally, it is okay to say, "Of course I wasn't turned on, because *I'm not like this*," without ever stopping to question one's motivations to say so. . . . I'm afraid if we ever want to make progress on this matter, we will have to have many, many more discussions like the one we had today. Sometimes, these discussions could be very ugly. We could end up at each others' throats. But it might be worth it.

Because I was worried that at this point in the class, students *were* about to end up at each other's throats, I became, like the publisher of the World Conference on Pornography, the censor of the visual material of the class. This actually only amounted to the cancellation of one screening, but the class experienced it as my retreat from the presentation of controversial material. I doubt that this was the right thing to do, but I was concerned that members of the class be able to keep talking to one another. I did, however, try to point out in discussion some of the fragilities of sexual identity and that what was at stake for a heterosexual man was not the same as what was at stake for heterosexual women in watching hard core. I appealed to psychoanalytic theory to explain what in heterosexual female gender identification is not threatened by seeing women in sexual connection and what in heterosexual male gender identification is threatened by seeing men in sexual connection. However, I made a decision not to press the comfort level of the class any further, thereby incurring the (fortunately temporary) wrath of the brave student who had precipitated our best, and our most disturbing, discussions.

We had a long discussion instead of another film. We continued to talk about pornography. We discussed and read about erotica. We had a debate and several guest lectures. Some students went on to see more pornography outside of class as they wrote their final papers, but we did not see any more pornography. I may have been guilty of pampering the sensibilities of "our guys," but my goal in offering the class had been to expose students to diversities of pornography and the dynamics of the genre so as to make them aware that the appeal to the censorship of pornography is an appeal to the censorship of diverse sexualities. I think everyone in the class saw that.

In the end, all students decided, in an anonymous evaluation, that pornography *could* be part of the university curriculum, though certainly not required. Some said it could be because they learned a lot about feminism, some because they learned about a popular film genre, some because it was intense and controversial and therefore engaging, some because it shed light on antiporn dogma, one person even said it changed his/her life and made him/her realize that pornography was not one "big Pavlovian turn-on." But by far the most frequent reason given had nothing to do with the film genre or the controversies of pornography—and everything to do with finding in those difficult and fraught class discussions of pornography an unexpectedly fruitful forum for the discussion of sex and sexualities: "It brings out all the issues that are addressed rather indirectly in other classes. It also offers the opportunity to be (at times painfully) honest—the journal was a real 'emotional outlet.'"

In a final class discussion, several students also suggested that what the class needed was simply more discussion of sexuality. As a final paper, one student designed a course that would mix science and pornography to achieve a kind of sexology. The one thing these students were not very interested in pursuing was thus what had motivated me to teach the class in the first place: the feminist debates and controversies surrounding pornography. To them, pornography was much more interesting as a springboard for discussion and demystification of the sex acts and sexualities we always seem to talk around in other contexts. This constituted my most important lesson from this class. My way into the teaching of pornography through the feminist controversies did not prove helpful in organizing an effective course, but it was my way in. Students tolerated this, but they were less interested in feminist position taking than they were in finding ways for talking about sex. What a course like this can give them are certain discursive ways of speaking sex: Freudian, Foucaultian, and feminist. Feminist perspectives—whether antipornography or anticensorship—did not impede this discussion if they were brought in at certain points, but they tended not to be useful when they determined the entire agenda of the class. In a second attempt at teaching this undergraduate-level class, I found that when I made less of a fuss about potential offense taken at the material—whether that offense be feminist outrage or male homophobia—none was demonstrated. The lesson here is that it can prove all-too-easy for a teacher to set up students to act out offense, but that dramatic demonstrations of offense are not useful to further discussion. I also learned that it was better to show contemporary pornography and diverse kinds of pornography early in a course lest students think they will only be regarding the more safely distanced "antique" and heterosexual varieties. Undergraduate students, even at Irvine, became more tolerant and more interested in diverse forms of pornography in my second version of the class. They became more adept at speaking sex while being respectful to one another. It could be that this was the inevitable result of the very process of on/scenity that I have been describing above; it could be that I was no longer signaling my own difficulty with the material; or it could just be that times had changed.

I have given up on framing the teaching of pornography primarily through feminist debates. At UC Berkeley I now teach occasional graduate and advanced undergraduate courses on pornography and other sex genres. It is comparatively easy to teach this material at such a notably liberal institution, where students often urge me to find more challenging—less normative and heteronormative—material, but it is still a challenge. I now believe that it was not wise of me to let students accept the challenge of creating better pornographies than those that already existed, as I did when I permitted a few students to write screenplays. Although I encourage students in every other sort of course to try their hands at "doing" the mode or genre we are studying, it is a mistake in the current climate for a teacher of pornography to do the same. It leaves one vulnerable to the charge of encouraging students to become pornographers; it may lead very young students into a world for which they are not prepared; and it can only bring oneself, and one's institution, bad publicity. It is already hard enough to justify the importance of this field of study to colleagues, administrators, and the general public; why complicate this difficulty with even the appearance of involving students in the profession? It is also worth noting that male teachers need to exercise special discretion in teaching this material because of long-standing presumptions, feminist and otherwise, that pornography is *for* men and only *about* women. I do not think this should deter male teachers, but it does mean that they need to take different sorts of precautions that are probably best acknowledged up front. A tone of frank sexual interest accepting the fact that sexuality and sexual representation have become compelling to all, but tempered by an awareness that we are still learning a proper pedagogy of pornography, seems the best course.

There are undoubtedly many other, and better, ways to frame the issues and debates of hard-core pornography than the route I have described here. This anthology, much of which has been written by a later generation of my students, suggests some of them. I dedicate this book to the experiment of that first undergraduate class.

Notes

1 He writes: "At $10 billion, porn is no longer a sideshow to the mainstream like, say, the $600 million Broadway theater industry—it *is* the mainstream" (Rich 2001, 51).
2 "Speaking sex," as I have argued in *Hard Core* ([1989] 1999), is the particularly modern compulsion to confess the secrets of sex described by Michel Foucault in his *History of Sexuality*. Pornography, I have argued, is one such discourse of sexuality. It is emphatically not a form of speech that liberates or counters repres-

sion. Speaking sex, and the related idea of on/scenity explained in the next several paragraphs, are reworkings of ideas from this book, especially pages 282–84 of the 1999 edition.

3 I discuss this episode in the 1999 edition of *Hard Core* (Williams, 285–86).

4 The same fate befell another talk by David Sonnenschein, whose very subject was the censorship of a number of extremely innocent photographs of a nude adult male next to a boy of about five years. The boy points inquiringly at the man's penis, looking at it with curiosity. In a subsequent picture, he looks at his own penis, then in another, back at the man's. The photos were shown in an art exhibit, then withdrawn when complaints about child pornography were registered. Subsequently, Sonnenschein was not able to print these photos in his book. He was censored again when the photos about which he was speaking, and which are referred to in his contribution to the world conference book as figures 1, 2, and so on, are simply missing. Once again, Sonnenschein's whole point was the complete innocence of the photos and the child's natural, comparative curiosity. See Sonnenschein 1999. In the case of my own contribution to the conference, I withdrew it from the volume when I learned that my talk would not be published with its illustrations.

5 See, for example, the discussion of the controversies surrounding the teaching of pornography in articles by Lord 1997 and Atlas 1999. See as well the controversies generated by Chicago School of the Art Institute professor Kelly Dennis (Letherman 1999) and Wesleyan professor Hope Weissman. David Austin (1999) has also written usefully about the use of pornography in the university classroom. More recently, and not very thoughtfully, see Abel 2001.

Works Cited

Abel, David. 2001. "Porn Is Hot Course on Campus." *Boston Globe*, August 25.

Atlas, James. 1999. "The Loose Canon." *New Yorker*, March 29, 60–65.

Austin, David J. 1999. "Sexual Quotation without (Sexual) Harassment? Educational Use of Pornography in the University Classroom." In *Porn 101: Eroticism, Pornography, and the First Amendment*, ed. James Elias et al. Amherst, N.Y.: Prometheus.

Barthes, Roland. 1981. *Camera Lucida: Reflections on Photography*. Trans. Richard Howard. New York: Hill and Wang.

Butler, Judith. 1997. *Excitable Speech: A Politics of the Performative*. New York: Routledge.

de Grazia, Edward. 1992. *Girls Lean Back Everywhere: The Law of Obscenity and the Assault on Genius*. New York: Random House.

Hunt, Lynn. 1993. *The Invention of Pornography: Obscenity and the Origins of Modernity, 1500–1800*. New York: Zone Books.

Leatherman, Courtney. 1999. "Conflict over a Divisive Scholar Combines Issues of

Art, Sexuality, and Teaching Style." *Chronicle of Higher Education*, August 13, A14–A16.

Lord, M. G. 1997. "Pornutopia." *Lingua Franca*, April-May, 40–48.

MacKinnon, Catherine. 1993a. *Only Words*. Cambridge, Mass.: Harvard University Press.

———. 1993b. "Turning Rape into Pornography." *Ms.*, July-August, 24–40.

Munk, Erika. 1994. "What's Wrong with This Picture?' *Women's Review of Books*, July-August, 5–6.

Rembar, Charles. 1969. *The End of Obscenity: The Trials of "Lady Chatterly," "Tropic of Cancer," and "Fanny Hill."* New York: Random House.

Rich, Frank. 2001. "Naked Capitalists." *New York Times Magazine*, May 20, sec. 6, 51–92.

Sonnenschein, David. 1999. "Sources of Reaction to 'Child Pornography.'" In *Porn 101: Eroticism, Pornography, and the First Amendment*, ed. James Elias et al. Amherst, N.Y.: Prometheus.

Williams, Linda. [1989] 1999. *Hard Core: Power, Pleasure, and "the Frenzy of the Visible."* Berkeley: University of California Press.

Yamashiro, Jennifer. 1999. "In the Realm of the Sciences: The Kinsey Institute's *31 Photographs*." In *Porn 101: Eroticism, Pornography, and the First Amendment*, ed. James Elias et al. Amherst, N.Y.: Prometheus.

Žižek, Slavoj. 1989. "Looking Awry." *October* 50: 31–35.

part 1

Contemporary Pornographies

How to Do Things with the *Starr Report*:

Pornography, Performance, and the

President's Penis

MARIA ST. JOHN

To *say* something is to *do* something.
—J. L. Austin, *How to Do Things with Words*

The . . . investigation, the . . . report . . . may have the over-all and apparent objective of
saying no to all wayward or unproductive sexualities, but the fact is that they function as
mechanisms with a double impetus: pleasure and power.
—Michel Foucault, *History of Sexuality*

The highest and the lowest are always closest to each other in the sphere of sexuality.
—Sigmund Freud, *Three Essays on the Theory of Sexuality*

✳ The insistent presence of sex in the American public domain came clearly
into focus during the highly publicized investigation into then president
Clinton's "physically intimate" encounters with Monica Lewinsky. Anyone
in the nation—or the world, for that matter—who read a newspaper, listened
to the radio, or watched television was privy to the details of the furtive sexual
encounters between the U.S. president and the White House intern. The
mainstream news media dealt in sex explicitly and relentlessly for the duration of the grand jury hearings. As Sasha Torres notes in her analysis of television news coverage of the proceedings, "television news organizations responded to the potentially contaminating proximity of their traffic in graphic
images to an illicit commerce in graphic sex by focusing on their own moral
embarrassment, constantly calling the scandal's details 'salacious,' 'lurid,'

'explicit,' 'sensitive,' 'embarrassing,' 'delicate,' 'sordid,' 'vivid,' and 'disturbing'" (2001, 107).

Rather than functioning to distance reporters from the material they professed to find so distasteful, however, such protestation served to implicate them in the intrigue. In the course of CBS coverage of an exchange between Clinton and Lewinsky, for example, Bob Scheiffer slipped wildly from the third to the first person, saying, "And again, they had sex of a kind. Once again, he stopped her before he was finished and said he didn't know me well enough, didn't trust me enough yet." Scheiffer stammered and complained to Dan Rather, "Dan, . . . it's very strong stuff" (Torres 2001, 108).

This "stuff" peddled by the news media was, in CBS correspondent Sharyl Attkisson's opinion, "not quite X-rated, but not G-rated either," yet ABC's Peter Jennings repeatedly referred to the *Starr Report* as "the hard report" (Torres 2001, 111). Hard core or soft? Titillating or tiresome? Salacious or silly? Consensus regarding the rating or characterization of the *Starr Report* would indeed prove difficult to reach. It is clearly more than just a document of Clinton and Lewinsky's grand jury testimony. It is also a record of our contemporary national relationship to material that would historically have been deemed pornographic.

In the introduction to this volume, Linda Williams posits the term *on/scenity* to describe "the gesture by which a culture brings on to its public arena the very organs, acts, 'bodies and pleasures' that have heretofore been designated ob/scene and kept literally off-scene" (4). This essay examines the products of Kenneth Starr's multimillion-dollar project to make a national spectacle of the president's penis. The American public became an audience as the illicit scenes that no one had actually observed (through keyhole, lens, or any other aperture) were spun into a "story" (or, as I will argue, a multitude of partial stories). What is the nature of this spectacle of spin, what kind of spectators did it make the nation into, and via what theoretical frameworks might it best be analyzed?

The Polymorphous Report

"The" *Report* attributed to Kenneth Starr is actually not a single, bound document, but a multimedia, mutating text, the boundaries of which are infinitely variable. It constitutes a polymorphous text/event. It exists in live, material, electronic, digital, print, and visual formats that occupy various temporalities, engage multiple audiences, and conform simultaneously, though imperfectly, to the representational conventions of a wide range of cultural forms, some classically designated as pornographic, others not. The *Report* includes transcripts of the grand jury proceedings, as well as the exhibits entered in this trial: a stained blue dress and the DNA kit linking it to Clinton, for example; a copy of *Leaves of Grass* given Lewinsky by Clinton; a letter opener given Clinton by Lewinsky; recovered deleted computer files; audiotaped telephone conversations (illegally obtained but entered nevertheless); White House records; photographs; thank-you notes; and other items of memorabilia.

The American public had been well aware of the *Report*'s compilation, and in 1998 it watched on television a scene described by Fedwa Malti-Douglas: "The awaited *Report* finally came into the world with much fanfare as Americans were shown two vans delivering thirty-six boxes of materials from Kenneth Starr's office." After all that, Malti-Douglas continues, "the printed version of Judge Starr's documentation, prepared by the House of Representatives, takes up less than two feet on a library shelf. And much of the material included, like excerpts from periodicals, is of dubious legal relevance" (2000, 2).

Nevertheless, the Government Printing Office promptly bound and reproduced this document for sale. It was also printed in any newspaper that would have it. At the same time, the House released a copy of the videotape of Clinton's grand jury testimony, and it aired on all major television networks. A number of servers made the report available on the Internet, and Simon and Schuster simultaneously published two versions of the material: an "extensive selection" and a shorter (559-page) "reader friendly" excerpt. Both books include the transcripts of the grand jury testimonies given by Clinton and Lewinsky.[1]

Starr's *Report* "reports" on this grand jury testimony of Clinton and Lewinsky, in the course of which they were obliged to report the details of their sexual exchanges. Clinton and Lewinsky's reports were induced in an elaborate scene of confession. Michel Foucault has suggested that "confession . . . remains the general standard governing the production of the true discourse on sex" (1978, 63). He elaborates, "We have . . . become a singularly confessing society . . . one confesses one's crimes, one's sins, one's thoughts and desires, one's illnesses and troubles . . . one confesses—or is forced to confess" (61). Foucault suggests that such force in fact constitutes a key element of confession: "The confession is a ritual that unfolds within a power relationship, for one does not confess without the presence . . . of a partner who is not simply the interlocutor but the authority who requires the confession, prescribes and appreciates it, and intervenes in order to judge"

(61). Starr was thus a key player in the scene of confession he orchestrated, as were the members of Congress who participated in the interrogation.

The *Starr Report* encompasses this (staged) live scene of confession, its unprecedented video documentation, and the television broadcasting of this footage, as well as the print and on-line versions of the transcripts from the hearings, and, in short, anything else Starr was inclined to toss into the thirty-six boxes marked "evidence" that he so theatrically delivered to Congress in anticipation of the hearings. Clearly, no singular theoretical framework would be adequate to the task of interpreting such an unwieldy cultural object. But one interdisciplinary field of study is practiced in the art of analyzing aesthetic objects as complex and multilayered, involving scripts and props, live encounters and video documentation, bodily exchanges and divergent speech acts. Such daunting collections of elements are the standard purview of performance studies.

Starr Performances

Andrew Parker and Eve Sedgwick have observed that as a result of the convergence in recent decades of various disciplinary tributaries, the field of performance studies has expanded "to embrace a myriad of performance practices, ranging from stage to festival and everything in between: film, photography, television, computer simulation, music, 'performance art,' political demonstrations, health care, cooking, fashion, shamanistic ritual" (1995, 2). In her forthcoming book, Shannon Jackson delineates the "disciplinary connections . . . between theatre studies and contemporary theories of performativity" that are in part responsible for this proliferation.[2] Both angles on the performance nexus—that is, spectacle-based (theater studies) and language-based (performativity) frameworks of analysis—are helpful in reading the *Starr Report*.

Neither Clinton nor Lewinsky auditioned for the roles in which Starr attempted to cast them. Neither one is a performer in the classical sense of the term; they have both spent their lives otherwise. And their speech in the context of the grand jury trials was coerced, not offered. Still, they comported themselves like pros (although Lewinsky, as I discuss below, played the ingenue), their performances on the stand were the subject of much scrutiny, and the liveness of the proceedings—their in-the-flesh quality— was something that Starr was at pains to capture, both through the video documentation of the event and through his inclusion of every stammer, cough, and hiccup in the transcript he disseminated.

William Jefferson Clinton was impeached. Confusion about this fact persists because in popular usage the term *impeachment* encompasses the impeachment trial and tends to be associated with removal from office, but as *Black's Law Dictionary* defines it, the verb *to impeach* means "to charge with a crime," and "impeaching a federal official, such as the President . . . requires that a majority of the U.S. House of Representatives vote to return at least one article of . . . impeachment to the U.S. Senate." This occurred in October of 1998. However, "even if an official is impeached," the definition continues, "removal from office does not occur unless two-thirds of the senators vote for conviction." Although the Senate vote in February of 1999 failed to produce even a simple majority in favor of convicting Clinton and removing him from office, the fact remains that, technically, he was impeached by virtue of being charged.

J. L. Austin has posited a term for speech acts (like impeaching) that *do* things (like impeach); he designates them "performative utterances." In his classic example of a performative utterance, he writes, "to utter the sentence . . . is not . . . to state that I am doing it: it is to do it. . . . When I say, before the registrar or altar, etc. 'I do,' I am not reporting on a marriage: I am indulging in it" (1962, 6). A good deal of Austin's analytic efforts is devoted to instances of performative utterances that fail to do what they ostensibly can. These he refers to as "unhappy" or "infelicitous" performatives.

The performative impeachment of Clinton prompted by Starr may technically have been successful, happy, and felicitous (Starr certainly got lucky with the president's semen); Clinton was impeached. But in the popular register, the project floundered. According to a December 1998 NBC poll, 70 percent of Americans opposed impeachment and removal from office.[3] In this sense, the impeachment was a flop.

The popular failure of the performative impeachment resulted in part from the success of the performances of both the president and the intern. They played it in very different ways—Clinton through withholding and Lewinsky through delivering—and it is impossible to know to what extent either was making conscious use of the rhetorical or presentational strategies they deployed. But their combined testimony held the nation spellbound, and ultimately, rather than being rejected as grotesques, the two figures inspired in many Americans a new sense of the carnivalesque.

It became clear throughout the interrogation that Clinton knew it to be a showdown, with words used as lethal weapons. His orations during the interrogation offer a model of phallic economy and monism. He repeats incessantly, "I revert to my former statement." When he is pressed to say whether his lawyer's statement that there "is absolutely no sex of any kind in any manner, shape or form" (Report, 366) between Clinton and Lewinsky, Clinton responds, "It depends on what the meaning of the word 'is' is" (Report, 387). Torres observes that certain commentators "seemed to find Clinton's formulation risible because of the ostensible obviousness of the meaning of 'is.'" In fact, Torres, suggests,

> the reason this phrase received so much air time was that the structure of Clinton's formulation . . . both proves and disproves his point. In [this] sentence . . . "is" actually means two things, working as a noun and a verb. Yet the sentence must depend on the putative stability of commonsense understanding in order to mean anything at all. Such dependence—the decision to strategically stabilize the meanings of words—constitutes the linguistic positivism of legal discourse, a positivism Clinton here simultaneously undermines and exploits. (2001, 106)

In another instance, Clinton resists being skewered by calling attention to the rhetorical context, rather than allowing it to remain naturalized and invisible. He says, "There's a videotape being made of this, allegedly because only one member of the grand jury is absent. This is highly unusual. And, in addition to that, I have sustained a breathtaking number of leaks of grand jury proceedings. And so, I think I am right to answer all the questions about perjury, but not to say things which will be forever in the historic annals of the United States because of this unprecedented videotape and may be leaked at any time" (Report, 435). Obviously, if he is going to "not . . . say things which will be forever in the historic annals of the United States" while the "unprecedented videotape" is rolling, he'll have to not say "things" at all. And to a remarkable extent, he manages this. The investigators bait him, but he doesn't bite. He submits to the interrogation, but withholds a sound bite.

If Clinton equivocates, Lewinsky blabs. I will discuss the effusive quality of Lewinsky's orality and some of its effects presently. But I would like here to suggest that her inappropriate chatter in the context of the sanctified, masculinized space of the grand jury trial was reminiscent of certain performance projects of the Life/Art movement of the 1970s, and in particular the interventions of certain feminist innovators. In *Living Art Situations* (1975), for example, Linda Montano challenged high/low, private/public, and aesthetic/nonaesthetic dividing lines by publicizing as a performance project a period of time during which she stayed home and documented her activity with neighborhood people. In *Feed Me* (1973), Barbara Smith created a boudoir environment in the San Francisco Museum of Conceptual Art and invited individuals to enter and interact with her. Many moments during Lewinsky's testimony echo aspects of such performance projects. Lewinsky complies energetically with the investigators' requests for copious accounts of the pedestrian movements and mundane details of personal lives. She takes seriously—and proceeds as though the investigators are inquiring in good faith about—the feminized realms of gossip, intrigue, and intimacy.

A particular moment of Lewinsky's testimony calls to mind Eleanor Antin's piece *The Sculpture* (1972), in which Antin photographed herself nude from four different sides every morning for forty-five days while following a strict diet. The piece commented on the phenomenon of the internalization of misogynist cultural surveillance and disciplining of the female body, but did this through a presentation that emphasized the monotony and ordinariness of these violent processes. The moment that seems to cite such feminist traditions is the one in which Lewinsky makes a point of bringing the feminized preoccupation with "looking skinny" into her testimony, making it clear that these are collective concerns, shared at least by herself, her faithless friend, and her family. Lewinsky testifies regarding the dress stained with Clinton's semen:

> I just wanted to say because I know that everybody here reads the newspapers and listens to TV that I didn't keep this dress [stained] as a souvenir. I was going to wear it on Thanksgiving and my cousins, who I always try to look skinny for because they're all skinny—and I know it sounds stupid. And when I told Linda [Tripp] I was thinking about wearing the dress [which would have entailed first washing it] she discouraged me. She brought me one of her jackets from her thinner closet. And so it wasn't a souvenir [I just never got around to wearing and therefore washing it].[4]

While additional stressors clearly contribute to the pulverized syntax and logic of this little speech, the desire to be perceived as thin, and the readiness to do some pretty strange things (keep two separate closets, dash off or not to the dry cleaners, etc.) to increase the chances of this, are operative for many American women, and Lewinsky, for whatever reasons, wants this on record. Lewinsky is not a feminist performance artist, but throughout her testimony she performs American femininity in ways that exceed the masculinist demands of the moment of confession she inhabits.

Audience with the President: Who's Interested?

Although the *Report* is ostensibly addressed to the members of Congress, the actual intended audience is far less circumscribed. Just as the *Report* inhabits infinite textual spaces and stages multiple scenes, it also coalesces many different audiences: viewers of a particular television station on a given evening, readers of one version or another of the printed matter, browsers alighting on the same server. Among the audience of critics and commentators, Alan Dershowitz represents a constituency undone by certain aspects of the *Report*. Dershowitz begins his book on the events surrounding Clinton's impeachment with the assertion that "the greatest constitutional crisis in modern American history [turned] on whether the President of the United States told a sex lie under oath and tried—unsuccessfully—to keep secret an improper sexual relationship." Dershowitz complains in the next sentence that "the titillating background to this crisis . . . obscured the profound issues of state . . . involved" (1998, 1). Dershowitz thus begins his book by positing a binary opposition between the "titillating" and the "profound" and aligns constitutional crises and matters of state with profundity, while casting titillation ("sex lies" and "improper sexual relationships") as irritating obstructions to profundity.

Profundity reappears again in the very next sentence, this time serving to align Dershowitz himself with that quality. He writes, "as a teacher and a practitioner of law, I have been profoundly interested in this conflict [among the Presidency, the Judiciary, the Congress, and . . . the Independent Counsel] from the beginning" (1). Dershowitz assumes that the grave may be clearly distinguished from the trivial, serious issues from prurient details, and matters of state from the matter of sex, as well as sex lies from other lies and proper from improper sexual relationships. The passage suggests further that Dershowitz himself, as a professor and a man of law, was always already "interested" in these distinctions and is authorized to categorize accordingly. But on closer examination something unusual about Dershowitz's description of the relation between what he sees as titillating and what he sees as profound becomes evident. Dershowitz writes that the "titillating background . . . obscured the profound issues." There is an odd configuration of space here, in which the background obscures what is presumably or rightfully in the foreground. Backgrounds might routinely compete with or absorb objects posited as being in the foreground, but obscure? The more readily conceivable formal problems pertaining to background and foreground include elements of a foreground being indistinguishable or barely distinguishable from their background, undecidability regarding positive and negative space, or the proverbial difficulty of sometimes seeing a forest for its trees. But it is difficult to imagine how a background can obscure what is in front of it. This spatial mix-up suggests that the issues Dershowitz is setting out to discuss refuse to order themselves neatly within the zones he assigns. Titillation won't stay in the background, and sex won't stay out of issues of state. As Foucault has suggested, the relation between power and sexuality must be imagined as "[tracing] around bodies and sexes, not boundaries not to be crossed, but perpetual spirals of power and pleasure" (1978, 45). Dershowitz describes even as he resists recognizing the mutual imbrication of pleasure and power theorized by Foucault.

Dershowitz's spatial disorientation and befuddlement in the face of these spiraling mechanisms of policing and producing sexuality and state power are understandable not only because, as a "teacher and a practitioner of law," he is indeed an interested party, but also because we were all implicated in the national production that was his object of study, and, as Lauren Berlant and Lisa Duggan remark in the opening to their book on the subject, the cultural moment in question "was a moment of astounding incoherence" (2001, 1).

Although dizzying for Dershowitz, the incoherence of the *Report* itself— its refusal to hang together—marks the very quality that enables it to accommodate so many audiences. The *Report* cites multiple representational conventions, addressing audiences defined not simply by the coincidence of their having stumbled on the same version of the proliferating *Report* but also by their literacy with respect to or affinity for a particular genre or form. These include, as I discuss in the concluding sections, pornographic forms. But the *Report* courts vanilla audiences as well.

There are, for example, the possibilities of reading the *Starr Report* as detective narrative or courtroom drama. In a paper on the subject of the *Report* delivered shortly after its release, Jonathan Lear cited an interview with Starr's mother, in which she recalled proudly the way her son used to shine his shoes while watching *Kojak*, a show for which he apparently had a passion.[5] The shining of the shoes struck Lear as a masturbatory action, but it also resonates suggestively with Freud's paper "Fetishism." Freud here describes a number of his fetishistic male patients, one of whom had happened on a certain shine on the nose of his sexual partner as the necessary condition of his arousal. Freud's broader argument is that a fetish stands in for the female penis that the fetishistic subject once assumed to exist and now refuses to give up on. Fetishism thus offers one solution to the problem of castration that the specter of sexual difference induces in the male subject. It is a primitive strategy of defense involving not repression, but splitting and divided belief. While a subject who has recourse to repression is perpetually vulnerable to the return of the repressed, and thus to guilt, the fetishistic subject has swept nothing under the rug and thus tends to be characterized by self-righteousness.

In describing the moment of crisis to which fetishism comes as a solution, Freud writes, "In later life a grown man may perhaps experience a similar panic when the cry goes up that Throne and Altar are in danger, and similar illogical consequences will ensue" ([1927] 1961, 153). Starr clearly feared—and tried to convince the nation—that both throne *and* altar were in danger during Clinton's tenure. The entire trial that sought to expel Clinton from office was presided over by the Senate chaplain John Ogilvie, who convened every session with prayers sanctifying the proceedings.

If the erotics of mastery through surveillance, inquisition, exposure, and condemnation drive the narrative for Starr, and accommodate an audience with similar predilections, Lewinsky's own fantasies, by contrast, appear, at least at first glance, to conform to the specifications of a bodice-ripper romance. Her testimony thus engages an audience inclined toward that genre. (I will argue presently that Lewinsky actually entertains conflicting fantasies.) She frets when in the presence of the grand jury that she cannot recount her love scenes in ways that sound "right" according, apparently, to the logic of this genre:

> A: We were in the back office and we were kissing, and I was—I had a dress on that buttoned all the way, all the way up and down.
> Q: To the neck?
> A: Correct. It was long and down to the, to my ankles, or whatever. And he unbuttoned my dress and he unhooked my bra, and sort of took the dress off of my shoulders, off my—I'm not explaining this right. So that he moved the bra so that my bra was kind of hanging on one shoulder and so was off. And he just was, he was looking at me and touching me and telling me how beautiful I was. (*Report*, 319)

If this description did not sound quite "right," Lewinsky may have been better pleased with her representational efforts in a letter she wrote to Clinton which was resurrected from a deleted file on her computer. She writes there, in keeping with the we-know-its-wrong-but-we-just-can't-keep-our-hands-off-each-other-even-if-it-ruins-us template of the bodice-ripper: "I cannot ignore what we have shared together. I don't care what you say. . . . I never would have seen that raw, intense sexuality that I saw a few times—watching your mouth on my breast or looking in your eyes while you explored the depth of my sex. . . . I don't want to breach your moral standard" (473). The specifications of the genre demand precisely that generous amounts of "breaching" occur, and that, president or not, Clinton's "moral standards" be invoked—and damned.

In addition to the romance novel, the *Report* has been associated with other related genres. A *Newsweek* article appearing as the events unfolded suggested that the entire narrative of Clinton's public and private life might be best understood as soap opera (Fineman 1998). And a number of commentators have had recourse to the term *melodrama* in attempting to categorize and characterize the events and their representation.[6] It seems to me that the *Report* does lend itself to being read in terms of all of these genres—a remarkable thing in itself, given the highly feminized status of some (melodrama, soap opera, romance novel) and the hyperbolically masculinized status of others (official/judicial document, courtroom drama, detective novel).[7] But there is another popular cultural form in terms of which Starr himself long ago insisted that such a document must be considered. In a 1987 *60 Minutes* interview with Dianne Sawyer, Starr said, "Public media should not contain explicit or implied descriptions of sex acts. Our society should be purged of the perverts who provide the media with pornographic material while pretending it has some redeeming social value under the public's 'right to know.' Pornography is pornography, regardless of the source." The suggestion from the horse's mouth, then, is that we read the report as smut.

Pornographies-in-Potentia

Approaching the *Starr Report* as a consumer of pornography entails special frustrations, however, even if it also yields certain pleasures. These frustrations result from the slipperiness of the *Report*, which as a text inscribes a multitude of conflicting desires and takes up and abandons multiple pornographic conventions. This gives rise to a pace and form of unfolding that precludes for most libidinal economies the kind of text-psyche-body sexual synchronization Osterweil (in this volume) posits as the conventional "aim of pornography." Although the *Report* may have brought only the roughest and readiest among us to orgasm on the first read, it (and the events it ostensibly documents) was, however, sufficiently cathected by others of us to prompt countless acts of cultural production, including casual and scholarly essays and books, as well as at least three porn videos: *Penetration on Pennsylvania Avenue* (dir. William Parker, 1998), *Scenes from the Oral Office* (dir. F. J. Lincoln, 1998), and *Deep Throat V: The Quest (Slick Willy Rides Again)* (dir. Bud Lee, 1998).[8] Such flights of fancy (both "high" and "low") are stimulated by the *Report*, perhaps even courted by it, but they are not consummated within it. Perhaps because of the interrupted status of these pornographies-in-potentia, the *Starr Report* adds up not to the damning evidence of a couple of individuals' guilt, but to a record of our unharmonious national on/scenity.

One of the frustrating aspects of reading the *Starr Report* as pornography results from the fact that rather than falling silently into line with present pornographic conventions (and thus rendering them invisible, as more cooperative cultural products do), it evokes conventions past. In a discussion of the history of pornography, Lynn Hunt examines the roots of modern pornography in political satire. She writes that political pornography "had a long lineage going back to Aretino [*sic*] in the sixteenth century, and it seemed to reach a crescendo in the last decades of the ancien regime in France." The "sexual sensationalism of ancien regime pamphlets," Hunt continues, "was used to attack the French court, the church, the aristocracy, the academics, the salons, and the monarchy itself." She explains: "Politically motivated pornographic pamphlets in the 1770s and early 1780s often denounced the supposedly excessive influence of women at the French court. Queen Marie Antoinette was the focus of much of this literature; pornographic pamphlets, couplets and ditties claimed to detail her presumed sexual misdemeanors, questioned the paternity of her children, and in the process, fatally undermined the image of royal authority" (1996b, 305–6).

Can we categorize the *Starr Report* as pornographic political satire? Certainly, this has been among the intentions of certain spokesfolk of the right since the beginning of Clinton's tenure. The outrage, for example, that Hillary Clinton's activity, visibility, and vocalness inspired in some evokes the scandalous pictures of influential women in the French court described by Hunt. The attempt to sell the Lewinsky affair—the attempt, in fact, to make a scandal of the affair—seems to offer a neat parallel to the (successful) attempts of French revolutionaries to bring down the powers that were by depicting their lowliness through pornography.

But there are also some important differences. Foremost among these is the fact that we, the people, did not take to the streets in disgust and outrage in response to our exposure to these presidential primal scenes. If the NBC poll cited above may be relied on as accurately representing U.S.

public sentiment, 70 percent of us, rather than supporting Clinton's impeachment, favored the "censure and move on" option.[9] And indeed, Hunt demonstrates that political pornography has not always expressed revolutionary sentiment, but has historically been deployed to conservative ends, as it was in this case. In a different essay in the same volume, Hunt writes that "pornography has a peculiar, even paradoxical relationship to democracy. In the sixteenth and seventeenth centuries, pornography was written for an elite male audience that was largely urban, aristocratic, and libertine in nature." In the eighteenth century, Hunt explains, "the audience broadened as pornographic themes entered populist discourses, a development given even greater impetus by the French Revolution. But the democratization of pornography was not a straight, one-way street." During the English civil war, Hunt continues,

> a royalist newspaper could use sexual slander to attack the revolutionary government, accusing it of being composed of cuckolds and fornicators who allegedly used words like "freedom" and "liberty" as passwords for entering brothels. Similarly, in the first years of the French Revolution of 1789, royalist papers and pamphlets used scatological and sexual insults to attack the new constitutional monarchy and, in particular, its more democratic supporters. Pornography was not a left-wing preserve. (1996a, 43)

Clearly Clinton's energetic opponents attempted to capitalize on any offense that his reputation as a draft-evading, marijuana-smoking, cunnilingus-performing swinger could inspire.[10]

The *Report*, then, reads ambiguously as political pornography. It certainly passes for a version of it at first glance. But the NBC poll cited above suggests that a popular on/scene response to sexually explicit material has taken the place of the popular "scandalizability" that, as Walter Kendrick (1987) asserts, has historically been productive of the entire category of pornography. Starr clearly did succeed in plugging Clinton into the porn circuitry of the cultural imaginary. (Or perhaps just amping up the voltage. I remember a poll early in Clinton's first term claiming that he was the man of the month most fantasized about by American women.) But that cultural imaginary proved to function according to the logic not of obscenity, which would have made scandal and exposé possible and socially exciting, but of on/scenity, resulting in the popular responses that ranged from being bored to being openly turned-on.

The *Starr Report* might be better placed within the realm of what Hunt designates as apolitical, commercial pornography. Aspects of the *Report*, for example, evoke conventions of the stag era of cinematic pornography. Specifically, the unfolding of the "narrative," if we can impose one on the series of sexual encounters between Monica Lewinsky and Bill Clinton, is repetitive, circular, and episodic, rather than classically linear. Linda Williams has described the brevity, lack of narrative coherence, and fragmentary character of stag films in ways that offer a historical conventional context for the furtive sexual contacts obsessively documented in the report. "In the primitive stag film," she observes, "the ending is typically abrupt, usually following a close-up" (1989, 72). Feature-length pornographic film, by contrast, is characterized by "greater narrative coherence of both the feature film as a whole and each of its sexual 'numbers.'" In feature-length porn films, Williams continues, "these numbers tend to be complete dramas of arousal, excitement, climax, and (usually) satisfaction that permit both the (male) characters in the film and the (usually male) viewers of the film to 'withdraw satisfied' after getting first into and then back out of the picture" (72).

Most of Clinton and Lewinsky's scenes come to abrupt endings. The scenes famously fail (this is a failure according to post-stag standards) to end in orgasm. They appear in the report as fragments reminiscent of close-ups that are cut and pasted obsessively into each investigatory session. They are more like loops repeating as the investigators crank their witnesses close-up than like stories emanating from elsewhere with the authority of self-coherence claimed by classic narratives of 1970s and 1980s film pornography. In fact, the narrativelessness of these scenes is laid bare by the battles to narrativize them differently. Lewinsky wants them to be scenes in a love story. Clinton wants to dismiss them as inconsequential contacts in the life of a busy man. Starr celebrates them as exposés of Clinton's immorality, abusiveness, deceitfulness, and corruption. The scenes themselves flounder pathetically between these appropriative projects.

The sexual material documented in the report strains at the edges of stag conventions. While it works within them in certain ways, it goes beyond them in others, and cites as well the set of conventions Williams describes in relation to feature-length cinematic pornography. She says, "Probably the most striking way that the feature-length hard-core film signals the narrative conclusion of sexual action . . . is through the new convention of external penile ejaculation—or, to use the jargon of the industry, the 'money shot'"(73). In most scenes, Clinton doesn't come. In two he does. The *Starr Report*'s efforts at narrativization, and the privileging of the money shot, are in evidence in the following exchange between Lewinsky and the grand jury investigators.

Q: The day you wore the blue cocktail dress—
A: It's not a cocktail dress.
Q: Okay, I'm sorry.
A: No, that's okay. I'm a little defensive about this subject. I'm sorry.
Q: How would you describe the dress?
A: It's a dress from the Gap. It's a work dress. It's a casual dress.
Q: With respect to that dress—
A: Right, I'm sorry.
Q: —you mentioned that you believe that there could be semen on it. Could you describe what you did with the President that led you to believe that?
A: We were in the bathroom and—can I close my eyes so I don't have to—
Q: Well, you have to speak up. That's the only—
A: Okay. We were in the bathroom and I was performing oral sex. I'm sorry, this is embarrassing. And usually he doesn't want to—he didn't want to come to completion.
Q: Ejaculate? (Kuntz 1998, 138)

The final question can be read as a command—to Lewinsky to spit it out, to Clinton to come, to the whole thing to conform to the emblematic convention of feature-length cinematic pornography. But to the extent that the evidence does conform, its rhythm, according to industry standards, remains highly unsatisfactory. The impatient investigator, who acts here as both a performer in the scene and a director, is reminiscent of the weary Ron Jeremy Susan Faludi (1995) describes as "waiting for wood" during a shoot when performer Zack Adams takes two hours to come. Exasperated, Jeremy steps from behind the camera into the scene and gets off himself.

In addition to the *Starr Report* evoking and frustrating the competing conventions of stag and feature-length porn film, it also excites and interrupts our expectations of video porn. This may be where Starr's plot backfired most. A tremendous amount of popular anticipation was generated around the release of the video—anticipation that resulted from and amplified the orchestrated association of the tape with pornography. And, as will be discussed presently, the visual version simply failed to deliver the goods.

Milking the Couples Market

Andrew Ross opens his essay "The Popularity of Pornography" with the following anecdote:

> Pornography from a woman's point of view? Yes, said the owner of my
> local video store, of course he could recommend some, and he rattled off
> the titles of a few of the more popular "couples" films currently being
> rented. Could he describe them? Longer, romantic sequences, with ap-
> propriate mood music, and lots of emphasis on feelings. Does this mean
> that there's no hard core? No, not at all, he said, and this time, his busi-
> ness instincts aroused, he leaned toward me, after a ritual glance over
> his shoulder, and proceeded to assure me, man to man, that the actors
> eventually did get down to the real stuff; it just took a little longer, and it
> was, sort of different (Ross 1989, 371).

Linda Williams has discussed some of the differences the heterosexual
couples market has made with respect to the conventions of cinematic pornography. She writes, for example, that "the pornographic marketplace is
now almost as eager to address women as desiring consumers as it once
was to package them as objects of consumption. . . . Women have entered
the pornographic conversation—not just as confessors and performers of
sex, but as readers and viewers who are increasingly addressed by the films"
(1989, 230). Williams identifies the primary influence of this market force
as being porn's "more earnest" inquiry into the question of women's sexual
pleasure. She suggests that the industry (profits because it) "takes more seriously the different nature of the woman's own desire and pleasure and accepts the challenge of helping her to achieve them" (233).

If, as I have suggested, the *Starr Report* plays like a stag film, while also
calling on feature-length conventions, and selling itself in a video age, it is
the demands of the couples market which pull most frantically at the shreds
of "evidence" the report embodies. Clinton's contortions of the definition of
sex certainly represent a lawyerly exercise in maintaining power, but they
find footing in a dominant cultural confusion around sexuality that stems
in large measure from conservative desires to have one's cake and eat it
too—to uphold patriarchal institutions of marriage, monogamy, and property, while managing to get some outside. Williams has described the ways
in which couples porn seeks to "uphold the ideology of monogamy" (236)—
and undergoes various narrative and ideological contortions in this effort.

The *Starr Report* squirms under the ideological pressure at stake in this quintessential problem of couples porn. While Clinton claims monogamy based on his insistence that the sex with Lewinsky did not constitute sex, Lewinsky nurses a fantasy of serial monogamy in which Hillary Clinton's title of first lady marks her place not in the White House, but in a sequence of marriages to Bill. She tells the grand jury, "After breakfast, in the car, I asked Mr. Jordan if he thought the President would always be married to the First Lady and he said, 'yes, as he should be.' And gave me a quote from the Bible. And a few—maybe a minute or so later, he said, 'Well, maybe you two will have an affair when he's out of office'" (Kuntz 1998, 219).

So much for Scripture! Lewinsky, undaunted, writes to Clinton later, "Bill, I loved you with all of my heart. I wanted to be with you all of the time. Most recently in London, I walked the streets thinking how content I would be to walk the streets at your side while you spoke of things past—filled the air and my soul with your knowledge of history" (464). These impossibly simultaneous defenses of monogamy in the course of practices of promiscuity, among other details, testify to the *Starr Report*'s embroiledness in the ideological problems of heteronormative couples porn.

Although Clinton resists speaking in the terms of couples porn, Lewinsky, in true amateur spirit, rises to the occasion. Her orality suffuses the proceedings when she is on the stand. She drinks a lot of water and asks to be excused to go to the bathroom a number of times, saying indelicately, "I have to pee." And she talks a lot. She is constantly being interrupted, redirected, reigned in by the investigators. Exchanges like this one are typical: "[The Witness]: Am I getting into too much detail? Mr. Emmick: Close" (232). She tries to be chatty: "The Witness: Time for a nap? Mr. Emmick [ignoring her quip]: Madam Foreperson, do we have a quorum?" (181). She tries harder: "Can you guys call me Monica? Are they allowed to call me Monica instead of Ms. Lewinsky? The Foreperson: If you say so. . . . Ms. Immergut [ignoring this request]: Ms. Lewinsky, there are two things I wanted to clarify. First . . ." (272–73). And of course she describes a lot of oral sex.

These descriptions are induced. As Foucault writes, "Society has taken it upon itself to solicit and hear the imparting of individual pleasures" (1978, 63). He elaborates in a passage that captures vividly the investigators' roles and stakes in eliciting Lewinsky's sex talk: "It is no longer a question simply of saying what was done—the sexual act—and how it was done; but of reconstructing, in and around the act, the thoughts that recapitulated it, the obsessions that accompanied it, the images, desires, modulations, and quality of the pleasure that animated it" (63).

Lewinsky not only complies with the inquisitors' demands, but does them one better; she *wants* her orgasms on record. When asked, "Did he bring you to orgasm?" Lewinsky would technically only have had to answer in the affirmative, but she says instead, "Yes, four times" (Kuntz 1998, 330). She stresses the "mutuality" of her sexual encounters with the president. She says, "It was mutual . . . I mean, it was in the course of being intimate. I mean, it was the course of having this kind of a relationship—sometimes he initiated it, sometimes I initiated it" (320). And again, "When we were together, it was fun. We would laugh and it would—we were very compatible sexually. I've always felt that he was sort of my sexual soulmate" (316). Lewinsky stresses the affectionate nature of these encounters, saying, "We were very affectionate . . . you know, we'd hug each other a lot. You know, he always used to like to stroke my hair. He—we'd hold hands. We'd smile a lot. We discussed a variety—you know, a wide variety of things" (276). We know, we know, we know. We know because these are the things that the shopkeeper tells us make heterosexual couples porn sell. We know because this is what contemporary porn industry understands straight women to want. But in addition to reciting many conventions of couples porn, Lewinsky's testimony challenges others.

In her history of the money shot, Williams discusses the historic significance of the film *Deep Throat* (dir. Gerard Damiano, 1972) and its implications for the gender politics worked out in the then newly emerging couples market. Williams writes, "for all its silliness and obvious misogyny, this movie attempts to perceive the different 'truth' of women's pleasure in ways unparalleled in previous film pornography" (1989, 110). And she suggests, via the theory of Luce Irigaray, that the film "represents a phallic economy's highly ambivalent and contradictory attempt to count beyond the number one, to recognize, as the proliferating discourses of sexuality take hold, that there can no longer be any such thing as a fixed sexuality—male, female, or otherwise—that now there are a proliferation of sexualities" (114). In her discussion of a sequel to *Deep Throat, Throat—Twelve Years After* (dir. Gerard Damiano, 1984), Williams says, "The one thing women in this film clearly do not want is fellatio followed by a money shot" (234), which Williams caricatures as "a penis in close-up ejaculating all over a woman's face and the woman acting like the semen is a gift from the gods" (231).

Lewinsky describes many scenes in which she fellates the president. And she describes many times her ongoing desire to have him "come to completion." When he does, she famously forgets to wash the drops of semen from her dress, almost as though the semen were, after all, a gift from the gods—to her. She is very active in her efforts to represent these scenes of fellatio in a way faithful to her experience of desire. She is asked, "Did you perform oral sex while he was on the telephone?" and she answers, "Yes. It was, it was — I think I'll just say, because for — there are a lot of people that could interpret that as being sort of a, that being done in a servicing sort of manner, and it was more done in a kind of an exciting sort of — I don't want to say erotic, but in a way that there was a kind of this titillating" (Kuntz 1998, 325). If Freud was right when he said that the unconscious holds no negatives, then Lewinsky does want to say erotic. In fact, she rewrites the history of heterosexual fellatio, suggesting, I assert, that the couples market jury is still out on the desirability and erotic politics of this scene.

Monica Lewinsky thinks she is professing her love for Bill Clinton, her good intentions, her patriotism. She thinks she is protesting the slander to which she has been subjected, the ill-treatment she has suffered at the hands of friends, lovers, the inquisitors, and the paparazzi, the terrible misunderstandings that have proliferated all around her. She wants to set the record straight. She wants to cooperate. She wants to believe. And so when the foreperson, on behalf of the investigators and the jury who have detained and questioned her for hours and days about anything their curiosities dictated, bestows on her "forgiveness" and flowers representing "a bouquet of good wishes that includes luck, success, happiness, and blessings," Monica cries and gushes, "Thank you. I appreciate all of your understanding for this situation and your — your ability to open your heart and your mind and your soul" (303). It was, of course, Lewinsky herself who did all the opening, but perhaps she did indeed open up more than the grand jurors had bargained for.

Strange Bedfellows

Has this discussion exhausted the list of conflicting desires inscribed in the *Starr Report*, the shapes it takes, or the fantasy audiences it engages? Certainly not. The forced/irrepressible speech of Monica Lewinsky tells at least two stories at the same time, one organized according to the logics of romance and repression, the other around an on/scene relationship to raunch. She says in the same breath (regarding the semen-stained dress Starr wants to cast under the sign of the scarlet letter), "It's a work dress. It's a casual dress." Casual work indeed! Clinton tells her at one point that if he gets elected for a second term, she can have any job she wants in the White House, and she quips "Well, can I be Assistant to the President for Blow Jobs?" Clinton allows, "I'd like that" (qtd. in Malti-Douglas 2000, 150).

But neither is what Clinton "likes" singular or simply heteronormative —

despite his lawyer, Robert Bennett's, assertion on CBS's *Face of the Nation* that according to a consulting urologist, "in terms of size, shape, direction, whatever the devious mind can concoct, the president is a normal man" (qtd. in Davis 2001, 96). Is the cigar Clinton fucks Lewinsky with really a cigar? If not, what are we to make of his subsequently putting it into his own mouth? On the other hand, if it is, does that liberate dildos from their undignified classification as fake penises? Might the very variability of things one can fuck and be fucked with be exciting in itself? And might the prospect of sucking these fucking things exercise its own appeal across the sexes?

Dana Nelson and Tyler Curtain assert that "something about the Clinton-Lewinsky relationship is definitely queer" (2001, 41). They celebrate their sex as sodomy and remind us that "one sexual act [in which Clinton and Lewinsky engaged] never made it to the surface of Starr's report: rimming." They continue, "Rimming, the licking or nibbling of the butt hole of one person by another, antiseptically referred to by Starr as 'oral/anal' contact, was never included in the body of the report, but lurked in multiple footnotes of the congressional reports" (46). Other commentators pick up on alternate fragments as fodder. Malti-Douglas likes the image of Clinton's secretary, Betty Currie, hiding under her very own bed the box of gifts Clinton bestowed on Lewinsky and suggests that the three constitute a ménage à trois.[11] She also identifies and analyzes the phone sex theme. She discusses the sexually explicit telephone conversations between Lewinsky and Clinton, but also draws out the implications of the telephone conversation Clinton is said to have had with Dick Morris while he, Clinton, was having sex with Lewinsky and Morris was "involved with a prostitute at the Jefferson Hotel," a scene that brings us to—*quatre!*[12]

Clearly, the count goes on. Starr himself exclaims, "I love the narrative!" (qtd. in Malti-Douglas 2000, 125). Foucault anticipated this affection, and described "the pleasure that comes of exercising a power that questions, monitors, watches, spies, searches out, palpates, brings to light; and on the other hand, the pleasure that kindles at having to evade this power, flee from it, fool it, or travesty it. The power that lets itself be invaded by the pleasure it is pursuing; and opposite it, power asserting itself in the pleasure of showing off, scandalizing, or resisting" (1978, 45). These mutually productive pleasures and powers proliferate in and around the *Starr Report*, making of it the very monstrosity Starr sought to expel. The impeachment notwithstanding, as an instrument for the reproduction of heteronormativity the *Report* failed.

With respect to coitus, the emblematic sex act of heteronormativity, Lewinsky says that she and Clinton tried it (albeit not in missionary position proper—they approached it standing up), but "it didn't really work" (qtd. in Malti-Douglas 2000, 153). Nor does it, as Freud intimated already in *Three Essays on the Theory of Sexuality*, do it for most of us. He writes, in a wonderfully on/scene moment of his own:

> By demonstrating the part played by perverse impulses in the formation of symptoms in the psychoneuroses, we have quite remarkably increased the number of people who might be regarded as perverts. It is not only that neurotics in themselves constitute a very numerous class, but it must be considered that an unbroken chain bridges the gap between the neuroses in all their manifestations and normality. . . . Thus the extraordinarily wide dissemination of the perversions forces us to suppose that the disposition to perversion is itself no great rarity but must form a part of what passes as the normal constitution. ([1905] 1953, 171)

At the dawn of the twentieth century, then, Freud posited a bridge spanning the imagined gap between normativity and perversion. Clinton also, of course, envisioned a bridge at the turn of his century and wished to lead the nation across it. It appears, however, that both the great divides and the connective possibilities are more multiple than this vision admitted, and we all cross our bridges when we come to them.

Notes

Many thanks to Linda Williams, Shannon Jackson, and Robin Silverman for helping me think through not only how to approach this material but why.

1   Throughout this chapter I work from Kuntz 1998, referring to it parenthetically as *Report*.

2   Jackson cautions that this relationship, although productive, is a "vexed" one that has been characterized by "tension and obfuscation" along with collaboration and insight.

3   NBC evening news, December 14, 1998.

4   Kuntz, 1998, 140. See Malti-Douglas's (2000) discussion of the stain in her chapter "Fall into the Gap," especially 109–11.

5   Lear delivered this talk at the San Francisco Psychoanalytic Institute. It was printed on September 28, 1998, under the title "Freudian Slip" in the *New Republic*, but unfortunately the *Kojak* anecdote was excised from the printed version.

6   See, for example, Berlant and Duggan 2001, 97.

7   For a discussion of the symbolism of the Clinton-Lewinsky affair in terms of the gender-bending that can be seen to operate in their pairing, see Nelson and Cur-

tain 2001. They write, for example, "Clinton's soft body is never quite masculine enough, just as Monica's soft white body is never quite feminine enough when it makes its claims on power" (46).

8 See Davis's discussion of *Deep Throat V* (2001, 91–94).

9 NBC evening news, December 14, 1998.

10 One of the rumors circulating about Clinton when he initially came into office maintained that he was an expert performer of cunnilingus. Minette Lehman took up this rumor in her performance *The Tongue* (1993), which played with the meanings of orality in a phallocentric political system.

11 See Malti-Douglas 2000, the chapter entitled "The Great Facilitator; or, How to 'Currie' Favor," esp. 74.

12 On phone sex, see Malti-Douglas 2000, 90–91 and 170–71. The Jefferson Hotel incident is discussed on 49–50.

Works Cited

Austin, J. L. 1962. *How to Do Things with Words*. Cambridge, Mass.: Harvard University Press.

Berlant, Lauren, and Lisa Duggan, eds. 2001. *Our Monica, Ourselves: The Clinton Affair and the National Interest*. New York: New York University Press.

Davis, Simone. 2001. "The Door Ajar: The Erotics of Hypocrisy in the White House Scandal." In *Our Monica Ourselves: The Clinton Affair and the National Interest*, ed. Lauren Berlant and Lisa Duggan. New York: New York University Press. 86–101.

Dershowitz, Alan. 1998. *Sexual McCarthyism*. New York: Basic Books.

Faludi, Susan. 1995. "The Money Shot." *New Yorker*, October 30, 64–87.

Fineman, Howard. 1998. "A Crisis at Home." *Newsweek*, December 21, 22–27.

Foucault, Michel. 1978. *The History of Sexuality: An Introduction*. Trans. Robert Hurley. Vol. 1. New York: Vintage.

Freud, Sigmund. [1905] 1953. "Three Essays on the Theory of Sexuality." In *The Standard Edition of the Complete Psychological Works of Sigmund Freud*. Trans. James Strachey. Vol. 7. London: Hogarth. 123–245.

———. [1927] 1961. "Fetishism." In *The Standard Edition of the Complete Psychological Works of Sigmund Freud*. Trans. James Strachey. Vol. 21. London: Hogarth. 149–57.

Hunt, Lynn, ed. 1996a. *The Invention of Pornography: Obscenity and the Origins of Modernity, 1500–1800*. New York: Zone Books.

Hunt, Lynn, 1996b. "Pornography and the French Revolution." In *The Invention of Pornography: Obscenity and the Origins of Modernity, 1500–1800*. Ed. Lynn Hunt. New York: Zone. Cambridge: Cambridge University Press. 301–339.

Jackson, Shannon. Forthcoming. *Professing Performance*.

Kendrick, Walter. 1987. *The Secret Museum: Pornography in Modern Culture*. Berkeley: University of California Press.

Kuntz, Phil, ed. 1998. *The Starr Report: The Starr Evidence*. New York: Pocket Books.

Malti-Douglas, Fedwa. 2000. *The Starr Report Disrobed*. New York: Columbia University Press.

Nelson, Dana, and Tyler Curtain. 2001. "The Symbolics of Presidentialism: Sex and Democratic Identification." In *Our Monica, Ourselves: The Clinton Affair and the National Interest*, ed. Lauren Berlant and Lisa Duggan. New York: New York University Press. 34–52.

Ogilvie, Lloyd John. 1999. *Opening Prayers: Impeachment Trial of the President of the United States January 7–February 12, 1999*. United States Senate document S. Pub. 106–18. United States Senate.

Parker, Andrew, and Eve Sedgwick, eds. 1995. *Performativity and Performance*. New York: Routledge.

Ross, Andrew. 1989. "The Popularity of Pornography." In *No Respect: Intellectuals and Popular Culture*. New York: Routledge. 171–208.

Torres, Sasha. 2001. "Sex of a Kind: On Graphic Language and the Modesty of Television News." In *Our Monica, Ourselves: The Clinton Affair and the National Interest*, ed. Lauren Berlant and Lisa Duggan. New York: New York University Press. 102–15.

Williams, Linda. 1989. *Hard Core: Power, Pleasure, and the "Frenzy of the Visible."* Berkeley: University of California Press.

Sex in the Suburban: Porn, Home Movies, and the Live Action Performance of Love in *Pam and Tommy Lee: Hardcore and Uncensored*

MINETTE HILLYER

As usual, I brought along my video camera. We weren't trying to make a porno, just to document our vacation. We watched it once when we returned home, then put it in our safe, a 500-pound monstrosity hidden beneath a carpet in my studio control room in the garage.

—Tommy Lee

✳ Probably the most explicit point of communion between pornography and the home movie, as ersatz genres of film production, is the promise that they both attempt to reveal the "truth." The idea that technology enables us to create documents of our experiences determines something of our response to watching pornography, much as it motivates our recordings of new babies or family holidays. In part, we could attribute this promise to the two genres' subjects. Both show facsimiles of intimacy and revelation; they seem to ease access to those things most fundamental to our humanity. This is not to propose that pornography, per se, traffics in a transcendental view of sex, or let's say, lovemaking. Nor is it to describe the full reach of porn, which like the home movie, engages complex and varied fantasies even as it sells "reality." Rather, if we see porn as transcendent, this should describe its ability to access live bodies, to get us closer to "real" action than real life allows. While closeness in pornography tends to the elimination of space (we can be closer, with other people), in the home movie we perhaps think of ourselves as eliminating time (we can be younger, or with those who are no longer here.) Given this, it is even possible to imagine that pornography and the home movie together represent a kind of generic idealization of recording technology, approaching what André Bazin described as the "guiding myth" of cinema: "Namely an integral realism, a recreation of the world in its own image, an image unburdened by the freedom of interpretation of the artist or the irreversibility of time" (Bazin 1967, 21). While both genres, as well as the video technology used to create them, call on this reality principle, the principle depends on the promise that these generic and filmic technologies may be erased.

My intention in beginning with this vision of pornographic uplift is not to suggest, however, that the genre of pornography represents the idealization of, and thus escape from, the so-called cinematic. If nothing else, pornography—like the home movie—itself proves too ambiguously cinematic to allow for this type of characterization.[1] Neither mode of production is easily separable from myriad other cultural products; similarly, their claim to "document" serves only to distance them from what is typically perceived as cinema, and to muddy the limits of their generic definitions. Meanwhile, this shared guiding myth no doubt serves as a perverse reminder that the two genres are often taken as radically incompatible—both in their social purpose and in their circulation as cultural products. Tommy Lee's description of his vacation tape in the quote above names it as "not porn," precisely due to the fact that it was a "home movie" (qtd. in Strauss 2001, 61). Nonetheless, the footage he describes, circulated as pornography, reportedly became the most watched home movie in recent history.[2] The tape's generic and technical markers—its cinematic qualities—then prove fundamental to determining and delimiting its cultural and social life. How do we account for the generic slippage or transformation—the "porning"—that this footage seems to undergo in its passage from the safe in the garage to hundreds of thousands of video stores and Web sites? What are the characteristics that inhere to the pornographic, as opposed to the domestic, and where do they occur? How do we negotiate the hierarchies of genre, spectatorship, and even "truth" engaged when these two different cultural products, with very different social lives, are conflated?

The Pamela Anderson/Tommy Lee sex tape, which began life as a home movie, happily—perhaps even effortlessly—contains all these questions. *Pam and Tommy Lee: Hardcore and Uncensored* (IEG, 1997) was released about a year after the couple's vacation tapes were stolen from their home safe in the second year of their marriage. It achieved immediate notoriety, in part because of the extremely public lives of its stars, the lead actress on *Baywatch*

and the drummer from Mötley Crüe. In addition to this, a barrage of publicity preceded the release, including the publication of stills in *Penthouse*
and on the Internet, legal action brought by the couple seeking to prevent
release of the material, and their discussion of the tape on the *Howard Stern
Show*. The tape is approximately fifty-four minutes long, only eight of which
show explicit sex. The remainder is padded out with the types of subjects and
images familiar from many amateur videos: the display of possessions and
people, the recording of holidays and unusual events. While the ratio of footage tends heavily toward the domestic, in the universe described by its movements, the domestic and the pornographic seem to work in partnership. The
tape's domestic credentials serve both to establish its authenticity—in an
environment populated by fake celebrity sightings and computer-generated
imagery—and to add an extra charge to its pornographic appeal.[3]

Nonetheless, viewed in its entirety, *Pam and Tommy* provokes a curious
mixture of boredom and titillation; or perhaps more precisely, a mixture of
boredom and titillation inflected in a different manner than that usual to the
experience of watching pornography.[4] Any exposure to publicity for the tape
ensures, given its slim quotient of hard-core pornographic action, that what
is pornographic in it is already familiar.[5] The tape's style and content plays on
a similar type of cozy recognition; its tone seems deliberately amateurish,
as though this were a quality as much of aesthetics as of its "genuinely" amateur creation. The narrative is divided and explained with intertitles naming
the location or situation in which the sequence was shot. In addition, a heavy
music track accompanies the sex scenes; a quasi–hard rock riff played on
guitars and synthesizer, perhaps meant to evoke the rock star personae of
its protagonists and also used in previews before the "main action." Other
than this, there is little immediate evidence of the distributing company's
hand in what could be described as the manipulation, or professionaliza-
tion, of the footage. Most particularly, this laissez-faire quality makes itself
felt in the narrative, which is sequential and opportunistic; it drifts through
days pitted with personal but ultimately inconsequential events. As such,
it resembles a classical home movie, if such a thing exists.[6] Although the
tape opens with shots of Pam at work on the set of her film *Barb Wire* (dir.
David Hogan, 1996), and a brief sequence shows Tommy rehearsing with
his band, the majority of the footage is of the couple relaxing. The longest
single narrative sequence shows their "first holiday": a four-day boat trip on
Lake Mead in Southern California, in which intertitles, but little else, distinguish the days. This section contains the most extended and most explicit
sexual scenes on the tape, including penetrative sex, masturbation, fellatio,

and frequent shots of the two naked. It is noteworthy that the sex shown in this part of the tape is the only sex taken to "completion," or climax, at least on Tommy's part. It also contains perhaps the most mundanely domestic imagery: a lengthy sequence shows Tommy fishing, and the couple also affirm their status as amateur enthusiasts by playing with an orange filter over the camera lens, again for an extended period.

For people watching the tape, these domestic sequences can prove frustrating. What type of pornographic pleasure could possibly derive from, for example, the couple's experiments with (video) technique? It is possible that one motivation for including this type of footage on the tape is the creation of a viable pornographic video product, the purchase of which guarantees some extra pleasure besides that provided by looking at pictures on the Internet. In this sense, the domestic really does function as padding to a more primary pornographic project. More compelling than this is the sense that the domestic features of the tape serve to cement the pornographic by providing an experience of a truly "integral realism." We know this tape (*Pam and Tommy Lee: Hardcore and Uncensored*) to be the genuine article in part because of the mundanity of some of its content. The effect that I mean to describe is a phenomenal one; that is, it is the reference back to the whole object of the original home movies, deposited in the safe, which guarantees authenticity. Accordingly, on-line references to the footage are very often couched in descriptions of "The Tape"—the "stolen video" (www.pamela-tommy-movie.com), "porn video" (www.clickheresex.com) or "Pamela Honeymoon video" (www.pam-tommy-video.com)—whether or not the sites are trading in a tape at all. In addition to the promise of liveness suggested by streaming video in this environment, video then also acts as shorthand for some original, authentic object; specifically, for the home movie this pornographic video purports to reproduce. Likewise, the pornographic tape, by retaining and even reemphasizing qualities of amateurism, suggests the possibility of our privileged entrance into a truly private sphere. The bad camera work and the boring stories the tape tells serve, in this way, to remind us that one or other of the two celebrities is always behind the camera; that—as we might like to imagine with other pornography—this time it really is just them, and us.

The (personal) charge that this intersection between the pornographic and the domestic provides thus also raises complicated questions about the public life of such private footage. That the couple sued IEG (Internet Entertainment Group), the company distributing the tape, for the amount of 90 million dollars, albeit unsuccessfully, gives some measure of such questions' legal and commercial significance. There are also significant and, to my mind, more interesting questions of culture at stake. While celebrity stalking through the visual media holds a certain fascination in and of itself, this alliance of the pornographic and domestic lives of a *Playboy* model and a rock star offers a mother lode of cultural possibilities. There is certainly something invasive, perhaps even something pornographic, in our contemporary access to the private lives of media celebrities. However, these particular celebrities can seem to play out their public lives, even in the names we attach to them ("*Playboy* model," "rock star"), as if they were characters in a pornographic movie. At the same time, the tape wields the fascinating promise of showing us that celebrities make home movies too. While the footage first circulated, following its theft from the couple's safe, as sexually explicit still images in *Penthouse* and then on the IEG "Club Love" Web site, as a video (*Pam and Tommy Lee: Hardcore and Uncensored*) its generic definition as pornography proves imprecise. The footage that cushions and surrounds the explicitly sexual content, and that makes up the bulk of the tape, marks it much more securely as a home movie of a type that anyone, some details of setting and behavior aside, could make.[7] In all its aspects— in what and who it represents, as well as how it represents them, in its circulation as a (discrete) cultural product, as well as in its generic transgressions and links to other cultural forms—the tape thus provides a rich opportunity to look at these "contaminated" modes of filmmaking and their broader social importance.

What Is a Porn Star?

I couldn't see the big deal: It's really just our vacation tape. There's only a little bit of fucking on there. That hasn't stopped Ron Jeremy, though, from trying to get me to make a fuck flick for him. I guess if my career ever fails as a musician, I can always be a porn star.
—Tommy Lee

Probably the clearest, or most encompassing, precedent for the tape is the subgenre of amateur porn, the conventionalized encounter between the pornographic and the domestic. Some theorists and spectators have argued that amateur pornography provides a psychologically truer, more intimate picture of the sex act than other types of porn; it is hard not to attribute this to its association with the authentic experiential load of the home movie.

As Patricia Zimmerman notes in her history of amateur film, amateurism, socially and historically, has generally functioned to safeguard and define the rationalization of the public sphere as something apart from our private lives: to deflect "the chaotic, the incoherent, and the spontaneous into leisure and private life so that public time could persist as methodical, controllable, and regulated" (1995, 11). As a consequence, the culture of amateurism, even as it "operates almost exclusively as consumption" (3), is defined in reaction to the organizing structures of capitalist production; it "materializes as a cultural reservoir for the liberal pluralist ideals of freedom, competition, fluidity among classes, upward mobility, and inalienable and creative labor—social relations dislodged from the economic by scientism, the division of labor, and the cult of expertise" (5). Amateur porn performers, according to this standard, should seem to be doing it for love; or, at least not for money. In particular, that their labor remains "inalienable" suggests that while we may see the amateurs striving, their work should appear natural or "spontaneous" as a consequence of their own enthusiasm or impulses, rather than the mechanical fulfillment of a task or role.

Hence, Bill Nichols, Christian Hansen, and Catherine Needham, for example, assert that amateur porn performers can achieve a degree of absorption in their own pleasure that liberates them from the alienating effects of representation. Essentially, they propose a different kind of relationship between performer and spectator than that in which those watching are radically other to those having sex. Even if strangers do eventually view the tapes, their argument suggests that the amateurism of this type of porn lies in somehow "keeping it in the family." This implies, in turn, the greater spontaneity of amateur porn performance, even its greater "naturalness"; the performers are "lost to the ideal spectator when they no longer tacitly arrange themselves as if at the behest of an invisible, orchestrating presence" (Nichols, Hansen, and Needham 1991, 226). If they perform for anyone, they suggest, they perform for a community of like-minded "participant-producers," couples all (227). The scenario which they propose, and which, they add, is "still dystopic" (227), seems based on a determination to vacate the position of "ideal" spectatorship, with all its implications of mastery over the gaze and "selfish" pleasures—and thus shift the emphasis from pornographic "spectacle," to "personal pleasure" (226), from representation back to the "truth" of the act itself.

Likewise, Peter Lehman, a more porn-friendly writer than Nichols, argues that if amateur video porn is not more "truthful" (in fact, he argues for its fictional qualities), it is nonetheless closer to a document than theatrical feature porn (1999, 359). By asserting that, even in narrative porn, "when the fucking starts" characterization "falls by the way," he suggests that a quality of the sexual act per se is the possibility for self-absorption and thus liberation from the cinematic (362). His subject, the "video porn *auteur*" Ed Powers, plays with this promise of authenticity by playing the role of "pro" to the "amateur" women he fucks. Both the titles of his tapes (for example, the *Dirty Debutantes* series) and certain of Powers's characteristic techniques (such as interviewing the women, or choosing women with "normal" breast size and bodies) convey the impression of amateurism (363). As Lehman notes, the documentary notion of authenticity in this context proves illusory; Powers's so-called debutantes are engaged in the performance of sex, just as the professionals are. Nonetheless, Lehman wishes to distinguish this "less developed" form from other, more cinematic pornography. Thus he argues that the psychological interaction that he notes in Powers's porn finds expression in an appropriateness of the generic image itself; that "we need to consider the less developed video forms as *moving porn back into a format* which is more closely aligned with many of its heterogeneous and fleeting pleasures" (361; italics mine).[8] In addition to this, the distinction he identifies between amateur and professional pornographic performance is one not based in the image but back in the "real world." As he concludes, the so-called amateurs do not "fuck like they do in their real lives"; he describes the imperative placed on female performers, in particular, to "look into the cameras, throw back their heads, pull back their hair, moan and groan, etc., in a way they think will turn men on and perhaps enable them to use this as a springboard to become 'pros'" (363–64).[9] This does not, however, offer an analysis that questions the categories of *amateur* and *professional* as much as it suggests, finally, that the women perform their amateurism. The promise of authenticity thus still haunts, and even enables, this analysis: somewhere, presumably in their real lives, people *are* having sex "like amateurs"—chaotically, incoherently, and certainly spontaneously. If the performance of sex provides an indicator of professionalism, then certainly the professional's oeuvre must be made up of the "number." By the same token, the specter of a professional performance of sex must be matched by something like an amateur experience of it. Thus the number meets up with just sex.

Perhaps a clearer example of the subgenre of amateur porn than Pam and Tommy's relatively glamorous tape is the tape known as *Tonya and Jeff's*

Wedding Night (1994), a video first sold to television by ex-Olympic figure skater Tonya Harding's ex, Jeff.[10] The tapes have in common the celebrity of their protagonists, as well as the violation implied in their public exposure. Much as Pam and Tommy's tape was stolen, Tonya was exposed to the public by her ex-husband. However, they differ in certain, significant ways. *Tonya and Jeff's Wedding Night* really does appear to take place on the night of their wedding, if only because it tells what could be described as the classical wedding-night narrative, which unrolls from the removal of the wedding gown, to the bedroom, to the postcoital slump.[11] The pornographic nature of the images differs markedly from those in *Pam and Tommy*: the majority of the tape consists of a single sex scene lasting approximately twenty minutes, framed in long and medium-long shot in two takes and set in a bedroom that appears to be either the couple's own or an unremarkable hotel room. In the version I watched, there was no extradiegetic music, or other added effects, and the quality is, in fact, generally worse than Pam and Tommy's tape, which had the advantage, known to all amateur enthusiasts, of being largely shot outdoors. Tonya and Jeff's tape is shot in fairly low light, and the soundtrack cuts in and out unexpectedly. Most relevantly, the nature of the couples' performances to camera differs markedly. While Pam or Tommy always hold the camera, after Tonya's initial striptease, during which Jeff introduces the notion of setting the camera up by the bed, these two place the camera on a tripod or similar surface and allow it to record them apparently uninterrupted.[12] Moreover, this tape contains more digressive talk during the sex act—either referring to the recording apparatus itself ("Are you sure it's not out of tape?") or to the domestic setting (the phone rings and momentarily interrupts them as they listen to the machine pick up.) Finally, the protagonists' bodies and the manner of their display appear more amateur (following Peter Lehman's description) than Pam or Tommy's; we do not get a very clear view of Jeff's penis, and Tonya's breasts are decidedly of a more "normal" size than Pam's.

The overall effect is that this tape in most ways seems more amateur than *Pam and Tommy*. While we know Jeff and Tonya to be celebrities in their lives outside the tape (well enough, in fact, to assume a first name basis), nothing in their behavior on tape marks them as such. Nor are they clearly marked as professional in their performance of sex. While *Pam and Tommy* offers greater visibility (more frontal displays, close-ups of penetration and oral sex), we apparently get to watch Tonya and Jeff having sex from beginning to end; as opposed to staging poses for the camera, it looks like they are really "doing it." In certain ways, they mimic the conventions of the porno-graphic display. They are certainly conscious of the camera's presence, albeit to varying degrees and at varying times, and they do stage certain actions for the camera: for example, they move it for a better shot, and Tonya displays the semen on her hand directly to camera after Jeff comes outside her. Even this scene, however, in no way resembles the "cum shot"' counterpart in Pam and Tommy's tape because we do not get to see Jeff come. All of this does suggest a degree of absorption in the sex act that could be described as amateur. Finally, however, it is perhaps the moments in which the recording camera is foregrounded that appear the most authentically nonprofessional; the suggestion that they record sex and subsequent setting-up of the camera, the display of Tonya's hand (and extra visual "proof" of sex), and most em-phatically, Tonya—dressed in jeans, postsex—shooting her husband watch-ing TV and then grinning delightedly directly into the lens before she passes out of shot to turn the camera off.

Pam and Tommy's amateurism, meanwhile, proves more difficult to pin down. Certainly, there are indications, most pronounced in the last and lengthiest sex scene in which Tommy comes on Pam's stomach, that they are performing sex for the camera. There seems to be no reason to suggest that this equates with a lack of sincerity on their part or, indeed, a desire to move on to careers as pros, though, as Tommy notes, the door is appar-ently always open (Strauss 2001, 61). It is conceivable that the presence of recording technology opened up a kind of pleasure in self-reflexivity; much as Richard Dyer has described the potential for users of porn to experience the "charge of cameras, crew, and me in attendance" (1994, 50), Pam and Tommy may get off at the sense of being spectators to their own sex. Their celebrity, however, adds an extra layer of reflexivity both to their own plea-sure, imagined in this way, and to that of other spectators. Chuck Kleinhans has suggested that "a plausible case could be made that although the couple had the obligation to sue to prevent distribution of the tape, the resulting publicity in fact was beneficial to their careers" (2001, 292). This may well be true. More interesting than their possible exploitation of this opportu-nity for publicity is the way in which their appearance performing sex might intersect with their other, "legitimate" performance careers. Again, I have no particular interest in the ways in which their careers already trafficked in sexual imagery, that is, it is not my intention to argue that it is a short step from the cover of *Playboy* to the cover of a porn video (although this is no doubt sometimes the case). However, it is worth noting the degree to which their legitimate work, in particular Pam's, was engaged, like porn, in the disciplining and display of the body. Likewise, Tommy's work, which he describes in *Rolling Stone* as responding to the need for attention of the little child within him (Strauss 2001, 62), originated in a degree of exhibitionism unusual even for a rock star.[13]

Most interesting about this is what it suggests about their relationship to the filmic image. For both Pam and Tommy it must, at some level, connote work. This is the fascination of knowing that celebrities make home movies: not that they have access to the same technology or the same repertoire of clichés as the rest of us, and only to some extent that they indulge in the same type of behavior. Most particularly, we are fascinated because we already know them by and as images. The first scenes on the tape, which show Pam on the set of her film *Barb Wire*, recall the hours of labor that go into creating and refining the celebrity body: all the shots we see of her working show her in hair and makeup. If this does not sound like work, neither, as Michael Sicinski notes elsewhere in this volume, does having sex. Our potential to forget the labor in this type of work is premised on just the type of reasoning that holds that "real people" can forget themselves in sex. The binaries line up, with the liberatory promise of the sex act, on one hand, and the repressive force of its representation, on the other. To argue that to represent sex truthfully implies an escape from representation is to suggest that the sex act constitutes a repository for genuine experience. Moreover, it is to deny any relations of power—any relations that could be described as social and not merely as human—in sexual relations in general.

What seems poignant, or perhaps even exploitative, about Pam and Tommy's tape, then, is the fact that their leisure, through a reinvestment and recitation of the image, transforms into work. While home movies, for the rest of us, serve to capture or create moments of celebrity, real celebrity, which is always only of the moment, easily becomes exploited by a reassignment of roles. The roles that Pam and Tommy were playing on ("our first") holiday are ones that according to some notions of common sense and, indeed, propriety, should rid this footage of the taint of the pornographic. As Chuck Kleinhans concludes his essay, flush with (their) married love:

> That the tape was stolen provides an excuse. That she was having sex with her husband is also a pardon. In fact, the overall effect of the entire tape is—counterintuitively—not a highlighting of the sensational parts, but a placing of newlywed sex in the context of love, affection, enthusiasm, mutual playfulness, and exploration. Two healthy people in a healthy re-

lationship. Tommy and Pamela are endlessly professing their love, clearly passionate, and devoted—exactly what is left out of pornography. (2001, 297–98)[14]

What he is pardoning, exactly, remains unclear, unless it is precisely the taint of the pornographic that attaches itself to this tape in its public circulation. As "devoted newlyweds," Pam and Tommy, like Jeff and Tonya, are not only allowed to have sex, they are publicly sanctioned to do so. In occupying this position of sexual and social power, their sex thus seems to escape the seeming untruths of representation and the "unnatural" contortions of the pornographic. In more ways than one, they represent an American success story.

If read in this way, the two tapes resemble another subgenre of the pornographic, couple's porn, which, as Heather Butler notes elsewhere in this volume, can seem to take on the role of educating its consumers about better sex, rather than simply indulging their fantasies.[15] Granted, couple's porn most typically refers to the porn's intended context of reception by (heterosexual) couples, something difficult to infer from the content of Pam and Tommy's tape. Regardless of denomination, however, the reception suggested above of these images showing couples and those intended for couples do share an important characteristic, namely, the attempt to resignify, (and therefore neutralize) pornographic imagery by its deployment in scenarios of romance.[16] By this standard, newlywed sex, in being "not pornographic," demands privacy. Lauren Berlant writes that the type of sex Kleinhans describes demarcates the one sexual "zone of privacy" in America; zone of privacy referring, here, to the literal space of a married couple's bedroom (1995, 382). Persons engaged in such sex are, therefore, engaged in the practice of "national heterosexuality": "Insofar as an American thinks that the sex she or he is having is an intimate, private thing constructed within a space governed by personal consent, she or he is having straight sex, straight sex authorized by national culture" (401). The invasion, or appropriation, of their leisure also suggests, in this configuration of social identity, that Pam and Tommy—practicing national heterosexuality—may have been having sex in public, but were invaded at home.

What Is Pornographic? Or, "See Pam Suck Tommy's Cock!"

Then, the judge in our video case shut Pamela and me down on every privacy issue and allowed the sale of the tape because he ruled that the content was newsworthy. It pissed me off because I don't ever want my kids to go to a friend's house and find a video of their parents fucking.

—Tommy Lee

In the first instance, the process of identifying this tape as "pornographic" must then rely on its marketing as such, both the most immediate and the most pervasive sign of its public presence. Nonetheless, an argument can be made for the pornographic nature of the footage itself. Those parts of the tape that do depict sexual behavior clearly meet the "prurient interest" test for obscenity based on "contemporary community standards" which Justice Brennan established in *Roth v. United States* in 1957 and which remains effective today.[17] Likewise, the fact that the bulk of the footage does not deal with sex in anything other than, at best, an anticipatory way, does not necessarily imply that the dominant theme of the material is not sexual. While the paucity of actual hard-core sexual action (again, eight minutes out of fifty-four) seems to confuse its generic definition, one could also argue that as a whole, the tape solicits and successfully provokes prurient interest in the more prominent domestic material via its intra- and extratextual associations with sex. At the time of making the tape, and its later release as pornography, Pamela Anderson was the lead actress on *Baywatch*, a television series mythologized for its almost complete disregard of narrative and characterization, or more precisely, for its frequent shots of swimsuit-clad lifeguards running in slow motion to the rescue of—well, *why* they ran wasn't ever very important. In the months after their wedding (Pam wore a white bikini), she was photographed lying naked on top of her bare-chested husband, himself well known for graphic sexual behavior as part of the glam metal band Mötley Crüe.[18] Pam's celebrity, from the date of her discovery at a football game in Canada, rose and fell (and still rises and falls) on her breasts. Given this, it is possible to argue that, applying contemporary community standards of the time, almost anything containing Pamela Anderson's image, and to a lesser extent that of her husband, appealed to prurient interest.

Nonetheless, its actual content tends to sully the tape's pornographic credentials. Expecting porn, it can prove disconcerting to discover just how little sex there is. If we resort to seeking the pornographic as a quality or characteristic of the stars themselves, would contemporary community standards recognize *Pam and Tommy*, the tape, as a discrete, distinctive pornographic object? Is this to suggest, moreover, that a life, or at least, a public life, can be pornographic? The definition of the tape is then also taxed, or at least confused, by the change it should apparently accommodate over time.

In this, the couple's own response to the tape as an object proves helpful. While they protested that they merely intended to document their vacation, their behavior after the fact—locking their footage away in a "monstrous" safe, in the garage and underground, no less—indicates that they recognized its illicit, off-scene qualities. In this, perhaps appropriately, their actions recall another, earlier definition of obscenity, the so-called Hicklin test, which held that the public circulation of obscene materials should be prohibited because of the damage such materials could cause to the "hitherto pure" mind of a putative "young person."[19] The tape is riddled with references to the family the two hope—in front of our expectant eyes—to start. In one of the first scenes of graphic sexual display, when the two ride in their Suburban truck on the highway going on holiday, Pam gives Tommy a blow job. Waving his penis in front of the lens, she says, "I get this for the rest of my life! Look kids! Mom is a happy camper!" before she laughs, saying "Oh!—I guess we're not going to show our kids this bit."

The recognition that this tape will be locked away, that it is "obscene," thus takes the form of an attempt to protect a truly putative young person—the couple's as yet unborn child. In this case, the "hitherto" pure mind has yet to reach consciousness. While the Hicklin test seems to propose a temporal progression—from an original, unsullied mind (a mind in a kind of state of grace) to its later corruption—this fact demonstrates the difficulty of locating stable moments before and after exposure. Much as it is impossible to claim that the tape has simply changed over time from being, in essence, a home movie to a porno, it is difficult to imagine, under these circumstances, a context for reception that is always already pure. The moment when the tape is most thoroughly enmeshed in the discourses of domesticity (even the couple's truck is (a) Suburban) is also the moment of pornography.

Finally, putting aside its historical provenance as porn, and its own historical trajectory (that is, the definitional change it undergoes between its conception and its public exposure), the tape is perhaps most emphatically made pornographic by an ahistorical, presentational quality of the image.[20] The pornographic, ultimately, seems to inhere in a kind of bare literalism, in "the act." The promise that we can "See Pam Suck Tommy's Cock" overshadows issues of intention or generic definition. Presumably, like Justice Potter Stewart, whose commonsensical opinion rounds out the triad of judicial dicta that may serve as our best official indicators of what constitutes pornography, we know it when we see it.[21] Web hits for sites displaying the footage of Pam and Tommy typically advertise it as porn in precisely these terms. If they go any further in their descriptions of the material, they tend to list the other sexual acts that you can see by purchasing or signing on. The description may include physical details about the couple (Pamela's "perfectly shaved pussy," Tommy's "huge cock"), but, probably unsurprisingly, will contain no reference to the domestic mundanity of the bulk of the video footage.[22] It is improbable that much of this more domestic imagery is even available on-line. As a consequence, the footage's public identity centers entirely around its pornographic acts, accommodating the literally presentational (Pam's pussy) only where it conforms to what we already know to be obscene.

This is to recall, however, that the home movie stands as perhaps the most hyperbolically presentational of genres. Pam shows us her husband's cock in the manner of any home video enthusiast ("This is my husband!"); likewise her house ("Look baby, this is our house!"); her dogs, and so on. While home videos tend to stage minor narratives, they most often engage in the display of objects, possessions, and acts. It is in this quality of display that the home movie's truth content, or relationship to the real world, makes itself apparent. It is also in quantifiable displays that the generic truths of pornography become most evident. The degree of coincidence between "generic verisimilitude" and "social or cultural verisimilitude" in pornography and the home movie can seem more pronounced than in other film genres since they are both based in the seemingly simple presentation of bodies, engaged in particular activities, before the camera.[23] As a consequence, both genres deserve little credit in the way of "cinematic," (that is, artistic or textual) qualities: they are often categorized as, at most, documentaries, and at least, as a type of behavioristic record. Nonetheless, as textual productions, they must be read, or made intelligible, with regard to other texts. Steve Neale, in his work on American film genres, cites Jonathan Culler's model for verisimilitude, or *vraisemblance*, which allows for ways in which "a text may be brought into contact with and defined in relation to another text which helps make it intelligible." The latter ranges from "the socially given text, that which is taken as the 'real world'" to "the complex *vraisemblance* of specific intertextualities, where one work takes another as its basis or point of departure and must be assimilated in relation to it" (Culler qtd. in Neale 2000, 33). Likewise, the notion of verisimilitude is itself subject to textual pressures. As Christine Gledhill writes: "The conditions of verisimilitude are not static but shift under the polemic of realism, . . . more precisely understood as that modality which makes a claim on the real, in a bid to redefine what counts as reality under pressure from struggles between established and emerging or resisting groups" (2000, 235). This quote proves useful in highlighting the dynamic relationship that generic texts create between textual and social claims to reality: while verisimilitude finds expression via textual norms ("realism"), it expresses, in turn, struggles between groups in the social world.

This analysis, which calls on generic definition as a means to access "society talking to itself" (Gledhill 2000, 238), again raises the possibility of a self-reflexive pleasure involved in viewing this tape (Dyer 1994, 54). In fact, this is something of a given; as my earlier analysis should show, naming, and viewing, the tape as pornography in this case provides a way of smoothing over the potential displeasure of its domestic content. It would be naive to suggest that viewers' pornographic pleasure in the tape genuinely derives from their surprise at "stumbling on" the private sex acts it contains. It nonetheless proves important, in considering the pleasures the tape might offer, to keep this promise of spontaneity in play. Despite a growing body of work that submits pornography to the same type of textual analysis as other film genres, a temptation to assume a greater social truth in porn still persists. This tends to grant the pornographic text a privileged access to reality—a claim to represent presence, or truth, as if for the first time each time, despite our tacit knowledge of the intertextual or generic qualities enabling us to recognize it as porn. It traffics in the pleasure born of this repeated violation. Gledhill's discussion of genre describes this "frisson of the boundary" as a characteristic pleasure of all genres' dual existence between the world of the text and the social world. As she writes: "Boundaries serve not only to separate and contain but also to constitute meeting points, instituting contact between spheres the dominant culture seeks to divide. Definition through differentiation brings new terrain into view. Desire is generated at the boundaries, stimulating border crossings as well as provoking cultural anxieties" (2000, 237). Porn, and amateur porn in particular, is premised as much on this illicit contact as on the illicit contact of its stars. It goes to the heart of pornography's vexed social status that it matters so much to us what may be shown. Thus viewers perceive a kind of circling relationship in the pornographic image between the social text taken for the real world and the intertext of the pornographic. Even as a text is deemed conventionally pornographic, and thus "not real," its "live" display secures its classification as pornography. Peter Lehman's assessment of the hard-core moment of the pornographic text—"What little characterization there is in the porn film quickly falls by the way when the fucking starts; we watch the actors fuck, not their characters"—sums up the complications in this position well (1999, 362). The specter of actors fucking suggests that porn retains one foot securely in a claim to social verisimilitude; indeed, the apparent loss of characterization here could point to a larger aspiration for the text to be taken not in relationship to but as itself the real world. The sexual act thus seems to be supposed to defeat not just characterization but qualities of representation: while we still watch actors, it is potentially unclear that we are watching a film.

Despite the porn film's apparently privileged relationship to reality, it remains unintelligible without reference to conventions found in other filmic texts. In her discussion of pornography as a genre, Linda Williams cites an instructional manual for would-be pornographers, which lists a series of sexual acts, in addition to the so-called money shot "deemed essential to a hard-core feature, circa 1977" (1999, 127). As Williams points out, "the guide is useful because it . . . goes to the heart of the genre's conventionality" (126). More consistently than for perhaps any other film genre, these conventions describe acts. The devices used to (re)present them (I mean here to include film and video technology, as well as narrative and stylistic devices) are, if not elided in the manner of Bazin's realist cinematic myth, made entirely workmanlike in the service of the act. By the same token, the direct presentational qualities delimiting pornographic numbers, so reminiscent of amateur home movies, have been reaffirmed by developments in video technology. If the sexual act was deemed definitive even of the "hard-core feature, circa 1977," the advent of cheap, portable video technology might be said to have enabled a pornographic refinement; a coming home for those pornographic conventions by which the primary demand on the filmic apparatus is that it record or document. This meeting of the domestic and the pornographic, revolving as it does around a principle of truth based primarily in access and visibility, was enabled not only by pornography's literal move into the home but also by a shared investment of the pornographic and the domestic in a different kind of image than that typically found in feature films.[24] As Constance Penley writes, in the eighties and nineties, the camcorder/VHS boom underwrote a wave of new "deliciously trashy" porn, "as producers threw off the 'quality' trappings of the golden era to start manufacturing product for the rapidly expanding VCR market" (1997, 101–2). What amounts to an apparent deprofessionalization of the image also renders the image less cinematic, less subject to artistic conventions, and, by association, apparently more concerned with the presentational act than its representation.

Which returns us to Pam and Tommy, or *Pam and Tommy*. To describe the footage as "the most watched home movie" of its time suggests that its generic classification serves as a function of its mode of production. The tape is a home movie because it was made—geographically, socially, and by virtue of the technology employed—"at home." By the same token, if there exists a moment at which the tape became porn, it was at that of its distribution and public display. The couple's practice of locking their tape away recalls not only the Hicklin test, and its attempts to police the street corners of public society, but the literal boundary exercises that continue to regulate, distinguish, and even ghettoize the pornographic as something alien and somehow threatening to the home.[25] Given the coincidence of representational strategies between the so-called porno film and the home movie in general, let alone their interdependence as manifested in the object of this tape, continued attempts to enforce a separation between the two might seem nothing more than an intellectual conceit.

However, these boundary exercises do have very practical consequences, ones that manifested themselves in what must have seemed a perverse fashion when Pam and Tommy were unable to prevent the distribution of their tape in part because the sex acts depicted occurred and were recorded in "public places" (Kleinhans 2001, 290).[26] Moreover, it is a commonplace to recognize that, by definition, a home movie and a porno film are not, or perhaps more accurately, should not constitute the same thing. If porn admits (indeed, sometimes encourages) trappings of domesticity, "home"—despite the fact that it now serves as the primary site for the consumption of pornography—is culturally defined as private, familial, safe, the opposite of pornographic. All this recalls that the generic definition of film texts proves revelatory of the social and cultural stakes in their production and reception. The difference between a porno film and a home movie does not simply lie in what it is called, but more profoundly, in what we understand it to be. To return to Gledhill: "Genre analysis tells us not just about kinds of films, but about the cultural work of producing and knowing them" (2000, 222). Perhaps the clearest means, in this case, of separating the home movie from the porno film, then, is to refer to the narrative and spectatorial conventions informing the tape as a whole. To do this is to state that, in one sphere, it constitutes porn, in another, a home movie—albeit also that these definitions stake their claims simultaneously. It is, appropriately, akin to dubbing the tape, to creating from one source two distinct, bounded objects, one of which we may name public and obscene, the other, private and domestic.

Nonetheless, if this distinction between genres or types of product calls for clear boundaries, within each genre these boundaries become readily obscured again. Both classifications—one private, one public—refer to the tape as a whole object, as a product to be recognized in terms of its circulation and its phenomenal existence in the world. In order for the footage to become pornographic in the ways described above, there also needs to be some quality of recognition or assertion, something intelligibly pornographic within the text itself. Which returns us to the notion of (phenomenal) truth as the public-private promise of the genre of pornography, and the private-public promise of the home movie. While the two genres on which this tape calls, and by which it is named and given social existence, propose a kind of originary relationship with the real world, in their actions on the tape itself they tend to restate the real as a quality of the image, and thus of citation. Likewise, the body, enmeshed in competing discourses of sexual and cultural identity, seems to stand both for and between us and the truth. If, as Michael Sicinski notes in this volume, the professional sex body "possesses an unmasterable physical density," the bodies portrayed in the *Pam and Tommy* tape become doubly unmasterable due to their double professional citation, a citation housed entirely in their physical bodies. The couple's celebrity acts as an extra density to the supposed truths of representation. At the same moment, these bodies—of porn stars, celebrities, newlyweds, and amateurs—represent for us multiple and multiplying roles.

At this point, it is helpful to recall that IEG also authored the footage as it circulates as porn. While it may well be "hardcore and uncensored," this does not guarantee that the footage is uncut, although what can feel like interminable scenes of Tommy fishing or the couple experimenting with lens filters certainly suggests this possibility. To recall the facts: *Pam and Tommy* contains approximately eight minutes of explicit sexual content, out of a total of fifty-four minutes. However, even the most cursory analysis of the tape shows that the first sex scene, in which Pam gives Tommy a blow job during a day-long boat trip for her birthday, is in fact misplaced in the narrative. From a shot of the couple beside a deck-top Jacuzzi, the tape suddenly cuts to Pam, shot from Tommy's perspective, kneeling on a bed fellating him. While the situation preceding this could certainly be described as sexual— the couple is naked, talking intimately—the footage itself is clearly lifted from a later, much more substantial sex scene, which takes place approximately forty minutes into the tape. This particular blow job does not take place sequentially during the day trip, but rather, as far as one can be certain, during the couple's four-day holiday on another boat.

Despite the fact that we cut abruptly from outdoors to indoors, and that certain relevant physical details change (for example, Pam's or the room's appearance), the scene does not necessarily seem out of place. At the least,

1. Pam Sucks Tommy's Cock. *Pam and Tommy: Hardcore and Uncensored* repeats this image out of narrative sequence to create a more coherent pornographic product than the amateurs alone have authored.

the scene seems no more out of place than the "generic verisimilitude" of pornography allows. The sex act here serves to so overwhelm its context that the latter in fact has little consequence; or, perhaps more accurately, context here becomes a textual reference, rather than an experiential one. The effect of spreading this scene through the tape by reediting or reinserting it likewise contributes to a kind of connotative spread, as well as containment. What was "just sex" becomes delimited and defined as a sexual performance, or number, by its sudden appearance as a speed bump or addendum to the narrative.[27] In this first scene, the use of slow motion accentuates this redefinition. The same means of isolating the sex act from its surroundings is also used in other scenes, most notably during a scene shot from Pam's perspective, in which the couple fucks on the deck of the (second) boat. Here, the sequence is repeated in its entirety, first in slow motion, then at regular speed. The principle of the act as a, or the, definitive element of porn in this way works directly on and in the image. Like the bodies of the stars that it portrays, the image here bears the burden of playing many roles. Moreover, as the tape progresses, the element of performance becomes more refined. In the last and most extensive sex sequence, it seems finally that the couple creates genuinely pornographic images "at the source" when Tommy, despite repeated references to their desire to have a baby, and at Pam's urging, comes outside and on top of her in a classically pornographic "money shot"—again, played in slow motion.

At the same time as these visual techniques tend to concentrate the tape's impact into discrete pornographic numbers, the effect of such sequences is to spread the pornographic through the material as a whole. In particular, the use of cheap synthesizer porno rock over the sex scenes serves to

establish associative links between explicitly pornographic and explicitly domestic sequences. While the music added by IEG does not only play during
sex scenes, its association with pornography is unmistakable. In fact, the
music seems to be used whenever diegetic music plays in the background;
thus for reasons of copyright, not protected under IEG's settlement with the
couple. When the music plays during nonsexual sequences, its effect is to
spread the off-scene, or the illicit, into the most domestic events. Most particularly, IEG's use of music here serves as a reminder of the commercial
imperatives of this enterprise—that while the footage per se shows little
evidence of planning, or even coherence beyond the strictly circumstantial,
what is at stake here is not the documenting of reality, but the creation of a
product, bound as much by conventions as by circumstances.

Accordingly, the recycling or reediting of footage within the tape serves
the very practical purpose of creating a legible and commercially viable pornographic product. Not only can we presume that the sex scenes, in their
unedited state, are much shorter than typical pornographic numbers, their
irregularity and lack of closure also serves to trouble the tape's generic classification. The distributing company's response—repeating and reemphasizing scenes depicting sexual activity—then seems a logical one in light of the
commercial problems this poses. To take just one example, without the insertion of what becomes the first blow job scene, viewers would be forced to
wait more than twenty minutes for any substantial sexual activity. Moreover,
the company's response to this problematic material is one which, while it
creates an untruth of the tape's narrative sequence, answers the lack with
a kind of generic truth. Thus IEG's response calls on tropes—on the repetition of figures of performance, which are, again, what we already know to be
pornographic—to answer to textual instabilities. The creation of porn out
of the footage emerges, in this way, as an exercise in time passing, both as
it answers to our expectations as consumers about the time spent watching
the tape and as it spreads the markers of the pornographic through the tape
by their repetition over time.

What I have referred to as the tape's historical trajectory—between the
safe and the video store, the home movie and the porno, or the private and
the public—thus also finds an expressive form in the passage of time within
the text. As Judith Butler writes: "By being called a name, one is also, paradoxically, given a certain possibility for social existence, initiated into a temporal life of language that exceeds the prior purposes that animate that call"
(1997, 2). Butler's subject of injurious naming, or hate speech, recalls the

purported injury to Pam and Tommy haunting this tape in its manifestation as pornography: its theft from their home, their attempts to stop its circulation in the public sphere, and even the invasion of their persons suggested by its continuing and proliferating public presence. Moreover, in serving to assert its generic classification, and thus boundaries for its interpretation, the insistent repetition of pornographic figures does work as a kind of name-calling, the definition of "a certain possibility for social existence." In as much as this seems to be creative of the tape as a particular kind of cultural product—as it is "made" pornography by repetition and recitation—this naming can be described as performative.

While the notion of performativity in porn is perhaps most familiar from Catherine MacKinnon's assertion that pornographic texts enact, or perform, real world violence on women, my interest lies rather with the generic or textual realities of porn (1993). If I am to argue that this particular example of pornography is performative, I must account for the fact that its performance is one that occurs in and of the image. In so doing, I am again following Butler when she writes that a performative speech act's success, or authority, remains inseparable from the conventions of the practice in and by which it occurs. "What this means, then, is that a performative 'works' to the extent that it *draws on and covers over* the constitutive conventions by which it is mobilized" (1997, 51). The insistent name-calling that pits *Pam and Tommy* with pornographic numbers garners its authority textually by pacing out the length—literal and figural—of the tape. The distributing company's manipulation of the "natural" or recorded time of the footage is perhaps the most blatant means by which it "draws on and covers over the constitutive conventions by which it is mobilized"; specifically, via the assertions of liveness and presentation of bounded sex acts that give pornography its generic identity. Although these qualities are (presumably) easily located in the tape in the raw, they also constitute conventions that intrude on the tape from the outside, from other pornography, in particular. If the literal repetitions in the tape suggest an excessive investment in the text, they also prove constitutive of the text as it is made pornographic—and whole. By the same token, the conventions that it draws on and covers over are not just pornographic but also domestic: the tape remains authentically interesting because it is authentically amateur. It is worth repeating that although the sex acts shown are recycled, they are also "real." The first mobilization of the pornographic, then, occurred in the home movie. In this way, the tape's porning does perform a kind of circling claim to "truth." If its first structuring referent, at the time of its making, was the (real-life) holiday, the creation of porn both turns the tape back on itself and sends it outward, into the world.

Notes

1 Hence my description of the two forms as ersatz genres of film production. The treatment of porn as a genre of film has proven historically significant in establishing its validity as a body of texts worthy of cultural criticism. For example, a significant feature of Linda Williams's argument in *Hard Core* is that moving-image pornography, from roughly the 1970s, or, what she refers to as the "classical" era on, became "more a genre among other [filmic] genres than . . . a special case" (1999, 120). Her argument for generic definition and similarity among pornographic films incorporates the processes of recycling and imitation seemingly so characteristic of pornography, today as in the 1970s. However, I would argue that the "genericness" of porn—or, more precisely, its status as a film genre—is, similar to that of home movies, often an aspirant one, or one based on a kind of contaminative practice tending to put generic definitions into a state of limbo. As Williams herself goes on to write in the epilogue to her book, added in 1999, the mode of production that seemed to represent the pornographic "has actually proven to be quite a brief aberration" (335 n. 28). To describe porn (along with the home movie) as an ersatz genre is therefore not to argue that it cannot constitute a genre, but merely that in its generic definition, pornography tends to the substitutive and the imitative. This reflects the illicit modes of production and distribution of these two practices, as well as their uncertain, "low cultural" historical development. Tellingly, the *New Shorter* OED gives as an example for the definition of *ersatz*, "as dehydrated and ersatz as TV" (*The New Shorter* OED, 847). As Constance Penley writes, "If Linda Williams' breakthrough was to get us to think of pornography as *film*, that is, as a genre that can be compared to other genres . . . the next logical step, it seems, would be to consider pornographic film as popular culture" (1997, 96).

2 Chuck Kleinhans describes the tape as "the most widely seen home movie since the Zapruder film of the Kennedy assassination" (2001, 1). Likewise, Web advertisements for the footage typically describe it as "the most famous" or "most seen" pornography in history. A recent Internet search for the words *Pamela Anderson* and *Tommy Lee* pulled up some 20,000 hits, the majority of which appeared to offer access to the footage, while most of the remainder at least discussed it.

3 See, for example, www.hardcore.com: "When is the last time you've seen a celebrity steer a boat with his massive cock?" This begs the question of whether Tommy Lee's celebrity is really the issue here. Obviously, however, his fame enables some extra reality effect; pleasure, then, is divided between the pleasure of arousal and the pleasure of recognition. This site, of the many I viewed on

the Internet, also contains perhaps the most coherent description of the "Pam and Tommy home video" tape. Typically, the sites, and links to them, intersperse breathless smut with the two celebrities' names. In May of 2001, for example, www.pamela-tommy-movie.com linked to: "pics pam sucking big cock photos porn video nude pussy fucking pictures naked celebs pam video sex video." In contrast to this, the hardcore.com text reads more prosaically: "Here is a list of some of the things you will see if you buy this video—

   —Pam suck Tommy's cock while he recklessly drives down the highway while towing their boat. Some very nice, close up shots of Tommys cock going in and out of Pamela's mouth.
   —Pam masturbate full nude on the deck of their boat in the open. She's shy at first, but Tommy cheers her on until she rubs her perfect shaved pussy for the camera.
   —Close up shots of Tommys cock going in and out of Pamela's shaved pussy while they take turns holding the camcorder.
   —Tommy Lee shooting his cum all over Pamela's stomach and tits then sits back and watches her rub it in.

There are some very comical scenes as well. When is the last time you've seen a celebrity steer a boat with his massive cock? Watch Pamela as she teaches you how to properly roll and smoke a joint. There are also scenes of their weird secret "alien" wedding that you have heard about. You name it, they did it." If anything, this description proves more expansive than is justified—certain of the so-called scenes described above, for example, last only a matter of seconds.

4 This relationship, between boredom and arousal, has been most thoroughly explored in avant-garde cinema. See Ara Osterweil's essay in this volume.

5 I'm thinking in particular of the shot of Pam sucking Tommy's cock, reproduced here, which assumes a semi-iconic status in publicity for the footage and is even included in an IEG preview/teaser on the tape before the home movie footage starts. As I will go on to discuss, this shot, or sequence, also assumes a structural importance through its insistent repetition.

6 Patricia Zimmerman dates the equation of amateur movies with "home"—in the figure of the nuclear family—and the subsequent exaltation of everyday details of living to the period from the 1920s to the 1950s, when amateurs were directed into models emulating Hollywood's narrative coherence and focus on action via the prism of everyday family life (1995, 66–67).

7 Clearly, this is not IEG's description. The tape is marketed as xxx-rated, as opposed to an R-rated version (*Pam and Tommy's Honeymoon*), presumably dealing more with romance than sex, which the company also released. However, their inclusion of the most banal domestic details in the X-rated tape indicates that these markers of domesticity are important in establishing a market and notoriety for it as porn. For the purposes of this study, I will refer only to the X-rated version, which I refer to as *Pam and Tommy*.

8 His argument appears motivated by Linda Williams's generic analysis, which, in highlighting "classical" feature-length porn, does not fully account for the trend toward a preeminence of "less developed" video forms of pornography. (See, in a similar vein, my note 1 above, and Tom Waugh's essay in this volume.)

9 In the *Dirty Debutantes* series Lehman describes, Ed Powers or his sidekick, Jake Steed, play "the pro." The imperative for men to perform, however, is arguably concentrated in the penis, thus lessening the demands placed on their eyes, hair, or other features.

10 The footage first played on television in 1994 and was sold to *Penthouse* and released as a tape in September of that year. It is currently available for purchase under this title as a *Penthouse* tape. I watched the footage as part of a compilation entitled *Pam and Tommy Lee Sex Tape*, which includes this footage and the "Rob Lowe Classic Sex Tape" as bonus footage. The tape is pretty clearly a bootleg. Much of the Pam and Tommy footage, for example, is described as "bonus" and "just discovered," although it merely repeats footage from the IEG tape. (This last section of the tape is, moreover, largely unwatchable thanks to dubbing protections which cause the image to cut out regularly.)

11 According to what seems to be her primary fan site, however (from the "Portland Ice Skating Society—New Zealand's own Tonya Harding fan club—Home of 'The Portlandian,' the net's premier source of Tonya news"), the tape is in fact cobbled together from three separate sex scenes, none of which were shot on her wedding night. See http://www.geocities.com/portice/tonyafaq.htm#wedvid. The site mentions "obvious continuity errors" as further proof; that these were not at all evident in the footage I watched is a hazard of watching illegal bootlegs, but one perhaps indicative of the special qualities of this type of film. While this might appear to negate much of my discussion of the tape, I would assert that since my interest lies with representational effects, as opposed to documentary "truth," the actual provenance of the footage is of less consequence than the manner in which it is deployed. See my discussion of the manipulation of raw footage below for more on this point.

12 See note 11 above. Chuck Kleinhans suggests that the tape resembles gonzo porn for this reason, although only in the scenes in which Tommy is holding the camera. While it is true that gonzo porn does not typically shoot from the woman's point of view, I am not sure that this serves to entirely reclassify the tape. Much of what Pam shoots is entirely focused on genital penetration, which could be from either perspective (Kleinhans 2001, 295).

13 Interestingly, Richard Dyer compares porn stars and musical stars in his discussion of self-reflexivity, arguing that they can be distinguished from movie stars in their common failure to easily reference cultural categories apart from the fact of their performance (1994, 55).

14 The most surprising thing about this passage is that the author's assumption of a "healthy" relationship here must be based solely on the fact of the couple's matrimony; or, possibly on the fact that they are not only married but also having

sex. As the couple's history has shown, if spousal abuse and repeated separation can provide any indication, theirs has been anything but a conventionally healthy relationship.

15 Note, by way of contrast, Richard Dyer's discussion of gay porn, in which he describes the notion that "anonymous sex, spontaneous, uncontrolled sex, sex that is 'just' sex, is more real than sex caught up in the sentiments that knowing one's partner mobilizes or sex which deploys the arts of sexuality" (1994, 51).

16 I am indebted to Maria St. John's discussion of Monica Lewinsky's portrayal of her pornographic encounters with President Clinton for this suggestion. See St. John's essay in this volume.

17 To quote from the decision, "Obscene material is material which deals with sex in a manner appealing to prurient interest, and the test of obscenity is whether to the average person, applying contemporary community standards, the dominant theme of the material appeals to prurient interest" (Kendrick 1996, 201).

18 The photograph is reproduced in *Rolling Stone*'s article on the couple's relationship, and a similar one appears on the cover of the magazine. It is noteworthy that the article is excerpted from a forthcoming biography not about the couple but about Mötley Crüe. Despite having dated their share of famous women, the other band members are scarcely mentioned.

19 The offence of such material lies both in its public circulation and in its content. "This work, I am told, is sold at the corners of streets, and in all directions, and of course it falls into the hands of persons of all classes, young and old, and the minds of those hitherto pure are exposed to the danger of contamination and pollution from the danger it contains." Lord Chief Justice Cockburn, *Regina v. Hicklin*, quoted in Kendrick 1996, 122. As Kendrick notes, this writing of the "young person" (and, I would add, his or her association with the infantilized lower classes) into law "still haunts discussions of pornography today" (123), most particularly as it raises the specter of an uncontrollable, obscene public sphere. See my discussion below.

20 In this much, the effect of the pornographic image could be compared to that found in the prenarrative cinema that Tom Gunning has famously termed the "cinema of attraction," which emphasizes spectacle over narrative continuity. It is also a reminder that pornography, in general, is overwhelmingly about showing; it is organized, in Linda Williams's terms, according to the "principle of maximum visibility" (1999, 48). Finally, the presentational quality of the image is one that refers back to the performance presented; the image and the act thus collude in presenting the appearance of something complete in itself and bounded from the other narratives surrounding it.

21 "I shall not today attempt further to define the kinds of material I understand to be embraced within that shorthand description; and perhaps I could never succeed in intelligently doing so. But I know it when I see it, and the motion picture involved in this case is not that." Justice Potter Stewart, *Jacoblellis v. Ohio*, quoted in Williams 1999, 319 n. 9.

22 Typically, the sites offer thumbnail stills, or, very occasionally, streaming video. As is typical of pornographic sites, access to the actual images depends on registering, and sometimes on paying a subscription fee (although this footage is now so ubiquitous that a significant percentage of sites advertise it as free). However, my interest here lies with the teasers we are exposed to before gaining access, which serve to establish the most public persona for the footage, including its manifestation as a VHS tape. These include, most relevantly, pages dedicated to describing the tape, as well as brief references couched in the sexual smorgasbord style typical of on-line porn sites. See note 3 above. The images were first displayed on IEG's "Club Love" site (www.clublove.com) which is also advertised in trailers on the video tape.

23 Although both genres often aspire to mimic or recreate more established narrative forms. See Zimmerman (1995, 64–89) on the home movie and Williams (1999, 120–52) on porn and the movie musical. I am taking the terms *generic* and *social verisimilitude* from Steve Neale's study of American film genre. He, in turn, takes them from Todorov. As Neale points out, "neither equates in any direct sense with 'reality' or 'truth'" (2000, 32).

24 For the purposes of my study, I have not looked at the stag film or other earlier forms of visual pornography, although it is possible that the stag film, in particular, deals in similarly presentational imagery as does the modern home movie.

25 See Juffer, in particular chapter 1, "Home Sweet Pornographic Home?"

26 Likewise, Tommy Lee notes that the couple proved unsuccessful in their bid to prevent distribution of the tape because it was ruled to be "newsworthy" (qtd. in Strauss 2001, 61).

27 I am grateful to Michael Sicinski for suggesting this analogy by example of his use of it to describe the opposite phenomemon; that is, the "unsexy" moments of porn, which he contrasts to the narrative gaps in Eadweard Muybridge's motion studies. See Sicinski in this volume.

Works Cited

Bazin, André. 1967. "The Myth of Total Cinema." In *What Is Cinema?* Vol.1. Trans. Hugh Gray. Berkeley: University of California Press. 17–22.

Berlant, Lauren. 1995. "Live Sex Acts (Parental Advisory: Explicit Material)." *Feminist Studies* 21, 2: 379–404.

Butler, Judith. 1997. *Excitable Speech: A Politics of the Performative.* New York: Routledge.

Dyer, Richard. 1994. "Idol Thoughts: Orgasm and Self-Reflexivity in Gay Pornography." *Critical Quarterly* 36, 1: 49–62.

Gledhill, Christine. 2000. "Rethinking Genre." In *Reinventing Film Studies,* ed. Gledhill and Linda Williams. London: Oxford University Press. 221–43.

Juffer, Jane. 1998. *At Home with Pornography: Women, Sex, and Everyday Life.* New York: New York University Press.

Kendrick, Walter. 1996. *The Secret Museum: Pornography in Modern Culture.* Rev. ed. Berkeley: University of California Press.

Kleinhans, Chuck. 2001. "Pamela Anderson on the Slippery Slope." In *The End of Cinema as We Know It: American Film in the Nineties,* ed. Jon Lewis. New York: New York University Press. 287–99.

Lehman, Peter. 1999. "Ed Powers and the Fantasy of Documenting Sex." In *Porn 101: Eroticism, Pornography, and the First Amendment,* ed. James Elias et al. New York: Prometheus. 359–66.

MacKinnon, Catherine. 1993. "Only Words". *Only Words.* Cambridge, MA: Harvard University Press. 3–41.

Neale, Steve. 2000. *Genre and Hollywood.* London: Routledge.

Nichols, Bill, Christian Hansen, and Catherine Needham. 1991. "Pornography, Ethnography, and the Discourses of Power." In *Representing Reality: Issues and Concepts in Documentary,* by Bill Nichols. Bloomington: Indiana University Press. 201–28.

Penley, Constance. 1997. "Crackers and Whackers: The White Trashing of Porn." In *White Trash: Race and Class in America,* ed. Matt Wray and Annalee Newitz. New York: Routledge. 89–112.

Strauss, Neil. 2001. "The Ballad of Pam and Tommy Lee, and Other Assorted Tales from the Mötley Crüe Dark Side, Told in the Words of the Men Who Did the Damage." *Rolling Stone,* May 10, 54–64, 98.

Williams, Linda. 1999. *Hard Core: Power, Pleasure, and the "Frenzy of the Visible."* Rev. ed. Berkeley: University of California Press.

Zimmerman, Patricia R. 1995. *Reel Families: A Social History of Amateur Film.* Bloomington: Indiana University Press.

Office Sluts and Rebel Flowers:

The Pleasures of Japanese

Pornographic Comics for Women

DEBORAH SHAMOON

✳ Hard-core pornography tends to be read as synonymous with film, video, and photography. Although Walter Kendrick in *The Secret Museum* (1996) demonstrates how in the nineteenth century the pornographic could be located anywhere, from ancient statuary to novels, accounts of porn in the twentieth century have tended to concentrate on the technological capabilities of film as the most appropriate medium for the pornographic imagination. In *Hard Core*, Linda Williams argues that hard-core pornography seeks to "induce and photograph a bodily confession of involuntary spasm" (1999, 48). Thus film pornography aspires to what Williams calls an aesthetic of "maximum visibility" (49), in which real bodies are seen performing real sex acts. However, in this formulation, the progression to ever more technologically advanced, mimetic art forms seems inevitable—from paintings to still photography to moving image, all in search of ever more faithful reproductions of "reality." Williams ends the book by wondering about the possibility of interactive porn in the form of video games or virtual reality, yet another step up the technological ladder. But must one limit the idea of maximum visibility to only the most mimetic of arts? Drawn pornography in the form of comic books, decidedly low-tech material, has continued to flourish in spite of the widespread availability of film and video porn. More specifically, pornographic comics have proliferated in Japan, while readership in the United States remains fairly small. Unlike film, comics cannot aspire to an extremely high degree of realism; however, the lack of popularity of comic book pornography in the United States has less to do with the limitations of drawing versus film than with the lack of an adult readership of comics in this country. In Japan, on the other hand, where comics, or *manga*, have a huge adult audience, pornographic comics constitute a large and significant genre. In the 1980s, a new genre emerged that has come to be called "ladies' comics" (*redezu komikku*), hard-core pornographic comics aimed at women in their twenties and thirties. I will argue that the success of ladies' comics as a genre lies in its ability to appeal to female readers through familiar generic conventions associated with girls' comics, but also in ladies' comics' use of maximum visibility. As Williams points out, one of the problems of film pornography is the invisibility of the female orgasm, as well as of penetration. Drawn pornography, however, has no such limitations. Thus drawn pornography in Japanese comics not so much lacks in realism as it depicts the different truth of the female body impossible to capture on film.

Japanese comic books, animation, and video games have become increasingly popular in the United States in the last ten years. Japanese comics in particular have gained an ever larger fan base not only for their high production values and variety of stories but also for their sexual content, which ranges from the mildly suggestive to the explicitly pornographic. The adult sections of American comic book stores now carry a large number of translations of Japanese hard-core comics, as well as an increasing number of homegrown imitations. Ladies' comics, however, have not yet been imported. Given that many American women still do not consume visual hard-core pornography of any kind,[1] it may come as a surprise that ladies' comics enjoy huge popularity in Japan, primarily among women in their twenties and thirties. As a genre, the ladies' comic is less than twenty years old, first appearing only around 1980, but already it has claimed a large portion of the massive, highly competitive comics market in Japan. Frederik Schodt estimates that ladies' comics magazines have a circulation of 103 million monthly, which amounts to about 10 percent of the total circulation of comics for adults, including nonpornographic ones (1996, 82).[2] Clearly, Japanese women have embraced this new genre, and there simply exists no parallel in U.S. popular culture.

So how is it that a genre of hard-core pornography for women has come to exist in Japan? In part, the answer lies in the specific cultural climate of contemporary Japan. Comic books, or manga, in Japan make for a popular form of entertainment not only for children but for adults as well, including women. As Sharon Kinsella points out in *Adult Manga*, while attendance at movie theaters has declined and rates of television viewing have remained level, sales of comics continued to rise throughout the 1970s and 1980s, and in 1993, the largest comic book publishers boasted profit margins that exceeded any company on the Tokyo stock exchange that year (2000, 40–42). Furthermore, there is a greater cultural acceptance of sexually explicit images in all kinds of comics. Kinsella writes, "In general pornography has not been as strongly compartmentalized in post-war Japan as it has in post-war America or Britain. Pornographic images have tended to appear throughout the media as well as in specifically pornographic productions" (46).[3] While the comics industry does distinguish between adult and children's comics, with hard-core or explicit images appearing only in the former, some nudity and sexual innuendo appear everywhere, even in comics for children and teens. In addition, a de facto relaxation of censorship laws has occurred throughout the 1990s, allowing for the sale of increasingly explicit material. Compared to their counterparts in the United States, comic book readers in Japan constitute a larger, more diverse audience, and also one more tolerant of pornographic images. In this respect, it seems only natural that the industry would seek to market pornographic comics to women as well as to men.

Ladies' comics have succeeded, however, not simply as a marketing ploy, but also because they are able to speak to female desire in a way appealing to Japanese women. How do ladies' comics speak to a female audience and formulate female desire? The answer to this question lies first, in an understanding of the ways in which ladies' comics relate to other genres of comics for women and girls and second, in looking at how the magazines themselves encourage a specific type of readership. A full understanding of the ladies' comics genre can explain some of the most salient features of the genre, including the display of the female body rather than the male and the prevalence of violence and rape. As a genre, ladies' comics are often overlooked as too lowbrow or trashy, even by Japanese comics critics such as Yomota Inuhiko and Natsume Fusanosuke, who barely acknowledge their existence. Critics who do examine ladies' comics, such as Anne Allison, tend to search out and condemn all aspects of them that are not pro-feminist. From an American standpoint, the label "comics by and for women" can prove a bit misleading: although most of the writers are women, and the comics are marketed specifically to women, ladies' comics do not present a vision of a sexually free, feminist utopia, nor are they radically subversive.[4] Ladies' comics do, however, represent real (or at least realistic) women actively pursuing their own sexual pleasure, taking the initiative in sexual experimentation and otherwise negotiating heterosexual relationships in a world of gender inequalities. In a small way, the characters' sexual adventurousness in the ladies' comics is subversive in a culture that still values sexual inexperience in females. More important, however, ladies' comics present an interesting example of female spectatorship and visual pleasure. The popularity of ladies' comics gives lie to the old myth that women are not visually stimulated and provides a much-needed example of how hard-core visual pornography for heterosexual women can come to exist.

There is little writing in English on the topic of ladies' comics, and what little there is tends to be very negative. One of the few critics to look at ladies' comics is Anne Allison, who devotes one chapter to *ero manga* (pornographic comics) in her book *Permitted and Prohibited Desires: Mothers, Comics, and Censorship in Japan* (1996). Allison begins the chapter by stating her intention not to take the reductive approach of antiporn feminists such as Andrea Dworkin and Catherine MacKinnon. However, because she uses a Freudian model of phallocentric power and desire to analyze the sex in pornographic comics, her conclusion does not veer far from the rhetoric of Dworkin and MacKinnon. Allison writes, "That ero manga are misogynistic is undeniable. That they embed and thereby foster an ideology of gender chauvinism and crude masochism is also irrefutable" (78). As evidence for these assertive claims, Allison cites examples from both ero manga for men and from ladies' comics, as if they belonged to the same genre. In a footnote she adds, "ladies' comics has emerged with narratives and images not significantly different from those in ero manga" (185 n. 11). If ero manga are so offensive and even harmful to women, and if ladies' comics are no different, why do women read them? Taking Allison's argument to its logical conclusion, one discovers the implication that Japanese women are blind to their own patriarchal oppression. Allison seems optimistic that once women gain more power in society, misogyny and masochism in comics will naturally disappear: "It is likely that this aspect of erotic comics (as well as of comics and mass culture in general) will change as more women enter the ranks of wage laborers and refuse to enter those of mother and wife" (78). In fact, ladies' comics have changed significantly through the 1990s, in spite of the fact that Japanese women continue to marry and have children. Allison's failure to understand the nature of ladies' comics not only results from her attempt to explain ladies' comics in terms of a phallocentric gaze but also from her assumption that all pornographic comics are essentially the same.

In fact, there is evidence that pornography for women works hard to differentiate itself from pornography for men in order for women readers to find it appealing. In *At Home with Pornography: Women, Sex, and Everyday Life* (1998), Jane Juffer, writing about American women's access to pornography, argues that the most important preconditions for women's enjoyment of pornography are aesthetics and access. Access, Juffer writes,

> is shaped by a number of conditions, including governmental regulation; education about technology, such as the Internet; financial resources to buy the technology, from subscribing to cable television to buying a computer; and the time and space in which to consume pornography amidst everyday routines such as work and child care. Furthermore, access is in part a question of content: to the degree that much pornography is still largely produced within the conventions of an industry that has for years catered mainly to male pleasures, access for women on their—albeit diverse—terms is still somewhat limited. (56)

In other words, access is not only a question of making pornographic videos available in woman-friendly stores; the content of the video itself must in some way address female desires—it must be something a woman wants to watch. Juffer claims that although the majority of pornographic videos and magazines remain aesthetically unpleasing to women, this does not mean that women do not consume sexually explicit entertainment. In the United States, pornography for women takes other forms, such as sex manuals and instructional videos for couples, lingerie catalogs, and especially romance novels and erotica. In fact, Juffer points out, the publication of erotic books, many of them aimed at a female audience, has risen by 324 percent in the 1990s (5). Literature, even sexually explicit literature, is far more accessible to women both as producers and as consumers, and it is aesthetically marked as feminine. Juffer writes, "Print erotica's claims to aesthetic value and the discourses that help produce this value outside the text facilitate the process of domestication through which women gain control over sexually explicit materials as readers within the spaces of their homes" (105).

Although Juffer uses the term *print erotica* to encompass publications as diverse as *Best American Erotica* and the Victoria's Secret catalog, she never once mentions comic books. This hardly comes as a surprise, given that women and girls make up only a tiny fraction of the already tiny audience for comics in the United States. A few erotic comics written by and for women do exist,[5] but as long as the comics industry as a whole caters only to a male audience and comics are only available in comic book stores, with their boys' club atmosphere, erotic comics will never reach a wide female readership in this country. Comics in the United States, pornographic or otherwise, lack ease of accessibility and aesthetic value for women. In Japan, on the other hand, comics readership is divided nearly equally between males and females of all ages, and comic book artist is considered a legitimate, even glamorous, career for a woman. Comic books in Japan are extremely cheap—the average cost lies between $3 to $4 for a magazine ranging from two hundred to seven hundred pages and containing over a dozen serialized stories. The more popular stories are later reprinted in paperback book form on higher quality paper, but the average price remains low, at only about $5 to $15. Japanese comics fall into clearly marked genres that tend to divide readers along the lines of gender and age, although all types of comic books and magazines are sold in the same stores. This includes ladies' comics, which are widely available in bookstores and newsstands. While women may hesitate to read pornographic comics in public (as men do), they do not have to think twice about buying them. Thus the success of women's erotic comics in Japan, as opposed to their almost total absence in the United States, derives from Japanese women's access to comics both as consumers and as creators.

As Juffer points out, however, material access is only part of the equation. Japanese women are more receptive to visual pornography because ladies' comics also prove aesthetically available to a female readership. More specifically, ladies' comics are not a female-oriented subgenre of porn for men. As a genre, ladies' comics arose from the genre of *shōjo manga*, or romance comics for teenage girls. Shōjo manga have been a major part of mainstream Japanese culture since the 1970s, when women artists began to write stories exploring the subjectivity of the girl protagonists. Since their inception, shōjo manga have been occupied with female desire. Depictions of sexual activity (albeit very discreetly rendered) have appeared since the early 1970s.[6] As the teenage readers reached their twenties and thirties, ladies' comics appeared as an adult offshoot of the shōjo manga genre. Although some differences exist in terms of plot, the artwork of ladies' comics maintains the recognizable traits of shōjo manga. This link with shōjo manga makes ladies' comics aesthetically pleasing and easily available to women. In fact, rather than grouping ladies' comics in the category of ero manga, as Allison does, I find it more useful to think of ladies' comics as a sexually explicit subgenre of shōjo manga. For this reason, a comparison of ladies' comics with shōjo manga proves more informative than one between ladies' comics and ero manga.

Looking at ladies' comics only in terms of porn for men can in fact lead to confusion. For instance, one of the most salient aspects of ladies' comics is the consistent display of the female body, almost to the exclusion of the male body. Superficially, this does not much differ from porn for men; the display of the female body is a standard generic trait of ero manga (and of hetero-sexual porn in general). The fact that display of the female body appears in ladies' comics as well is one of the reasons Allison assumes the two genres to be the same. However, what may appear visually similar can, in the context of different audiences and different generic expectations, have radically different meanings. In ero manga, the female body is displayed for the enjoyment of the male reader, while in ladies' comics, the display of the female body arouses the sexual desire of the female reader through the endless play of difference and similarity between her and the characters.

To understand how this works, let us take a closer look at the genre of shōjo manga. Although the genre today encompasses an ever widening array of stories, making generalization difficult, most shōjo manga still bear at least some resemblance to the classics that defined the genre in the late 1960s and early 1970s. At that time, a group of young women cartoonists took over the genre of girls' comics, previously run largely by men, and began producing comics that spoke intimately to the desires and concerns of teenage girls.[7] The change was nothing short of revolutionary. While many of the comics they produced were for the most part frothy romances of young girls and boys finding their "one true love," the stories examined in detail the inner psychology of the girl protagonists. In order to visually portray the interiority of the characters, shōjo manga artists developed a radically new style of visual expression, which has now become standard throughout the shōjo manga genre. Some of the methods they developed include the large eyes with many highlights, as well as the use of flowers, clouds, and abstract designs as background motifs to reflect the characters' emotions. Another widely used technique is the montagelike arrangement of panels, including liberal use of empty space and the superimposition of characters or text outside the borders of the panels. In *Why Manga Are Interesting*, an analysis of the narrative structure of Japanese comics, Natsume Fusanosuke points out that the purpose of the art in shōjo manga is not to depict an action taking place over time, but to illustrate the emotions of the characters; for this reason, montage is preferable to an orderly progression of panels (1996, 166). Close-up renderings of the main characters' faces appear frequently, often partially superimposed over the action, accompanied by text recording the character's thoughts. In long scenes in which the "action" is nothing more than two people talking, variations in frame size, angle, and point of focus are used to give the scene more dramatic weight. All of these design innovations draw the reader's attention to the image of the female protagonist for the purpose of sympathizing and identifying with her.

One of the most recognizable visual characteristics of shōjo manga is the superimposition of a full-length view of a character along the side of the page. This type of composition also appears in ladies' comics. The figure usually is not a direct part of the action and dialog in the accompanying panels, but appears as a visual echo of the action on that page. Often this visual arrangement introduces the main character, or shows her off in a new outfit, with flowers in the background to emphasize her beauty. But in "Study of Shōjo Manga," Mizuki Takahashi argues that this constitutes more than simply a display of fashion. As Takahashi points out, "In shōjo manga that do not feature 'adventure,' the depiction of the upper part of the body or face overwhelmingly occupies most of the panels, as the expression of feelings is more important than the action of the body" (1999, 34). In other words, shōjo manga are always in danger of becoming visually monotonous because the stories generally do not contain much physical action. Showing the full figure not only adds visual interest to the page but also encourages the reader to see the main character as literally full and complete. Takahashi writes, "By the full-length body image, the reader confirms the body of the character and can identify with her personality and atmosphere" (35). Shōjo manga feature a consistent and marked display of the female body in order to encourage readers to identify with the female characters.

The art in ladies' comics is aesthetically marked as feminine by its relation to shōjo manga, which includes as a generic feature the consistent display of the female body. The design conventions of shōjo manga encourage the reader to see the characters as the self, not as other. This is not unique to shōjo manga, but is a part of the nature of the comic book medium itself. In other forms of visual narrative that rely on photographed images, such as film or video, the viewer tends to approach the character on-screen as the other. But as Scott McCloud points out in *Understanding Comics* (1993), the more generalized or iconic quality of the drawn face has the effect of drawing the reader in. McCloud writes, "When you look at a photo or a realistic drawing of a face, you see it as the face of another. But when you enter the world of the cartoon, you see yourself . . . the cartoon is a vacuum into which our identity and awareness are pulled, an empty shell that we inhabit which enables us to travel in another realm. We don't just observe the cartoon, we become it" (36). McCloud also points out that Japanese comics, which often juxtapose a simply drawn figure against a more detailed background, emphasize this effect. No less than any other manga genre, shōjo manga also often show iconic or "cartoony" characters in a detailed, realistic physical environment. According to McCloud, this contrast encourages the reader to identify with the characters. In this case, the tendency of the reader to experience the drawn character as the self complements shōjo manga's exploration of the subjectivity of teenage girls.

There is yet another possible reason for the absence of male bodies in ladies' comics. Again, the answer may lie in the relation between ladies' comics and shōjo manga. While many shōjo manga stories feature girl protagonists seeking heterosexual romance, some shōjo manga artists, concurrent with the aesthetic innovations of the early 1970s, began to write stories about homosexual love among teenage boys. These *bishōnen*, or "boy-love," comics constitute a distinct subgenre of shōjo manga, but share all the same visual elements (not surprisingly, since the same artists created them). Midori Matsui, in her 1993 essay "Little Girls Were Little Boys," argues that although the characters of bishōnen comics are boys, the girl readers experience the characters in the same way as they do the protagonists of heterosexual romances, that is, as the self, not as other. Not only are the boy-boy comics visually similar to girl-boy comics, they share thematic similarities as well. The story usually focuses on adolescent romance and an exploration of the characters' interiority. Furthermore, the boy characters often look extremely feminine, with large eyes, long flowing hair, and ectomorphic bodies. Matsui writes, "It was apparent that the boys were the girls' displaced selves; despite the effeminate looks that belied their identity, however, the fictitious boys were endowed with reason, eloquence and aggressive desire for the other, compensating for the absence of logos and sexuality in the conventional portraits of girls" (178). In addition to homosexual boy-love, many shōjo manga feature stories about boys and girls who cross-dress or who magically change sex. All these types of characters give teenage girls the freedom to imagine themselves as acting beyond the strictures imposed on them in Japanese society. Not surprisingly, shōjo manga featuring homosexual boys or girls dressed as boys were the first to show the characters in bed together (Fujimoto 1998, 47).

Boy-love comics have grown increasingly popular in the last twenty years, and (like ladies' comics) have become more sexually explicit as their fans have grown up. Hard-core boy-love comics, known as *shota-con* or *yaoi* comics[8] are now widely available in bookstores, comic book stores, and on the Internet. While the circulation of the most popular yaoi comics magazine, *June*, is only 100,000 per month, significantly less than that of ladies' comics magazine *Amour* at 430,000 (Schodt 1996, 123, 127), most yaoi comics are written by amateurs and sold or traded outside the professional manga industry or posted on the Internet. In fact, the term *yaoi* is almost synonymous with amateur comics.[9] It is difficult to know exactly how the readership of boy-love comics compares to that of ladies' comics; boy-love may in fact be the more popular genre. On the other hand, boy-love stories are not segregated from other shōjo manga comics, and the borders between yaoi, shōjo manga, and ladies' comics are quite permeable, so in all likelihood, most readers enjoy both homosexual and heterosexual stories. While ladies' comics favor images of female characters, Japanese women who want to look at hard-core pornographic images of idealized male bodies have no shortage of material.

Boy-love comics also feature a strong fantasy element, which can prove empowering, as well as potentially unsatisfying. Many boy-love stories have a fantastic, historic, or futuristic setting. The fans themselves make no secret of the fact that boy-love comics constitute a form of escapist fantasy. Mark McLelland quotes from the home page of a yaoi fan: "[Boy-love] comics are an imaginary playground in which I can flee the realities of everyday life" (2001). As Matsui suggests, while transference of the girl reader's identity onto the boy character can provide a powerful means for girls to access their sexual desires, the leap of imagination required for such a reading can also prove detrimental. Matsui writes, "The Japanese boy-love comic, in its most imaginatively ambitious mode, is a remarkable amalgam of the feminine and the adolescent imagination.... Yet this transgressive play can easily slide into self-indulgence, an intellectual equivalent of drug-taking" (1993, 194). Self-indulgence does seem to have taken over the genre: the current trend in yaoi comics favors endlessly repeating sex scenes over plot and character development, and parody or appropriation of existing texts over originality. On the other hand, ladies' comics provide a realistic alternative to the endless play and fantasy of boy-love comics.

While even the earliest shōjo manga, particularly of the boy-love variety, included depictions of sexual activity, the transition from chaste to pornographic images has been gradual. While there is no ratings system (such as there is with film in the United States), the distinction between the merely suggestive and the truly hard-core, not surprisingly, seems to lie in the explicit rendering of genitalia. In the 1990s, new shōjo manga magazines aimed at girls in their late teens and early twenties, such as *Dessert* and *You*, advertised the stories' sexual content on the cover. The main difference between these new shōjo manga stories and those of the 1970s seems to be the emphasis on casual sex in lieu of romance; however, the sex act itself is still not explicitly rendered. Pornographic stories never appear alongside less explicit ones in the same magazine. Ladies' comics, which not only show but highlight the characters' genitalia, remain a distinct genre. In this regard, at least, ladies' comics show some similarity with the conventions of ero manga. Both genres make use of the selective veiling of genitalia in order to evade censorship, although enforcement of the law has become increasingly lax. The little white or black squares that once covered drawings of genitalia have now shrunk, become transparent, and, where necessary, changed shape to triangles, thin strips, or tiny dots, to the point where they now emphasize rather than conceal the anatomy, and pubic hair, which was once forbidden, now sprouts lushly. While shōjo manga may hint at sexual activity, ladies' comics, like other hard-core comics and films, purport to reveal that action in every detail.

The fact that ladies' comics are drawn and not filmed, however, has a significant impact on the viewer's experience of the text. In *Hard Core*, Linda Williams argues that one of the pleasures of watching film or video pornography derives from the opportunity of seeing the truth of the body, what she terms the "frenzy of the visible." She writes, "Hard core desires assurance that it is witnessing not the voluntary performance of female pleasure, but its involuntary confession" (1999, 50). Whatever the premise of a porn movie, the actors are really having sex, and much of the emphasis in porn films lies on demonstrating the reality of the filmed sex act. In comic book pornography, obviously, this effect is not possible. Instead, these comics have opted for other types of visual pleasures. One advantage of comics is that only the imagination of the artist can limit the action. Many Japanese pornographic comics and animated films have taken advantage of that fact, showing acts that would be either illegal, such as pederasty, or events that would be impossible in real life.[10] Much of ero manga for men has tended toward the fantastic, showing bodies that are increasingly superhuman in ever more bizarre settings. The image of an impossibly buxom heroine being penetrated by a tentacled alien has become clichéd in porn comics for men. In the case of ero manga, part of the visual pleasure seems to involve pushing the human body to extremes, exploring the point at which it can no longer be recognized as human.

In ladies' comics, on the other hand, with their emphasis on reality and the real sex lives of their readers, part of the visual pleasure seems to derive from an aesthetic of maximum visibility. This represents a significantly different kind of visual pleasure from that found in the hard-core films and videos Linda Williams analyzes. As Williams points out, the "frenzy of the

1. Maximum visibility in ladies' comics. The insert in the upper right corner reveals the hidden action of the larger image. In this case, the woman's clothes have also become temporarily transparent. From "My Most Perverted Evening" [Watashi no ichiban etchi na yoru], by Kado Motomi.

visible" has historically been tied to gender issues: "The animating male fantasy of hard-core cinema might therefore be described as the (impossible) attempt to capture visually the frenzy of the visible in a female body whose orgasmic excitement can never be objectively measured" (1999, 50). While male pleasure in hard-core cinema involves showing the erect penis and ejaculation, the physiology of the vagina makes female pleasure and orgasm much more difficult to represent on film. For this reason, comics are perhaps better able to depict female pleasure. While drawings may not be able to reveal the "truth" of the real body in the way film can, drawings can show things that would not be visible on film, in particular vaginal penetration. In ladies' comics, bodies are frequently made transparent, such that penises, fingers, and sex toys become visible even inside the body (figure 1). In fact, the convention of leaving the genital area blank or very quickly sketched can add to this effect. One common convention is to show a penis extended in blank space, but dripping with juices and inserted through an oval opening. The reader familiar with the aesthetic conventions of ladies' comics instantly understands that this is not a penis in thin air but inside a body. In this way, perhaps this aesthetic of maximum visibility in drawn pornography is uniquely accessible to women, because it can depict female genital stimulation in ways not possible in film.

Ladies' comics magazines encourage strong identification between the readers and the characters of the stories and demonstrate ways in which women can express and act on their desires. Ladies' comics not only address a female audience by using the shōjo manga art style but also encourage a continuity of sexual experience between the fictional stories and the readers' real lives. For the most part, the stories are "realistic" (that is, not science fiction or fantasy) and are set in recognizable, contemporary Japan. The characters appearing in the stories are very similar to the women whose letters appear in the back of every issue: unskilled office workers and housewives in their twenties and thirties, single or recently married, and without children. At the back of every issue, a questionnaire asks readers to report which stories they liked and disliked, and what sorts of stories they want to see. These kinds of questionnaires are commonly included in comics and books of all kinds in Japan. But ladies' comics magazines go one step further, encouraging readers to write down their real-life sexual experiences and opinions, which are then published in later issues. The February 1999 issue of *Labien* features a long article on techniques for cheating on one's husband, with advice from several readers. An issue of *Fizz* from the same month has articles discussing the results of a questionnaire about the pros and cons of one-night stands, instructions for arranging threesomes, and a "reader's vibrator report." On the whole, the magazines encourage a continuity of sexual experience beyond simply reading the stories.

The same issue of *Fizz* mentioned above also contains two manga stories supposedly based on the true experiences of readers. The first is "My Most Perverted Evening" [Watashi no ichiban H na yoru] by Kado Motomi, based on the experiences of Kishiwada Mayumi (age twenty-four). The story revolves around a girl (named Mayumi) who gets caught having sex with her boyfriend on a crowded train. Although Mayumi swears off exhibitionism at the end of the story, the last frame indicates that she and her boyfriend will continue their sexual experimentation. The second story is entitled "Neighborly Love" [Rinjin'ai] by Nagaya Yōko and based on the experiences of Yamashita Ryōko (age twenty-three). The plot centers around a newly wed couple who move into a new apartment complex. The wife is seduced by a neighbor, who eventually initiates the couple into the joys of swinging. Like the previous story, this one also ends with the promise of future pleasures. While it is possible that these "true stories" are, in fact, fiction, the events of the narrative are plausible and take place in locales commonly associated with casual or illicit sex in modern Japan, such as the crowded train. The use of the readers' (supposedly) real names and ages encourages identification and possibly even imitation. Even more explicitly than in shōjo manga, the ladies' comics reader is encouraged to think of the characters as the self, not as other. In addition to the stories, the magazines carry ads for pornographic videos, sex toys, and phone sex services all explicitly marketed to women. The stories claim to reflect the lives of real readers, while the surrounding articles and advertisements encourage the reader both to enter into dialog with the text by writing letters and to seek out sexual gratification in real life.

Ladies' comics magazines indicate what type of reader they address, but they also point to a theory of desire. Of course, while any reader may approach the text in unpredictable ways, I am less interested in how an individual might read than in how the text presents itself and how it theorizes female sexual desire. One typical ladies' comics story is "Second Party for Two" [Futari no nijikai][11] by Madono Yuki, the lead story in the February 1999 issue of *Labien*. The story begins with a young woman, Mikami, at a party with a group of coworkers, when one of the men in the group, named Kubo, persuades her to slip off to a hotel with him instead. At the hotel, Mikami, a married woman, suddenly has second thoughts, but Kubo jokingly says he will not allow her to go home until she masturbates in front of him. She complies, telling herself that she has no choice, and while Kubo watches, she brings herself to orgasm. There follow several pages of the couple enjoying oral and anal sex, but in spite of her demands, Kubo refuses to bring her to orgasm again, claiming that since she is married it would not be right. Instead, he urges her to call her husband and tell him that she will be home soon. She makes the call, but tells her husband that she is going to a second party and will come home late. When Kubo asks why she no longer wants to leave, she points to her wet vagina and demands that he satisfy her. Now having permission to play, Kubo penetrates her with a vibrating cell phone wrapped in a condom. After many more pages of such teasing, she again demands that he penetrate her, again displaying her wet vagina as proof of her desire for him. He at last complies, and they enjoy a simultaneous orgasm. The story ends with them kissing and promising to meet again for another "second party."

Scant as the characterization is, the story still reveals some information about Mikami and Kubo, as well as their desires. Mikami clearly emerges as the main character—she is the character whose thoughts we read and who has the most visual salience in close-ups. Obviously for both characters, much of the erotic excitement comes from transgressing a taboo, in this case, cheating on the husband, but it seems clear that for Mikami, desire also arises from her own body. When they first arrive in the hotel room, Kubo attempts to get her in the mood by kissing and holding her, but she resists. After she masturbates, however, she is suddenly demanding: she wants him to penetrate her. He keeps her in suspense for most of the story, and the methods that he uses (anal sex, fingering, the cell phone) at first cause her shock and embarrassment. However, it is clearly her pleasure that is of primary narrative and visual importance; that Kubo also reaches orgasm seems almost secondary, and readers rarely see his penis. Also, in spite of the casual nature of this encounter, the story highlights the emotional bond between them. Mikami insists that Kubo ejaculate inside her, as proof of this bond (a common trope in ladies' comics), and afterward checks to make sure that she indeed finds his semen inside her vagina. It may seem like stating the obvious to emphasize that this text revolves entirely around bodies, although it is not just the interaction but the individual body itself that generates sexual desire. The implication is that desire is something that Mikami already possesses; she merely has to access it by exciting herself.

Mikami's desire arises from her interaction with her own body, but how is that desire indicated visually? One of the central problems of all pornography is how to depict female sexual excitement. As in other forms of visual pornography, depicting female arousal and orgasm proves problematic because there is less physical evidence; specifically, there exists no direct female equivalent to erection and ejaculation. To circumvent this, ladies' comics emphasize vaginal wetness as a sign of female arousal, and frequently female characters use it as a demand for satisfaction.[12] The wet vagina takes on a significance comparable to that of the erect penis. While it may be going too far to state that phallic power accrues to it in a larger cultural sense, within the framework of the story, the wet vagina serves as proof of the woman's arousal and a demand for satisfaction. As befits its symbolic significance, the wetness is typically overdetermined. Fluids gush forth in a tide of unbridled sexual excitement in the many repeated close-ups. Characters, both female and male, gesture toward it, touch it, and talk about it in every story. Wetness is further determined in the beads of sweat and saliva that soak the characters in nearly every story. The wet vagina also represents a demand that must be satisfied. In "Second Party," when Kubo asks Mikami why she does not go home to her husband when she has the chance, she displays her dripping genitals and demands that he drive her

もうビショビショなのよ！ひどいじゃない…っ

メチャクチャにしてよ…っ!!

2. Mikami displays her wet vagina. She says, "I'm already totally wet! Drive me wild!" From "Second Party for Two" [Futari no nijikai], by Madono Yuki.

wild (figure 2). Thus concurrent with the proof of the woman's arousal is the perceived necessity of satisfying such arousal in that site, that is, through penetration, which forms the climax of every story.

In "Second Party," as in many of these stories, penetration to the point of orgasm often constitutes the climax of the narrative, but far from being a display of phallic power (as the climax of porn for men often is), in these scenes the male is nearly absent. As is typical of shōjo manga, the female character, Mikami, has greater visual salience than the male. In part, this serves to fix her as the main character in the story—the repeated close-up views of her face, along with the disclosure of her thoughts, indicate that hers is the primary viewpoint in the story, and her emotions inform the text. The story offers extensive close-ups of her body, specifically her sexual organs, almost to the exclusion of the male. However, it is not just his penis that is left out of the picture but often Kubo's entire body. We only see his body parts as they relate to her pleasure. Kubo's eventual penetration of Mikami is depicted in a single panel that takes up the entire page. The large size of the image highlights this moment in the narrative, but here Kubo is completely absent (figure 3). The only sign of his presence comes in the form of speed lines at her vagina, indicating the rapid in-and-out motion of his penis. Realistically, at least part of his body would be visible in this position, but except for the speed lines, he remains absent. Furthermore, considering the way in which ladies' comics often emphasize maximum visibility of penetrating organs, it seems somewhat surprising that Kubo's penis suffers reduction to a few brief lines. Three pages later, when Mikami reaches orgasm, we again see a

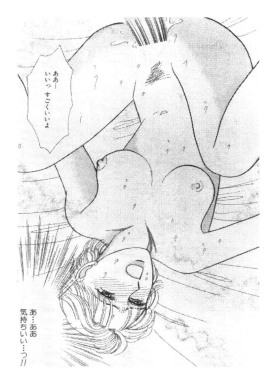

3. The penetration scene: the woman's body is fully visible while the man is reduced to a few abstract lines. She says, "It feels so good!" From "Second Party for Two" [Futari no nijikai], by Madono Yuki.

large close-up of her alone, with Kubo's presence only abstractly indicated in a spray of ejaculate. As the story progresses and Mikami approaches satisfaction, Kubo becomes more and more marginal, until he disappears entirely in the moment of orgasm. In fact, this curtailment of the male body appears with surprising consistency. In many ladies' comics, the climax of the story has the full-page panel showing the act of penetration with the man's body partially or wholly obscured. However, what is most consistently absent is not his penis but his face, whereas the woman's face is always shown, and often repeated in close-up (figure 4). This arrangement of the bodies and faces seems to indicate that the female orgasm, and the woman's fulfillment of her desire, holds greater importance than the man's. While proof of desire begins with the vagina, it ends with the face.

"Second Party for Two" does not seem to support Anne Allison's assertion that the pleasure of pornographic comics is about the possession of the female form by the gaze of the reader, and that the female characters derive pleasure only from pleasing men. Mikami's desire for Kubo is preexisting, which is why she has gone to the hotel with him in the first place. The action

4. Another penetration scene in which the man's face is hidden, in this case, by a close-up of the woman's face. She says, "Aaah! I'm coming!" From "Office Slut" [Ofisu reijo], by Mizuki Misato.

in "Second Party for Two" begins with a scene of female masturbation to the point of orgasm. This act, even though it is brought to culmination, does not satisfy or end Mikami's desire, but rather begins it. Her sexual emotions are only given free play after she has aroused herself. In this way, she seems very similar to the reader of ladies' comics, who arrives at the text with desire in need of stimulation. Identification between the reader and Mikami is not merely a matter of becoming her, but of the interplay between the similar positions of the real and fictitious woman. Readers are certainly encouraged, through the letters, questionnaires, articles, and ads, to be sexual like the characters in the stories. However, even if a reader imagines the female protagonist to be real, rather than possession, it seems more likely that her goal would be identification. A woman reading "Second Party" probably does not want to *have* Mikami, but to *be* her.

Another example of the importance of the female body for informing female pleasure and the persistent absence of the male is the February 1999 lead story in *Fizz*, "Rebel Flower" [Ran no hana] by Azuma Katsumi. It begins with a wealthy, proper young wife named Kaoru who feels sexually inhibited with her husband. She accidentally observes her husband engaging in sadomasochistic sex play with a maid and realizes that she wishes to play the role of the masochist like that woman. Immediately after her discovery she masturbates, which, as in "Second Party," serves to activate her desire. Her first act in exercising her newfound sexuality is to have sex with another man, a gardener named Yamazaki. Again, we see the familiar full-page panel of the female protagonist being penetrated by a man whose face remains out of view (figure 5). Her thoughts read, "Even as we were rubbing together, I forgot that Yamazaki even existed. The sensation of my flesh became my whole existence." After this, she is ready to take on with her husband the sexually uninhibited role she had previously only imagined. Not only the theme but the narrative of this story features the display of female pleasure in order to arouse female pleasure. It is an exploration, not of the other, as in pornography for heterosexual men, but of the self, or what may potentially become the self. Much as the woman in the story says that all she feels is herself, the reader, engaging her own desires with the text, is occupied with pleasuring herself.[13]

The story "Rebel Flower" also introduces the theme of female masochism, which appears in several (but not all) of the stories in *Fizz* and *Labien*. The idea of women finding pleasure in submission and coercion, even in fantasy, appears politically problematic to some feminist critics. The presentation of female masochism is the primary reason Anne Allison found ladies' comics so disturbing, and why she saw no difference between ero manga and ladies' comics. Allison relies on a psychoanalytic theory of spectatorship, one in which men look and women are looked at, and one which leaves no possibility of female spectatorship. For this reason, Allison finds that not only the female character but also the female reader is forced to become a masochist, taking pleasure only in her own submission to phallic power. In such a reading, the presence of female masochism in ladies' comics can be no more than a symptom of society's misogyny. But is it really impossible for women to take pleasure in looking at other women? This kind of pleasure does seem to be operating in shōjo manga, in which the repeated depiction of girl characters serves to encourage identification between the readers and the characters. An understanding of the structure of the ladies' comics genre can account for the prevalence of masochistic fantasies while still accounting for the agency of the readers.

Fujimoto Yukari offers one explanation of the role of female masochism in ladies' comics in a 1992 essay titled, "The Shape of Women's Desire: Women's Sexual Fantasies as Seen in Ladies' Comics" [Onna no yokubō no

全身が山崎を
抱んでいるのに
沸上がる快感は
打ち消しようも
ない

こすれ合うごとに
山崎の存在さえ
忘れ

肉の感覚だけが
私の存在になった

5. Kaoru has her first satisfying sexual experience with Yamazaki, the gardener. The text represents Kaoru's thoughts: "Even though my whole body refused Yamazaki, I could not deny the sensations that arose in me. Even as we were rubbing together, I forgot that Yamazaki even existed. The sensation of my flesh became my whole existence." From "Rebel Flower" [Ran no hana], by Azuma Katsumi.

katachi: Redezu komikku ni miru onna no sei gensō]. Fujimoto identifies herself in the essay as both a feminist critic and an avid reader of ladies' comics since they first appeared in the 1980s. Refusing to accept that masochism is nothing more than a disguise for the oppression of women, she contends that taking a masochistic stance provides a powerful means for the female character to access her own sexual desire. Fujimoto writes that most ladies' comics stories follow a specific pattern: the female protagonist meets with a "man of destiny," who introduces her to the world of deviant sex. While the woman is at first afraid and resists, the man overpowers her, usually through rape, bondage, and humiliation (73). According to Fujimoto, that the woman be completely overpowered is necessary to her sexual awakening. Only when she is overcome, and feels there is no way she could resist, can she surrender herself to pleasure without feeling that she has become "dirty" (74). Linda Williams notices the same dynamic in American sadomasochistic film and video porn: "For only by playing the role of the 'good girl' that is, by pretending to be good and only coerced into sex—does the woman who is coerced and punished get the 'bad' girl's pleasure. She gets this pleasure *as if* against her will and thus *as if* she were still a good girl" (1999, 209).

Looking at ladies' comics in comparison to the broader genre of shōjo manga may also help explain the prevalence of rape stories. Within the realm of romance comics for girls and women, sexual encounters between characters had been depicted since the mid-1970s, for the most part only in boy-love comics, however. As Fujimoto points out, scenes of sex and even rape in boy-love comics are more palatable to readers because boys, unlike girls, do not need to worry about possible pregnancy or the necessity of remaining virgins until they marry (1998, 144). Thus, she suggests, sex scenes, sometimes involving violence, became common in boy-love comics. Not only is it more plausible to read about boys, rather than girls, exploring their desires, but because of the fantasy element of the boy-love genre, it also appears less threatening. The female readers indulging in the fantasy of boy-love comics are free to imagine love and sex in a sentimental, idealistic way. McLelland quotes from a yaoi magazine suggesting reasons for the great popularity of boy-love comics: "Some reasons suggested include, 'you are attracted to a pure kind of love,' and, 'you wish to wrap yourself in the joy of love'" (2001). Most boy-love comics foster an aesthetic of purity, even when depicting hard-core sex acts. Heterosexual romance, by comparison, is distinctly more threatening. Compared to the pure (that is, imaginary) love of boy-love comics, heterosexual sex seems frightening and dirty. Masochism and rape fantasies provide one method of allowing the female characters to engage in dirty acts without themselves becoming dirty, and without owning the desires depicted.

While a masochistic stance serves as a method for attaining sexual pleasure, it is not the only route to pleasure. In the stories from the 1980s and early 1990s that Fujimoto examined, masochism seemed to be the preferred theme, but a decade later, interest in the topic seems on the wane. While consensual s/M play appeared in some of the stories in the February 1999 issues of *Fizz* and *Labien*, hardly any instances of the rape, violence, and humiliation Fujimoto describes occurred. A more common theme was that depicted in "Rebel Flower," where a woman actively seeks the masochist role, rather than having it thrust on her. Furthermore, many stories did not feature masochism at all, and many also presented sexually aggressive women. True, many of the female protagonists, like Mikami, put up a vestigial display of resistance and shame. For instance, there is the conceit that Kubo will not allow her to leave until she masturbates, but within the story, this type of coercion is portrayed as more of a game. When Kubo gives Mikami the opportunity to leave, she of course chooses to stay, and it is her own arousal that causes her to overcome her shame and fully embrace her "bad-girl" identity.

This shift away from the need for masochism results from the evolution of ladies' comics as a genre to include a more overtly acknowledged female-centered sexual desire. Romance fiction in the United States underwent a similar shift away from the use of rape as a device for accessing female sexual desire. In *The Romance Revolution*, Carol Thurston relates the decline of rape fantasies in romance to women's increased access to means of satisfying their own desires: "Though without conscious intent or plan, in rejecting rape as sexual fantasy the great majority of romance readers had freed themselves to recognize and embrace the role of erotica in developing their own identity, and ultimately a sense of self" (1987, 26). Interestingly, she adds in a footnote that Japanese romance is still replete with violence and rape, and she wonders, "It will be interesting to see if the evolution of the Japanese romance consumer follows the pattern of the American consumer, particularly whether most Japanese readers also will in time reject the rape fantasy and violence" (219 n. 2). Thurston wrote this in 1987; just over ten years later, it seems that this is exactly what has happened. This is not to suggest that Japanese women lag ten years behind American women in terms of sexual liberation. In fact, the shift away from rape fantasy in comics happened without a drastic change in the status of Japanese women. Rather, what this suggests is that the genre of ladies' comics has matured to the point where realistic, hard-core depictions of female sexuality are accessible and pleasing to female readers, and this maturation of genre has taken place in a relatively short time.

Within the world of ladies' comics, even tropes that seem familiar from genres of porn for men can take on different meaning. Dismissing ladies' comics as yet another example of patriarchal oppression, as Anne Allison does, is a disservice to both the comics and their readers. An understanding of the genre of ladies' comics and its links to other related genres proves crucial to comprehending the content of individual stories and the appeal of the genre as a whole. In this case, the display of the female body does not serve to make the woman into an object to be viewed and possessed, but to encourage the female reader's sexual experimentation. The magazines hearten the female reader to think of the female characters as the self and to imagine ways in which the reader and the character could be one and the same. This is not to suggest that ladies' comics are truly subversive or revolutionary; most stories might be read as heteronormative or as reinforcing the patriarchal system. I do not believe, however, that the value of any example of popular culture necessarily lies in its ability to incite revolution. In the case of ladies' comics, their very existence denies many common myths about pornography, such as that women are not visually stimulated and that hardcore pornography necessarily proves harmful to women. Ladies' comics provide a unique example of what heterosexual women might find pleasure in looking at.

While it is heartening from a feminist perspective to see texts that speak to female desire, it is perhaps impossible to separate ladies' comics from their culture of origin and to make the same texts available to American women. Ladies' comics could only have arisen within a culture that already had a large female readership of comics and a genre aimed at them. If the aesthetics and access to comics were more female-friendly, American women might in fact find a new medium for expressing their own sexual subjectivity. The fact that such texts exist at all, however, does have significant implications for the analysis of other types of visual media and implies that film and video are not the only media appropriate to the pornographic imagination.

Notes

1 As Jane Juffer astutely notes, American women's preference for print erotica, particularly romance novels, over film or video pornography does not derive

from the fact that women are less visually stimulated than men, but from the cultural conditions in which all these genres have developed. Romance novels have been historically more available to women than hard-core videos, although this is slowly changing (1998, 5).

2 By way of comparison, note that Laura Kipnis cites the peak circulation of *Hustler* at around 2 million (1999, 125).

3 Some critics, such as Sandra Buckley, attribute this to the sexually open climate of the Edo period (1600–1864) and make associations between modern porno-graphic comics and Edo-period erotic woodblock prints called *shunga* (1991, 164). This essentializing view ignores the fact that Japanese artistic traditions, as well as sexual mores, underwent a profound shift after the country opened to the West in 1864. In fact, from the time of the Meiji Restoration through to the ultranationalist fervor of World War II, pornographic images and texts were severely censored. Claiming that the proliferation of pornographic comics from the 1960s to the present is somehow related to the tradition of shunga seems as absurd as attempting to analyze contemporary American video porn in light of eighteenth-century pornographic novels such as *Fanny Hill* or *My Secret Life*.

4 As in other genres of comics for women and girls, the writers/artists tend to be women who are close in age to their readers, and who have similar values and experiences (Fujimoto 1991, 54). On the other hand, most editors are men, and they exert some control over the types of stories their female staff writes. For a description of the sometimes antagonistic relationship between comic book editors and writers, see Kinsella 2000, 162–201.

5 For example, see *The Desert Peach* by Donna Barr, *Meat Cake* by Dame Darcy, *Naughty Bits* by Roberta Gregory, *A Distant Soil* by Colleen Doran, and *Mystery Date* by Carla Speed McNeil, all of them remarkably talented artists doomed to obscurity by the inaccessibility of their chosen medium.

6 Fujimoto Yukari cites the first heterosexual "bed scene" in shōjo manga as ap-pearing in *Love Game* by Ichijō Yukari in 1972 (1998, 46). In the page Fujimoto reproduces, a naked boy and girl embrace, with the boy lying on top of the girl such that their genitalia are shielded from view. The image is static, as is typical of most renderings of bed scenes from that era. According to Fujimoto, merely the suggestion of sexual activity was enough to create a great emotional impact on teenage readers at the time (46). Another common technique is to leave the lower half of the body out of the frame when showing characters naked in bed together.

7 The most famous of these are Hagiō Motō, Ōshima Yumiko, Ikeda Riyoko, Take-miya Keiko, Ichijō Yukari, and Yamagishi Ryōko, known collectively as the Year Twenty-Four Group (Nijuni Nen Gumi) because they were all born in the year 1949, or *Shōwa* 24 in the Japanese calendar. Unfortunately, very little of their work has been translated into English.

8 The term *yaoi* is an acronym for the phrase "YAmanashi, Ochinashi, Iminashi,"

meaning "no climax, no conclusion, no meaning," so called because many of these comics forsake plot in favor of desultory love scenes between male characters. It has been suggested as a joke, however, that yaoi really stands for "YAmete, Oshiri ga Itai," "Stop, my butt hurts!" (McLelland 2001, 3). The term *shota-con* is a variant of the term *loli-con* for "Lolita complex" comics, a genre of porn comics for men featuring young girls. Shota is a common Japanese boy's name, thus shota-con indicates porn comics featuring young boys.

9   In terms of their amateur status and their depiction of homosexual male sex for female pleasure, yaoi are quite similar to American slash fiction. Like slash fiction, yaoi stories also tend to be plotless, derivative, and parodic.

10 The fact that pornographic comics are drawn obviates one of the antiporn feminists' objections, namely, that pornographic films are necessarily exploitative of the women who appear in them. Still, they would probably find small comfort in this suggestion at best.

11 *Nijikai* literally means "second party." The most common pattern of socializing in Japanese cities is to go out in a large group to a restaurant, then after dinner to break off in smaller groups to other locations—usually a bar or karaoke box— for a second party, then a third, and so on until morning.

12 While it may seem overly obvious to locate female desire in the vagina, this is not necessarily what one sees in other pornographies. It took the American porn industry years to realize the importance of the clitoris. For example, see *Deep Throat* (dir. Gerard Damiano) which locates female desire in the mouth.

13 As Williams points out in *Hard Core*, the image of the masturbating female is relatively new in Western pornographic films and represents a shift to the depiction of female pleasure, as well as of a new kind of woman, one not in desperate need of a man (1999, 109). It is important to remember, however, that these films arose from a culture that has historically harbored an intense fear and loathing of masturbation, especially female masturbation (see Bennett and Rosario 1995). In Japanese culture, on the other hand, while female masturbation is undoubtedly naughty, a sign of an active libido, it has never been pathologized. Images of women masturbating show up regularly in ero manga as well, with relatively little comment or anxiety. This cultural difference has perhaps made it easier for a masturbatory literature to be marketed to women.

Works Cited

Allison, Anne. 1996. *Permitted and Prohibited Desires: Mothers, Comics, and Censorship in Japan*. Boulder, Colo.: Westview.

Azuma Katsumi. 1999. "Ran no hana" [Rebel flower]. *Fizz*, February, 3–50.

Bennett, Paula, and Vernon A. Rosario II, eds. 1995. *Solitary Pleasures: The Historical, Literary, and Artistic Discourses of Autoeroticism*. New York: Routledge.

Buckley, Sandra. 1991. "Penguin in Bondage: A Graphic Tale of Japanese Comic

Books." In *Technoculture*, ed. Constance Penley and Andrew Ross. Minneapolis: University of Minnesota Press. 163–93.

Fujimoto Yukari. 1991. "A Life-Size Mirror: Women's Self Representation in Girls' Comics." Trans. Julianne Dvorak. *Review of Japanese Culture and Society*, 4, 19: 53–57.

———. 1992. "Onna no yokubō no katachi: Redezu komikku ni miru onna no sei gensō" [The shape of women's desire: Women's sexual fantasies as seen in ladies' comics]. "Porunogurafi" [Pornography], *Nyū Feminizumu Rebū* [New Feminism Review] 3: 70–90.

———. 1998. *Watashi no ibashō wa doko ni aru no? Shōjo manga ga utusu kokoro no katachi* [Where do I belong? The shape of the heart as reflected in girls' comics]. Tokyo: Gakuyō Shobō.

Juffer, Jane. 1998. *At Home with Pornography: Women, Sex, and Everyday Life*. New York: New York University Press.

Kado Motomi. 1999. "Watashi no ichiban etchi na yoru" [My most perverted evening]. *Fizz*, February, 107–50.

Kendrick, Walter. 1996. *The Secret Museum: Pornography in Modern Culture*. Berkeley: University of California Press.

Kinsella, Sharon. 2000. *Adult Manga: Culture and Power in Contemporary Japanese Society*. Honolulu: University of Hawaii Press.

Kipnis, Laura. 1999. *Bound and Gagged: Pornography and the Politics of Fantasy in America*. Durham, N.C.: Duke University Press.

Madono Yuki. 1999. "Futari no nijikai" [Second party for two]. *Labien*, February, 3–40.

Matsui, Midori. 1993. "Little Girls Were Little Boys: Displaced Femininity in the Representation of Homosexuality in Japanese Girls' Comics." In *Feminism and the Politics of Difference*, ed. Sneja Gunew and Anna Yeatman. St. Leonards, Australia: Allen and Unwin. 177–96.

McCloud, Scott. 1993. *Understanding Comics: The Invisible Art*. New York: Harper Collins.

McLelland, Mark. 2001. "Why Are Japanese Girls' Comics Full of Boys Bonking?" *Intensities: The Journal of Cult Media*. Available at www.cult-media.com/issue1/CMRmcle.htm

Mizuki Misato. 1999. "Ofisu reijo" [Office slut]. *Fizz*, February, 77–106.

Nagaya Yōko. 1999. "Rinjin'ai" [Neighborly love]. *Fizz*, 151–82.

Natsume Fusanosuke. 1996. *Manga wa naze omoshiroi no ka: Sono hyōgen to bunpō* [Why comics are interesting: Their vocabulary and grammar]. Tokyo: Nippon Hōsō Shuppan Kyōkai.

Natsume Fusanosuke and Takakuma Kentarō, eds. 1995. *Manga no yomikata* [How to read comics]. Tokyo: Bessastu Takarajima.

Schodt, Frederik L. 1996. *Dreamland Japan: Writings on Modern Manga*. Berkeley, Calif.: Stone Bridge.

Takahashi, Mizuki. 1999. "Study of *Shōjo Manga*: Analysis of Representations and Discourses." Ph.D. diss., University of London.

Thurston, Carol. 1987. *The Romance Revolution: Erotic Novels for Women and the Quest for a New Sexual Identity*. Urbana: University of Illinois Press.

Williams, Linda. 1999. *Hard Core: Power, Pleasure and the "Frenzy of the Visible."* 2nd ed. Berkeley: University of California Press.

Yomota Inuhiko. 1994. *Manga genron* [Comics theory]. Tokyo: Chikuma Shobō.

Going On-line: Consuming

Pornography in the Digital Era

ZABET PATTERSON

✳ On July 3, 1995, before the rise (and fall) of the so-called Internet revolution, *Time* magazine shocked its readers with one of the first mass-media exposés on the prevalence and dangers of on-line pornography. The opening paragraph begins its panicked inquiry into cyberporn by stating, "Sex is everywhere these days—in books, magazines, films, television, music videos and bus-stop perfume ads. It is printed on dial-a-porn business cards and slipped under windshield wipers. It is acted out by balloon-breasted models and actors with unflagging erections, then rented for $4 a night at the corner video store" (38). But the accompanying illustration did not show unflagging erections or ballooning breasts. On opening to the story, readers were instead confronted with an image of a naked man, his arms and legs wrapped around a keyboard and computer monitor, seeming to dissolve into the screen.

Within this admittedly strange and startling image, with its formless room, its featureless everyman, its computer glowing with a blistering, apocalyptic light—we can begin to discern the visual tropes that would become mobilized around the issue of Internet pornography. It is a visual rhetoric of anxiety specifically located at the rapidly evolving interface between corporeal body and computer screen. It is an anxiety concerning the possible lack of control and autonomy of that body when confronted with this technology. On the level of sexuality, it figures the relationship between body and networked computer as peculiarly and unwholesomely dissolute. The image displays a sociocultural panic over what we might term "correct object choice"—here a man, ostensibly failing to find a suitable "other," is solipsistically collapsing into himself in mastubatory pleasure.[1] This solipsistic collapse is one engendered by the new technology. The "body" of the computer clearly replaces the body of another human. And herein lies the ostensible "danger" of cyberporn as seen by *Time* magazine[2]: the danger of the dissolution and fusing of man into machine, or perhaps, man into "network."[3] It is an understanding of the relationship of body and networked computer as potentially, peculiarly, and unwholesomely dissolvent of the subject. Simultaneously, though, we also see the danger of a sexuality mediated and transformed through the digital screen.

In part because it is so clearly symptomatic of the anxieties evoked for a certain audience when confronted with the issue of Internet pornography, this image offers a useful place to begin interrogating the topic of Internet pornography. It gestures toward important questions of proximity and identification by specifically staging the *corporeality* of the encounter with pornography, as well as the corporeality of the encounter with the computer. Here, it is the encounter with the computer that proves consuming; the rest of the room fades out, for both the man and the viewer. This staging also leads us to question the viewing of the pornographic image itself, in unexpected ways. The screen image within the image—the screen on-screen— turns out to be a curious blind spot; the "image" of pornography is either unimportant or unshowable. The absence of the image proposes that it is impossible for us, as outside viewers, to ever really see what the man is seeing; it suggests that the encounter with pornography, and the encounter with technology, may not allow for an easy, distanced critical spectatorship. Further, it suggests that, for this audience, an understanding of the relationship to the computer is reached indirectly, through a confrontation with the pornographic image: the relationship to the computer itself remains a nonseeing one, imbricated in the nonseeing of the pornographic image. Thus it would seem that this gesture of looking away makes for a critical element in viewing either porn or technology.

Cyberporn, in this image and its imagination, offers a new ordering of sex and the body, one scripted through a particular logic of networked computer technology. This image, and the article it accompanies, was produced when the Internet had not yet become an established fact for much of the audience and when the graphical World Wide Web had not yet assumed its present ubiquity. Digital technology was perceived as threatening the integrity of the users' bodies, and the issue of so-called cybersex could be seen as a kind of summa of these fantasies and fears. Today, questions and concerns about the relationship between the body and technology have largely dropped out of mass-media discussions, which increasingly assume computer technology as a given. As Lev Manovich points out, "the speed with which new technologies are assimilated in the United States makes them 'invisible' almost overnight: they become an assumed part of the everyday existence, something which does not seem to require much reflection" (Manovich 2003, 13). But in some sense, to analyze Internet pornography is necessarily to return to these larger questions concerning the Internet itself as well as the particular mediation of embodied visual experience to which the computer user is subjected.

Categorization and the "Truth" of Desire

The pornographic image can be a particularly dense semantic site, but it is one which functions only in and through a direct visceral appeal to the body. Much of the academic writing on pornography sees this direct address to the body as grounding both its limitations and possibilities. The appeal of the pornographic image is importantly corporeal, and images become effective as porn to the extent that they elicit certain bodily sensations, almost involuntarily. Yet cyberporn, in its engagement with the technological site of the Internet and the material interface of the computer, presents a range of novel issues and problems for our investigation of this coporeal dimension. To interrogate Internet pornography, we must begin by considering the ways in which the organization of on-line pornographic discourses function to guide, if not overtly discipline, their targeted subjects.

The massive metasites of cyberporn are organized to provide a near instantaneous mass mediation and dissemination of sexual representation. In theory, this wealth of images would seem to offer a truly emancipatory scenario allowing subjects to project their virtual selves into a seemingly endless variety of scenarios and environments, and to embody an infinite variety of freely chosen subject positions, roles, and desires. Yet, in reality, what cyberporn tends to offer—especially with a rapidly consolidating market—is an environment in which desire and subject position are produced as "truths" of the self through a discourse of categorization and classification. Images are available to the viewer only through the negotiation of an elaborate schema in which sexual desire is produced through the sequencing of fixed subject positions always and only defined in relation to each other. A subset of the cyberporn industry is devoted to the categorization and classification of these images and Web sites; these sites present categories of images, laid out in tables or allowing so-called key term searches. The "click here if you're gay!" button, like the "s/м" button, indicates a technology of desire both productive and regulatory. These buttons do allow for a kind of limited role-playing, but it is one in which the "exploration" is always already constrained by a logic requiring instantly recognizable cues, cues frighteningly regularized under the dictates of maximum efficiency and maximum profit.[4] Part of the captivation of cyberporn is that it allows images to be managed and categorized so readily, allowing the subject to assimilate and emulate a particular subject position while retaining the hallucinatory promise of fluidity. The "contract" and financial exchange entailed by "clicking through" to a Web site, or in signing up for a particular site, then, forces this schema of classification to become fixed through acceptance and repetition.

Embodiment and Technologic

The question of discipline returns us necessarily to the more specific question or problem of the technological apparatus of the computer and how the intersection between pornography and the computer operates on the body. How do we begin to address this curious imbrication—so dramatically figured in the *Time* magazine image with which we began—of the human body and the computer apparatus?

Though seemingly obvious, a crucial and often unstated aspect of any technology is its material specificity—the way one cannot engage with the Internet except through the computer as a specific kind of material object or instrument with which the user has to interact in certain habitual ways. In the course of this interaction, repetitive practices concretize into a particular citational chain, one which becomes embedded both within a particular personal and more general social history. Vivian Sobchack refers to this incorporated logic as a "technologic." In "The Scene of the Screen," she claims that representational technologies, such as the computer, convey their logic in two ways: first, through the representations they display; and second, through the manner in which they latently engage our bodies. For Sobchack, technological analysis must take place on these two levels simultaneously, and any given technologic text must be read not only hermeneutically but also "through our perceptive sensorium, through the materiality (or *immanenent mediation*) of our own bodies. . . . The perceiving and sensing body is always also a *lived-body*—immersed in and making social meaning as well as physical sense" (2000, 139).

Considering Internet pornography in this light leads us to read collections of on-line images through the framework of a technologic always already reflexively incorporated by the viewer. This suggests not only that the habits of looking at Internet pornography are as constitutive of the viewing experience as the images themselves but, likewise, that these habits of looking insistently participate in inscribing power relations and social relations directly onto the body of the subject through gesture and repetition.[5] These physical habits of looking—of pointing and clicking, of pushing the refresh button on Webcams, of the delays and frustrations of opening and closing windows—as well as the representational assumptions these habits entail, push the viewer into a particular kind of interaction with the Internet, one that not only reflects but reinscribes social relations. We might consider these material habits, following Judith Butler's reading of Pierre Bourdieu, as "a tacit form of performativity, a citational chain lived and believed at the level of the body" (Butler 1997, 155). This is not to say that any given technology demands a certain practicum, any more than it automatically reproduces preexistent social relations, but rather that it "generates dispositions which *incline* the social subject to act in relative conformity" with those relations (Butler 1997, 155).

The insistent appeal of the pornographic image necessarily offers us a denser understanding of the insistent mechanisms with which particular technologics incline the body. In some sense, an analysis of on-line pornography must begin with the framework of this technologic and an examination of the physical apparatus through which pornographic images are encountered because the physical apparatus of the computer, and the material habits it requires, places the viewer in a relationship with the images in Internet pornography that differs significantly from the viewer's relationship to other types of pornography.

Delay and Deferral: Body and Interface

The question then becomes one of the body's relation to the screen as a material object and as a space of representation. Information on the World Wide Web does not simply appear—it must be found. This process of searching can help us to clarify significant aspects of the interface, and the particular logic and habitus such searching provokes.

It is important to note that a substantial difference exists between being a "member" of a pay porn site and simply surfing for porn on the Web; and regardless of the growth and gross income of porn sites, many (if not most) people who look at porn on-line are not members of pay sites. Thus, from the perspective of the average viewer, a primary experience of looking for, and eventually at, cyberporn is precisely one of frustration and waiting.[6] The promise of cyberporn is one of immediate gratification, yet the technological systems of the Internet, as well as the interfaces of cyberporn sites, necessitate delay: the delay of logging on, the delay of finding a site, the delay of "signing through" the initial contract, the delay of having the thumbnails load, and then, finally, the delay of waiting for the selected image, sequence of images, or video segment to appear. A high-speed connection may decrease this delay, but cyberporn constantly pushes the boundaries of bandwidth; as soon as the technology can immediately deliver full-frame images, streaming video comes on offer, with slower load times. Even with a high-speed connection, there is still often delay on the side of the site delivering the content. The technologic of the computer forces these sequential acts of waiting and looking and waiting to become habit, and in so doing, it inscribes repetition and delay as pleasures of a different order. On some level, there is indeed a limit to what the viewer will willingly put up with in order to get what he or she wants, and as such, delay can become frustration. But *Web surfing*, a telling term, offers its own pleasures, regardless of the frustration porn sites both understand and provoke; the structure of many porn sites seems to both direct and cater to the viewer's desires for delay and deferral by allowing the process of searching to exist under the aegis of the goal of "getting what they want," but in excess of it. Specifically, the floods of images and the enormous range of selection on any given pay site are there for a reason, and the reason seems to be precisely this process.

One might see this delay as intensifying the pleasure of the eventual visibility of the object by causing the object to acquire an illusory inaccessibility. But it makes more sense to see the satisfaction as taking place in the deferral of satisfaction itself. Seen in this light, the goal exists in part to allow the subject, or a portion of the subject, to rationalize the pleasure of surfing. To imagine the goal, then, is to project into a moment of perfect satisfaction—and the obtaining of a perfect image, one completely adequate to the subject's desire. But in comparison to this imagined perfect image, every image will always remain inadequate, and so the "search" continues. Psychoanalysis generally, and Jacques Lacan's particular articulation of the impossibility of fulfilling one's desire,[7] articulates this point and its implications for subjectivity at some length. But common sense tells us that part of the pleasure in Web surfing is the pleasure of motion and movement either toward an unknown object or away from a boring desk job. The nearly perfect image, the one that comes closest to approximating one's desire—the group-sex shot with the not-too-busty redhead bent over in the front, perhaps—still only offers momentary satisfaction; in fact, images close to one's desire can provoke anxiety because they might cause the end of Web surfing. The subject is faced with a choice—will this be the last image? Even if the viewer knows he or she is unlikely to find one better, he will often continue on, forgoing the pleasures of the known for the pleasures (often through frustration) of the unknown. The user constantly shifts on to new images—and in this process, new delays—in an endless slippage of desire in which part of the pleasure derives from habitual repetition and habitual deferral.[8]

Amateur Pornography

An interrogation of on-line pornography's imbrication in a particular technological apparatus necessarily leads us to a particular interrogation of on-line pornography sites, sites which, however much they may share, each constitute a specific field of application. The remainder of this inquiry will investigate the viewing mechanisms and structures of identification as developed in a specific subgenre—that of on-line "amateur" pornography. The shifting relationship between viewer and object inaugurated by cyberporn most clearly becomes evident in the category of amateur cyberporn. Beyond its immediacy, the key offer of the Internet for pornography would seem to be a sense of interactivity, which brings with it a sense of shared space and a collapse or disavowal of distance. The amateur subgenre most significantly engages with the opportunities for "interaction" and "self-production" offered by the Internet. With on-line amateur porn, we are watching, as if in a petri dish, the shifting nature of the relationship between viewer and woman-as-spectacle.

The bulk of pornographic imagery on-line is professionally produced—including, at this point, the bulk of so-called amateur porn, at least on the corporatized Web sites. Amateur porn on-line takes its visual language and textual cues in part from amateur videos, a genre which exploded in the middle of the 1980s—a case of couples doing it for themselves and distributing their homemade efforts through swap services. These efforts eventually made it to video store distribution, and the professional porn industry was quick to capitalize on the trend, which elevated previous drawbacks such as slapdash lighting, low production values, and wobbly camera movements from liability to aesthetic and financial asset. The Internet seemed to reposition this co-opted DIY aesthetic in crucial ways—an initial ease of distribution, and the possibility of "swapping," extended to the possibility of "interaction" between the producers and consumers of this pornography. The central frisson in amateur porn lies in its articulation of a certain proximity to the life of the spectator—and amateur Internet porn promises to make that proximity even more proximate.

There is a wide spectrum of material on the Web that could be classed as amateur pornography, ranging from camgirls who show a little skin periodically to professionally produced shots of the same airbrushed and implanted women one sees on "professional" porn Web sites. The images, then, are set apart by the rhetoric that surrounds them: these women are billed as your neighbor, your boss, your sister-in-law.

SIGNING IN

When you sign up as a member of a $39.95-per-month amateur porn site, such as amateuruniversity.com or karasamateurs.com, you enter an enclosed area positioning itself as an exclusive club. Oddly enough, some of these clubs look like nothing so much as graphically enhanced Web portals. Once "inside," members are greeted by an elaborate menu—they can look at new or archived photos, watch videos, read erotica, chat in the chat room, chat with a stripper performing a private real-time Web-cast show, gamble, shop, read an advice column, or look at erotic cartoons. The lower portion of the screen sometimes links to nonerotically oriented services: news headlines, magazine articles, or free email accounts. Much like Web portals such as Yahoo!, the sites are structured to become a habit and a community. It offers full service, one-stop shopping—all your Internet needs at once. The space of the Web site becomes a familiar, even domestic "place."

Amateur porn Web sites provide some specific menu options that work to position them as amateur sites; these include personal letters, biographical information, on-line diaries, and Webcams. The personal letters address the viewer directly, inviting him into the space of the Web site or detailing the amateur's life; on-line diaries are another way for the viewer "to get up close and personal."

These viewing mechanisms offer a space of very particular, limited interaction; in their persistence across corporatized Web sites, they allow the viewer to enter into a relationship with the women shown that is simultaneously real and phantasmatic. It is the articulation of a space of public privacy that the viewer both enters and maintains at a distance. The viewing mechanisms available on a number of amateur porn Web sites foreground the idea that consumers of pornographic images are purchasing a fantasy of private access to a person; the specifically pornographic character of these images constitutes only a small part of the total "interaction". It is an inter-action that comes to take on the character of a fetishistic disavowal, an "I know, but nevertheless . . . ." Critically, this relationship is grounded in seri-ality and repetition and the sense of proximity these characteristics serve to generate. It is a "relationship" based on and created through the purchase of intimacy, and this one-way intimacy constitutes, over and above the prurient imagery itself, a substantial part of what is being sold in amateur Internet porn, and hence a substantial part of what people are looking to buy.

A DAY IN THE LIFE

At Kara's Amateurs, "Members now have access to see what our Amateurs are all about. Spend a day of their life up close and personal! Go through our Amateur's daily schedule and see what they are up to. From the time they wake up, their walk in the park, to their sex life!" This section, called "A day in the life . . . ," is promoted as an exclusive attraction, but it func-tions much like the Webcams and simulated Webcams available on other sites and as such clearly demonstrates the everyday dynamics of the "en-counter" with the amateur in Internet pornography. The amateur's day is divided into segments scheduled as appointments in a so-called date book. Some appointments are explicitly theatrical—the model will take a shower, masturbate with a vibrator, or have sex with the delivery boy—but many are not. The nontheatrical segments show more clearly what is at stake here: the abolition of the spectacular in favor of other models of relationality.

These appointments, or events, showcase the particular temporality of Internet pornography, as well as how it is framed and articulated by the spe-cific mechanisms and limitations of the Internet. Importantly, the tempo-rality of the date book is one of routine; it draws on the staging of amateur Webcams, where live, twenty-four-hours-a-day access means that the viewer can constantly check in on the performer's life or keep the performer's image in constant sight on the computer desktop. The "A Day in the Life . . ." videos participate in this rhetoric of liveness, presenting the frame as a win-dow.

The day's events are further subdivided into brief segments of streaming video. This might seem a purely technological constraint, but the elabora-tion of these individual segments resembles the elaboration of "chapters" in the now ubiquitous DVD format, and this allows for a familiar exercise of control over the interface. And yet this desire to control the time of the video is not in fact complementary. With streaming video, viewers can pause the stream to create a still shot blurred with traces and ghostlines but, crucially, they cannot time-shift to fast-forward or rewind. To re-view a particular sequence is to begin again. Time thus becomes a sequence of discrete "chapters" or events—this is the logic of television before TIVO or the VCR, and it is a logic closely related to that of event and reality television, offering the sense of presence generated by an "implicit claim to be live" (Bolter and Grusin 1999, 188). Casting itself in this rhetoric, the necessarily low-res quality of the streaming video thus becomes a further guarantee of liveness, rather than an eruption into an awareness of the video as image. The low-res images visually reference Webcams offering continuous live broadcast, generally of still images, refreshed at rates measured in seconds or minutes. Webcam images are marked by low resolution, and are attractive precisely because of the level of "intimacy" they offer—a sense of presence guaranteed by what is perceived as a privileged relationship to the real. The low-res images themselves come to signify this privileged relationship, a signification only enhanced by their similarity to the image sequences obtained from video surveillance cameras, which have a similar claim to liveness.

Click on the 6 P.M. appointment in "A Day in the Life of Chandler," and blonde and tan Chandler leans into the camera to declare "now we're gonna go eat some sushi. We'll have some sake, get a little toasty, gonna be a lot of fun." The camera follows her as she walks into the restaurant and sits down next to a mirror. The camera is then positioned at a diagonal angle to her; part of the time she talks directly to the camera, and part of the time she talks away from it, to someone who would be sitting across the table from her. She is not alone in the film—when the sake is set down, there are two glasses—but all you see of her companion is his hand reaching for the sake.[9] The visual rhetoric of this sequence, as seen in figure 1, teases the viewer with a situation somewhere between voyeurism and direct address. The tease lies in the fact that you're not there, but you might as well be. The hand on the sake translates, with a slight hitch of dislocation, to the spectator's hand on the keyboard and the mouse.[10] Here, you are present to the space Chandler is in, more directly than in conventional narrative film (pornographic or otherwise) because you are solicited as a participant in this space. But you necessarily experience the situation and its pleasure in a thrown and almost robotic state, comfortably deprived of the necessity of action.[11] A second type of presence, then, is offered when Chandler ad-

1. A typical capture from "A Day in the Life of Chandler" on the Kara's Amateurs Web site.

dresses the camera directly. In this model, the viewer does not enter into the space of the screen, but the figure on the screen is present to and in the space the viewer inhabits.

Click on the first appointment in "A Day in the Life of Chandler," and Chandler stretches, rubbing her eyes and yawning as she rolls over in bed. Her makeup is already perfect, and she waves and smiles, saying "Hi! So are you waiting to follow me around? I'm very excited that you're coming with me. I've got a lot of errands to run, but I want you to come and watch me." She leans over and turns on the light, whispering conspiratorially that she needs to take a shower. "You still watching me? Watch me get in the shower. . . . Do you like watching me? Waking up in the morning?"

But the viewer does not, and would not want to, answer "yes." To answer would be to foreground his status as desiring, and hence, as lacking. That lack is exactly what this sequence is designed to recompense. The viewer's lack, his need, is proposed by Chandler's first question, which situates him as *waiting* for her, to wake up, to act. But this lack is announced only to be deferred, taken on by the woman with her claim to be excited that the viewer is going to accompany her throughout her day. Her "I *want* you to come and watch me" thus becomes understood by the viewer as "I *need* you to come and watch me," serving to displace his own need entirely. The event of the encounter proceeds through this dialectic of recognition. Through this play of recognition the woman acknowledges, produces, the element of lack only to take it onto herself, thus foregrounding the spectator's anxiety so much the better to relieve it. Her language accentuates the way in which this displacement of lack—a lack the spectator is aware of but fetishistically disavows— is itself one of the key sources of pleasure and excitement here.

In this encounter, a substantive portion of the fantasy seems to be the feeling, on the part of the viewer, that he is necessary to the woman on the other side of the camera; that she needs the viewer to be looking, in such a manner that the looking enables her pleasure. It is a fantasy which, as we have seen, emerges out of the spectator's own desire, his own lack—and the need to displace that lack. Displacing his needs and desires onto Chandler, he moves from a position of lack to one of overflowing plenitude. Chandler can exist by the grace of his look. She needs him, and he is able to fulfill her need. This differs from the relationship the viewer develops with an exhibitionist Web site such as Jennicam, however, because here the relationship is sustained entirely on the side of the spectator. This projection nourishes a more overarching vision of the woman as lacking, but more directly, it works to sustain a relationship in which the viewer, and the viewer's look, is needed by the images on the other side of the screen.[12]

"Reality"

The dynamics of this type of encounter, and the sense of presence it provokes, can be partially explained through what Jean Baudrillard terms the "frisson of the real." As he describes the filming of the Louds, the family whose lives were broadcast in the 1971 PBS series and ur-scene of reality TV *An American Family*, the producer's triumph was to say 'They lived as though we were not there'. An absurd, paradoxical formula—neither true nor false: utopian. The 'as if *we* were not there' being equivalent to 'as if *you* were there' (1994, 28). He goes on to say that it was "this utopia, this paradox that fascinated the twenty million viewers, much more than did the 'perverse' pleasure of violating someone's privacy. In the verité experience it is not a question of secrecy or perversion, but of a sort of frisson of the real, a frisson of vertiginous and phony exactitude, a frisson of simultaneous distancing and magnification. . . . There one sees what the real never was (but 'as if you were there')."

In Baudrillard's description, the pleasure of the reality TV experience lies not so much in the voyeurism of the viewing, and the power relationship that would imply, as in the way that the screen makes an impossible real available for encounter. The viewer is aware of the necessity of televisual mediation and its inevitable transformation of the depicted lives, but still disavows it in order to take pleasure in the microscopic exactitude of what is shown and the magnification of the minutest details. This magnification is of a different order altogether than that of the film screen, in which the image is literally enlarged into a physical spectacle. With reality TV, the television screen begins to operate as a transparent window, showing a reality always already impacted by the structuring of televisual mediation.[13]

Baudrillard's discussion of reality television allows us to understand that in Web-based, amateur pornography, viewers are witnessing an abolition of the spectacular itself through a collapse of subject and object and of the poles of activity and passivity. It is no longer a question of watching but of a hallucinatory "being there" while knowing that one is not "there" and that, in fact, there is no "there" there (i.e., no reality apart from its mediation.) This then presents a different type of subjectivity, a subjectivity for which the problem is, as Žižek puts it, not the possibility that "Big Brother is watching, but the possibility that Big Brother is not watching."[14]

The abolition of the spectacular is further at stake in what viewers often articulate as the central draw of the amateur image—that it shows "real bodies" experiencing "real pleasure." This desire is figured oppositionally to the supposed artificiality of more general pornography, in which "it's all fake." A teaser to one site's hard-core amateur porn states, "I have another friend who used to shoot Glam Porn Shots for a major men's magazine (you've heard of it). Eventually he became bored and when the opportunity to shoot amateur girls having sex came along, he jumped at it (wouldn't you?). He says that nothing gets him harder than watching those innocent girls lose all control." The loss of control of the amateur is contrasted to the control of the professional—and it is the loss of control that guarantees the realness of the sex. It also demonstrates the type of access at issue here—the photographer (and, by extension, the viewer) is turned on by seeing something the girl does not necessarily want to reveal, something that goes past the performance of sex. The pleasure, then, comes from the "real" pleasure of the other. This begins to show a way in which the viewer desires a direct and involuntary somatic reaction on the part of the performer, which lines up rather neatly with the direct, and somewhat involuntary, somatic reaction provoked in him through identification.

Interpassivity

In attempting to assess the nature of these new mediations of subjectivity, we cannot help but return to that traditional guarantor of subjectivity itself —the concept of free choice. We often find this compensatory rhetoric and narrative of free choice, a cornerstone of American cultural ideology, inhabiting precisely those situations that, on a basic structural level, admit of little or no choice at all. In the contemporary media landscape, we consistently encounter paeans to the promise and potential of media "interactivity," yet it remains often unclear how much substantive interaction is taking place, and whether we would even want it if it were.

Interactivity allows the user to break out of a relationship in which he stares passively at the screen and is acted on, as is supposed, in this particular rhetorical and theoretical constellation, to be the case in ordinary film and video spectatorship. An interface is considered interactive to the extent that it functions to return control to the user (Bolter and Grusin 1999, 33.) In "On Totalitarian Interactivity," Lev Manovich points toward an analysis of the illusory nature of choice in many interactive situations—after all, the viewer is only able to select from a limited number of producer-created options. Paradoxically, this "choice" can have a proscriptive effect, even as the viewer is given a highly illusory sense of control.

Žižek goes beyond a critique of the lack of choice in many interactive situations by proposing the term *interpassivity* as a "shadowy supplement" to interactivity, postulating it as a necessary correlative to "interacting with the object, instead of just passively following the show" (1997, 112). In a relationship of interactivity with the object, the object performs a certain type of work for the viewer. Interpassivity is a similarly transferential relation to an other, but one in which the other not only does the work for the viewer but also enjoys or believes in the viewer's place. Žižek's typically heterogeneous examples include the canned laughter of sitcoms, the Tibetan prayer wheel, and the VCR. Critically, there are two aspects to this: in the first, the other takes over the dull, mechanical aspect of routine duties; and in the second, the other takes over the duty to enjoy, a demand placed on the subject by the superego. This transference constitutes a passive action, but it also constitutes a deferral of this very passivity. The term *interpassivity* pushes us toward a different understanding of the type of work that goes on in looking at Internet pornography, and it also articulates a different understanding of the ways in which technologics have already been incorporated.

In the "A Day in the Life . . ." segment with Chandler, presence is negotiated through a particular dynamic of transference. Throughout the segment, there is a sense of the woman, Chandler, performing actions *for* the viewer. Through Žižek, we might instead consider Chandler to be performing *in the place of* the viewer. This, then, is the relationship he refers to as interpassivity.

In the viewer's relation to on-line amateur pornography, three objects "work" for the subject: the camera, the computer, and the woman in the picture. This logic of transferred work is traced, imagistically, in a still image from Kara's Amateurs, in which we see a woman, Kitty, sitting on a toilet, masturbating, while another woman films her. Given the expectation that Internet porn incites masturbation, the initial identification seems to be a cross-gendered one of pleasure; the viewer takes pleasure in the woman's pleasure, in the way in which it incites his own. The pleasure of the spectator is also offered to the viewer through an identification with the woman using the camera to film, even as the viewer uses the computer to view. This is further complicated by an intrasite intertextuality; the video filmed within the photograph is also available to the viewer. It is another "A Day in the Life . . ." video, this one for Kitty. Given the process of emulation that emerges as one of the hallmarks of the computer/Internet experience, objects become radically conflated here; it is not that they represent each other, but rather that, through the logic of digitalization, they become each other. The camera is a type of digital video camera in which the image is not seen through a viewfinder, but is, rather, displayed for the viewer on a screen, in the process of filming. The computer is capable of emulating a video player, to display the "A Day in the Life . . ." video, and through this logic is capable of being a camera displayed as already a video player. Following this logic, Webcams cause the computer to function as a camera, not just as the display of the outlet of a camera. This creates a slip, or an elision between the two tasks or events. Instrumentality and use are key here, rather than any quality of the object. This fact positions objects as somewhat fluid, and the ensuing confusion about the specificity of tasks and labor becomes part of the logic of the computer, which has been reflexively incorporated into the body.

A number of potential identifications are set up for the viewer here, but the two primary ones are the enjoyment of Kitty masturbating and the enjoyment of the photographer, who is in control. Both of these figures are simultaneously subject and object, and simultaneously passive and active. And the viewer's relationship to both of them is one of transference; the spectator is able to displace his "work" of spectating onto them, as well as his passive enjoyment. In this scenario of interpassivity, we are pushed toward being conscious of pleasure as itself a type of work, a realization that seems particularly critical in the case of pornography, in which what we are seeing, and taking pleasure in, is bodies at the work of pleasure. This also allows us to conceive a radically different notion of the type of enjoyment available to the viewer in pornography, one particularly applicable to on-line pornography. In this scenario, both women are performing this work of viewing and enjoying for the subject, as are the computer and the camera. And, again, in amateur pornography, this enjoyment on the part of the woman is exactly what people articulate as the critical point of their interest. What this suggests is a situation in contemporary culture in which people displace their enjoyment onto others; that what they enjoy seeing in pornography is not necessarily the impulse toward masturbation, but precisely the experience of seeing, and having, someone else enjoying in their place.

Critically, though, in amateur porn, the enjoyment is not just sexual. These women do it all—they masturbate *and* water the plants *and* walk the dog *and* take college classes. Amateurs are not just experiencing sexual pleasure for the viewer; they are eating sushi, baking cookies, and buying pizza with and for him. This further extends the concept of interpassivity and its relationship to sexual pleasure because, in amateur porn, these secondary activities become primary—they mark the crucial difference of amateur porn. This suggests that the process of intimacy and identification is cemented by the somatic identification of one body experiencing sexual pleasure and sexual arousal with another body experiencing the same thing, only on a computer screen—but that the sexual activities are somehow less important than the other activities. It suggests the possibility that even the graphic sexuality within amateur porn exists mainly as an incitement for subjective identification with the performer, for this ever-fuller sense of participation with that performer's life, and that it is this ever-elusive relationship, in effect, that itself becomes the obscure object of desire. Yet this relationship is, as we have said, thoroughly mediated through a technology which itself holds a kind of affective charge. We will never understand Internet pornography as long as we consider the networked personal computer as a mere tool through which we access the sexually explicit graphics, for in so doing, we miss the ways in which our sexual desires are being mediated through the pleasures of the technology itself, and the particular fantasies it has on offer.

Going On-line . . .

Pornography is going on-line. And not just pornography—music, television, even mainstream films are increasingly downloaded over the Internet and viewed on personal computers. What was previously a marginal behavior is emerging as a mainstream practice. As it does, film and cultural studies needs to attend to the material specificity and the embedded cultural history of this particular interface. Yet any such account must consider the fact that the Internet, and the computer technologies that underscore it, are inherently unstable, constantly shifting and evolving. The instability of these objects is compounded by an instability of subjects, caught in the flux of technological change, capital exchange, and inscribed power relations. Any history or mapping of the Internet—or of Internet pornography—will thus be a snapshot of a particular place and a particular time. This exploration of amateur Internet pornography is thus necessarily a partial and contingent account.

Pornography is currently prevalent on the Internet not simply because it allows the quick and easy distribution and private consumption of erotic images, but because the affective charge of pornography is linked to, and redoubled by, the affective charge attached to new and perpetually renewed computer technology. Pornography changes once it is positioned on the computer; the attraction of cyberporn becomes in part the attraction to and fascination with what we perceive as the vastly new possibilities for subjectivity that technology seems to offer. There is a fascination with the continually shifting capabilities of the computer as a relatively new apparatus for displaying images, both still and moving. Not inconsequentially, there is always a link between pornography and advancing technologies of representation, and the specifically hybrid representational space of the networked computer interface is no exception. This essay has tried to introduce some of the complex fantasies of identification and interaction that are arising at this particular intersection of technology and pornography.

On-line amateur porn impels us to consider the newly hybrid space of the computer as it redraws the boundaries that operate within and around private, or domestic space. As the television has become larger, and living rooms have been transformed into home theaters, the computer has become smaller and more personal—it has become a private enclave within the domestic or corporate sphere. This becomes evident in operating systems such as Microsoft Windows and Apple's os x, and internet portals such as AOL, which allow multiple users to each log in to their own space. In these systems, changes to the color scheme or the desktop pattern are meant to stand in for the 'ownership' or delimitation of a private space on the computer. This private space *within* a public environment (even the privacy of the individual family member vis-à-vis the family) then opens out onto a larger space of the Internet, a space which is itself importantly both public and private. These interface technologies are transforming our received understanding about the very nature and division of what is private and what is public.

This transformation is key to understanding how and why Internet pornography has largely replaced magazine pornography, but it is also critical in understanding the way in which the computer functions as a space of encounter, or space of "liveness." This space of liveness is aligned with Webcams, but it is also linked to the function that digital camera images have come to serve in current culture. John Seely Brown was recently quoted in the *New York Times* stating that "We're beginning to take pictures not to keep them around, but to reach out and touch someone with them, to extend the moment, that sense of presence" (Hafner 2002). It is not only a matter of mapping our old conceptions of private space and the public sphere onto the Internet, but of the potential, even the necessity, of generating new kinds of spaces and encounters.

Notes

1   It is important to note that the gender of the figure here, while somewhat ambiguous, is necessarily, and presumably male. This would be a different article if it were evidently a woman wrapped around the computer screen. However, in this particular technological panic, it is assumed that computers, and their potential, or requisite contamination are a masculine problem, much as it is assumed, by this article and by culture in general, that the lure of pornography in particular, and technology in general, is directed toward men. Because the mainstream pornographic websites that I will be addressing presume a male viewership, this paper will follow this assumption. However, it is important to note that this assumption has a normative agenda, one that works to efface the female spectator of online pornography, as well as the female user of computer technology. This double effacement of women might be read as a defense, on the part of the heterosexual male imaginary, against the radical social possibilities that the Internet might seem to provide.

2   An overview of the dubious methodology behind this article can be found in Mike Godwin's "Fighting a Cyber-Porn Panic," in *Cyber Rights* (2003, 259–318).

3   If the personal computer and its connection to the World Wide Web represents in some way the entry of the public sphere into the domestic space of the home, or rather, the possibility that the soul of the domestic space might be turned outward toward a networked public sphere, there seems to be a cultural fear about promiscuity and adultery in play as well. What desires can this (potentially married?) man (or woman) have which are not satisfied by his home life? What does it mean that these desires might, for once, not have to be simply repressed, but could find some kind of expression on-line? Could this expression possibly be legitimate, and what would this do to the "space" of the domestic nuclear family? As is often the case, new technologies come to figure old social and cultural anxieties, giving these anxieties new avenues for expression.

4   The space of the Internet is generally considered in dematerialized rhetorics

but it exists only by means of large, expensive machines that exist in physical space. The reality of countries prohibiting access to certain sites or the way the structure of the Internet increasingly follows the dictates of large corporate conglomerates will play an ever increasing role in our experience of this particular cultural site. As such, it seems critically important not to lose sight of the larger field of a corporatized social technology into which Internet pornography occurs. Presented through a particular technological apparatus, pornographic images are embedded in networks of production and consumption and informed by particular social conditions.

5 This is informed, as I believe Sobchack's piece is critically informed, by an understanding of Bourdieu's conception of the habitus as developed in *The Logic of Practice* (1992).

6 But as I will argue, even members of pay sites are not freed from the logic of delay and deferral. It is simply transformed and imparted in different ways.

7 This concept is developed, in particular, in Seminar 7 and Seminar 11.

8 This information is taken from anecdotal evidence, personal experience, and interviews conducted in the chat rooms of various porn sites.

9 The hand reaching for the sake is both obviously white and obviously male. This gestures toward a presumed audience, but also works to reinforce and reiterate the limits of this exclusive identification.

10 While the analogy is not exact, we might trace out a relationship between the sense of presence here and the telepresence video games offer, particularly in cut sequences, in that viewers are pushed into inhabiting the screen space as a ghostly, mediated other.

11 This dynamic becomes evident even more dramatically in the "virtual lap dance" feature available at www.danni.com, where in a number of shots from Crissy Moran's lap dance, the camera offers the point of view of a man receiving a lap dance — in one video to the point of showing "location" shots of "your" lap, clad in nondescript jeans.

12 This is not a dialectic limited to amateur sites, although it is more clearly foregrounded there. This dialectic, and the displacement it serves, becomes evident in the chat rooms and Webcam setups that make for prominent features on "professional porn Web sites, from the personal sites of Jenna Jameson and Briana Banks to "Danni's Hard Drive," which tells its viewers, "when you become a member, you have the opportunity to truly interact with the women of your dreams."

13 Baudrillard's statements are made even more apropos by the current explosion of the reality television genre, which has been paralleled by an explosion in on-line Webcams and journals, often accompanying one another. For the users, these on-line journals frequently articulate a public space of privacy, which dismantles traditional conceptions of the public sphere. People write in them without seeming to realize that what they say is public, and available through Internet search engines, and then are shocked when parents and colleagues at work

read these journals, to real-world effect. "It's my private journal!" they say. "If he wasn't going to treat it as such, he shouldn't have read it!"

14 One of the participants in MTV's reality TV show, *The Real World*, interviewed in the *New York Times*, stated that it was "easy to get used to" being watched for four months by a network of television cameras and went on to say that "now, not having a mic and camera feels weird to me." ("Designed to Pry," 20).

Works Cited

Baudrillard, Jean. 1994. *Simulacra and Simulation*. Ann Arbor: University of Michigan Press.

Bolter, David Jay, and Richard Grusin. 1999. *Remediation: Understanding New Media*. Cambridge, Mass.: MIT Press.

Bourdieu, Pierre. 1992. *The Logic of Practice*. Trans. Richard Nice. Palo Alto: Stanford University Press.

Butler, Judith. 1997. *Excitable Speech: A Politics of the Performative*. New York: Routledge.

Elmer-Dewitt, Philip. 1995. "On a Screen near You: Cyberporn." *Time*, July 3: 38–45.

Godwin, Mike. 2003. *Cyber Rights: Defending Free Speech in the Digital Era*. Cambridge, Mass.: MIT Press.

Hafner, Katie. 2002. "Turning the Page." *New York Times*, May 3.

Lacan, Jacques. 1981. *The Four Fundamental Concepts of Psycho-Analysis*. Trans. Alan Sheridan. New York: W. W. Norton.

———. 1992. *The Seminar of Jacques Lacan, Book VII: The Ethics of Pyschoanalysis*. Trans. Dennis Porter. New York: W. W. Norton.

Lane, Frederick. 2000. *Obscene Profits: The Entrepreneurs of Pornography in the Cyber Age*. New York: Routledge.

Leland, John. 2001. "Designed to Pry: Building a Better Fishbowl." *New York Times*, June 21.

Manovich, Lev. "On Totalitarian Interactivity." *Rhizome Digest*, October 11, 1996.

———. 2003. "New Media from Borges to HTML." In *New Media Reader*. Ed. Noah Wardrip-Fruin and Nick Montfort. Cambridge, Mas.: MIT Press. 13–25.

Sobchack, Vivian. 2000. "The Scene of the Screen." *Electronic Media and Technoculture*, ed. John Thornton Caldwell. New Brunswick, N.J.: Rutgers. 137–55.

Žižek, Slavoj. 1997. *The Plague of Fantasies*. London: Verso.

part 2

Gay, Lesbian, and Homosocial Pornographies

Homosociality in the Classical American Stag Film: Off-Screen, On-Screen

THOMAS WAUGH

Seduced by A. Prick
Directed by Ima Cunt,
Photographed by R. U. Hard

✳ The 1927 American stag film *Wonders of the Unseen World*, whose pruri-ently succinct credits I have borrowed for my epigraph, got it wrong. In fact, Mr. Prick was the real director and Ms. Cunt only the star performer, while Mr. Hard, the state of whose arousal is solicitously queried through-out, was and is the spectator addressed. For it is no secret that there are many more cunts than pricks in front of the camera in this film, and in the Ameri-can stag cinema in general—that distinctive corpus of approximately 2,000 films of a total duration of perhaps three hundred hours produced between 1915 and 1968 that is the subject of this essay.[1] It is equally without ques-tion that behind the camera and in the audience there are pricks, and only pricks. Not only are most of the anonymous male artists during the heyday of the stag fanatically focused on the female organs but they also, in most cases, do everything in their power to avoid showing male organs, to keep those pleated flannel trousers on.

There is nothing surprising in this avoidance, for the stag filmmakers who supplied the lively clandestine market of itinerant projectionists and all-male audiences anticipated that great American pop culture tradition of genital aphasia of the postwar era, shaped by censorship, yes, but also by shame and disavowal. This tradition would reach its zenith in the 1950s with Russ Meyer and *Playboy*,[2] which for the first two decades of its history meticulously banished not only Ima's cunt from its airbrushed photographic iconography but, more significantly, all hints of the male body, especially the eyes and penises to which the "bunnies" were addressing their "R. U. Hards". Take *Smart Alec* (1953), for example (some say the 1953 apogee of the American stag tradition), a film that miraculously does not even acknowledge that the male protagonist (who is lithe, blond, and tanned if you *really* look hard) actually *has* a penis, and fights as hard to avoid getting it in the frame as squeamish leading lady Candy Barr struggles to avoid sucking it. This is what I still remember from my experience thirty years ago on first seeing this film with a rowdy group of college boys who, smothered by Barr's sixteen-year-old mammary amplitude, did not seem to notice the hero's castration . . . but that's another story.[3] Throughout *Strictly Union* (1917), the protagonist Mr. Hardpenis may well have had his personal reasons for keeping his voluminous overalls on, but the tenacious drapery of most of his peers, as well as the unceremoniousness of male disrobings when they do occur in the stag film corpus—whether off-screen (e.g., *Inspiration* [1945]) or via jump cuts (e.g., *The Hypnotist* [1931]; *Fishin'* [1941])—form part of a consistent pattern of denial.

At the same time, the general corpus of the American stag film demonstrates the obsession of patriarchal culture with the elusive Ms. Cunt, with "figuring and measuring" the unknowable "truth" of sex—making the female sex speak, as Linda Williams might put it (1989)—with penetrating women's bodies and their erotic pleasure.[4] But stag films fail remarkably in this endeavour. *Playmates* (1956–58), in which a lit cylindrical lightbulb is inserted in the protagonist's vagina, offers both an extremist parody of this desperate search for truth and a demonstration of its futility. However, what these movies ultimately succeed in doing instead is illuminating both the fleshly pricks they try so hard to avoid showing, or show only incidentally, and the symbolic phallus—in short, masculinity. This is my objective in the present essay: to demonstrate how the stag films, both on-screen and off-screen, are tenaciously engaged with the homosocial core of masculinity as constructed within American society, inextricably spread out over what Eve Kosofsky Sedgwick calls the "homosocial continuum" (1985).

Only rarely does this question of masculinity erupt explicitly in the stag film corpus. Two films draw attention to the pattern elsewhere by their deployment of an exceptional trope: in the remarkably similar denouements of *An Author's True Story* (1933), and *Goodyear* (1950s),[5] two worldly wise stag heroines pause and diddle thoughtfully with flaccid and spent pricks, shown unusually up close, as if to ask not only "R. U. [No Longer] Hard?" but also "what is this that has caused so much narrative and social commotion?" The *Goodyear* performer even shakes her head—sadly? bemusedly?—as she looks at the unprepossessing organ. The cartoon *Buried Treasure* (1925) is the only other site of what I would call an overt interrogation of masculinity, availing itself exuberantly of the resources of animated metaphor and deconstruction. This nonphotographic (i.e., graphic and iconic, rather than indexical) "western," with its penile sword fights and visual jokes about buggery, crab lice, impotence, castration and prostitution, offers the only hint of the *problematization* of sex that Williams would diagnose in a much later corpus, seventies hard core, the only anticipation of the screen-size blow-ups of monstrous, detachable pricks in *Deep Throat* (dir. Gerard Damiano, 1972) and its ilk. In the corpus of American stags made between 1915 and 1968, there are thus only a few moments of explicit reflection among more than three hundred hours of unconscious masculinity on display in spite of itself.

I am not denying that some evidence of women's subjectivity also flickers against the grain of the stags. Across the screen divide come occasional *glimpses* of female subjectivity in different forms: pleasure (the rare unmistakeable female orgasm identified by diarist Glenway Wescott in a 1949 stag screening as "the female finally lifting in a kind of continuous kiss of the entire body from head to foot," [1990, 266]); camaraderie (especially with other women, e.g., nude bathing *à trois* in *Getting His Goat* [1923], but also with men, e.g., the extraordinarily congenial and natural conversation the skinny-dipper in *Fishin'* has with her farmboy conquest); generous professionalism (the *Nun's* [1958] expert fingers irresistibly drawn back to the anus of her humping Fabian-haired lover); distraction (the most important thing the star of *Kensey Report* [sic, c. 1950] has on her mind at the end of her performance is to frantically brush off her flouncy, black New Look cocktail skirt); and, yes, disgust (the buxom blonde with the heap of Betty Grable ringlets grimaces and wipes her face after an unforeseen ejaculation in *The Dentist* [c. 1947]). Admittedly, these films were presumably directed by men and ultimately sutured within the framework of male subjectivity. But the spontaneous, "natural" resonance of these gestures I have described, in relation to the self-conscious awkwardness of most of the nonprofessional performances throughout the stag corpus, gives them a behavioral authenticity that stands apart. But these instances, notwithstanding a certain revisionist identification with stag women by "bad girl" feminists of the 1980s,[6] are idiosyncratic moments that seep almost by chance through the continuous fabric of male subjectivity.

Aside from these chance flickers of documentary "truth" in this paradoxical, primitive, and innocent art form that seeks cunt and, as I will show, discovers prick, what do we learn, then, directly but mostly indirectly of men? The whole mosaic of underground erotic film and its spin-off genres does more than expose men's gazes and gestures, and even the occasional full-shot male body. It also exposes the spectrum of male sociality, the experience of having a penis (and being white) in the first two-thirds of the twentieth century.[7] For in front of and behind the camera, on the screen and in the screening room, this spectrum radiates in all its ambiguities and over-determinedness, however hermetic, abstract, individualized, and displaced the narratives are. A. Prick lives in packs.

In the rest of this brief essay, I would like to examine this spectrum of male homosociality that is the object, setting, and vehicle of Mr. Prick's prolific and obsessive work. Or, I would like to lay bare, as John H. Gagnon and William Simon (the only social scientists I know to have studied the stags' subcultural milieu, no doubt aware that they were witnessing the swan song of the stag) put it back in 1967, the "primary referent of the films in this instance [which] is in the area of *homosocial* reinforcement of masculinity and hence only indirectly a reinforcement of heterosexual commitments" (Gagnon and Simon 1973, 266).[8]

Let's start with the pack in front of the screen. In 1976, Al Di Lauro and Gerald Rabkin, the chief stag historians in a still sadly untrodden field, embellished our picture of this crowd in its North American variant, active from the interwar period through the fifties. Participant observers, it is implied, Di Lauro and Rabkin vividly evoked the small-town stag parties, Legion smokers, and fraternity clubhouse parties with film programs run by furtive traveling projectionists carrying suitcases of reels (54–57). Gertrud Koch has assembled the only slightly more bountiful documentation, mostly German, on the audience in Europe and Latin America, found chiefly on the brothel circuit and having an accessory relation to the trade in *real* flesh (1990).[9] These historical accounts emphasize the interactive, collective nature of spectatorship in both Old World and New (the Americans' imagined dialogue runs "Hey Joe, look at the jugs on that broad!" [Di Lauro and Rabkin 1976, 25], while the German equivalent, less speculative, describes "shouts, consoling voices, grunts, applause and encouraging cheers" [Kurt Tucholsky, qtd. in Moreck 1956]). In fact, no direct quotes by participants are available from any continent, and, to my knowledge, no oral histories.

The fragmentary evidence of both milieus remains frustratingly nonspecific, unreliable, moralistic, and condescending. But what else can we expect for any domain of popular culture, much less one whose preservation has been doubly whammied by both cultural stigma and illicit status?

Williams justly chides Di Lauro and Rabkin for their feminist-baiting indifference to the unequal economy of gender difference underlying the turn-on trade, and for their nostalgic sentimentalization of the homosocial vocation of the stag screenings (Williams 1989, esp. 58, 92). I would agree with Williams about the fundamental insufficiency of any project to historicize in a nonfeminist manner the commodification of sex and sexual representation that proliferated in Western culture both before and during the sexual revolution. Think about why so many male performers, unlike most of their leading ladies, wear masks and disguises, and how abject it must be to get fucked by a man wearing a mask (or absurd—the heroine of *Inspiration* [1945] can't stop laughing at her partner's Groucho Marx glasses and mustache).

But in fact, Di Lauro and Rabkin's summary of the acculturation and initiation role of the group screenings, extrapolated from the findings of Gagnon and Simon, is itself quite unsentimental and to the point. They stress above all the tensions, anxieties, avoidance, and embarrassment of the group experience, the "forced bravado of laughter and collective sexual banter," and the obligation "to prove to their fellows that they were worthy of participating in the stag ritual" (Gagnon and Simon 1973, 266). No wonder the inquiries about tumescence were à propos, as were the fast and furious intertitle jokes that knowingly revved up the bravado and banter and bandaged over the vulnerability of the male libido. (Culinary images were a favorite; for example, over the fellatio trope in *Strictly Union* are the titles "Going downtown for lunch" and "Cocktail sauce.") And as for the bonhomie of men getting hard *together*, Di Lauro and Rabkin seem hardly sentimental at all—since they are in denial about the whole thing. Sentimentality is something I myself may well be guilty of, however, for to me, as for many "objective" observers who lean toward the homo end of the homosocial spectrum, the collective rituals of male homosociality are blatantly and inescapably homoerotic (a truth the so-called physique films of the fifties and sixties succeeded in marketing, but we'll come back to that).

In getting together to collectively get aroused—if not off—at the spectacle of Ima Cunt, the stag spectators reenacted some of the basic structural dynamics of the patriarchy, namely, the male exchange in women, in this case the exchange in fantasies and images of women. Those club-rooms were the scene, lubricated by alcohol and darkness, of what Sedgwick defines as homosocial desire, "the affective or social force, the glue, even when its manifestation is hostility or hatred or something less emotively charged, that shapes an important relationship [between men]" (1985, 2; see also 1–26). The screenings enabled all the affective infrastructure and institutional support for that desire, from rivalry, competition, and heckling to procuring, matchmaking and cheerleading, from tandem or serial sharing of women's bodies to their collective repudiation, from the mutual ego reinforcement that Gagnon and Simon identified as a main dynamic of the fraternal Elks Club settings, to the functions of instruction, mentorship, and initiation that characterized the frat-house environment (1973, 266). Above all, the specularization of homosocial desire is in place, in the screening room and on the screen: men getting hard pretending not to watch men getting hard watching images of men getting hard watching or fucking women. It is interesting that Dr. Kinsey, the pioneering sex researcher who dramatically revealed the homoerotic within the sliding scale of the homosocial (himself immortalized by the stags in both *Kensey Report*, a year or two after his "report," and *Kinsey Report* [c. 1960], a decade later), was intensely aware, as a collector himself, of stag movies as an element in the erotic socialization of American (white) men. But in the long list of individual and private erotic stimuli that Kinsey included in his questionnaires, he asked respondents about the use of the stag film as an object of arousal, but apparently did not think to ask them about the *context* of erotic stimulation, about the same-sex collective public sharing of these cine-heteroerotic stimuli (Kinsey, Pomeroy, and Martin 1948, 23, 65).

The prevailing assumption in the historical accounts, including Gagnon and Simon's, Di Lauro and Rabkin's, and Williams's, is that peer conformity rigidly policed group membership in the homosocial spectatorial setting and that proof of membership was required (at least in the North American milieu; European and Latin American brothels, according to the skimpy anecdotal evidence available, would have been much more tolerant of diversity, with a price and room for every fetish and perversion that could pay, multiplexes before their time).[10] However, in retrospect, none of the authors carry their image of male stress and vulnerability to the point where it undermines their assumption of monolithically uniform masculinity. None allows for the traumatized silence I felt when I saw *Smart Alec* with my dormitory peers in 1968 and the queer difference I and others must have felt. Extrapolating back through the decades, it is impossible not to imagine that difference was not present in all of those classic all-male audiences. Not only difference but also dissemblance, the deceptive performance of belonging.

Significantly, the only positive firsthand vintage account of the straight stag experience that I have tracked down, one that diverges from the self-righteous dismissals quoted by Koch and the Americans, is by another complicit but objective queer, Glenway Wescott. This man of letters rapturously described in 1949 the hydraulics and poetics of the male and female genitals as they meet, the unattractiveness of the featured couples notwithstanding (1990, 266). No dissemblance occurs in his report, not only because he was writing in his diary but also because he had not seen the stag package at a semiprivate homosocial smoker. He had seen it at a private gay men's party, an option increasingly viable for both straights and nonstraights during the postwar boom in home-movie technology.

What about homosociality *on-screen*? The screen, like a mirror, reflected many of the same dynamics unfolding in the screening room. In particular, I am thinking of the significant proportion of films depicting homosocial behavior in a literal way, for example, to name only ten, *The Aviator* (1932), *The Bellhop* (1936), *Broadway Interlude* (1931–33), *Dr. Hardon's Injections* (1936), *Emergency Clinic* (1950), *Grocery Boy* (1944), *Merry Go Round* (1950s), *Mixed Relations* (1921), *Paris after Dark* (1947), and *While the Cat's Away* (1950–55). In such films, men share women, men get off watching men with women, men help men with women, men supplant men with women, men procure women for men, and so on. And I am not even referring here to the small corpus of films that show explicit homoerotic behaviors in the context of heterosexual relations, a feature of stag films much more common in Europe than in phobic America. I have discussed these films elsewhere in terms of both queer authorial participation in stag-film production and, perhaps more important for this essay (in the absence of historical evidence of a queer *American* A. Prick), of the inoculatory function and freak-show operation of queer discourses in homosocial culture (1996, esp. 309–22).[11] In other words, regardless of whether queers produced or performed, for the spectator who watches the sexual other perform, for example, the drag queen in *Surprise of a Knight* (late 1920s) or the black male cocksucker in *A Stiff Game* (1930s), the meaning is "I am not like that." Complementary to my initial discussion of the homoerotic stags are the recent advances by such researchers as Jonathan Ned Katz and George Chauncey in the historicization of evolving and diverse conceptions of masculinity that prevailed in the period of the classical stags. In certain contexts, these conceptions, according to Chauncey, "allowed . . . men to engage in casual sexual relations with other men, with boys, and, above all, with the fairies themselves without imagining that they themselves were abnormal" (1994, 65; see also Katz 1995).

Perhaps the most interesting stag plots in respect to homosociality are those narrative triangles in which two male accomplices or rivals express their bonding through a joint female partner. In *An Author's True Story*, a variation on the artist-and-muse formula, a tormented proto–Barton Fink writer conjures up, and then spies on, his girlfriend for inspiration. He catches her red-handed betraying him with a Valentino-type lover, but significantly lingers at the keyhole until their debauch is played out. Only then does he rush the guilty couple, pummel his exhausted, nude rival into unconsciousness (or is it depletion . . . or submission?), and proceed to supplant the interloper in the heroine's embrace. The new couple is cushioned on the languorously spread-out and very becoming body of the gigolo (who peeks once or twice to get his own look at the acrobatics unfolding on his abdomen). The climax then images a three-way relation of intense intimacy and tactility, concluding, as I've mentioned, with an unusual visual articulation of the finally softened penis. Who is getting off on (literally) whom?

Another example from the next decade, *The Photographer: Fun and Frolic in the Studio* (1940s), is curiously self-reflexive about both the homosocial triangle and a triangle of representation engaging the male image-maker/spectator and the heterosexual performers. An excitable male photographer, fully clothed, is directing a porno shoot starring a seasoned Jean Harlow–type blond and her butch and tattooed but somewhat passive male partner. The couple seem to need a lot of coaching, and much guidance, both verbal and manual, is provided by the *metteur-en-scène*, in between his fussy attention to the lights and camera. The blow job phase of the operation seems to require special attention on the part of the photographer, and his solicitous identification with the ministrations of the heroine is quite palpable. I wondered while watching whether this was a case of standard projection/transference or whether this film would turn out to be another homoerotic buried treasure. But no, the photographer finally declares, somewhat exaggeratedly, his own horniness and receives his share of "Jean Harlow"'s oral attention, but almost as an afterthought, without any disrobing. Here the triangle formula is all but explicitly built on the binary of opposing models of masculinity, including that of the artsy-type fairy. Is the perfunctory final denouement, the "heterosexualization" of the photographer, added

134 THOMAS WAUGH

as an unconscious disavowal of the difference within masculinity that otherwise resonates from the frame?

A final triangular example, of the fifties this time, appears equally "perverse": the wife in *While the Cat's Away* entertains her lover in the wood-paneled family abode, but cleverly pushes him into the closet when her husband comes home unexpectedly, and horny, as it turns out. The lover ends up watching the married couple have sex from the closet vantage point, and two emphatic shots, including the final image of the film, show him standing masturbating through the half-open door (fully clothed, naturally). What is the object of this wanker's voyeuristic pleasure . . . and the object of the director/spectator's? And do they know? How to disentangle these complex circuits of desire, sight, and performance played out by characters/performers and spectators/performers, even putting aside the anachronistic reading that fin de siècle viewers should resist applying to the final title, but won't: "I wonder if that guy ever got out of the closet?"

No doubt the old-fashioned class politics of the encounter between movie women and male spectators are less ambiguous than these unanswerable questions around the sexual politics of male-male desire. Between stag screen and stag audience, one discerns not only a narrative/visual match but also a political synchronicity. Departing from a monolithic view of the masculinity of A. Prick requires us to investigate his class and ideological particularity. Gagnon and Simon define the class sensibility of the smoker audiences as "upper lower and lower middle class" (boy-next-door Elks, remember, not elite Rotarians), and the frat boys may be thought to share some of this social positioning by virtue of student status (rather than their probable future class identification as managers, professionals, and owners). In any case, recurrently surfacing through all the ribaldry and innocence of the stags is a palpable but amorphous populist resentment. This sensibility crystallizes not so much in the direct class references in the stags (although doctors, intellectuals, bankers, and bosses often come off rather badly) and not so much in ethnic/racial terms (although the demographic uniformity of the audience erupts occasionally in racist and xenophobic humor and stereotype, for example, the addition of racist jokes about Asian sexual anatomy and Asian American social types in the American subtitles to the French *Le ménage du Madame Butterfly* [sic; 1920]). This sensibility crystallizes most concretely in gender terms. It cannot be denied that detectable misogynist discourses inflect the more idealizing or fetishizing representations of Ms. Cunt. How else to account for the edgy eroticizations of the insatiable nympho (*Strictly Union*); the treacherous adulteress (*Dr. Hardon's Injections, While the Cat's Away*); the duplicitous cockteaser, castrator, and avenger (*Getting His Goat*); and, above all, in the character of the prostitute?

The hooker presides over the entire corpus of stags in a generalized way, inflected by the familiar hypocritical class-centric contempt for the working girl since the audience undoubtedly assumed the female performers to be sex workers—and most clearly they often were as much, just as their inept male partners were assumed to be, and visibly were, amateurs. (In fact, pursuing this documentary reading, the stag corpus may well be the best visual ethnography of sex workers in America during this period.) Many of the performers were decades older and less trim than the prevailing ideal of the sixteen-year-old Candy Barr, adding the complication of age to the misogynist economy at play around the sex worker.

On a literal level, the hooker is incarnated specifically in character types who exchange sex for money, not desire, in films from *The Casting Couch* (1924) to *Artist's Model* (1945) to *The Payoff* (1950s; the narrative hook for this item is the rent, as far as I can make out). Few literally drawn prostitute characters appear in the stag stories as such, but the recurring exchange of money and services implies that most female characters are candidates. This element of populist male blame which channels the stresses of masculinity awakened by the stag-film setting, this social scapegoating attached to the attractive/repulsive lumpen femme fatale, of course makes for a familiar element in popular and high art of the period. But neither the arts nor the social sciences progressed much further than Kinsey, with his exemplary refusal to moralize and his conclusions that the mythology of prostitution proved more significant than its actual operation and that actual contact with female sex workers by white American males was class-inflected (frequency inversely proportional to rising social/educational level). If Kinsey was right, and upper lower- and lower-middle-class American men were more exposed to prostitutes than their "betters," this would at least partly confirm why a class-homogeneous audience like the Elks or American Legion, situated within a gynophobic and erotophobic culture and focused on a narrative form descended from the punitive logic of the dirty joke, might fixate its transgression anxieties and guilt on the lumpen hooker character (just as reform movements and venereal disease panics had done for a century). A sour flavor adheres to the representation of these dozens of efficient and sportsmanlike workers in the stags—in the mocking intertitles and jokey endings that invite heckling, in the mechanical mise-en-scène of genitals and meat shots, in the contempt for the seller but not the buyer, in the indifference of the metteur-en-scène to the women's pleasure. Can one detect in these on-screen and off-screen dynamics an ancestor of the class resentment and the embrace of obscenity and gross-out as populist revolt that Laura Kipnis (1993) has dissected so brilliantly in *Hustler* magazine of the seventies and eighties? I would bet on it, but this is clearly a subject for further research.[12]

I have left for last one small body of erotic films tangential to the stag film proper but very relevant to it: the "physique" cinema, mail-order homo-erotic films that came into being only as the stags were on their last leg after World War II. Here again, the order of the day is difference and dissemblance (queer lust disguised as exercise films), rather than the rambunctious honesty of the stags and rather than class resentment focused on the lumpen hooker, a kind of idealized class fetishism of proletarian muscle (Waugh 1996, 255–73). Not surprisingly, physique films do not care very much about Ima Cunt—at least not directly—and concern themselves overwhelmingly with A. Prick and R. U. Hard (though they are never allowed to show the penis except under clinging fabric, and only abs and pecs were hard).

In many ways, the movies of Bruce, Bob, and Dick (Bellas, Mizer, and Fontaine, respectively, major auteurs of the genre) shared the swaggering innocence and small-format, one-reel primitiveness of their predecessors, reinventing the voyeuristic cinematic gaze and narrative as they evolved. In other respects, fittingly, these mail-order posers and wrestlers have more in common, formally and contextually, with the burlesque teasers, the Betty Page leg art/fetish prancers, and other peripheral licit and semilicit genres of their age. All were hiding behind legal, artistic, scientific, political, medical, and sports justifications—or playing with such justifications, working winkingly (and wankingly) within the law of their day. All had to maneuver within the gray border zones of the licit rather than the no-holds-barred underground of the stags. The price of licit status is of course very high, not only in terms of the posing straps that prevented the genital choreography forming the centerpiece of the stags but also politically, in terms of self-hurting camouflages (the alibi of bodybuilding as a denial not only of eroticism but also of self) that place the physiques in a totally different category of illicitness from the stags' missionary-position conformity. The judicial record of producers and customers alike (the wily physique mogul Bob Mizer may have brushed off his run-ins with the law, but collector Newton Arvin was destroyed)[13] exist to remind us of the physiques' outcast status. Both filmmakers and buyers were marked not only by the stigmas of sex and kitsch but also by the ostracism and the enforced closet in an age of criminalized sodomy and witch-hunts by police, psychiatrists, and politicians. Directors and audiences usually managed to surmount these problems with the humor and resilience of the oppressed. These films were not made for the Elks!

Nevertheless, like the stags, the physique films were made by men for men about men, and thus they, too, center around the specularization of masculinity, and fall along the spectrum of homosociality. The physique films, although almost entirely merchandized to individual mail-order customers, addressed collective, interactive groups as much as they did furtive solo wankers. Physique pioneer Dick Fontaine vividly recalls the raucous private parties in Manhattan lofts at the start of the fifties which served as the testing ground for his own early work (1991), and, at the end of the decade, Arvin's prosecution was wholly predicated on his intent to "exhibit" his collection to his friends.

Does an iconographical overlap between the two sets of films exist? Only a few character types walk back and forth between the stags and the physiques (the odd bellhop, repairman, live-model artist, burglar, and Oriental[ist] potentate). Stags never took any interest in prisoners, gladiators, sailors, bikers, athletes, bodybuilders, or cowboys—farmboys maybe, but that derived from the heritage of earlier erotic folklore. And the physique artists understandably never felt drawn to doctors or sex researchers with flabby bodies and sedentary desk jobs. Any overlap resides mostly in the homosocial codes and formulas: rivalry and sharing, display and specularization, trickery and triangles, crescendo and release. And the logic of surrogacy, fetish, and tongue-in-cheek coding—from frenzied wrestling as a knowing simulacrum of fucking to fun with spears and guns and boots—is of course unique to the Aesopian exigencies of working above ground but under the still Comstockian U.S. Postal Services.

The opposition between stags and physiques is neat, set by the glue of transgression: on the one hand, illicit films about licit desire and, on the other, licit films about illicit desire. Admittedly, during the pre–sexual revolution heyday of the stags, the Hays days of the Hollywood Production Code, the stags' specialty acts of adultery, prostitution, and sex—extramarital, nonreproductive, oral, female-initiated, interracial, and group—were in fact officially illicit or "deviant." Yet a patriarchal culture founded on the double standard of male promiscuity and female monogamy unofficially bolstered them. Ironically, the physique movies' cult of all-American masculinist icons, all of them of the boys-next-door type—however illicit their coy orchestration of double meanings really was—seems on the surface the epitome of populist respectability, the overstated yearning of the pariah to belong. Were any of the stag genres and their grungy hetero spin-offs more abject and transgressive than these ballets of clean-cut marines and glistening jocks? Each corpus in fact engaged in dialogue with the other about precisely those fuzzy boundaries between the licit and the illicit, between the homoerotic and the homosocial. The stags could ultimately overlook the fuzziness in their anxious innocence, but the physique movies knew exactly what the problem was, how to exploit it—and how to *celebrate* it.

Comparing, then, the stag corpus and its physique underbelly, one is overwhelmed by how much social status and audience infrastructure differently determine the iconographies of desire. But, in fact, the two genres were moving in similar directions at the beginning of the sexual revolution in the fifties, both of them poised nervously on the same homosocial continuum of desire. Both were also eagerly embracing new technologies, 16 mm, 8 mm, soon super-8, and eventually that electronic panacea that was still a gleam in the producers' eyes in 1968, home video. Thanks to these technologies, both traditions penetrated the domestic sphere, the physique films through aboveground mail order, the stag films through under-the-counter sales (the days of the itinerant projectionists had passed). Both stags and physiques in mutated form would also erupt into the hard-core features of tenderloin theatrical circuits in the late sixties and early seventies—the entrenchment of homosocial male eroticism in the marketplace of the commodified sexual revolution. These two interrelated corpuses, these mosaics of homosociality, these ethnographies of A. Prick and R. U. Hard, thus reentered the public patriarchal sphere together, arm in arm, pricks in hand.

Notes

This essay was originally published, in a somewhat different form, in *Sexualities* 44, 3 (2001). For their support in this research, the author wishes to thank Oksana Dykyj, Chuck Kleinhans, Matthew Yokobosky, the Kinsey Institute for Research in Sex, Gender, and Reproduction, the Whitney Museum for American Art, Quebec's Fonds pour la Formation de Chercheurs et l'Aide à la Recherche, Concordia University, as well as the anonymous readers at *Sexualities*.

1 This is my conservative estimate of the size of this corpus, extrapolated from the most reliable filmography available, in Di Lauro and Rabkin 1976. The question arises, of course, of whether a group of films produced over more than half a century, encompassing both professional studio productions in 35 mm and their amateur 8 mm descendants, could constitute a "corpus" in any useful sense. However, I insist on the coherence of this body of work, despite its obvious evolu-

tion over time, for three reasons: the continuity of its thematic and iconographic content; the continuity of its clandestine but commercial status throughout this period; and, finally, the finality of its termination by the emergence of explicit sexual cinema in the licit public marketplace around 1968.

2   Russ Meyer may well be identified in popular memory with his films of the late 1960s, but his first breakthrough hit, *The Immoral Mr. Teas*, appeared in 1959.

3   I tell this story, along with many others, in Waugh 1996, 2–3.

4   Williams (1989) treats classic stag films in chapter 3, "The Stag Film: Genital Show and Genital Event," of her definitive monograph on heterosexual film pornography of the seventies and eighties.

5   *Goodyear* is unusually prophetic in its focus on condoms, hence the title.

6   Such refreshing rereadings of vintage hetero erotica first surfaced in f.a.c.t. Book Committee 1986.

7   Nothing is apparently known about the circulation of stag movies within African American circuits, the occasional black character in the corpus notwithstanding (approximately a dozen black men or women appear in American stag films seen by the author).

8   The passage quoted is a slightly more detailed, updated 1973 version of an earlier description first published in *TransAction* magazine in 1967 (July–August) and assembled in Gagnon and Simon 1970, 144. Gagnon and Simon offer astute observations about the audience scene and intervene politically in the debates about pornography at the height of the sexual revolution; but, like many empiricist social scientists, they are less astute when actually watching the screen (*if* they did so) and are guilty of observing that the stag film "is rarely more than a simple catalogue of the limited sexual resources of the human body" (1937, 144), a statement whose every adverb, adjective, and noun can be shown up as utterly wrong by screening even the most basic selection of stag films.

9   Other than Koch, Williams, Gagnon and Simon, Di Lauro and Rabkin, and the original Kinsey research triumvirate, another principal source on the stag cinema is Knight and Alpert 1965–69. See especially "The Stag Film," *Playboy*, November 1967, 154–58, 170–89. See also Waugh 1996, chap. 4, "'(Oh Horror!) Those Filthy Photos': Illicit Photography and Film," esp. 309–22. A question: Does it support my thesis about homosociality that most of the major literature on stag history has been written by male buddy teams?

10 See my discussion of the pansexual atmosphere of the pre–World War II European brothel sexual culture in *Hard to Imagine* (1996, 285–322).

11 The corpus analyzed consists of approximately fifteen pre–World War II films, about ten European, five American, and one Cuban.

12 One model for such research might be Theweleit 1987, a study of post–World War I German protofascist male culture and politics which offers a fascinating historical analysis of the relation between class-based social anxiety and misogynist representations,.

13 Newton Arvin (1900–63), a Smith College professor and National Book Award winner, was allegedly at the center of a "smut ring" broken up by the Massachusetts authorities in 1959. At issue was a collection of physique magazines, photos, and movies (Martin 1994).

Works Cited

Chauncey, George. 1994. *Gay New York: Gender, Urban Culture, and the Making of the Gay Male World, 1890–1940*. New York: Basic Books.

Di Lauro, Al, and Gerald Rabkin. 1976. *Dirty Movies: An Illustrated History of the Stag Film, 1915–1970*. New York: Chelsea House.

F.A.C.T. Book Committee. 1986. *Caught Looking: Feminism, Pornography, and Censorship*. New York: Caught Looking.

Fontaine, Richard E. 1991. Interview with the author, June.

Gagnon, John H., and William Simon. 1970. "Pornography: Raging Menace or Paper Tiger?" In *The Sexual Scene*. New York: Aldine.

———. 1973. *Sexual Conduct: The Social Sources of Human Sexuality*. Chicago: Aldine.

Katz, Jonathan Ned. 1995. *The Invention of Heterosexuality*. New York: Dutton.

Kinsey, Alfred C., Wardell B. Pomeroy, and Clyde E. Martin. 1948. *Sexual Behavior in the Human Male*. Philadelphia: W. B. Saunders.

Kipnis, Laura. 1993. "(Male) Desire and (Female) Disgust: Reading *Hustler*." In *On Sex, Capital, Gender, and Aesthetics*, ed. Kipnis. Minneapolis: University of Minnesota Press. 219–42.

Knight, Arthur, and Hollis Alpert. 1965–69. "The History of Sex in the Cinema." *Playboy*.

Koch, Gertrud. 1990. "The Body's Shadow Realm." Trans. Jan-Christopher Horak. *Jump Cut* 35: 17–29.

Martin, Robert K. 1994. "Scandal at Smith." *Radical Teacher* 45 (winter): 4–8.

Sedgwick, Eve Kosofsky. 1985. *Between Men: English Literature and Male Homosocial Desire*. New York: Columbia University Press.

Moreck, Curt. 1956. *Sittengeschichte des Kinos*. Dresden: n.p.

Theweleit, Klaus. 1987. *Male Fantasies*. Vol. 1, *Women, Floods, Bodies, History*. Trans. Stephen Conway. Minneapolis: University of Minnesota Press.

Waugh, Thomas. 1996. *Hard to Imagine: Gay Male Eroticism in Photography and Film from Their Beginnings to Stonewall*. New York: Columbia University Press.

Wescott, Glenway. 1990. *Continual Lessons: The Journals of Glenway Wescott, 1937–1955*. Ed. Robert Phelps with Jerry Rosco. New York: Farrar, Straus and Giroux.

Williams, Linda. 1989. *Hard Core: Power, Pleasure and the "Frenzy of the Visible."* Berkeley: University of California Press.

The Cultural-Aesthetic Specificities of

All-male Moving-Image Pornography

RICH CANTE AND ANGELO RESTIVO

✳ Over the course of the 1990s, the applicability to all-male pornography of the analytic model developed by Linda Williams in her 1989 book *Hard Core* has been the basis for much discussion in film and cultural studies, as well as in gay and lesbian studies. While a number of analyses of gay porn have appeared since then, none has really gotten to the crux of the underlying complications.[1] For us, the crucial point is that in all-male moving-image porn, space and spatial mapping take on a distinctly important role. In other types of pornography, these dimensions are not relevant to the same extent, or in the same ways.

In staging any sex scene for the camera, a moving-image text invariably indexes social space. In making that action "take place," it thus indexes fantasy space too. When the action is male-male sex, the spaces in which it transpires can never constitute neutral backdrops. This results from the fact that the acts themselves are non-normative, whether one conceives the non-normative as a violation of patriarchal law, or, more experientially, as the excess attached to feeling different and acting like an outsider. Therefore, visually recorded male-male sex acts are always situated in relation to a public via mechanisms distinct from male-female acts, even when their setting is a private space, such as a house or an apartment. This constitutes a key aesthetic dimension of the history of all-male moving-image pornography. Its cultural importance persists to the present because, despite all the gains made in public acceptance and increased visibility, homosexual acts—

as well as their witnessing—still force the subject to situate itself in relation to publicity, one way or another: "I'm gay"; "I needed money"; "I was drunk and horny and didn't know what I was doing, but I'm really not gay"; "I was 'experimenting'"; "I'm not sure what I am"; and so on. Each of these phrases aspires to performing this mapping function relative to the public sphere or some section of it, though each one does it differently.

This mandate toward spatiality is exactly where the cultural and aesthetic specificity of all-male moving-image pornography resides, exactly what makes it different from other sorts of porn. But it is not just to be conceived as a symptom of larger discursive and ideological formations, or of the workings of those formations. After all, in its continual reinscription of all the spaces surrounding us, all-male pornography at some point also *becomes* the field for the (utopian) reinvention of the world eternally promised by identity politics. Gay porn thereby presents the cultural critic with the complicated task of untangling the intricate knots connecting real historical beings not only to real historical spaces but also to the imaginary "subjects" of historical discourse networks—as well as to the phantasmatically charged spaces where history is retroactively imagined to have played itself out, and where it will presumably continue to play itself out in the open book that is the future.

This shift in the terms by which we understand the importance of all-male porn has especially broad political ramifications in an era of media globalization. Within the more specialized realm of critical theory, understanding the phenomenon's essential nature in terms of space leads us away from the impasses of representationalism and away from the reliance on cognitively conceived social "effects." This is good. Tendencies toward both representationalism and effects-fixation are currently preventing media, sexuality, and cultural studies from appropriately articulating and thinking through all-male pornography's complex relations to the lives of huge numbers of real men who have sex with men.

Think of it this way. You can pick up any gay-oriented magazine and find advertisements for resorts, sex clubs, and travel agencies. Such ads typically present a group of exquisitely chiseled, beautiful men in a more or less erotic tableau at some sunny locale. In fact, the San Fernando Valley hardcore production and distribution company All Worlds Video now regularly advertises the clothing-optional Palm Springs resort it owns and operates on its VHS tapes and DVDS, prior to the beginning of the features. These ads explicitly state the likelihood of bumping into a porn star at the All Worlds Resort. They also image the very spaces that so often appear in the features themselves, many of which are shot at this or similar Palm Springs resorts. These advertisements in this way aspire to "proving" the likelihood that the men patronizing the place will have certain sorts of looks. But they do this in a blatantly counterintuitive manner. Of course, having imagined yourself in the picture, you might well travel to the resort or club, only to find that you consider 30, 50, or even 95 percent of the club's patrons physically repugnant.

This is not simply a question of "reality" versus "fantasy" that is mobilized for the spectator, though. For it will happen that among the sexually adventurous in the larger cities, many gay men will indeed transform themselves—not just by working out but also by shaving their genitalia and torso, getting certain haircuts, growing facial hair in certain patterns, purchasing particular types of swimwear, picking up certain phrases and tones of voice, and so on—so that the spaces they actually traverse will effectively begin to conform more and more closely to that which is the proper representational ground for their own manufactured images. Just like the content of these somatic, sartorial, and vocal styles, this figure/ground relationship itself is continually (re)constructed by recourse to gay male pornography and its numerous activational intertexts. And this continual construction of and in real space occurs as much in the realm of fantasy as in the realm of reality.

When thinking specifically about gay pornography, one cannot help but be struck by a particular historical "coincidence." The emergence of feature-length hard-core pornography in the United States occurred in the relatively fresh wake of the Stonewall rebellion. The latter is the transformative event that, in the most popular historical schema, inaugurates contemporary gay liberation politics in the United States. But in no sense is such a coincidence self-evidently logical or predictable, even in the more specialized case of the emergence of the all-male pornographic feature. Nor are any chains of cause and effect that might undergird that predictability necessarily apparent or plausible nowadays. This partly derives from the fact that Stonewall, besides being an "event," is/was first and foremost a complicated *site*, embedded within grids of spatial, social, and power relations in lower Manhattan circa 1969 (and to this day). This fact reiterates the centrality of public space to gay sexuality in the United States. It brings to the fore the crucial role that gay porn could suddenly play in liberation politics, as newly activist historical subjects began to transform themselves, the spaces of their lives, and their imagined pasts and futures relative to the (new) horizons of such politics. The templates for these transformations had to come from somewhere.

In late capitalism, though, they also had to lead somewhere. So when

these historical actants developed ways of understanding such self-transfor-
mations in political as well as personal terms, they concomitantly went out
to purchase all the necessary equipment. Some of that equipment was pornography, and the spaces traversing pornography's insides and outsides lay
at its commodifiable core. This is due precisely to that two-way traversal's
effectiveness in allowing us to imagine myriad personal and social possibilities and in complicating the historical schemas that could potentially thwart
the plausibility, "exclusiveness," and pleasure of any such specific imagin-
ings in the first place.

   In this two-part essay, the first section further explores the implications
of these observations, questioning the general relation of this historical convergence to its lingering connections to the everyday lives of real people. The
second section comprises a self-consciously close analysis of Jack Deveau's
1977 film *Night at the Adonis*. (Historically, we are still not very far beyond *Deep Throat* [dir. Gerard Damiano, 1972] here in terms of narrative
filmic style.) For reasons that will become clear as the second section proceeds, we have chosen this film to exemplify what a politically engaged,
relatively close reading of a pornographic text might look like once we re-
focus moving-image exegetical practices through the lens of our observations from the first section—and when we more fully tease out their historiographical complications too.[2] In other words, we are concentrating on
space here because it seems to us the most readily currently available conceptual means for traversing pornographic textuality (and its boundaries)
in the course of using the idiosyncratic aspects of such textuality to analyze
connections between aesthetics, culture, society, history, and politics. On
the evidence of the texts themselves, we will explain why space now clearly
seems central to the way men take their pleasures from all-male moving-
image texts. And we will illustrate why it now seems clear that space has continually been a key component of these pleasures throughout post-Stonewall
gay American history—though for tellingly different reasons, and in tellingly different ways, at distinct moments during this period.

In his recent book, *The Trouble with Normal: Sex, Politics, and the Ethics of
Queer Life*, Michael Warner argues that gay politics must understand pornography not only as part of a public culture of sex, but also as part of a
culture of public sex. He writes: "There is very little sense in this country that
a public culture of sex might be something to value, something whose accessibility is to be protected. Even when people recognize the combined effect

of privatization initiatives—and in New York the effect is widely acknowledged—they find it difficult to mount a principled defense of a public culture of sex. Instead, they fall back on free speech arguments" (1999, 171).[3] He continues: "The very concept of a public sexual culture looks anomalous because so many kinds of privacy are tied to sex. . . . In fact, the legal tradition here tends to protect sexual freedom, in general, by privatizing it. And now it also reserves privacy protection primarily for those whose sexuality is already normative" (173).[4] Warner proceeds to discuss an argument made by gay philosopher and critical legal theorist Richard Mohr. For Mohr, sex is in some sense "inherently privatizing" of certain sorts of environments, and thus should be legally protected as such no matter where it occurs. His argument rests on the idea that sexual experiences always exclude the world of everyday social status and individual will since their "special somatic states of arousal, and their altered sense of personhood and its intimate relations, combine to remove people from the common order while they are so engaged" (Warner 1999, 175).

In his 1988 book *Gays/Justice*, Mohr writes:

> Many people find orgies and backrooms and bathhouses not to be private. This view is wrong, for if the participants are all consenting to be there with each other for the possibility of sex polymorphic, then they fulfill the proper criterion of the private in the realm of the sexual. If, as is the case, sections of gay cruising zones of parks at night have as their habitués only gay cruisers, police cruisers, and queer bashers, then they too are private in the requisite sense; and, in the absence of complaints against *specific* individuals by others, arrests should not occur there for public lewdness in general. (qtd. in Warner 1999, 175–76)

The issue here boils down to the fact that, as Warner puts it, "the practice of public sexual culture—including both cruising and pornography, among other realms of practice—involves not only a world-excluding privacy, but also a world-making publicness." (1999, 177) For Warner, that world-making publicness proves central to what we call gay culture.

Consider, for instance, the following itinerary of a typical workday: stop for a morning cappuccino and newspaper; run to the health club at noon for a quick swim, sauna, and shower; duck into a department store after work to buy a shirt and some underwear; take the leisurely route home, stopping occasionally to look in store windows; and then lay around watching a video while waiting for a pizza to be delivered. This scenario changes in important ways as soon as one assumes the subject of this itinerary to be a gay man. From the beginning, feature-length all-male filmic porn was deeply invested in narratologically and imagistically "gaying" such itineraries of everyday life. The aim has been not only to make "us" finally visible in the college locker room, the high school classroom, the army barracks, the city street, and so on. The goal has also been to keep continually open all of these everyday spaces to the myriad transformative potentials that develop once we are indeed visible there, in considerable numbers. In fact, it should be remembered that, until very recently, it was pretty much only in gay pornography that we could regularly see representations of gay men at all. Indeed, pornography remains the one genre where, in numerical terms, gayness is unquestionably *much, much* more commonly represented than in any other category of U.S. moving-image product.

Warner's argument for the value of a public culture of (gay) sex lies partly in the consumer chain of gay male–owned and/or –oriented businesses, of which porn shops, and other stores that sell or rent porn, are an important component. According to Warner, these businesses keep each other alive in a neighborhood like Manhattan's West Village — paradigmatically, on Christopher Street. They provide a convenient spatial circuit for, say, our abovementioned itinerary, where gay men can also continuously *see each other* in the process of their individual rounds. Taken together, such circuits also play key roles in, for instance, AIDS and safer-sex activism. This "networking" occurs in myriad and complex ways, not just via the disbursement of information at any individual venue, but precisely because people can traverse each other's itineraries. In turn, the existence of this consumer chain presumably benefits the entire country as well as the more specific subculture with which the space is intimately entangled. As long as the AIDS epidemic is conceived as a "public" event that can and should be controlled in its reach, for the good of the public, such wider benefit would presumably accrue.

This is just one of the reasons for which Warner's "world-making publicness" becomes central to all-male porn. The gravitation toward such publicness lies at the heart of all-male moving-image aesthetic conventions because public space lies at the heart of men's relationship to moving-image pornography in the post-Stonewall gay ghetto. Even the gay spectators who do not reside in these ghettos participate in their construction by, as well as their representation in, the pornographic texts themselves. Changes in all-male textual conventions over time — along with the multidetermined reasons for these changes and the mechanisms by which the changes occur — are thus as inherently political as is the transformation over time of a street like Christopher Street via the processes such as gentrification and rezoning.

In their coauthored article "Sex in Public," which appeared in the influential 1998 "Intimacy" issue of *Critical Theory*, Warner and Lauren Berlant usefully transpose into different terms these dilemmas involved in accounting for—and formulating policy and/or legislative arguments via-à-vis—this dialectic between world-excluding privacy and world-making publicness. Berlant and Warner attempt to formulate a language for discussing "sex as it is mediated by publics," even where "these publics don't (as with pornography) have an obvious relation to sex." Their discussion involves "not necessarily acts in the usual sense," but "queer zones," "other worlds estranged from heterosexual culture," and "more tacit scenes of sexuality like official national culture—which depends on a notion of privacy to cloak its sexualization of national membership" (547).

In attempting to describe and imagine the place of such things in a context where "the heterosexual couple is no longer the referent, or the privileged example, of sexual culture," Berlant and Warner end up arguing that our citizenry's common, or "public," modes of distinguishing between public and private are heteronormative from the start. For Berlant and Warner, such modes of distinction "link intimacy only to the institution of personal life" (551). They "make sex seem irrelevant or merely personal" (551), so that "intimate life becomes the endlessly cited *elsewhere* of political public discourse" (550). As a result, "[a] complex cluster of sexual practices gets confused, in heterosexual culture, with the love plot of intimacy and familialism that signifies belonging to a society in a deep and normal way" (554). "Making a queer world," on the other hand, "has required the development of kinds of intimacy that bear no necessary relation to domestic space, to kinship, to the couple form, to property, or to the nation" (558).

For example, consider a widely used Web site, www.crusingforsex.com. Cruising for Sex illustrates the ways in which Warner's specific conception of a public culture of sex, and a culture of public sex, varies from any such "nongay" understanding of each. The Web site also illustrates how the differential between such understandings becomes crucial to the workings of all-male pornography. It is not, as one might assume, those general aspects of pornography that have always presumably given it its "infotainment" dimension that are primarily at issue in the all-male case. Pornography's pedagogies of sexual hygiene and public health, its fascinating ethnographic "quirks," and its aid in the supposedly transcontextual human search for "better sex" are, in the all-male case, beside the point.

The Cruising for Sex Web site is indeed full of the hard-core images, and links to more hard-core images, so characteristic of many Internet porn sites. But it is the very different sort of "public sexual function" conceptually unifying this site that sets it apart from other forms of porn. The *cruising* in *cruising for sex* refers not just to the process of Internet surfing. In an act of symptomatic linguistic condensation, this site's name links the act of masturbatorially surfing the Internet (back?) to the search for quick, anonymous sex in the physical world. In fact, the Web site presents itself as "adding value" to what's "already out there" by simultaneously facilitating both of these search processes.

Besides all the conventional digital porn available at the site, its original selling point—presumably, the crux of its reputed commercial success—is its extensive international, area-by-area listing of public places in the real world where men can supposedly hook up for fun. From a particular strip of boardwalk in Lebanon (yes, *that* Lebanon) to the Shop Rite parking lot in your own Long Island town, this archive busts out all over with listings of such venues. Yet the site's most ingeniously interactive feature is that its users can review all of these cruising places in detail on message boards, while "chatting" about them both synchronously and asynchronously. This promises visitors less trouble finding the sometimes off-the-beaten-path locations. It helps them know what to expect once they get there. Often, it even instructs them in precisely how to (covertly) act in order to find what they want once there. These reviews of public sex places can be continually updated, and added to, over time. For instance, so-called heads-up postings can be generated when police target an area. And notes can be posted when commercial establishments have suddenly closed down, or when everyone has evidently stopped swinging through a particular "Park and Ride" at the tail end of their suburban Saturday nights.

A typical posting, about a health club in Chicago, reads: "Upscale gym with lots of twenty and thirty-something professionals. Hot mix of gay and straight men looking for spontaneous action in the locker room during non-peak hours. Can always find jackoff buddies in the steam room. I have taken a number of hot gay and straight dicks up my ass in the showers." Notice the shift from the "thick description" of the first three sentences to the confessionality of the last. Also, notice the suspicious seamlessness with which that transition occurs. The phrase "hot gay and straight dicks" seems either a rather telling poetic error of adjectival reference or a highfalutin poetic technique, take your pick. Either way, the idea that such things exist, and that one can discern their differences during anonymous action, is an interesting one, to say the least. In this literary light, what does a commentary such as the one above actually (purport to) register? Here's another run-of-the-mill post, about a different Chicago gym: "It has recently become more cruisey on weekday afternoons, especially Fridays. The clientele is largely white and black, and usually pretty hot. I've had fantastic sex in the steam room three times, once with three other guys watching and a guy watching the door. There is also a toilet by the pool that is usually deserted. Strongly recommended."

After reading enough of these reviews, one begins to wonder to what degree the site's users should take seriously the underlying pretensions to spatial and temporal all-knowingness. Alas, it is not uncommon to see writers adapting questionably erudite points of view on all sorts of things; points of view that top even tearoom sociologist Laud Humphreys' notable ability to obtain supposedly exhaustive amounts of empirical "data." Nor is it uncommon to see a glowing review of the action at a hot cruising site immediately followed by a very different sort of posting dated a few days or weeks later. In the second posting, the writer reels in anger, warning others about having made a long and complicated trip only to find that the place was "troll city," or completely deserted, or out of business. In fact, it may well seem highly unlikely to the writer that this place *ever* saw serious action. (And this makes him even angrier!)

One begins to wonder about the extent to which the real and the virtual become confused in these posts, and why. The cunning "planting" of comments by business owners seeking to encourage (or discourage) the pilgrimage of gay patrons, and by people like men who literally live next door to public parks, is always possible. But the fantasies of the cruisers prove just as germane to such confusion. For, apparently, part of the basic pleasure of Cruising for Sex lies in this slippage between the actual, the virtual, and the phantasmatic in the contemporary experience of space.

It is partly because of this slippage that these "performances of description" so often veer toward pornography in the strictest etymological sense. As is clear from the confessional post about the gym shower, such textuality often comes notably close to the "written reportage of whores" from which the word *pornography* originally derives. This constitutes precisely the sort of writing that is designed to be "read with one hand," and maybe even remembered with one hand once a visitor actually goes to a physical cruising site. (In referring to the use of the computer mouse, Rousseau's old formulation becomes even more resonant.) Indeed, this Web site's use of the material of digital technology remains skewed toward the verbal rather than the visual, though visitors will, of course, also find a few surveillance camera links at cruisingforsex.com, as well as plenty of animated banner ads. Perhaps the importance of the site's repeated will to literally give image to its potential "amateur reporters," via its prominently displayed "cruiser of the week area," relates to this relatively archaic slant toward the written word. In this area, one user is selected for a special profile from the many who post their images along with descriptions of themselves, their locations, information about how and when they use the site, and so on. In a way, these postings equal the "author photos" so crucial to any explicit published memoir and to the history of such writing, as well as to the moving-image textual forms that eventually developed from that literary genre.

The always already dubious nature of pornography's "empiricism" is of course one of its most overarching characteristics, and the source of some of pornography's overarching pleasures. But a particular textual double movement seems to characterize cruisingforsex.com. The site aspires to record ostensibly independent external spaces, as well as conditions supposedly preexisting the acts of inscription that document them on the Web. But this commercial Internet venture also aspires to (re-)incarnate that external world in this act of representation, and through acts of representation in general. In this sense, the text aims to bring about a (new?) state of affairs only *perhaps* already latent in the world of the viewer before his encounter with the text. These competing aspirations are involved in the Web site's phantasmatic workings in ways rife with a different type of social struggle than those of heterosexual pornography's related, oft-discussed pornotopic dimensions.

Frances Ferguson has discussed the relevant theoretical issue in her analysis of pornography's function in sexual harassment. The "vanishing mediator" (the representation itself) for the activation of such public spaces does not simply trace "supposedly-already-having-existed" past activations of such spaces and thereby become one entry in an archive of them. For Ferguson, the representation itself also demands that *you*, the text's addressee, somehow morally "act" in receiving it. At minimum, this action lies in the "movement" of your "beliefs" about even the most supposedly material, unchangeable dimensions of the world: namely, its spaces. This "movement" within the addressee—the investment of desire in those spaces, and in the objects that inhabit them—is provoked by the encounter with the text (Ferguson, 1995). It is a change (in)voluntarily affected in your continual constitution as subject of, and subject to, all the chains of signification that converge not only at such texts but at all of the spaces that the text shares with the world at large.

Exactly what are we talking about here? On a data-gathering venture into one of the most heavily trafficked men's rooms at a state university that one of us recently visited—a bathroom listed, naturally, on cruisingforsex.com —we found a wall in one of the stalls that was (predictably) covered by sex graffiti. There were erotic "stories," some set in that very men's room ("I Fucked a Sigma Alpha Epsilon here") and some set elsewhere, such as the one written by an also ambiguous-with-the adjectival-reference author who reportedly got it on with his "French T.A." in the latter's office. There were also announcements of meeting times, instructions for initiating action ("tap foot for BJ!"), general exclamations of sexual longing, and the requisite cornucopia of erotic pictograms. But the following piece from a completely different genre immediately jumped out. Not only was it written in thick, black magic marker ink on a mostly blank area of one of the stall walls but its final word was underlined (in fact, underlined twice): "WHAT IS WRONG WITH YOU PEOPLE??? THIS IS A *BATHROOM*."[5] Underneath this perplexingly sincere inquiry—in a relatively meek, plain-old pen script more typical of the rest of the stall's writing—was this solitary reply: "No, it's not. This is a gay tea room, you FUCKING IDIOT!"

Thomas Laquer has recently argued that pornography arises as modernity's way of economically managing the very difficult-to-commodify threat of "imagination." It does this by transforming "Onanism" into the ("modern") act of "masturbation." Pornography gives "object" to the immaterially private meanderings of the onanist, a process made possible by print culture's instantiation of the private/public divide via its implicit conception of "publication" (2003). The writing on these bathroom walls, and on cruisingforsex.com, does not merely document battles over space finally fought at the intersection between homosexuality and the "publication" of such masturbatory flights of fancy. The writing *enacts* such battles.

Both operations are representative of what all-male textuality *is* and what all-male textuality *does*, to use Frances Ferguson's useful distinction. In the case of the men's room and the case of the Web site, this "graffiti" is ostensibly designed for anyone who might happen on its location and read it. In this sense, such writing qualifies as being pornographic: it has been written to be published (i.e., for an anonymous, or mass, readership).[6] Yet such textuality is also always addressed specifically to *you*, its particular reader. For it is always *you in particular* who might be just the exact type of person the text's author is looking for: the one for whom "meeting here for BJ at 4 P.M." is perfectly convenient, or the one who just happens to unknowingly use that one deserted shower stall over by the pool at the gym because you're so shy about your body—and thus are perfectly "positioned" to be lured into some scenario or another. For this reason, there is a discontinuity embedded within these publications that perfectly exemplifies what Michael Warner means when he argues that, paradoxically, one's awareness of oneself as a member of a "minority" is inextricably bound to one's recognizing oneself as an element of the anonymous "mass." Of course, this discontinuity is closely tied to the advent of modern ideology as capitalism's preferred method of self-management (Warner 1997, 389).

It is precisely this tension between anonymity and self-recognition that we discern in the spatial logics of all-male porn. On the one hand, it seems to aspire to activating space and reinscribing relations between publicness and privateness "indiscriminately," or in ways in line with whatever might motivate a particular individual to notice the texts in the first place. (Straight men presumably don't *have to* read the writing on the walls, right?) On the other hand, in the process of interpellating its subject—whether via the Internet or via good, old-fashioned writing on walls—all-male pornography directs its energies toward imagining a space where homosexuals will *not* have the same sort of discontinuous perceptions of themselves that, by definition, constitute the subject of mass publicity. Consequently, all-male pornography is utopian in a strictly spatial sense. That is, it is utopian in its own uniquely troubling way.

Director Jack Deveau's 1977 filmic feature *Night at the Adonis* suggests the importance of injecting these and surrounding considerations into any given historical period of gay porn and gay culture. Largely filmed on location at Manhattan's legendary Adonis theater—an early twentieth-century midtown movie palace somewhat typically turned porn theater—this film presents a formally documentary-like record of the style of the post-Stonewall urban gay male subject and its spaces. For instance, the film even outrageously includes a cut-in that seems straight out of a seventies "labor documentary": a close-up of the half-eaten corned beef sandwich that is the makeshift dinner of the interesting black woman who busily but coolly tends the titular theater's ticket booth.

Night at the Adonis presents us rather directly with the cultural spaces that porn texts were, like various other (commercial) texts, complicit in marketing and selling, along with the model of the subject implicitly attached to them. The film's loose, somewhat fluid narrative quality, together with its mobilization of fantasy via the text's positioning of itself as just a hair's breadth removed from the rest of the sensorium that was gay male New York at the time, make the film stand out as being a perhaps symptomatic, rigorously gay historical document and cinematic text. Indeed, the film itself seems designed to encourage us, one or two generations later, to imagine *Night at the Adonis* as actually having played at the Adonis theater in 1977. This is an imagining in which the events on the screen and the events in the movie theater would, in a rather odd realization of André Bazin's "myth of total cinema," coincide not just with each other but also with the very representation of that coincidence within *Night at the Adonis* itself.

Such a "mind-blowing" thought experiment brings us back to a central fact about all visual pornography: structures of fantasy here enframe the visual field, so that the presumed convergence of "reality" and diegesis can come about only through the self-consciousness mediating the intervention of fantasy. This is the case with the Cruising for Sex Web site and the "tearoom" walls too, though the difference of their operations from the film's lies partly in the different physicalities surrounding these other texts, and partly in the distinctions of materiality that characterize print, digital media, and film. In *Night at the Adonis*, this enframing process works at the level of narrative and, more specifically, in the construction of cinematic space in the sex scenes themselves. Sound plays a particularly important role in this process.

In keeping with the by then already established conventions of pornographic narrative in general, the film is organized around a series of vignettes. Most of these are designed to enframe the sex numbers in what amounts to the "blended" narrative/number typology that Linda Williams pinpoints in *Hard Core* (1989). For example, the film has as one of its central characters a seasoned urban gay who is left alone in the city when his lover goes on a business trip. Unable to locate the barber with whom he had earlier had a post-haircut sexual liaison (on the barber chair), and too restless to spend the evening reading Jonathan Katz's newly published *Gay American History*—an excuse he scornfully uses to ward off the boorish advances of his lothario coworker/adversary (Jack Wagner) at the leather shop around the corner—this character ends up at the Adonis theater for the night. This is a decision contrivedly marked by his early uttering one of the film's key tag lines: "Oh well, there's always the Adonis." The irony of this line is that while it identifies the Adonis merely as a space of last resort, the very fact that the theater is "always there," always publicly available, apparently charges it with its essential phantasmatic richness in the first place, paradoxically making the theater into a destination in and of itself. This clearly relates to the fantasy value with which the "private" technology of television had already overlaid our "public" spaces of narrative film exhibition well before *Deep Throat*'s commercial success ever left its mark.

Another of the most prominent characters in this multicharacter film is "the new kid." At the film's outset, he has just been hired to tend the concession stand and perform various other odd jobs at the theater. It is interesting that his story initiates the narrative because none of these duties is sexual. This pre-Reaganite Reagan baby—he has majored in "gay businesses," apparently an ambiguous joke even in 1977—is the only one of the male characters who does not engage in sex during the film. In contrast to the aforementioned experienced, urbane character left alone in the city for the weekend, the new kid presumably has no idea that "there's always the Adonis" when the film begins. (Even though he somehow managed to find a job there.) So he must be trained in great detail for his new duties, and very meticulously initiated into the workings of the "sawhorse" venue by a more seasoned employee. This structures a striking sequence whose editing works to position the spectator in a classically "all-knowing" voyeuristic position—a position from which the spectator can seamlessly "see" all of the theater's sexual geography. The spatial logic of this sequence will then guide the film's episodic investigation of the sexual geography outside the theater as well, finally placing especially tenuous boundaries on its overall story space.

The implications of this sequence warrant a more detailed analysis. But the opposition created by the text's fixation on the experience/innocence binary as one of its points of narrative origination brings us first to the issue of gay tutelage. This issue is itself closely allied to our claim that gay male pornography differs from straight pornography precisely insofar as its public/private phantasmatics are somehow different. Like the "open secret" of homosexuality itself, the sex at the Adonis is at once well known and, nonetheless, invisible to the untutored eye. The process of "opening one's eyes" to the nature of cruising in such places is then strictly correlative to the process of coming out in the logic of the historical period that surrounds this film. Both potentially involve a process of self-transformation that simultaneously and fundamentally transforms all of the spaces one inhabits once one has received a "sentimental education." However, here, in contrast to the novelistic coming-of-age tradition, that education is not really very "sentimental" at all. Not only does it not involve "love" for the new kid's educator; it seems to involve no feeling at all on the new kid's part, for either that educator or the greater system of institutions his tutor represents.

The detached commercialism of this process is what provides the film with its tonal idiosyncrasy as pornography. The tutored's desire is never visibly or conventionally performed as having been mobilized, and yet he serves as the organizing sensibility for the text and repeatedly functions as an anchor point for the viewer's gaze. Though it could be argued that his desire has been mobilized and signified in the "negative" sense, via the character's disinterest, this would seem even more unusual in a work of gay pornography. And given the other tendencies of this particular text, that argument would prove especially implausible. Ultimately, the resulting hermeneutic quandary is not all that surprising, though. The ending of the film ties its plot structure—and, via that, the strange detachedness of its overall aesthetics—to the consciousness of this particular character, by ending as he locks up the theater and bids all his coworkers farewell until tomorrow. In other words, it is the "night of his own world" that organizes the text. This is a narrative strategy that will seem even more contradictory as our discussion proceeds, and even more indicative that something of substantive sociocultural significance lies behind the troubled signifiers of this character's unusually (un)complicated affective arc.

As the worker who knows the ropes takes the new employee on a tour of the theater, and they move into the space of theater from the lobby, we briefly get to watch snippets of a film within the film, a scene from the feature presumably being projected at the Adonis theater. In a touch of wicked humor, a short "documentary" about ancient Egyptian fertility cults is playing at the moment. This depicts a young, well-endowed "Egyptian" stroking himself to ejaculation while a voice-over narrator talks in some detail about Isis, Osiris, and other mythical figures of that order. Meanwhile, the two employees have gone to an upper balcony, where they can get a view not only of the screen but, more important, of the lower balcony. There, the spectators of the porn within the porn perch against the walls and balcony rail, in various states of apparent arousal. As the experienced employee's voice-over explains to the newcomer the various clone styles of the regulars below, the camera singles out each patron as he alternately stares at the projected documentary and surveys the glances of the other characters. All the while they are fondling themselves and, ultimately, exposing themselves until various contacts between them begin.

Meanwhile, the camera seamlessly detaches itself from strict enchainment to the point of view of the touring employees. The survey of the theater now becomes sonically organized, and much more loosely organized too, by the phantasmatic frame provided primarily by the seasoned employee's voice-over. The resulting redoubling of voice-over sound—the disembodied voice of the documentary narrator echoes within and through the voice-over of the diegetically embodied employee/guide—here performs a critical function. Within the cavernous, fictive space of the movie palace, the voice-over of the porn within the porn is highly reverberant. Bouncing off the walls of the theater space, it becomes a kind of ("Egyptian"!) sonic envelope enclosing all of the characters. By indiscriminately "seizing" the spectators in the text in this manner, it allows for equivalencies and exchanges to develop between the pornographic images on the theater screen and the various points of view on the theater balcony. This pushes toward the construction of a kind of radically democratic sexual space later realized in the film's extended men's room orgy scene as the theater men's room is a space to which the projected film's sound conspicuously carries over, European-style. However, it never becomes clear whether or not viewers should take this sonic carry-over as diegetic. Hence, a similar promise of this "(in)voluntary seizure" of the sonic is simultaneously offered to the theatrical audience of *Night at the Adonis* itself.

Let's think about this contextually for a moment, considering the overarching sound aesthetics of the low-budget porn film of this period. In *Night at the Adonis*, we find several distinct characteristics of the (primitive, three-track) sound mix, characteristics in some cases appropriated from New Wave, avant-garde, and documentary filmic practices of the 1960s. First, the number of shots with synchronous sound is kept to a minimum, being reserved for pieces of dialogue the director presumably considers key. These sync shots are cut into ones taken without sound, though no attempt is made to preserve the ambience of the space in the process: when the sync sound drops out, so too does the ambient sound. Only the cheaply produced and repetitive music is used to smooth over the resultant intermittent quality of the ambience. Second, there is no sound-effects editing. Sound effects exist only as they have been captured by the sync sound recording, making their status as "sound effects" interestingly dubious. For example, we can hear the turnstile as patrons enter the theater in medium close-up in this particular film, but the soundtrack provides no accompanying footsteps.

Similarly, when the camera cuts to a close-up of keys attached to a character's belt loop, we cannot hear the jangle of the moving keys because the shot is taken and presented without attached sound. Significantly, the key-sporting character is simultaneously, just as we cut to that close-up, described in the organizing voice-over as "the jangler." This strangely identifies him visually and linguistically primarily with a sound effect conspicuously absent from the film's soundtrack. In fact, the seasoned employee's voice-over even goes on to add—in the slightly-too-difficult-to-pull-off sort of double entendre that has befallen so many porn actors over the years— that the jangling keys mean that "you can always tell when he's coming." If, as Linda Williams (1989) has established as crucial in her model of hetero- sexual porn, it is the sound of the woman's orgasm that allows the viewer of this period to know that *she's* coming (or, at least, is "genuinely" turned on), we are here brought up against the issue of a fundamental redundancy that characterizes all-male porn. Insofar as sound is "liberated" in the all-male text from the necessity of providing such evidence, or from the necessity of providing it for the same reasons—since in the all-male case each partici- pant can ejaculate, or at least display an erection—its usage in the articula- tion of space, and in cementing the various spaces of the narrative together, becomes excessively charged with some other function.

In this sense, perhaps the most interesting trait of *Night at the Adonis*'s soundtrack lies in its profligate use of semisync sound.[7] Utilized often in the sex numbers of the period, and especially in group and orgy scenes, this consists of the improvised-in-postproduction mishmash of moans, breath- ing, gasps, cries, and what we call "pornoperformative vocalizations" (para- digmatically, "Suck that dick!" and "Fuck that ass!"). Such sounds only re- motely, intermittently, and randomly appear to actually "sync up" with any character's performance of particular actions, or even with any mouthings of the sounds themselves. Conventionally unanchored from their sources in this way, such vocatives function more like music than dialogue. This gives a further sort of incidental plausibility to Williams's wry use of the musi- cal term *number*. Together with narrative techniques such as those used by *Night at the Adonis* to introduce its characters—and to thereby articulate the text's own underlying discourse on character (which arises partly from its reflexivity, as well as from its complex plays with indexicality)—these low- budget sound techniques finally result in a soundtrack that is highly stylized aesthetically and very interesting to interrogate for its cultural generative mechanisms, as well as its technological ones because that stylization makes this interrogation very tricky.

To the extent that *Night at the Adonis* constitutes a typical all-male text from this period, though, what must be noted is that such techniques are decidedly *not* here mobilized to produce the kind of "Brechtian distance" usually associated with avant-garde counternarrativity or counterreferen- tiality.[8] (Not even in the way similar techniques are mobilized in, say, *Deep Throat.*) Instead, we are here talking about a distantiation self-consciously posited by the text's narrative scheme as requisite for its phantasmatically intimate availability as a pornographic text in the first place. A crucial question for reception theory—as a previous writer about related issues such as John Champagne seems to already implicitly know—becomes precisely how the spectator is positioned by this imperfect sound mix. It makes sense to assume that both producers and audiences recognized these aspects of the mixes as imperfections, but accepted them as inherent to the genre's pleasures nonetheless. But again, this acceptance occurred for different reasons, and via different discursive operations, in the all-male case than in the case of heterosexual film porn.

In the balcony sequence discussed above, it can be argued that the redoubling of the voice-overs has the effect of naturalizing, in advance, the very semisync sound techniques which "will have been used" in all of the sex numbers by the end of the film. Once its attention moves from the pornographic "documentary" within the film into the narrative space of the theater, *Night at the Adonis*'s images change in their ability to register spatiality. But they continue to be enclosed by the sonic envelope of the reverberant documentary narration. The "voice of pornography" embodied by this documentary, then, continues to seize the spectators within the text otherwise only intermittently connected to the images through vision. Of course, this has been proposed as the essential characteristic of televisual sound, for example, in Rick Altman's description of television sound as the umbilical cord linking the wandering domestic glance to the TV set (1986).

However, such an analogy does not quite work here. The enveloping, non-localized sound floating through the cavernous spaces of the movie palace creates something much more similar to what Michel Chion calls the "sonic aquarium" (1991) in relation to the Dolby mix. By seizing spectators equally and indiscriminately, the sound of the movie creates the "democratic" space for sexual possibility within *Night at the Adonis*. Put another way, the sound of the pornographic film is (generally) posited within the film as giving ultimate voice to the utopian sexual possibilities of pornographic space. It thereby takes over the role of any actual bodily sound connected to a viewed sexual event. Given that all of the "public" sex scenes within this film have inscribed within them at least one person who is only watching, this presence of the movie-within-the-movie sound works to continually posit this space, despite all the film's other tendencies toward the indexical, not as real space but as phantasmatic space. Or, at least, to posit this space as the sort most conventionally thought of as private. In other words, given the ostentatious nature of this aporia, there is always only a fantasy connection between the viewed sexual acts and the enveloping sound, whether the sound is presumed to come from "within" the staged scene or from outside it. Rather than being understood merely as an effect of the conventions and the technology underlying it, this contradiction could be taken as actually motivating, or at least facilitating, the adaptation of such sound conventions and technology in all-male porn films in the first place.

But this issue of a radically democratic sexual space at once brings us to the more general question of historicity, and the historicity of gay male subjectivity in particular. This, we can recall, has already been hinted at in the film itself, in its emplacement of the monumental 1976 publication of Jonathan Katz's book *Gay American History* into its plot as an alibi, and into a central character's apartment as a diegetic object too. The details of Katz's rewriting of American history are set aside for another time, of course, as the interest of this era of pornography lies, instead, primarily in the old maxim that "history is made at night." The film's title already addresses this view: history is made at *Night at the Adonis*, to be more specific. In this regard, it becomes especially interesting that the world outside the Adonis theater (and, by implication, perhaps the world outside of pornography itself) is rendered mostly as a world of missed encounters.

This idea seems to motivate the "disinterest" of the Reaganite rookie in the theater's proceedings for all but financial reasons. With the exception of the barber-chair liaison that originates one character's quest, and eventually does reach complete closure, none of the other characters seem really able to connect in the "real world" within the film. The telephone, in particular, becomes a vehicle for these missed encounters. With this narrative fixation on the phone, sound once again becomes decisive in mapping these eternally blocked attempts at connection. The characters on the other end of the line are either (literally) absent, or, if they are present, then only as disembodied voices registered in tinny, one-dimensional sound via over-the-top "macho" performances that contrast decisively with the voices and reverberant sounds inside the movie theater.[9]

Another recurring, and related, motif in the film is that of the young "kept-boy" character's trying to connect with his businessman "daddy" via that pre–cellular age hustler's indispensable tool, the New York City public phone booth. At one point, he provocatively tells the ridiculously authoritative and well-established sounding disembodied voice of "Daddy" that he's on his way to the Adonis theater in order to "give away what you pay me so much for." Significantly, the one character unable to reconnect with his barber buddy by telephone does end up bumping into him at the Adonis. And the kept boy, after abandoning himself to the men's-room orgy, ends up getting his "daddy" to take him back. Yet these happy "private" couplings become possible only after the narrative makes each of its major characters pass through public space. The maxim, "there's always the Adonis," then, asserts that it is "publicity"—the essential relation to a public—that is, by the time feature-length all-male filmic porn exists, central to gay subjectivity.[10] In other words, it is a passage through a public "gaze" that allows one to decode, and thus to open up, all the key phantasmatic landmarks in the iconography of gay male porn itself: the locker room, the gym, the office, the park, the pizza delivery system, the plumber or UPS guy arriving at the door, the prison, and so on. A major in "gay businesses" is perhaps no longer necessary to learn these ropes even in 1977, this film thus implies. It is for this reason, in part, that the line reads as such a joke to begin with, and part of the reason why the "new kid" remains such a blank from start to finish, even though he functions as the text's organizing sensibility.[11] He has already passed through precisely what we expect to have *witnessed* him pass through, or at least to have *passed through with him*, by the time the interaction between narrative and number that constitutes the all-male moving-image text has concluded.

By film's end, the Jack Wrangler character has also replaced the tag line, "there's always the Adonis," with his snide but acute quip, "So this is gay American history, huh?" He utters this rhetorical question as he catches in the throes of the bathroom orgy the coworker who had earlier spurned him at work by snootily saying he was planning on staying home to read Katz's new book that night, while his lover was away on business. To make matters "worse," Wrangler finds his desired coworker going at it in the Adonis theater bathroom with the very barber with whom Wrangler himself has just gotten it on somewhere in the theater's rafters. This replacement of one cliché by another, then, finally unifies the entire space that the film aspires to totalize as the index of just the sort of publicity always ultimately traversed in the pleasures of all-male moving-image pornography.

In other words, even when an all-male pornographic scenario is set in a private space—for example, two "straight" boys bounding into an apartment after a morning jog and stripping out of their sweaty clothes, or two "cousins" secretly perusing *Playboys* together—there is always a passage through a phantasmatic public that, precisely, allows the decisive connection to happen. Furthermore, this moment of passage cannot finally be registered in gay porn. It can only be mysteriously indexed. This comes into evidence again and again by the arbitrary, awkward, and unsatisfying way gay scenarios present this passage through publicity.

Now, the arbitrariness of porn's passage into sex is evident in hetero-sexual porn as well. We only need to think of the contrivance that has a plumber arriving and a door being opened by a woman in a negligee. How and when will the sex begin? Soon enough and predictably enough. One of the related observations Linda Williams makes in *Hard Core* (1989) is that the old crisis of needing to "break into song" is another thing that connects the porn film to the musical. But we are discussing something slightly differ-ent here. Specific to all-male porn, inherent in both its aesthetic terms and its sociocultural functions, is the necessity of a passage through an imag-ined public gaze where what is at stake in the encounter is precisely one's position within the greater *socius*, something never at stake in the same way in heterosexual porn. What is also at stake here is the point of "narrative wager" differentiating such moments in the all-male texts from those in other sorts of pornography. The number is automatically overlaid by narra-tive in a unique way because there is a supplemental question about what will happen when there are two bodies with two penises. Who will, and/or who won't, get penetrated?

It is through this specifically male-male issue, the question of who will or will not "get fucked"—and through its relationship to the passage through publicity—that yet another dimension of the historicity of *Night at the Adonis* is linked, in a clearly overdetermined way, back to the matter of space. This is the trope of the movie palace as historical "ruin." Certainly it is a truism that, by the 1970s, the movie palaces of the old urban centers had become economically unviable. This situation was itself overdetermined by declin-ing and/or demographically changing movie audiences since the 1950s, the abandonment of urban centers by the middle class, the social antagonisms made visible in the 1960s, and so on. For instance, a film like Martin Scor-sese's *Taxi Driver* (1976) vividly paints a hallucinatory picture of a Manhat-tan in ruins. In that film, pornography seems to have invaded all of the "use-less" and abandoned spaces of postmodern urban capitalism not yet ready to be made residential or legitimately commercial. In retrospect, we can see this uneven development as having been governed by a large-scale reorga-nization of capitalism toward dispersed, transnational modes of production and consumption.

In this regard, we could say that the Adonis theater's status as ruin is exactly what allows us to open up to history any narrative that presents the place to us. As Fredric Jameson's work argues, inscriptions of historicity like those in and around *Night at the Adonis* are what allow us to "cognitively map" structural relations—which would otherwise remain invisible, as would the ideological mechanisms that do/do not present them to us—into all of the spaces transecting the text, its cognate historical documents, our present phantasmatics, and their contexts.[12] For, in *Night at the Adonis*, what exactly stands opposite the ruin of the movie palace, to occupy the position of avatar of some emergent culture? It is the gay male subject itself: a form of subjectivity that, most significantly, is already thoroughly imbued with pornography. Or at least thoroughly shot through with pornography's possibilities for rethinking the dominant (and dominantly frustrating) positings of the public/private divide in post-1950s America. Therefore, the most telling symptomatic detail of *Night at the Adonis* remains the new boy's aloofness from sex. The new employee sublimates sex for something better: getting ahead in a new world order. As such, he anticipates the central role the newly constructed gay male subject will (unwittingly) play in the coming gentrification of the ruins, a process integrally connected to the political programs of Thatcherism/Reaganism he now represents. This character anticipates a "representation" of the male homosexual that will be continually embodied by porn in the video era, and which is perhaps even more important to the workings of dominant, heterosexual capitalism than any larger thing we might delineate, believe in, and optimistically call gay subculture (let alone gay history).[13] For, in the end, this is an individual who *seems* at least partly to have brought on himself the very historical predicament of Giuliani-era New York that is the subject of so much impassioned debate over so-called gay spaces today.

This is why we should not take *Night at the Adonis*, even in all its idiosyncrasy, as a peculiar case. It is entangled with a large range of issues that all-male pornography saliently continues to work through, on some level, for people in the throes of history: that is, people in the throes of desire who are charged with the duties of navigating its spaces. As we move into a new century of transnational media flows and media convergence, all-male porn ever more expansively remaps the world as a literal and a figurative place. In the process, it inherently demands our continual reimagination not just of ourselves and our relationships to each other but of that eternal navigation process itself.

Notes

1 This includes work by Richard Dyer, Thomas Waugh, Earl Jackson Jr., John Champagne, and Daniel Harris, among others.
2 We offer this sort of close reading partly in response to John Champagne's rea-

sons to "stop reading films," at least via older exegetical methods, in the essay "Stop Reading Porn!" (1997).

3 In saying that "in New York the effect is widely acknowledged," Warner is perhaps dubiously estimating the overall barometric pressure among the city's gay men about the effects of Giuliani-era policies and initiatives not only in Times Square but also in the West Village itself.

4 With his statement that "and now it reserves privacy protection primarily for those whose sexuality is already normative," Warner specifically means in the aftermath of the *Bowers v. Hardwick* decision.

5 In other words, it looked as though the magic marker was carried into the bathroom specifically in order to write this message in an appropriately "urgent" style.

6 Considered in the context of a mode of public/private relationality not necessarily organized by heteronormativity, then, the idea that pornography is always inherently "published" runs completely counter to an assumption structuring so much cultural debate about it. This is the notion that, as Alan Soble has put it, "pornography is nonpropositional," which structures many such debates in both its positive and its negative forms. At least in the case of all-male pornography, the propositions porn does make are clearly about the context of its immediate reception. This becomes most evident in the bathroom-wall examples, where a text problematizing certain public/private oppositions must always already invoke the very normativity it wishes to transgress. See Soble 1991.

7 Filmmakers usually call this "fake sync" or "slop sync."

8 This holds especially true due to the number of other releases of so-called theater films during the 1970s, including *Bijou* (dir. Wakefield Poole, 1972), *The Back Row* (dir. Jerry Douglas, 1972), and others. This ultimately became a legendary subgenre. The recent packaging of Chi Chi LaRue's remake of *The Back Row* along with the original as a dual cassette (or DVD) boxed set lends typical evidence of the lingering importance of this subgenre.

9 This especially reminds us of the decharacterized men's voices used in 1970s pop music. At the outset of disco diva laments, this sort of male voice sometimes functioned as a point of comparison, and departure, for that of the female singer. The male voice saying "hello" over the phone line at the outset of Carol Douglas's historically contemporaneous hit "Doctor's Orders," and the (textually absent) voice that Donna Summer has purportedly heard "On the Radio," provide just two examples. A related use of filmic, heterosexual porn sound comes in the form of Harry Reems's laughably "clinical" Dictaphone readings throughout what is probably the most narratologically inventive segment of *Deep Throat*.

10 Here we are using the word *publicity* as the preferred translation of the term *Öffentlichkeit*, an English term adopted by Peter Labanyi in his translation of Kluge and Negt 1988. As is the case with many philosophical terms taken from German, no connotationally precise English equivalent exists.

11 For a particularly interesting and self-conscious recent riff on the centrality of

this passage through publicity to both narrative and number in all-male porn, see *Betrayed* (dir. John Rutherford, 1999), the film carefully chosen as the heavily publicized comeback vehicle of 1980s *Falcon* star Kevin Williams. Here the overarching narrative is not just structured as a series of sexual opportunities that keep literally showing up on the bourgeois Hollywood Hills doorstep of the main character while his live-in lover is out of town, opportunities, it turns out, that his traveling lover orchestrated. (To keep his stay-at-home "true"?) Even more interesting, the series of arrive-at-the-door trysts culminates in a backyard "gang rape" sequence where all the men penetrating the Williams character do it with strap-on dildos, so that the publicly manufactured objects magically and impossibly displace their real penises during the penetrations! Gay privateness—in the realm of the monogamous romantic, as well as the realm of the anonymous sexual—is here imaged and narrated as achievable only through the ever more novel, continual, and redoubled symbolic insertions of the public. For more on the function of this passage through publicity in pornography at other historical moments (the age of video and the era of transnational porn, respectively), see Cante and Restivo 2001 and 2003.

12 While Jameson discusses the issue of cognitive mapping at the end of the celebrated essay on postmodernism (1991), we are thinking here of the specific ways in which his methods of close reading themselves become a kind of cognitive mapping process. See, for example, the readings offered in Jameson 1995.

13 It might seem as if the emergence of video (where sound and image are married from the beginning) as the dominant mode of porn production would alter the sound/image conventions described here. But, strangely enough, these conventions are very often retained. The work of Kristen Bjorn proves exemplary in this respect. Perhaps the most internationally legendary of the porn directors of the 1990s, Bjorn consistently uses fake sync and (albeit much more sophisticated) enveloping sound mixes in his tapes, while at the same time working in a transnational and "postidentitarian" context. For a detailed analysis of the implications of Bjorn's work, see Cante and Restivo 2003.

Works Cited

Altman, Rick. 1986. "Television/Sound." In *Studies in Entertainment: Critical Approaches to Mass Culture*, ed. Tania Modleski. Bloomington: Indiana University Press. 39–54.

Berlant, Lauren, and Michael Warner. 1998. "Sex in Public." *Critical Inquiry* 24, 2: 547–67.

Cante, Rich, and Angelo Restivo. 2001. "The Voice of Pornography: Tracking the Subject through the Sonic Spaces of Gay Male Moving-Image Pornography." In *Key Frames: Popular Cinema and Cultural Studies*, ed. Matthew Tinkcom and Amy Villarejo. New York: Routledge. 207–28.

———. 2004. "The 'World' of All-Male Pornography: On the Public Place of Moving-

Image Sex in the Era of Transnationalism." In *More Dirty Looks: Further Essays on Gender, Pornography, and Power*, ed. Pamela Church-Gibson. London: British Film Institute Publishing.

Champagne, John. 1995. *The Ethics of Marginality: A New Approach to Gay Studies.* Bloomington: Indiana University Press.

———. 1997. "Stop Reading Porn! Film Studies, Close Analysis, and Gay Porn." *Cinema Journal* 36, 4: 76–98.

Chion, Michel. 1991. "Quiet Revolution . . . and Rigid Stagnation." *October* 58: 69–80.

Dyer, Richard. 1990. "Coming to Terms." In *Out There: Marginalization and Contemporary Culture*, ed. Russell Ferguson et al. Cambridge, Mass.: MIT Press. 289–298.

Ferguson, Frances. 1995. "Pornography: The Theory." *Critical Inquiry* 21, 3: 670–95.

Harris, Daniel. 1997. *The Rise and Fall of Gay Culture.* New York: Hyperion.

Jackson, Earl, Jr. 1995. *Strategies of Deviance: Studies in Gay Male Representation.* Bloomington: Indiana University Press.

Jameson, Fredric. 1995. *The Geopolitical Aesthetic: Cinema and Space in the World System.* Bloomington: Indiana University Press.

———. 1991. *Postmodernism, or, the Cultural Logic of Late Capitalism.* Durham, N.C.: Duke University Press.

Kluge, Alexander, and Oscar Negt. 1988. "Excerpts from *The Public Sphere and Experience.*" Trans. Peter Labanyi. *October* 46: 60–80.

Laqueur, Thomas. 2003. *Solitary Sex: A Cultural History of Masturbation.* New York: Zone Books.

Mohr, Richard D. 1988. *Gays/Justice: A Study of Ethics, Society, and Law.* New York: Columbia University Press.

Soble, Alan. 1991. "Defamation and the Endorsement of Degradation." In *Pornography: Private Right or Public Menace?*, ed. Robert M. Baird and Stuart E. Rosenbaum. Buffalo, N.Y.: Prometheus. 96–111.

Warner, Michael. 1997. "The Mass Public and the Mass Subject." In *Habermas and the Public Sphere*, ed. Craig Calhoun. Cambridge, Mass.: MIT Press. 377–402.

———. 1999. *The Trouble with Normal: Sex, Politics, and the Ethics of Queer Life.* Cambridge, Mass.: Harvard University Press.

Waugh, Thomas. 1996. *Hard to Imagine: Gay Male Eroticism in Photography and Film from their Beginnings to Stonewall.* New York: Columbia University Press.

Williams, Linda. 1989. *Hard Core: Power, Pleasure, and the "Frenzy of the Visible."* Berkeley: University of California Press.

What Do You Call a Lesbian with Long Fingers? The Development of Lesbian and Dyke Pornography

HEATHER BUTLER

Pay attention please; I'm inviting you to move to a new *king*dom
—Clarice Lispector

✳ This essay attempts to identify different historical trends, styles, motives, and developments within the subgenre of lesbian pornography.[1] It offers an examination of the signification of lesbian pornography, as well as of its relationship to more mainstream pornographies, and traces the historical progress/ion of lesbian pornography, while also locating certain significant nonlinear developments. Through the investigation of a handful of cinematic lesbian sex acts and actual pornographic films from 1968 to 2000, I analyze the various permutations of the butch/femme dyad, the dildo, the concept of authenticity, and the idea of creating through representation a discursive place/space that is coded as a specifically lesbian zone. This space reinforces not only the idea of authenticity but also the very legitimacy of lesbian sexuality in and of itself, as well as the idea of lesbian pornography.[2] I cannot provide an exhaustive account of all that has been done in the last thirty years within the realms of lesbian-themed exploitation film and lesbian pornography. Rather, in isolating certain films that stand out to me in particular, I examine their attempts to authenticate lesbian sexuality through representation, as well as to interpellate the potential lesbian viewer. In the process, I address some heterosexual porn in an effort to locate moments of intertextuality, in addition to those marking lesbian pornography's direct challenges. These challenges made within the genre of lesbian pornography illustrate a more mainstream movement made by lesbians toward an autonomous and accurate representation of both lesbian sex acts and lesbian sexuality.

My essay takes its title from a joke I heard several years ago: "What do you call a lesbian with long fingers?" The punch line, "well hung," would suggest a lesbian's fingers are her most valuable sex tools—the equivalent to a penis. These fingers, which also serve as a penis substitute (or rather, *substitutes*), therefore apparently can only be contemplated in terms of male anatomy, in which size matters most.[3] In the hetero cosmos, the lesbian does not exist as a discrete being, and lesbian sexuality seems to serve as a comical substitute, with her sex tools merely serving as referents to the heterosexual counterpart. The "lesbian," as she is typically represented in heterosexual pornography, is most often used as a warm-up for sex between a man and a woman.

This type of representation does not occur solely in the realm of pornography; we can also find it in mainstream cinema, personal experience,[4] and heterocentric society in general. The "one-sex" model, which tends to privilege male sexuality at the expense of female sexuality, is reinforced even further not only when women are perceived as *ce sexe qui n'en est pas un*,[5] but when lesbians simply become relegated to the sphere of "boys." In lesbian pornography, the joke mentioned above is discursively and visually played out and played on through role-playing and name-calling, especially dirty talk, and thus is subverted and even inverted. It is not the lesbian who is the butt of this joke, as we will see, but rather the heterosexual male, and while this joke intends to aggressively assault the lesbian and her sexuality, it actually reveals the fragile and insecure apparatus working the one-sex model and exposes the idea of monolithic sexuality as both inadequate and unnecessary. Lesbian pornography inherently uncloaks the impotence behind the phallic model and proposes alternatives to simply "taking it" or "faking it." Since biological limitations, such as an impending ejaculation, do not necessarily contain lesbian pornography, it does not have to preoccupy itself with or become imprisoned by the idea of showing telos. As a result, lesbian desire can be actively explored in ways not articulated within the heterosexual model of pornography. Lesbian pornography could be said, in fact, to be the practice behind the theory.[6] Desire between women is (really) articulated, lesbian subjectivity and lesbian bodies are realized and represented (no joke!), and pornography is reconceptualized and reinvented in very important ways.

In all of the films that I discuss, the butch, and, with one exception, the butch/femme dyad, is present to various degrees. The figure, or idea, of the butch is and has always been *the* visible marker of lesbianism.[7] She quite possibly both constitutes the most important icon of lesbian visibility and one of the most important icons in lesbian history; with the figure of the butch, the lesbian gains maximum visibility.[8] As we will see, the butch de-stabilizes any fixed notions of gender that we might have had concerning masculinity and femininity. She gives these notions new significance and new expression, and she ultimately overthrows heterohegemony. Because of the butch's inevitable visibility, and because our cultural knowledge has given us the tools to identify and recognize her *as* butch, I argue that the butch authenticates lesbian pornography, even if only superficially. She thus answers more to the need (which is not gender-specific) to "see sex" and to see some kind of proof that sex is indeed taking place. In her very being, the butch offers "proof," for she wears her sexual preference the way most of us wear clothes. She is the certificate of authenticity in lesbian pornography for lesbians; she turns the screen into a potentially safe space for the visual representation of lesbian desire; and she inspires trust in her lesbian view-ers. Without necessarily being convinced of "real" pleasure or a real orgasm, the viewer may nevertheless acknowledge a lesbian authenticity through the figure of the butch. At the very least, viewers might feel assured that the hypervisible status of the butch, as well as of the butch/femme dyad, effec-tively destabilize any and all notions of heteronormativity.[9] In doing so, both can provide us with new ways of viewing pornography (the rules obviously change with the representation of same-sex desire; as we will see, the rules change even more when "lesbian" becomes lesbian).[10]

A Man's Worst Enemy, a Woman's Pride and Joy

The King (dir. Looney Bear, 1968) is one of many sexploitation-era films that purport to deal with the topic of lesbianism.[11] Within the genre of sexploi-tation, lesbianism constituted merely one of many "dirty" topics liberally explored, if only to titillate the targeted male viewer with brief images of female breasts, buttocks, and bellies. Where *The King* seems to deviate from the sexploitation model of lesbian-themed films is in its disarming and even sincere attempt to represent lesbians as authentic people. The majority of the sexploitation films I have watched typically depict lesbianism as some-thing that happens to women who have been victimized by men; a phase in a young girl's sexual development *before* she moves on to boys; an afternoon activity between bored and neglected housewives; a lurid account about depraved and deviant individuals who hopefully end up dead; or as the subject of "earnest inquiry" in the form of a "mocumentary" complete with a vulgar appropriation of psychoanalysis and phony statistics.[12] *The King* notably refuses to depict lesbianism in any of these ways, but, rather, offers an earnest attempt to represent lesbianism as an actual choice not contingent on heterosexuality and a lifestyle that remains discrete from the heterosexual imperative.

The King begins (and ends) with a rather long poem—evocative of the limericks of the early stag films, as well as of the square-up ("a prefatory statement about the social or moral ill the film claimed to combat")[13] of early exploitation films—about the joys of lesbianism, and more specifically about the joys of a stereotypical butch/femme setup. A photomontage of female body parts taken from pinup photos (typically breasts, beaver shots, legs, and bottoms) illustrates the poem. The film's protagonist is an African American woman named Carol, who lives with her two white roommates, Joan and Mickey, aka the "King." Carol works as a secretary to a frizzy type named Ms. Jerner, and the film begins with a sexual encounter between the two ("I know I won't mind working late hours at *this* job!"). Carol returns home from work to find the King lounging (she has no day job; she's a king, that's a full-time job). The King begins to whip Carol for apparently stealing some money, but the whipping dissolves quickly into an embrace and then some light petting. This scene immediately establishes the stereotype of the bulldagger and her femme—the cruelly unpredictable sadist and the insatiable, passive masochist. As a butch, Mickey is rather subtle. She does not in any way conform to a recognizable notion of a butch aesthetic; she has long hair, carries a purse, and bears a strong resemblance to Janis Joplin (who was, in fact, perceived as butch by heterosexual standards). She does, however, conform to the representation of the "butch," the "bulldagger," or the "dyke" within the genre of sexploitation. That is, she is *named* or classified as butch, and this is discursively reinforced throughout the film, regardless of the fact that she does not look much different from the other "femme" women (figure 1).

When Joan comes home, she gets undressed and joins Carol and Mickey; eventually Carol is pushed aside, and Mickey and Joan make out exclusively. Carol finds herself displaced in favor of Joan, and in the voice-over narration, she expresses her sexual frustration and anger.[14] A series of dreams and flashbacks presents Carol's insatiable same-sex desire in sexual encounters (and failed attempts) with other women. Eventually, the three lesbians go to

1. A butch and her femme in *The King.*

Cherry Grove (the place where "things are the way they're supposed to be: the women with the women and the men with the men"),[15] and after a wild night of smoking, dancing, and making out, Carol leaves the trio in favor of Ms. Jerner, and the King is deposed. It is also important to note that much of what could be considered pornographic is really just voice-over narration. That is, there are no actual representations of sex acts on-screen; they are aurally invoked by the disembodied narrator, and there is little coherence between what is said and what is shown. It is also important to note that the narrator sounds perpetually aroused; whether she describes exactly how she takes her clothes off or how the three get to Cherry Grove, she always sounds "ready" for something never actually represented on-screen, though it is described, and often in minute detail.

In his 1999 book *"Bold! Daring! Shocking! True!" A History of Exploitation Films, 1919–1959*, Eric Schaefer discusses mode of production and style in a typical exploitation film. While *The King* was made in 1969, and would be classified as sexploitation rather than exploitation, its mode of production equals that of the exploitation films preceding it. The problems inherent in most exploitation films, such as the lack of continuity, tacky style, bad acting, and cheap scenery, all resulted from a specific mode of production, something we have come to see as one of the genre's defining characteristics (48). There is little to no continuity within *The King*: one minute Carol is wearing a bikini, and the next minute a long-sleeved sweater; they say that they are at Cherry Grove, yet the beach is littered with heterosexual couples and small children; one minute they have no clothes on, and in the very next cut, they are all in the exact same positions, but dressed. In addition, films such as these often recycled stock footage from old films, which might explain the several odd cuts to unexplained (negative) images (cops beating up patrons of a bar, an ugly white man screaming, a race car, a sailboat) that have absolutely nothing to do with the diegesis. *The King* was obviously made on a shoestring budget, using stock music, recycled footage, sparse sets, and what Schaefer calls a "hyphenate" (meaning that the same person wrote, directed, and produced it, as well as providing the narration). It adheres completely to the mode of production of a typical exploitation film.

But *The King* manages to distinguish itself from other sexploitation films in its refusal to engage in the popular views of lesbianism as either a phase, an inferior substitute to heterosexuality, or just deviant behavior. In this refusal, *The King* resists its own genre and can be read as a truly deviant representation of the classic sexploitation film and as a forerunner to lesbian pornography. *The King* remarkably seeks to interpellate an exclusively lesbian audience from the very beginning. The film represents lesbian desire as discrete from heterosexual desire by attempting to create an authentic queer space on-screen—these lesbians live in the Village in New York City and spend their weekends at Cherry Grove, both historically queer spaces. Like its more mainstream British counterpart, *The Killing of Sister George* (dir. Robert Aldrich, 1968), and, to a lesser extent, the more notorious sexploitation films by Radley Metzger and Joe Sarno, it contains stereotypical representations of a butch as aggressive, sadistic, and even predatory. It also contains a relationship with a passive, subservient, and even unsatisfied femme, who eventually leaves her butch for another woman. The use of the butch figure as an authentification device appears as a sort of "clichéd but necessary" stereotype; it provides an easily identifiable marker of lesbianism.[16]

I use *The King* as a starting point for my discussion of lesbian pornography because this film attempts to represent an exclusively lesbian desire that, unlike Aldrich's more mainstream representation, does not portray lesbian sexuality as pathetic, pathological, or disgusting. In fact, *The King* portrays lesbian sex and lesbian sexuality as the only choice, which then contains other choices. (A piece from the closing limerick-like poem almost taunts the female viewer: "Take heed the rest of you, for soon you may surrender, if at any time you've had any doubt deciding on your gender, remember—are you a king or are you a queen, or are you like me, an in-between thing?") I view this film not as explicitly representative of lesbian pornography, but rather as an ultimately positive genesis, and though it is fraught with complications, including an incoherent narrative, it constitutes an important document for tracing the development of the visual representation of lesbian erotics within the genre of sexploitation cinema.

In the so-called golden age of pornography (the 1970s), no distinct lesbian presence is to be found in the industry. One possible explanation for the lesbian lacuna might be the fact that lesbian separatism remained in full swing throughout the 1970s and into the early 1980s, and making pornography for lesbians and by lesbians was not on the agenda. However, there is no shortage of woman-to-woman sex scenes in mainstream heterosexual pornography (or what I like to call the "lesbo-jelly" in the hetero-donut). Typically, the "lesbian" number serves as a warm-up for the "real" thing, that is, sex with a penis that will eventually ejaculate.[17] *Behind the Green Door* offers a perfect example of this type of pornography, for the soon-to-be-insatiable Maid Marilyn is licked, fondled, rubbed, and even *comforted* by several women in preparation for the bigger numbers (all heterosexual) that will follow.[18]

In my research on 1970s pornography, I did find a rather compelling "lesbian" presence that warrants some attention: her name is Georgina Spelvin. Notorious for her work in the classic *The Devil in Miss Jones* (dir. Gerard Damiano, 1972), Spelvin was an extremely prolific porn star throughout the 1970s and into the 1980s, and although she began her career rather late for her profession (she was already thirty-six when *The Devil in Miss Jones* was made in 1972), both her unconventional appearance and her notable acting ability made her a remarkably successful figure in mainstream pornography. She was typically cast as a celibate spinster type who has a sexual awakening and then becomes an oversexed, kinky sex fiend and often meets a tragic end (suicide and eternal damnation are two examples). In two of her films, *Sleepyhead* (dir. Joe Sarno, 1973) and *The Private Afternoons of Pamela Mann* (dir. Radley Metzger, 1975) the "lesbian" sex scenes do not only remain discrete from the heterosexual sex scenes; they are also not presented as a warm-up for what will "come" later. *Sleepyhead* tells the story of the celibate writer Bernice, played by Spelvin, who reawakens sexually on reuniting with her ex-lover Nancy, a sexually promiscuous photographer played by Judith Hamilton, who also stars opposite Spelvin in both *3 A.M.* (dir. Robert McCallum, 1975) and *The Devil in Miss Jones*. Both women go on to seduce Bernice's Bible-banging younger sister Tracey (Tina Russell), whom they "convert" from Christianity to lesbianism. The film includes a painfully long orgy scene, but the real action occurs in the other bedroom, occupied by Bernice, Nancy, and Tracey. *Sleepyhead* focuses on sex acts between women, and the sex that does occur between men and women is always part of a larger orgy sequence, where the woman-to-woman action is greater than that of woman to man (in one orgy scene, there are four women and one man). The film ends with Nancy replacing Bernice with the latter's younger and more conventionally attractive sister, whereupon Bernice takes off with the Bible and a David Cassidy look-alike. Though we cannot classify this film as lesbian porn, its depiction of lesbian sex as neither a warm-up to hetero-sexual sex nor a pathetic imitation of it, its sexual transformations of the three female protagonists, its primarily gynocentric narrative, and its queer ending (Tracey leaves Jesus for a lesbian!), not to mention the passionate per-formance of Georgina Spelvin, make for a surprisingly queer heterosexual porn.[19]

The Private Afternoons of Pamela Mann, in contrast, constitutes a com-pletely conventional example of 1970s porn. Organized around a thread-bare narrative about excessive voyeurism, there is almost nothing within this film that deviates from convention, save one sex scene between Spel-vin and Barbara Bourbon (who plays Pamela). It is the longest sex scene in the film (over ten minutes), and it contains three different types of music, soft-focus shots of facial as well as vaginal caresses, conversation, smiles, and hard-core sex acts. There is cunnilingus, vaginal and anal penetration (with fingers), and tribadism; there are no faked orgasms, and there are no penises. Sex between two women is neither relegated to the realm of nonthreatening caresses and giggles, nor is it a freak show of body oil and multiple vibrator penetration, like the 1977 "lesbian" pornography *Aerobi-sex Girls* (dir. Bruce Seven). This sex scene stands out from the others in the film in many ways: not only does it last longer than Pamela's hetero encoun-ters; these two women are actually friends. (Spelvin plays a hooker, with the Pamela character as her therapist. Pamela is performing a "cleansing" of Spelvin, which actually consists of smoking pot and having sex.) In the midst of what is supposed to be a serious discussion about the hardships of prostitution, the two have sex. The scene does not concern itself with the representation of authentic telos; the two women simply enjoy one another for ten minutes, and then the scene is over. The representation of lesbian sex is again discrete, and it does not conform to excessively passive activity, nor does it border on the freakish; it in fact provides a rather lyrical synthesis of the hard and soft elements of sex.

The work of Georgina Spelvin does not hold significance because she was a lesbian or a lesbian porn star, because that was not, in effect, the case.[20] There is, however, something very butch about Spelvin. Though her films typically paint her as a lonely, frigid spinster, she always "butches up" to be-come sexually assertive, as well as sexually receptive. Her work is notable be-cause it consistently escapes the typical lesbian setup so prevalent in main-stream pornography; that is, we get to see lesbian sex acts discrete from the heterosexual acts that surround them. We also get to see the synthesis of hard-core sex and "soft" intimacy reminiscent of nonpornographic cinema. We get to see a less conventional, somewhat older female body aggressively assert itself through active sex with other women, and we get to see "good" acting on the part of Georgina Spelvin. Though this might not constitute lesbian pornography, it certainly deviates in the right direction.

The most significant piece of lesbian pornography I looked at from the 1980s is a film entitled *Erotic in Nature* (dir. Cristen Lee Rothermund, 1985). It is extremely indicative of what had been happening (politically, socially, culturally) among lesbians in the 1970s and 1980s, and it constitutes one of the first attempts to create a lesbian presence in pornography as *different*; that is, as distinctly nonheterosexual in its emphasis on the more erotic aspects of lesbian sexuality.[21] The film begins with shots of a very athletic, young lesbian chopping logs out in the country. She is topless, clothed only in running shorts and hiking boots. She is very tan, slim, and beautifully muscular. She chops logs, does push-ups and stretches, gazes at her body in a mirror, and listens to her radio while she prepares for a date.[22] The camera focuses almost obsessively on her musculature. The film periodically cross-cuts to the image of another woman (relation as yet unknown) who masturbates with a red dildo and a red rubber hose in an outdoor bathtub. This woman is slim but curvy, and the camera lingers obsessively on her curves in much the same way it lingers on the muscles of the other lesbian. She has long, blond hair and is naked except for a red beaded necklace and a pair of sunglasses. Her fingernails are painted red, and she has one nipple pierced. We hear a voice-over moaning along to the music, a sort of "tribal" rhythm of drums and pipes, as she masturbates first with the dildo, then with both the dildo and the water hose, until she orgasms. After their respective "work-outs," the women meet up for dinner, which, of course, takes place outside, "in nature."

Erotic in nature has a double meaning. The first indicates that the majority of the scenes occur outside, around and in water, under the sun. The brown and strong bodies roll around in the grass, under trees. Nature is glorified and celebrated (think mother earth–goddess, chthonic ecstasy). The setting also has connotations of the remote, the separate, as in lesbian separatism or lesbian love life outside of hetero cities and hetero city limits, in an untouched zone where lesbians can express themselves freely and, although the scenes are shot out in the open, privately. Then there is a second meaning of *erotic in nature*: lesbian sex and sexuality as erotic in their very nature. Sex between two women is depicted as natural, wholesome, healthy;

2. A lesbian sex scene taken from *Erotic in Nature.*

rather than being deviant, it is sensual, an experience that glorifies and cele-brates female bodies. Everything appears normal, as a part of nature, and of the body, and as a completely positive process (figure 2). There is no trace of "deviancy" in either the surroundings or in what the film represents as lesbian desire.[23] It is romantic and soft, like trees and breezes and birds and clear, pure streams—all fluid lesbian sexuality. There is no hint of tension or anxiety toward or about men or heterosexuality. Nor is the relationship be-tween the two women set up as an oppositional and/or sadomasochistic one, such as we saw in *The King*, for example. Nevertheless, a soft butch/femme dyad does exist, but it is oh-so-subtle (the butch figure is really more *ath-letic* than butch and, like her femme counterpart, wears jewelry and makeup and has extremely soft features, so that no one would probably ever call her "sir" or throw her out of the women's bathroom). Nor does any butch/femme role-play occur. The femme uses a dildo exclusively for onanistic purposes. The dildo, it is worth noting, has a deep red color and matches the femme's necklace (it also looks to be made out of crystal rather than silicone).

In its cinematic treatment of the lesbian body, *Erotic in Nature* in some ways resembles its mainstream counterpart, *Personal Best* (dir. Robert Towne, 1982). A similar athletic aesthetic is present in this film, which in fact charts the affair and subsequent breakup of two female athletes as they train for the Olympics. In both *Personal Best* and *Erotic in Nature*, athleticism and athletic female bodies become eroticized within the representation of lesbian sex, and the lesbian body and overall aesthetic is depicted as ath-letic, rather than butch. Unlike *Personal Best*, however, *Erotic in Nature* is exclusively lesbian; that is, there is no trace of the heterosexual anxiety, the "pre-verbal, pre-oedipal narcissism" so explicit, depressing, and suffocating in *Personal Best* (Williams 1986, 150). The lesbian spectator does not have to worry that a man will wander onto the set and replace the butch in *Erotic in Nature*, which is in fact what eventually happens in *Personal Best*.[24] Actual sexual intimacy exists between Kit and Chris, the protagonists of *Erotic in Nature*, while the sexual intimacy between Tori and Chris in *Personal Best* is limited to arm wrestling, tickling and giggling, and light, nonthreatening stroking. Nevertheless, something in *Erotic in Nature* has gone seriously awry: the film does not give a fulfilling representation of a sex act. Rather, the camera lingers lovingly on contorted, twisting, rolling, and often posing bodies and lesbians who giggle and caress, run fingers through hair, and gaze lovingly into one another's eyes. The voice-overs (the film has no dialogue)[25] emphasize how *different* and *exciting* and *new* this relationship is and how *perfect* the sex is, and yet it is difficult (primarily due to the way the film is shot) to ascertain what exactly the two are actually doing. So while the camera does attempt to represent two lesbian bodies engaging in lesbian sex, it is not initially clear what exactly that means, or even what that should look like. For example, in one scene, Kit gets on her knees behind Chris, who is on all fours, and Kit begins to move back and forth very slowly as if she were perhaps penetrating Chris with a dildo, yet she is not penetrating her, nor is she actually rubbing up against her. While Chris has a look of absolute ecstasy on her face, *there is nothing happening* other than two female bodies slowly knocking into one another. I do not mean to imply that pleasure cannot be had as a result of two female bodies moving together to the rustic call of nature; rather, I simply want to stress the fact that no penetration or tribadism seems to actually occur. There is then a quick cut back to the familiar shots of contorted, twisting, rolling female bodies. Eventually, explicit sex acts do occur between the two women, but, perhaps not consciously, this film emphasizes the very difficulty involved in the representation of lesbian sex acts, and the difficult position of lesbians in the porn industry in the late 1980s and early 1990s. The film also seems more invested in the image of lesbian sex as a "positive" and even nonthreatening and nonviolent reciprocal exchange than it is in the representation of actual sex acts. Perhaps it indicates an ideologically motivated intention on the part of the filmmakers to reinforce the idea that sex between women—and lesbianism itself—is "natural."[26]

This film reeks of a different kind of "coming out": namely, coming out of the aftershock of 1970s lesbian feminism, as well as out of the sex wars of the early 1980s.[27] Any behavior possibly linked to the masculine or the aggressive (at the time, these seem to have been considered as one and the same) was considered verboten to lesbian sexuality and destructive to the goals of lesbian feminism. Both Judith Halberstam and Carol Vance discuss the effects of the antipornography position, which, rather than developing into a lesbian call to arms for sex education or an attempt to revitalize and even queer the world of porn, settled into a moralistic, essentialist, and suffocating view of sex as always already perverse (see Halberstam 1998, 136–40; Vance 1992). For many lesbians, the butch/femme dyad was evocative of heterosexuality, a pathetic and even oppressive imitation of the male/female unit. When viewed as role-play, it was seen as objectifying and therefore as counterproductive and even devious, as were other sex-related activities that both heterosexuals and gay men enjoyed, such as s/m, strip shows, bathhouses, X-rated movie theaters, bar culture, and cruising. *Erotic in Nature* marks one of several attempts in the mid-1980s to represent lesbian sexuality,[28] while it also tries to move away from certain reified notions of female sexuality espoused by cultural feminists of that period. For example, the rhetoric of that period held that lesbian sex did not make for an incredibly important issue on the feminist agenda, that feminists should concentrate on "real" social issues instead, and that certain types of representation were to be avoided, namely, the pornographic, which objectified women within the heterosexual, patriarchal configurations from which lesbians sought to escape. Although *Erotic in Nature* marked a step toward the representation of what Linda Williams calls "diff'rent strokes for diff'rent folks," it still seems to contain remnants of the fear that heterosexual sex might pervert lesbian sex and appears to espouse the notion that certain sex acts did not or could not belong in the representation of lesbian sex. However, these fears, and the prohibitions that resulted from them, were on their way out—and fast.

Life in the Fast(er) Lane: Dyking the Lesbian

In 1984, Susie Bright, Nan Kinney, and Debbie Sundahl (aka Fanny Fatale) published the first issue of a lesbian-centered erotica magazine called *On Our Backs*. The title of the magazine is both a play on and an explicit challenge to its radical feminist predecessor, *Off Our Backs*, a feminist journal that began in 1970 and held most of the opinions regarding sex and pornography I mentioned earlier. *On Our Backs* represented not only a challenge to the antipornography views of the most vocal feminists of the 1970s and 1980s but also a fierce move toward higher visibility for lesbians and lesbian sexuality. One year later, Kinney and Sundahl formed Fatale Video (still in business) and began making lesbian pornography. Some of their first videos featured rough sex, dirty talk (words previously disdained, such *cunt, dyke,* and *fuck*, became reintegrated into the lesbian lexicon), the use of dildos and vibrators, elaborate s/m fantasy sequences, and female ejaculation scenes.[29] In 1990, Debbie Sundahl made a lesbian porn film called *Suburban Dykes* (a contradiction in terms if ever there was one!), starring Nina Hartley, Pepper, and Sharon Mitchell. In my opinion, this film marks yet another important stepping-stone, another triumphant coming-out story (this time I use the metaphor in both senses of the word), in the history of lesbian pornography. As the title intimates, the idea of lesbians and lesbian sexuality has become normal: lesbians now live in the suburbs, are in their mid-thirties, attractive, and feminine, in fact. They have regular jobs, a hot tub, and monogamous marriage-type setups; they are doing quite well. They no longer have to live in a big city in order to meet other lesbians; they are financially stable, they are not perverts, they are your neighbors, they throw little lesbian parties, they eat hot dogs, and they fuck. Their sex lives become dull, familiar, and, like any "married" couple, they need new sexual outlets to keep that "spark" long-term couples often lose (in the lesbo-lingo articulated by the film, it is called "the lesbian bed-death syndrome"). The lesbians here grew up and came out under the protective wing of cultural feminism. Eventually, they left that behind and cancelled their subscription to *Off Our Backs* in exchange for *On Our Backs*, though they do not engage in any of the "deviant" sexual behavior that the magazine condones. Not yet, at least.

In a scene from *Suburban Dykes*, Nina and Pepper are relaxing in their hot tub after another fun-filled lesbian get-together. In a moment of absolutely brilliant dialogue, which sets up everything that follows, Nina says something to the effect of, "Wow, what a party! I don't think there's anything left but two dead hot dogs!" The two then begin to discuss some friends who seem on the verge of breaking up. Their friends are experiencing the "lesbian bed-death syndrome" because one of them is apparently not sexually adventurous enough. Nina proceeds to bring up the idea of phone sex (apparently a friend tried it), but Pepper, who has idealistic ideas about relationships, firmly resists the idea: "If you are really in love, the sex will stay hot." In her opinion, "lesbian bed death" is "just a phrase to sell a book," but Nina convinces her to try the phone sex nevertheless. Nina then follows up with a confession of her own: during the party, she spied on two of their friends having sex on their weight bench in the garage. There is a flashback to a sex scene, a porn within a porn, between two butchy women who engage in rather fierce penetrative sex, fingers only.

Nina has set the scene in every way. She brings up the threatening "lesbian bed-death syndrome" and follows this by several unconventional, even taboo, but sexy scenarios such as phone sex, voyeurism, and rough sex. All of this is coupled with snuggles and dirty talk, and as she tells Pepper the sex story, she dons white, lacy lingerie and cuddles up to Pepper, dressed in cotton jockeys, cooing, "I wished it was you taking me with that kind of passion." Nina then passes Pepper the telephone. Pepper of course makes the call and is connected to a dominatrix type called "Mistress Marlena." Nina again plays the role of audio-voyeur, and while she listens to the exchange between Pepper and Mistress Marlena, she does not verbally participate.

The phone sex escapade deserves some attention; for it is here that we can gain a better understanding of where the "typical" (read: suburban) lesbian *was*, sexually speaking. First of all, we find out that Pepper considers herself butch, which might come as a surprise to the viewer. Pepper is stereotypically less femme than Nina, but she does not conform in any way to the aesthetic idea of butch; she has long dark hair, shaved legs and armpits, long fingernails, and very soft features. She is only *comparatively* butch: Nina's lingerie is *more* feminine; Nina's fingernails and pubic area are *more* manicured; Nina's hair is *more* styled and sprayed than Pepper's; Pepper's voice is slightly deeper; she wears no makeup or fingernail polish; and her style of dress is *more* masculine than Nina's. We then discover that this couple does not engage in dildo-play or role-play of any kind. Pepper tells Mistress Marlena that they do, however, use vibrators, and Mistress Marlena scoffs at their obvious ignorance: "Oh *that's* right! Dykes don't like cocks!" Mistress Marlena then confesses that she, in fact, is wearing a big dildo, and that Pepper is going to, among other things, suck it. The camera then cuts to Mistress Marlena, allowing the viewer a half-profile shot of her, in which we see her as a slightly feminine dominatrix type, who is not, in fact, wearing the big black dildo, but is instead slapping it up against her thigh. This dirty talk arouses both Pepper and Nina, who has been keeping one eye on Pepper the entire time, watching how she reacts to the idea of a dildo, of being penetrated, and to dirty cock talk, and both of the women eventually orgasm through masturbation, Nina with a big pink vibrator and Pepper with her hand (figure 3). After they hang up, Nina teases Pepper by calling her a "pervert,"[30] while Pepper teases Nina, calling her a Peeping Tammy, and then they both agree to move on to bigger and better things, namely, an escort service, where they can rent a big bad butch (or a bull-dyke), and this is where things really get kinky (or dykey).

The big bad butch (Sharon Mitchell), who turns out to be a bit more butch than they had imagined, then comes over and provides these two lesbians

3. Nina and Pepper engage in phone sex with Mistress Marlena in *Suburban Dykes*.

4. Sharon educates Nina and Pepper in *Suburban Dykes*.

with a lesson in dyke sex; that is, dildos, emphatic safe-sex education, dirty talk, and butch/femme role-play (figure 4). In Sharon Mitchell's butch persona, we see the almost parodic return of the "butch-style" lesbian: black leather, no makeup, short, slicked-back hair, edgy urban-style clothing (in contrast to the conventional clothing of Nina and Pepper), an exaggerated swagger and smirk, gold chains, and carrying what I have come to recognize as *the* cinematic marker of the old-school butch, a motorcycle helmet. Initially stunned by Sharon's appearance (Pepper only *thought* she was butch, and maybe for the suburbs, she was), Nina and Pepper are only too eager to wave bye-bye to their vibratory vanilla sex as they welcome everything that Sharon pulls out of her big black bag, especially the big, lavender dildo. This becomes everything lesbian pornography could not be; this becomes dyke porn. I differentiate here between "lesbian" and "dyke" porn: dyke porn is exactly what lesbian porn should have been, but could not be. Dyke porn is safe-sex savvy and not afraid to appropriate sex acts once considered definitive of heterosexual and gay male pornography, such as penetration, dirty talk, rough sex, and role-playing, to name a few. Anything once considered off-limits, perverted, or inappropriate (for either political or personal reasons) is now up for grabs—literally. In addition, dyke porn differentiates itself from its heterosexual and gay male counterparts in its staunch declaration and performance of safe sex. These characteristics remain constitutive of dyke porn up to the present day.

I see Sharon Mitchell's big bad butch as more than a return to a familiar and loveable lesbian stereotype; I see her as a sort of lesbian superhero as she provides Nina and Pepper with this cathartic experience of sexual enlightenment, which enables Pepper to transition into what is obviously about to become her role. The rather traditional notions of femme as passive and butch as active still cling to this film, for although Nina orchestrated the whole scene, it is Pepper who actually *does* all of it. Also, Sharon refers to Nina as Pepper's wife, and Sharon fucks Nina, not Pepper, while it is Pepper, and not Nina, who eventually fucks Sharon. In the last scene of the film, a "changing of the guard" occurs: the dildo is handed to Pepper, who makes the transition into her new role not through sex with Nina, but through sex with Sharon (Pepper penetrates the big bad butch as Nina cheers her on). It seems important to note that Pepper initially gets interested in calling the escort service because of her positive phone-sex experience, during which the idea of being penetrated by a dildo arouses her. Yet as the final sex scene suggests, Pepper will be the penetratrix, not the penetrated.

The problems presented in this film illustrate what lesbians were up against during the post–sex wars, postseparatism, and even postassimilation era: how should lesbians have sex? How *do* lesbians (real ones) have sex? Do lesbians like to watch other lesbians have sex, and, if so, how should that sex be (re)presented? Is it acceptable to recognize the presence of fierce, erotic, aggressive, and possibly perverse (perverse *for lesbians*, of course) desire? Is it then acceptable to represent this desire visually? What makes for a pleasing representation of lesbian desire? How does one successfully film hot lesbian sex? It is through the butch persona that this new lesbian, or *dyke*, sexuality becomes "normalized." That is, it has become acceptable to engage in various types of "deviant" sex-play (no lesbian membership cards will be revoked if one straps on a dildo and talks dirty cock talk to one's lover), and these sex acts are represented as positive through the very positive image of, and ironic homage to, the butch lesbian persona.

Looking (and Staying) Hard: Difference and the Dildo

One of the nice things about being a dyke is getting to choose the size of your dick.
—Rachel Vernon, *On Our Backs*

Numerous questions, concerns, and debates surround the dildo and whether it *fits* in lesbian sex (see Findlay 1999). Is it a penis substitute? Is it a male stand-in? Is it a phallus? Is it a fetish? Can it feel? Does it feel good to her? Is it erotic? Can it be castrated? Should I castrate it? Am I castrated? Do I have penis envy? Do I have phallus envy? Do I have a fetish? Do I want to be a man? Is this the only way to have active sex? Is it perverted? Am I a pervert? Do I look stupid wearing it? Should I read more Lacanian theory? Should I read a feminist's interpretation of Lacan? Should I castrate Lacan? Am I experiencing a form of castration just by reading Lacan? Should I be wearing the dildo while I read Lacan? All of these questions are entirely valid, yet they, and much of the scholarship I have read concerning the dildo, consistently fail to mention what seems to me its most important quality: the fact that the dildo functions as a pleasure-giver, not a pleasure-seeker. Unlike its male "counterpart," the dildo does not ejaculate, does not lose its erection, can come in most any size, color, and even shape and, *most important*, the dildo is detachable.

The dildo represents one aspect, or one accessory, rather, of lesbian sex, which neither begins nor ends with dildo penetration, and although the wearer is associated with a more active, or "masculine," role than the one being penetrated, this association is only somewhat accurate. For while the dildo-wearer might do the thrusting, it is the recipient of the dildo penetration who counts most. According to Cherry Smyth, "it is the 'butch/top's' aim in lesbian sex to give the 'femme/bottom' complete satisfaction, while the penis is often the only satisfied genital in heterosexual porn" (1990, 157). In my opinion, the very notion of the dildo displaces several Lacanian ideas concerning the phallus and phallic power in important ways. For example, if one were to regard penetration as a particularly phallic act, or as "the phallic act *par excellence*" (Reich 1999, 260), then she, Judith Butler (1993), Marjorie Garber (1992), Sue-Ellen Case (1993), Teresa De Lauretis (1994), and others would all be correct in their various assertions that the phallus does indeed belong to any and everyone, that the phallus is not the penis, but, rather, a detachable, performative, even phantasmatic object that nobody owns and that everybody can play with, wear, or discard. This actually makes perfect sense in the context of dyke porn. Although there is role-play and the words "cock" and "dyke dick" are often used in sex scenes, the dildo is never intended as a substitute for or an indication of any primordial lesbian lack. The lesbians in this porn make no effort to disguise exactly what they are doing, namely, playing. They do not try to "really" pass as men.[31] If that were the case, none of the lesbians would be wearing bright pink or sparkly gold or vibrating, bunny-shaped dildos. Dildos are *accessories to* the lesbian sex act; they are in no way requisite.

One might be able to convincingly say that there is no phallus in the Lacanian sense;[32] that the dildo or the fingers, or whatever object one might use in order to penetrate, is not in fact a phallic object, and that the very idea of the phallic is displaced when the desire represented is lesbian. If one wants to speak in terms of the Lacanian phallus, then one could say that the lesbian both is and has the phallus, potentially speaking. In keeping with the idea that there is indeed a phallus that penetrates, and that the lesbian does indeed have it—whether it comes in the form of a dildo, long fingers, a tongue, or any other object—Lacan's formulation of the phallus would not be effective or illustrative as a representation of lesbian desire. Lacan's formula, and the subsequent feminist critique of its formulation,[33] implies that the phallus belongs to the man, yet the lesbian with her object of penetration can perform all of the same things that the penis/phallus can perform during the sex act, *except for one very important thing*—she, or rather her dildo, does not ejaculate.[34] She does not have to ejaculate, she is not biologically predisposed to ejaculating, the object she uses to penetrate her partner (who may, in fact, ejaculate), though it may be attached to her body in some way, is not beyond her control. It is dependable, adjustable, and controllable.

This stands in direct contrast to the end of a typical sex scene in heterosexual pornography, in which a man will ejaculate on some part of the female body. The man always comes on the woman, be it in her eyes or mouth or on her breasts, belly, or ass. Ejaculation on the woman's face is referred to as a "facial," thereby describing this act as a beneficial and even luxurious process for the female receiver. Facials *exfoliate, rejuvenate*, and *hydrate*. Facials are supposed to keep the skin from aging, they do not leave behind a sticky residue, and they moisturize without clogging pores. Facials are mostly expensive, a luxurious and self-indulgent practice, although now one can purchase them at drugstore costs in bottle form (they also come as nifty towelettes). Semen becomes more than glorified male piss; it becomes an alpha-hydroxy infused substance that replenishes, nourishes, soothes, healing dry, wrinkled, female skin. And female protagonists in heterosexual pornography, because they apparently do not orgasm in a way that is conducive to the principle of "maximum visibility" (Williams 1989, 48–49), turn, for the most part, into cum-catchers, and there is little attempt to represent female pleasure in any form other than a smiling or ecstatic face dripping with semen.[35]

It is logical, then, to say that the strap-on dildo provides the kind of agency to a woman (or two women) that a man's penis simply does not. In this case, it would also be logical to say that the lesbian has more sexual agency wearing a strap-on dildo than the male has with his perpetually premature ejaculator. Therefore I propose that the Lacanian phallus has as its telos not penetration, but rather ejaculation. This gives a whole new meaning to the word *lack*; for one could argue that there is no lack in lesbian sexuality, that the real lack is in Lac(k)anian psychoanalytic theory, which gives us little more than premature ejaculate. I will return to the topic of the dildo in my discussion of three more films, all of them made within the last four years.

Dyke Porn Gets a Face-Lift and Goes Urban: Shar Rednour, Jackie Strano, and other San Francisco Lesbians

Dyke porn in the late 1990s saw more radical changes, among them younger and more urban bodies, extensive dildo- and role-play, nonmonogamous sex, dirty talk, and a continuation of the safe-sex education themes which emerged in the early 1990s (specifically in the work of Debi Sundahl and Fatale Video). In 2000, s.i.r. (which stands for Sex, Indulgence, and Rock 'n' Roll) Production released *Hard Love/How to Fuck in High Heels*, a double feature written, directed, and produced by Shar Rednour and Jackie Strano (both of whom star as well). Rednour and Strano are a lesbian couple from San Francisco who are actively involved in the sex industry through video production, spoken word, books, and even as sex educators for Good Vibrations, as well as for the dyke community in San Francisco.[36] Their porn is actually the first to receive attention from the world of mainstream pornography (Rednour and Strano won the "Best All-Girl Feature" Award from Adult Video News). In this double feature, we see younger dykes who live in San Francisco engaging in all kinds of safe sex with multiple partners. The cast is a multiracial group of women in their late twenties and early thirties; they come in all shapes and sizes, are tattooed, pierced, hair-dyed, and often glittered.

The first feature, *Hard Love*, consists of a rather simple narrative: a recently separated couple, who each have new partners, end up in bed together after some fierce post-breakup dyke drama/trauma (figure 5). *How to Fuck*

5. Post-breakup makeup sex in *Hard Love*.

in High Heels is a mock behind-the-scenes feature based on a spoken word piece by Shar Rednour, which actually toured nationally with a group of poets called Sister Spit. It contains clips from her live performance, as well as actual demonstrations of how to fuck and be fucked while wearing high heels. At the end of the video, there is a mock commercial called "How to Pick Up Girls," hosted by Fairy Butch (who lives and works in San Francisco), which takes place at the Lexington (a real dyke bar in San Francisco), in which dykes use tired old one-liners on other dykes and either get lucky or get rejected. By the end of the commercial, all the dykes have gotten lucky and are all making out with one another in the bathroom. At the very end of the scene comes a humorous interpellation of the viewer and a simultaneous plug for the bar: "So come to the Lexington, San Francisco's *only* dyke bar, where every night is ladies' night," and the address and phone number of the bar are provided.

The idea of real dykes living and working and playing in a real dyke space is one of the film's main themes, as is the use of local dykes in the film (Phyllis Christopher, a local photographer, as well as Fairy Butch, author Michelle Tea, and recognizable employees from the Lexington and other local businesses). The film authenticates dyke presence/reality by co-opting an already established dyke community in San Francisco. This authentic dyke presence is portrayed as a little slice of reality predicated on a preexisting dyke cosmos already in full orbit. Rooted in place, this project potentially constitutes an intimate affair for a dyke viewer from the Bay Area. It is also very effective in its presentation of the young, urban dyke.

In *Hard Love*, the butch penetrates the femme with her dildo (or her "dyke dick," as it is called), but in *How to Fuck in High Heels*, Shar (and one other femme) penetrate one another with dildos. While there is a representation of all types of sexual interaction between dykes, penetration with a dildo being one way among others to signify dyke pleasure, the tape does in fact adhere to certain conventions. For example, no butch-on-butch action occurs, and the only time that a femme penetrates a butch, she uses her fingers. Dildo penetration (or rather, the dyke who penetrates) is always concerned with the woman penetrated; there is a constant need for affirmation. "Is this ok?" and "Does this feel good?" are two questions asked repeatedly and with apparent sincerity throughout the film. This type of verbal affirmation is not a priority in heterosexual pornography, where pleasure is typically located on the side of the penetrator, while proof of that pleasure primarily "comes" in the form of an ejaculating penis. On the dildo difference, I quote Jackie Strano, who in a personal correspondence in the spring of 2001 kindly elaborated on what *exactly* the dildo meant to her. It is

> a pleasure tool, an extension of my energy, attached to my clit, it is something that does not become flaccid or shrivel up . . . it exists to make a woman come, to give her pleasure . . . and does not come out or come down until she says it does according to her orgasmic wax and wane, not mine as a man's basic physiology would dictate. Also, I can adjust girth, length, shape, etc., according to my partner's needs and desires and not leave her stuck with just one option. Dildo play is part of the complete sex act not the pinnacle or finishing off as in straight sex.

The dildo is not only an effective pleasure tool; cinema can also easily represent dildo sex. Both partners' hands and mouths are free to talk and touch, and both bodies can be seen clearly. Dildo sex as it is represented in this film, is never concerned with actual orgasm (the only times even slight attempts are made to suggest orgasm take place during a fisting scene and a masturbation scene). None of the scenes end with orgasm; in fact, orgasm does not seem to be a preoccupation in this film. Pleasure is represented as authentic through a mutually communicative experience, and the film preoccupies itself with the representation of dyke desire and dyke sex, in its various manifestations, as well as an attempt to suggest an authentic dyke space outside of the diegesis.

KEEPIN' IT "REAL": *SAN FRANCISCO LESBIANS*

> True dykes right off the street! They're incredible and they're real!
>
> —box cover of *San Francisco Lesbians*

I take the series of amateur dyke porn entitled *San Francisco Lesbians* as a perfect example of what I call "keepin' it 'real.'" Each tape contains three to four shorts; each short is usually fifteen to twenty minutes long, and one nonprofessional lesbian director directs all of the shorts on each tape. These brief pieces vary enormously, from sex with fruit to blow-up dolls that come to life to sex with pregnant lesbians, all kinds of fetishes, and every body type, race, and personal style imaginable, so that the idea of real dyke sex becomes, to a certain extent, exoticized.[37] The typical setup goes as such: either the director or one of the actresses will introduce the tape as "featuring real San Francisco lesbians," and then she will introduce and briefly summarize each short. Often the director will also function as a character in one of the shorts (as if we needed further assurance). There is always an introduction, and there is always some sort of statement of authenticity: "My friends— real San Francisco lesbians," or "Let's go see what my lesbian friends are up to," and my personal favorite, "I had so much fun last time, I decided to bring a whole new group of friends—all San Francisco lesbians," offer three such examples. The shorts are shot on video, either in small apartments or small informal spaces (never in a studio), with primarily natural lighting, and little to no script. The actresses often burst into giggles, accidentally acknowledge the presence of the camera, or can be seen looking off into nondiegetic space; viewers often witness uncomfortable silences or unexplained noises. This series resembles the dyke porn discussed above, except that it is amateur and its strategies of authenticity differ slightly; we have no actual indication that these are, indeed, San Francisco lesbians, save an occasional poster featuring the Golden Gate Bridge (they never party with Fairy Butch at the Lexington, for example). Rather, we get to see the often uncomfortable but painfully "real" interactions between lesbians, which at times border on improvisation.

The most remarkable example of pornography I saw in the *San Francisco Lesbians* series was a beautifully awkward butch-on-butch anal sex scene— the *only* butch-on-butch scene I found in *any* of the dyke porn I screened— in which both dykes wear strap-ons, though only one, the "more butch" of the two, gets to penetrate (figure 6). This short clearly illustrates an attempt, however futile, to represent visually *authentic* lesbian desire and an authentic lesbian sex act. There is embarrassed and victorious laughter; there are mishaps (dildos that slip out unexpectedly, a dyke who almost takes a tumble off of the bed, dykes who say the wrong lines); there are awkward silences; there is even blushing; and there is sweating without the hot lights. There is also the safe-sex plug, which has become a staple in dyke pornography since *Suburban Dykes*, as well as the kind of dirty talk I found to be quite typical in most of the contemporary dyke porn I viewed. What proves most

6. A rare butch-on-butch sex scene from *San Francisco Lesbians, Volume 7.*

compelling about this dyke porn—most contemporary dyke porn, in fact—is the attempt to create a fantasy of authenticity—utopian in its scope, yet strangely admirable, always optimistic, and almost believable (as a fantasy, it is totally believable, as a reality, it keeps one hovering).

HOW TO SEDUCE A BUTTHOLE:
BEND OVER BOYFRIEND (LISTEN AND LEARN)

In 1998, Shar Rednour, director of *Hard Love* and star of *How to Fuck in High Heels*, directed an educational/instructional film addressing heterosexually identified couples entitled *Bend over Boyfriend: A Couple's Guide to Male Anal Pleasure*. Produced by Fatale Video, the film stars Dr. Carol Queen, author of *The Femme and the Leather Daddy*, *Real Live Nude Girl*, and *Exhibitionism for the Shy*, and her partner Robert Morgan, who conarrates the film. The film also features two other heterosexually identified couples, and Miss Behavin', a sexy M.D. who pops in from time to time to give us important medical advice concerning safe anal-sex practices.

From the very beginning, viewers are aware that this video addresses specifically heterosexual couples who have little or no expertise in the area of anal play (we know this because the two couples on-screen are watching the same video we are all watching at home). Although Carol Queen explicitly states at the beginning of the film that this video lends itself to people of any sexual preference, it is indeed a video addressed to heterosexual couples, in an attempt to educate and inform. We might view this video as the closing of a porn circle that began with the stag film, which purported to "educate" men about, among other things, female sexuality. *Bend over Boyfriend*, along with many other educational videos made, for the most part, by females (Annie Sprinkle's *Sluts and Goddesses Video Workshop* (1992), Nina Hartley's series of *How to* videos, all of the *s/m How to* videos, as well as countless other how-to series) constitutes a radical attempt to (re)educate people in the art of sex and sexual expression. These videos have paramount importance. Through them, the topography of porn can change. They also offer a place where the female presence in pornography can really exact influence (these educational videos are primarily made by females; this one in particular was made by lesbians).[38]

In this video, the female viewer is addressed as a potential penetratrix and her boyfriend as the penetrated. In a moment of humorous dialogue, men are metonymically reduced to their buttholes when the "young lady viewers" are advised to be extra gentle: "Remember you are trying to seduce a potentially interested but possibly reluctant butthole." The all-important penis is replaced by the more important dildo (we have already established the advantages of a dildo). It is important to note, however, that the penis is not ignored; like the dildo, the fingers, the breasts, and the mouth, it becomes a part of the entire sex act without becoming its focus. The women in the video "butch up," so to speak, in order to occupy the more active role of penetratrix previously occupied exclusively by their boyfriends (figure 7). Carol Queen thoroughly educates them on the art of communication. I find this part absolutely illuminating, and tragically absent from any of the heterosexual porn I have ever seen. Carol Queen comments that being communicative might be a "new thing" for the "ladies," who are probably "not used to" communicating what they want/don't want from their men, but can, and must, listen, while their men voice what *they* want, for anal sex obviously warrants more communication than more conventional hetero sex. Queen even expresses hope that this communicative effort might have some influence on one's regular, noncommunicative sex life. Participants in the film talk about the advantages of gender-play that can be involved in this type of hetero sex through the use of the dildo, the fingers, and the tongue. They also talk about the various types of sex toys available for this type of play, where to find them, and, in typical dyke fashion, they offer a constant show-and-tell of safe-sex practices. It is interesting to note that the sexual techniques and practices advocated in this film made for heterosexually identified couples are primary components of queer sex. As in the previous films discussed in this essay, the idea of orgasm again becomes displaced in favor of "merely" representing new and exciting ways to have sex.

What is especially innovative about this video, besides the fact that heterosexually identified females anally penetrate men and that the penis holds even less importance here than in lesbian pornography, if that's possible,

7. In *Bend over Boyfriend*, Carol Queen straps it on and teaches anal sex for heterosexual couples.

is its educational component. *Bend over Boyfriend* much resembles the contemporary lesbian pornography I viewed. Like its lesbian counterparts, it advocates a conscious commodification of sex toys and safe sex, thereby effectively displacing the commodification of female bodies that typically occurs in most heterosexual porn. I am not excusing the fact that commodification does occur; the variety of dildos displayed and the copious amounts of lube used to lubricate them is, to say the very least, excessive. One might even be tempted to read this video as an extended commercial for Good Vibrations, and sex toys in general. The idea that one might purchase sexual pleasure is certainly not a new one, but it is refreshing to see that the silicone purchased in these videos comes in the form of a detachable dildo (usually encased in a condom), rather than in the form of breast implants, as one might expect in mainstream porn. The film serves as an example of lesbians instructing heterosexuals on new ways of sexual expression. *Bend over Boyfriend* also gives another example of lesbians inserting themselves into the development of pornography, thereby changing its educative role. If pornography does indeed have educational value—and certainly many people do watch it to learn about sex and sexuality—what do its viewers learn by watching *Deep Throat* (dir. Gerard Damiano, 1972) or *Behind the Green Door* (dir. Mitchell Bros., 1972), or a more contemporary version, such as Michael Ninn's 1996 *Shock*? What are lesbians and heterosexually identified women learning by watching these videos? My guess is that they are learning next to nothing except how to "fake it" and how to "take it." (Lesbians are learning that they make a nice jelly for the hetero-donut, but that they do not really exist in the heterosexual cosmos as lesbians; in fact, real lesbians don't have sex/look at porn/strap-on dildos/have dirty thoughts.) If lesbians attempt to educate (and notice I did not say *appropriate* or *revise* or *reread* or *interpret*) the hetero mass, they not only contribute something authentic to this world that would completely exclude them otherwise but they make their *own* desire more visible as well.

This essay began as a tentative offering of a way to look at the historical presence and evolution of the lesbian's participation within the genre of pornography. I wanted to trace certain staples of the lesbian experience throughout the last three decades, look at some of the bigger struggles she has faced, and watch the porn that she has made during and after those various struggles. I also found it necessary to look at a video not explicitly made for lesbians, but made by them, in an attempt to see lesbian presence in a not-necessarily lesbian (but certainly queer) context.[39] If the notions of sex and its representation are reexamined and reworked, and even retaught, in completely new ways from the point of view of someone whose visibility has been marginalized, ignored, or grossly simplified in reference to (the dominant) male sexuality, what can be done outside of the realm of sex? I do think that this lesbian effort answers to a call for "diff'rent strokes for diff'rent folks," as well as to ideas about the on/scenity of pornography, and I think that, potentially, we could go even further with this were we to acknowledge the on/scene qualities inherent within the dominant ideologies in which we work (or that work us) and the pornographic potential embedded within them. This inadequacy is only one of many. If we continue to work within those impotent and inadequate paradigms predicated on inauthentic models of subjectivity, we remain drenched in little more than premature ejaculate. How much longer should we continue to fake it? How much longer will we watch as other females fake it? When will the very idea of faking it cease to be acceptable to women?

Notes

I would like to thank the classes of Film Studies 240 and Film Studies 108, Albert Ascoli, Mia Fuller, Jake Gerli, Judith Halberstam, Nguyen Tan Hoang, Jade, Alix Ogilvie, Eric Schaefer, Deborah Shamoon, Barbara Spackman, Jackie Strano, and, most important, Linda Williams.

1   I use *lesbian pornography* not exactly interchangeably with *dyke porn*, but more on that shortly.

2   Much has already been done on lesbian pornography in general, and on certain specific films. Although I do not enter into dialogue with much of the preexisting scholarship on lesbian pornography, I attempt to supply a thorough bibliography throughout the footnotes of this essay.

3 This is not the only joke of this kind. There are several others, which take the tongue as well as the fingers as penis substitutes.

4 Mine, for example. I have heard this joke from several lesbian friends, who, through their giggles, have never been able to explain *why* they laugh, but have only been able to say that they find it "stupid but funny."

5 This phrase was coined by Belgian philosopher Luce Irigaray in her book of the same title (in English, *This Sex Which Is Not One*). "This sex" would be the female sex, which does not exist, or cannot exist, in a world modeled and controlled by and for men and their dicks. Female sexuality is and has always been trapped, in fact, in the androcentrically structured and motivated parameters of language, psychoanalysis, and philosophy (Irigaray 1977).

6 A play on Robin Morgan's infamous formulation, "pornography is the theory, rape is the practice." See Morgan 1980, 139.

7 I do not mean to imply that the butch aesthetic is monolithic; this will become obvious as these films, and the butches in them, are discussed.

8 In visual culture, "before there were lesbians, there were butches." (Halberstam 1998, 186). Also, according to June Reich, "Butch/femme offers a rich history for talking about bodies, identities, and agential politics in a way that hopefully furthers the work of breaking down multiple oppressions" (1999, 255).

9 As Judith Butler (1991) writes, "In both butch and femme identities, the very notion of an original or natural identity is put into question; indeed, it is precisely that question as it is embodied in these identities that becomes one course of their erotic significance" (123).

10 There are, of course, other ways to make lesbian sexuality or lesbian reality visible besides the butch/femme dyad. This is simply the original lesbian stereotype, and probably one of the only sure-fire ways to "publicize" one's lesbian status.

11 The film begins with a poem, which has my subtitle here as one of its lines. It continues, "after her, any girl will reject any boy."

12 There are hundreds of sexploitation films that take the topic of lesbianism as a theme. The "bored housewife" theme, in which two women play around while their husbands are at work, seems to have been the most popular. See *Sin in the Suburbs* (dir. Joe Sarno, 1964); *Odd Triangle* (dir. Joe Sarno, 1969); and *Just the Two of Us* (dir. Barbara Peters, 1970). For lesbianism as a phase in a young girl's sexual development, see *Twilight Girls* (dir. André Hunebelle, 1961); *Therese and Isabelle* (dir. Radley Metzger, 1967); *To Ingrid My Love, Lisa* (dir. Joe Sarno, 1968); and *That Tender Touch* (dir. Russell Vincent, 1969). For lesbianism as a result of victimization, see *Dominique: Daughters of Lesbos* (dir. Peter Woodcock, 1967). For lesbianism as utterly deviant and often fatal, see *The Girl with the Hungry Eyes* (dir. William Rotsler, 1967); *A Bride for Brenda* (dir. Tommy Goetz, 1968); *She Mob* (dir. Alfred Sack, 1968); and *Vibrations* (dir. Joe Sarno, 1969). For the "mocumentary," see *Chained Girls* (dir. Joseph Mawra, 1965).

13 This formulation comes from Eric Schaefer in this volume. For a very thorough historical account of the development of the exploitation film, see Schafer 1999.

14 Judith Halberstam does a brief but nice reading of both the butch imagery and the racial politics implicit within this film (1998, 204–5). She also helped me to locate this film.

15 Cherry Grove serves as a marker for queers and queer space. It is a resort town about fifty miles outside of New York City that was first "colonized" by gays and lesbians in the 1930s and became the first actual gay and lesbian town. See Newton 1993.

16 See Halberstam 1998, chap. 6. In her discussion of the image of the butch in film, Halberstam remarks, "the stereotype, the image that announces identity in excess, is necessarily troublesome to an articulation of lesbian identity, but also foundational" (177).

17 I did find one entirely "lesbian" porn, entitled *Aerobisex Girls* (dir. Bruce Seven, 1977), in which leotard- and leg warmer–clad girls first aerobicize and then pour vegetable oil all over one another and anally and vaginally penetrate each other with very large, brightly colored, handheld dildoes. Eithne Johnson (1993) does an incredible job dealing with this film.

18 For more on *Behind the Green Door*, see Williams 1989, 156–66.

19 See the Gerli essay in this collection for an elaboration on queer heterosexual porn.

20 Since the beginning of mainstream porn, all female porn stars are bisexual, and all male porn stars are heterosexual. This means that in mainstream pornography, we get to see women fucking each other, but it means nothing more than that, and we will never see two men fuck each other.

21 Lillian Faderman (1991) briefly discusses this film: "Tigress productions made the film *Erotic in Nature*, which, although advertised in lesbian pornographic magazines, promised the reader to go beyond pornography: not only does it 'steam with pleasure,' according to the producers, but it also 'exults in beauty and displays a tenderness which we feel will *warm your hearts*'" (258; emphasis mine).

22 In a moment of absolute semiotic brilliance, there is a shot of young butch drying off and wrapping herself up in a beach towel decorated with high heels.

23 To quote Linda Williams, from a personal correspondence, "There is that one pierced nipple!" I actually agree and view that one pierced nipple as a sort of metaphor for the entire film: while not *exactly* devious, it is somewhat transgressive of the typical 1980s lesbian aesthetic. The film as a whole cannot exactly be described as deviant, yet it is somewhat transgressive.

24 In *Personal Best*, the lesbian relationship essentially constitutes a phase, something experimental, a college fling, that Chris outgrows in favor of a more mature heterosexual relationship. She graduates not only from college but also from an immature, incomplete lesbian relationship. As in mainstream pornography, les-

bianism here is merely a warm-up, or practice (or, in the case of *Personal Best*, training) for the real thing.

25 There was one phrase I actually heard Kit say, which was, "Ooohhh, you're so strong!"

26 I owe this observation to Linda Williams, who saw a connection between this type of ideological move and the type that frequently occurs in heterosexual pornography, when nothing sexually stimulating is happening to the woman, yet she appears to be experiencing some sort of ecstasy in her face.

27 For a more in-depth account of this, see Faderman 1991.

28 There were, of course, other attempts. *On Our Backs* was created in 1984, as was *Bad Attitude*, another lesbian sex magazine. Several production companies (Tigress, Lavender Blue, and Blush) also attempted to represent the spectrum of lesbian desire (some more tame than others). Overall, however, the sleaze factor remained pretty low.

29 Since this is one of the only lesbian-owned and -operated producers of pornography, much has already been written on various videos, and I will not discuss the work that has been done here. See Conway 1996; Johnson 1993; Smyth 1990; and Williams 1992.

30 I love the fact that a lesbian calls her partner a pervert for wanting to be penetrated (historically, a woman would be considered a pervert simply for being a lesbian. Now, however, a lesbian can be considered a pervert for wanting what is considered a "heterosexual" and, therefore, perverted sex act).

31 For that, see the very nonpornographic book *Stone Butch Blues* by Leslie Feinberg or Annie Sprinkle's film *Linda/Les and Annie* (1989), where Annie's transgendered lover definitely attempts to pass as a man, but not through the use of a dildo.

32 I use Lacan's formulation of the phallus as it is articulated in his essay "The Signification of the Phallus" (in Lacan 1977, 281–91).

33 Particularly the work done by Grosz 1990.

34 I will not discuss female ejaculation in this paper, as this is an entirely different ejaculatory situation. I am merely acknowledging it because it does indeed exist, and is important in terms of lesbian sexuality as a whole, but it cannot be compared to and does not pertain to my discussion of male sexuality. It is only important to note that so far, female ejaculation is shown to occur on the part of the woman being penetrated, and not on the part of the penetrator.

35 My reading of the orgasm in heterosexual porn has been informed by Patton 1989.

36 They have recently made another porn film entitled *Sugar High Glitter City*, which was released after this essay was written.

37 According to the back of the boxes, "what distinguishes this series from other 'all-girl action' flicks is that these are real dykes—with all the bohemian kink and enthusiasm for which San Francisco is notorious. You'll see butches, femmes,

grunge babes and hippie chicks all playing hard with multiple dildoes and beau-coup anal sex."

38 For a fabulous reading of another lesbian-centered educational film, *Safe Is Desire* (dir. Blush/Fatale Video, 1993), see Conway 1996.

39 To quote Emmanuel Cooper: "Much, if not all, queer culture is concerned with aspects of social transgression, whether involving a variety of same-sex relationships, and/or cultural confrontations . . . also . . . the rejection of fixed notions of sexuality" (1996, 14).

Works Cited

Bright, Susie. 1990. *Susie Sexpert's Lesbian World.* Pittsburgh, Pa.: Cleiss.

Butler, Judith. 1991. *Gender Trouble: Feminism and the Subversion of Identity.* New York: Routledge.

———. "Imitation and Gender Insubordination." 1991. In *Inside/Out: Lesbian Theories, Gay Theories,* ed. Diana Fuss. New York: Routledge. 13–31.

———. 1993. *Bodies That Matter: On the Discursive Limits of "Sex."* New York: Routledge.

Case, Sue-Ellen. 1993. "Towards a Butch-Femme Aesthetic." In *The Lesbian and Gay Studies Reader,* ed. Henry Abelove, Michele Aina Barale, and David Halperin. New York: Routledge. 294–306.

Clover, Carol J. 1992. *Men, Women, and Chainsaws: Gender in the Modern Horror Film.* Princeton, N.J.: Princeton University Press.

Conway, Mary T. 1996. "Inhabiting the Phallus: Reading *Safe Is Desire." Camera Obscura* 38: 133–62.

Cooper, Emmanuel. 1996. "Queer Spectacles." In *Outlooks: Lesbian and Gay Sexualities and Visual Cultures.* Ed. Peter Horne and Reina Lewis. London: Routledge.

De Lauretis, Teresa. 1994. *The Practice of Love: Lesbian Sexuality and Perverse Desire.* Bloomington: Indiana University Press.

Faderman, Lillian. 1991. *Odd Girls and Twilight Lovers: A History of Lesbian Life in Twentieth-Century America.* New York: Columbia University Press.

Feinberg, Leslie. 1993. *Stone Butch Blues: A Novel.* New York: Firebrand.

Findlay, Heather. 1999. "Freud's Fetishism and the Lesbian Dildo Debates." In *Feminist Theory and the Body: A Reader,* ed. Janet Price and Margrit Schildrick. New York: Routledge. 466–76.

Fuss, Diana, ed. 1991. *Inside/Out: Lesbian Theories, Gay Theories.* New York: Routledge.

Garber, Marjorie. 1992. *Vested Interests: Cross Dressing and Cultural Anxiety.* New York: Routledge.

Grosz, Elizabeth. 1990. *Jacques Lacan: A Feminist Introduction.* New York: Routledge.

Halberstam, Judith. 1998. *Female Masculinity.* Durham, N.C.: Duke University Press.

Hart, Lynda. 1998. *Between the Body and the Flesh: Performing Sadomasochism*. New York: Columbia University Press.

Horne, Peter, and Reina Lewis, eds. 1996. *Outlooks: Lesbian and Gay Sexualities and Visual Cultures*. London: Routledge.

Irigaray, Luce. 1977. *Ce sex qui n'en est pas un*. Paris: Éditions de Minuit.

Johnson, Eithne. 1993. "Excess and Ecstasy: Constructing Female Pleasure in Porn Movies." *Velvet Light Trap* 32: 30–49.

Lacan, Jacques. 1977. *Écrits: A Selection*. Trans. Alan Sheridan. New York: Norton.

Morgan, Robin. 1980. "Theory and Practice: Pornography and Rape." In *Take Back the Night: Women on Pornography*, ed. Laura Lederer. New York: William Morrow. 134–40.

Munt, Sally, ed. 1998. *Butch/Femme: Inside Lesbian Gender*. London: Cassell.

Nestle, Joan. 1987. *A Restricted Country*. Ithaca, N.Y.: Firebrand.

Newton, Esther. 1993. *Cherry Grove, Fire Island: Sixty Years America's First Gay and Lesbian Town*. Boston: Beacon.

Patton, Cindy. 1989. "Hegemony and Orgasm: — Or the Instability of Heterosexual Pornography." *Screen* 30: 100–13.

Reich, June. 1999. "Genderfuck: The Law of the Dildo." In *Camp: Queer Aesthetics and the Performing Subject*, ed. Fabio Cleto. Ann Arbor: University of Michigan Press. 254–65.

Schaefer, Eric. 1999. *"Bold! Daring! Shocking! True!" A History of Exploitation Films, 1919–1959*. Durham, N.C.: Duke University Press.

Smyth, Cherry. 1990. "The Pleasure Threshold: Looking at Lesbian Pornography on Film." *Feminist Review* 34: 152–59.

Straayer, Chris. 1996. *Deviant Eyes, Deviant Bodies: Sexual Re-orientations in Film and Video*. New York: Columbia University Press.

Vance, Carol. 1992. "Negotiating Sex and Gender in the Attorney General's Commission on Pornography." In *Sex Exposed: Sexuality and the Pornography Debate*, ed. Lynn Segal and Mary McIntosh. London: Virago. 29–49.

Williams, Linda. 1986. "Personal Best: Women in Love." In *Films for Women*, ed. Charlotte Brunsdon. London: British Film Institute. 146–54.

———. 1989. *Hard Core: Power, Pleasure and the "Frenzy of the Visible."* Berkeley: University of California Press.

———. 1992. "Pornographies On/Scene: Or, Diff'rent Strokes for Diff'rent Folks." In *Sex Exposed: Sexuality and the Pornography Debate*, ed. Lynne Segal and Mary McIntosh. London: Virago. 223–65.

Wittig, Monique. 1992. *The Straight Mind and Other Essays*. Boston: Beacon.

The Gay Sex Clerk: Chuck Vincent's Straight Pornography

JAKE GERLI

✳ In the context of any current critical discussion of moving-picture pornography, Chuck Vincent would appear to inhabit one of the most contradictory predicaments of cultural production imaginable. Vincent was a gay man who directed straight pornographic films in the late 1970s and early 1980s. Based on these facts alone, the immediate impulse may be to view his career as a tale of the closet, of cinematic failure and/or commercial servitude. In fact, he made his films as an openly gay man living in the gay metropolis of New York City. His films were celebrated by the straight pornographic industry to the point that he was successful enough to start his own production company, Platinum Pictures in 1981.[1]

Vincent was respected within the straight pornographic film industry for bringing what was perceived as a touch of unprecedented quality to porn.[2] His most notable successes, *Roommates* (1981) and *In Love* (1983) attempted to blend hard-core sex with strong cinematic narrative and high production values. Both films received awards from the Adult Film Association of America and the Critics' Adult Film Award committee.[3] They also attracted attention from more mainstream audiences at the box office. *Playboy* reviewed *Roommates* alongside *Das Boot* (dir. Wolfgang Petersen, 1981), *My Dinner with André* (dir. Louis Malle, 1981), and *Tragedy of a Ridiculous Man* (dir. Bernardo Bertolucci, 1981). *Roommates* also merited a review in *Cineáste*. Circulating in both the traditional realm of pornographic consumption and the more respectable arena of art house taste, Vincent's pornographic features of the early 1980s aimed to garner maximum box office attention. At a time when the golden age of porn shot on 35 mm seemed to be coming to an end due to dwindling box office receipts attributed to the rapid rise of video production, the industry saw Vincent's crossover attempts as examples of how to keep feature-length porno alive on film and in the theater.[4]

Vincent's films constitute pornographic films onto which an evolving industry projected its anxieties and desires. After the success of *Deep Throat* (dir. Gerard Damiano, 1972) made the industry realize that pornography could attract a respectable bourgeois audience, continual efforts were made to expand and retain that audience. In the early 1980s, with decreasing attendance at the porno box office due to the rise of video, the struggle for an audience became more pronounced. The pornography industry wanted to create a hybrid product capable of crossing over to more mainstream audiences and of expanding the range of exhibition venues for pornography. Porn made a bid for the mainstream as it fashioned an image of itself as a classy affair.[5] By emphasizing narrative, acting, editing, mise-en-scène, and costumes alongside meat and money shots, Vincent's films provided a working model for the sectors of the pornographic film industry that wanted to add some classical value to their productions.[6]

If one watches Vincent's films in the present, it becomes apparent that high production values are not their only distinguishing feature. These values are motivated in their consistent employment to accomplish aesthetic and narrative distortions of heterosexual sex troubling the utopian aspirations of generic straight pornography. Often, the straight numbers in Vincent's films depict "bad" sex, or deemphasize sex in order to focus on other aspects of the production.[7] These breakdowns might be viewed as instances of inept filmmaking or as confirmation of the alleged impossibility of mixing explicit sex with the drives of narrative. Instead, I would contend that they constitute queer strategies of representing heterosexual sex. If straight sexuality is the norm from which queer sexualities deviate, Vincent subjects one of the grounding graphic elements of straight sexuality found in pornography—the fantasy of utopian heterosexual intercourse as encountered in pornography—to a destabilizing set of cinematic operations. Straight sex in Vincent's films is questioned, viewed with indifference, and even degraded. Vincent's films do not stop there, though. Exclusively bad sex would not make good porn. His films take visible heterosexual acts from the low point he establishes for them and puts them back into more diverse and potentially queer arrangements in order to create new affective trajectories.

These queer arrangements provoked extreme responses in both contemporary reviews of Vincent's films and in the historical accounts of straight pornography that include him. In the minds of straight critics, Vincent's films either incite discussions of the transcendence of pornography and sex, of alternative utopias, or they prompt condemnation and revulsion. In all of these instances, Vincent's queer visions of straight sex clearly prompt heterosexuality to question itself. Vincent's films interrupt the industrialized naturalization of heterosexual privilege and problem solving that marked the genre of straight porn at the time and that continues to inform the production of heterosexual pornography today. The straight porn industry's willingness to accept and to celebrate Vincent's productions circa 1982 reveals a system of production in crisis that was willing to embrace alternative, queer strategies in the name of survival. For a brief time, straight porn entertained a queer look and saw it as an innovation that could possibly rescue existing models of 35 mm feature production.

Queer Methodology

In thinking about how to frame the queer strategies exhibited in Vincent's films, I draw on Richard Dyer's 1991 historiographical essay "Believing in Fairies." In it, Dyer explains the methodology behind his book-length study of gay and lesbian film, *Now You See It* (1990). A history of gay and lesbian film may seem paradoxical in itself because gays and lesbians have historically remained without a dominant industry geared toward self-representation. Rather, queer filmmakers have often been forced to work within the margins of straight filmmaking. Dyer's effort to recover their contributions and the energies that animated them requires a more general, multiple theory of authorship that both affirms the constructed nature of the author and pays attention to the way in which film authors work "with (within and against) particular codes and conventions of film and with (within and against) particular, social ways of being lesbian or gay" (1991, 187). Teasing out historical examples of gay and lesbian agency means reading films quite carefully in order to apprehend the instances where film form manifests same-sex desire. From there, one can begin to think about the particular and historical "social ways of being lesbian or gay" that these contested signs affirm and to which they attest.

Vincent's films do exhibit significant textual peculiarities that attest to a director working "with (within and against) particular codes and conventions of film," but they present few affirmative depictions of same-sex desire because Vincent was not making films for a gay or lesbian audience. He labored to produce a straight cinematic product. In this way, Vincent's films inhabit a cycle of production and circulation that is almost the inverse of Dyer's model. Vincent found himself as an out gay mediator between straight performers and technicians and straight audiences, rather than as a worker within a straight industry leaving traces of same-sex desire in his or her films for gay and lesbian audiences. As a director of straight pornographic features, though, Vincent still had to work with the demands of the genre. Although he was culturally out as a filmmaker, Vincent stood at the margin of all straight margins in a generic and semiotic sense. He had to depict heterosexual sex, while at the same time excluding screen representations of the types of sex he participated in as a gay man, preserving gay sex in his films as the "structuring absence" of straight pornography. Vincent's films are in no way explicitly homosexual, but they do introduce some queer elements that question the terms of straight sex put forth by heterosexual pornography.

Narrative

In her study of the generic parameters of straight pornography made during the 1970s and 1980s, *Hard Core*, Linda Williams observes that "in cinematic hard core we encounter a profoundly 'escapist' genre that distracts audiences from the deeper social or political causes of the disturbed relations between the sexes" (1999, 154). Heterosexual porn proposes utopian symbolic solutions to actual sexual tensions within the social construction of heterosexuality. In order to elaborate this type of symbolic resolution, though, hard core must evoke the very anxieties it seeks to address. In various forms, straight pornography repeatedly plays out a dialectic of real sexualized social relations evoked in narrative and imaginary solutions depicted in the pornographic "numbers." This dialectic rests at the end of the feature with a utopian negotiation of power and pleasure between men and women partners. Hard core thus "adhere[s] to the principle that sexual pleasure still offers the best solution to all the problems afflicting the sexual realm" (170).[8]

If the genre of straight hard core begins with a problem and proceeds to a solution, Vincent's films proceed from entirely different narrative premises. Sexual utopias are either never achieved or, if they are, they are realized in passing as part of a scrambled chronology that does not celebrate them as teleological solutions to sexual problems. For example, *Roommates*, a rough remake of Jean Negulesco's *The Best of Everything* (1959), tells the story of three working women who live together in New York City. Amidst discrimination and disappointment in work, they try to find some sexual satisfaction. After a few high points, the film ends with the roommates leaving one another. Only the actor Joan (Veronica Hart) finds a sexually satisfying relationship. The advertising assistant and former prostitute Billie (Samantha Fox) tarries with a potential Mr. Right (Jack Wrangler), but loses him when he marries another.[9] The third roommate, Sherry (Kelly Nichols) is exploited as a model by the fashion industry and raped by a technician from one of her photo shoots (Jamie Gillis), who becomes obsessed with her. There is no realization of sexual pleasure capable of resolving the exploitative dimensions of the single women's corporate work situations in *Roommates*. The film ends with a lonely shot of Billie as she accepts a phone call from a potential tenant.

The narrative trajectory of *In Love* deviates from the generic patterns of straight hard core in another extreme fashion. A utopian vision of sex is presented at the beginning of the film, rather than at the end. Andy (Jerry Butler) and Jill (Kelly Nichols) meet by chance in Key Largo in the summer of 1962 and have a three-day affair depicted in a montage of multiple sexual scenarios and swelling music. At the end of the three days, Andy must return to his wife, and Jill ventures out into the world to seek her fortune. They decide not to keep in touch. The rest of the film is devoted to depicting the next two decades during which they live separate lives. Despite their mutual promise to forget one another, their lives are filled with longing for each other. None of the other sexual encounters they have live up to those three days in Florida. By placing the utopia of sexual fulfillment at the beginning of the film, *In Love* poses utopian sex as a problem in and of itself. The loss of utopia constitutes the narrative problem around which the film revolves. This problem is preserved even at the end of the film, when Andy and Jill finally find one another. There is no climactic lovemaking scene that restages their remembered fulfillment. *In Love* renders sexual utopia as a memory of a lost time or as simply a dream.

Style

The opening number of *In Love* that establishes the lost utopian feel is quite unusual for the pornography of the time. The sense of utopian sex ultimately derives from the cinematic manipulations of editing and voice-over, rather than the performance of the actors. The sequence alternates between several scenes, creating a transcendent sense of time and place. Scenes of Andy and Jill fucking in two different boats are intercut with shots of them having sex in a bedroom. These numbers are juxtaposed with frames of surrounding nature and of Andy and Jill enjoying themselves on the dance floor and on bike rides. Melodramatic instrumental music and dubbed voice-over dialogue hold the seven-minute montage together. While images of Andy and Jill fucking and having a good time from disparate times and places flash across the screen, the characters attest to the greatness of the sex and the intensity of their love on the soundtrack. The emphasis on the postproduction elements of editing and sound in this sequence downplays the importance of the actual images of Andy and Jill fucking. The graphic images cease to have any primary significance. Rather, they derive most of their energy from the way in which they have been arranged in postproduction.

As Jerry Butler recalls in his autobiography *Raw Talent*, the tone of the shoot differed markedly from that of the finished sequence. There was not much chemistry between him and Nichols. He remembers: "I never really enjoyed working with Kelly, and I found her to be very tedious. What saved me was the fact that most of the sex scenes were very stylized. (We had one long sex scene in a rowboat!) Because you couldn't see a lot of ins and outs, you couldn't tell I wasn't totally erect" (1989, 91). Butler readily admits that his performance in *In Love*—particularly in the rowboat episode of the opening number—was lackluster. In Butler's estimation, Vincent rescued his performance with heavy postproduction stylization. While Butler's comments suggest that style serves as a device compensating for a subpar performance, Vincent's films appear to privilege stylization as an organizing principle, rather than a rescue strategy. Although there are no other readily available testimonies to the production methods used by Vincent other than Butler's, at the textual level it is clear that Vincent's pornographic films consistently supplement sexual numbers with flourishes of cinematic technique. Style in his films comes to dominate and mediate the "real" of the sexual performances.

Vincent's consistent emphasis on style in the sexual numbers produces two complementary trends toward depicting straight sex in his films. In general, both techniques downplay actual sexual performances to integrate them into more complex dramas of affect and power. The first tendency in Vincent's films is toward disengagement with heterosexual sex acts, questioning the importance of the acts in and of themselves. Vincent extracts hard-core sex from a utopian fantasy world and places it in a more nuanced emotional realm, often of hurt and humiliation. The second trend in his films is to supplement straight sex with a queer look. His films deemphasize the straight sex act in order to put it in surprising, different contexts, where it becomes part of new erotic investments.

Disengagement and Critique

In a general assessment of what it was like to work with Vincent as a director, Butler evokes a sense of how Vincent would engage specifically with the hard-core sex scenes in his films: "I've mentioned earlier that Chuck is gay. There's nothing wrong with that, but how can a guy who's a softball expert coach a hardball team? There are similarities, but it isn't the same game. Sometimes Chuck seems very sheepish about heterosexual sex" (1989, 270). Butler remembers that Vincent could be "sheepish" about directing straight sex, highlighting a slight embarrassment or reluctance at the heart of Vincent's cinematic vision. While Butler attributes this to a certain inability on the part of Vincent to engage with heterosexual sex because he was gay, I would like to think about this reluctance as a strategy of representation, rather than an inherent shortcoming. As the example of Vincent's *Bon Appétit* (1980) attests, he was capable of directing hot straight sex comparable to that found in other straight porn of the time.[10] The relative indifference to sexual performance in the later films such as *Roommates*, *In Love*, and *Jack and Jill 2* (1984)—a memory of which prompts Butler's more general commentary about Vincent—can be seen, then, as a defining stylistic element.

The exemplary instance of a stylized detachment from straight fucking in Vincent's films occurs in an early scene in *In Love*. After departing from the three days of bliss with Andy, Jill has moved to San Francisco. The film finds her living with her boyfriend Kip (Michael Knight). They go out to a bar, where there is an open mike. From a shot of a poet performing on stage, the film cuts to what is presumably an afternoon in the near future. The shot begins focused on a window. It slowly tracks left, revealing a radio broadcasting a baseball game (figure 1). Vaguely sexual moans can be discerned on the soundtrack, muffled by the ambient sound of the radio. The shot continues to track to the left, revealing the space of the apartment. The camera glides past a set of French doors dividing the living room of the apartment from the bedroom. Behind a chair and a guitar in the foreground, one can barely make out two bodies writhing in the midst of some sexual encounter. In this scene, which develops into a hard-core number, sex only becomes a wholly apparent part of the scene as it emerges from the background. As much hiding the sex from view as revealing it, this establishing shot signifi-

1. The beginning of the distanced tracking that introduces the sexual number between Janet and Kip in *In Love*.

cantly downplays the sex act by making it a single element in the surrounding clutter of the apartment. Advancing at its own pace in vivid contrast to the frenetic thrusting in the background, the camera distinguishes itself in a marked fashion from the performers and what they are up to. Even after it stumbles on the performers, it continues to keep its distance, pursuing its own trajectory. This play with disengagement from the sexual numbers acts as a tease, of course, but it also provides an interruption that opens up possibilities within the pornographic feature for being critical about straight sex. The sheepishness of Vincent's films becomes a resource for the dramatic rethinking of the premises and pleasures of straight sex.

Roommates, for instance, from the beginning declares itself a film that intends to question the arrangements and fantasies underlying straight pornography. It opens with a scene in which Ted (Josh Andrews) rapes his acting student Joan. Prior to this number, the film begins with a detached sequence that shows how Joan and Ted separately commute to a rural motel to rendezvous away from Ted's wife. At the motel, it soon becomes apparent that this is the occasion for a long good-bye. Joan has decided to give up school to pursue a career in New York City. While Joan talks of her hopes to succeed in New York, Ted begins to undress her. She protests but he shuts her up by sticking his dick in her mouth and then forcing her to have genital sex with him. The sex is quick, brutal, and a torture to watch. With every piece of clothing that is removed, the film cuts to a slightly different angle, but it maintains the blank stare of a cold medium shot. The scripted maneuvers of sex advance monotonously in time toward a coerced genital goal, making the sexual number an exercise in duration, rather than arousal. Finally, a poorly lit close-up of the missionary-style penetration gives way to an exterior come shot. Ted rolls over, off the bed, and into his pants in a moment.

He's out the door, telling Joan that he has to be somewhere for an appointment, but that he will call her when he visits New York. The film cuts to an isolating long shot of her holding herself, naked and alone.

Clearly not a utopian realization, sex is depicted in this opening scene as a mechanical step-by-step process bound up with emotional and professional pressures, which ends in humiliation and loneliness. The final shot of Joan alone on the bed condenses the depressing conclusion. It is unusual for movie-picture pornography to end a sexual number with a reaction shot, especially one that radiates such disappointment and vulnerability. The sense of violation is underscored by the long duration of the reaction shot. Instead of cutting away to the next sexual scenario capable of producing some euphoria, as if this initial bad sex was just a stumbling block on the road toward more euphoric realizations, *Roommates* dwells with an abandoned and hurt individual who has been coerced into sex in an entirely unerotic way.[11] The sexual problem that *Roommates* begins with is not exclusively one of pleasure that has to be worked through in order to discover the ideal sexual scenario, but rather a problem with the power relations that form the basis for the heterosexual fantasy. By explicitly making the patriarchal student-teacher relationship and its abuse a part of its opening scene, *Roommates* underscores and performs the coercive power relationships at the heart of the scenario, rather than using the sex as a way to escape from and symbolically resolve the contradictions of Joan and Ted's relationship.

Extending this critical attitude beyond the opening sequence, *Roommates* makes this demystification of heterosexual sex its feature-length project. The film's most fully developed engagement with the coercive aspects of patriarchal fantasies of heterosexual sex occurs later in the film in a scene that centers around the former prostitute Billie and her current boss Marv (Bobby Astyr). Marv knew Billie when she had sex for money and continues to put her in situations where she must "entertain" clients in order to keep her legitimate job working for him at an advertising agency. Near the end of the film, Marv forces Billie to service him too. During a commercial shoot for the cat food Pussy Treats, Marv pulls Billie into the bathroom, unzips his pants, and forces her to her knees. The sequence begins focused on the filming of the commercial, where a crew tries to force a handsome white cat to eat Pussy Treats. What seems to be an otherwise simple commercial take is frustrated again and again by the feline, who refuses even to nibble the Pussy Treats. The cat is verbally encouraged, poked with a broomstick, thrown toward the food, and dragged on a leash (figure 2). While all of this is happening, the film intersperses shots of Marv's verbal attempts to coerce

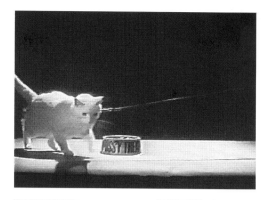

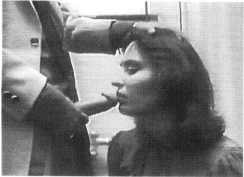

2. The cat that doesn't want its "Pussy Treats" (from *Roommates*).

3. Marv imposes his own "treat" on Billie in *Roommates*.

Billie into giving him a blow job. Finally, he decides to force her into the bathroom for her own "pussy treat." As they exit, the film cuts to a shot of the cat, which has been coerced into eating the cat food like a good kitty should. There is applause from the male crew.[12] Meanwhile, Billie and Marv reach the bathroom, where he pulls out his dick and shoves it into her mouth (figure 3). He promptly comes in her mouth. She refuses to play the part of the good pussy and spits his come all over his shoes, which he had been polishing with great care in a previous scene.

The cat food commercial functions as a commentary on the forced sex in the bathroom. Both the cat and Billie are told what they allegedly want by a group of men or a man. Both "pussies" are supposed to want their respective "pussy treats"—cat food or cock and come—and to perform the pleasure of ingesting them. Relentlessly poked and prodded, the cat is made to digest what it clearly does not want. Billie is likewise pressured into ingesting what she clearly abhors. By juxtaposing this sex scene with the takes of the cat, *Roommates* again frames straight sex as an activity that comes out of a hierarchical relationship in which a male superior is able to impose himself on a female subordinate. The film depicts this familiar scenario as ugly and ludicrous. It makes about as much sense as forcing a cat to eat cat food.

Furthermore, in that the cat is engaged in the production of a moving-picture commercial, its labor conditions not only comment on the gendered labor conditions Billie endures as a production assistant but also on the labor condition of performers in pornography. Porn actors are paid to operate on allegedly natural impulses for sex, much like the cat is supposed to eat to assuage its hunger. Performers in pornography are also supposed to produce allegedly involuntary or natural reactions—the "truths" of the body—rather than indulging in any sort of artifice that detracts from this process of revelation.[13] By staging a commercial within a film, *Roommates* uses a baroque device to comment on porn's tendency to avoid artifice in its numbers. By criticizing and denigrating these performance practices as metaphorically couched in coercive relationships, *Roommates* hints that straight porn expects a form of automation from its performers like that the commercial producers expect of the cat. Straight porn, in other words, does not acknowledge, much less explore, the artifice of sex. While working within the genre of feature-length heterosexual porn, *Roommates* critiques the genre for not indulging in the full range of affective and dramatic possibilities capable of animating and extending its sexual fantasies.

Queer Rearrangements

Judging by the titles *Roommates* and *In Love*, these films are intent on depicting forms of affect other than just getting off. One makes the bonds between people sharing a living space its central feature, while the other takes romance as its premise. By describing relationships that evolve between people, the titles of these films stray from the trends of the era's straight porn feature titles, which focused on anatomical parts, individual capacities, or exceptional characters.[14] While *Roommates* and *In Love* attempt to describe different relationships dramatically, they also make attempts to elaborate new forms of sexual desire and pleasure within the context of straight porn.

Both the opening utopian scene of *In Love* and the Pussy Treats episode discussed above made their interventions into the pleasure-giving capacities of the straight number by employing montage. Montage in the first instance offered a way of salvaging a utopian feeling from a series of lackluster sexual numbers. In the latter episode, parallel montage drew a comparison between the coerced cat and the abused assistant. In other portions of the films, montage and other more complex forms of editing (depicting a relay of looks) becomes a way of opening the sexual number up to other erotic investments, reorganizing the straight number to displace it in a queered fashion.

The erotic life of things and of setting becomes all-important in a scene from *In Love* in which Andy fucks his boss's wife Elaine (Samantha Fox). Having lost Jill and returned to the Jiffy Hamburgers business in New York, Andy has begun to concentrate on his career. He hopes to please Elaine so she will encourage her husband to make Andy vice president. They meet at a festive New Year's Eve party, and Elaine pulls Andy into a back room for a quickie away from the prying eyes of Andy's wife Melinda (Veronica Hart). Andy and Elaine are dressed to a tee—he in tuxedo, she in a shimmering silver-and-white dress. They settle down on a fur coat draped across a bed. Despite Andy's unassertive protests that his wife is in the next room, Elaine unzips his fly and begins to suck him off. At this point, the film starts to cut back and forth between the sexual number that develops and the party in the adjacent living room, where Melinda can be seen worriedly looking around. The plodding, light jazz of the party's band filters through the cross-cut sequence. Andy and Elaine move from cock sucking to fucking, as Andy begins to thrust in time with the dull music. When the sequence cuts back to the party, the bandleader interrupts the music to begin the New Year's countdown. With the release of the New Year's balloons, Andy pulls out and shoots his load all over Elaine's stomach. The cheering and the release of the New Year's balloons coincide in a shared climax with the come shot. Andy says a quick good-bye and rushes out of the back room to the dance floor, where he embraces Melinda and begins to dance with her to the music the band has struck up again.

By paralleling the pornographic rush to the come shot with the New Year's countdown, this sequence campily points to the conventionality and inevitability of the former. This sequence underscores the repetitive nature of heterosexual genital sex as depicted in straight porn. But the montage also makes this number part of a larger cinematic and erotic unit. By acknowledging the cycle of conventionality in which this sequence intervenes, the sequence is able to put these clichés into new erotic arrangements. The shots of Melinda in the adjacent space of the party act as reaction shots, drawing the spectator out of the back room where Andy and Elaine fuck and back into the realm of the party. There, people are dancing, singing, drinking, and, most important, looking good in their elaborate costumes. Boas, frills, and sequins abound on the women, and the men looking fine

4. The erotics of fur enveloping sex in *In Love.*

in their nicely tailored tuxedos. The attention to the costuming in the party portions of the sequence draws attention to the rather incredible setup of Andy and Elaine's number. Elaine is the most spectacularly dressed of all the guests, her beaded dress sparkling with sequins borders. Andy wears a fitted tuxedo and his hair glistens with an elaborate pattern of artificial highlights. When they fuck, they do not remove their clothing. The packaging of the performers becomes an essential erotic part of the number, reciprocally eroticizing the costumes and grooming of the guests at the party. The erotic supplement of the clothing becomes even more of an essential element in the sex when Elaine lays Andy down on the fur coat in the back room. As she begins to suck his cock, the camera assumes an angle that makes it look like the fur is enveloping the performers (figure 4). Then, Andy and Elaine switch positions, so that she is spread out on the coat. As he starts to fuck her, the film cuts to a low angle shot that would seem to focus in on the site of penetration. But it also partially obscures Elaine behind the fuzzy edges of fur coat, making it look as if Andy could be having sex with the mink as well as Elaine.

This scene is queer in the sense that it puts the conventional straight sex act into proximity with the erotic life of things, making those things part of the performance. Andy and Elaine do not strip to grant maximum visibility of their bodies to the viewer as in most straight porn of the era, but rather retain their costumes and include them in the act. The pleasures of this scene come not exclusively from their corporeal connection, but through the link made between the moment of sexual coupling and the rest of the party. This is accomplished through the crosscutting and the clichéd countdown, but, most important, through the forms of dress.

Costuming in general is the realm of production where Vincent seems to have invested most of his own economic and erotic energies when making his straight porn films. The attention paid to costuming in *In Love* is extraordinary for a porn film. The film spans a twenty–year period and goes to great pains to differentiate each of the historical moments it traverses through costuming and setting. This attention leads me to believe that a significant portion of the film's $750,000 budget (enormous for a porn film at the time) was spent on costuming.[15] More subjectively, Butler recalls that Vincent consistently emphasized costuming at the expense of a proper straight sexual ambiance and sometimes to the detriment of sexual numbers.[16] In Butler's estimation, the type of attention Vincent devoted to the costuming of women did not achieve the proper "*tasty*" look required by straight porn. Instead, the way Vincent dressed women was "pretty" (1989, 270–71). A queer aesthetic asserts itself in the costumes of the women in Vincent's films, disrupting the look of patriarchal heterosexual eroticism.

Butler also remarks that Vincent "always dressed [him] very nicely" (271). The presentation of male bodies in Vincent's films is always more meticulous than in straight porn of the era. Men in Vincent's films are not flaccid, skinny bodies attached to big dicks, but comparatively sexy devils put erotically on display through their clothing and grooming. Butler is always done up with makeup, tailored clothes, and cute outfits. The real attention to the male body in Vincent's films, though, manifests itself with respect to Jack Wrangler. A frequent star and guest star in Vincent's productions, Wrangler is always the best dressed and most coifed. It is on the body of this former gay porn star that the most explicit manifestations of gay desire in Vincent's films can be read.[17] At the beginning of the hard-core feature *Voyeur* (1984), for instance, Wrangler becomes the center of erotic attention at the expense of the woman in the opening scene. A cabbie (Robert Bullock) drives around New York City in search of fares. A man (Wrangler) flags down the driver and hops into the back of the cab with a woman. He tells the driver to keep driving while she unzips his pants and begins to suck him off. A complex relay of looks ensues as the cabbie is torn between keeping his eye on the road and looking through the rear-view mirror at the action on his backseat. The action in the back is shot from a low angle, which makes Wrangler's cock look like a majestic object rising out of his pinstripe suit. As he shoots his come all over the backseat, it becomes apparent that this dick is the object of the cabbie's insistent rear-view gaze. The driver slows the cab, and the man kicks the woman to the curb. As he zips up his fly, he leans into the front of the cab and tempts the cabbie with a vague but lucrative business proposition—something about investigative work that could help the cabbie exercise the police skills he learned on the force but is no longer able to use because he was discharged for embezzling. The film cuts away from the rest of their cab ride. Having made it amply clear that the cabbie enjoys watching the man getting his dick sucked and that the man is aware of the cabbie's look and gets off on the cabbie watching him, this scene can be understood as an acknowledgment of a homoerotic bond between them. Although mediated by the discarded figure of the woman and the alibi of business, the result is not unlike a gay pickup, although the sex between men never makes it to the screen.

Straight History and Reception

As I have tried to demonstrate, Vincent's films break apart straight erotic clichés, supplement straight sex with elaborate costuming and curiosities of the mise-en-scène, and hint at gay desires. For whom, though, were all of these forms of "deviance" staged? It is unlikely that there was ever a queer audience for Vincent's films.[18] An archive of straight reception does exist, though. Histories of straight pornography, contemporary reviews, and an industry statement all attribute a degree of significance to Vincent's pornographic productions. Despite their agreement on the importance of the director and his films, however, these responses cannot agree on *why* he must be remembered. Nevertheless, his films consistently inspire strong feelings across the spectrum of evaluative writing. Because straight critics cannot fully account for the particularities of Vincent's films, the latter provoke either thoughts of transcendence and lost utopian possibilities, or they incite violent disavowal and rejection. The responses vary as commentators try to grapple with the difference his films represent.

In reviewing the critical literature, I think the best place to begin is in the relative present, where the historical reception of Vincent's films appears the most divided. Luke Ford spends a chapter of his *History of X: 100 Years of Sex in Film* (1999) celebrating the fact that straight pornography did not follow Vincent's lead. Ford dismisses Vincent's pornographic films because of their emphasis on narrative and production values. These elements constitute aberrations when seen from the perspective of contemporary video pornography, devoted as it is to wall-to-wall sex, which Ford sees as the proper historical realization of male desire. To Ford, narrative and production values make sex unsexy because they deviate from the male desire for exclusively graphic sex. From his point of view, then, Vincent's relevance to porn history derives from the fact that he provides a stunning example of what not to do. "Through [his] noble failures, Vincent helped turn porn in the opposite direction of his approach: Rather than more story and character development, X-rated movies since Vincent have concentrated on sex," Ford writes (160). By emphasizing cinematic elements other than graphic episodes of interlocking bodies, Vincent represents what had to be negated in order for straight porn to achieve its telos in the present day.[19]

Ford takes his cues from Steve and Elizabeth Brent's assessment of the film in the *Couples Guide to the Best Erotic Videos* (1997). The Brents, however, give Vincent's "failures" a more positive spin. They imbue *In Love*, for example, with an incredible degree of nostalgia: "If you're a newcomer [to pornography] . . . don't rent this film first. Save it for after you've seen some of the modern examples so you can appreciate what might have been if the forces of repression and censorship had never won their community-standards platform and banished sexuality from mainstream filmmaking" (qtd. in Ford 1999, 160). Here, the Brents offer a sophisticated account of how Vincent's films might be thought of in terms of the history of pornography. It is not that the films did not conform to the "male" desire of which pornography is merely the graphic realization, as Ford would have it, but that Vincent's films sought to challenge and to change the social value attributed to pornography. Vincent did not want to dwell in the porn ghetto, but rather attempted to develop a pornographic aesthetic that would work for both porn audiences and mainstream audiences. With pornography presently out of mainstream theaters, the Brents frame Vincent's films as symbols of a lost past they can appreciate in the nostalgic tense of "what might have been."[20]

This conditional and virtual critical tense indicates not just another opinion about Vincent's films. It also traces the historical mode that Vincent's films inhabit relative to the type of history of straight pornography critics like Ford attempt to write. Both Ford and the Brents insist that Vincent's films are historical in some sense, but that they do not fit into an otherwise linear historical narrative of straight pornographic film's development. While Ford's strategy is to write Vincent's films off as instances of pornographic film production significant only because they serve as warnings of how not to make pornographic films, the Brents see in them lost possibilities capable of improving porn and making it a more widely appreciated cultural form. The Brents are unable, however, to give an account of these possibilities. In this respect, Vincent's films are fundamentally undecided cultural products that resist any definite status. Although they tell stories of straight sex and offer representations of straight sex, they constitute troubling anomalies without any definite place in the history of straight porn.

This lack of historical place for Vincent's films despite their manifest content of straight sex and straight stories suggests that the critics are dimly aware that something exceeds the overtly visible in his films. Vincent's films put straight sex on the screen in a fundamentally different way. As I have tried to argue, this difference is a queer one. In contrast to the historians who have relegated Vincent to the realm of anomaly, contemporaries to Vincent did not dismiss or refuse to engage fully with this queer quality. Some saw the difference at the heart of Vincent's productions as capable of rejuvenating the pornographic feature in the early 1980s.

This faith in the innovative capacities of Vincent's features is best expressed in *Dirty Looks* (1982), a feature-length compilation of sex scenes from his previous films that Vincent made to promote the release of *Roommates*.[21] Two of the most dedicated promoters of straight porn during the early 1980s host this montage of highlighted scenes: Al Goldstein, the publisher of *Screw* magazine, and Gloria Leonard, the publisher of *High Society* magazine, narrate *Dirty Looks*, setting up each scene and praising the arousing capacities of Vincent's films and the talent of the performers he employs. Rivals in publishing, they stage an act that makes it clear they will agree to do the show together only out of mutual admiration for Vincent. It quickly becomes apparent, though, that they are not just hosting the film anthology out of respect. They have also come to Vincent to acquire a degree of respectability previously unavailable to them.

Dirty Looks begins with the arrival of Goldstein and Leonard at the apartment where their hosting will take place. He is dressed in a tacky sweater with a wolf on it—identifying him with the iconic sexual predator. She wears a leopard-print dress, projecting an image of chintzy but sensuous sexuality. Immediately, they begin to bicker, trading insults, four-letter words, and bad jokes. They eventually agree to set aside their differences and host the show out of respect for Vincent. They play the first clip. After a highlight from *Jack and Jill*, where Fox and Wrangler fuck on a hardwood floor, the film cuts back to Goldstein and Leonard. They have changed into formal wear. More strikingly, their speech—which now appears to be fed to them via prompting cards off-screen (this is made evident by their straying looks off-screen and by their sometimes stilted speech)—has undergone a complete transformation. They use much more refined vocabulary than their previous "obscene" speech. Additionally, Goldstein and Leonard demonstrate a high degree of cinematic literacy. They applaud actors' performances, promote drama in sex films, and quote from reviews in addition to praising the hotness of the sex scenes they present. The setting also changes as Goldstein and Leonard move from an area near the apartment's back door (or an area that has the feel of a back room) to a living room equipped with a finely upholstered couch, dark wood, a bar, and an antique lamp. Through Vincent's script, his costumes, and his set composition, Goldstein and Leonard are given an air of formality and respectability. They reciprocate by promoting Vincent's films, saying that they admire the director's work because it depicts hot sex while incorporating drama, performance, and production values.

Goldstein and Leonard openly articulate that the stakes they have in Vincent's films are rooted in a shared desire for increased aesthetic quality. This is reinforced by the costume change, the migration in the mise-en-scène, and the elevated sense of cinematic style. As I have tried to demonstrate, these aspects of production are also linked to a distinct queer displacement of straight sex in Vincent's films. This analysis suggests that for a time, the straight porn industry was willing to see its product "queered" in an effort to produce innovations capable of creating a more viable and popular cultural product. Looking back on this moment, I would like to affirm it as a time when straight porn was willing to open itself up to a queer revision. A gay man found a way to change the terms of straight pornographic feature films and to establish himself as an admirable auteur of straight porn. Looking into the hidden realm of production, this instance begs further inquiry into the role of gay workers in producing straight pornography, a presence recently given attention through the character of the boom operator Scotty (Philip Seymour Hoffman) in *Boogie Nights* (dir. Paul Thomas Anderson, 1997).[22] As examples, Vincent's films also open up more general cultural questions about the role erotics straying from heteronormative ends play in straight porn. At the most general level, the willingness of the industry to welcome and celebrate films such as Vincent's point to a largely unexplored but nevertheless intimate relationship between changes in industrial conditions and changes in sexual mores, desires, and subjectivities. In some sense, the Meese Commission was right when it stated that "the history of pornography has yet to be written" (U.S. Department of Justice 1986, 233). It would seem that this declaration applies especially to our recent past.

Notes

1   Unfortunately, I do not have any legal documents attesting to the founding of this company in 1981. But 1981 is the first year in which Platinum Pictures is credited as the production company in the titles of a Vincent feature (*Roommates*).

2 Jerry Butler, one of the best-known male stars of the period recalls that "in the early 80s, Chuck was one of the first people to give adult films class and charisma. He shaved the ugly corners off pornography" (1989, 83–84). Dick Hebditch and Nick Anning remember Vincent as one of the ten best and most consistent directors of pornography's golden age in their history of the straight porn industry of the late 1970s and early 1980s (1988, 195).

3 *Roommates* won the following Adult Film Association of America (AFAA) awards in 1982: Best Film, Best Director (Chuck Vincent), Best Actress (Veronica Hart), Best Supporting Actor (Jamie Gillis). This information is available at us.imdb .com/Tawards?0083007 and was last accessed April 6, 2003. In 1983, the AFAA awarded Kelly Nichols its Best Actress award for her performance in *In Love* (us.imdb.com/Tawards?0085719).

4 In an interview with *Variety* in 1988, Vincent recalls 1982 (the year between *Roommates* and *In Love*) as a landmark year for the conflict between film and video in the straight porn industry. "The market for adult films started slipping around 1982 and in the past three years has dried up. . . . Five years ago the video companies such as VCA and Caballero would typically advance $40–60,000 for the video rights to a theatrical porn film. Then roughly two years ago they stopped making offers—they decided they could do four shot-on-video programs themselves for the cost of video rights to a single theatrical film" (qtd. in Cohn 1988: 3, 26).

5 *Variety* was willing to agree with the crossover aspirations of *Roommates*: "While pic's lack of a Hollywood major pedigree may lead to it being dismissed as porn, 'Roommates' deserves a shot at mainstream audiences." ("Roommates" 1982b, 24). Echoing *Variety* with a more aesthetic inflection, *Playboy* affirmed that "*Roommates* deserves to be judged as a real movie—rare on the porn scene in recent years—that places credibility above crotch level" ("Roommates" 1982a, 36).

6 Rick Marx, screenwriter for *Taboo* and *Roommates*, recalls in 1988 that "the fundamental difference between now and several years ago is that back then we wanted to make a real picture—which people would enjoy and had the possibilities of attracting the crossover, mainstream audience. The best shot we had at this was Chuck Vincent's 'Roommates' in 1981, which I co-wrote" (qtd. in Cohn 1988, 26).

7 By "bad" sex I mean to refer to representations of sex that do not engage their viewers in a pleasurable fashion. This typology includes scenes with unerotic coercion at their heart, flatly photographed and edited scenes in which the action is difficult to see and repetitive, and scenes in which the performers clearly are not into each other.

8 Borrowing from Dyer's work on the film musical, Williams ventures that pornography exhibits a similar narrative/number structure. The number inevitably provides the "solution" to problems that spring from the contemporary social reality and that are evoked and framed by cinematic narrative, whether they be

the realities of capitalist oppression or the general woes of heterosexual union (as in the case of the musical), or the more specific psychosexual ills of heterosexual desire and pleasure (as in the case of pornography). The number can either do this by appearing as a *separated* utopian moment that provides an escape from these anxieties, or it can function as an *integrated* spectacle that more directly confronts social problems and "solves" them in a much more ambivalent fashion. Both run in a vicious circle, either by offering capitalist solutions to antagonisms created by capitalism, or by offering sexual resolutions to sexual problems. See Williams 1999, chap. 6. My contention is that Vincent evokes the problems, but does not offer any satisfactory solutions because his numbers fail to embody straight utopian sexual fantasies.

9 It should be noted that Jack Wrangler was quite a famous gay porn star who abandoned his gay porn career to work in straight porn. See Wrangler's autobiography (Wrangler and Johnes 1984) for a more complete story. Wrangler's place in Vincent's work will be discussed in more detail below.

10 *Bon Appetit* shares a lot of narrative and stylistic similarities with *The Opening of Misty Beethoven* (dir. Radley Metzger, 1975) although without the educational aspect of the plot. Like *Misty Beethoven, Bon Appétit* is the story of a down-on-her-luck woman who becomes part of a high-class international sex contest. Faith (Kelly Nichols) caters a party for rich socialites and becomes involved in their contest to see who can seduce the ten best lovers in the world. The prize for the winner is $250,000. Her companion photographer Scott (Randy West) must catch her in the act on film as she conquers the ten best lovers. Each lives in a different international city, so Faith and Scott travel the globe, offering an excuse to show location shots from Paris, Munich, New York, and other scenic cities around the world. In the end, Faith and Scott discover they are the best sexual matches for one another. The pornographic numbers throughout are varied, erotic, and seem to have only ever-increasing pleasure as their aim.

11 As Williams contends in *Hard Core*, bad sex is a structuring principle of straight feature-length pornography, but only insofar as it establishes the erotic problem that the rest of the film seeks to resolve through its ever more ecstatic numbers. *Roommates*, on the other hand, depicts the problem as one more of heterosexual sex itself, rather than a narrative conceit. It provides no specific problem that must be worked through, and it does not solve any problems. Rather, heterosexual sex in all of its many scenarios is depicted as rife with problems. See Williams 1999, chap. 6.

12 This scene is also an allusion, I think, to a scene in François Truffaut's film about making a film, *Day for Night* (1973). At one point in Truffaut's film, a cat similarly holds up production. The cat in *Day for Night* is supposed to eat from a breakfast tray two lovers have left outside their bungalow, becoming a metaphor for the gentleness and tenderness of the lovemaking. In the world of the film production company, finally getting the cat to perform is an affirmation of the magic of cinema (they similarly cheer). This allusion seems to work in two complemen-

tary but contradictory fashions. On the one hand, it mocks the art cinema of Truffaut by bringing it down to an utterly commercial level (in that in Vincent's film the "film within a film" is a commercial shoot). On the other hand, the quotation seems to be a way for *Roommates* to make a claim to a more legitimated form of cinema beyond pornography and its relatively low production values. Both tendencies appear to inform Vincent's film. His productions consistently demonstrate and test B movie economic limits as he works within budget but tries to elevate the artistic cache of his productions.

13 Peter Lehman, for example, has analyzed the affinities pornography shares with the documentary quest for truth. He calls porn "a kind of documentary" that encodes a particular patterned attraction taken for a fantasy of reality. Lehman's discussion focuses on gonzo pornography and other hybrid ethnographic-pornographic films. Other writers, such as Bill Nichols, Christian Hansen, and Catherine Needham have commented more generally on the truth-seeking impulses pornography shares with the ethnographic quest for truth. And Linda Williams has explicitly framed straight pornography as a quest for the "truth" of bodies and pleasures. See Nichols et al. 1991, Lehman 1999, and Williams 1999, esp. chap. 1.

14 For example, anatomical features: *Deep Throat*; capacities: *Insatiable* (dir. Godfrey Daniels, 1980), *Raw Talent* (dir. Larry Revene, 1984); characters: *Debbie Does Dallas* (dir. Jim Clark, 1978), *The Devil in Miss Jones, Flesh Gordon* (dir. Michael Benveniste and Howard Ziehm, 1974), *The Opening of Misty Beethoven, The Resurrection of Eve* (dir. Mitchell Bros., 1973).

15 Butler offers this figure as the budget for *In Love* (1989, 304). A significant portion of the film's budget must have also been spent on location shooting, since it takes place in a number of real settings including Miami, New York City, and San Francisco.

16 The full quote from Butler that I am basing these observations on runs over two full pages in his book. An edited version that brings out the most significant aspects runs as follows (I quoted the part about "sheepishness" above): "*Jack & Jill 2* was another movie I did for the famous, ever-ready Chuck Vincent. It was a three- or four-day shoot and was a typical Chuck Vincent movie. That means there was a lot of dilly-dallying and fussing with costumes. . . . My sex scenes in *Jack & Jill 2* were odd, but not really hot. I've mentioned earlier that Chuck is gay. There's nothing wrong with that, but how can a guy who's a softball expert coach a hardball team? There are similarities, but it isn't the same game. Sometimes Chuck seems very sheepish about heterosexual sex. He does care about the look and the presentation of his works, and he always dressed me very nicely, but he seemed a little confused about how to dress women. In *Jack & Jill 2*, for example, the women wore picture hats and frilly dresses—pretty, but not . . . *tasty*" (1989, 270–71).

17 It should be noted that another significant "broaching" of gay desire occurs in an explicit fashion in *Roommates*, although this appearance is quickly recuper-

ated into the heterosexual dynamics of the film. After moving to New York City, Joan meets a charming young man named Eddie (Jerry Butler) at an audition. They become fast friends, and he is very up front about identifying himself as gay to her. In one scene, they picnic at the docks down by the South Street Seaport. Two guys are standing at the end of the peer. After checking out their asses, Eddie suggests that he and Joan go introduce themselves. He calls dibs on the guy on the left. The scene ends at this point with them thoughtfully finishing their lunch. Importantly, a gay desire is voiced and not depicted as strange or punishable. Soon, though, Eddie's sexuality is subject to revision by the narrative. He and Joan inevitably jump into bed. By the film's end, it is unclear if Eddie is a sensitive straight guy who was experimenting, bisexual, or a gay man who is doing some experimenting of his own.

18 Although, as Samuel R. Delany's memoir of Times Square attests, straight porno theaters were often used by men as places to engage in sex with other men. See Delany 1999.

19 Ford is an unabashed misogynist when it comes to pornography. He views women's desire as insignificant to the history of straight pornography. To Ford, contemporary video pornography with constant sex is a telos that acts as a graphic realization of an eternal male heterosexual lust. Vincent does not fit into the progression pornography has gone through in order to reach this high point because he injected too much "reality" into his productions, and "reality . . . is rarely sexy" (1999, 159).

20 For a legal and economic history of the times, which focuses on the role the Motion Picture Association of America played in driving pornography out of the mainstream (thereby saving Hollywood), see Lewis 2000.

21 *Dirty Looks* includes scenes from *Bang Bang* (1975), *Dirty Lily* (1977), *Bad Penny* (1978), and *Jack and Jill* (1979), and ends with a scene from the upcoming *Roommates*.

22 Scotty also has, of course, a much more metaphorical function in the film. He stands in for the homoerotic gaze disavowed and mediated in much straight porn directed at straight male audiences.

Works Cited

Bonavoglia, Angela. 1982. "Roommates." Review of *Roommates*, dir. Chuck Vincent. *Cineáste* 12, 2: 43–45.

Brent, Steve, and Elizabeth Brent. 1997. *Couples Guide to the Best Erotic Videos*. New York: St. Martin's Press.

Butler, Jerry. 1989. *Raw Talent: The Adult Film Industry as Seen by Its Most Popular Male Star*. Buffalo, N.Y: Prometheus.

Cohn, Lawrence. 1988. "Pornmakers Surface in Mainstream: HV Quickies Speed Demise of Genre." *Variety*, March 9, 26.

Delany, Samuel R. 1999. *Times Square Red, Times Square Blue*. New York: New York University Press.

Dyer, Richard. 1990. *Now You See It: Studies on Lesbian and Gay Film*. New York: Routledge.

———. 1991. "Believing in Fairies." In *Inside/Out: Lesbian Theories, Gay Theories*, ed. Diana Fuss. New York: Routledge. 185–201.

Ford, Luke. 1999. *A History of X: 100 Years of Sex in Film*. Amherst, N.Y.: Prometheus.

Nichols, Bill, Christian Hansen, and Catherine Needham. 1991. "Pornography, Ethnography, and the Discourses of Power." In *Representing Reality: Issues and Concepts in Documentary*, by Bill Nichols. Bloomington: Indiana University Press. 201–28.

Hebditch, David, and Nick Anning. 1988. *Porn Gold: Inside the Pornography Business*. London: Faber and Faber.

Lehman, Peter. 1999. "Ed Powers and the Fantasy of Documenting Sex." In *Porn 101: Eroticism, Pornography, and the First Amendment*, ed. James Elias et al. Amherst, N.Y.: Prometheus. 359–66.

Lewis, Jon. 2000. *Hollywood v. Hard Core: How the Struggle over Censorship Saved the Modern Film Industry*. New York: New York University Press.

"Roommates." 1982a. Review of *Roommates*, dir. Chuck Vincent. *Playboy*, June, 34, 36.

"Roommates." 1982b. Review of *Roommates*, dir. Chuck Vincent. *Variety*, February 17, 24.

U.S. Department of Justice. 1986. *Attorney General's Commision on Pornography Final Report*. 2 vols. Washington, D.C.: GPO.

Williams, Linda. 1999. *Hard Core: Power, Pleasure, and the "Frenzy of the Visible."* Exp. ed. Berkeley: University of California Press.

Wrangler, Jack, and Carl Johnes. 1984. *The Jack Wrangler Story; or, What's a Nice Boy Like You Doing?* New York: St. Martin's.

part 3

Pornography, Race, and Class

The Resurrection of Brandon Lee:

The Making of a Gay Asian

American Porn Star

NGUYEN TAN HOANG

✳ In an article in the Asian American pop culture zine *Giant Robot*, jour-nalist Claudine Ko recounts her search for Brandon Lee. She refers not to the son of Bruce Lee, who gained cult stardom after dying mysteriously and tragically at a young age while shooting *The Crow* (dir. Alex Proyas, 1994), but the *other* Brandon Lee, the gay porn star. Ko reports on rumors that Brandon the porn star had been discovered while delivering Chinese food to a gay porn set. As the story goes, the director asked to see his egg roll and was so blown away by the sight that he immediately cast Brandon in a porn video. Later on in the article, Ko tracks down Chi Chi LaRue, one of the best-known directors in gay porn, who straightened out the story. The drag queen director claimed to have discovered Brandon Lee at a gay bath-house in Los Angeles. Impressed by Brandon's good looks and ten inches of manhood, she brought him to Catalina, the popular gay video company, which promptly signed him on, and the rest, as they say, is history.[1]

I am not particularly interested in ascertaining which version of the story about Brandon's discovery is true. Rather, what I find compelling is the way the two versions can be read as emblematic of how the image of Asian men in gay porn has shifted with the appearance of Brandon Lee.[2] Before Brandon, Asian porn actors played the roles of karate masters, Chinatown grocery boys, or their cousins, Chinese food delivery boys, which is to say, they served as representations of racialized sexual stereotypes. In his videos, Brandon Lee is frequently portrayed as West Hollywood boyfriend material, having both mundane roles and pornotopic professions such as real estate agent, young man who inherits a gay brothel, army recruit, porn star, and, most commonly, as West Hollywood twink.[3] In other words, Brandon Lee is just another random (American) gay guy one could easily find cruising in a West Hollywood bathhouse. He has left his parents' grocery store in China- town and is living in sin with his white boyfriend in the gay ghetto. This movement from one ghetto to another parallels Brandon Lee's transition from ethnic-niched to mainstream gay video pornography.

In his seminal article, "Looking for My Penis: The Eroticized Asian in Gay Video Porn," Richard Fung observes that dominant Western discourses on race and sexuality posit a racial/biological spectrum that attributes to blacks a hypersexuality and relegates Asians to the opposite extreme of asexuality, according to "quantifiable levels" of sexual activities, primary and secondary sexual characteristics, and sexual attitudes. Fung argues that these racial- ized sexual stereotypes have "permeated the global popular consciousness" (1991, 146), as exemplified in Western popular visual culture such as tele- vision and advertising. For example, in Hollywood films, Asian women are restricted to the roles of Lotus Blossoms passively catering to the sexual appetites of white men or depicted as aggressive, conniving Dragon Ladies conspiring with evil Fu Manchus. In contrast, Asian men are portrayed either as harmless wimps and nerds or as threatening kung fu masters; both types are seen as undersexed and feminized. Consequently, Fung asks, "If Asian men have no sexuality, how can we have homosexuality?" (148).

In his analysis of gay male porn videos employing Asian actors—the one arena where Asian men engage in explicit homosexual sex—Fung interro- gates the "role the pleasure of porn plays in securing a consensus about race and desirability that ultimately works to our disadvantage [as Asian men]" (158). He describes the feminization of Asian men in gay porn within the context of minority power relations. Looking at the work of Vietnamese American porn actor Sum Yung Mahn, Fung demonstrates how the repre- sentation of Asian men focuses on their submission to the pleasure of white men. In these tapes made in the mid-1980s, Asian men almost always adopt the bottom role in relation to a white top. In *Asian Knights* (dir. Ed Sung, 1985), the only exception where an Asian top fucks a white bottom, the Asian character is portrayed as serving the white man domestically and sexually as a houseboy.[4]

The intended audience for these Asian-themed videos is primarily gay white men. A sex scene between two Asian men in *Asian Knights* is edited to conform to the point of view of a white man. What appears to be an Asian-

Asian sexual scenario is undercut when a white man enters the scene and occupies the center of the sexual attention, much the way the male enters into a "lesbian" number in heterosexual porn. Most significantly, in these tapes the white male fear of being fucked is displaced onto the bodies of Asian men. A scene in *Below the Belt* (dir. Philip St. John, 1985) has an Asian actor step temporarily into the role of a white character in order to articulate his anxiety about getting fucked. In this sequence, the Asian male body substitutes for the white male body to receive the punishment represented by anal sex.[5] Fung emphasizes that "the problem is not the representation of anal pleasure per se, but rather that the narratives privilege the penis while always assigning the Asian the role of bottom" (1991, 153).

Despite the recent critical attention and popularity of Asian male actors in Asian cinema and its successful crossover into Hollywood (represented by such actors as Jackie Chan, Jet Li, and Chow Yun Fat, and directors such as Ang Lee and John Woo), the representation of Asian men as sexually appealing scarcely figures in mainstream American popular culture. In the realm of explicit sexual representation, one finds that in marked contrast to the overwhelming presence of Asian and Asian American women in heterosexual pornography, there is a notable absence of Asian American men, let alone a "named" straight male Asian American porn actor.[6] Thus the popularity of Brandon Lee as a gay Asian American porn star represents a startling and unique achievement that demands special attention.

Brandon Lee is the only Asian American porn actor with the distinction of having a *Best Of* video compilation. Starting in 1997, at the ripe age of eighteen, Brandon began acting in gay videotapes marketed for an Asian niche market in Catalina's Far East Features series, in such popular titles as *Asian Persuasion* (dir. Josh Eliot, 1997), *Fortune Nookie* (dir. Chi Chi LaRue, 1998), and *Asian Persuasion 2* (dir. Josh Eliot, 1998). He then quickly crossed over into mainstream gay porn, appearing in *Dial "S" for Sex* (dir. Chi Chi LaRue, 1998), *Stag Party* (dir. Chi Chi LaRue, 1998), *Harley's Crew* (dir. Chi Chi LaRue, 1998), *Big Guns 2* (dir. Josh Eliot, 1998), *Throat Spankers* (dir. Josh Eliot, 1998), and *Peters* (dir. Dane Preston, 1999).[7] I am interested in looking at the racial "packaging" of Brandon Lee in the Asian videos, where he is depicted as "American" in relation to his Asian costars, and how this process changed in the mainstream videos, where he is the only Asian (and frequently the only person of color), while his racial and ethnic difference is not remarked on. I will argue that the making of this gay Asian American porn star is accomplished through the coding of Brandon Lee as an assimilated (Asian) American. And of course, I would be remiss if I did not mention the fact that he is also popular for being a fierce top, which, as Richard Fung has shown us, represents a very significant departure for an Asian actor in the world of North American gay porn. In other words, the case of Brandon Lee the porn star shows how American masculinity underlies topness, which then confers the status of gay porn star. His work serves as an exemplary "border study" of the conflicting categories of "American" and "Asian" as they are enacted and performed in top and bottom sexual roles in contemporary gay video porn.[8] Through the star-text of Brandon Lee, I trace a history of how these two highly unstable categories have been constructed in mutual opposition to one another as a consequence of political, economic, and social forces, and I delineate the ways in which the "absolute" difference between Asian and American finds expression in terms of sexuality and gender.

To better contextualize and understand the shift in the racialized sexual coding of Brandon Lee, it is necessary to consider how Asian men have been positioned historically in American society. As numerous scholars in Asian American studies have observed, formations of gender and sexuality fashioning the image of Asian men and women in the United States cannot be considered apart from Asian American history. These factors include labor history, patterns of immigration, bachelor societies, exclusion and antimiscegenation laws, female prostitution, Orientalist exoticization, emasculation of men, and hyperfeminization of women. As Yen Le Espiritu has noted, "America's capitalist economy wanted male workers but not their families" (1997, 17). The necessity of housing, feeding, and educating the workers' families cut severely into profit margins. Since women and children were considered nonproductive, they were not welcomed. Racist immigration laws did not allow Chinese men to bring their wives from China or to send for them from the United States. Antimiscegenation laws—based on the fear of Asian men as sexual threats, as sex fiends able to attract white women—revoked the citizenship of white women who married "aliens ineligible for citizenship" (Wong and Santa Ana 1999, 178). These exclusionary laws thus resulted in forced bachelor societies. Unequal employment opportunities restricted Asian men to menial and unskilled labor, such as cooks, waiters, laundry workers, and domestic workers, or what is traditionally deemed "women's work."[9] Existing outside of heteronormative gender roles and patriarchal family formation, Asian men conformed to what Robert G. Lee, borrowing from Marjorie Garber, calls "the third sex,"[10] or "a gender of imagined sexual possibility" (Lee 1999, 85). Lisa Lowe has commented on the historical imbrications of race and gender in the legal discourse of citizenship as it affected the Asian American subject:

> Racialization along the legal axis of definitions of citizenship has also ascribed "gender" to the Asian American subject. Up until 1870, citizenship was granted exclusively to male persons; in 1870, men of African descent could become naturalized, but the bar to citizenship remained for Asian men until repeal acts of 1943–1952. Whereas the "masculinity" of the citizen was first inseparable from his "whiteness," as the state extended citizenship to nonwhite male persons, it formally designated these subjects as "male" as well. (1996, 11)

Lowe's concise explication shows that U.S. citizenship originally confers the status of maleness, of masculinity, predicated on whiteness. Since Asian laborers were excluded from this subject-citizen status formulated as masculine and white, they were seen as "emasculated" and "feminized."

Writers in the Asian American cultural nationalist movement of the seventies took up the historical baggage linking Asian (American) masculinity with effeminacy and emasculation. The Asian American literary response to the emasculation of Asian American men involved a reinscription of conventional constructions of masculinity propped up by heteronormative cultural nationalist discourse. The work of Frank Chin and his colleagues in the 1975 anthology, *Aiiieeeee! An Anthology of Asian-American Writers*, forcefully asserts and vehemently prescribes an ideal Asian American subject-citizen.[11] As various Asian American feminist critics have asserted, this subject-citizen based on a particular brand of "authentic" masculinity simply apes the dominant version of patriarchal and familial norms and "[prescribes] who a recognizable and recognizably legitimate Asian American racial subject should ideally be: male, heterosexual, working class, American born, and English speaking" (Eng 2001, 209). The defensive move of asserting an identity premised on an overarching emphasis on the domestic space of the nation demonstrates a reaction against the historical relegation of Asian Americans to the status of perpetual foreigners and unassimilable aliens.[12] Hence the legal discourse linking U.S. citizenship with white masculinity, as Lowe described it, is coterminous with the *Aiiieeeee!* group's positing of an ideal Asian American subject based on the same hegemonic version of masculinity, heterosexuality, American citizenship, and facility with the English language. These two historical forces exerting influence on popular understandings of Asian American masculinity—one state-produced and the other in resistance to the state's regulation—should be kept in mind as we look at how Brandon Lee's image is consistently coded as American, which in turn enables his rise as a top Asian American porn star. But before zooming in on Brandon's racial packaging in the porn videos, we need to consider another major intervention in the visual representation of Asian masculinity in mainstream American popular culture.

Dance of the Little Dragon:
"Remasculinization" and Transformation

It is not insignificant that an Asian American porn star takes as his "nom de porn" the name of Brandon Lee, son of martial arts superstar Bruce Lee. This choice of name clearly activates the one "positive" place Asian men occupy within the American popular imagination. This cinematic genre is set within a visual economy where Asian men are seen as physically powerful, energetic, graceful, and sensual. Yvonne Tasker has noted the importance of a "remasculinization" of Chinese national identity in the star-text of Bruce Lee.[13] The cultivation of the hard and muscular fighting body counteracts the view of Chinese men as soft and delicate, and thus foregrounds a Chinese national identity based on a macho muscularity. Tasker recounts a scene in *Fist of Fury* (dir. Wei Lo, 1972),[14] in which a Chinese go-between, a traitorous character affiliated with the Japanese martial arts school, comes to the Chinese school to offer a challenge by taunting the students there as the "Sick Men of Asia." Responding to this insult, Lee's character goes to the Japanese school and defeats the students there to proclaim that he and his Chinese schoolmates are not sick men. Tasker writes, "This assertion of nationalism is very clearly inscribed through the revelation of Lee's body— as he ritualistically removes his jacket—so that discourses of masculinity and nationhood are complexly bound up together in his star image" (1997, 318).

In addition to these textual operations expressing a masculinist, nationalist agenda, audiences of Lee's films also respond to their anticolonial narratives.[15] Unlike American interracial male buddy films, where the conflict is couched in terms of class antagonism, the conflict in Lee's films comes from outside threats represented by colonial forces. For instance, in *Fist of Fury*, the Japanese school occupies the role of foreign threat and enemy, while in *The Way of the Dragon* (dir. Bruce Lee, 1972),[16] the villains are Italian gangsters who threaten to destroy a Chinese family restaurant. Lee's films became popular not only with Asian audiences but also with black and white working-class audiences in the United States, as well as with Third World viewers because they functioned as fantasies of empowerment.[17] *Enter the Dragon* (dir. Robert Clouse, 1973), a coproduction between a Chinese film company and Warner Brothers, inverts this anticolonial theme by having Lee play an agent working for the British government fighting against a James Bond–type Chinese villain named Han. Stephen Teo has pointed out that the film "conveys the West's antipathy towards Lee's nationalism . . . [and] shows a sullen and sulking Lee forced to submit to the West's perception of him as a mere action hero" (1997, 117).[18]

Another important element animating the star image of Bruce Lee is the centrality of his transformation from a dull, shy nerd to an intense, sexually charged martial arts fighter. Lee's invisibility as a Chinese man, as a common working-class character, functions as a disguise before the moment of conversion. The films build suspense by "teas[ing] the audience," which eagerly anticipates the thrilling moment when Lee can no longer hold himself back. Stuart Kaminsky argues that this holding back highlights the moment when Lee's character refuses to continue "to be a respectable working-class ghetto resident. . . . His resolve disappears when his family is attacked and destroyed and he sees that being a good worker and loyal citizen has ruined him" (1976, 63). Finally forced to fight, he abandons the "acceptable route of behavior" and throws off all self-restraint. He removes his shirt and exposes his muscular body, shows off his hidden strength, and exhibits his amazing "fist of fury" (Tasker 1997, 317).[19]

Lee's visual, physical transformation from nerd to martial arts hero is accompanied by a concomitant verbal transformation, the change from an awkward, naive country bumpkin delivering generic, unremarkable dialogue to the explosive emission of his famous cries, wails, and shrieks. These animalistic sounds suggest brute, physical exertion, the release of pent-up rage and energy, and an involuntary bodily "truth," but paradoxically they also reveal the excessive theatricality of the overdubbed sound as a series of constructed sound effects. Tasker attributes this audio excess to an eruption of the sensuousness of the body, disrupting the usual connection of Lee's films with aggression (1997, 320). Furthermore, the notoriously inept English dubbing of most of Lee's films (and Chinese martial arts films in general) explicitly marks them as low-budget foreign movies, underscored by the poorly synched dubbing of "high" formal English with a "low" cultural product.[20] Moreover, the kung fu films also appeal to the lower bodily senses of immediate gratification, eliciting verbal calls, cheers, and applause from their viewers.

The kung fu film's solicitation of the spectator's direct bodily engagement, inspiring awe, thrill, suspense, and amusement, calls to mind similar responses to another cinematic genre; the structural resemblances between the martial arts film and the musical prove striking. The two genres possess two primary corresponding features: the first concerns their emphasis on realism, while the second focuses on their reception by audiences. Bruce Lee's innovations to the kung fu genre include the injection of more realism into the martial arts performances. He was one of the first to promote the use of martial artists, rather than actors, in his films.[21] Skill and expertise took precedence over a pretty face. Lee often employed his own students, including Chuck Norris, Dan Inosanto, and Kareem Abdul-Jabbar, as his movie opponents. He rejected the industry's "unrealistic" and manipulative utilization of trampolines and cables to depict characters jumping and flying. Instead, like the dance numbers in musicals, long shots of full bodies in "total performance" were favored over frequent cuts and close-up inserts, thus "proving" to the audience that "they were watching genuine kung fu instead of camera deceptions" (Chiao 1981, 33).

Hsiung-ping Chiao observes how Lee's "kicks, turns and elbow movements of kung fu intrinsically resemble dance steps" (34). She draws a parallel between Gene Kelly's "life-is-music" worldview to Lee's analogous "life-is-kung fu" worldview. The physicality and athleticism of their performances —dance for Kelly and kung fu for Lee—define their "ultimate self-expressions." Referring to the tension exerted on the male body subjected to the audience's "admiring gaze" in the martial arts film and in the musical, Tasker remarks: "In Western culture, dance is constructed in opposition to fighting. It is also linked to the feminine, and often explicitly to images of male homosexuality. It is important to note though that this does not mean the *feminization* of the male dancer, a formulation that operates within a simple gender binary. Rather, dance offers the possibility of occupying a feminine position that involves, as with the martial arts film, an explicit location of the male body on display" (1997, 320). While Tasker is careful not to fall into an essentialist (and heteronormative) description of the male dancing body as automatically feminizing, for the *male* dancer an intense anxiety is triggered by the association of dance with the specters of femininity and homosexuality. Writing on *Singin' in the Rain* (dir. Stanley Donen, 1952), Carol Clover describes the Gene Kelly–Donald O'Connor dances as "muscular, apparently impromptu, unrestrained, exuberant, . . . in which the interest lies to a considerable extent in the athletic feats of the (male) body: how fast the feet, sinuous the twists, high the jumps" (1995, 726).[22] While

Gene Kelly's dance can be described as "martial," the martial arts of Bruce Lee aspire to the graceful qualities of dance. Various commentators have remarked on the fact that Lee was the first martial arts actor to place great importance on choreographing fight sequences. Like a dance choreographer in the musical, Lee frequently choreographed the battle sequences of his own films.[23] But the feature that most reflects the connection between Lee's martial moves and dance gestures is the frequent use of slow motion for the fight sequences. In the final, climactic confrontation with the Russian archvillain Petrov (Robert Baker, Lee's real-life personal bodyguard) in *Fist of Fury*, the fighting "stops" while Lee is shown gyrating his arms in delicate circles; this intense moment of arrested spectacle is depicted in slow motion and with optical printing, which register the multiple traces of his arm movements across the screen.[24]

Another point of likeness between the musical and the martial arts film is the way they address their audience. Both Kelly's and Lee's performances are often directed *at* the camera, which acts as a surrogate audience. For example, dance numbers often unfold on a stage set where the camera stands in for the missing audience. In the same way, Lee's kicks at the camera in *The Way of the Dragon* are shot from the point of view of his opponent, thus interpellating the viewer quite directly into the fight sequence. Additionally, audiences of musicals and kung fu focus on and appreciate performances, rather than quality of plot. The fight scenes function not as mere interruption of narrative by spectacle, but actually represent the crucial element for the propulsion of the narrative. Because kung fu is affirmed as the resolution to all conflicts in the films, the fight scenes "become the real force carrying the narrative flow" (Chiao 1981, 35). The special attention to the martial arts sequences, set off from the rest of the film textually and through audience expectation, supports Kaminsky's suggestion that performance represents the "essence of the Kung Fu film" (1976, 57).

The most striking feature of the Bruce Lee star image in relation to our present discussion of the eroticized representation of Asian men is his portrayal in the films as an ascetic, sexually naive, and repressed working-class hero. His relationships with women in the films remain platonic and without any sexual tension. In *The Way of the Dragon*, the main female character is his cousin, who first doubts Lee's ability to help her fight against the Italian gangsters. Once she sees him in action, however, she develops a soft spot for him; but their relationship stays on a tender, familial level. The asexuality of the Lee character becomes especially pronounced in a sequence from *Enter the Dragon*. In a brothel scene, while Lee's cohorts John Saxon and Jim

Kelley readily pick out several women from a lineup to join them for the night, Lee requests only one woman to come to his room. This "prostitute" turns out to be a fellow secret spy; needless to say, no romance ensues between them. Hsiung-ping Chiao (1981) has observed that sex in the Bruce Lee oeuvre is seen as the "corrupting force" associated with decadence and linked with brothels, prostitutes, and slave trafficking. Lee's films subscribe to a puritan sexual morality, continuous with traditional Confucian values. Yvonne Tasker (1997) has called attention to the fact that while the martial arts genre, like the American western and the action film, allows for the traditionally taboo looking of men at other men, Western critics' overemphasis on the aggression of Bruce Lee's films relegates the sensuous and homoerotic force of his performances to the background.[25] In addition, Tasker suggests that another mechanism of displacement occurs in these films, whereby racially marked bodies customarily acting as screens "for the projection of a range of fantasies, come into intimate physical contact" and take on the function of "deflect[ing] anxieties around their implicit homoeroticism" (318). Nevertheless, a contemporary viewer, who may already be cognizant of the work of recent Asian male action actors such as Jackie Chan, Chow Yun Fat, or Jet Li, can still be struck by the awesome sexual intensity of Lee's on-screen presence, which remains uneclipsed by the other Asian actors working today. Chiao comments on the way in which audience reception undercuts the desexualization of Lee's fictional characters at the thematic level:

> Puritan sexual morality have [sic] been paradoxically decoded by audiences as sexual stimulants. . . . It has been pointed out that his fights resemble sexual behavior. The open-legged posture before attacking, the slow-motion shots of his tense body, and the expression of excitement and elation intermingle to imply sexual provocation. The subtle tie between violence and sex thus transcends the overt layer of sex-inhibition and becomes emotional retribution for Lee's ill-fated destiny and plight (1981, 40–41).[26]

Finally, Bruce Lee is figured as a solitary, individual hero. In his films, frequent close-up inserts and fast zooms of his intense face punctuate the fight sequences, offering brief pauses between the dazzling fight choreography and expressing his surveillance of his surroundings and the movements of his opponents. While he is supposed to be on the side of the people, visually he is not shown as a part of the crowd, but as a unique and spectacular fighter in the spotlight (41).

Like the masculinist project of the martial arts film genre, the question of remasculinization in gay Asian American pornography occupies a central place in our discussion of Brandon Lee. As indicated above, Richard Fung has charted the ways in which male sexual potency is very much racially inflected in Western pseudoscientific and popular discourses on sexuality. Whereas the black man's savage hypersexuality is "proven" by his big black dick, the asexual Asian man possesses nothing "down there." Positioned as passive bottoms, "Asian and anus are conflated" (1991, 153). Hence, Brandon Lee's claim to porn-stardom as an exclusive top and as the instigator of sexual activity in his videos challenges the dominant view of Asian men in gay porn as forever bottoms. Brandon's remasculinization in gay porn videos creates a space in which he plays a performer who acts on the bodies of other men, in the narratives of videos, as well as outside of them, in the reception of the tapes.

Parallel to Bruce Lee's shift from nerdy country bumpkin to powerful kung fu master, the transformation in gay pornography takes place when the motivating porn narrative gets established and the sexual episodes begin to unfold. In the case of Brandon Lee, the transformation from asexual Asian man to porn star comes at the thrilling moment when he finally exposes his "hidden" asset. In the words of the *Adam Gay Video Directory*, which details his contribution to any video he appears in: "He can act, he's good sex, he's a top, and in case you hadn't noticed . . . that dick" (2000, 52). While the kung fu movie builds up the viewer's anticipation of the moment when Bruce Lee finally decides to fight, gay pornography provides only minimal buildup leading to the performance of sex and thus offers the viewer little in the way of suspense. The gay porn viewer bypasses even the most skeletal narrative framing by simply fast-forwarding and/or rewinding to the hottest parts of the tape. One gay Asian viewer describes his viewing habit: "I just zoom to the sex scenes. I zoom through all the stuff where there's no sex happening and I stop at the sex scene and watch for a bit to see if I think it's exciting. If it's not, I zoom to the next" (qtd. in Fung 1993, 362). The selective mode of concentrated *and* distracted viewing, the fast-forwarding and zooming in to where the real exciting sexual performance is happening, calls to mind the kung fu viewer's anticipation of the moment when Lee exposes his muscular upper body and demonstrates his masterful martial arts skills.

Accompanying Bruce Lee's exhibition of powerful and visually stunning movements is the "involuntary" eruption of convulsive grunts and wrathful yells, which evoke intense rage and piercing sensuality. The overdubbing of Bruce Lee's films at these impassioned moments echoes the porn convention of post-dubbing dialogue and sex sounds, such as generic dirty talk and repetitive moans in gay pornography. The porn soundtrack offers evidence of authentic sexual pleasure, provides proof of the final delivery of satisfaction, and adds realism by fleshing out the visual performance. But, as in the martial arts movie, the low-budget, lack-of-synch, and poor verbal performance also exposes the sex sounds as fake and unbelievable. Nevertheless, in Brandon Lee's Asian porn videos, the heavily accented English and the slow, awkward, and sometimes unintelligible delivery of lines by his Asian costars accentuate their limited facility with the English language. This lack of a perfect match between the audio and visual tracks paradoxically fits into the thematic of the porn narrative, which is premised on the foreignness and exoticism of the Asian actors. In other words, their poor English actually enhances the Orientalist authenticity the tapes hope to achieve.

In my discussion above on the structural similarities of the musical and the kung fu film, I propose that performance commands more attention than narrative complexity in both genres, in their textual operations as well as in audience reception.[27] At the risk of stating the obvious, I suggest that most viewers of gay porn concentrate on the spectacle of gay sex rather than on the role of the sexual numbers in working through narrative conflicts. For example, in a review of a recent porn video in the San Francisco gay weekly, *Bay Area Reporter*, critic John F. Karr faults a video for its "overwrought plotting," which, he claims, "stifle[s] the spontaneity of the sex act, distancing the performers from the naturalness they need to bring to sex." To get a sense of what he means by "overwrought," in the next paragraph Karr complains of a video which "*drowns* in plot scenes of *five-minute* duration" (2001, 35; emphasis mine). While there are structural correspondences between the martial arts genre's focus on the amazing battle scenes and gay video pornography's spotlight on sex sequences, it is important to note that the extreme episodic structure of the latter contains much less of an organizing narrative than the kung fu film. In fact, recent mainstream gay porn productions from Falcon Videos, such as *Absolute-Arid* (dir. John Rutherford, 2000) and *Absolute-Aqua* (dir. John Rutherford, 2000), have no explicit narrative framework; their sexual activity is united only by the fact that they take place in a natural environment, the desert and the beach, respectively.[28] To be sure, as in all fantasy, the scene where the sex occurs holds great significance and erotic purchase, as can be seen in gay porn's (re)appropriation of homosocial spaces—locker rooms, mechanic's garages, college fraternity houses, military barracks, and prisons—as the "stages" where sexual fantasy unfolds. However, the narrative motivation (one might say "silly excuse") leading to the sex is often extremely formulaic. Indeed, any regular gay porn viewer can attest to the predictable yet enjoyable manner in which characterization and narrative setup frequently serve as unconvincing pretense in order to get to the real matter at hand, the sex.[29]

Another marked contrast between the genres of martial arts and porn is their point of view in relation to the eroticized imaging of Asian male bodies. Whereas the sensuality of Bruce Lee is produced by the viewer's resistant reading, going against the grain of the narrative, the homoeroticism of Brandon Lee constitutes the central element of his status as a gay porn actor.[30] However, as stars commanding "top" billing (one an international martial arts superstar, the other a porn star in the smaller realm of gay male popular culture), both figures are set off narratively from the characters surrounding them. A "respectable working-class ghetto resident," Bruce Lee nevertheless transcends his downtrodden status through the performance of martial arts virtuosity. While Lee is presented as a man of the people who fights against imperialist forces, he stands out from the swarms of Asian male bodies that fight alongside him or, more often, get beaten up by him. Similarly, Brandon Lee remains a recognizable, "named" actor, a fierce top among the nameless hordes of interchangeable Asian bottoms.[31] Though Brandon is one among other men of the "Asian persuasion," he is marked off as different: he is an American real estate agent to the Japanese house buyer; he is the new owner of the boy brothel, where other Asians are sex workers; he is a porn star, a role model for another Asian character's porn ambition. These multiple differences are premised on an imbalance of power based on a higher economic, social, and cultural status. These power differentials relate to factors of nationality (Americanness), race/ethnicity (unfixed, unstable), age (youth), size (dick, muscle), language (English-speaking), and region (West Hollywood),[32] all of which contribute to his star status and top position. In what follows, I will look more closely at these various components that go into the making of this gay Asian American porn star.

The Making of a Gay Asian American Porn Star

Asian Persuasion opens with a scene of Brandon Lee and his boyfriend Brad Davis Mikado awakened in bed by a phone call. The caller is a client who wants to see a house in the Hollywood hills that Brandon, the real estate agent, is trying to sell. Before Brandon leaves, Brad makes comments about the sexual nature of Brandon's job, which requires meeting strange men at empty houses. Brandon denies entertaining any sexual possibilities and suggests that Brad, who is in the pool cleaning business, probably has more opportunities for sex with *his* clients, charges that Brad also denies. Immediately, the viewer notices that the framing narrative of the video revolves around the two main characters' professions, what they do for a living.[33] Brandon is boyish, clean-cut, well built, middle-class, and relationship-oriented. Most important, he is an (Asian) American. In the following scene, we see Brandon, dressed in a pink Hawaiian shirt, finish showing the house to an older Japanese man.[34] The scene begins with Mito saying, "I like it. The neighborhood's great. And it's large." He looks down meaningfully at Brandon's crotch. Brandon responds, grabbing his crotch, "Yeah, it is large. And it gets bigger when somebody's lips are around it." The Japanese man proceeds to suck Brandon and then gets fucked by him. Mito's comment about largeness refers first to the neighborhood and the house, then to Brandon's cock, and we can infer from the context—a Japanese buying property in California—that the term also connotes the spaciousness of America in general. Throughout the scene, the sex is punctuated by Mito's broken, heavily accented English emphasizing the big size and hardness of Brandon's cock, crudely narrating how it acts on him: "Big cock. You've got big cock"; "I feel your hard cock"; and "Your dick makes me come!" On the other hand, Brandon's verbal expression is limited to generic moans and stock phrases like: "Oh, baby, feels so good" and "Yeah, baby, suck it." In this scene, the position of top is aligned with Brandon's coding as an American, associated with his Valley Guy English, youth, butchness, muscularity, and big dick, in relation to the bottom's broken English (hence marking him as non-American), older age, femme-ness, skinny build, and smaller dick. Although the Japanese client may belong to a higher class—he is a potential buyer of the property—in the world of gay porn, other factors, such as physical endowment of muscle and genitalia, confer greater status than wealth. The other Asian actors in the video are the pool boys who work for Brad's pool cleaning company, playing the roles of working-class immigrants.[35] None of them gets to fuck the two white special guest stars, well-known actors Mike Nichols and Sam Crockett.

The portrayal of Brandon's Asian costars as working-class foreigners/immigrants also occurs in *Fortune Nookie*, another tape in Catalina's Far East Features series. In this tape, Brandon plays a young man who has inherited a fortune from a recently deceased uncle (figure 1). The problem is that the

1. Brandon Lee's young and charming face (from *Fortune Nookie*).

white lawyer, Jacob Scott, refuses to tell him what the fortune is unless Brandon pays him legal fees. Brandon protests desperately, "But I have nothing! . . . Lawyers suck." To which Scott replies, "Yes, we do." Thus Brandon finds himself "coerced" into having sex with Scott in order to receive his fortune. Scott, dressed in a gray suit, orders Brandon to take his clothes off and perform for Scott's pleasure.[36] The fortune turns out to be a brothel, where the sex workers are Asian men. They are managed and mistreated by a vicious white drag queen—dressed up in bad Japanese geisha drag—named Pixie (Vida de Ville). The Asian boy prostitutes are forced into working there for economic reasons. One of them, Niko Time, complains to Pixie that he wants to quit; but she reminds him that he has nowhere else to go. Tishiro Ho tells his coworker Erik Tenaka that he fears Pixie will fire him. Ho worries about his job security, especially since he has two kids to support. After taking over the whorehouse, Brandon tries to make friends with Time, who also fears losing his job. Brandon tells him, "I have a new job for you." Time replies, "Okay, let's get it over with." But what Brandon has in mind is giving Time the pleasure of firing the bitchy Pixie. They bond over this expulsion of the drag queen. Time agrees to have sex with Brandon and gets fucked by him. But unlike his previous scene with a white client (Paul Morgan), the sex with Brandon is coded as "consensual."[37]

Sexual coercion and consent in *Fortune Nookie* are directly thematized around class-inflected power relations. Whereas Brandon is coerced into having sex with the tie-wearing white lawyer (who tells him, "You have a lot of fees to work off, boy. . . . I'm pretty expensive"), after inheriting the brothel, Brandon occupies the position of power over Niko Time and the other Asian boy prostitutes. This tape makes a direct connection between lack of money and power and the necessity of performing sex for money.

Though he is poor at the beginning of the video, Brandon's inheritance affords him a promotion in the economic and sexual hierarchy. On the other hand, the status of the foreign, immigrant sex workers under his charge remains unchanged. Sex in *Fortune Nookie* is tied to economic necessity, not utopian fantasy, sexual expression, or "free" choice. In addition, the use of Asian actors with heavy accents and FOB (fresh-off-the-boat) appearance gives *this* viewer an uncomfortable awareness of the coincidence/overlapping of the actors' "real-life" situation with their characterizations in the porn narrative. Their actual low economic position and tenuous immigrant status resonate with their characters' marginalized positioning as sex workers threatened with unemployment. As bottoms in the political, sexual, and representational economies, the actors get fucked (and fucked over) by white American tops, porn directors—and eroticized as such by viewers of the video. This dynamic corresponds with what Richard Fung has described as the lack of an empowering subject position for the gay Asian porn viewer: "I may find Sum Yung Mahn attractive, I may desire his body, but I am always aware that he is not meant for me. I may lust after Eric Stryker and imagine myself as the Asian who is having sex with him, but the role the Asian plays in the scene with him is demeaning. It is not that there is anything wrong with the image of servitude per se, but rather that it is one of the few fantasy scenarios in which we figure, and we are always in the role of servant" (1991, 158).

Here I want to sound a word of caution against the uncritical embrace of Brandon Lee, a big-dicked Asian American butch top, as *the* answer to what Asian American and other politically progressive gay porn fans have been waiting for. For although his work does invert the passive houseboy-bottom paradigm critics like Fung have protested against, this new and improved "positive image" of the Asian American top comes about at the expense of relegating other Asian men to the same old, tired, abjectified position of unassimilable, forever bottomhood. Though the Asian penis has been found, there are only a few inches of it to go around, or it comes to resemble another white pink dick, tinted yellow.

Even though I have been discussing the Americanization of Brandon Lee in relation to his Asian costars, it is noteworthy that a similar process is at work in the mainstream gay videos that he appears in as well. *Big Guns 2* is a generic Catalina gay video taking the military as a sexual background. Porn star Steve Rambo begins the tape by introducing the cast through a voice-over, read as if from a journal entry. While conventional descriptions of white, macho, army-porno types comprise most of the voice-over characterizations, descriptions of the men of color in the tape exploit racial stereo-types. For instance, Rambo describes the three black men as one group. (Tellingly, the sex scene with the three men is segregated; they do not appear in any other scene with the other actors.) The three blacks are portrayed as hypersexual studs; Rambo's voice-over makes references to a "six-foot-five monster of muscle and a tool between his legs that would make anyone's knees weak" and "a chest as hard as a rock and lips that could make a dead man come when he puts them into action." One Latino character is described as "streetwise from East L.A.," while another is said to possess a "burrito [that] was jam-packed with sour cream [and] was constantly being munched on." Whereas the black and Latino actors are ascribed racist characteristics, Brandon's Asianness is not explicitly commented on: "And finally there's Brandon. You might call him our mascot. I guess when you're as youthful-looking and cute as he is and feature a giant, fucking dick to boot, everyone wants to be your friend." There are no crass references to his egg roll, teriyaki sauce, smooth, hairless skin, or his Oriental exoticism. The video begins with everyone being awakened in boot camp by Brandon's moans while masturbating. Taking his role as mascot seriously, Brandon here acts as the instigator of the orgy action that ensues. Not only is he portrayed as just another army recruit, he is painted as a special member of the unit, someone who gets along with everyone *and* who everyone can get off to. In addition, it is also significant that before the video even begins, Brandon appears with Rambo in a public service announcement encouraging viewers to practice safe sex. The PSA functions as a paratext that further constructs Brandon as a porn star.

Although one could argue that the phrase "youthful-looking and cute" does not play off any Asian markers, a closer (and more anal) reading uncovers the connection between age and size that conventionally animates a specific popular American conception of Asian men. Various critics have highlighted the way in which Bruce Lee's small stature operates as a disguise —for instance, as a harmless, naive bumpkin—which contrasts with and intensifies the moment of transformation when he finally exhibits his spectacular fighting skills. Part and parcel of this revelation of agility coupled with sensuality is the pairing of Lee with huge opponents, such as Robert Baker in *Fist of Fury*, Chuck Norris in *The Way of the Dragon*, and Kareem Abdul-Jabbar in *Game of Death* (dir. Robert Clouse and Bruce Lee, 1978). This contrast in size produces in the audience the pleasure of seeing Lee's small, lithe body performing high kicks and knocking down his big opponents. For marginal audiences whose relationship with Lee's image is based on a primary identification, which is to say, an identification with a more perfect hero who "ultimately triumphs" despite extended duress and suffering, visual pleasure comes from watching the victory of the small and downtrodden over the giant, menacing other. In the same way, the uniqueness of Brandon Lee surfaces in references to his big dick. Numerous commentators have registered surprise and pleasure at the sight of such a dick on a small Asian man. Josh Eliot, the head director at Catalina who has directed Brandon in several videos, recalls being impressed by his cute face, but his great surprise came at the first sight of Brandon's dick, which inspired Eliot to add another scene for Brandon in *Asian Persuasion*. The porn magazine *Adam Gay Video xxx Showcase* puts it this way, "18-year-old Brandon has a hard-on almost as big as he is" (Lawrence 1998, 45). While this comparison stresses the large size of his cock, the comment implies that he has a small body out of proportion with his dick. Consequently, it mobilizes the image of Asian men as small and youthful. Hence the choice of vocabulary in "youthful-looking and cute mascot" in *Big Guns 2* does indeed call forth the picture of Asian men as boyish and youthful-*looking*, thus conjuring up the notion of a hidden disguise, of the Asian face as a mask: they might look youthful, but they're really not. This false appearance of youthfulness implies, nevertheless, that Asian men are not quite men, being neither manly nor masculine.[38] In *Fortune Nookie*, Jacob Scott, the white lawyer, comments repeatedly on the size of Brandon's big, hard cock, as if indicating a mild shock. He articulates in detail what he wants Brandon to do, telling him to show him the big dick and to stick it up his sweet little ass. The ultimate controlling bottom, Scott commands Brandon to get his cock hard so he can fuck Scott with it. But most striking, Scott repeatedly calls Brandon "boy." After asking Brandon whether he wants to fuck him like a man or like a boy (Brandon breathlessly responds, "Fuck you like a man"), Scott cranes his neck around and barks directions and orders while getting fucked by Brandon: "Fuck me hard. Yeah, harder! Fuck me like a man. C'mon, harder. That's a boy. Faster. That's it. Good boy!" While getting fucked like this, Scott is naked except for the tie that continues to hang loosely around his neck, signifying his "superior" position. The dynamics of this scene complicate any easy attribution of topness/fucker to masculine power and exceed the simple connection of bottomhood/fuckee with feminine passivity. Even though Scott gets penetrated, he remains in control, administering orders, but also visually and verbally dominating the sexual activity.

In spite of the fact that so many commentators both inside and outside the videos keep remarking on the size of Brandon's penis—which "ranges" from 8.5 to 10 inches, depending on which source one believes (based on visual evidence from the videos, I would say the former)—it must be pointed out that in the world of gay pornography, the size of Brandon's dick is not that extraordinary. The exaggeration and hype around Brandon's sizeable equipment, I would contend, can be attributed to its attachment to the body of an Asian man. As suggested in the *xxx Showcase* citation, the big dick attached to the body of a five-foot-seven Asian man is considered out of proportion. This question of weight-to-height proportion does hold a positive valence in the gay male sexual marketplace, judging from the frequent invocation of this requirement in personal ads in gay newspapers and on gay Web sites. Another, even more famous example of a relatively short porn actor with a weight-height-proportional body nicely setting off his humongous genitals is Jeff Stryker. However, we never hear remarks that Stryker's dick is out of proportion with his body *or* that it is as big as he is. Creative camera angles can easily correct any anomalous pairing of actors that might expose the secret of the vertically challenged yet well-endowed porn actor. A moment of mild shock and surprise registered for me when I watched Brandon Lee in a four-way scene from *Dial "S" for Sex*. He is standing next to Sam Crockett and merely reaches Crockett's shoulders. This medium long shot is held only for a minute or two before switching to a low angle underneath their cocks. From this worm's-eye view, Lee and Crockett, standing side by side, appear to be the same size; photographed this way, their similar stature thus implies their status as peers, as equal participants in the sexual scenario, objects of desire standing upright while getting their cocks serviced by kneeling partners (figures 2 and 3).[39]

The living room in which this four-way orgy from *Dial "S" for Sex* takes place is the same setting and actually the *exact set* for another of Brandon's videos, *Stag Party*. It is a typical southern California bungalow living room with French doors opening up onto a sunny backyard or balcony. This setting typifies most of the settings of Brandon's other videos—the middle-class, gay, white milieu of West Hollywood. As I suggested above, this constitutes a significant shift from the ethnic ghettos where previous Asian-themed porn videos were based.

Daniel Tsang, in a discussion of the mise-en-scène of recent gay Asian videos, has noted the prevalence of the vague, timeless space of a remote land in the majority of these tapes. These fantasies of the sensuous East, of "lands far away from urban life," position the viewer as either an actual or a virtual sex tourist. Tsang observes how the unmarked, unspecified "hotel rooms in unnamed cities or countries" in which the videos are filmed sug-

2. Brandon Lee, Sam Crockett, Brian Hawke, and Drew Andrews (clockwise from left) enjoy each other in *Dial "S" for Sex*.

3. In this shot from *Dial "S" for Sex*, Brandon Lee and Sam Crockett appear to be the same height.

gest the use of underpaid actors from Third World countries (1999, 474–75). Christopher Ortiz, writing about gay videos featuring Latino/Chicano men, has proposed that these tapes rely on racialized sexual fantasy by "[framing] their objects of desire within already culturally familiar codes" (1994, 84). Latino/Chicano porn titles exploit locations such as prisons, warehouses, restaurants, kitchens, and Latino/Chicano neighborhoods (i.e., the barrio). Whereas mainstream gay porn videos show characters fantasizing about performing specific sex acts set in specific pornotopic locales, the fantasy structure underlying the Latino/Chicano tapes depends on the exotic differences of race and ethnicity, even when these videos do not locate themselves explicitly in ethnic ghettos. Echoing Tsang's description of timeless, unlocatable Asian hotel rooms, Ortiz comments, "The bed that is not part of a recognizable setting reduces Afro-American men and Chicano/Latino men to their sex" (84). Though I previously described the secondary role of narrative in gay pornography, I feel it is still crucial to look at the racially marked motivation of the staging of sexual fantasies in the Brandon Lee videos. In other words, the viewer of a video like *Asian Persuasion* is not just watching sex between men, but what the bodies and the sex with/between Asian men look like. The racial and ethnic coding of the actors occupies a central place in the sexual fantasy.[40] For example, watching the excerpt of a sex scene between Brandon Lee and Brad Davis Mikado in the *Best of Brandon Lee* compilation, one entirely misses the point that Brad Davis is supposed to be read as Asian in this video. Seen outside the original context (*Asian Persuasion*), Brad Davis appears as just another white porn actor. The logic of these tapes bespeaks the need to exoticize/eroticize racial difference by conjuring up a generic, slapdash Orientalia that, paradoxically, aims to reference vague notions of cultural authenticity. Consequently, we see credits in chopstick fonts, East Asian names, and characters having sex for money in settings like Chinatown, Hong Kong, or Bangkok. Or, as Tsang notes, even when they are set in a no-place like anonymous hotel rooms in nameless countries, we are aware that this document of "fantasy" depends on the fact that the actors come from somewhere else, not from here in the United States, but from an ahistorical, unspecified Orient.

Along this same line, the text for the video box packaging of *Fortune Nookie* is written on white elongated rectangles made to resemble paper strips from fortune cookies: "You will travel soon to the Far East for a pleasurable experience you won't forget"; "Your love for men of Asian persuasion will increase and intensify"; and so on. The second-person address replicates the phrasing of fortune cookies, but also positions the viewer as not of the Asian persuasion—a Western (and most likely) white viewer. The video promises to deliver the Far East to the viewer or to bring him there virtually, thus confirming Tsang's point that the ideal viewer of these tapes is the sex tourist. However, though it does not explicitly announce it, the setting of *Fortune Nookie* seems to be contemporary Los Angeles. We can deduce this from such clues as exterior shots of a Silverlake neighborhood, the use of a white drag queen to play the role of the bitchy madam, Pixie, the southern California architecture, "guppie" furnishings, and the kitschy porno-set decoration of the rooms. Similarly, *Asian Persuasion* mobilizes references to the Far East in its video box packaging: "Do you need some persuading to experience a far east encounter? How about letting 8 ½ luscious inches make up your mind? How about smooth supple chested men giving you their eager, far east cocks standing firm in sweet scented nests of jet black hair. Super-hung Catalina discovery Brandon Lee has what it takes to persuade you. Just in case you need it!" The punning on the word *persuasion* activates two levels of meaning. The first refers to belonging to a religion or, in this case, a racial group, while the other meaning is a play on the verb *persuade*, implying a sexual seduction.[41] While one can appreciate the cleverness of the double entendre and the gimmicky rhyming, this emphasis on the viewer's *needing to be persuaded* to try a "far east encounter," to find Asian men desirable, to buy the video, depends on the "common" view of seeing Asian men as undesirable and unsexy. The video box text must provide evidence—such as "8 $\frac{1}{2}$ inches" of "far east cocks standing firm," "smooth supple" chests, and "nests of jet black hair"—in order to persuade the potential (white) porn consumer to lust after Asian men. Again, like *Fortune Nookie*, *Asian Persuasion* is actually set in contemporary Los Angeles, as we can see from the exterior shots of the L.A. skyline in the credit sequence, in the "house in the hills" that Brandon shows the Japanese buyer, and the fancy southern California home where Brad and his pool boys go to work cleaning pools. What the discrepancy between video packaging and actual diegetic setting suggests is that even when Asian men are removed from the ethnic ghetto of Chinatown and placed in the generic porno locales of West Hollywood, in conventional, pornographic historical time and space, they are still seen as carrying the timeless, mysterious, mystical Orient with them. Their inscrutable, exotic sexuality continues to hold hidden, unexploited "Far East" pleasures unknown to the white man.

In contrast to the persistent emplacement of Asian men in sexual encounters that can take place only in the Far East, Brandon Lee's crossover into the mainstream of gay porn videos concomitantly allows him to travel outside of the ethnic ghetto once and for all and set up residence in the contemporary urban gay male ghetto of West Hollywood. These tapes simply portray Brandon as a West Hollywood twink whose Asianness is never commented on. In *Dial "S" for Sex*, Brandon comes home to find his white boyfriend, Drew Andrews, jerking off while talking on the phone with an anonymous caller. Brandon and his boyfriend proceed to have sex together, and they are later joined by two (white) friends who drop by unexpectedly for a four-way orgy. At the end of the scene, we find out that Brandon came home on a lunch break and must go back to work. Before doing so, he reminds his boyfriend, "Don't forget that Mitch is coming by to pick up those papers. Don't forget to call him, okay? Gotta go. Bye." Neither the preceding sex scene nor anything that comes after narratively motivates this line. Its only purpose, it seems to me, is to establish Brandon as a regular guy living in generic pornotopia, in a tame coupledom occasionally spiced up by kinky sex. In *Stag Party*, Brandon plays one of the guys at a straight stag party, where participants watch straight porn videos while waiting for a female stripper to show up. Bored with the scene, Brandon goes into the bedroom to seduce another young partygoer, Sandy Sloane, who has passed out from too much drinking. These two twinks have sex in the bedroom, while the older men in the living room end up releasing their pent-up sexual energy in a group orgy. The only features that mark Brandon and Sloane off from the rest of the men at the party are their boyish looks and smaller size; their exclusion from the massive orgy seems to turn on these two differences of physical appearance. The video that locates Brandon most firmly in the West Hollywood gay scene is *Peters*, a porn remake of the Winona Ryder vehicle *Heathers* (dir. Michael Lehmann, 1989). Brandon plays the Winona/Veronica character, here called Daniel Sawyer. This typical American name erases any connection to a "Far East" identity. After throwing up on one of the Peters at an "exclusive" sex club, Chandler rebukes Daniel/Brandon and threatens to reject him from his West Hollywood in-group by telling him, "Might as well move to the Valley, Daniel."[42] Another reference to the West Hollywood gay world is invoked when Daniel/Brandon and his cohort Jack Long (who plays the Christian Slater role) make a rendezvous with the two bullies Buzz and Rahm at the Hollywood Spa, the largest gay bathhouse in Los Angeles. Taken together, these narrative elements demonstrate how Brandon Lee's appearance in mainstream gay porn recodes him into just another gay pornotopic character, carousing within the central space of gay, white, male, affluent West Hollywood. The color-blind casting of Brandon in the starring role of Daniel Sawyer in *Peters* signals the most extreme instance of his legitimation as an American.

In a context dominated by white, American, masculine physical perfection, what is it about Brandon that has enabled him to enter into the segregated world of mainstream gay pornography? I propose that Brandon's crossover is made possible by a certain degree of racial instability accruing to his star image. This ability to penetrate into the mainstream forms part and parcel of an undecidable (inscrutable, unfixed) Asian ethnicity.

In addition to their name, the other "coincidence" between Brandon Lee, cult star of *The Crow*, and Brandon Lee, porn star of *Fortune Nookie*, is their racial ambiguity. The son of Bruce Lee was hapa (half-Asian, half-white), a fact seldom mentioned as a result of Hollywood's typecasting of Brandon Lee as a martial arts actor. Consequently, most commentators are invested in establishing a patriarchal lineage and emphasizing the connections between father and son (the "Little Dragon" and "Son of the Dragon"). The racial/ethnic ambiguity of Brandon the porn star proves a bit trickier. For example, he first appeared in a gay porn video entitled *Glory Holes of* L.A.

(dir. Bianco Piagi, 1997) under the name of Sean Martinez. It was not until his second video, *Asian Persuasion*, that he took on the name Brandon Lee. In the context of mainstream gay video pornography, where young, white, well-built actors are the unquestionable norm, any departure from this type represents a "special niche," a context in which differences such as race become heavily commodified.

The "trouble with Asians" is the difficulty of telling them apart. But, as Richard Fung has noted, in the world of gay video porn, it is not necessary to discriminate the "minute" differences among Asians—he mentions national flags and martial arts schools. Rather, it suffices to connote cultural authenticity by conjuring an all-encompassing Orientalia. Thus most Asian actors have East Asian, or more specifically, Japanese-sounding names, such as Tenji Mito, Hiro Sukowa, Erik Tenaka, and Niko Time. Other actors take on Japanese first names and Chinese last names, like Tishiro Ho. Others Orientalize their names for an Asian tape, as in the case of Brad Davis Mikado and Jean Russo Chen. The former usually goes by Brad Davis in his other videos. The addition of "Mikado" implies a "hidden" Japaneseness in his person. Josh Eliot, director of *Asian Persuasion 1* and *2*, suggests the practical necessity of using "not quite Asian" actors like Davis in the Asian-themed videos in order to safeguard against the risk of Asian actors changing their minds and reneging on their commitment to appear in a video on the day of the shoot.[43] This bit of extratextual information notwithstanding, I think that the mixed-race reference in these actors' names also exploits the exoticism traditionally associated with interraciality in the United States. This transgression draws on the historical taboo, threat, and punishment against miscegenation. For instance, Gina Marchetti has called attention to Hollywood cinema's depiction of Eurasians as evil, deceitful, and dangerous. In the context of gay porn, the bi-/multiculturalism of mixed-race actors also provides a form of "the-best-of-both-worlds" exoticism, invoking difference but also similarity—threat and spice, as well as comfort and familiarity.

Far from being merely camp and kitsch (like the short, butch names taken on by white actors), naming in the Asian-niche videos plays a large role in the racial packaging of the tapes, since the producers are selling eroticized-exoticized racial and ethnic difference. Quentin Lee, who played Peekay Chan in *Shanghai Meat Company* (dir. Tony Chan, 1991), claims that the white producers of the video gave themselves Asian names in the credits in order to sell it as an authentic "by-Asian-for-Asian" videotape. Along these same lines, we can appreciate Brandon Lee's assumption of a recognizable Asian American name from a recent cult martial arts celebrity. This choice of name exploits the cultural association of Asian men in the popular imagination with the kung fu action genre. Inadvertently, he may have conjured up the racial ambiguity of the real Brandon Lee as well.

My friend John told me that his friend John ran into Brandon the porn star at a gay Asian club in L.A. (appropriately called Persu*asian*). John's friend spoke to Brandon and found out that his real name was also John and that he was "really" Filipino. Since acquiring this crucial bit of information through hearsay gay gossip, I have been able to ascertain the "fact," indirectly, from a forwarded e-mail from another Brandon Lee fan who claims to have received an e-mail from Brandon/John himself confirming his Filipino ethnicity. (He "remains" American; according to a gay video guide I consulted, Brandon/John was born in Mobile, Alabama, on March 18, 1979.) If we take Brandon/John's Filipino identity to be true, I propose that Brandon's previous appearance in gay porn as Sean Martinez reveals an attempt to present himself as a Latino, hence drawing on the closer association of Latinos/Chicanos with hypersexual appeal.[44] After deciding to appear in Asian-themed videos, it seems very significant that Brandon/John would choose a porn name aligned with East Asian and Asian American connotations. In the United States, there is an automatic association of Asia with East Asia. The Far East/East Asia axis grounds the Orientalist fantasies of gay pornography. To support this observation, I mention here, in addition to the Brandon Lee titles, several others in Catalina's Far East Features series: *Pacific Rim* (dir. Mitchell Dunne, 1997), *With Sex You Get Egg Roll* (dir. Peter Romero, 1999), and *Chew Manchu* (dir. Mark Jensen, 2000). In the discourse of Oriental sexuality—based on an *ars erotica* (erotic art), with its connotations of Eastern repression covering over kinky sexuality—the sexuality of Filipinos does not figure strongly. Regarded as dirty and impure, too mongrelized and Westernized from four hundred years of colonial contact with Spanish and American cultures, Filipinos are excluded from this exotic framework.

In an article about the taxi dance halls in Filipino immigrant communities of the 1920s and 1930s, Rhacel Salazar Parrenas (1998) refers to the threat posed by the interracial mingling between the "little brown monkeys" (the male Filipino laborers) and "white trash" (women who worked at these dance halls) to the hegemonic American discourse around racial purity represented by the eugenics movement. Jinqi Ling has noted that the classification of Filipinos as U.S. nationals and as Malays (rather than Mongolians) in the same period allowed Filipino men relative freedom of movement and interaction with white women.[45] Ling writes, "The invention of Filipino males' threatening sexuality is thus bound up with white men's concern about securing their social power, a concern brought to the point of crisis by Filipino workers' participation in the labor movement" (1997, 319). My brief references to Filipino male labor history in the United States aim to emphasize the historical coding of Filipino men as sexual threats to white American manhood. Along with the "corruption" of the Philippines by Western colonial forces, the image of the Filipino male as an "irresistible stud" prevented the incorporation of Filipinos into the exoticized, feminized, and domesticated (*because* distant and elsewhere) discourse of Orientalist, racial fantasies. It is this particular, historically inflected, racialized sexual dynamic that forces the transformation of John X to Sean Martinez—identities couched in the threatening, opaque, and vexed framework of Filipino American sexuality—to the more culturally intelligible (and easier-to-consume) Brandon Lee.

In his essay "Written on the Face: Race, Nation, Migrancy, and Sex," David Palumbo-Liu, looking at American social scientific discourse of the 1930s, explores how assimilation into American society was thought to enact both somatic and psychic transformation in the immigrant's body. Citing the work of anthropologist Franz Boas and the federally sponsored Immigration Commission, Palumbo-Liu shows how this discourse asserted that presence on "American soil" brought about changes in the European immigrant's head form. For instance, the European Jew's round head elongates, while the southern Italian's long head transforms into a shorter length. Whereas the faces and bodies of Eastern European and Mediterranean immigrants were amenable to appreciable changes once in the United States, "'orientals' . . . were not susceptible to such transformation, no matter how intense or lengthy their exposure" (1999, 86). Thus the Immigration Commission believed Asians should be excluded from the nation since they were seen as unalterably foreign and unassimilable. Palumbo-Liu discusses the work of sociologist Robert E. Park, who suggested that Asians could erase the physical signs of racial difference, and thus assimilate into the nation, through intermarriage with white Americans. Interestingly, Palumbo-Liu also cites Albert Palmer's *The Oriental in American Life* (1934), which claims, contra Boas and the government report, that American life did indeed affect the Asian body. In addition to noting the increased height of the American-born children of immigrants, Palmer remarks, "Changes in eyelids and eyelashes are also evident, but the most noteworthy adjustment is in the shape of the mouth and the general openness and responsiveness of the countenance. . . . [S]ooner or later, an enlightened and intelligent American public opinion will discover that . . . the Oriental masks are looking more and more like

American faces" (qtd. in Palumbo-Liu 1990, 90). Twenty years later, in the fifties, the long process of intermarriage advocated by Robert E. Park to biologically efface racial difference was rejected in favor of the more immediate technology of plastic reconstructive surgery to speed up what before would take generations. In the terms of this medical discourse, the "'narrow' eyelid [of Asian people] betrays 'dullness,' 'stupidity,' 'passivity'" and gives the impression of the Asian face as an inexpressive mask, as if hiding behind a disguise (90). By creating a "double-eyelid" and a higher bridge for the flat nose, the face is "opened up" and "a new 'person' emerges" (100). As a result, the physical reconstruction also ensures an attendant psychical transformation, thus making one's interior conform to the new Americanized face. Significantly, plastic surgery cannot turn Asian subjects into white Americans; they are transformed, rather, into white *ethnics*. They resemble Mexicans or Italians; their facial mimicry remains "not quite, not white."

Adapting the insight from Palumbo-Liu's very rich essay, I contend that the conventionally handsome face of Brandon Lee functions as a product of a "mongrelized" Filipino American interracial mixing after many generations. The colonial and imperialist legacies of the Philippines have produced what some of my Filipino friends jokingly refer to as a "mutt," a mixture comprised of indigenous Filipino, Malaysian, Chinese, Spanish, and American biological and cultural, somatic and psychical ingredients. One can "see" this "mutt" mixture reflected on the face of Brandon Lee as a set of hybridized, Westernized facial features: most meaningfully, the double eyelid, the tall nose bridge, and the brown skin. It is also this "un-place-able" face that permits a crossing of ethnicities. Because "all Orientals look the same," the face of Brandon animates a variety of racial connotations, going from John X to Sean Martinez to Brandon Lee. John, Sean, and Brandon's ability to *pass* resides precisely in exploiting this "hidden" disguise of the exotic, inscrutable Asian mask in order to put forth a legible, real, average American face.[46] As my friend John, a hapa, points out, "Compared to the other Asian guys he's with in the videos, he's definitely a better watch. The other guys usually aren't cute. . . . They make funny noises when Brandon Lee fucks them and have that annoying Asian edge to them—kind of like my brethren that I shy away from at gay Asian clubs."[47] In contrast to the "closed," slanted, single-lidded eyes and foreign, FOB demeanor of his Asian costars with their often unintelligible verbal recitals, Brandon's open American face is "a better watch," and the viewer can understand him and relate to his Valley Guy accent without great effort. Furthermore, doesn't the register of surprise and pleasure at seeing an "American" dick attached, out of proportion, to the face and body of an Asian American man, doesn't this attention, blown out of proportion—on what are after all only eight and a half prime inches of cut meat—indicate another *pass*port? Isn't this big (enough) dick the appeal and the prerequisite, the *pass* for admittance into the world of white gay mainstream pornotopia? Is this the dick that is finally big enough to rival, and with which to fuck, white men?

Pinups, Porn Stars, FOBS

In her essay on the 1991 Asian Pacific Islander Men's Calendar, Sau-ling Wong offers a critique of the project which seeks to contest the image of Asian men as asexual "geeks and nerds" by focusing on Asian men's "virility and sexuality." Wong observes that by rejecting one set of "negative stereotypes," this sincere and earnest intervention inadvertently reinscribes another set seen as more "positive," that of the model minority. Conforming to its politically progressive stance, the calendar presents "real," sexy Asian American men by depicting a group of pan-ethnic, respectable, professional men who have successfully assimilated into American society. They are all college-educated; most possess impeccable activist credentials; and all are hard at work on their respective careers. The calendar represents sexy Asian male bodies in the mode of arty erotica by deploying the codes of black-and-white studio portraits and tasteful seminudes; thus it distances itself from any association with the crass, colorful beefcake of pornography. Wong writes:

> In the process of dissociating itself from the soft porn aspect of the pinup genre, the denerdification project of the APIM calendar cannot help invoking—*and reinforcing*—precisely the discourse that it claims to contest [namely the model minority myth]. . . . [It] replicate[s] a rather one-dimensional, consistently class-biased portrait of the Asian American male: urban, college-educated, upwardly mobile, white-collared or black turtle-necked. Conspicuously absent are grocers, waiters or blue-collar workers whose physically demanding work, I imagine, must be conducive to muscular development without benefit of Nautilus machines. (1993, 68)

One can see clear parallels between the privileging of the sexy, urban, college-educated, middle-class Asian American male over the unassimilated grocer, waiter, and blue-collar worker in the APIM calendar and the making of Brandon Lee as a desirable West Hollywood twink in contradistinction to his less-than-appealing Asian costars with their working-class status, Chinatown address, bad accent, bad hair, flat face, small dick, and propensity for bottomhood. My preceding analysis of the star-text of Brandon Lee has repeatedly foreground its insistence on the construction of Brandon as an assimilated American and as a masculine top, qualities which accord him the status of gay (Asian) American porn star. One important lesson to be learned from the foregoing discussion is the limited potential of reversing the paradigm of the passive, Oriental, skinny, houseboy bottom by replacing it with one claiming that Asian men are *really* active, American, big-dicked, butch tops. In other words, by linking sexual dominance and desirability with porn stardom, topness, and hegemonic white American masculinity, one risks relegating Asian men again to the same position of sexual submission and abjection, with its reinscription of anonymity and bottomhood.[48] In addition, this essentialist and binary coding of white American/top and foreign Asian/bottom serves to further foreclose any consideration of the pleasures and agency of the bottom, whether white, black, Latino, or Asian. To be sure, a more critical consideration of the dynamics of top and bottom would trouble any easy equation of topness with masculinity and dominance and bottomhood with femininity and passivity.

In his book *Racial Castration*, David L. Eng offers a new model for critically intervening in the Asian American cultural nationalist project centered on a homophobic, misogynist, heterosexual male subject-citizen. In the place of Frank Chin and his colleagues' assertion of an Asian American identity based on the domestic and the national, Eng articulates a transnational and diasporic critical methodology for understanding the complexity of Asian American subject formation at the turn of the century. Instead of a whole, pure, and heroic male subject, Eng proposes the concept of a split subjectivity, divided between "over here" and "over there." This suggestion for broadening the scope of Asian American studies is politically necessary as we take into account the ongoing interpenetrations between the United States and the Pacific Rim in transnational capital, immigration, and labor. Eng reminds us that we cannot adequately understand patterns of migration and immigration from places like Vietnam, South Korea, and the Philippines without taking into consideration past and present neo-imperialist practices perpetrated by the United States in these countries. In addition, the fact that the majority of Asians living in the United States are foreign-born speaks to ongoing social, cultural, economic, and political connections between "over here" and "over there" for many contemporary Asian American subjects. Eng writes, "If earlier Asian American cultural nationalist projects . . . were built on the political strategy of claiming home and nation-state through the domestic and the heterosexual, a new political project of thinking about these concepts in Asian American studies today would seem to center around queerness and diaspora—its rethinking of home and nation-state across multiple identity formations and numerous locations 'out here' and 'over there'" (2001, 219).

What I find extremely provocative about Eng's formulation is the political necessity and productive strategy of thinking about the politics of Asian American sexuality and identity beyond the borders of an American context. While I understand the need to assert the claim of Asians as Americans, *without* the hyphen, in the face of our being seen as unassimilable aliens, an overly defensive gesture of disavowing any connections to Asia runs the risk of "whiting" us out entirely and fails to capture the complexity of our collective histories. In looking at the more positive and progressive depiction of Brandon Lee as Americanized, we can see how this is accomplished at the expense of the business-as-usual, Orientalist marking of other Asians as being forever foreigners, exoticized and repudiated, and presented as forever bottoms for the white sex tourist's consumption. Instead of the usual focus on the Asian male as the object of somebody else's fantasy, of the body that is *acted on* by another, the proposal to think about identification and desire beyond white masculine homonormative configurations of the nation-state might entail a challenge to place the gay Asian American male *immigrant*-subject at the center of the pornographic fantasy scenario. This does not mean creating and prescribing more politically palatable positions for the Asian subject as either a butch top, a controlling bottom, or a bland, versatile, polymorphous sexual performer. Rather, it aims to mobilize, in a self-reflexive manner, a multiplicity of sexual scenarios where the Asian American immigrant figures as the central desiring subject, all the while retaining and exploiting the sexual turn-on of power differentials. As queer experimental video artist Wayne Yung—born in Hong Kong, raised in Edmonton, living in Hamburg—expresses it:

Myself, as a potato queen [Asian who dates white men], or at least right now as a potato queen, I would really be interested in seeing gay white men on screen who somehow expressed desire for Asian men but in a way that would turn me on as an Asian. That would mean a guy who wasn't into dominating me or making me submissive or stereotyping me basically. That could be sexy too, true, but I guess the only way to get around that is to have producers, writers and directors create the porn they would want to see as gay Asian men. (qtd. in Cho 1998, 62)[49]

Family Reunion: Blood, Cum, and Tears

I would like to end by staging a fantasy scenario of my own, from my position as a queer Asian immigrant-spectator invested in the production of a gay Asian American male immigrant pornography. In this fantasy sequence, the long-dead father, international cult martial arts hero Bruce Lee, is reincarnated in order to meet his illegitimate gay son, porn star Brandon Lee. By reading the exhibition of Bruce Lee's martial body alongside Brandon Lee's pornographic one, I wish to challenge the commonplace view of the martial arts genre as a threatening and violent arena stripped of all sensuality and eroticism. Conversely, juxtaposing Brandon's pornographic positions next to Bruce's martial arts moves brings back the *difference* of Brandon's performance as an Asian American porn actor. The first fantasy clip is drawn from Brandon's video *Asian Persuasion 2*. The scene shows Tommy Lin, an aspiring porn star, seated in the waiting room of Catalina Video watching Brandon Lee, the porn star, perform a solo-jerk on the TV monitor. Brandon directly addresses Tommy (and by implication, the porn viewer), throughout his masturbatory performance. In this scene, a great deal of pressure is exerted between his position as the top—the subject acting on the viewer—and as bottom—as the object of someone else's desire. While on his stomach humping a pillow, Brandon looks at the camera: "I want my ass eaten out really good. . . . Nice tongue in my hole." He fingers and spreads his hairless asshole. But then he shifts from this bottom position (getting eaten out) to top: "Bend your knees so I can fuck you. . . . I need a tight ass for my cock." However, what we immediately see is his spread butt cheeks. At the end of the scene, he turns over on his back, shoots on his own face, and ends by wiping his cheeks and eating his own cum, while looking directly at the camera (figure 4). The second clip shows Bruce Lee in his final showdown with the evil Chinese villain, Han, in *Enter the Dragon*. In this film, Lee is recruited by the British government to enter Han's martial arts tournament in order to investigate Han's female sexual slavery ring and heroin trafficking. While Lee agrees to be sent as a secret agent, he is also there to avenge the death of his sister. In the final confrontation, Lee tells Han, "You have offended my family. And you have offended the Shaolin Temple." During their final face-off, Han claws Lee's face and naked torso with his

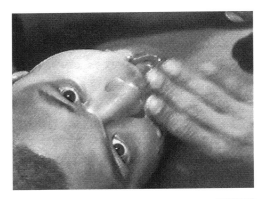

4. Brandon Lee swallows his own cum in *Asian Persuasion 2*.

5. Bruce Lee tastes his own blood in *Enter the Dragon*.

metal-bladed prosthetic hand. In response, Lee wipes the blood from his mid-torso wound and licks the blood, all the while sustaining intense eye contact with Han (figure 5). After performing a high kick to Han's face, Lee lands on his feet, stands upright, and forcefully spits out the blood.

Bruce Lee's dramatic tasting of his own blood signifies an acknowledgment of his body as clawed, wounded, suffering—the hardness of the muscle-bound body finally penetrated. The touching and licking of his own blood, while emphasizing the body in pain, powerfully express his lifeblood, the reinvigoration of his physical strength. The menacing shrieks and grunts also call to mind the aggression of a wild animal that has "tasted blood." The licking represents a challenge to the opponent, a retrenchment of masculine power, and his ultimate triumph over pain. By contrast, Brandon's ejaculation indicates a sign of authentic satisfaction and pleasure. But complementary to Bruce Lee's bloodthirsty gesture, his coming in his own mouth suggests a recycling of Brandon's own man-juice, of his virility. It also recalls the practice of ingesting one's partner's cum in the pre–AIDS era gay porn of the seventies, where the act signals sexual passion at the end of a sex scene. In the context of the post-AIDS solo-jerk, the eating of cum represents a resignification of risk and sexual taboo associated with the exchange of bodily fluids. The scene thematizes the importance of masturbation and the important role of pornography in affirming this sexual practice in the age of AIDS.[50] Most significantly, however, as with Bruce and his blood, Brandon's ingestion of his own cum points to the destabilizing of his body as hard and impenetrable. Yet while Bruce Lee's ingestion of and spitting out blood indicates an acknowledgment of the body's porousness, it simultaneously recuperates this vulnerable moment into a demonstration of how this body endures and triumphs over the violation. Conversely, Brandon's self-facial dramatizes the enormous pressure brought to bear on the racially inflected fantasy of an Asian top porn star performing for another Asian man who desires him and desires to be like him. Moreover, the coming and shooting on his own face can be seen as a complex negotiation of the way in which an Asian American top porn star must also accommodate and submit to the desire of a white spectator. Finally, the fact that this transpires in a scene where an Asian man is performing sexually for another Asian man points to the new, liberatory possibility of our desires finally being addressed, for and toward one another. And yet this invocation of a self-conscious "sticky-rice" (Asian-into-Asian) scenario within a highly mediated scene—through the separation of porn viewer (Tommy Lin) from porn star (Brandon Lee) on the TV screen—suggests that sex between Asian men remains a self-contained, narcissistic, and ultimately solitary masturbatory practice; it remains an impossible, pornographic fantasy.[51]

Notes

I would like to extend my gratitude to Linda Williams for her invaluable support of this project from its inception. I would also like to thank Thomas Waugh, Eve Oishi, Jake Gerli, Minette Hillyer, Doug Au, and Dredge Byung'chu Kang for their helpful suggestions on how to clarify and strengthen my arguments.

1   Throughout the essay, I frequently refer to Brandon Lee the porn star by his first name (instead of his last name as convention dictates) in order to prevent confusion with the other major Lee figure in my paper, Bruce Lee. More significantly, by using "Brandon," I wish to foreground the Americanness of this forename over the more Chinese-sounding surname "Lee." As I argue, the American coding of this first name is essential to this porn actor's legibility as a porn star. Calling a man by his first name draws on an association with youth, another element that is central to Brandon Lee's image. In addition, my use of "Brandon"

alludes to the practice in fan cultures (including gay male porn fan culture) of referring to celebrities by their first names, as if stars were just ordinary next-door neighbors instead of extraordinary fantasy objects endowed with beauty, talent, wealth, and renown. In adopting this same practice, I register my position not merely as a distanced critic of this porn actor's work, but also as an avid fan.

2 Brandon Lee may not be the "first" gay Asian American porn star. Hapa (half-Asian, half-white) stars like Jordan Young have been quite successful and even more prolific. However, these stars have never been explicitly coded as Asian, but instead have appeared only in mainstream gay videotapes.

3 Gay slang for a generic, cute, boyish young man, implicitly coded as white.

4 Conducting close readings of only three videos in his essay, Fung restricts his analysis to American-made videos with Asian themes because the Japanese and Thai productions "come from cultural contexts about which I am incapable of commenting. In addition, the fact that porn from those countries is sometimes unmarked racially does not mean that it speaks to my experience or desires, my own culture of sexuality" (1991, 164). I adopt an approach similar to Fung's in my analysis of Brandon Lee's videos. Writing in 1991, Fung considers the work of "the only Asian to qualify as a gay porn 'star,'" who goes under the names of Brad Truong or Sam or Sum Yung Mahn. Below I explore the importance of names and the naming of Asian American porn actors in a more in-depth manner.

5 The scene in question has Robbie, a white karate student, telling a fellow class-mate his sex dream about their karate teacher, Greg. In the dream, shown as a cutaway, Greg rescues Robbie from "an evil samurai." As part of his expression of gratitude, Robbie lets Greg fuck him. While Robbie appears as himself (that is, white) in the video up to this point, during the fucking scene, he "turns Japanese": Sum Yung Mahn plays Asian Robbie in the bottoming sequence.

6 Darrell Y. Hamamoto locates one rare instance of an appearance by an Asian American man in the porn film *Once upon Annette* (dir. Annette Haven, 1978). Hamamoto writes: "A White woman (Tina Orchard) and her mate (James Fong) are shown blithely romping through a meadow, both wearing only animal skins, in Neanderthal fashion. As pseudo-Sinitic music plays in the background, the couple pause to caress each another [*sic*]. Across the way, a similarly clad White caveman (David Blair) spies the couple making out. He sneaks up on the two and, shouting caveman gibberish (the inter-title translation reads, 'Eat Chinese — and half-hour later you want more'), runs off the Yellow man with a club before he can deposit Asian genetic material into the White woman" (2000, 74).

7 Although two of the directors of Brandon Lee's videos remain the same (Chi Chi LaRue and Josh Eliot) and there is an overlap in the time of production (1997–98), the crossover I am suggesting has less to do with Lee jettisoning one market/audience for another over a period of time. Instead, I am arguing that there exists a shift in the casting and coding of his image from the Asian-themed videos to the mainstream productions. The relatively small size of the gay porn industry and its rapid production schedule allow for the simultaneity of

Brandon Lee's appearance in both the Asian-themed and mainstream tapes, or rather, their contemporaneous release on the market. I shall argue below that it is precisely the (il)legibility of this porn actor's racial coding that makes possible his cross-appeal to both mainstream and Asian-niched audiences. His racially mixed face and body make him desirable to both white and Asian men.

8 The concept of *border cases* comes from Valerie Smith, who uses it to describe "issues that problematize easy assumptions about racial and/or sexual difference, particularly insofar as they demonstrate the interactions between race and gender" (1990, 272). Thanks to Eve Oishi for bringing this term to my attention.

9 Similar racist, exclusionary immigration policies and the legal frameworks maintaining them existed in Canada as well. See Richard Fung's impressive experimental documentary, *Dirty Laundry* (1996), for an imaginative exploration of the homoerotic bonds between Chinese men usually suppressed in conventional, heteronormative accounts of bachelor societies in late-nineteenth-century Chinese immigrant communities in North America.

10 The term *the third sex* originates from the German gay movement in the nineteenth and early twentieth centuries. Magnus Hirschfeld and his colleagues in the sexual emancipation movement, the Scientific-Humanitarian Committee, believed that lesbians and gay men represented a "third sex," or an in-betweenism, due to their difference from "real" (read heterosexual) women and "real" men. This term has been self-consciously reclaimed by modern-day gays and lesbians to articulate a queer radical politics and activism. An interesting example of this tendency can be seen in a popular dyke punk band from Olympia, Washington, which calls itself The Third Sex.

11 In their violent repudiation of the image of Asian men as effeminate sissies— "closet queens like Charlie Chan and . . . homosexual menaces like Fu Manchu" (qtd. in Eng 2001, 34)—Chin and his colleagues sought to reclaim and recover a lost Asian American masculinity premised on an "original manhood that is U.S.-centric and thus derived from a historical and mythological context of early Asian immigrant laborers," as seen in romanticized western figures like the "adventurous cowboys," the "indomitable pioneer," and the "brawny working-class laborer laying the railroads" (Wong and Santa Ana 1999, 191).

12 For example, we can see how the conflation of Asian Americans with Asians was cruelly enacted with the incarceration of Japanese Americans during World War II. In April 2001, the same dynamic was played out in the American responses to the U.S. spy plane–Chinese fighter jet standoff, in which American talk show hosts called for the internment of Chinese Americans and boycotts of Chinese restaurants.

13 While I look at the complex coding of Brandon Lee as an (Asian) American at length below, it is worth noting that the dominant perception of Bruce Lee as a *Chinese* martial arts superstar is not altogether accurate. Bruce Lee was born in 1940 in San Francisco, California, to a Eurasian mother and a Chinese father (who was touring with the Cantonese Opera Company). Lee's family returned

to Hong Kong when he was one. He began his film career as a child actor in Hong Kong, appearing in films from the late 1940s through the 1950s. When Lee turned nineteen, his parents sent him back to the United States due to his street fighting and also in order to retain his U.S. citizenship. At twenty-one, he enrolled at the University of Washington and studied philosophy. In 1964, his stellar performance at a karate championship in Long Beach, California, led to a "discovery" by William Dozier, the producer of the television series *Batman*. In 1966–67, he appeared on American television as Kato in *The Green Hornet*. Although cancelled in the United States, the TV show made Lee a huge star in Hong Kong. In 1971, on a return trip to Hong Kong on family business, Lee was offered a starring role in a movie, an offer he readily accepted. The film, *The Big Boss* (dir. Wei Lo, 1971), became a phenomenal success in Hong Kong. In the same year, he was rejected for a role in an American TV series (later broadcast as *Kung Fu* [1972], which featured the white actor David Carradine). It was not until after the immense success of two additional Hong Kong productions (*Fist of Fury* and *The Way of the Dragon*) that Hollywood's Warner Brothers decided to capitalize on Lee's box office draw by collaborating on a coproduction with a Chinese film company. Ironically, Lee died under mysterious circumstances one month prior to the release of *Enter the Dragon*, the film that established him as a worldwide superstar and instant cult hero.

14 This was Lee's second film; it was also released as *The Chinese Connection*.

15 I don't mean to suggest that *all* of Lee's films should be read as "anticolonial." For example, in his first kung fu feature film, *The Big Boss*, Lee's character, Cheng Chiu-on, and his cousins are employed as (presumably illegal) migrant workers at an ice factory in Thailand; the villain in the film is their drug-trafficking boss. Thus the narrative conflict against a tyrannical oppressor is couched in terms of class.

16 The film was released in the United States as *Return of the Dragon*.

17 Commenting on the appeal of the kung fu genre to the black American audience, David Desser observes how "kung fu films offered the only nonwhite heroes, men and women, to audiences alienated by mainstream film and often by mainstream culture. This was the genre of the underdog, the underdog of color, often fighting against colonialist enemies, white culture, or the Japanese" (2000, 38). Jachinson Chan and Gina Marchetti have argued that the violence in Bruce Lee's films can be read as a metaphor for the Vietnam War, in which the small Asian underdogs battle successfully against the technologically advanced American imperialists. See Chan 2001, 87–88. For another interesting account of the African American reception of kung fu cinema, see Ongiri 2002.

18 For a more thorough discussion of the nationalism of Bruce Lee's films, see Teo 1997 and Fore 2001, 117–22.

19 An interesting instance of how this buildup of suspense sometimes backfires is *The Big Boss*. In this film, Lee's character has promised his family that he will give

up fighting; tension mounts in different scenes where he witnesses rowdy young men inflict abuse on innocent people around him, yet he must restrain himself. Contemporary viewers' comments on the Internet Movie Database about the film complain of the "agonizingly slow" pacing of the first half of the movie, due not only to the poorly constructed story line and badly dubbed dialogue but primarily because Bruce Lee doesn't "kick ass" until halfway into the movie.

20 Kwai-cheung Lo asserts that Bruce Lee's films were dubbed in Mandarin at first release due to the Hong Kong Cantonese film industry's competition with Mandarin films at the time. The English dubbing in the American prints thus represents a second translation from the Cantonese original. In the same article, Lo also offers a novel reading of Lee's famous shrieks. As part of his wider argument about "Hong Kong identity . . . derived from an ambivalent emotional attachment to a fictional China," Lo interprets Lee's animalistic verbal eruption as a "hole" in this "new symbolic center for identity construction": "Though Lee's mouth is moving, the shrieks do not come from a particular source or a subject. The animal-like voice is all pervasive and free-floating, unfixed to any definite visual object on the screen. . . . Disembodied, this animal voice, this sound from nowhere, seems to have a life of its own, even as it is, conversely, looking for a body to fill out" (1996, 111).

21 In the 1950s, Kwan Tak-hing, famous for his portrayal of the Cantonese kung fu legend Wong Fei-hung, was also a highly trained martial artist who performed realistic, well-choreographed kung fu sequences on-screen. Stephen Teo maintains that Wong Fei-hung is the prototype for Bruce Lee's characters in the 1970s (1997, 51).

22 In fact, Clover refers to a television program produced in 1955 in which Kelly establishes direct connections between dance moves and the sports moves of such "hardy" American male sports as baseball, football, boxing, and basketball in order to counteract the "stigma of effeminacy" that has always been attached to dance (1995, 726).

23 Chiao has called attention to the "dance-like choreography" of Lee's movies, in which the solo number corresponds to the sequence where Lee performs with the nunchaku, the duet is analogous to the final showdown with the archvillain, and the chorus numbers resemble the fight scenes with hordes of disposable opponents (1981, 34).

24 The strobing effect setting off this climactic sequence finds a neat parallel with 1970s pornographic films' formal exhibitionism (e.g., the fireworks). Both straight and gay porn films from this era employ such innovative and then–avant-garde techniques as slow motion, optical printing, and repetition from multiple camera angles in order to build up and lengthen the climactic money shot. For example, the Mitchell Brothers pulled out all the stops during the unforgettable final money shot in their classic *Behind the Green Door* (1972); they exploited such visual pyrotechnics as extreme slow motion, superimpositions,

continuous dissolves, psychedelic colors, and solarization, effects worthy of the most celebrated of the American avant-garde filmmakers. I am indebted to Linda Williams for suggesting this interesting formal parallel.

25 It is important to note that Lee's films *do* contain extreme violence. One infamous scene of Lee sawing a man's head open and another showing him sticking his fingers into the villain's torso from *The Big Boss* had to be edited out of the U.S. version of the film in order to escape an X-rating. Nevertheless, I agree with Tasker's perceptive critique that Western critics' exclusive attention to the gory violence in his films is used to offset and disavow the homoeroticism of Lee's handsome face, on-screen charisma, and his half-naked body under duress.

26 However, the issue of Bruce Lee's "asexuality" is complicated by the fact that Chinese codes of masculinity (*wu*, or martial masculinity) stipulate that involvement with a woman indicates weakness, "losing control," for a martial arts hero. Thus "manliness" in Chinese contexts becomes translated as "asexual" in Asian American critical analyses of Bruce Lee. Thanks to Chris Berry for bringing the Chinese archetype of wu masculinity to my attention. The complex cultural and historical codings of Asian and Asian American masculinities suggest the necessity of situating discussions of Asian American masculinity and sexuality in a transnational context, something that I am unable to undertake here due to space constraints. See Louie 2002.

   I understand the muting of Lee's sexual intensity as a recontainment of the threat posed by Asian male sexuality (for example, as part of the same process of the Asian male body's policing we saw in antimiscegenation laws and employment discrimination in nineteenth-century North America). Lee's virile, powerful presence is tolerated (indeed, celebrated) precisely because it remains untainted by the domain of sexuality. The uncorrupted, puritan asexuality of the naive country bumpkin sets Lee off from the crowd and precludes any sexual contact with either women *or* men. In his chapter on Bruce Lee as a Chinese American male object of desire, Jachinson Chan rereads Lee's asexuality in terms of sexual indeterminacy and "ambi-sexuality." He notes that while Lee's nationalistic masculinity is posed against the traitorous effeminacy of the homosexual characters, Lee's character does not reject outright the (homo)sexual objectification of his body. Chan points out that in fact both female and gay male characters sexualize Lee's body in the films; yet because he does not commit "himself to any form of sexual union, Lee exhibits an ambi-sexuality that is characterized by an indeterminate sexual identity" (2001, 78).

27 In *Hard Core*, Linda Williams establishes connections between the genres of the musical and the feature-length heterosexual porn film. However, the direct transcription of Williams's generic formulation to gay porn would be tenuous due to the negligible role of narrative elaboration in contemporary gay videos.

28 In "Coming to Terms," Richard Dyer famously argues that narrative forms the basis of gay pornography. He maintains that there is narrative even in the most

minimal pornographic loop: the narrative drive toward coming. While in complete agreement with Dyer's important analysis and groundbreaking critique of the central thrust of gay pornography (and male sexuality in general) as being fixated on "visible coming," I am underscoring the lack of narrative *elaboration* in gay porn videos in comparison with kung fu cinema.

In spite of its advertised premise, *Absolute-Arid* actually has only one scene set in the desert; the other scenes take place in pastoral landscapes. Interestingly, *Absolute-Arid* received the Best All-Sex Video award at the Adult Video News "Gayvn" Awards in 2000. The inclusion of such an award category bears out my point regarding the secondary role of narrative in recent gay video porn. It is also worth noting that two of Falcon's recent popular titles, *Out of Athens—Parts 1 and 2* (dir. John Rutherford, 2000)—shot "on location" in Greece—are loose porn remakes of the Matt Damon homosexual thriller *The Talented Mr. Ripley* (dir. Anthony Minghella, 1999). However, reviews of this two-part video (TLA Video Web site's reviews at www.tlavideo.com offer a typical example), like most gay porn video reviews in general, focus almost exclusively on the sexual performances—the physical pairings and permutations among the well-known and up-and-coming actors—and give the story line only lip service.

29 In his experimental videotape, *Let's Just Kiss + Say Good-Bye* (1995), artist Robert Blanchon reedits 1980s porn videos in order to retrieve and reenvision these moments of narrative before and in between the sexual numbers, moments when these appallingly bad actors—with their feathered hair and pastel muscle shirts —deliver their dreadful lines of dialogue. Backed by the popular title song (recorded in 1976 by the Manhattans), the pornographic found footage—in its new, campy juxtapositions—evokes the bittersweet, "innocent" interstitial period between the wild sexual abandon of the gay seventies and the tempered grimness of the AIDS era of the eighties and nineties. Blanchon's recathexis of early 1980s gay pornography bespeaks a certain poignancy in "saying good-bye" to an important period in the history of gay sexuality in the United States, and it also serves as a memorial and tribute in its bid of farewell to the unnamed, forgotten actors in the porn videos who passed away as a result of the AIDS pandemic.

30 The link between martial arts, or more specifically, Bruce Lee, and pornography (albeit heterosexual) is casually made in Paul Thomas Anderson's *Boogie Nights* (1997). In a footnote to his article, Darrell Y. Hamamoto cites this link as "a breakthrough of sorts, [whereby] the exclusion of eroticized Asian American men in the dominant media is subverted" (2000, 82). In the film, Mark Wahlberg's porn actor character, Dirk Diggler, idolizes Bruce Lee and performs "karate chops" in front of the dressing room mirror before his porn shoots.

31 The explanatory power of juxtaposing Bruce and Brandon Lee next to each other resides in the fact that both represent border cases in which overlapping signifiers of "Asian" and "American" are expressed through performances of masculinity, violence, and sexuality. On the one hand, Bruce Lee's overt sexuality is sublimated into a visual display of masculine power in his struggles against

unjust, oppressive domination. As we shall see below, in the case of Brandon Lee, sexuality is the alleged focus, but the top-bottom positions in the sexual scenarios mask other cultural articulations. Both figures represent rare cases of virile Asian (American) male subjects, yet the two actors embody the enduring inequalities and contradictions between popular understandings of *Asian* and *American*, terms historically and culturally articulated through constructions of gender and sexuality. These two Asian (American) male stars, then, are symbols representing American popular culture's inability to accommodate a masculine, desiring Asian male subject in cultural narratives invested in viewing "Asian" and "American" as two unintegrated and incommensurable cultures. Most significantly, their status as exceptional, masculine Asian (American) media figures requires that the full range of sexual possibilities accruing to their images must ultimately be muted and contained: Bruce Lee through the overemphasis on the violence of his martial arts, Brandon Lee through the contradictions underlying his "passive autoerotic topness." (For an elaboration on this point, see especially my discussions below of *Fortune Nookie* and *Asian Persuasion 2*.) I am grateful to Eve Oishi for her help in fleshing out and making explicit these important connections between Bruce and Brandon Lee.

32 In my use of *West Hollywood* throughout this essay, I wish to mobilize the full range of connotations associated with this term in the popular imagination; that is, West Hollywood—like the Castro in San Francisco—has come to stand in for a specific "brand identity" or "gay lifestyle" constituted by a set of features such as race (whiteness), economic class (upper middle class), gender (male), body and fitness consciousness (gym-bunny), and attitude/worldview ("southern California" superficiality), features that construct this sexual minority not only as an extremely profitable consumer demographics for corporations but also as a shorthand expression used within the gay community to reference a certain type of gay male identification. In this manner, *West Hollywood* exceeds the physically demarcated zone of this southern California city denoted by "region" and instead signifies what Thomas Waugh has noted as an "intra-sexual identity/class/subculture." I am grateful to Waugh for bringing this critical point to my attention (personal communication, April 23, 2002).

33 The characterization of Brandon Lee and Brad Davis Mikado by their professions in this first scene signals another key departure from earlier gay male porn videos with Asian actors analyzed by Richard Fung. Fung observes that the "occupations of the white actors are usually specified, while those of the Asians are not. The white actors are assigned fantasy appeal based on profession, whereas for the Asians, the sexual cachet of race is deemed sufficient. In *Asian Knights* there are also sequences in which the characters' lack of 'work' carries connotations of the housewife or, more particularly, the house boy" (1991, 162). While it is interesting to take note of the "promotion" of Asian men from unpaid house boys to more respectable occupations (such as pool cleaning businessmen and real estate agents), a class-inflected sexual hierarchy based on the charac-

ters' professions can be discerned in the newer videos, as we shall see below in my discussions of *Asian Persuasion* and *Fortune Nookie*.

34 We assume the character is supposed to be Japanese from the earlier credit sequence, which informed us that his name is Tenji Mito.

35 Except for Brad Davis Mikado and Broc Hiyashi, the other two Asian actors, Hiro Sukowa and Tishiro Ho, speak with pronounced accents.

36 In response to Scott's aggressive commands, Brandon strips naked and poses in different positions (standing, bending over, sticking up his ass) while Scott remains clothed, rubbing his cock through his business suit trouser. After an extended sequence of Scott's dirty talk and Brandon's bodily display, Scott finally goes down on his knees and shows that lawyers indeed *do* suck.

37 Whereas the sex between Brandon and Time is mediated through class inequalities, another Asian-Asian scene in the same tape mobilizes the "transgression" of sex with straight men. The sex scene between two of the sex workers, Erik Tenaka and Tishiro Ho, occurs right after the viewer is told that Ho engages in sex work in order to support his two kids. This portrayal of Ho as a lower-class immigrant family man "forced" into having sex with men for money invokes the sexual frisson and taboo connected to the gay male fantasy of seducing an allegedly impossible object of desire, namely straight men, into gay sex.

While the sexual turn-on of straight men is a common feature in gay pornography of the seventies, it has since been abandoned (or deployed only infrequently) and discredited as enacting a politically incorrect sexual scenario based on an internalized homophobia. It is important to note that in addition to the historical coding of straight men in gay male subculture as working class, or trade, they are also often marked as racially other. As Christopher Ortiz points out, "One pervasive stereotype in gay pornography is the desire to be fucked by the Black or Chicano/Latino stud who does not reciprocate and may even be straight. . . . The fantasy of the straight macho Chicano/Latino man who fucks 'me' (a white man) allows for sexual relations between two men and at the same time excludes the Chicano/Latino man from being framed as a member of a gay community" (1994, 39).

If Ho is coded as straight and engaging in homosexual sex for economic reasons, what motivates his sex scene with a fellow worker? The attempt to depict Ho as a macho straight man in this scene—in order to reference his desirability for Tenaka and, by implication, the viewer—remains unconvincing in that his acting does not succeed in projecting a hetero-butchness; his voice is soft and hesitating, while his body type and gender style connote a boyish and femme quality. In order words, he does not "measure up" to the clean-cut, all–(Asian) American, masculine image of Brandon Lee.

38 Of course the word *mascot* itself already mobilizes political and racial connotations. In the United States, Native Americans have been protesting for years against the use of indigenous peoples as mascots, nicknames, symbols, and logos by various sports teams, for example, the Washington Redskins, the Cleve-

land Indians, and the Golden State Warriors. Thanks to Dredge Kang for bringing this point to my attention.

39 An interesting difference between the star image of Brandon, an Asian American porn star, and other mainstream white gay porn stars can be seen in a product "tie-in" that follows the video *Chew Manchu*. Though Brandon does not appear in the video, he is shown on the box of the "Samurai Penis Pump," a "prop"
used in the video. (The tag line is "As Seen in 'Chew Manchu.'") The Orientalist
marking of Asian male sexuality is neatly condensed in this sexual aid. Whereas
white gay porn stars like Jeff Stryker and Ryan Idol endorse "life-sized" dildos
cast from their own penises, Brandon Lee—though allegedly possessing a cock
too big for his own body—is used to sell a "hollow" device for the purpose of in-
flating the user's/viewer's penis. The use of Brandon in this ad conjures up two
possibilities revolving around the question of spectatorial desire and identification. Either Brandon has acquired his big dick by using the Samurai Pump, and
the intended consumer (a less-endowed porn viewer) desires to attain Brandon's
big dick by employing the pump; or Brandon is naturally well endowed and the
intended consumer can become like him by purchasing this equipment.

40 I am drawing on Ortiz's perceptive reading of gay Chicano/Latino porn videos
and adapting it to the Asian American videos. Discussing *Soul and Salsa* (dir.
Frank Jeffries, 1988), Ortiz writes: "The text, then, is structured so that the fantasy is not only that of watching men perform specific sexual acts with each
other, but that the spectator watches racially coded men—Afro-American and
Chicano/Latino men—engage in sexual acts with one another. The text provides
an idea of what sex between hot men of color might possibly look like" (1994,
84–85).

41 Of course the term also activates the word *Asian* embedded in *persuasion*. This
assonance has been creatively deployed by at least one (now defunct) gay Asian
club in Los Angeles, which calls itself Persuasian. The simple change in spelling
constructs the club as a queer Asian space where Asian men are the objects of
"pursuit"—by white men as well as by other Asian men.

42 In this West Hollywood context, and in hip L.A. parlance in general, the San Fernando Valley represents the social death of the dreaded suburbs.

43 Due to space and time constraints, I am unable to sufficiently explore the reasons for the lack of Asian actors in gay pornography. In addition to Josh Eliot,
Chi Chi LaRue also bemoans the difficulty of finding Asian actors: "Now it's very
hard to find Asian models. . . . They're very private. I think maybe they're worried, maybe their culture doesn't condone this kind of thing, maybe Asian guilt,
like Catholic guilt. That's why they'll come and do one or two films and they'll
disappear" (qtd. in Ko 1999, 85). Similarly, Oggi, an Asian American producer-
director of Exotic Videos, suggests, "It would take me forever to find models
here; that's one reason why I don't make them in the U.S. . . . The ones I interview, sometimes they will chicken out. When it gets right down to production,
they get scared. Asians aren't very brave, not like (non-Asian) American people

who don't care. What if my friends or parents see it?" (qtd. in Ko 1999, 85). Whether the paucity of Asian actors in gay porn can be attributed to cultural difference or the lack of demand (and adequate rewards) for them, I would reject the individualist and psychological explanations of guilt and timidity. Though he does not provide any "hard evidence" or theoretical elaboration, Hamamoto attributes the lack of Asian men—or what he refers to as the "exclusion of the Yellow man from video porn"—working *in front* of the camera to the "pervasive White-supremacist race/sex/power ideology": "The absence of Asian American men in video porn has nothing to do with having the 'right equipment' and the 'desire' to be in the business. The reason is found in the obdurate anti-Asian racism of the dominant society, which is reproduced intact by the thematic conventions of U.S. video porn" (2000, 75). Although I agree with Hamamoto's politically based diagnosis, I still wonder about the dismal show of Asian men in American porn, an industry riddled with niched and specialty markets always ready to exploit "sexual novelties."

44 The name Sean Martinez may also be read as Filipino, though I do not think most American porn viewers are savvy enough to be cognizant of the tremendous influence of Spain on Filipino culture. In spite of the fact that Oh Man! Studios' synopsis of *Glory Holes of L.A.* identifies Sean Martinez as an "Asian newcomer" on their Web site, I would contend that a viewer watching the tape without this extratextual information might not automatically make the assumption that Sean Martinez should (only) be read as Asian, let alone specifically Filipino.

45 That is, up until riots broke out in communities like Watsonville, California, where white men killed Filipino men for attracting white women at taxi dance halls.

46 See Stuart Gaffney's fascinating examination of another, even higher-profile queer Filipino mestizo in his experimental video, *Cunanan's Conundrum* (1997). Gaffney's brilliant reading of the mixed-race gay serial killer considers how this hapa's chameleon-like ability to "pass" and to "pass himself off" as many different identities troubles and defies traditional racial, ethnic, class, and gender categories. The media simultaneously portrayed Cunanan as white, Cuban, Arab, and Filipino, as well as a man who might be dressing up as a woman. During the FBI manhunt, Cunanan sightings were reported from all over the continental United States and Alaska. Cunanan, because he "looked like anyone of us," was spotted everywhere, yet he successfully eluded capture. An ironic note in light of my discussion at hand is the fact that Cunanan committed suicide by shooting himself in the face; his positive identification was ascertained through his fingerprints. According to Gaffney, the threat represented by this racially and ethnically illegible serial killer was read as a "natural" expression of his "deceitful" hapa Filipino identity (born of a Filipino American father and an Italian American mother) and was further attributed to his pathological, s/m-inflected, predatory homosexuality.

47 John Wirfs, personal e-mail. April 26, 2001. A big shout to John for recount-

ing his Brandon Lee sighting to me and for sharing his perspective on the porn star.

48 The fact that an Asian American gay porn star must be set off in clear opposition to the Oriental FOBs in these videotapes demonstrates the decisive part that Brandon Lee plays in maintaining border divisions (Asian/American, bottom/top), even as he embodies their blurring.

49 Throughout this essay, I have argued that the ideal viewer constructed by the Brandon Lee videos (and Asian-themed gay video pornography in general) is a gay white man. However, the insertion of my own experience and reactions to these tapes in these pages—in addition to my citations of Richard Fung, Wayne Yung, and my friend John—do offer some evidence that there exists an active gay Asian audience intellectually engaged with (and getting off to) this pornography. My personal interest in explicit sexual representation (of which gay moving-image pornography occupies a central position) arises from my own experimental video practice concerning issues around queer Asian American sexuality and identity as they intersect with and are articulated through popular cultural productions (e.g., Hong Kong pop stars, high-fashion supermodels, Vietnamese American popular music). More specifically, my attraction to Brandon Lee comes out of my previous artistic work on the politics and pleasures of sticky-rice (Asian-into-Asian) desire, explored in my videos 7 Steps to Sticky Heaven (1995), and Forever Bottom! (1999). Presented as a pseudoinstructional "workout" video, Forever Bottom! gently pokes fun at the notion of Asian men as passive bottoms in gay sex. Instead of proffering the more "positive" corrective that Asian men are "really" butch tops, I embrace the pleasures of unrepentant bottomhood by presenting a humorous look at the insatiable appetite of an Asian boy bottom who "gets fucked" everywhere (in the shower, in the kitchen, on the carpet, on the balcony, on the front lawn, at the park, on the beach, in the car). Through parodic performance and repetition, I mount a critique as well as a celebration of the politics of queer Asian bottomhood. The question of recentering the desiring Asian immigrant-spectator is dealt with in my videotape PIRATED! (2000). In this work, I employ pirated footage from such diverse sources as The Crimson Pirate (dir. Robert Siodmak, 1952) with Burt Lancaster, Querelle (dir. Rainer Werner Fassbinder, 1982) with Brad Davis, and Vietnamese American music videos, in order to rewrite the official account of my boat escape from Vietnam in the late 1970s. In place of a linear and coherent documentary narrative, this experimental video imaginatively transforms my personal tale of perilous escape as a young boy into one about homoerotic fantasies about Thai pirates and German sailors, fantasies reenacted and performed by me and my friends on a California beach. Working against the nostalgic notion of finding oneself by going back (to the motherland), the restaging of my "formation of identity" takes place on the high seas, during the boat journey, an in-between queer space/time not to be found again or recaptured, but only reimagined and relooped.

As these brief comments regarding my own art video practice intimate, the most sustained interventions into the arena of homoerotic Asian American visual representation at the turn of the century have taken place in the realm of queer experimental film and video. In the place of an amateur or commercial practice, something akin to a queer Asian American "counterpornography" seeking to muddle the mono-vision of the white sex tourist's gaze, the realm of low/no-budget queer Asian experimental film and video constitutes the one key area where the problematic depiction of the Asian male body in gay video porn comes under interrogation. It is also where more alternative and complex—not to mention smart, campy, and sexy—accented voices and "slanted visions" (to invoke a title from Ming-Yuen S. Ma) are articulated and mobilized. In addition, venues such as lesbian and gay film festivals around the world, Asian American (and Asian Canadian) film festivals, and the few remaining nonprofit alternative art exhibition spaces continue to lend support and offer exposure for this critical work. Some of the most exciting film- and videomakers engaged in these issues include Richard Fung (*Dirty Laundry*, 1996), Wayne Yung (*The Queen's Cantonese*, 1998; *Field Guide to Western Wildflowers*, 2000), Stuart Gaffney (*My Lover's Aunt Porn*, 2000; *Transgressions*, 2002), Ho Tam (*Season of the Boys*, 1997; *99 Men*, 1998; *Matinee Idol*, 1999), Michael Shaowanasai (*Exotic 101*, 1998; *To Be . . . or Not to Be: The Adventures of Iron Pussy III*, 2000), and Ming-Yuen S. Ma (*Slanted Vision*, 1995; *Sniff*, 1997).

On recent queer Asian American experimental film and video, see Oishi 2000. For a brief overview of queer Asian American cinema and the politics of curating such work in Asian American film festivals, see Han 1998.

50 This crucial point about the affirmative relationship of gay porn and masturbation (as a "reeducation" of desire) in the AIDS era is eloquently made by Richard Dyer in the conclusion of his essay "Idol Thoughts": "The most exciting thing of all about porn is that it affirms the delights of that most common, most unadmitted, at once most vanilla and politically incorrect of sexual acts, masturbation" (2002, 202).

51 My conclusion does not attempt to take issue with Dyer's valuable observation regarding the validating role of gay porn in promoting the "safest sex" of all, masturbation. What I am contesting is how this specific porno encounter between two Asian American men, one in which the Asian American porn star directly acknowledges and solicits the gaze and the desire of another Asian American viewer, can only be represented at a "once-remove," in a technologically mediated fashion via the *mise-en-abîme* of the porn viewing situation: the imaginary Asian American porn viewer at home watching Tommy Lin, the porn character, watching Brandon Lee, the porn star, playing (with) himself. It is worth noting that while Brandon Lee gets off by shooting on his own face and mouth, Tommy Lin does not reach orgasm. A white male Catalina Video office worker—who can be seen as part of the white gay porno-industrial apparatus—suddenly appears (conveniently right after Brandon Lee's cum shot on the monitor) to inform Lin that the producer is ready to see him, thus causing Lin's *onanismus interruptus*.

Works Cited

Adam Gay Video Directory 2001. 2000. Los Angeles: Knights Publishing.

Chan, Jachinson. 2001. *Chinese American Masculinities: From Fu Manchu to Bruce Lee*. New York: Routledge.

Chiao, Hsiung-ping. 1981. "Bruce Lee: His Influence on the Evolution of the Kung Fu Genre." *Journal of Popular Film and Television* 9, 1: 30–42.

Cho, Song, ed. 1998. *Rice: Explorations into Gay Asian Culture and Politics*. Toronto: Queer Press.

Clover, Carol. 1995. "Dancin' in the Rain." *Critical Inquiry* 21: 722–47.

Desser, David. 2000. "The Kung Fu Craze: Hong Kong Cinema's First American Reception." In *The Cinema of Hong Kong: History, Arts, Identity*, ed. Poshek Fu and Desser. Cambridge: Cambridge University Press. 19–43.

Dyer, Richard. 1992. "Coming to Terms: Gay Pornography." In *Only Entertainment*. London: Routledge. 121–34.

———. 2002. "Idol Thoughts: Orgasm and Self-Reflexivity in Gay Pornography." In *The Culture of Queers*. London: Routledge. 187–203.

Eng, David L. 2001. *Racial Castration: Managing Masculinity in Asian America*. Durham, N.C.: Duke University Press.

Espiritu, Yen Le. 1997. *Asian American Women and Men: Labor, Laws, and Love*. Thousand Oaks, Calif.: Sage.

Fore, Steve. 2001. "Life Imitates Entertainment: Home and Dislocation in the Films of Jackie Chan." In *At Full Speed: Hong Kong Cinema in a Borderless World*, ed. Esther C. M. Yau. Minneapolis: University of Minnesota Press. 115–41.

Fung, Richard. 1991. "Looking for My Penis: The Eroticized Asian in Gay Video Porn." In *How Do I Look?*, ed. Bad Object-Choices. Seattle: Bay. 145–68.

———. 1993. "Shortcomings: Questions about Pornography as Pedagogy." In *Queer Looks: Perspectives on Lesbian and Gay Film and Video*, ed. Martha Gever, John Greyson, and Pratibha Parmar. New York: Routledge. 355–67.

Hamamoto, Darrell Y. 2000. "The Joy Fuck Club: Prolegomenon to an Asian American Porno Practice." In *Countervisions: Asian American Film Criticism*, ed. Hamamoto and Sandra Liu. Philadelphia: Temple University Press. 59–89.

Han, Ju Hui Judy. 1998. "Creating, Curating, and Consuming Queer Asian American Cinema: An Interview with Marie K. Morohoshi." In *Q & A: Queer in Asian America*. Ed. David L. Eng and Alice Y. Hom. Philadelphia: Temple University Press. 81–94.

Kaminsky, Stuart M. 1976. "Italian Westerns and Kung Fu Films: Genres of Violence." In *Graphic Violence on the Screen*, ed. Thomas R. Atkins. New York: Monarch. 46–67.

Karr, John F. 2001. "Flip-Flopping Fun." *Bay Area Reporter*, March 29, 35.

Ko, Claudine. 1999. "My Search for Brandon Lee." *Giant Robot* 14: 83–85.

Lawrence, Doug. 1998. "Asian Persuasion." *Adam Gay Video xxx Showcase*, May, 45.

———, ed. 2001. *The Films of Josh Eliot*. Los Angeles: Knights Publishing.

Lee, Quentin. 1993. "Between the Oriental and the Transvestite." *Found Object* 2: 45–66.

Lee, Robert G. 1999. *Orientals: Asian Americans in Popular Culture.* Philadelphia: Temple University Press.

Ling, Jinqi. 1997. "Identity Crisis and Gender Politics: Reappropriating Asian American Masculinity." In *An Interethnic Companion to Asian American Literature*, ed. King-kok Cheung. New York: Cambridge University Press. 312–37.

Lo, Kwai-cheung. 1996. "Muscles and Subjectivity: A Short History of the Masculine Body in Hong Kong Popular Culture." *Camera Obscura* 39: 105–25.

Louie, Kam. 2002. *Theorising Chinese Masculinity: Society and Gender in China.* Cambridge: Cambridge University Press.

Lowe, Lisa. 1996. *Immigrant Acts: On Asian American Cultural Politics.* Durham, N.C.: Duke University Press.

Oishi, Eve. 2000. "Bad Asians: New Film and Video by Queer Asian American Artists." In *Countervisions: Asian American Film Criticism*, ed. Darrell Y. Hamamoto and Sandra Liu. Philadelphia: Temple University Press. 221–41.

Ongiri, Amy Abugo. 2002. "'He Wanted to Be Just Like Bruce Lee': African Americans, Kung Fu Theater, and Cultural Exchange at the Margins." *Journal of Asian American Studies* 5, 1: 31–40.

Ortiz, Christopher. 1994. "Hot and Spicy: Representation of Chicano/Latino Men in Gay Pornography." *Jump Cut* 39: 83–90.

Palumbo-Liu, David. 1999. "Written on the Face: Race, Nation, Migrancy, and Sex." In *Asian/American: Historical Crossings of a Racial Frontier.* Stanford, Calif.: Stanford University Press. 81–115.

Parrenas, Rhacel Salazar. 1998. "'White Trash' Meets the 'Little Brown Monkeys': The Taxi Dance Hall as a Site of Interracial and Gender Alliances between White Working Class Women and Filipino Immigrant Men in the 1920s and 30s." *Amerasia Journal* 24, 2: 115–34.

Smith, Valerie. 1990. "Split Affinities: The Case of Interracial Rape." In *Conflicts in Feminism*, ed. Marianne Hirsch and Evelyn Fox Keller. New York: Routledge. 271–87.

Tasker, Yvonne. 1997. "Fists of Fury: Discourses of Race and Masculinity in the Martial Arts Cinema." In *Race and the Subject of Masculinities*, ed. Harry Stecopoulos and Michael Uebel. Durham, N.C.: Duke University Press. 315–36.

Teo, Stephen. 1997. *Hong Kong Cinema: The Extra Dimensions.* London: British Film Institute.

Tsang, Daniel. 1999. "Beyond 'Looking for My Penis': Reflections on Asian Gay Male Video Porn." In *Porn 101: Eroticism, Pornography, and the First Amendment*, ed. James Elias et al. Amherst, N.Y.: Prometheus. 473–77.

Wayne, Bruce, ed. 2000. *Gay Adult Video Star Directory.* Laguna Hills, Calif.: Companion Press.

Williams, Linda. 1989. *Hard Core: Power, Pleasure, and the "Frenzy of the Visible."* Berkeley: University of California Press.

Wong, Sau-ling Cynthia. 1993. "Subversive Desire: Reading the Body in the 1991 Asian Pacific Islander Men's Calendar." *Critical Mass: A Journal of Asian American Cultural Criticism* 1,1: 63–74.

Wong, Sau-ling Cynthia, and Jeffrey J. Santa Ana. 1999. "Gender and Sexuality in Asian American Literature (Review Essay)." *Signs: Journal of Women in Culture and Society* 25, 1: 171–226.

Skin Flicks on the Racial Border:

Pornography, Exploitation,

and Interracial Lust

LINDA WILLIAMS

The question of interracial sexual relations remains virtually untouched.
— Jane Gaines

✳ It has been argued that the so-called classical cinema is regulated by a
semiotics of race relations posited on a single prohibition: "No nonwhite
man can have sanctioned sexual relations with a white woman" (Browne
1992, 8). Yet this prohibition is now regularly flouted, if not in today's Hollywood, then in that parallel universe in the San Fernando Valley where a line
of contemporary pornography labeled "interracial" aims specifically at violating precisely the taboos that once reigned supreme in Hollywood. Videos
with titles like *Black Taboo, Black and White in Living Color, Black Meat, White
Cream, White Dicks/Black Chicks, White Trash, Black Splash, Color Blind*, and
South Central Hookers speak about racial differences in sex in ways that elsewhere in the culture have often remained unspeakable. The loudest thing
they say is that *Crossing the Color Line* (to invoke yet another title) can be sexually exciting, especially the line between black and white that had been most
firmly erected by America's history of chattel slavery. If Hollywood has been
lacking in "honest and open explorations of the complexities of interracial
sexual attraction"(Gates 1991, 163), pornography and sexploitation cinema
have at least been willing to explore what more polite forms do not.

Racialized Sexuality

Abdul JanMohamed has coined the term *racialized sexuality* to designate the field in which Michel Foucault's familiar "deployment of sexuality" joins with a less familiar "deployment of race" (JanMohamed 1992, 94). Racialized sexuality is constructed around and through the policing of an (unequally permeable) racial border. Unlike "bourgeois sexuality," which emerged through a compulsive discursive articulation, "racialized sexuality" has been characterized by a "peculiar silence" (94). While Foucault teaches that bourgeois sexuality was articulated through the intersection of techniques of confession and scientific discursivity, racialized sexuality in the United States was more occulted, grounded as it was in the "open secret" of the white master's sexual desire for, and sexual use of, the female slave (104). JanMohamed argues that this sexual relation, which implicitly acknowledged the slave's humanity, threatened the maintenance of the racial other in a subservient position. "Unable or unwilling to repress desire, the master silences the violation of the border and refuses to recognize, through any form of analytic discursivity, the results of the infraction. This peculiar silence prevents the development of the kind of confessional and 'scientific' discursivity central to the deployment of sexuality as Foucault defines it" (104). The hypersexualization of the black body (male and female) in some ways parallels the "hysterization" of the white woman's body: both are represented as excessively saturated with sexuality. However, the discursive exploration of the female body ultimately integrates that body into the social body, while the discursive silence and lack of confession about sexual relations with the racialized other has aimed at segregating it from the social body. JanMohamed thus argues that racialized sexuality constitutes an inversion of bourgeois sexuality; where bourgeois sexuality is driven by an analytic will to knowledge, as well as an empiricist discursivity, racialized sexuality is driven by a will to conceal its mechanisms and a reliance on unempirical stereotypes (105).

The situation JanMohamed describes may be true enough for the era he describes (his essay centers on a reading of Richard Wright's *Native Son*). What happens, however, when the racialized body becomes the subject of pornography's unique brand of confession? If, as I have argued (1989), pornography seeks to confess the discursive "truths" of sex itself, what happens when racialized bodies are asked to reveal their "truths"? In this case, the "peculiar silence" that JanMohamed so aptly describes can turn into a noisy confession. In contemporary video pornography, the pleasures of sexual-

racial difference once the province of white masters have become commodified, mediated, and available to all.[1] Not unexpectedly, the power differentials of that original relation inform them.

Consider a contemporary porn video, marketed under the rubric "interracial": *Crossing the Color Line* (dir. Gino Colbert, 1999). Like most examples
of hard-core pornography, it presumes to confess the so-called truths of
sexual pleasure. But, unique to the subgenre of interracial pornography, it
speaks the once-silenced, taboo truths of racialized sexuality. The video consists of a series of interviews followed by sexual performances between African American and white performers who "frankly" discuss their feelings
and observations about race in the porn industry. The interview sections are
earnest and full of liberal sentiments of equality and the unimportance of
race; the sex sections are intensely erotic, often "nasty," and contradict the
preceding liberalism by a fascination with racial difference. Sean Michaels,
a handsome African American with a shaved head and athletic build, begins
in an initial interview with a complaint about racism in the industry and
concludes with an appeal to progress: "Young ladies in our industry, white
or black, are told that if you work with a black man you will probably have difficulty getting a job or gig dancing on the road in Southern states. . . . Okay,
well, if that's the truth, then what about the rest of the continent? . . . Sure,
the South is the South, we know this, but things are changing and they have
changed . . . if we don't wake up as a people, we are going to be left behind
by the rest of the world in the progression of our minds and our very souls."
Next, a white female porn performer, Christi Lake, speaks: "I think people
believe interracial sex is taboo just because of the Old South. The plantation
owner getting a hold of black females and such. They could do it, but no one
else, and so it was always kept taboo. I don't believe that, though. Having
sex with a person of another color is very exciting, very erotic. I look at the
person inside, not outside."

Both Michaels and Lake speak about the outdated taboos of the Old
South, and Lake explicitly asserts the contemporary ethic of color blindness. Yet these supposedly outdated taboos against interracial sex inform
and eroticize the subsequent sexual performance between them, proving
not that Lake looks "at the person inside" but quite the contrary: that "sex
with a person of another color is very exciting." Thus liberal, verbal protestations of the ethic of color blindness in the interviews give way to a dirty
talk common in porn video performances. Lake, in particular, noisily articulates a sexual pleasure taken in the observation of racial differences linked
to sexual differences. Sometimes this racialized sexuality becomes clearly

visible, as when Lake's verbal ejaculation, "fuck my tight, pink little pussy with your big black dick," can be seen in the form of an actually pinkish "pussy" next to Michaels's truly long, truly black-colored "dick." Sometimes, however, it is a suggestion not literally visible, as when Lake says, "put your spit in there and make it all wet and mix in with my white juices." Not all of the interracial sexual performances in this video verbally articulate such an overtly racialized sexuality, but once we have been cued by this first number to look for racial-sexual differences, such differences, visible and invisible, articulated and nonarticulated, seem to emerge. Thus, in the next interracial pairing, following similarly earnest interviews—this time between a white man, Mark Davis, and a black woman, Naomi Wolf—the usual visual pleasure of exaggerated gender difference typical of heterosexual pornography becomes complicated by race. When we see, for example, a pinkish penis and balls slapping up against a dark pubis, or creamy white ejaculate on black female skin, it is no longer just sexual difference that we see, but a racial one.

What does it mean to watch such comminglings of raced bodies? In a genre that tends to suspend narrative in order to scrutinize the sights and sounds of interpenetrating bodies—tongue in mouth, mouth around penis, penis in vagina or anus, hand on pubis, and so on—what does it mean when these bodies are not only differently gendered but also differently raced? And if it is possible to say that the pleasures of heterosexual pornography have something to do with the differences of gendered bodies, is it possible to say that pleasure can also be taken from the sight of differently raced bodies interpenetrating? Why is this once-forbidden commingling, as Lake puts it, "very exciting, very erotic"? Finally, is it possible to articulate the formal pleasures of the color contrast without sounding like or becoming a racist?

Pornography, because it has so long existed in determined opposition to all other forms of mainstream culture, has often become the place where sex happens instantaneously. Pornotopia is the land, as Steven Marcus once wrote, where it is "always bedtime," (Marcus 1974, 269) and where the usual taboos limiting sex are very easily overcome. Couples fall into bed at the drop of a hat, and nothing impedes the immediate gratification of myriad forms of sexual pleasure; the taboos that circumscribe and inform sex acts in the real world just melt away. Because it is always bedtime in pornography, the genre can often seem determinedly opposed to the generation of erotic excitement. *Erotica* is a term frequently opposed to pornography, often by antipornography feminists to contrast a tame and tasteful female pleasure to a more gross and violent porn. However, this contrast belies the fact that both forms of representation ultimately aim at sexual arousal. What may more usefully distinguish the two terms, then, is the way taboo functions in each. Pornography as a whole defies the taboos against graphic representations of sex acts, but it often chooses not to inscribe these taboos into the truncated narratives of its fantasy scenarios. Erotica, in contrast, inscribes the taboo more deeply into its fantasy. Thus erotica is not necessarily more tasteful or tame than pornography (witness the grossly transgressive literary erotica of Georges Bataille, also the great theorist of transgression), nor is it without explicit imagery (witness the explicit but tasteful film and video erotica of Candida Royalle), but it does inscribe the tension of the forbidden into its fantasy.

If pornography is the realm where nothing impedes the immediate enactment of easily achieved and multiple forms of sexual pleasure, then erotic forms of pornography are those in which the taboos and prohibitions limiting pleasure are, at least vestigially, in force often in order to enhance the desire that overpowers them. Eroticism in pornography thus depends on the continued awareness of the taboo. This is one reason why interracial pornographies can sometimes have an erotic charge that other forms of pornography do not.

To transgress a taboo is certainly not to defeat it. Georges Bataille argues that transgression is the flouting of a taboo that fully recognizes the authority and power of the prohibiting law: "Unless the taboo is observed with fear it lacks the counterpoise of desire which gives it its deepest significance" (1957, 37). Prohibitions thus often provide an element of fear that enhances desire. In much of what follows, I will be arguing that it is fear — the fear once generated by white masters to keep white women and black men apart — that gives erotic tension to interracial sex acts which in "ordinary," nonracialized pornography often become rote.[2]

The interviews in *Crossing the Color Line*, then, invoke the prejudices of the Old South as if they were passé. But in the sexual performances that follow, these passé stereotypes make the violation of the color line more vivid and dramatic. Awareness of these taboos and stereotypes lends erotic tension to the performance of the sex acts. The video takes the (unequally enforced, weakened) "taboo observed with fear" to elicit the "counterpoise of desire." To the extent that such pornography acknowledges the color line informing the taboo, it works against the contemporary goal of color blindness now operant in U.S. culture.

Whether this attention to racial difference makes for a good or a bad thing—in pornography or elsewhere—is a matter for debate. On the one hand, "recognizing" racial differences can seem to be, and sometimes is, synonymous with racism itself (Pascoe 1999, 482). On the other hand, in a culture now so determined to be officially blind to racial differences that it has created a new kind of taboo around their very mention, it can seem excitingly risqué to notice differences of skin tone, ass or lip shape. On one level, then, interracial pornography's refusal to be color-blind points to the obvious fact that as a culture, Americans are not so much color-blind as, as Susan Courtney puts it, "color-mute": we take note of racial differences, much as we take note of sexual differences, but unlike sexual differences, racial differences are not supposed to be noticed.[3] Ample female posteriors, for example, are often celebrated in "black" and "interracial" videos; Caucasian features can also be racialized. In *Crossing the Color Line*, for example, white male or female skin tone seems to exist *for* its contrast to black, and black skin exists for its contrast to white. Sometimes this contrast remains imaginary: "White pussy"—which actually registers as a pink color not visually all that different from the interior pink of African American women—nevertheless seems racialized in its contrast with the black penis. "White cock"—which registers considerably darker than the rest of the variously toned skin of white men, and therefore as not dependably lighter than the penises of all men designated black—nevertheless seems racialized in contrast with the darker skin of the black woman. An even more impressive contrast is offered in the white man's pink lips and the black woman's dark-haired pubis. Contrast, real or imagined, is what makes these comminglings so stunningly dramatic.

Contrasts are also invoked between men in this, and other, interracial videos. For example, we cannot help but note the hirsute quality of the white man, Mark Davis, who has sex with the black woman, Naomi Wolfe, in the second episode, compared to the smoothness of the black man, Sean Michaels, in the first episode. Nor can we fail to notice that Davis's lighter-toned penis is shorter—though thicker—than Michaels's, and also uncut. (Of course, both penises are oversized by any but pornographic standards.) If the white man's penis is (comparatively) small and the black man's is (comparatively) large, which is the norm? Pornography as a genre has its own, changing, norms. The large black penis once given by the white master as a reason for white women to abhor and fear black men is today valued by all in the world of interracial pornography. One thing is clear, however; though blackness and whiteness are articulated as racially and sexually saturated differences, they are articulated differently. The black woman does not articulate her pleasure in the "whiteness" of the white man's cock, as the white woman articulated hers to the black man. Only the black man and the white woman's sexual-racial differences are singled out. This is the case both for those differences that can be registered visually and those that are only imaginary.

All of the above racial differences remain more or less unmentionable in polite discourse because of their associations with racial stereotypes. Once used to elicit fear and revulsion that would enforce separation, these stereotypes are now used to cultivate desire across the racial border. It would be a mistake, certainly, to consider the mere flouting of an increasingly anachronistic color line as a progressive act, especially if we accept Bataille's notion that we actually honor transgressed taboos in their transgression. What, then, can we say about the deployment of racial stereotypes in the erotic excitement of crossing the color line? Do these stereotypes do further harm to people of color and should they be eschewed? Must we agree, for example, with Frantz Fanon that sexual stereotypes of black men, born of white fear, continue to reduce the black man to an "epidermalized" racial essence?

Racial Fear and Desire

Frantz Fanon has famously written about the experience of being interpellated as a raced being when a white boy points to him on the street to say, "Look, a Negro. . . . I'm frightened" (1967, 112). In this classic description of the power of the white gaze to reduce the black man to an epidermalized phobic essence, Fanon sees negrophobia as a form of white sexual anxiety. The white gaze sees the organ of black skin and immediately feels fear. According to Fanon, the deepest cause of this fear lies in the reduction of the black man to a penis, which ultimately constitutes a pathological projection on the part of the white man of his own repressed homosexuality (170). The white man's fear is thus, to Fanon, also his desire. Yet, as Mary Ann Doane (1991, 221) has shown, the specific instances of negrophobia analyzed by Fanon tend to ground the pathology of this projection especially in the white woman. The white woman's fear of rape by a Negro is viewed as an "inner wish" to be raped: "It is the woman who rapes herself" (Fanon 1967, 179). Pathology thus marks the white woman's desire for the black man. Fanon similarly pathologizes the black woman's desire for the white man. Yet, as Doane shows, Fanon does not equally pathologize the black man's desire for the white woman. Indeed, he does not find anything in his behavior that is motivated by race. This man is simply a typical "neurotic who by coincidence is black" (Fanon 1967, 79).

Fanon's (unequal) condemnation of the epidermalization of racial fear and desire is understandable given his quest for revenge on the system that so fixes him. But his protestation that the man of color's desire is not itself racially influenced remains unconvincing. It is as if Fanon's response to the negative stereotype of the oversexed black man can only be to create another set of negative stereotypes: the oversexed white woman and the undersexed white man (a repressed homosexual to Fanon). Originally writing in 1952, Fanon, for good reason, cannot conceive of a world in which epidermal difference would become a commodity fetish grounded in the very fear expressed by the child who once hailed him. Nor can he admit that this fear-desire might exist (unequally but powerfully) on both sides of the racial border. He thus cannot imagine a black man's desire for a white woman as grounded in a fear that enhances desire.

Kobena Mercer's much later (1994) attempt to analyze his own, black and gay, attraction-repulsion to Robert Mapplethorpe's photographs of nude black male bodies offers an intriguing new take on Fanon's notion of epidermalization.[4] Mercer's initial reaction to Mapplethorpe's photos in the (in)famous *Black Book* (1986) follows Fanon's example and dismisses them as stereotypical objectifications grounded in the phobia of the hypersexed black male body. He quotes Fanon: "The Negro is eclipsed. He is turned into a penis. He *is* a penis" (Mercer 1994, 185). Mercer thus accuses Mapplethorpe of a fetishistic objectification of the black male body. In the much-discussed photograph, *Man in a Polyester Suit* (1980), showing a penis protruding from the fly of the eponymous suit, he objects to the conjuration of the large penis as a "phobic object," evoking "one of the deepest mythological fears and anxieties in the racist imagination, namely that all black men have huge willies" (177). Mercer argues that Mapplethorpe's camera fetishizes the black male body, masking the social relations of racial power between the well-known artist and his anonymous subjects and oscillating between sexual idealization of the racial other and anxiety in defense of the white male ego (178). This racial fetishization is ultimately Mapplethorpe's way, Mercer argues, of splitting belief, of saying "I *know* (its [sic] not *true* that all black guys have huge willies) but (nevertheless, in my photographs, they do)" (185).

In a second article, however, Mercer opts for a more contextualized reading of the photograph's aesthetic and political value and for a revision of the very notion of racial fetishism as a necessarily bad thing (190). Here, he complicates his earlier discussion of the fetishized "big black willy" as part of the "psychic reality of the social relations in which our racial and gendered identities have been historically constructed" (191). Mercer now allows that fetishized (gay male) erotic representations are not "necessarily a bad thing." Interestingly, he names as his reason that, like the point-of-view shots in gay male pornography, they are "reversible" (185)—the object of the gaze can look back. Because the gendered hierarchy of seeing/being seen is not so rigidly coded in homoerotic representation, Mercer can justify Mapplethorpe's objectification of the big black willy. Fanon's argument against the epidermal fixing of the black man by the white man and the white woman had been to say that the irrational fear of the black man's sex actually constituted pathological desire, a pathology from which the black man himself was exempt. In contrast, Mercer's own homosexual (and intraracial) desire *for* the same black penis that the white photographer desires leads him to question the very pathology of fetishism. Torn between seeing the black man's sex as desirable and seeing it as a phobic object, Mercer fails to see that it is the tension between fear and desire that marks the special appeal of these photos, whether the taboo transgressed is that forbidding same-sex desire or that forbidding interracial sex.[5]

Mercer admirably introduces a rich ambivalence into his reading of these images, claiming that it is not possible to say whether such images reinforce or undermine racist myths about black sexuality. Nevertheless, he wants to think that the homoeroticism of these images is capable of shocking viewers out of the stable, centered subject position of the straight "white male subject" (192). He thus comes close to saying that because Mapplethorpe's photographs come from within a shared community of homoerotic desire, and because Mercer himself writes from a similar perspective, these images do not offer a "bad" kind of racial fetishization, even though, from the perspective of Mapplethorpe's desire, they still objectify the blackness (if not the same-sexedness) of the black models' "willies." Does this mean that a progressive, taboo-breaking, same-sex desire can absolve interracial lust of its own bad history of fetishization? Mercer, who has already gone a long way in probing these difficult issues, does not further elaborate.

Mercer's argument evades, but also evokes, the important question of whether the phobic fetishization that once fixed Fanon is still present in the new desiring fetishization. I argue that it is, but that now it works in the service of fueling a pleasure that has become more complex, a pleasure that serves more than the white former masters. Jane Gaines (1992), for example, in a complex response to Mercer's essay, has called for a better understanding of the "full diversity" of Mapplethorpe's *Black Book*, by which she means the full diversity of the readers of its images (27). Gaines suggests that straight black women, straight white women, and gay black men have all derived different kinds of pleasure from these pictures and that the actual sexual preferences of these models—whom Mercer presumes to be gay—are irrelevant to the fantasies they may generate (29). Her point is that there are many taboos that inform the fantasies of sexual and racial couplings and that the furor and ambivalence over these photos suggest that many people, gay and straight, black and white, who once only feared the appearance of the "big black willy," are now becoming educated in its desire.

I would add that this "education of desire"—I borrow the term from Richard Dyer (1985, 131)—occurs along with the rise of aboveground hardcore pornography in the seventies and eighties. As is well known, this pornography has enshrined the penis—of whatever hue—as a commodified object of desire. Such commodification occurs in different ways across the racial border, but it now includes the black man's own repertoire of sexual postures vis-à-vis the white women he once had good reason to fear. Indeed, the real historical change, as Jane Gaines demonstrates, is the simple fact of the circulation of a book of photos whose main raison d'être is the display of this once fear-inducing, now desire-inducing, sexual object. Thus while white supremacist stereotypes certainly inform the fascination with the black penis in these photos, we may not need to have recourse to Mercer's intelligent, but also highly defensive, arguments to "save" Mapplethorpe's black male nudes from Fanonian-style disdain. Mercer, for example, argues that the "commonplace stereotypes" of pornography can create, when mixed ironically with high art, a "subversive recoding of the ideological values supporting the normative aesthetic ideal" (1994, 199). In this light, racial fetishism becomes not a "repetition of racist fantasies but a deconstruction of the ambivalence at play in cultural representations of race and sexuality" (1994, 199).

I am full of admiration for Mercer's willingness to rethink his earlier condemnation of racial fetishism. I am a little suspicious, however, of his argument about the "subversive recoding" of both the high art ideal and the low pornographic stereotype because it tends to elide the fact that both the high and the low are not simply ironic but capable (to different degrees and in different ways) of arousing desire.[6] The real point of the combination of traditions in Mapplethorpe, I suggest, is not the shock of the juxtaposition, but that both are so frankly erotic. What Mercer seems not to recognize fully in his much-revised and extremely important argument is that the phobic deployment of the stereotype of the black man's sex had already been transformed by popular culture, not Mapplethorpe's art, into an ambivalently mixed bag of stereotype and fetishistic valuation in which fear, desire, and envy blended. It is precisely the erotic appeal of this racialized sexuality around which Mercer's essay seems to dance. The gist of his fascinating and honest argument with himself might come down to something like this: If Mapplethorpe's photos were viewed only by (straight) white viewers, then they might easily be accused of fixing and negatively fetishizing black men in their very blackness and hypersexuality. But the context of viewing is everything. Black viewers of these bodies, and gay viewers of these bodies, and black gay viewers of these bodies, and women viewers of all races and sexual orientations now exist in a culture that has not only denigrated and "fixed" the black man negatively in his sexuality but has also celebrated his erotic power in the familiar poses of a macho black power. Racial fetishization is today not the same as the fixing to which Fanon objected. As Mercer notes, the statement "the black man is beautiful" takes on different meanings depending on the social subject who says it: white or black woman, white or black man, gay or straight. Beauty is indeed an important component of Mapplethorpe's photos. But it may be more pertinent to alter the statement to "the black man is sexy," for beauty in this case leads to an acknowledgment of desire. The black man is sexy in this instance in the way he is sexy in contemporary interracial pornography: in the stereotypical, racialized characteristics of black skin and large penis. These characteristics now inspire ambivalent mixes of fear and desire in a much wider range of subjectivities than Mercer originally conceived (including, as Gaines points out, white women and black women). Those who transgress taboos that proscribe either interracial or same-sex desire may experience an ambivalent mix of fear and desire that is part of these images' appeal.

If we are willing to acknowledge that interracial lust evolves out of the taboos initially imposed by the white master, but which now serve to eroticize a field of sexuality that is no longer his sole province, then we begin to recognize the validity of varieties of commodification in contemporary visual culture, and not only in much-discussed, high art incarnations. But what if we now turn to a decidedly "low" example of interracial lust, which no one could call high art and which is not even attempting, like *Crossing the Color Line*, to counter the racism of the porn industry, but which seems vigorously to embrace its crudest stereotypes?

Let Me Tell Ya 'bout White Chicks (dir. Dark Brothers, 1984) is a porn video that became notorious, and popular, for its articulation of all the stereotypes and clichés of racial difference. Since its release in 1984, when it won the XRCO Best Picture award, it has acquired something of a cult status and has, unlike many other porn titles, been subsequently reissued as a "classic." The video box proclaims it "The Original Interracial Classic." Its director, Gregory Dark, is a white man who also pioneered hip, politically incorrect "New Wave" straight porn and then briefly turned his hand to interracial pornography in the mid-1980s. Dark proudly proclaims that "you will not find one sensitive moment in any of my work." (Bright n.d., n.p.). Like Spike Lee's *Jungle Fever* (1991), it unearths the most regressive sexual stereotypes of taboo desire. Unlike Lee, who chooses to tell his version of the story from the perspective of an upwardly mobile black man who momentarily succumbs to "jungle fever" and then learns better, Dark revels in the black male enthusiasm for the ever more outlandish conquest of "white chicks." The tone is set with this opening rap:

> White chicks! They're so hot and pretty, they get down to the real
>   nitty-gritty.
> White chicks got this attitude, they ain't happy 'till they get screwed.
> Give me five on the black hand side, there's nothing as sweet as a little
>   white hide.
> When I see black chicks on the street, I know white chicks got them
>   beat.
> Got to get some fine white pussy, feel so wet and tastes so juicy.
> Got to get some fine white chick, give her some of my big black dick.
> White chicks!

In the film, a group of low-life black men—a pimp, some petty thieves, and one slightly more respectable figure whom I will call the resister—sit around in a bedroom, bragging about their sexual conquests of "white tail." Each narrated conquest is viewed in flashback. Each consists of an intrusion into a perceived white, upper-class realm (actually only mildly upscale southern California kitchens, bedrooms, and bathrooms), until the final number, which occurs in the funky bedroom the men occupy. Typically, the episodes begin as robberies and then turn into opportunities for sex with exceedingly willing white women. Conspicuously absent from the video are white men. By behaving like the stereotypes that white men have made them out to be— lazy, lawless, and sexually insatiable—these black men take a crude revenge on the unseen white man.

The pimp figure begins the bragging, extolling the virtues of white over black women. The resister disbelieves him, saying at one point that white women make his stomach turn. His buddies spin fantasy after fantasy to convince him, and finally, in the last number, they break down his resistance by offering him a white woman on his very own bed. Before he is finally won over, however, he confesses his fear of white women. Indeed, one could say that the entire drama of this video (such as it is) rests on the ambivalence of this one black man toward the white woman he has historically been blamed for desiring. The sex scene with which the film concludes, and indeed all of the outrageous sexual fantasies of black men "boning" eager white women, might thus be construed as a counter to this fear. Bataille's statement about the relation of fear to desire again proves relevant: "Unless the taboo is observed with fear it lacks the counterpoise of desire which gives it its deepest significance" (1957, 37). The taboo observed with fear resides in the very real fact that black men were once justly afraid of white women for the danger they could cause. White racists also have been known to fear that white women would, if they tasted sex with black men, never "come back." Both fears inform the racialized sexual fantasies performed in this video. However, fear is not, as it was for Fanon, the dominant emotion. It now is Bataille's "counterpoise of desire"—the tension that enhances desire.

On one level, then, we can describe *Let Me Tell Ya 'bout White Chicks* as the racist white male fantasy arguing that black men are animals and that the white women who go with them are sluts. The pleasure taken in this depiction of their sex acts could be called the pleasure of seeing the white woman sullied by the animalistic appetites of the black man—appetites which the white man has historically projected onto the black man. In this case, the white man is not directly implicated in the nastiness except as its onlooker and, of course, as the main author of the fantasy. The black man who acts the part of the animal and the white woman who proves herself to be a slut by going with the black man may also be flouting the taboos of white supremacy for the very pleasure of the white men whom we know to be the dominant consumers of pornography and the writer, director, and producer of this video.

On another level, however, this video can play as a black male sexual fantasy. Narratively, the "me" who tells "ya" about white chicks is a black man talking to other black men, telling tall tales of the obliging availability of white women who crave sex with, and pay money to, low-class black men for their sexual services. On this level, the video can be viewed as a straightforward black male fantasy that takes pleasure in acting out what was once the white man's worst nightmare. On yet another level, however, it is possible to see that even the eponymous white woman might take pleasure in watching her counterparts have down-and-dirty sex with a primitive other. One thing at least is clear: while it is not in the least politically correct, this fantasy offers an eroticized transgression of a variety of racialized perspectives. The one racialized perspective studiously ignored, however, is that of the "black chicks" unfavorably compared to the "white chicks." A companion video, *Let Me Tell Ya 'bout Black Chicks*, by the same writer, director, and producer, would appear to have rectified the imbalance of insult, but it is lost.[7] However we judge the racist stereotypes at work in these films, it would seem that by the time of their release, interracial forms of lust had begun to refunction the more purely phobic kinds of reactions to racial-sexual stereotypes. On both sides of the color line, men and women who watched these videos could participate in the "ambivalences" described by Mercer.

Let Me Tell Ya 'bout White Chicks thus neither constitutes a "subversive recoding of the ideological values supporting the normative aesthetic ideal," as Mercer claims for readings of Mapplethorpe, nor is it a pure "repetition of racist fantasies." It does not function, as did Reconstruction and Progressive Era racial fantasies, to keep black men in "their place." Rather, it represents a new kind of racial pornographic fantasy come into being due to America's history of racial oppression but not a simple repetition of these past racist stereotypes. Like *Crossing the Color Line*, the video reworks the phobic white fear of the black man's sex, and the related fear of the white woman's animalistic preference for that sex, into a pornographic fantasy that may have originated from but is no longer "owned" by the white man. Is it then a positive or negative stereotype? Perhaps the conventional language of stereotypes fails us in the attempt to analyze the refunctioning that has occurred around this phobia. For the phobia's original purpose was to prevent precisely the kind of black male–white female couplings celebrated in these videos.

The problem in thinking about stereotypes, as Mireille Rosello has pointed out, is our stereotypes about them (1998, 32), leading to a lack of precisely the sort of ambivalence noted by Mercer. Rosello argues that stereotypes are important objects of study not because we can better learn to eliminate them from our thinking, but rather because they cannot be eliminated. Stereotypes persist, and perhaps even thrive on, the protestations against them; the louder the protest, the more they thrive. Instead of protest, Rosello offers a nuanced study of the changing historical contexts of stereotypes. Something like this seems to be what we need in our understanding of stereotypes of interracial lust as well. To forbid all utterance or depiction of the stereotype of the originally phobic image of the large black penis is to grant it a timelessness and immortality that it does not really possess. Once uttered, however, a stereotype does have an enormous power to endure. Racial stereotypes especially, as Homi Bhabha has noted, take on a fetishistic nature as a "form of knowledge and identification that vacillates between what is always 'in place' as already known, and something that must be anxiously repeated . . . as if the essential duplicity of the Asiatic or the bestial sexual license of the African that needs no proof, can never really, in discourse be proved" (1994, 66). In the perpetual absence of proof (say a random sampling of penis size and actual sexual behavior of black men), there is no truth to the stereotype. But precisely because there is no truth the claim must be repeated. Rosello, however, argues that the refunctioned repetition of stereotype shows what happens when what the culture thinks it knows comes in contact with the stereotyped person's reaction to that supposed knowledge. In this case, the "iteration" of the refunctioned stereotype does not deny it, but uses it in historically new ways that are more erotic than phobic. In other words, the racial stereotype of the big black "buck" that right-thinking Americans have now come to label as unjustly "negative" (but have in no way eliminated as a vacillating form of knowledge and belief) has ceased to function in the same way it did when the Klan was riding. It has ceased to so function precisely because it has, in the intervening years, been refunctioned to different ends by black men who have willingly occupied the fantasy position of the hypersexed black man in order to instill fear in the white man and to counter the older stereotype of the passive Uncle Tom.[8]

The typical argument against stereotypes is to say that "real" people do not resemble them. But as Steve Neale (1979–80, 35) and Jane Gaines (1992, 27) point out, it is almost never actually "real people" who are asked to offer the antidote to harmful stereotypes, but an imaginary ideal that can serve as a "positive image" for stigmatized minorities. Harmful, negative stereotypes are not measured against the real but against the culturally dominant ideal. Jane Gaines quotes Isaac Julian and Kobena Mercer on this point: "It's not as if we could strip away the negative stereotypes of black men . . . and discover some 'natural' black masculinity which is good, pure and wholesome" (Gaines 1992, 27; Mercer and Julien 1986, 6). Historically, then, the negative stereotype of the oversexed black buck was countered in the late 1950s and early 1960s by the positive stereotype of the supercivilized (handsome but never overtly sexual) Sydney Poitier. But this desexed image of the black man was in turn countered by more explicitly sexualized—"bad"—images of black men produced in reaction to the perceived passivity of the Tom figure. Thus the reappearance of the stereotype of the black buck in the post–civil rights era does not represent a return to a *Birth of a Nation*–style stereotype. Stereotypes, if we follow Rosello, do not simply repeat. The very emergence of this figure, in a newly aboveground, post–civil rights era pornography, would seem to provide evidence that the older function of what Foucault calls the deployment of power through "systems of alliance" and a "symbolics of blood" (1978, 147) indeed does give way to a newer deployment and analytics of sexuality. But like so much else in Foucault, these two modes of power are intertwined.

A stereotype that once functioned to frighten white women and to keep black men in their place (as in JanMohamed's stereotyping allegory), now functions to solicit sexual desire in the form of a transgressive, pornographic tale. However, this arousal remains propped on the original phobic stereotype aimed precisely at prohibiting the very sexual commerce depicted. Are black men and white women kept any less "in their place" by this sexual fantasy whose point of origin is the power of the white man? I would argue that the white man's power remains the pivotal point around which these permutations of power and pleasure turn. The sexual fantasies depicted primarily constitute rivalries between white and black men. The agency of white women, and black women even more, is difficult to discern. Nevertheless, there is a big difference, as Tessa Perkins has observed, between "knowing" racist stereotypes and "believing" them (qtd. in Gaines 1992, 27). I suggest that pornographic and erotic fantasies of interracial lust rely on all viewers, male and female, black and white, *knowing* these stereotypes. Although nothing necessarily rules out their also *believing* them—that is, they can certainly be interpreted in a racist manner—the pleasure taken in pornographic depictions of interracial lust does not depend on believing them. It would seem that what is involved instead is a complex flirtation with the now historically proscribed stereotype operating on both sides of the color line. Thus the very taboos that once effectively policed the racial border now work in the service of eroticizing its transgression.

"Fear of [and Desire for] a Mandingo Sexual Encounter"

We have seen that a mix of fear and desire lies at the heart of interracial pornography's erotic tension. The resister figure in *White Chicks* who admitted his fear of white women was also, inadvertently, admitting his fear of white men. White men, for their part, have historically feared black male prowess, even while (and as a means of) exercising sexual sovereignty over black women. White male fear of the black man's sexual threat to white women has been the ostensible reason, as JanMohamed notes, for countless acts of violence against black men. What we see in the above examples of interracial pornography is that this fear has now been iterated in a new way. Where it once operated in a more exclusively phobic mode to keep the black man and the white woman apart, now its reversal in pornographic fantasy shows how the stereotype informs the erotic tension of representations of interracial lust. I do not mean to suggest, however, that a racialized mix of fear and desire informing contemporary pornography now renders it totally innocuous. Quite the contrary. One of the worst riots of recent American history was precipitated by the phantasmatic projection of one white man's racial-sexual fear, envy, and resentment grounded in just such a scenario of interracial lust.

When the white Los Angeles police sergeant Stacey Koon saw a powerfully built black man holding his butt and gyrating his hips at a white female highway patrol officer, he claimed to see a lurid scenario of interracial sex that then triggered the beating of Rodney King. Koon's reading of King's pornographic gestures is described in his book, *Presumed Guilty*.

> Melanie Singer . . . shouted at King to show her his hands. Recognizing the voice as female, King grinned and turned his back to Melanie Singer. Then he grabbed his butt with both hands and began to gyrate his hips in a sexually suggestive fashion. Actually, it was more explicit than suggestive. Melanie wasn't so much fearful as offended. She was being mocked in front of her peers. . . . Control and common sense were cast aside. Melanie's Jane Wayne and Dirty Harriet hormones kicked in. She drew her pistol, and advanced to within five feet of the suspect. (Koon 1992, 33–34)

In the original manuscript of this book, however, Koon had offered a slightly different version of his reason for intervening, stressing this time not Singer's "offense" but what he called her "fear of a Mandingo sexual encounter" (Fiske 1996, 145). In a May 16, 1992, interview with the *Los Angeles Times* after his acquittal in the first (state) trial, Koon tried to explain what he meant by these words, which were eventually eliminated from the book: "In society there's this sexual prowess of blacks on the old plantations of the South and intercourse between blacks and whites on the plantation. And that's where the fear comes in, because he's black." Koon's phrasing is worthy of note: he uses the word *intercourse* rather than the word *rape* that his logic of imputed fear seems to imply. Yet he clearly wants it to appear that he was saving the white woman from a fear-inducing black "sexual prowess." It is not clear whether he realizes that "intercourse between blacks and whites on the plantation" historically occurred almost entirely between white masters and black slaves. Most likely, he is attempting to subscribe to the Reconstruction era myth of the helpless white woman in need of rescue from the lustful black man by a heroic white man (himself).[9] But the scenario no longer fits. Koon's improbable imputation of sexual fear to the six-foot-tall and highly professional Melanie Singer at the moment King was surrounded by no less than eight highway patrol officers with drawn guns says more about his own sexual insecurities regarding the competence of the female cop who threatens to usurp his own authority. The vacillations in his story are telling: in one version he attributes sexual fear to Singer; in another version mere offense. It is clear that in both cases, fear and offense are not only a projection of an actual sexual threat onto King but a form of punishment enacted on Singer for having the gall to place herself in the "Dirty Harriet" position of a male officer. The real fear for which he also punished *her* by taking over the arrest may very well be that she was a perfectly competent cop doing her job arresting a speeder.

At the same time, however, Koon's use of the phrase *sexual prowess of blacks* intimates something of white sexual envy of black men; it is hardly a phrase old-fashioned racists like Thomas Dixon or D. W. Griffith would have invoked. This envy, I suggest, is inherited from a much more recent legacy of pornography and exploitation cinema that has culminated in the fantasy depictions of interracial lust cited above. While Stacey Koon would like us to believe that Singer's "fear of a Mandingo sexual encounter," caused him to initiate Rodney King's beating, his motives differed from Dixon and Griffith's brand of racism. Like them, he wants to keep black men and white women in their place. But unlike them, he seems aware of the various ways in which the fantasy of the black male sexual threat to the white woman has also become material for overtly titillating scenarios.

One clue to his different deployment of the figure of the "black beast" may lie in Koon's peculiar use of the word *Mandingo*—which designates, along with the variant *Mandinka*, a tribe of African warriors—instead of *black* or *African* or any of the other available animalistic epithets apparently used by police before and during King's beating. This word signals Koon's own semiconscious acknowledgment that the scenario he invokes has since the 1970s become something more than the white patriarch's fear of the pollution of his own racial line by a hypersexual African slave and the subsequent loss of control over "his" women. *Mandingo* does not mean to Stacey Koon's generation what *African* meant to Dixon and Griffith's. One reason may be that in

1975, a popular sexploitation film with the very title *Mandingo*, which Stacey Koon is old enough to have seen as a teenager, had already refunctioned the older scenario of white female fear in the face of black male lust. Stacy Koon's overreaction to King's grabbed butt and gyrated hips may have unleashed the same kind of overkill as the ride of the Klan, but the raced and gendered fear that Koon attempted to project onto Melanie Singer was no longer a historically believable emotion. This is one reason for its excision from the manuscript of his book and its replacement with the word *offense*. But in saying "fear of a Mandingo sexual encounter," Koon also invoked a white female *desire for* that encounter as depicted in the film of the same name. For Richard Fleischer's 1975 film is most famous for its depiction of a white mistress's taboo-breaking seduction of her husband's Mandingo slave.

As noted above, one component of the legacy of Black Power in American popular culture since the sixties has been to fight the stereotype of the emasculated Tom with gestures of black male virility. From the virile stances of the Black Power movement proper, to Eldridge Cleaver's claims to have raped white women in *Soul on Ice*, to an array of early seventies blaxploitation films which *Mandingo* followed, to the Black Power–derived poses of *Mandingo* itself, the defiant gesture by which the black man asserts his virility in the face of a white dominated world has become as automatic a reflex as "rescuing the white woman" was to Stacey Koon. Perhaps if we could begin to understand the reach of the sexual-racial fantasies that fuel the relations between the races at so many levels, we might better understand not only the reasons Stacey Koon grabbed his taser but also the reason Rodney King "grabbed his butt" in the first place.

We thus need to understand Stacey Koon's fateful projection onto Melanie Singer of a "fear of a Mandingo sexual encounter" as a nexus of extremely ambivalent, highly stereotypical white and black sexual fear that Koon certainly wanted to see reaching back to the mythic plantation, but which actually joined mainstream popular culture in the 1970s. It is the emergence of this mixture of racial fear and desire that I would like to examine now. As we have seen, the racially inflected hard-core pornography examined in the last section rests on the old, purely phobic, picture of the threatening, hypersexual black male. In these films, white myths of the Old South come into contact with post–civil rights era assertions of black power and black sexual potency. But how do they actually interact? We can see the effect of this interaction in the catastrophic collision of the two reflexively macho gestures described above: the reflexive gesture with which Rodney King asserts his defiance of the law by adopting a "sexually provocative" pose vis-à-vis a white woman police officer; and the reflexive gesture of beating the black man in order to "rescue" a white woman who was never really in danger. I would suggest that neither of these reflexes constitutes a pure repetition of the past: the macho bravado of King's response to Singer's order is as deeply conditioned by the very same 1970s popular culture that Stacey Koon inadvertently invokes when he says the word *Mandingo*. The macho bravado of Koon's response, which wants to see itself repeating a gesture of heroic rescue out of the mythic white supremacist past, is also deeply conditioned by the imagination of a "Black Power" sexual prowess. The word *Mandingo* seems to function as a screen memory—a memory that both recalls and blocks out unresolved questions of interracial sex and violence percolating in the culture since the 1970s. It would therefore behoove us, before trying to say too much more about Stacy Koon and Rodney King's fantasies, to examine the film titled *Mandingo* as a way of excavating a moment in American culture when mainstream audiences, black and white, began to find titillation—not just danger—in depictions of interracial lust.

Mandingo

Mandingo is not a pornographic film, but for many viewers who did not yet venture into the porn theaters of the era, it came close. Reviewers unanimously viewed it as an exploitative potboiler and a work of lurid "trash."[10] Directed by Richard Fleischer in 1975, and a big hit at the box office, *Mandingo* has only recently begun to receive its critical due.[11] Nor does this rather expensively produced film directly belong to the category of blaxploitation films. However it is best understood, as Ed Guerrero (1993) argues, in relation to them. *Blaxploitation* was Hollywood's word for an exploitation of both race and sex that became popular, and economically important, to the very survival of Hollywood in the early and mid 1970s. Often breakthroughs for black directors, Blaxploitation films typically offered contemporary reworkings of outlaw and detective genres set in the inner city with contemporary jazz scores and tough, sexually desirable black heroes who displayed sexual prowess toward both black and white women (the Isaac Hayes theme song for *Shaft* [dir. Richard Roundtree, 1971] sings of the "black private dick that's a sex machine for all the chicks"). *Mandingo*, in contrast, is set on a plantation of the Old South, was directed by a white man, and has a primary white hero. But like the blaxploitation cycle, it portrays black struggle against racism while also celebrating black male sexual prowess. Also like blaxploitation, it became popular with the same black urban audiences who played such a major role in Hollywood's recovery from economic slump in the early seventies.[12] The film represents a new post–civil rights, post–Black Power view of the coercive sexual relations of slavery, but one which also takes a frankly lurid interest in those relations. Finally, *Mandingo* presents interracial sexual relations not only as compellingly erotic but also systematically in relation to the different economic situations of white masters and mistresses and black male and female slaves. It thus represented a revision of the most recent incarnation of the plantation genre—a type of pulp fiction already predicated, sans Black Power message, on a certain lurid fascination with black/white sexual relations.

The film is one part gothic sexploitation, one part blaxploitation, and one part philosophical treatise on the Hegelian bond between master and slave. The story concerns a young white master (Perry King) who openly enjoys his *droit du seigneur* with a particular female slave while, unbeknownst to him, his sexually unfulfilled white wife furtively enjoys the sexual services of his prize Mandingo "buck." Here, Kyle Onstott's lengthy 1957 novel about interracial sex on the plantation has been overlaid with a post–civil rights celebration of black power that systematically revises *Gone with the Wind*–style clichés of the plantation melodrama.[13] The plantation, presided over by the young master's enfeebled patriarch (James Mason), is a breeding farm for slaves. When the young master discovers that his new wife is not a virgin, he turns to one of his previous slave "bed wenches" and develops a romantic relationship with her.[14] Sex between master and slave is not in itself presented as transgressive, though the romantic nature of this relationship is. Out of jealousy and frustrated desire, his wife then orders her husband's prize Mandingo to service her sexually in a prolonged sex scene. When she later gives birth to a mixed-race child, the master kills it and poisons her.

The one thing the film is not, however, is what Stacey Koon's conflicted memory seemed to want it to be: a lesson teaching white women to fear the "sexual prowess" of black men. Rather, it teaches that these transgressive relations of racialized sexuality are the only relations that have any emotional force in a film otherwise structured by totally instrumental uses of both white and black flesh. But the part of the film that Stacey Koon really ought to have remembered is its conclusion. For when the white master seeks revenge on his slave for having had sex with his wife, his excessive violence,[15] like Koon's, leads to civil unrest—in this case a slave revolt.[16]

Mandingo's black male revenge on the white master marks the film as a post–civil rights era expression of black power. The film systematically revises happy black servility with equal parts of black rage and illicit sexual desire. There are two major interracial sex scenes. They are not the first interracial sex scenes offered up for prurient, as opposed to phobic, interest in mainstream American cinema, but they are the most sustained and the most provocative in their challenge to plantation genre precursors.[17] Both entail transgressive erotic recognitions across racial difference.

The first scene shows the young master on a visit to another plantation where he and his traveling companion receive slave women for the night. Although he has previously been shown to have matter-of-fact breeding relations with a female slave, the kindly Hammond here responds differently. Sickened by the sadistic treatment of one of the women by his traveling companion, and responding to the fear shown by Ellen, the woman he has been given, he retreats into the next room with her. But the kiss his companion has planted on "his" woman in violation of the code against real intimacy between the races has also repulsed him. Ellen, for her part, is shaken by the rough violation of her fellow slave, afraid of her own violation (she is a virgin), and intrigued by Hammond's vulnerability, symbolized by a childhood injury that has left him lame. He reciprocates her kindness toward his lameness by telling her that if she does not want to stay she needn't. During the scene she stands above him. Andrew Britton has argued that Hammond's abrogation of his mastery then leads to Ellen's desire to please him, suggesting "not the submission of a servant but the emotional commitment of a lover" (12). Britton, who mounted the first major defense of the film, argues that Ham and Ellen thus overcome their differences: she overcomes the fact that he is master, and he overcomes the fact that she is a slave, as well as his revulsion to the idea of kissing a slave on the mouth.

Where Britton argues that Ellen's "color and status become irrelevant for Ham" and that he "renounces mastery" (12), I would argue that the abrogation of mastery can never be complete; its residue, in fact, is what marks the scene's erotic tension.[18] Indeed, if we look at how master and slave get to the point of their dramatic first kiss, we see that difference and mastery are never truly overcome. For example, even though Ham tells Ellen that she is free not to service him, and even though he invites her to "put your eyes on me; look at me straight into my eyes," she resists: "I can't. Niggers don't." Although Britton argues that Ham then more gently *asks* her to look at him, and that when their gazes meet they overcome their differences, I suggest that the shift from demanding to asking does not overcome mastery or negate difference. Ellen is never truly free to refuse a master and her color and status do not become irrelevant for Ham. Rather, they become relevant in a new way. If Ellen's desire coincides with her need to please the master, so much the better. But when Ham says that she needn't service him, she reassures him with words whose sincerity we cannot ascertain: "I like you, sir. I want to please you." Ellen's *apparently* willing recognition of Hammond as a man, not a master, elicits a corresponding recognition of Ellen as a woman, not a slave, when he finally overcomes the revulsion to kiss her on the mouth. But the recognition figured by the multiple kisses that end the scene is never free of the powered and raced differences that fuel its eros.

In their own way, however, these kisses are revolutionary, especially if we recall Abdul JanMohamed's (1992, 104) argument that sexual relations between master and slave do entail potentially subversive recognitions of humanity. In *Mandingo*'s larger narrative, this transgressive kiss initiates a chain of events that threatens the entire institutional edifice of slavery by exposing the homology of the black (male and female) slave's position as chattel and the white mistress's position as breeder for the master's seed. For this kiss precipitates the wife's sexual envy and her own much more transgressive violation of the taboo against interracial intimacy when she has sex with Hammond's Mandingo slave, Mede. The repercussions of that sex act will in turn precipitate the master's Stacey Koon–like overkill, which in turn sparks a slave revolt. Thus while it is possible to say that "common humanity" becomes recognized in these transgressions of the racial border between master and slave, the recognitions take place *through* and *because of*, not *despite*, erotically charged racial differences.[19]

It is almost impossible not to see the sexual encounters between master and slave and mistress and slave in terms of racialized versions of Hegel's scenario of the dialectic of recognition between the lord and the bondsman that has proven so influential in postcolonial studies. In this Hegelian turn, I am especially indebted to Celine Parennas Shimizu (2000), whose paper on *Mandingo*, "Master-Slave Sex Acts: *Mandingo* and the Race/Sex Paradox" has clarified many of these issues for me. Hegel's description of the relation between the bondsman and the lord in *Phenomenology of Spirit* (1977) concerns the philosophical problem that "the one"—the "ego subject" or "I" of human self-consciousness—must relate to the "ego object" of the other in order to achieve its identity and become itself. Hegel frames this relation to the other in terms of desire—ultimately the desire of "the one" for recognition by "the other." Although Hegel's sense of desire is never, as Jane Gaines notes, sexual, there is a strong sense of the bodily confrontation between sameness and difference in his discussion of how the bondsman or slave becomes an object for the lord or master which eminently suggests the sexual scenario (Gaines 2001, 62). The Hegelian dilemma of mastery lies in the fact that the more complete it is, the more the master fails to achieve genuine self-consciousness. For the master needs to be recognized by an independent will or consciousness, which is precisely what he has not granted the slave. Thus the master's very power frustrates the recognition of his own will and consciousness by an independent other. Jessica Benjamin calls this dilemma the dialectic of control: "If I completely control the other, then the other ceases to exist, and if the other completely controls me then I cease to exist" (53). Only in mutual recognition can the two become what Hegel calls actively universal subjects.

Hegel's paradigm may offer a way of conceiving forms of recognition extended to forms of racialized and sexualized subjugation inherited from American slavery.[20] Judith Butler's (2000) recent interpretation of both Hegel and Jessica Benjamin rejects the notion of a mutual recognition that functions as normative ideal of an inclusion of the other by the self. According to Butler, the kind of overcoming of difference that we saw Britton argue above with respect to *Mandingo* would constitute an example of the easy and overly optimistic interpretation that she challenges in Benjamin.[21] In contrast, Butler stresses a version of the master/slave recognition that sees both as running the risk of destruction. But this risk of destruction also proves, she argues, constitutive of the self. It is a recognition grounded in difference and instability. Butler's argument is complex and nuanced, ultimately challenging Benjamin's dyadic concept of desire with a more multiple—heterosexed, homosexed, and unnamably sexed—triad. I only take from it the basic paradox that recognition does not overcome difference or destruction but is, rather, grounded in both. I find this Hegelian reinterpretation, along with Shimizu's, helpful for understanding the nature of the erotic recognition that occurs between Ham and Ellen and that their kisses symbolize. In a film in which sex acts have functioned in the economic interests of the master, these transgressive, interracial sex acts do not, as Andrew Britton would have it, overcome difference. Rather, they offer a perversely exciting form of sexual-racial recognition-in-difference.

This negativity of a destructive difference offers an important qualification for understanding erotic forms of recognition whose very eros is grounded in racialized differences of power. Consider, for example, the second big moment of interracial lust depicted in this film, that between the aptly named Blanche (Susan George), the sexually frustrated plantation mistress, and Mede, the Mandingo wrestler (the boxer Ken Norton). Blanche had disappointed Hammond by proving—due to sexual abuse by her older brother—not to be a virgin on marriage. When Ham purchases Ellen and then turns to her for love, elevating her to quasi–mistress status, Blanche seeks revenge by seducing her husband's slave. On a steamy afternoon, dressed in her white nightgown, with long blond hair falling down nearly to her waist, a half-drunk Blanche orders Mede to her bedroom to sit on her bed—a move which momentarily equalizes the difference in their height when she stands before him, making it possible for each, as in the previous master/slave "recognition," to look into the other's eyes. First, she threatens him with his master's wrath: if he does not do what she wants, she will claim to have been raped by him. But since such coercion will only make her like Hegel's master, she then entreats: "Mede, ain't you ever craved a white lady before?" With this shift from terrorizing command to an entreaty that addresses his own desire for the other, she kisses his unresponsive lips, caressing the sides of his face and looking him in the eye.

It was at the point of just such an interracial kiss that the previous "love" scene between Ham and Ellen faded out. Here, however, the kiss begins a prolonged seduction that climaxes in a soft-core depiction of mutual orgasm. Considered simply as a sex scene, it proves no more transgressive than a great many of its era; considered as an interracial sex scene, it pushes the envelope, an effect enhanced by Maurice Jarre's gothic music. Blanche slowly removes Mede's shirt and pulls him up from the bed to stand, towering over her. Embracing the full length of his body she reaches her hand down his chest and toward his groin. A reframed shot of their upper bodies shows both of them looking down in that direction. With this allusion to Mede's involuntary sexual response to her coercive "seduction," Blanche begins to undress him (figure 1). This gesture leads her, eventually, to kneel at his feet as if in abject submission to a virile response that she nevertheless controls. From behind Mede's back, we see a powerfully built black man, naked buttocks prominently displayed, with a white woman kneeling at his feet. This scene clearly puts Mede's body, not Blanche's, on display. Standing once again, Blanche now removes her clothes and embraces him, rubbing her face with its long blond hair against his naked chest.

At this point, Mede finally begins to respond voluntarily to her seduction. His arms embrace her and she smiles. Taking "control," he lifts her briefly up and then onto the bed where he lies on her. Once again, it is his body, especially his buttocks, that is on display as the camera glides along its length to reveal her feet caressing his thighs. Suddenly, as if remembering that she should be in charge, Blanche reverses this arrangement and climbs on top, for the first time in the scene revealing the upper part of her own naked

1. In *Mandingo*, Blanche undresses Mede. His body, not hers, is on display.

body. Immediately, however, Mede puts her back under him, and trembles as if in the grips of orgasm that gives the appearance, if not the guarantee, of mutuality. The scene ends with a languorous crane shot pulling up, revealing his body sprawled on top of hers with her legs spread-eagled beneath him.[22]

What kind of Hegelian recognition can we see in this scene? First of all, it is literally one that runs the "risk of destruction" by keeping in play a negativity—a possibility of obliteration that is the very source of its erotic tension. Indeed, both mistress and slave will die as a consequence of this sexual-racial recognition. The very death at the master's hand with which Blanche threatens Mede, will be delivered to them both. The intense eroticism of the scene derives not merely from the explicit (relative to previous, nonexploitation Hollywood films) details of their sexual relations—reference to Mede's off-screen erection, nudity, shuddering orgasm—but from the way his body itself becomes a battleground between fear and desire. Here is another permutation of the fear of, and desire for, the racial other. But where Ellen risked destruction in refusing to satisfy her master, Mede risks destruction both ways—in refusing to satisfy his mistress *and* in satisfying her.

Judith Butler writes,

The self in Hegel is marked by a primary enthrallment with the Other, one in which that self is put at risk. The moment in "Lordship and Bondage" when the two self-consciousnesses come to recognize one another is, accordingly, in the "life and death struggle," the moment in which they each see the power they have to annihilate the Other and, thereby, destroy the condition of their own self-reflection. Thus, it is at a moment of fundamental vulnerability, that recognition becomes possible and becomes self-conscious. (2000, 287)

Butler's interpretation of the achievement of Hegelian self-identity through a relation to the other that runs the risk of destruction suggests, in contrast to Jessica Benjamin, that the price of self-identity is, paradoxically, self-loss. To be a self, according to Butler's reading of Hegel, is not to "enjoy the prerogative of self-identity" but to be *ek*-static, cast outside oneself, to become other to oneself. Thus Butler resists the sort of "happy" interpretation of recognition that sees it as an incorporation of the difference of the other into the one. Her challenge to Benjamin is to think about the desire for (and the desire of) the other beyond the complementarity of the dyad—master/slave, self/other—to consider the ways in which a third term intervenes.

In the various scenarios of interracial lust we have discussed thus far, both in pornography and here in a film thought to "exploit" (soft-core) sex in pornographic ways, the different interracial permutations of lust—those of the white woman and the black man and those of the white man and the black woman—contain a nonpresent third term that haunts the scene. This is the putatively "proper," same-race partner whom the spectacle of interracial lust can be said to betray. When the black woman and the white man recognize and desire one another across their differences, this recognition is nevertheless haunted and erotically animated by the missing figure of the black man, who finds his very masculinity and virility jeopardized by his exclusion. It is also haunted by the missing figure of the white woman deprived of a partner because of the white male's interest in the "othered" woman. Similarly in the sexual-racial recognition of the white woman and the black man, it is the jealous white man who represents the absent third term and who has his masculinity (and mastery) put in jeopardy by his exclusion. To a lesser degree, the second scenario is also haunted by the black woman who loses a potential partner to the myth of superior white womanhood.

These exclusions are not equal, however. The white man has much more power in his absence to structure the scene in which he does not act than does the black man, the white woman, or the black woman. And for this reason we might say that the transgression inherent in the sex scene between the white woman and the black man is greater and therefore more erotic. The point, however, is that the interracial recognition taking place never occurs only between the two figures present in the scene and that this mutual but unequal recognition is animated, in different ways, by the desire and jealousy of an absent third person. As Butler suggests, "If desire works through relays that are not always easy to trace, then who I am for the Other will be, by definition, at risk of displacement" (2000, 284). Thus "part of what it means to recognize the Other" is to recognize that "he or she comes, of necessity, with a history that does not have oneself as its center" (285). The lame white master who looms so large in the Blanche/Mede recognition, the sex-starved white mistress who looms so large in the Ham/Ellen recognition, are what give these erotic recognitions their sexual charge. They are the (unequally) powerful, white, transgressed-against figures whose very absence structures the erotic tension of the scenes. The black woman who would be the "appropriately raced" partner for Mede, and the black man who would be the "appropriately raced" partner for Ellen, do not have the same power to constitute a force in the scene as their white counterparts. The transgression, in other words, is perceived as against the dominant white power: the large power of the white master and the much smaller power of the white mistress. The "hotter" the sex, the greater the transgressed-against power.

Both Blanche and Mede put themselves at risk in their enthrallment with each other. The "hot sex" that ensues is not a gesture of each "including" the other in his or her unity or oneness or humanity. Rather, it constitutes a dangerous giving over of the self to the other, one never "freely" given and never achieving complementarity. Yet Blanche and Mede *do* recognize one another in sex through the very power differentials of their (similarly but unequally) enslaved conditions. If their recognition flouts the key sexual taboo of chattel slavery, it is also informed by it. Indeed, the sexual encounter between Blanche and Mede is erotic in a way that the more romanticized relationship between Hammond and Ellen is not—precisely because the component of fear is greater. Fear of one another and fear of the white master are both palpable in the white mistress's and the black slave's bodies. Erotic tension unlike that seen in any previous Hollywood film manifests itself especially in Mede's body, which becomes a battleground of fear and desire.[23] Because Blanche is less conflicted in her desire for the "Mandingo" sexual encounter—since she, in effect, has less fear and more desire—her body is less eroticized than Mede's (though it is more eroticized than Ellen's whose "proper" mate has no social power). Blanche and Mede recognize one another not in their common humanity, not in their unique individuality, but precisely across racial and sexual skin and hair differences displayed in a sex act that flirts with but at least momentarily holds "destruction in check" (Butler 287). And their erotic relation is haunted by the power of the white master who is not there.

Obviously one can only take Hegelian readings of interracial sex in this film so far. While Butler is interested in what Hegel has to teach about the notion of the self, I am interested in what her reading of Hegel's master-and-slave scenario can teach us about cinematic representations of erotic excitement. I simply hope that this mining of insights can point to new ways of reading moments of erotic recognition informed by fear and transgression. For it is fear, finally, that fuels the erotic fantasy of *Mandingo*. Stacey Koon got that much right.

The sex scenes in *Mandingo* need to be understood not only for their ambivalent political celebration of black male and white female sexual power and pleasure but as a new kind of mainstream visual pleasure—a pleasure explicitly and knowingly derived from flirting with taboo. In 1975, amid the tumult of a mainstream film industry seeking to appeal to younger and more racially and ethnically diverse audiences, interracial lust became a new commodity, acknowledged not for the first time, but in a way that explicitly foregrounded the context of the master/slave dynamic of power as an erotic pleasure grounded in the taboos it transgresses. *Mandingo*, a film that ranked sixteenth at the box office, helps us recognize the emergence of the peculiar conjunction of Black Power, cinematic sexual explicitness, and self-conscious revisions of white myths of the Old South into a quasi-mainstream popular culture.

Behind the Green Door

But, of course, not only *Mandingo* ventured into this taboo territory. I would like to conclude this essay by returning to a "classic" work of film pornography that has already been much discussed as pornography but very little as interracial sex. It is the early *Behind the Green Door* (dir. Mitchell Brothers, 1972), and the scene in question is the film's first heterosexual sex act. As far as I can determine, this is the first American feature-length hard-core film to include a major interracial sex scene; yet, as far as I can also determine, this sex scene has gone unnoticed by critics.[24] A woman named Gloria (Marilyn Chambers) has been abducted and placed on a stage where a series of men will ravish her before an elegantly dressed audience wearing masks. A frightened Gloria is led on stage, disrobed, stroked, kissed and

fondled by a group of black-robed white women in seemingly ritual preparation for her first sexual "number." Suddenly a spotlight directs attention
to a green door at the back of the stage. A barefoot black man (the boxer
Johnny Keyes, here anticipating the later Ken Norton in *Mandingo*) emerges
through the door dressed as a pornographic version of the African savage. He
sports an animal-tooth necklace, facial paint, and yellow tights with a hole in
the crotch from which his semi-erect penis already protrudes. The "African,"
as if just let out of a cage, tentatively approaches the brown-haired white
woman, not exactly stalking her but as if led to her by the magnetic pull of
his projecting penis. She is held on the floor of the stage by the robed women
who direct him to her spread legs. As the African performs cunnilingus,
the robed women look on intently and massage Gloria's body while some
members of the cabaret audience begin to masturbate. The scene builds as
cunnilingus gives way to penetration and Gloria begins to respond to the
rhythms of the African's thrusts, the initial hushed silence giving way to jazz
music.

The scene is intense, with both the white woman and the black man displaying initial reticence and then abandon. As pornotopia—the place where
it is always time for sex—the scene does not portray the moment of sexual-
racial recognition as the same dramatic battleground between fear and desire as does *Mandingo*. Like all hard-core pornography, it turns to explicit
sex acts very quickly, though an erotic tension much more intense than
our examples discussed earlier from the 1980s and 1990s distinguishes the
scene. This sex scene marks, for the feature-length, on/scene genre of pornography, the first moment in which the blatant invocation of taboos against
interracial lust become a way of adding drama and excitement to hard-core
pornography's usual celebration of easy polymorphic perversities.

Here again a white woman and a black man display highly theatricized
mixtures of fear and desire as each slowly gives him- or herself over to the
sexual-racial other. The face paint, animal-tooth necklace, and crotchless
tights emphasize the racial difference of the African in contrast to the white
woman he ravishes. This is not, like *Mandingo*, a scene in which the mistress has a measure of power over her slave. The African trappings seem designed to assert the animal power of the black man against the more servile
iconography of the slave. Yet the African is no more in charge of the sexual
show than he was in *Mandingo*, and once again the specter of the white man,
the absent third term, haunts the performance. Although the black man
finds himself in the more typically masculine position of ritualized "rav-
isher," he is obviously subject to the power that orchestrates his entrance and

exit. Nevertheless, the film resembles *Mandingo* in its depiction of the black man's desire tinged with fear, and in its theatrical performance of an interracial sex act as a form of commodified visual pleasure. In both cases, this pleasure consciously plays on racial and sexual stereotypes—of the hypersexed black man and the sexually voracious white woman. It is worth noting that the excitement of this particular performance is not measured in the usual close-ups of penetration and money shots, but in a sustained rhythmic give-and-take, in which "recognition across difference" is paramount. Although we see their entwined, whole bodies gyrating, the camera also frequently holds tight on their faces as they look one another in the eye, kiss, and thrust in increasingly fast rhythms until Gloria suddenly closes her eyes and stops, as if unconscious, and the African slowly withdraws. We see his still-erect penis as he pulls it out and walks back to the green door from which he entered.

Earlier hard-core pornography in the form of stag films had occasionally played on stereotypes of African animality.[25] But no feature-length theatrical film shown to sexually and racially mixed audiences in "legitimate" theaters had ever displayed these kinds of sexual-racial stereotypes for the primary purpose of producing sexual pleasure in viewers. This certainly does not mean to say that these films do not traffic in stereotypical depictions of African animality (or, indeed, white female purity—let's not forget that Marilyn Chambers began her career as the Ivory Soap girl) suddenly transformed into insatiable lust. However, it is to say that the effect of the portrayal of animality differs quite markedly in a generic world that celebrates lust and the fetishes enhancing it.

It is certainly true that white men can still deploy the quasi-taboo relation of the stereotypically hypersexual African man and the white man's stereotypically pure white woman as cautionary tools to maintain the sexual-racial hierarchy of white man over black man and white woman. Nevertheless, as we have seen, the fact that the hypersexual black man no longer features as a purely phobic object in the shared cultural imaginary deeply complicates such deployments. He has become, rather, a familiar element in erotic sexual fantasy producing visual pleasure for an audience that can now include—and does include in the case of the diegetic audience in *Behind the Green Door*—white men, black men, white women, and black women, and a wide range of other sexualized and racialized beings. In 1972, this black man is thus very different from what he had been. A fear that had kept black men and white women "in their place" now began to fuel an eroticism bringing them together, not in a happy mutual overcoming of difference, but running the risk of destruction by tempting the outrage (however vestigial) of the excluded third term.

Conclusion: "In the Blink of an Eye."

This essay has worked backward from a 1999 example of the fully commodified category of interracial porn, marketed as such, to a 1972 classic of pornography that preexists the emergence of interracial porn as a marketed category, but that appears to be the first example of the pornographic commodification of interracial sex acts in aboveground feature film. The 1975 film *Mandingo*, while not an example of interracial pornography proper, has nevertheless permitted us to probe some of the deeper questions of power and pleasure in depictions of interracial lust. What conclusions can we now draw from these examples?

All depictions of interracial lust develop out of the relations of inequality that have prevailed between the races. They grow out of a history that has covertly permitted the white man's sexual access to black women and violently forbidden the black man's access to white women. The racist and sexist assumptions that underlie such unequal access to sex have generated forms of pornographic sexual fantasy with an important purchase on the American sexual imagination. To recognize the racism that has generated these fantasies does not suggest that the function they fulfill today is racist in the same way. Nor is it to say that it does not participate in aspects of an increasingly outmoded racial stereotyping. This, indeed, is the lesson of the historicity of the stereotype. Distasteful as some of the stereotypes that feed these fantasies are, I hope to have shown that the simple charge of racism is increasingly imprecise when we talk about visual pleasures generated by depictions of interracial lust. Tessa Perkins's distinction between knowing and believing racist stereotypes seems worth remembering: the excitement of interracial lust—for both blacks and whites—depends on a basic knowledge of the white racist scenario of white virgin/black beast. But the pleasure generated by the scenario does not necessarily need to *believe* in the scenario. Rather, we might say that there is a kind of knowing flirtation with the archaic beliefs of racial stereotypes.

It would seem, then, that the racialized sexuality described by Abdul Jan-Mohamed is not always as silent as he claimed, at least not recently and at least not within the realm of pornographic and exploitation discourse. The pleasures of sexual-racial difference once available to white masters alone are now more available to all, though not equally to all. Black female viewing pleasure, it would seem, is the least well served by these newly racialized, noisy confessions of pleasure. Kobena Mercer writes, "Blacks are looked down upon and despised as worthless, ugly and ultimately unhuman. But in the blink of an eye, whites look up to and revere black bodies, lost in awe and envy as the black subject is idolized as the embodiment of its aesthetic ideal" (1994, 210). As I have been trying to argue, aesthetic ideals are deeply imbricated in the sexual desirability of this "black subject." And the change to which Mercer refers may not have exactly occurred within "the blink of an eye." Rather, as we have seen, it has occurred through a somewhat slower, three-decade-long process of re-aestheticization and positive sexualization, in which low forms of exploitation and pornography have played an important part.

Notes

Thanks to Jane Gaines for enabling this essay in the first place and to Celine Parrenas Shimizu for many stimulating conversations and for sharing her pioneering paper on *Mandingo* with me. Thanks also to Elizabeth Abel, Karl Britto, Heather Butler, Anne Cheng, Noel Carroll, Lawrence Cohen, Susan Courtney, Tom Gunning, Ralph Hexter, Michael Lucey, Ara Osterweil, and Steven Schneider for helpful comments. And special thanks to Rich Cante for a chance to say some of this out loud for the first time.

1 They are not, of course, *equally* available to all. Jane Juffer, writing about women's consumption of pornography in the home, notes that access to pornography is radically different for women when compared to that of men (1998, 5, 107).

2 For Bataille, this violation of prohibition constitutes a violent jolting out of discontinuous existence—a moment that puts the individual in contact with the continuity of death, which orgasm, often referred to by the French as *le petit mort* (little death), approximates. This jolt transgresses the law but does not defeat it (1957, 30–39).

3 I am indebted to Susan Courtney for the illuminating adjective *color mute*, which seems to me a useful description of the post–civil rights era dilemma of so much racial discourse: no one is blind to visible racial differences, but the practice of politely ignoring them produces a condition of muteness that often impedes the ability to deal with racial inequality. The term does not appear in Courtney's forthcoming book, *Hollywood Fantasies of Miscegenation*, but derives from that book's insights.

4 Mercer published an initial article attacking Mapplethorpe in 1986, and a second article, revising the first, in 1989. He then combined them in the 1992 "Skin Head Sex Thing: Racial Difference and the Homoerotic Imaginary." My notes are taken from his most recent revision, in his 1994 book, *Welcome to the Jungle*.

5 Of course the real issue may be, as Jane Gaines (1992) has pointed out, who is reading, and finding erotic pleasure in, the *Black Book*: Mercer and other gay black friends; white gay men, like Mapplethorpe himself; white women; or black women? Only the latter could be said not to transgress some racial or sexual border.

6 See, for example, Nead 1992, Dennis 1995, and Freedberg 1989.

7 The Dark brothers are white, as is the script writer, who writes under the pseudonym Antonio Pasolini. Pasolini claims that these videos were written with the intention of being as politically incorrect as possible. The companion video, *Let Me Tell Ya 'Bout Black Chicks*, was about the slightly less taboo sexual relations of low-class white men and black women. It apparently contained scenes of white racists extolling the parallel virtues of "black chicks" and their special appeal to white men. Though the taboos against crossing this color line are historically less in force, in this instance, apparently the use of white characters in KKK uniforms pushed many buttons. It was thus this video, not *White Chicks*, that was selected for indictment during the Reagan era, resulting in the disappearance of *Black Chicks* from all shelves. Even the writer claims not to be able to obtain a copy (personal phone interview with Antonio Pasolini, March 2001).

8 For a further discussion of this issue from the point of view of white supremacist mainstream American culture, see Williams 2001.

9 It is worth noting that in these two different accounts, Koon wildly vacillates between two competing images of the white woman cop: one casts her, somewhat improbably, in the Lillian Gish role of defenseless white woman cringing before the "black beast," while the other casts her as a trigger-happy Dirty Harriet trying to fill a man's shoes. I write about the racial melodrama of this fantasy of the endangered white woman in the white male imagination in my 2001 book *Playing the Race Card: Melodramas of Black and White from Uncle Tom to O. J. Simpson*.

10 On May 7, 1975, *Variety* wrote: "Schoolboys of all ages used to get off on Kyle Onstrott's novel of sexploitation sociology, 'Mandingo,' and now, thanks to Paramount and producer Dino De Laurentis, they still can. Richard Schickel follows suit in *Time*, dismissing the film's luridness: "Most of the suspense in *Mandingo* is generated by the unconscionable amount of time it requires for the blonde mistress of Falconhurst to invite into her bed the handsome black slave . . . her husband purchased to improve the breeding stock down in the quarters. Until this moment we cannot be certain that the movie is going to employ *every* cliché of antebellum melodrama" (1975). In the L.A. *Times*, Kevin Thomas (1975) called it "this year's trash masterpiece" whose "condemnation of slavery" is "but an excuse to project the most salacious miscegenation-inspired sex fantasies ever seen this side of an X rating."

11 Several critics have made recent claims for the film's importance. Andrew Britton has made the earliest, and most auteur-centered, claim for the film's im-

portance as a work of art, as opposed to a crass work of exploitation, which marked the film's original critical reception. Robin Wood (1998) has followed suit. Ed Guerrero (1993) places the film more or less within the tradition of blaxploitation, but does not make the same kind of claims for its importance. And Celine Parrenas Shimizu, in an unpublished paper entitled "Master-Slave Sex Acts: *Mandingo* and the Race/Sex Paradox," to which I am much indebted, has explored its connections to the Hegelian dilemma found in "Lordship and Bondage."

12 The cycle of blaxploitation began with *Sweet Sweetback's Baadasss Song* (1971) and was followed by *Shaft*, *Superfly* (dir. Gordon Parks, 1972), and a range of action-sex films set in the ghetto. They were closely followed by a cycle of female-centered action-sex films such as *Cleopatra Jones* (dir. Jack Starrett, 1973), *Coffy* (dir. Jack Hill, 1973), and *Foxy Brown* (dir. Jack Hill, 1974).

13 The elegant way in which the film reworks the luridness of both previous traditions is encapsulated in the cover of the novel's paperback edition, which, in turn, took its cue from the film's posters. On one cover, cleverly parodying the pose of Scarlett O'Hara in the arms of Rhett Butler in the posters for *Gone with the Wind*, we see the white master sweeping his black slave girl off her feet; in the next, we see the Mandingo "buck" sweeping his white mistress off her feet. See Wood 1998.

14 The novel is considerably less romantic: the young master is never really enamored of his wife and is already involved in a more than merely procreative relationship with his slave "wench."

15 He not only shoots him, but pushes his wounded body into a boiling cauldron with a pitchfork. The slave who picks up the gun at the end had been taught to read by Cicero, the revolutionary slave who is hung midway through the film, but not before delivering a speech in which he berates his fellow slaves for their servility and invites the masters to "kiss my black ass."

16 A house slave grabs a gun and kills the old master before running off. The young master is left mourning the body of his father, bereft of wife and child, while Muddy Waters sings the blues.

17 A frequently cited precursor to both this film and the urban genre of blaxploitation is the James Brown/Raquel Welch love scene in *100 Rifles* (dir. Tom Gries, 1969). Henry Louis Gates briefly cites it as Jim Brown making "wild and passionate love to Raquel Welch," (1991, 163), although Ed Guerrero (1993) notes that the fact that Welch was cast as a Mexican tempers this scene (79). The Brown/Welch scene has none of the frisson of the *Mandingo* scene. Indeed, when Gates writes that it is "safe to say that the frisson of miscegenation has never been treated in American film with either intelligence or candor [until Spike Lee's *Jungle Fever*]," he clearly had not seen *Mandingo*.

18 Andrew Britton describes it as "one of the most beautiful and moving love scenes in the cinema," arguing that the beauty of the union lies essentially in its fra-

gility, as the couple is "united in their horror at the other man's use of another human being for a personal satisfaction . . . which denies and degrades their humanity" (1976, 11).

19 Celine Parrenas Shimizu writes of this scene: "The two who struggle against each other's difference instead affirm each other's insufficiencies and dependencies within a system of dehumanizing brutality" (2000, 16).

20 Celine Shimizu offers an intriguing, and somewhat more hopeful, argument that something like a subversive mutual recognition momentarily occurs in both this scene and in a later sex scene between the female mistress and her black slave before violence and subjugation reemerge: "Sex both ensures slavery and undermines it in a complicated formulation of power" (2000, 20). While she may be right about the (briefly) subversive nature of these recognitions, it is worth asking on what basis this recognition is made. Shimizu seems to suggest that it is grounded in a common humanity, that subject and other find themselves, at least momentarily, reflected in one another despite their differences. Intersubjectivity is thus conceived here as an overcoming of difference, a discovery of sameness with radical, "self-fashioning" potential able to undermine the structure of slavery. My argument inclines more toward the notion that the eroticism is fueled by the taboo, but that recognition keeps in place a destructive difference and aggression.

21 Butler differentiates Benjamin's ideal of recognition in which "destruction of the self is an occasional and lamentable occurrence, one that is reversed and overcome in the therapeutic situation and that does not turn out to constitute recognition essentially" (Butler 2000, 274). Her own description of the ongoing process of recognition reads Hegel differently to argue that recognition cannot "leave destructiveness behind" (274), as if recognition was not also a form of aggression.

22 Shimizu says that as Blanche strips Mede of his clothes, she also strips off her mastery. However, her "mastery" has never been the same as her husband's, proof of which is given in the fact that what she risks in having sex with Mede is not what her husband risks in having sex with Ellen: her very life. Ellen is "sleeping up"; Blanche, like her husband, is "sleeping down," but, unlike him, at real cost.

23 This is not the first extended representation of interracial lust in Hollywood. A case could be made for the shower sex scene in *Shaft*, and even for the sex scene between Jim Brown and Raquel Welch in *100 Rifles*, both mentioned by Henry Louis Gates as rare moments of interracial sex. However, the sex in *Shaft* remains purposefully casual, and in *100 Rifles* it is arguably portrayed as occurring between two persons of color (Mexican Indian and African American). *Mandingo*, however, appears to present the first important scene of interracial lust in Hollywood cinema that inscribes the taboo against it into the very scene that transgresses it. It is thus also, in the Hegelian sense, the one film that portrays the difficulty of recognition.

24 I include my own, racially unmarked discussion in *Hard Core* (1989, 157).

25 A stag film from the twenties, entitled *Darkie Rhythm,* had an African American woman roll her eyes to the rhythm of the black male's thrusts.

Works Cited

Bataille, Georges. 1957. *Erotism: Death and Sensuality.* Trans. Mary Dalwood. San Francisco: City Lights Books.

Bhabha, Homi K. 1994. *The Location of Culture.* New York: Routledge.

Bright, Susie. N.d. "Inter-racial and Black Videos." Unpublished manuscript. Courtesy of author.

Britton, Andrew. 1976. "*Mandingo.*" *Movie* 22. 1–22.

Brown, Nick. 1992. "Race: The Political Unconscious in American Film." *East-West Film Journal* 6, 1.

Butler, Judith. 2000. "Longing for Recognition." *Sexuality and Gender Studies* 1, 3.

Courtney, Susan. 2004. *Hollywood Fantasies of Miscegenation.* Princeton: Princeton University Press.

Cromer, Mark. 2001. "Porn's Compassionate Conservatism." *Nation,* February 26, 25–28.

Dennis, Kelly. 1995. "Playing with Herself: Feminine Sexuality and Aesthetic Indifference." In *Solitary Pleasures: The Historical, Literary, and Artistic Discourses of Autoeroticism,* ed. Paula Bennett and Vernon Rosario II. New York: Routledge.

Doane, Mary Ann. 1991. "Dark Continents: Epistemologies and Racial and Sexual Difference in Psychoanalysis and the Cinema." In *Femmes Fatales: Feminism, Film Theory, Psychoanalysis.* New York: Routledge.

Dyer, Richard. 1985. "Male Gay Porn: Coming to Terms." *Jump Cut,* March.

Fanon, Frantz. 1967. *Black Skin, White Masks.* Trans. Charles Lam Markmann. New York: Grove.

Fiske, John. 1995. *Media Matters: Race and Gender in U.S. Politics.* Minneapolis: University of Minnesota Press.

Foucault, Michel. 1978. *The History of Sexuality. Vol. 1: An Introduction.* New York: Pantheon Books.

Freedberg, David. 1989. *The Power of Images: Studies in the History and Theory of Response.* Chicago: University of Chicago Press.

Gaines, Jane. 1992. "Competing Glances: Who Is Reading Robert Mapplethorpe's *Black Book?*" *New Formations* 16 (summer): 24–39.

———. 2001. *Fire and Desire: Mixed Race Movies in the Silent Era.* Chicago: University of Chicago Press.

Gates, Henry Louis, Jr. 1991. "Jungle Fever; or, Guess Who's Not Coming to Dinner." In *Five for Five: The Films of Spike Lee.* New York: Workman Publications. 163–69.

Guerrero, Ed. 1993. *Framing Blackness: The African American Image in Film.* Philadelphia: Temple University Press.

Hegel, G. W. F. 1977. *Phenomenology of Spirit*. Oxford: Oxford University Press.

JanMohamed, Abdul. 1992. "Sexuality on/of the Racial Border: Foucault, Wright, and the Articulation of Racialized Sexuality." In *Discourses of Sexuality*, ed. Donna Stanton. Ann Arbor: University of Michigan Press.

Juffer, Jane. 1998. *At Home with Pornography: Women, Sex, and Everyday Life*. New York: New York University Press.

Julian, Isaac, and Kobena Mercer. 1986. "True Confessions." *Ten* 8, 22.

Koon, Stacey. 1992. *Presumed Innocent*. New York: Regency Publishing.

Mercer, Kobena. 1987. "Imaging the Black Man's Sex." In *Photography/Politics: Two*, ed. Pat Holland, Jo Spence, and Simon Watney. London: Comedia. 61–69.

———. 1991. "Skin Head Sex Thing: Racial Difference and the Homoerotic Imaginary." In *How Do I Look? Queer Film and Video*, ed. Bad Object-Choices. Seattle: Bay. 169–222.

———. 1994. *Welcome to the Jungle*. New York: Routledge.

Nead, Lynda. 1992. *The Female Nude: Art, Obscenity, and Sexuality*. New York: Routledge.

Neale, Steve. 1979–80. "The Same Old Story: Stereotypes and Difference." *Screen Education*: 32–35.

Pascoe, Peggy. 1999. "Miscegenation, Court Cases, and Ideologies of 'Race' in Twentieth-Century America." In *Sex, Love, Race: Crossing Boundaries in North American History*. Ed. Martha Hodes. New York: New York University Press.

Perkins, Tessa. 1979. "Rethinking Stereotypes." In *Ideology and Cultural Production*, ed. Michele Barrett et al. London: Croom Helm.

Review of *Mandingo*. 1975. *Variety*, May 7.

Rosello, Mireille. 1998. *Declining the Stereotype: Ethnicity and Representation in French Cultures*. Hanover, N.H.: University Press of New England.

Rubin, Gayle. 1984. "Thinking Sex: Notes for a Radical Theory of the Politis of Sexuality." In *Pleasure and Danger: Exploring Female Sexuality*, ed. Carol Vance. New York: Routledge and Kegan Paul. 267–318.

Schickel, Richard. 1975. "Cold, Cold Ground." *Time*, May 12.

Shimizu, Celine Parrenas. 2000. "Master-Slave Sex Acts: *Mandingo* and the Race/Sex Paradox." Unpublished Manuscript.

Thomas, Kevin. 1975. "Sadism Down on the Plantation." *Los Angeles Times*, May 22.

Williams, Linda. 1989. *Hard Core: Power, Pleasure, and the "Frenzy of the Visible"* Berkeley: University of California Press.

———. 2001. *Playing the Race Card: Melodramas of Black and White from Uncle Tom to O. J. Simpson*. Princeton, N.J.: Princeton University Press.

Wood, Robin. 1998. *"Mandingo*: The Vindication of an Abused Masterpiece." In *Sexual Politics and Narrative Film: Hollywood and Beyond*. New York: Columbia University Press.

Crackers and Whackers:

The White Trashing of Porn

CONSTANCE PENLEY

White Trash Theory

✳ Before getting into my topic—porn's predilection for white trash looks
and tastes—I want to say something about the benefits to one's theoretical
formation that can accrue from growing up white trash. This brief comment
does not mark a digression from my topic because it was precisely my white
trash upbringing that gave me the conceptual tools to recognize this predilection, as well as the language to describe and explain it. I cannot imagine
any better preparation for grasping the intricacies of contemporary theory
and cultural studies than negotiating a Florida cracker childhood and ado-
lescence. I understood the gist of structuralist binaries, semiosis, the linguistic nature of the unconscious, the disciplinary micro-organization of
power, and the distinguishing operations of taste culture long before I left
the groves of central Florida for the groves of academe. At the University
of Florida in Gainesville, the University of California at Berkeley, and the
École des Hautes Études en Sciences Sociales in Paris, I encountered the
ideas of Ferdinand de Saussure, Claude Lévi-Strauss, Roland Barthes, Louis
Althusser, Jacques Lacan, Michel Foucault, and, somewhat later, Michel de
Certeau, and Pierre Bourdieu. In those ideas I immediately recognized the
home truths of white trash or, as Barthes would say, white trashnicity.

How does such theoretical precociousness emerge in cracker culture?
Consider, for example, the intense conceptual work involved in figuring out
the differential meanings of white trash—what it is because of what it is not,
a regular down-home version of honey and ashes, the raw and the cooked.

A Southern white child is required to learn that white trash folks are the lowest of the low because socially and economically they have sunk so far that they might as well be black. As such, they are seen to have lost all self-respect. So it becomes particularly unseemly when they appear to shame-lessly flaunt their trashiness, which, after all, is nothing but an aggressively in-your-face reminder of stark class differences, a fierce fuck-you to anyone trying to maintain a belief in an America whose only class demarcations run along the seemingly obvious ones of race.

If you *are* white trash, then you must engage in the never-ending labor of distinguishing yourself, of codifying your behavior so as to clearly sig-nify a difference from blackness, which will, in spite of everything, express some minuscule, if pathetic, measure of your culture's superiority, at least to those above you who use the epithet *white trash* to emphasize just how beyond the pale you are. This is hard going because the differences between the everyday lives of poor blacks and poor whites in the rural South are few and ephemeral. I am not denying the difference of race—and of how that difference is lived—but am trying to point to the crushing weight, on all those lives, of enduring poverty and the daily humiliations that come with it.

Even someone with as impeccable white trash credentials as my own can recall only one "distinction": white people don't eat gopher, but blacks do (gopher is crackerese for a variety of land turtle). Perhaps I remember the socioanthropological distinction gopher/not gopher because it intersected with so many other distinctions marked by race, gender, and economic class which would, as I came to realize, both help and hinder me as I grew up and out into the world.

I made money as a kid by catching the slow-moving gophers in the white-owned groves and selling them for a quarter each to my teenage cousin Ricky, already a reprobate but a shrewd entrepreneur. Ricky would turn around and sell the gophers for fifty cents in East Town, the black neigh-borhood where I, as a white girl, was not allowed to go. I progressed from being grateful to my cousin for giving me the odd quarters to chafing at the restrictions on my mobility and my own budding entrepreneurship. This was especially so after Ricky had rounded up a crew of gopher catchers from whose labor he was able to extract for himself at least as much as the mini-mum wage Disney pays its workers now toiling on our old hunting grounds.

But crackers are not always content merely to learn the complex strata-gems of maintaining the tenuous distinctions of white trash culture; they sometimes go beyond that understanding to devise the critical method of using white trash against white trash. The epithet *white trash* can be deployed in a similar way to the original usage of *politically correct* within left circles, where a group would adopt the phrase to police its own excesses. My brother and I had a favorite game, which was to try to figure out which side of the family was the trashiest, our mother's Tennessee hillbilly clan or our father's Florida cracker kin. The point of the game was not to come to a definitive conclusion (we agreed it was pretty much a toss-up), but to try to selectively detrash ourselves, to figure out just how trashy we were so as to monitor and modify our thinking and behavior as much as possible. We vied to amass the most self-humiliating family statistics by claiming for mom's or dad's side the greatest number of cousins married to one another, uncles sent up the river for stealing tv sets, junked cars on blocks in the front yard, converts to Jehovah's Witnesses, or grandparents who uttered racist remarks with the most vehemence and flagrancy. Why my brother and I came to want to engage in this funny but painful detrashing project is a long story that must wait for another day, but the fact that we created this game demonstrates that white-trashness does not just involve the effort to make distinctions in response to a label coercively imposed from above ("Hey, at least we don't eat gopher!") but can also offer a prime source for developing the kinds of skills needed to grasp the social and political dynamics of everyday life.

Growing up white trash, then, can give one the conceptual framework for understanding the work of distinction and the methods of criticism. But the real advantage lies in the way that upbringing helps a nascent theorist grasp the idea of agency and resistance in an utterly disdained subculture whose very definition presumes it to have no "culture" at all (Genovese 1972, 565).[1] The work of distinction in white trash can be deployed downward, across, but also up, to challenge the assumed social and moral superiority of the middle and professional classes.

White Trash Practice

Considering the ways that white trash can be deployed up as a form of populist cultural criticism brings me to pornography. We already have several good discussions of the class nature and class politics of pornography, although the research on earlier periods is more extensive than that on the products of today's commercial industry. The contributors to Lynn Hunt's *The Invention of Pornography: Obscenity and the Origins of Modernity, 1500–1800* (1993) give a wealth of examples of the way pornography was used during that period to challenge absolutist political authority and church doctrine, variously linked as it was to freethinking, heresy, science, and natural philosophy. In *The Literary Underground of the Old Regime*, Robert Darnton (1982) describes the workings of the eighteenth-century literary underground, a counterculture that produced smutty, muckraking, libelous literature and images that mocked and eroded the authority of the Old Regime. In *The Secret Museum: Pornography in Modern Culture*, Walter Kendrick (1987) argues that nineteenth-century pornography had no typical content of its own, but consisted solely of dangerous and seditious images and ideas that the ruling classes wanted to keep out of the hands of the presumably more susceptible lower orders. Defense attorney Edward de Grazia's *Girls Lean Back Everywhere: The Law on Obscenity and the Assault on Genius* (1992) tells story after story of early and mid-twentieth century attempts to defend books such as *Ulysses, Tropic of Cancer, An American Tragedy, The Well of Loneliness, Howl*, and *Naked Lunch* against the efforts of the state, the police, and religion to ban this material from public and popular consumption.

But where are the defenders of contemporary works like *Tanya Hardon, The Sperminator*, or *John Wayne Bobbitt: Uncut*? The more mass-cultural the genre becomes, and, it seems, the more militantly "tasteless," the more difficult it is to see pornography's historical continuity with avant-garde revolutionary art, populist struggles, or any kind of countercultural impulses. Add the feminist antiporn polemic, and this low-rent genre appears unredeemable artistically, socially, or otherwise. Exceptions do get made, of course, for quality politically oriented gay male videos, such as Jerry Douglas's *Honorable Discharge* (1993), about gays in the military; Candida Royalle's so-called couples erotica; Fatale's lesbian-made videos for lesbians; and educational porn, which includes Gay Men's Health Crisis's safer sex videos or porn star and feminist Nina Hartley's guides to better fellatio and cunnilingus. But within mass-commercial videos, the great majority of the titles are seen to merit little critical, much less feminist, interest.

Two writers have suggested why this might be the case. In "The Popularity of Pornography," a chapter of Andrew Ross's *No Respect: Intellectuals and Popular Culture* (1989), he argues that the feminist disdain for pornography constitutes a Victorian holdover, a conditioned middle-class female revulsion for anything associated with the lower orders, a revulsion that leads directly to, as Judith Walkowitz (1980) has shown in the case of nineteenth-century feminism, the political strategy of legislating an outright ban (the temperance movement) or engaging in moral reform and public hygiene efforts (getting prostitutes off the street and into "proper" jobs as maids and factory workers).

Laura Kipnis builds on Ross's argument about feminism and the class politics of porn in "(Male) Desire, (Female) Disgust: Reading *Hustler*" (1992). She tells us how she made herself overcome her revulsion for the magazine to be able to sit down one day and actually look at it. Kipnis discovered that this most reviled instance of mass-circulation porn is at the same time one of the most explicitly class-antagonistic mass periodicals of any genre. *Hustler*, she found, was militantly gross in its pictorials, its cartoons, its editorials, and its political humor—with bodies and body parts straight out of Rabelais—all put to service in stinging attacks on petit-bourgeoisie-hood, every kind of social and intellectual pretension, the social power of the professional classes, the power of the government, and the hypocrisy of organized religion. Although Kipnis remains grossed out by *Hustler*, her reading of the magazine gives her and us an invaluable insight into the class-based reasons for that revulsion and the social and political uses of grossness. She carefully points out, however, as Darnton does in his study of the eighteenth-century French literary underground, that the libertarian politics here cannot always or necessarily be described as progressive; still they serve an important role in questioning repressive and pretentious assumptions of morality and authority. You can be sure that if Newt Gingrich is *Hustler*'s "Asshole of the Month," Oprah Winfrey will have the honors next time (as they did, in consecutive months, in 1995).

What Kipnis calls *Hustler*'s grossness could also be characterized as an ingenious deployment of white trash sensibilities. Don't look to this magazine for the kind of witty and bitter barbs that issue forth from the mouths of Bertolt Brecht's working-class antiheroes. When *Hustler* maneuvers into class position, it stations itself firmly on the bottom of the sociocultural chain of being. Its deliberately stupid humor, savaging of middle-class and professional codes of decorum, its raunchiness and sluttiness all scream white trash. But this kind of lumpen bawdiness is not unique to *Hustler*. It pervades contemporary mass-commercial porn, as well as the entire history of U.S. porn production, far more so than does the "classier" tone of *Playboy* and *Penthouse*.

To me and to the students I teach in a course on pornography as a popular American film genre, the most striking feature of the films we survey, beginning in 1896, is the ubiquitous use of humor, and not just any kind of humor, but bawdiness, humorously lewd and obscene language and situations.[2] Up until the late sixties, the predominant form of pornographic film was the short, usually black-and-white, anonymously produced film known variously as the stag film, the blue movie, or the smoker, so called because of the smoke-filled rooms where men would gather for clandestine screenings. In a recent sympathetic evaluation of Linda Williams's *Hard Core: Power, Pleasure, and the "Frenzy of the Visible,"* the (yes, I'll say it) seminal book on pornographic film, Peter Lehman worries that she misses some crucial aspects of porn by overestimating the importance of narrative structure and neglecting the role of "fleeting moments of humor in porn" (Lehman 1995, 3).[3] His argument about the relatively greater importance of "fragmentary pleasures" over narrative resolution proves persuasive, but his assessment that there occur only "fleeting" moments of humor in porn falls short. Stag films are full of humor, and the narrative, which, as Lehman notes, is often more vignette than fully developed story, is itself structured like a joke. And here we are talking about really bad jokes, ranging from terrible puns to every form of dirty joke—farmer's daughter, traveling salesman, and Aggie jokes. Of course, not all of the sexually explicit films of this period exhibited the bawdy, farcical character of the stags. The short peep show loops consisted of earnestly direct views of sexual action with little setup and no story. But the majority of the few hundred American stag films made for collective male viewing depended on this popular brand of humor. This holds especially true for the pre–World War II films made on the edges of the entertainment world, thus sharing the qualities of both burlesque and silent film comedy.[4]

Given the enormous success of the feminist antiporn movement—and their strange bedfellows, the religious right—in shaping the current prevailing idea of porn as nothing but the degradation of women and the prurient documentation of the most horrific forms of violence waged against women, it may prove difficult to recognize that the tone of pornography—when one actually looks at it—is closer to *Hee Haw* than Nazi death camp fantasies. Also difficult to recognize, because it so goes against the contemporary typification of porn as something *done to* women, is that the joke is usually on the man. And if the man is the butt of the joke, this also contradicts Freud's description of the mechanism of the smut joke, in which any woman present at the telling of the joke will inevitably be its butt.

On the Beach (a.k.a. *Getting His Goat*) is a classic stag film from 1923 that illustrates both the kind of humor and the level of commentary on masculinity found in the typical stag film of the era. The narrative follows that of a practical joke played on a hapless man. The man (Creighton Hale, better known as the professor in D. W. Griffith's *Way Down East* [1920]) is daydreaming while leaning on a fence at the beach. He accosts three playful, flirtatious women who come walking by and agree to have sex with him, but only through a hole in the fence. The punning alternate title of the film tells you what's coming next: what the man believes is "the best girl I've ever had" is a goat the women back up to the hole in the fence. The women take all his money, which he happily gives, and dance laughing down the beach. At some unspecified time later, the three women are again walking along the beach. On spying the erstwhile daydreamer, one tucks a pillow under her dress to simulate pregnancy, and the women again extract money from the bewildered man, once more "getting his goat." The women in the film are not portrayed as motivated by some intrinsic female evil but rather by a kind of charming mischievousness, and the man is shown deserving what he gets because of his sexual and social ignorance. "Watch your step. There's one born every minute," says the final intertitle in a cautionary address to the male audience not to be fools to their own desires.

One can trace the low-level humor of many stag films back to the bawdy songs and dirty jokes that inspired them. If Linda Williams's breakthrough was to get us to think of pornographic film as *film*, that is, as a genre that can be compared to other popular genres like the western, the science fiction film, the gangster film, or the musical (porn's closest kin, she says) and studied with the same analytical tools we take to the study of other films, the next logical step, it seems, would be to consider pornographic film as popular culture. We would then be able to ask what traits pornographic film shares with the production and consumption of a whole range of popular forms.

Reading through Ed Cray's *The Erotic Muse: American Bawdy Songs* (1992) makes one aware, for example, of the similarity between the lyrics of the dirty song tradition and the plots of stag films. Anticlericalism is big, of course, in both bawdy songs and porn films, as it is in the endlessly recyclable joke, "Did you hear the one about the priest and the rabbi . . . ." Cray tells us that songs about licentious ecclesiasticals proved so popular that English obscenity law evolved from court actions to suppress them.[5] In the several versions of the bawdy song "The Monk of Great Renown," the monk engages in rape, anal intercourse, and necrophilia. The somewhat tamer stag films that I have seen prefer to attack the hypocrisy of the clerical class by having the priests and the nuns get it on in all sorts of combinations. Most of the anticlerical films were imports from France or other heavily Catholic countries, except for the American classic *The Nun's Story* (1949–52). Beginning in the fifties, stag films, especially in the United States, shifted from attacking the priesthood to mocking the mores of the new professional classes, which they depicted as exploiting professional power for sexual purposes in films such as *The Casting Couch* (1924), *The Dentist* (1947–48), *Doctor Penis* (1948–52), and *Divorce Attorney* (1966–67).

Surprisingly (although why should it be?), stag films also share with bawdy songs an emphasis on female agency, with the woman both initiating sex and setting the terms for the sexual encounter. In "The Tinker," and related bawdy songs, the housewife cajoles the workingman into having sex first with her and then all the other women in the house, but she turns on the tinker when he decides to screw the butler too. In one stag film from the late teens or early twenties (provenance and title uncertain), two women undress, drink wine, and fondle each other. One says to the other, "I brought Jacques," and straps on a dildo. A few moments later, an intertitle tells us that the hairdresser is at the door. One woman fellates the hairdresser while he works on the other woman's hair; they then pull him into a three-way. In another film of the same period, two women are out mushroom hunting in the woods and come across a penis poking through the underbrush. They examine the penis with a magnifying glass before deciding that they have discovered a new species of mushroom. An intertitle tells us that "the mushroom was enjoyed in all kinds of sauces," and we then see the two women, and the naked man revealed to be attached to the penis, in various combinations. In *Goodyear*, from the forties, a man and a woman are sitting on a couch when the woman pulls a condom out of her bag and demonstrates its use to the man. After a blow job, intercourse, and another blow job, the woman flips the man's limp penis from side to side, shaking her head with disappointment. In *The Wet Dream*, from the Horny Film Corporation (also from the late forties or early fifties), the woman in the man's dream will not let him get on top after she's been on top of him. He finally does manage to get on top, but only after she has put a French tickler on him, presumably for her pleasure. This film also ends with the woman's disappointment with the man's now completely limp penis. In one of the best-known stag films of all times, *Smart Aleck* (1951) with Candy Barr, she refuses to go down on the man, especially when he starts to force her. She gets up in disgust and calls a female friend who does want to have oral sex with the man. While that's going on, Barr gets back into the scene to get the man to go down on her. Here, as in "The Tinker," the woman orchestrates the sexual activity.

The theme of the penis run amok makes for another important trait shared by the bawdy song and the stag film. Such penises appear, for example, in meldings of the bawdy ballad and the sea shanty, where you get descriptions like, "With his long fol-the-riddle-do right down to his knee" (Cray 1992, 35), or, "Hanging down, swinging free. . . . With a yard and a half of foreskin hanging down below his knee" (36). The tinker rides to the lady's house "with his balls slung o'er his shoulder and his penis by his side" (31), but he gets in trouble by fucking the butler when he is supposed to be fucking all the ladies and, in another variant, fucks the devil. Wayward and wandering giant organs abound in everything from fraternity songs, "Do Your Balls Hang Low?," to cowboy and Vietnam-era lyrics about efforts to exert some control over the penis, such as, "Gonna Tie My Pecker to My Leg" (336–37, 192–93).

Animated films of the stag era, unconstrained by physical reality, managed to depict the amok penis better than live-action films. *Buried Treasure* (ca. 1928–33) features Everready Hardon. Poor Everready's penis runs off on its own, gets bent and has to be pounded back into shape, goes after a woman but accidentally fucks a man, and runs into the business end of a cactus, among other, often painful, mishaps. In *The Further Adventures of Super Screw* (also ca. 1928–33) the hero's penis is so big that he must drag it along on the ground, where it gets bit by a dog and then run over by a bus. While his penis is in a sling at the hospital, a nurse decides to cut his gargantuan member down to size. After they have ribald sex, he goes into the lab and starts screwing a chimp who impales him on its own giant penis. After returning to the operating room to get his penis restored to its original dimension, he finds an ape to screw. Since the producers and consumers of these films were unquestionably male, the ubiquity of this theme of male humiliation demands accounting for in some way.

Laura Kipnis points out that in *Hustler*, much as we have seen in the films, jokes, and songs noted above, sex emerges as an arena of humiliation for men, not as one of domination and power over women: "The fantasy life here is animated by cultural disempowerment in relation to a sexual caste system and a social class system" (1992, 383). Rather than offering the compensatory fantasy found in the more upscale *Penthouse* and *Playboy*, where the purchase of pricey consumer goods will ensure willing women and studly men, *Hustler* puts into question a male fantasy that represents power, money, and prestige as essential to sexual success; "the magazine works to disparage and counter identification with these sorts of class attributes on every front" (383). *Hustler* puts the male body at risk, Kipnis says, which helps to account for its focus on castration humor and ads addressed to male anxieties and inadequacies, such as advertisements for products promising to extend and enlarge penises. *Hustler* and other deliberately trashy magazines (my favorite is *Outlaw Biker*)[6] are the print progeny of stag films and related forms of smutty folklore.

Ed Cray underestimates the centrality of bawdy humor to the porn film when he contrasts what he sees as the lack of prurience in folk balladry to the dearth of humor in pornography. Although he recognizes that folk balladry can easily veer toward the pornographic, and does so often, he is not as ready to acknowledge that pornographic titillation can incorporate bawdiness; "pornography is rarely humorous," he says (1992, xxviii). But ribald humor seems equally important to the two forms and, moreover, bawdy songs often prove much wilder sexually than porn films. Only the animated films can play with the kind of hyperbolically exaggerated body parts and wildly impossible sexual positions that are a staple of the bawdy song. It would be more accurate to say that both popular forms are fundamentally based in a kind of humor that features attacks on religion (and, later, the professional classes), middle-class ideas about sexuality, trickster women with a hearty appetite for sex, and foolish men with their penises all in a twist—when those penises work at all.

It is illuminating to see which forms or figures from popular culture stag films cite to reinforce these themes. The soundtrack added to *The Casting Couch* is a recording of Mae West's riff on the importance of education, where she gives a man a lesson in mathematics: "Addition is when you take one thing and put it with another to get two. Two and two is four and five will get you ten if you know how to work it." Subtraction is when "a man has a hundred dollars and you leave him two." Another film of the same era, *The Bachelor Dream*, ends with a shot of *Mad Magazine's* mascot Alfred E. Neuman.

While it is true that stag films borrowed heavily from the oral culture of joke telling, it is also important to note that the films, in the way male audiences consumed them, themselves became part of oral culture. The American Legionnaires, Shriners, and Kappa Sigs counted on the films' humor to help them manage a relation to the sex on screen and to each other, a kind of "comic relief" regulating the viewing's guilt and discomfort. No film exists without its audience, but this holds especially true for the stag film because the back talk and verbal display the film sparks form an integral part of the film experience. *Hard to Imagine*, Thomas Waugh's 1996 history of gay male photography and film, briefly suggests that such humor may have appealed to gay men in the audiences as well, even though it has long been recognized that the linguistic antics surrounding the films traditionally functioned to shore up the homosocial heterosexuality of the audiences against any hint that a bunch of men looking at penises together were gay (319–20). Waugh thinks it would be a reach to claim that stag film humor reflects a gay camp sensibility, but he does believe that "the stag film's coy mixing of levels of cultural affectation with sexual innuendo and vulgarity would not have fallen on deaf gay ears" (320). If Waugh found few gay male films among the stag films he researched, he still thinks it possible that gay pleasures were nonetheless to be found in both the straight stag films and the oral culture that embedded them.

Although porn is usually conceptualized and debated as a stigmatized "other," completely beyond the moral and cultural pale, its desires, concerns, and uses do not differ that markedly from those found in other popular forms throughout U.S. history. Here, I took the example of bawdy songs, but those other forms include the dirty jokes told everywhere, everyday in offices, on playgrounds, and now in faxes and on the Internet. Folklorists like Alan Dundes and Gershon Legman tell us that smutty joke telling is the warp and woof of American working life, a kind of humor that constitutes a major form of symbolic communication expressing and forming our changing ideas and anxieties about a number of issues, but especially sexuality and the relations between the sexes.[7] Other closely related popular forms are *America's Funniest Home Videos*, *Mad Magazine*, and WWF wrestling, which, like porn, is a physical contact sport requiring a similar suspension of disbelief.

When my course on pornographic film was protested by the local antiporn group (based in local churches) and Pat Robertson in a *700 Club* special on godlessness in public schools, it became clear that my critics most feared that studying pornography as film or popular culture would normalize it. That's why Pat Robertson called my course "a new low in humanist excess," right after making the wonderfully curious statement that "a feminist teaching pornography is like Scopes teaching evolution."[8] And if the antiporn people followed the culture wars, they would also know that another danger lurked for them beyond the threat of normalization: the risk that scholars who take popular culture seriously might start asking of porn what they ask of all other forms of popular culture. These questions would include: "What is the nature of the widespread appeal?" "To what pleasures and ideas do these films speak?" "What desires and anxieties do the films express about identity, sexuality, and community, about what kind of world we want to live in?" "What kind of moral, social, and political counterculture do the producers and consumers of porn constitute?"[9] If the study of porn as film and popular culture reframes its subject as a relatively normal and socially significant instance of culture, this goes a long way toward disarming those who depend on its typification as sexual violence to crack down on moral and political dissidence. But enough of cracking down; let's get back to the issue of cracking up.

The bawdy humor, at the expense of the man, tends to drop out of porn films only during the so-called golden age of 1970s big-budget, theatrically released, feature-length narrative films like *Behind the Green Door* (dir. Mitchell Bros., 1972), *The Opening of Misty Beethoven* (dir. Radley Metzger, 1975), *The Resurrection of Eve* (dir. Mitchell Bros., 1973), and *The Story of Joanna* (dir. Gerard Damiano, 1975). In an era in which the makers of adult films were trying to respond at once to the sexual revolution, women's lib, and the possibility of expanding their demographics beyond the raincoat brigade and fraternal lodge members, the narratives began to center, albeit very anxiously, around the woman and her sexual odyssey. While there are some eruptions of egregious punning and willfully vulgar humor in these "quality" films meant for the heterosexual dating crowd (for example, Linda's friend in *Deep Throat* [dir. Gerard Damiano, 1972] who asks the man performing cunnilingus on her while she leans back and puffs away on a cigarette, "Do you mind if I smoke while you eat?"), they are far more "tasteful," even pseudoaristocratic, in their demeanor and depicted milieu than the great majority of films from the earlier stag era. But the stag films, which Linda Williams characterizes as lacking in narrative and more misogynistic in their "primitive" display of genitals and sexual activities than the golden-age pornos, may not come out as misogynistic as Williams says if we can recognize them more as strong popular joke structures than weak film narratives.

What I have observed is that as porn films "progressed" as film, technically and narratively, and began to focus on the woman and her subjectivity, they became more socially conservative, losing the bawdy populist humor that so often centered around the follies and foibles of masculinity. And while it is true that stag films usually just peter out, so to speak, without any narrative closure, such closure may not prove so desirable. Most of the golden-age pornos have closure, all right: like Hollywood films, they end in marriage or some other semisanctioned kind of coupling, while the stag films are content to celebrate sex itself without channeling it into the only socially acceptable form of sexual expression—heterosexual, monogamous marriage. It may also be that insofar as the golden-age films focus on women's sexuality and subjectivity, the pat solution of the marriage ending may have constituted an attempt to resolve the anxieties those films inadvertently raised in the course of a narrative about women's new sexual and social freedoms.

Fortunately, in the eighties and nineties, porn films got trashy again as producers threw off the "quality" trappings of the golden era to start manufacturing product for the rapidly expanding VCR market. Suddenly, many more people, women included, could consume porn, and many more people could produce it, even those who lacked money, technical training, or a sense of cinema aesthetics. Sure, there will always be pretentious auteurs in porn, as everywhere else, such as Andrew Blake and Zalman King, but during those two decades, amateur filmmaking ruled. So popular, in fact, were amateur films that the professional adult film companies started making fake amateur films, "pro-am," in which recognizable professionals, even stars, would play ordinary folks clowning around the house with their camcorder. As porn became deliciously trashy again, it coincided with a new female media deployment of white trash sensibilities against the class and sexual status quo not seen since the goddesses of burlesque reigned. Roseanne, Madonna, Courtney Love, Brett Butler, and Tonya Harding would certainly make the list, but it should be extended to include some significant male talent.

Howard Stern and Mike Judge (the creator of *Beavis and Butthead*) would have to rank among the most ingenious such deployers, with *Saturday Night Live's* Wayne and Garth in the running, but not really, because their raffishness is shot through with too much redeeming sweetness. All of these white trash theorists and practitioners understand the politically strategic value of making a spectacle of masculinity. Jeff ("You're a Redneck If . . .") Foxworthy, offers, by comparison, just a soft celebration of hick manhood.

When James Garner called Howard Stern "the epitome of trailer trash," Stern responded, in his typically scatological fashion, "I can't believe this guy wants a war with me. He should be busy worrying if he's gonna have a solid bowel movement." We know, of course, from Stern's now two best-selling memoirs that neither his parents nor his own Long Island suburban family live in a trailer. His nontrash origin goes to show that you do not have to be white trash to use white trash sensibilities as a weapon of cultural war, although the fact that white trash's rocket scientist, Roseanne, grew up so solidly trashy reinforces the argument that early training counts. In a real shocker, feminist artist and critic Barbara Kruger came out as a Howard Stern fan and defender, on the cover of *Esquire* no less, claiming that his "sharp, extemporaneous brand of performance art, his unrelenting penchant for 'truth'-telling, serves as a kind of leveler: a listening experience that cuts through the crap, through the deluded pretensions of fame, through the inflated rhetoric of prominence. . . . Zigzagging between self-degradation and megalomania, political clarity and dangerous stereotyping, temper tantrums and ridiculously humble ingratiation, he is both painfully unsettling and crazily funny" (1992, 95).

One feminist friend, who has long admired both Kruger's art and her critical writing, expressed dismay and disappointment that Kruger could defend such a sexist, racist homophobe. Is this postfeminism ad absurdum, she wondered. A couple of weeks after the shock of seeing Kruger's *Esquire* article, my friend called to tell me that she had been up late the night before and channel-zapped into something called "The Lesbian Dating Game." As she marveled at the funniest, most nonjudgmental representation of lesbians she had ever seen on television or in the movies, she was chastened to realize that she was watching—and loving—the *Howard Stern Show*.

Laura Kipnis argues that *Hustler* publisher Larry Flynt's obscenity trials did more to ensure First Amendment protection for American artists than any of the trials prosecuting much more culturally legitimate works of art and literature. In the same vein, Howard Stern's trashiness does more to counter the angry white men of America's airwaves (and elsewhere) than any liberal commentator because he targets precisely that masculinity that perceives itself to be under attack from all sides, a masculinity no longer sure of its God-given privilege and sense of entitlement so long taken for granted in law, government, and religion. Stern puts his body on display— phobic, farting, flailing—a male body lashing out at all the feared others— women with beauty, smarts, and power; strong, sexually confident blacks; those men with the kinds of superior qualities that attract women but who willfully choose to be gay. He also makes it clear that he wants more than anything to *be* those others and to *be with* them. Feeding his hysteria, then, is his not having a clue how to pull that off. Who, after all, wants a skinny, neurotic (if not psychotic) white guy "hung like a pimple"? *This* angry white man gives us a brilliant daily demonstration of what that anger is all about. Rush Limbaugh and his ilk dress up their anger in the trappings of a (male) rationality and knowledge. Howard Stern needs all the trailer-trashness he can muster to cut through the false decorum of that unexamined fury.

Beavis and Butthead, too, have never lived in a trailer, but they did burn down a trailer park. And the shabby den in which they watch TV makes Roseanne's house look like an Ethan Allen showroom. All of the pundits and parents who worry about kids mimicking these two delinquents have either never watched the show or have no idea of the way kids watch TV. Instead of simply modeling themselves after Beavis and Butthead, kids use these cartoon lumpen to teach themselves a very important social fact: that the only people who get to be that stupid and live are white guys, and they just barely do. A sure sign that *Beavis and Butthead* detractors do not know the show itself is that they never mention the role of Daria (called "Diarrhea," of course, by Beavis and Butthead). Daria is the smart, hardworking little girl who knows that she cannot afford stupidity and is more often than not the audience for the boys when they are variously humiliated by their out-of-control bodies or their sudden recognition of the limits of their stupidity.

Although the use of gross, dumb humor has undergone heavy censoring in the television version of *Beavis and Butthead*, the two boys' trashiness still thrives in the album and comic book format. In *The Beavis and Butthead Experience* (1993) they get to play air guitar with Nirvana, sing along with Cher, and party on the Anthrax tour bus. The point of their greatest abjection comes when a member of Anthrax shows Beavis and Butthead some girly photos and Beavis runs off to the bathroom with them, where it becomes apparent to Butthead and the band members that Beavis does not know the difference between shitting and coming. The more you get to know of Beavis and Butthead, by the way, the more you realize that Butthead has a few more IQ points than Beavis, of both the intellectual and emotional kind. The relatively (only relatively) greater awareness of Butthead means that he is often able to offer a critical perspective on their polymorphously perverse antics, to a lesser extent than Daria, of course, because he is, after all, a full participant in them.

For example, in the second issue of the *Beavis and Butthead* comic book the two young chicken-chokers decide that it would be cool (that is, not suck—see Lévi-Strauss, Bourdieu) to sneak into the morgue of a funeral home. The following dialogue ensues:

> *Butthead*: Whoa! Huh-Huh-Huh Look at all th' stiffs? They're . . .
> *Beavis*: . . . NAKED! Heh-Heh-Heh. Yeah . . . there's *one* stiff on that slab . . . and one in my pants. Heh-Heh.
> *Butthead*: Uhhh . . . I'm afraid I've got some bad news for you, Beavis . . . Huh-Huh. These are all naked GUYS!
> *Beavis*: Oh . . . Heh-Heh. Yeah, I forgot! Heh-Heh.

Beavis's sexual orientation is only one of many things he cannot quite keep track of, and Butthead is always there, not to straighten him out, but to remind him of the price to pay if he fails to achieve standard issue masculinity, as if Butthead stood a chance himself. If Howard Stern takes on the psychopathology of angry white men, Mike Judge addresses the panicky arrogance of these horny, pale adolescents as they try to figure out what, as white guys, they are entitled to, even though they know (or Mike Judge and we know) that they have zip going for them other than what used to be the automatically privileged white guy status. Where Beavis and Butthead fail, is that they do not even know how to work the one advantage they sort of have. They also remain incapable of noticing when Judge throws in their path a way out, a possible ally, but Beavis and Butthead fans do not.

The first story, "Dental Hygiene Dilemma (Fart 1)," March 1994, of the first *Beavis and Butthead* comic starts off with an extended homage to feminist performance artist and NEA Four member Karen Finley. The two boys pull up their bikes to a small store called Finley's Maxi-Mart which seems to sell only yams, recalling the yams that the artist stuffed up her vagina in one of her many performances on the powerful desires of women and the social and psychical wounds inflicted on their bodies. Beavis and Butthead cheat an elderly man, a customer at Finley's Maxi-Mart, out of his money and his yams. "Diarrhea" walks by (perfect timing) and chides the boys for their cruelty while explaining the idea of karma to them, trying to get them to understand that their stupid actions will have consequences for them later.

Mike Judge would have been even more appreciative of Finley's strategies for attacking the sexual and social status quo had he known then the details of the second censorship scandal she would be involved in. In early 1996, Crown Publishers cancelled its contract to publish Finley's decidedly Beavis and Butthead–like parody of domestic tastemaker Martha Stewart's *Living* when they found it just too gross with its tips on coffin building, rude phone calls, and cuisine that mixes Oreos, Ring Dings, and beer. For Valentine's Day, Martha Stewart recommends choosing chocolate with care, since taste varies considerably: "Choose Valrhona chocolate from France or Callebaut from Belgium." Finley, of course, is almost as well known for smearing chocolate on her nude body as for the yam insertion trick. Crown, also Martha Stewart's publisher, decided that graciousness and grossness do not mix.

Jesse Helms is more right than he knows when he calls Karen Finley's work "pornographic" because so much of the sensibility of her performances and writing, like that of Howard Stern and Mike Judge, arose from the porn world's now decades-long use of trashy, militantly stupid, class-iconoclastic, below-the-belt humor. But I have no interest here in demonstrating porn's trickle-up influence on art and media, even if it proves illustrative to chart just how large that influence is.[10] Rather, I want to show that the male popular culture that is pornography constitutes a vital source of countercultural ideas about sexuality and sexual roles, whether or not the more legitimized areas of culture pick up those ideas.

One of contemporary porn's most brilliant organic intellectuals has to be Buttman, John Stagliano, the white trash Woody Allen, who has made a score of films documenting his travels and travails as he goes around the world (and Southern California) seeking the perfect shot of a woman's perfect ass. Buttman gets mugged, evicted, bankrupted, rejected, and ridiculed—all in his single-minded quest for perfection. Licking ass, caressing ass, ogling ass, and only occasionally fucking ass, if the woman insists, Buttman does for anal fetishism what Woody Allen does for neurosis—and it's not always a pretty picture. In thrall to his obsession, things get even worse when he does not stay true to his own fetishistic commitments. In *Buttman's Revenge* (dir. John Stagliano, 1992), the erstwhile ass worshiper falls on hard times after foolishly trying to branch out by making a disastrous "tit film." No longer a star, he is rejected by his business associates and friends, and he ends up living on the street, although the others later relent and help him with his comeback by surprising him with Nina Hartley, celebrated for having the most beautiful ass in the business. As in so many stag films, the man, this time Buttman, is the butt of the joke.

In her 1983 *The Hearts of Men*, Barbara Ehrenreich constructs a history of male rebellion against the status quo from the cold war era through the seventies, and men's production and consumption of porn deserves a place in that history. The gray flannel rebels, the Playboys, the beats, the hippies— they all tried to conceive of less restrictive versions of masculinity, ones not subject to the alienation of the corporate world, alimony-hungry wives, dependent children, monogamy, or mortgages. Ehrenreich appreciates the impulse fueling much of this masculine refusal, but she faults all of the various strategies for either disregarding or blaming the woman. When we put porn into this history, we find a male popular culture that, by contrast, neither disregards nor blames the woman in its attempt to renegotiate the sexual and social status quo, a male popular culture that devotes itself—to a surprising degree—to examining the hearts of men. What's in the hearts of men according to porn? A utopian desire for a world where women are not socially required to say and believe that they do not like sex as much as men do. A utopian desire whose necessary critical edge, sharpened by trash tastes and ideas, is more often than not turned against the man rather than the woman.

How else to explain that *John Wayne Bobbitt: Uncut* (dir. Ron Jeremy, 1994) is practically a feminist chef d'oeuvre? The year 1995 proved a glorious year for the white-trashing of porn, to which much credit must first be given to Tonya Harding. The porn industry could not resist recreating Tonya's story again and again, including circulating the wedding night videos that her ex-husband put up for sale to the highest bidder. Of the several porn takeoffs of the scandal on ice, the best has to be *Tanya Hardon*, which revels in "Tanya's" trashiness over and against "Nancy Cardigan's" pseudo–upper-classness. Tanya and her husband Jeff shove empty beer cans off the kitchen counter to fuck while planning how to wreck Nancy's skating career with a blow to the knee. Although one could point out how reminiscent this scene is of Roman Polanski's brilliant rendering of the eroticism inherent in the Macbeths' roll in the marital bed as they plot the killing of the king, that wouldn't be the point, now, would it? *Tanya Hardon* celebrates Harding's white trash verve over Kerrigan's refined pathos ("Why *me*, why *me*?"), but also the whole genre's love of white trash sensibilities to deflate upper-class pretensions and male vainglory. In the best scene in the film, which has fairly high production values for an adult film—there are even insert shots of a skating rink—Tanya has stolen Nancy's boyfriend and is sharing him with another skater in the rink's dressing room, when Nancy walks in on the threesome. Aghast yet riveted, she blurts out, "Why *not* me, why *not* me?" but Tanya is so mean she will not let her join in. Jeff, of course, is dead meat by this time, having hooked up with the Beavis and Butthead of henchmen to carry out the knee-whacking operation.

Former porn star Ron Jeremy's direction of *John Wayne Bobbitt: Uncut* provides viewers with the epitome of how white trash can be deployed to criticize male attitudes and behavior. Given the chance to tell "his own story," the on-camera Bobbitt does not realize that the film is telling a story about his story, and it is not flattering. The deeply dim ex-marine, called Forrest Stump by *Esquire*, narrates and reenacts the night his wife, Lorena, cut off his penis and doctors labored for nine and a half hours to reattach it. The ever-so-slightly fictionalized aftermath of the surgery shows women every-where, from Bobbitt's hospital nurses to the porn stars he meets because of his new celebrityhood, avidly pursuing sex with him to find out if "it really works." It sort of does.

Early on in the video, we see Bobbitt and his buddies at a nude dance club, drinking beers and ogling the performers. When he arrives home, late and drunk, and falls into bed, Lorena (played by Veronica Brazil) is already asleep after a hard day's work at the nail parlor. He climbs on top of his sleepy wife who rouses only to complain about the late hour and his drunkenness and to tell him clearly that she does not want to have sex with him. He pays no attention to her refusal, screws her for a few seconds and then, just as Lorena is starting to wake up and get into it, falls off and passes out. The unhappy and sexually frustrated Lorena muses to herself for a while before leaving the bed to get a knife. Standing over her unconscious husband, she tries repeatedly to wake him, to get him to respond to her needs, before she resorts to cutting off his penis in despair at his insensitivity and inattentiveness. (Because contemporary porn will not show even a hint of violence, we get no special effects of the penis being cut off but only, hilariously, a shot of her hand clutching the severed penis and the steering wheel as she flees the house in her car.)

Although the film offers a sometimes disparaging portrait of Lorena — for example, showing her stealing money from her boss at the nail parlor — the film's sympathies lie with the wife whose husband thinks marital rape is how a man has sex with his wife. The more we see of John on screen, the more we hear his attacks on Lorena and his rationalizing of the faults in their marriage, the deeper a hole he digs for himself. Julie Brown's 1995 HBO spoof of *Lenora Babbitt* was, by contrast, much less sympathetic to a Lorena it portrayed as entirely unreasonable in her demands for mutual sexual satisfaction. So, too, Brown's companion spoof of *Tonya Hardly* exhibited little of the affection for the skater's trashiness found in *Tanya Hardon*. In both HBO stories, it is the women who get their comeuppance, not the men. It is also noteworthy that Julie Brown's version, the supposedly more progressive, even avant-garde rendering of these characters and events, offers a racial stereotyping of Lorena — Carmen Miranda with a blade — much more blatant than anything found in the porn version.

Radical sex writer Susie Bright says she cannot believe John Wayne Bobbitt permits the screening of this video because it demonstrates for all the world to see that "this man does not know how to give head to save his life," and indeed he doesn't.[11] Nor is he good at much else. In one unscripted scene in the film, where two women labor mightily to get John hard — without much success — and he seems to be tentatively trying out cunnilingus, Ron Jeremy walks into the scene and begins expertly giving head to two other women he has brought onto the set. Lore has it that Bobbitt did not know the director was going to put himself into the movie; he certainly did not know Jeremy's plans for shamelessly upstaging him, the supposed hero of this video. Next, and in pointed contrast to Bobbitt's scarce tumescence (his two fluffers are clearly flagging at this point), Jeremy whips out his own much larger and fully functioning penis, which he applies immediately, and again expertly, to the female talent. Jeremy may have lost his porn star looks, staying behind the camera these days for good reason, but here he reappears on screen to make a pedagogical point, to remind us that porn's expertise, what it promises to teach us, is good sexual technique.

What's the moral of *John Wayne Bobbitt: Uncut* for men? If you don't learn better sexual technique and start being more sensitive to your partner's needs, you're going to get yours cut off too, and, what's more, YOU'D DESERVE IT! Who would have thought that the porn industry would give us the nineties version of Valerie Solanas's *SCUM Manifesto*, brilliantly disseminated in the form of a tacky, low-budget (by Hollywood standards) video sold and rented to millions of men? That tackiness also takes aim at Hollywood. The center of commercial adult film production is North Hollywood and Northridge, making those two shabby cities the tinny side of Tinseltown. The adult industry so loves producing knockoffs of Hollywood films that it is impossible to keep track of all of them. The knockoffs cannot be intended simply to ride the coattails of popular Hollywood films because most consumers know that the porn version seldom has much to do with the themes, characters, and events found in the original film. What is more likely, as Cindy Patton says of films such as *Beverly Hills Cocks*, *Edward Penishands*, and both gay and heterosexual versions of *Top Gun* (*Big Guns*) is that they are meant as "an erotic and humorous critique of the mass media's role in invoking but never delivering sex." (1996). I would add the gay male film *The Sperminator* to her list because of the way it rewrites *The Terminator* to expose the closeted homoeroticism of so much Hollywood film (Kyle Reese and John Conner get together to "sperminate" the Sperminator.) In the new videos, Patton says, types of sex are rarely presented as taboo in themselves, only as representationally taboo—what Hollywood or television is unwilling to show. With Hollywood under attack by the family-values crowd and liberals and conservatives alike clamoring to V-chip to death television's creativity (the industry having immediately caved in), porn and its white trash kin seem our best allies in a cultural wars insurgency that makes camp in that territory beyond the pale.

Notes

1 In *Roll, Jordan, Roll: The World the Slaves Made*, Eugene D. Genovese (1972) argues that white trash folks have no culture of their own because it is entirely borrowed from poor blacks. He, too, as I did, claims that the everyday lives of poor blacks and poor whites are very similar, and were so even during the period of slavery. But he credits those similarities to a massive poor white appropriation

of black culture, seeing in white trash culture a degraded form of black food, religion, and language. He even says that white trash folks lacked the desire for literacy and education so strong in black culture. Genovese would not, then, buy my argument, admittedly a slightly tongue-in-cheek one, that growing up white trash offers one of the best possible preparations for a theoretical and political engagement with the world. To do so, he would first have to acknowledge the productively creative hybridity of white trash culture in its exchange with black culture, as well as the corresponding capacity for white trash social agency, both of which he disavows in his book. Genovese does, however, have a fascinating and persuasive account of the origins of *white trash* as an epithet. He believes black slaves derived the term, but their hostility toward poor whites was fostered by wealthy landowners wanting to prevent any interracial unity that might be turned against a system oppressing both blacks and whites. Like the epithet *fag hag*, then, it is meant to drive a wedge between natural allies.

2   I have taught the course on pornographic film since 1993 in the Department of Film Studies at the University of California, Santa Barbara. I would not have been able to put together a historical survey of the genre without the help of the Institute for the Advanced Study of Human Sexuality in San Francisco, which provided many of the films and much-needed historical information on producers, venues, and collateral industries such as magazine publishing and sex toy manufacturing.

3   Thanks very much to Linda Williams and the students in her fall 1995 "Pornographies On/Scene" class at UC-Irving, where I first tried out the arguments in this essay that I had been developing with the students in my class at UC–Santa Barbara.

4   The figures on the number of stag films are understandably not as reliable as one would want. At this point, I am relying on the fact that the few researchers working on the stag film all use approximately the same figures, which are based on Kyrou (1964) and Di Lauro and Rabkin (1976). Di Lauro and Rabkin base their figures on their own viewings in Europe and America, Kyrou, the Kinsey collection, Scandinavian catalogs from the sixties and early seventies, and the catalog listings of a private collector who did not want his identity revealed. Thomas Waugh says these figures match what he has found thus far: "The corpus of the stag film seems to include about two thousand films made prior to the hardcore theatrical explosion of 1970, of which three quarters were made after 1960. Of the group made prior to World War II, which is the present focus, I have found documentation for only about 180, about 100 American, 50 French, plus a sprinkling of Latin American, Spanish, and Austrian works" (1996, 309).

5   Ed Cray does not neglect women's talent for bawdiness. He collects, for example, the songs known among sorority women as the rasty nasty, with lyrics celebrating the women's nastiness and sluttiness, such as "We are the Dirty Bitches" (1992, 351–52). For further evidence of this talent, he refers the reader to Green (1977).

6 Thanks to Deborah Stucker for her analytical insights on *Outlaw Biker* and its role in the creation of a lumpen or working-class sexual and social counterdiscourse for women and men.

7 Beyond Dundes and Legman (1975), see also Hill (1993), which has a good discussion of class bias in joke theory in chapter 7, "At Witz End." He shows Freud's (failed) attempt to separate the high-minded "Witz" from the lowly "Komik."

8 The special on godlessness in public schools was broadcast in April 1993.

9 For a discussion of pornography as a moral counterculture, see Abramson and Pinkerton (1995), especially chapter 7, "Porn: Tempest on a Soapbox."

10 For porn's influence on contemporary art see Frecerro (1993), on Madonna and 2 Live Crew; Elizabeth Brown, "Overview of Contemporary Artists Interacting with Pornography," a lecture for the Sex Angles Conference, at the University of California–Santa Barbara, on March 8, 1996; and Williams (1993).

11 Susie Bright made this comment in "Deep Inside Dirty Pictures: The Changing of the Guard in the Pornographic Film Industry and American Erotic Spectatorship," a lecture she gave at a conference entitled "Censorship and Silencing: The Case of Pornography" at the University of California–Santa Barbara, on November 5, 1994.

Works Cited

Abramson, Paul R., and Steven D. Pinkerton. 1995. *With Pleasure: Thoughts on the Nature of Human Sexuality.* New York: Oxford University Press.

Cray, Ed. 1992. *The Erotic Muse: American Bawdy Songs.* Urbana: University of Illinois Press.

Darnton, Robert. 1982. *The Literary Underground of the Old Regime.* Cambridge, Mass.: Harvard University Press.

Frecerro, Carla. 1993. "Unruly Bodies: Popular Culture Challenges to the Regime of Body Backlash." *Visual Anthropology Review* 9, 2: 74–81.

Genovese, Eugene D. 1972. *Roll, Jordan, Roll: The World the Slaves Made.* New York: Vintage.

De Grazia, Edward. 1992. *Girls Lean Back Everywhere: The Law on Obscenity and the Assault on Genius.* New York: Random House.

Di Lauro, Al, and Gerald Rabkin. 1976. *Dirty Movies: An Illustrated History of the Stag Film, 1915–1970.* New York: Chelsea House.

Dundes, Alan, and Pagter, Carl R. 1975. *Urban Folklore from the Paperwork Empire.* Austin, Tex.: American Folklore Society.

———. 1987. *When You're Up to Your Ass in Alligators: More Urban Folklore from the Paperwork Empire.* Detroit: Wayne State University Press.

Ehrenreich, Barbara. 1983. *The Hearts of Men: American Dreams and the Flight from Commitment.* New York: Doubleday.

Green, Rayna. 1977. "Magnolias Grow in Dirt: The Bawdy Lore of Southern Women." *Southern Exposure* 4, 4: 34–45.

Hill, Carl. 1993. *The Soul of Wit: Joke Theory from Grimm to Freud*. Lincoln: University of Nebraska Press.

Hunt, Lynn. 1993. *The Invention of Pornography: Obscenity and the Origins of Modernity, 1500–1800*. New York: Zone.

Kendrick, Walter. 1987. *The Secret Museum: Pornography in Modern Culture*. New York: Viking.

Kipnis, Laura "(Male) Desire and (Female) Disgust: Reading *Hustler*." 1992. In *Cultural Studies*, ed. Lawrence Grossberg, Cary Nelson, and Paula Treichler. New York: Routledge.

Kruger, Barbara. 1992. "Prick up Your Ears." *Esquire*, May, 94–99.

Kyrou, Ado. 1964. "D'un certain cinéma clandestine." *Positif* 61/62/63: 205–23.

Legman, Gershon. 1968. *Rationale of the Dirty Joke: An Analysis of Sexual Humor, First Series*. New York: Grove.

——. 1975. *No Laughing Matter: Rationale of the Dirty Joke: An Analysis of Sexual Humor, Second Series*. New York: Breaking Point.

Lehman, Peter. 1995. "Revelations about Pornography." *Film Criticism*. 3–15.

Patton, Cindy. 1996. *Fatal Advice: How Safe Sex Education Went Wrong*. Durham, N.C.: Duke University Press.

Ross, Andrew. 1989. *No Respect: Intellectuals and Popular Culture*. New York: Routledge.

Walkowitz, Judith. 1980. *Prostitution and Victorian Society: Women, Class, and the State*. New York: Cambridge University Press.

Waugh, Thomas. 1996. *Hard to Imagine: Gay Male Eroticism in Film and Photography from Their Beginnings to Stonewall*. New York: Columbia University Press.

Williams, Linda. 1993. "A Provoking Agent: The Pornography and Performance Art of Annie Sprinkle." In *Dirty Looks: Women, Pornography, Power*, ed. Pamela Church Gibson and Roma Gibson. London: British Film Institute. 176–91.

——. 1999. *Hard Core: Power, Pleasure, and the "Frenzy of the Visible."* Berkeley: University of California Press.

part 4

Soft Core, Hard Core, and the Pornographic Sublime

Pinup: The American Secret Weapon
in World War II

DESPINA KAKOUDAKI

✳ Apparently nobody had noticed that the day/date calendar of 2002 was perfectly aligned with the year 1963, until the staff at Goodtime Publishing saw an opportunity to sell some inventory that had never made it to the market. Starting in the summer of 2001, copies of the undelivered "1963 Girl-a-Week and Joke-a-Day" pinup calendar began selling on eBay, while later in the year five hundred copies were shipped out as a gift to the United States Special Forces in Afghanistan. As the publishers note, after thirty-eight dormant years, the calendars became especially necessary then for two reasons: first, because unlike what is currently available, the 1963 pinups represent a nostalgic and innocent sensuality; and second, because "they are the SYMBOL OF FREEDOM AND OPPORTUNITY, AMERICAN WAY OF LIFE AND INNOVATION" ("Five Hundred" 2001). The company also notes that is has reserved one calendar "for Osama Bin Laden in case he voluntarily surrenders."

The two claims made by Goodtime Publishing about the effect and relevance of the pinup in times of war seem like common sense nowadays. Indeed, critics often accept as a given the pinup's political relevance because of its representation of sensual innocence and its embodiment of patriotic values. These associations result from the fact that the American pinup as a genre is indelibly linked to the Second World War and the role it played as a talisman of patriotic action. It is as if the 1940s pinup wrote a new origin story for the genre. Just as World War II presents the last war that now seems morally clear, so the 1940s pinup also appears classic, mainstream, patriotic, innocent—and morally clear.[1]

The pinup's near domination of the mainstream visual landscape during World War II has interrupted our understanding of its long history before and after the 1940s. The resulting episodic trajectory is perceived in a convenient division of three eras: the pre-1940s pinup (mostly related to advertisements or soft-core erotica), the 1940s pinup (American and innocent), and the post-1940s pinup (published in men's magazines and increasingly pornographic). This, of course, presents far from an accurate history of the genre, but it does make for an attractive mythology. Even given the exponential intensification of pinup illustration after the war, and the long and diverse careers of many World War II pinup illustrators, the pinup in the classic sense always refers back to the 1940s. We are also now seeing an explosion of new pinup art. The Internet has functioned as a huge pinup library, making images from the past available to newer artists and audiences, and creating more demand for contemporary versions.[2] With work spanning from mainstream to hard-core, contemporary pinup artists such as Hajime Sorayama (1983, 1984) and Olivia de Berardinis (Berel, 1993) have expanded the possible modes of the pinup, and have also allowed a wider range of explicit sexual representation into the mostly soft-core vocabulary of the genre (figure 1). But again, these artists share the public fascination with the wartime pinup: they mine the iconography of the 1940s incessantly, often reinvigorating specific poses or techniques, or adding more explicit sexual scenarios and a newer type of body to the mainstream forms developed by George Petty and Alberto Vargas in *Esquire* magazine.[3]

And yet despite the new interest in the form, the classic art of the illustrated female pinup from the war years still poses important questions on how we understand the intersections of pornography, technology, politics, and culture. The intense appropriation of the pinup by the military-industrial complex, which itself emerged in its contemporary form at the time, has not been previously examined. It is a strange relationship, mingling propaganda with pornography, new technology with ideas of naturalness, and the glorified "American Girl" with xenophobic and homophobic sentiments. Precisely because the pinup mode is always potentially mainstream, or is often remembered as if it is/was mainstream, pinups alert us to the semantic flexibility of pornographic images. Compared to our contemporary visually explicit and hard-core genres, the illustrated mid-twentieth-century pinup is tame and, I would claim, not easily readable. This is because the pinup's function and cultural relevance were completely revolutionized in

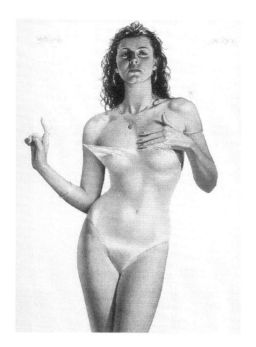

1. *Pin-up.* A contemporary pinup
by Hajime Sorayama, from the
Pin-up series, 1984. Recent
artists represent pubic hair and
nipples. Copyright 2003 Hajime
Sorayama/Artspace/Uptight.

the 1940s, to the point where we can no longer see its historical development
clearly and cannot make out how it relates to our contemporary debates
about pornography. How innocent or pornographic was the 1940s pinup?
How patriotic was it? What made it patriotic? How did its patriotic function relate to its pornographic potential? And why is the hegemonic memory
of the pinup as an equivalent of American values so difficult to challenge?
In what follows, I want to explore how the sexual content of the pinup was
used to promote a patriotic agenda in order to then elucidate how the pinup
became hegemonic in the 1940s and what it did from that central cultural
position.

The multiple definitions of the pinup, from pornographic to nonpornographic, or from marginalized to mainstream, give us a special insight
on how sexually explicit visual genres work and how they negotiate the
boundaries between public and private pleasure, as well as public and private viewing. Despite its association with soft-core pornography and men's
magazines through the 1930s, in the war years, the pinup functioned as a
patriotic and family-oriented register of Americanness and became the premier vessel of pro-war propaganda (figure 2). The mainstream, patriotic use
of the pinup in the 1940s marks a transition between older advertising prac-

2. *V is for Victory.* The Varga Girl, *Esquire*, April 1943. One of the most famous military pinups of the 1940s, the Varga Girl is wearing a type of military uniform and carries a trumpet as a literalization of the "call to arms." Here, the V-sign is replicated in the insignia on her arm, and her neckline as well.

tices and the new realities of multimedia consumerism: the pinup emerges as an expansively versatile visual product, appearing in men's magazines, in women's magazines, on war posters, in adult or pornographic publications, musicals, cartoons, mainstream movies, and popular songs. Much of the energy of the time—its vitality, patriotism, family values, and ideals— were deemed to be contained in the pinup, and were consciously considered as its central features. The varied pinup venues of the 1940s effectively say: "This girl, this style of illustration, this idealization, is so fundamental to our society that we feel it actually represents us." How does a visual genre become so potent? How can it navigate such political and representational challenges? The wartime pinup constitutes a state-initiated, propagandist, mainstream image, while the pre-1940s and the postwar pinups are seen as "secular" or "civilian" texts: not state-sanctioned, not specifically patriotic, and not specifically American. What disrupts the historical continuity of the pinup as a genre is its aberrant patriotic ideological function during the war, in contrast to the assumed "normal" function of pornographic images—the idea being that the latter cannot have ideological uses or implications. Instead of isolating the mainstream role of the pinup during World War II as an aberration in its otherwise pornographic history, we should consider it as a poignant case study for exploring the cultural functions and political appropriations of sexually explicit and pornographic texts. As a matter of fact, the pinup works as a patriotic image not because it is clean-cut and mainstream, but because it channels the excitement of an explicitly sexual scenario into nonpornographic media.

The American pinup comprises a variety of representational modes and visual genres, and more important, a range of pornographic engagement. Beyond the first obvious distinction between illustrated and photographic images, and between images depicting primarily male or female models, the pinup style depends on two main stylistic features. First of all, pinups usually depict one body in its entirety. This body may be male, female, ambiguously gendered, overtly transsexual, hybrid, only part human, completely nonhuman, and so on. It is usually not depicted in a sexual encounter with another body, and as a result, most pinups are soft-core. But the image nonetheless contains sexual content, and this content may be overt, as with the work of contemporary artists who push the soft-core limits, or covert, as in versions of the pinup we would consider mainstream. Other factors such as pose, captions, clothing, facial expression, level of nudity, or level of genital exposure may affect the mainstream presence of an image. The second main stylistic feature of the pinup results from the genre's focus on the potential sexual energy of the single body. The figure depicted usually has a direct eye-line connection to the implied viewer, and this imagined mutual recognition between viewer and model gives the pinup its characteristic allure and sexual content. Other implied or intertextual clues may give us specific details about the imagined sexual or voyeuristic encounter between the image and the viewer. The usually submerged layer of sexual connotation in the classic pinup constitutes a central feature of soft-core genres in general. In the case of the World War II pinup, it is a layer both visible and potentially dismissible, making it possible for the same image to be acceptable in a variety of publications and to evoke numerous levels of pornographic identification. On the other hand, the erotic layer is exactly what makes the pinup effective as propaganda.

For example, the participation of the pinup in the American war effort is the theme of a short MGM cartoon titled "Blitz Wolf" (dir. Tex Avery, 1941). As with other wartime cartoons, "Blitz Wolf" retells the story of the Three Little Pigs in a war context: the Big Bad Wolf is Nazi Germany, the Three Little Pigs are Americans, and blowing the houses down is done with a variety of tanks and machine guns. The third Little Pig is thoroughly prepared for war through barricades, anti-aircraft cannons, and war bonds. In one of the final showdowns, the Wolf points a cannon, with the words "King Size" on it, in the direction of the Little Pig's house. He fires a bomb. In alarm, the Little

Pig reaches down in its trench, gets out a copy of *Esquire* magazine (with the logo very visible), opens it (presumably to the centerfold "Esquire Girl"), and shows it to the approaching bomb. The bomb stops in midflight to look at the image, seems very impressed, whistles appreciatively, and immediately retreats. It returns with ten other bombs, its friends, and they are all first fascinated and then defeated by the *Esquire* image. The bombs look at the pinup centerfold in awe, whistle, and make catcall sounds, and then . . . drop to the ground, apparently deactivated.

Even though we do not see the image deployed as a weapon in the cartoon, the meaning of the scene is in line with the public articulation of the pinup's role in the war. The pinup is viewed as a talisman, an image that has power over things. What it depicts, how it works, and why it is effective remain slightly mysterious in the cartoon, thus replicating the evasive public explanations of the period. Most accounts describe the pinup in terms of its American wholesomeness and innocent charm and explain its military function as "boosting morale." Even in family-oriented magazine settings, such as in *Family Circle*, there seems to be a blind spot about the pinup's overt sexual allure and an investment in nebulous patriotic talk and idealized versions of "it's for the boys." In its parodies of attack and defense, "Blitz Wolf" is more explicit about the functionality of the pinup. The pinup helps the war effort because of what it depicts (which we don't get in the cartoon but we can easily supply), and by the ways in which it can be used. Instead of setting the interaction between the pinup and its viewer in a domestic context (the "American Girl" as viewed by the American soldier), this cartoon depicts the pinup as viewed by the enemy and functioning as a weapon. The pinup averts the enemy's bomb by eliciting an erotic arousal, which in this case is represented as male vulnerability. However, the same erotic arousal is exactly what the euphemistic "morale" hopes for when the pinup is viewed by "the/our boys."

In its many double entendres, the cartoon is completely conscious of the phallic representation of military equipment and the imaginative connection between military equipment and military personnel (bombs do not get aroused but bomb operators do). To literalize this: In the very next sequence, the Little Pig's cannon has gotten tired and falls limp to the ground. The Little Pig picks it up tenderly, gives it some "B-12" vitamins, and the cannon stands erect again and resumes firing. Even though it is not a pinup that revives the tired cannon, the proximity of the two scenes seems telling. To be effective as a pro-war text, the cartoon has to make a connection between civilian money and military equipment (represented by the vita-

mins, which are named to resonate with airplane, tank, and bomb types—
B-17, B-27, B-52, and so on) and to equate military equipment with military
prowess. The connections between the pinup and erotic arousal, and arousal
as a figure for prowess, go without saying. The pinup works through its
weird blend of a specifically feminine but also phallic and military American power. As the cartoon implies, we want "our boys" to be in a state of
military and sexual erectness/arousal, and we want our enemies to be emasculated, detumescent, or "spent." The pinup can create both desired effects.
As an image for domestic consumption by military personnel, it can concentrate and focus sexual energy, transforming it into military energy or
patriotic (but also sexual) arousal. As an image directed against one's enemies, the pinup can channel this sexual energy (now relocated from the
idealized female form to the military/sexual response it evokes) and use it
as a weapon. "The boys" are basically instructed by the cartoon to channel
their erotic response to the pinup into aggression toward the enemy. Instead
of being a figure of sexual release (through masturbation, for example) the
pinup here becomes equated with the pent-up frustration pretty common
in army barracks, a frustration that (in the patriotic version) calls not for personal pleasure but for military action (figure 3). This patriotically channeled
sexual energy is a standard feature of military representation. It glorifies
"our boys," who are too focused on the war to masturbate to pinups, though
of course it is for the express purpose of sexual release that "we" supply them
with so many sexually explicit texts.

The cartoon takes for granted that viewers understand the pinup as the
transformer of sexual energy into a weapon, and this becomes useful in
negotiating a more tenuous relation between civilian money and military
success. Both weapons used in "Blitz Wolf," the pinup and the B-12 vitamins,
negotiate technological and social necessities. They dispel the threat of the
enemy's unknown technological advances in weaponry and at the same time
provide a visually persuasive argument for the need for more weaponry. The
"domestic" call for aggressive weapons manufacturing is hidden under the
pinup's sexual allure: used as a defensive mechanism, the pinup obscures
the fact that bombs usually answer other bombs. Other versions of this staple
of military propaganda would proclaim that "they" have aggressive technology, while "we" have values, thus hiding the fact that both sides may be
using equally inhuman and destructive weapons. The pinup image functions as a euphemistic and allegorical representation of military machinery,
and it is depicted communicating and fighting with other machinery—not
with viewers whose lives and fantasies animate the illustrated body and are

3. *Target for Tonite.* The Varga Girl, *Esquire,* military edition, March 1944. Notice the insignia of the Air Force transformed into a hair ornament.

hurt by the war. The cartoon encounter between the bomb and the pinup thus rescripts the technological encounter between armed enemies as an erotic encounter and literalizes the sexual language of war and capitalist in-vestments: spending, outspending the enemy, and being spent. Since the state of sexual arousal is what gives "us" potency at war, the B-12 vitamins function in two ways: In relation to military equipment, the vitamins serve as a reminder that one needs to invest in military technology. In relation to military personnel, they represent the ability of the pinup to inspire sexual response. In the iconography of pro-war propaganda, the pinup's ability to excite can indeed function as a central ideological register.

The military appropriation of the pinup, and the military claim on civilian money, start even before the United States enters World War II, and are then directed toward the "home front." At stake here is not military performance, but military preparedness: the American public has to be persuaded that the war mobilization effort is worthwhile. Major image-makers of the time, especially film studios, voluntarily produced a massive amount of moralistic tales in an attempt to reorient that nature of "American" values, especially again in relation to money. One such example, *The Spirit of 43* (dir. Jack King, 1943) shows a confused Donald Duck fighting both his "zoot-suiter" persona, asking him to be "American" and have some fun, and his "Scrooge Mac Duck" persona, reaffirming the "American" value of thrift. Donald is befuddled: the post-Depression market depends on increased consumption. However, the tale soon explains the actual moral necessity: Donald must save his money in order to be able to pay all his taxes on time, so that the U.S. military can build the necessary weapons to fight the war. The last image of the film contrasts the swastika-shaped door of a nightclub with a brick wall made of U.S. bonds, with the blasting message: "Spend for the Axis, or Save for Taxes." But what looks like an ideological transition from an iconography of leisure to one of "traditional" values, actually constitutes a redirection of private money into government and corporate control. In truth, Donald is not asked to save his pennies, but to invest them in the U.S. government. Other animated films similarly repeat this amended mantra of capitalism. A cartoon titled "All Together" (dir. Walt Disney, 1942), for example, has no narrative plot except for an extraordinary parade of airplanes, bombs, battleships, and guns. The infinite procession of these machines is the only guarantee of victory according to the voice-over narrator. In the technological horizon, huge letters appear, urging viewers to "Buy More . . . and More . . . and More . . . US War Bonds."

Pinups in *Esquire* magazine indeed reference the need for military investments and military action overtly. Some pinups become patriotic because the girl wears some element of military uniform or insignia (figure 2), or because of a sign in the image that dedicates it specifically to a patriotic purpose or audience. The two favorite signs have two distinctive audiences: "To the Guy Who Buys G.I. Bonds" addresses civilian supporters of the war effort; "Target for Tonite" (figure 3) is designed for enlisted men, who should be staying "on target." The pinup therefore proves central to the public relations necessities launched by the war effort. The encounter of the pinup and the bomb in "Blitz Wolf," especially from my contemporary point of view, has uncanny connections to accounts that a pinup of Rita Hayworth was attached to the nuclear bomb dropped on Hiroshima.[4] But why does one of the largest military machines of the century need this connection with an image? What is the political and military effect of implicating the beautiful woman in the business of ugly war? Why are sexy women called "bombshells"? Why are nuclear experiments (on Bikini Island) reimagined as a new two-piece bathing suit? To answer these questions and to elucidate the specific advantages of the pinup as a medium for propaganda, we have to explore how the pinup comes to a hegemonic ideological position as a pro-war text, mainly through its abilities to represent sublime abstractions and to animate military machinery.

The connection between the pinup and new technologies constitutes a fundamental feature of its stylistic development. The pinup as a visual genre is connected to advertisement and popular illustration styles dating from the mid-nineteenth century. It has its roots in *cartes postales* (postcards) of exotic places, art nudes, portraits of actresses of the burlesque theater, erotic photographs, "Little Egypt" and the hoochie-coochie dances of the Chicago Fair in 1893, cigarette cards, early movie posters, and the cancan. In the 1890s, revolutions in printing technology allowed even small magazines to carry illustrations. Images of stage and burlesque actresses and "French" models emerged on a variety of printed promotional materials, from cigarette cards to theater posters. From an art historical point of view, the pinup is a massive recycler of popular and commercial representation. Its precursors, advertising entities such as the Gibson Girl and the Christy Girl, identified the commercial potential of the New Woman. Similarly, in a direct pairing of beautiful women with new machinery, the Kodak Girl and the Typewriter Girl established the association in advertising of the female body and new technologies. Indeed, every important technological object of the twentieth century—from bicycles, cars, trains, vacuum cleaners, electric lamps, and motorcycles to airplanes, tanks, and computer networks—has been explained, publicized, and advertised through intimate, often sexualized representations of a beautiful, smiling girl.

Soft-core images such as the pinup have a wide range of cultural uses because of their ability to both "pass" for mainstream images and to retain the excitement and explicit sexuality of their pornographic component. They are thus supreme in their ability to initiate public interest in new media or art forms, new technologies, and social conditions. Calendars, posters, advertisements, illustrations, magazine covers—all the places and functions that can now be occupied by anything (a racing car, a horse, a landscape)—at one time or another only featured "beautiful girls." The presence of the smiling young woman is often what actually initiates and animates these various spaces, media, or print forms before anything else can occupy them.[5] In order to see how the pinup functions as war propaganda, we have to understand how a context associated with beautiful girls can become occupied by heavy machinery, weapons, or cars—favorite pinup topics in the 1940s and since. Is there any connection, affinity, or transference of erotic allure between these pinup themes? Mark Gabor takes this for granted when he defines the pinup in an all-encompassing way: "A pinup can represent whatever we love, want to love, or want to have. Any printed image that can be hung on a wall could conceivably be regarded as a pinup" ([1972] 1996, 23). He later redefines this mainstreamed pinup in more specifically erotic terms: "A pinup is a sexually evocative image, reproduced in multiple copies, in which either the expression or the attitude of the subject invites the viewer to participate vicariously in or fantasize about a personal involvement with the subject" (23). If this is the case, we have to account for the representation of machinery pinups. On a surface level, the definition works: if the pinup is of a motorcycle, one can fantasize about owning one; if it is of a film star, one can imagine being a film star or being with a film star. However, this simplification does not help us understand how a motorcycle can be posed to look sexually alluring, or whether part of the fantasy might involve having sex with a motorcycle! Critics fail to respond to this challenging possibility: that what makes pinups of machines sexually alluring and what makes pinups of young women sexually alluring may be connected. The young woman and the "impersonal" machine are related in the social public space.

Precisely because of the pinup's mainstream presence and more or less hegemonic social position, it can function as a domesticating context. As we see in the work of the two most successful pinup illustrators of the 1930s and 1940s, George Petty and Alberto Vargas, the pinup can create an everyday image of telephones as sexual enablers or humanize tanks and airplanes, as it did during World War II, through the connection of the Petty pinups with the telephone, and the Vargas pinups with the airplane. Petty's insistence on the telephone as a necessary prop becomes outdated all of a sudden, in the middle of the most amazing proliferation of pinup images. Why? One way to understand the succession of Petty by Vargas is to see the Vargas pinup as an abstraction of the feeling of flight. Since flight was registered as sublime at the time, the pinup on the airplane or on the page succeeds most when resonant with the desire to fly: first to fly as a pilot in the mobilization years, but later also to fly away, or transcend the grimness of war. This transition from one pinup prop/representation to another, from the telephone to the airplane, is our clue to how pornographic images interact with technology, innovation, and cultural change.

The word *pinup* does not emerge until the early 1940s, and what it refers to solidifies stylistically at about the same time. The pinup evolved out of advertisements and cartoons in *Esquire* magazine in the 1930s, and it is in these ads and their creation of the glamorous girl that we can see why the pinup can gather together capitalist and military meanings. Begun as a quarterly in September 1933, *Esquire* became a monthly magazine due to its amazing success. One of the first men's luxury magazines in the United States, it addressed the "New Leisure" audience of fashionable, mobile, middle-class men. In 1933, perhaps the worst year of the Depression, it cost fifty cents (at the time, most magazines cost ten cents, and a good sirloin steak cost eighteen cents a pound). Its contents revolved around new fashions for men, "coated" with editorials, cartoons, advertisements, and some journalism. The pictorial luxury of the magazine was evident in its many pages of full-color ads and cartoons. Within two years, the circulation of *Esquire* rose to a staggering 600,000.[6]

George Petty was involved in the illustration of *Esquire* from the beginning. He was a masterful airbrush artist, whose submission had just been selected as the poster for the 1933 Chicago World's Fair. In his advertisements for Old Gold cigarettes and other products, he first developed a cartoon style depicting a young, beautiful, and glamorous girl, often accompanied by an older and visibly rich patron. In one of these early cigarette ads, the scene shows the older man sitting in an armchair and reading a newspaper, while the beautiful girl, looking bored, leans on an oversized pack of Old Gold cigarettes. The ad copy describes both the problem and the solution: "Hitched to a Humdrummy? . . . Light an Old Gold." The rather schematic and round older man, often called "the old geezer" by the staff at *Esquire,* was a standard image/logo of the magazine, and it is still referenced in its contemporary logos and illustrations. In this context, we witness a dialogue between the male figure, the female figure, the product (seen in this case in a surreal scale), and the viewer. It is indeed tempting to see the ad copy as the viewer's words or thoughts projected into the ad. In other words, "Hitched to a Humdrummy?" is short for "Are *You* Hitched to a Humdrummy?" as the text addresses the woman in the illustration.

By 1939, the ad copy involved a variety of double entendres and puns. George Petty's most popular line of advertising illustrations, for Jantzen swimsuits, uses such puns to eroticize the setting of the advertised encounter. In one ad, two figures, one male and one female, both in Jantzen swimsuits, address each other with: "You Have a Good Line Darling, But Your Jantzen Lines Are Better." This caption creates a scene where either one of the figures of the illustration may be "coming on" to the other. As in the cartoons, we also see an interaction between male figure, female figure, product, and text in the ads. Petty's trademark white background constituted an unprecedented innovation, as was his habit of leaving parts of the drawing unfinished. Petty was a shrewd businessman and always kept all reproduction rights to his work and name. He often resold paintings to more than one publication, sometimes with small changes. As the style he defined became more and more recognizable, so did his name, and his success was immense. As early as 1935, his daughter Marjorie, then fifteen years old, was well known as the model for all his illustrations. She often received letters of thanks or admiration and was interviewed and featured in magazines.[7] The way in which Petty recycled his paintings contributed significantly to the name and style recognition of the specific form he created.[8] But the fact that the same painting from 1934 exists in the public sphere as advertisement, poster, or cartoon until the late 1940s makes it hard to trace when Petty's style changed.

Responding to readers' comments that the "girl and geezer" plot was getting old, *Esquire* editor Arnold Gingrich asked Petty to "leave the geezer out" of the illustrations sometime in 1935. The October 1935 issue of *Esquire* was the last to feature the glamorous young woman and the "aging cartoon Romeo" (Austin 1997, 36). In November 1935, what we now recognize as the setting of the classic pinup came into being. It is an illustration of a single female figure rendered on a white, unpainted background. Petty's biographer relates that the telephone that consistently accompanies this female figure emerged when Marjorie took a call in the studio: "This innocent action raised that lowly instrument of communication from the depths of utility to the height of glamour" (36). Adopting the telephone as an ever-present prop allowed Petty to get rid of the male figure in the advertisements and posters.

The phone was not new as a prop in sexually alluring illustrations. As early as 1922, young Alberto Vargas used early telephone models in his illustrations, and such telephonic references feature prominently in soft-core imagery. For Petty, the telephone became a necessary feature, however, and after its inclusion, the structure of the pinup image solidified once again. Now, the female figure is alone, looking toward the viewer. The ad text may address her, or may reflect what she tells the viewers, and the product is often described in terms of her outfit or the setting of the illustration. One beautifully illustrated Petty girl looks alluringly toward the viewer while apparently saying (both to us and to an unseen companion on the standard Petty telephone): ". . . but don't forget the Pepsi Cola." It is unfortunate that most reproductions of pinups from that era crop the text or caption in order to appear more "classic," thus displacing the relationship between the female figure, the text, and the viewer that is so fundamental to the history of the pinup. The titles, captions, or headings accompanying the girl function as verbal cues, and they usually solicit and establish a relationship between the viewer and the figure: a kind of talking back reminiscent of the cartoon settings. In advertisements, the text is standard product promotion, if with sexual puns. In the full-page or double-page (centerfold) Petty illustrations in *Esquire*, the text often relates to seduction and revolves around recognizing the double entendre. For example, a 1937 illustration of a glamorous woman talking on the phone in a black dress and transparent black hat was published unchanged in two contexts. As an advertisement for Green River Soda, with the caption "Picks me up—How about you?" the focus lies on the telephone communication as a setting for product information, but with the "pickup" it is also present as a seductive reference. As a full-page Petty Girl illustration in *Esquire*, the very same painting appears with the caption "Well, we could go to the opera, Mr. Hammond, if you insist on preliminaries." Obviously, the meaning of the exchange is now explicitly sexual, with the female figure in the position of the sexually inviting and uninhibited partner.

The recurrence of the same image in many settings and with many captions is an important factor in understanding the pinup. An illustration originally used for Coca Cola, Best Form underwear, or Jantzen could then be transported into a sexual setting through a caption or title, and the phone proved absolutely necessary to these transformations. One of Petty's paintings, which was selected as the poster for the 1937 Miss America Pageant, later appeared in *Esquire* with the caption: "I said 'no' and he said 'why not?' —He had me there. . . ." Other captions create a sexual, money-grabbing, pleasure-girl persona for the Petty Girl. In mainstream ads, the person she is talking to on the phone remains unidentified, and the pun of the text revolves around the product ("picks me up"). In *Esquire*, the person she is talking to on the phone is usually suggested by the captions as a friend or lover (or sometimes as a friend who hears her confessions about a male friend or lover), and the puns of the text create an identifiable sexual setting. The captions may appear from "her" point of view or as something an assumed male voice is saying about her. Petty himself never supplied these captions; they were created by the magazine editors (often as a bet), and they produce a secondary plane of meaning that is age-, class-, race-, and gender-specific. The invisibility of the person the woman is talking to facilitates the varied uses possible for each image. Petty involves all the elements required for an intimate communication in the visual rendering of the image, but he leaves the terms of this intimacy up to the context.

As a result, it is not the illustration itself but the caption that creates the male-specific or female-specific context of the Petty Girl. This does not suggest that these discourses are truly different or mutually exclusive. A mainstream audience may not understand the pinup as a pornographic image because it is missing the continuity of seduction plots supplied by the cartoons and captions of the men's magazine. Even though soft-core pornography is often invisible and "passable" in the mainstream media, in the context of men's magazines, the sexual plots of these figures emerge clearly. It would be much easier if we could identify the function of the pinup through a visual pornographic vocabulary (certain poses or certain clothes), but for this soft-core, almost mainstream genre, the pornographic element is slightly off-site. It is created by an interaction between the image, the caption, the magazine context, the assumed or implied viewer, and a rhetoric of female exclusion. So-called men's magazines sell on the basis of that rhetoric, as they imagine a female-free space or readership. Understanding contexts as male-specific and female-specific does not imply the opposition or separation of public domains, especially since in the 1930s and 1940s they are not really separate. Both then and now readers and viewers have no trouble occupying all these discourses and "getting" the jokes. But this division helps account for the kind of address to the viewer the pinup engages. Viewers understand the terms of the address, and those terms are usually gender-specific. The *same* image (metaphorically in terms of stylistic presentation, but also often literally because of the practice of reprinting pinups as advertisements) can have a number of possible meanings. It can be a wholesome American Girl on a recruitment poster, a sensible middle-class girl in an ad for women's clothing in women's magazines, a glamorous actress in an announcement for a theater or film event, and a fantasy girl in a pornographic illustration. The address is created by all the information attached to the image, and the captions prove central. Often, the etiquette of "who is talking to whom" is again context-specific: in mainstream advertisements, films, or posters, the viewer describes or talks to the Petty Girl. In pornographic or cartoon contexts, the Petty Girl may be addressing the viewer. Despite the cultural amnesia that covers pinups when it comes to their pornographic potential, these two modes of address solidify the reception of the image as a selectively mainstream or pornographic genre.

The Petty Girl therefore emerged out of a very specific advertisement/cartoon structure. In a way, André Bazin's post-war statement that the pinup is not a pornographic or erotic image simply replicates the way pinups were understood by the general public at the time (Bazin 1971, 158). It seems surprising, for example, that there was no widespread objection to the public fact that Petty's adolescent daughter served as the model for these scantily clad figures. The "innocent" generic evolution of the pinup out of a humorous environment allowed it a mainstream presence that explicit images would not be able to enjoy in later years. The "wholesomeness" of the pinup was further guaranteed by the father-daughter collaboration, which at the time sparked no moral concerns. Marjorie Petty's public presence as the model added a "family-style" quality to the pinup, perhaps even to *Esquire* magazine. When Alberto Vargas took over as the main illustrator of *Esquire* in 1940, after increasing friction between the editors and George Petty, the editors objected to the fact that his main model was his wife, Anna Mae. They set Vargas up with a fifteen-year-old model, Jeanne Dean, who served as his main model for most of the war years. One reason behind this decision may be that Anna Mae, who had been a Ziegfeld Girl in the 1920s, represented a different kind of female beauty to them. Anna Mae was a redhead with ethereal, pale blue eyes, tall, slim, and, as a former dancer, muscular. As a Ziegfeld Girl, she probably resonated with the worldly knowledge of the glamorous women of the 1930s. Jeanne Dean and Marjorie Petty were shorter, more voluptuous, and had black hair and blue eyes. They were both very young when they started modeling, which contributed to an ideal of "vivaciousness and innocent sensuality" (Robotham 1995, 16), while their "girl-next-door" persona also aligned them with middle-class femininity. The editors' insecurity signals a slight change in the social reception of the pinup, which motivated their efforts to keep things as mainstream and innocent as possible. One cannot underestimate how important it was that Vargas follow the Petty paradigm and satisfy the desire of the editors to supplant one innocent young woman (as the identifiable model) with another. But primarily, it seems to me, the sexual connection between the artist and the model has to be dispelled before the illustration can appeal to a wide audience. The incest taboo rescues the Petty-Marjorie collaboration from ever appearing sexual. A husband-wife team cannot live up to the ideal of the pinup girl as a young, innocent if provocative, and potentially available sexual entity.[9]

The other component of the Petty Girl that Vargas was asked to imitate and incorporate into the new Varga Girl was the presence of the telephone. So specific and powerful was the iconic connection between the glamorous girl and the phone that one critic says: "It reached the point in the late thirties and forties that one couldn't see a woman talking on the phone without thinking of the Petty Girl" (Austin 1997, 36). With the telephone, we see one of the many permutations of the link between a pornographic theme and a new technological process. As an object, the telephone was associated with a specifically female voice from the very beginning, through "hundreds of thousands of high school–educated, middle class young women, who served as human telephone switches" (Lipartito 1994, 1075). These so-called Hello Girls provided an excellent workforce: they were educated, disciplined, supportive of each other, polite to irate customers, and single. On marriage, they had to leave the company and give up their high salaries and professional knowledge. The resulting five-year turnaround of female operators deterred the unionization of telephone workers, despite their highly publicized strikes between 1905 and 1920 and the public support of their rights.[10]

The telephone was consistently presented as a feminized/sexualized technological object, partly due to its association with a young, attractive female workforce, the telephone operators, who presented a "mobile" class both socially and perhaps morally. These single, newly urban women stood at the core of business communication, and, as a result, very close to the "male" sphere. Their control of the rapidly expanding telephone networks caused many attempts to automate the switching process, resulting in "girl-less" networks—which did not become the norm mostly because the AT&T and Bell companies refused to participate in this technological innovation.[11] AT&T did not start automating its switching process until the 1920s, and even then, in very small increments. One of AT&T's World War I posters, titled "Where Woman's Service Looms Large," features a young woman with arms stretched out holding a telephone over a map of the United States. But as is often the case in women's labor history, as the image of the female operator became publicized and idealized, women's actual control of this medium diminished. The poster copy aims to change the image of the female operator from a fundamental to an occasional labor force, by stating: "War gave woman her supreme and glorious opportunity to enlarge her field of service. She won her share of the laurels for patriotic achievement."[12] As was also the case with women's participation in heavy industry and manufacturing during World War II, when major corporations praised female workers for their patriotic work, they implied that for women this kind of work only held relevance during times of war. By the time George Petty created his phone-related advertisements for Bestform and other brands, the woman on the telephone was a private user, not a professional operator, even though women operators were still the norm in most cities. Such representations validated the established perception that a telephone had a female voice, but they also helped transform this voice from the professional action of a worker to the leisure activity of a glamorous girl in a private setting. In other words, instead of talking *through* her (where she is the facilitating presence), the pinup allows viewers to fantasize talking *to* her. The female operator in this case is implied as an available sexual entity: her presence as a voice is rendered sexual while denying her presence as a worker at the same time.

Petty's use of the telephone as a pinup prop was so consistent that telephone receivers became a necessary iconic referent for the pinup in general. When Vargas replaced Petty at *Esquire*, the chief editor gave an interview for *Newsweek* in September of 1940, announcing the arrival of "a new siren — the Varga Girl, who displays the same seductive curves, murmurs over the same telephone, and looks for all the world like the twin sister of the Petty Girl" (Austin 1997, 80–81). Given the anxiety of the editors over the replacement of Petty by Vargas, their insistence on the "same" telephone and the "same" girl comes as no surprise. Vargas was asked to imitate Petty's style, which at first demanded depicting the figure on the phone. As we can see in figure 4, however, there are fundamental differences. Instead of leaving the telephone as one of the unfinished parts as Petty always did, Vargas makes the receiver a focal point by giving it the most contrasting color. Both Petty and Vargas are interested in transparency. For Vargas the outline of the figure is slightly diffuse, and barely emerges from the yellowish background. Where Petty sets the figure on a single perspectival layer, Vargas positions her on a sharp diagonal, and plays with perspective to elongate the legs even more. Finally, in an added attempt to keep the pinup illustration as mainstream as possible, the Varga Girls appear not with a cartoon-style caption, but with a poem by Phil Stack (printed at the lower right corner of the image). Here is the poem for this first Varga Girl of October 1940:

> *Love at Second Sight*
> Irene, I just called up to let you know
> That I am signing off that guy from Butte,
> Though his intentions may be pure as snow
> The way that cowboy rumbas isn't cute!
> He says it's pretty lonely in New York
> And here is one for Ripley to endorse —
> The other night when we were at the Stork
> He called up home and asked about his HORSE!
>
> What's that you say . . . for me to hold on tight?
> Speak louder! This connection isn't clear . . .
> Oh Boy! You're sure that Winchell has it right?
> SIX SILVER MINES! How interesting my Dear!

AS RICH AS THAT? He surely doesn't show it . . .
MY GOD! I've been in love and didn't know it!

The poem creates a clear plot for the illustration and answers a number of questions: she is in New York, for example, she went out with a guy from Butte, and she is talking to her friend Irene about it. The title, "Love at Second Sight," functions as a reference to the fact that this is a "new" girl: readers of *Esquire* who were "in love" with the Petty Girl will have to adjust their affections. The persona created for the Varga Girl through the poem is consistent with the Petty Girl's outgoing, money-grabbing, and sexual character. The same point-of-view division identified with the Petty Girl exists here as well: poems that appear as/through her voice create a more explicitly sexual plot than poems in which someone else is addressing her.[13]

The presence of the telephone therefore creates a viewer-inclusion theme for the pinup, which is accentuated by the increasing necessity to have the image look directly at the assumed viewer. Despite the public character of the *Esquire* promotions, if there was a fundamental premise for the pinup in the 1940s, it was the idea of private address and possession—which seems surprising when each image was distributed in unprecedented numbers, and when each image had numerous imitations. The distribution of the famous Betty Grable pinup amounted to about 20,000 photographs *a week* in 1942 and through the war years. Grable was often congratulated for her role in the war—she was "supreme among the army of curvaceous pin-up queens who helped win the war" (Stein 1974, 143–45). When these images were annexed to the war effort, new props emerged to contain the patriotic referent. For example, the styling, pose, and design of the Varga Girl in figure 4 are almost identical to a Varga Girl published four years later in the middle of the war effort. But by then, the sexually explicit context of "Love at Second Sight" had been transformed into a patriotic one. Instead of having an idle conversation on the phone, the Varga Girl addresses the viewer with a direct appeal, asking him (because now she is appealing to a specific "guy") to support the war financially: she holds a sign that advertises war bonds.

Esquire magazine was one of the first mainstream media outlets to put into practice the new public relations strategy that equated being American with being pro-war. In 1939, David Smart, the Chicago editor of the magazine, made an agreement with the U.S. Armed Forces to produce an extra edition and distribute it to the troops free of charge. The monthly "military edition" contained no advertisements and by 1942 had a circulation of 300,000 copies.[14] For *Esquire*, the decision to become pro-war was

4. *Love at Second Sight.* The first Varga Girl to appear in *Esquire*, October 1940. Stylistically, this painting is closer to Vargas's work from the 1930s, when Anna Mae was still his model.

connected to a circulation crisis. A recession in 1938 dropped the circulation numbers of this highly successful magazine from 728,000 to about 550,000. This forced Smart to make rebates to advertisers and implement a new rate structure. As George Petty's biographer Reid Steward Austin writes: "What better serum for *Esquire*'s flagging circulation than total mobilization?"[15] On the other hand, annexing the pinup to the war effort proved inspiring and effective for the Armed Forces as well. In December 1942, Alberto Vargas (by then the main *Esquire* illustrator) received a letter from the U.S. Coast Guard, thanking him for painting pinup girls in uniforms: "This is really going to be of great help to us, since recruiting is getting away to a very slow start" (qtd. in Robotham 1995, 23). The relationship between the U.S. Armed Forces and *Esquire* had obvious marketing advantages for both.

In his patriotic illustrations, Vargas added a new technological referent to the pinup through tropes of flight and emergence. As artists, both Petty and Vargas were concerned with the challenge of painting the nude body. In descriptions of their technique, collected by Reid Steward Austin, it is clear that both Petty and Vargas focused on creating the color that rendered the perfect caucasian skin tone (which was always a secret recipe) and on ensuring the success of the illusion of body parts (which was meticulously planned).[16] Painted bodies have to create the illusion of roundness, belying their flat surface. In other words, they have to succeed in emerging from their background and appearing three-dimensional. Both artists used the airbrush, which functions differently from other paint media, since it has no contact with the canvas. The airbrush, or spray gun, discharges "liquid paint by means of air pressure. Altering the setting enables one to apply the paint to the surface in a finer or coarser jet" (Toman 1993, 4).[17] Because it distributes paint as a sprinkled cloud, the airbrush is an excellent tool for creating surface tension: a viewer can experience the subtle succession of tonal quality, without perceiving a boundary between colors or brushstrokes. The paint thus "lands" on the canvas as a film, without necessarily covering previous paint layers.

The language of flight and of elusive, almost invisible layers is fundamental to the pinup. For one, Petty and Vargas created unprecedented effects with the airbrush, which had previously mostly been used to *remove* curves and cleavage from photographs. They reversed the medium to *reveal* curves emerging out of the page. Both artists use this presentational shift self-consciously. The transparent clothes, barely distinguishable skin tone, and unfinished body parts of their figures show an engagement with the narrative of the female body materializing through a seemingly blank page. In a Petty pinup, this narrative of emergence is engaged through the contrast between finished body parts and unfinished outlines. After initial pencil sketches, Petty always started his paintings with a red outline of the figure. Everything was outlined in red, including the eyes, hair, and clothing, regardless of the final coloring of the composition. He then attached a protective frisket (a transparent adhesive film) to this outline in order to protect the paper background and all body parts not to be airbrushed. These parts remained unfinished. He considered whatever clothing was to be painted on as a color layer, and he usually distributed the latter very thinly so as not to cover the figure's skin tone. Transparent clothes therefore became the norm. Petty's technique created four planes for the figure: the white or beige paper background, the red outline body parts, the fully rendered body parts, and the "dressed" body parts. Petty seemed deeply invested in the choice between body parts rendered in absolute realism and ones completely left undone. Often the boundary between the two is a strikingly liminal space. Petty obviously had the ability to do realistic, lifelike representations. His insistence, therefore, to always remind viewers that the woman existed but as paint on a surface has to be considered as a self-conscious response to the challenges of the medium.

Petty focuses on slippage, but between strictly enforced divisions. Vargas, on the other hand, redistributes these divisions between fully rendered and unfinished parts. While Petty insists on making the face especially lifelike, for example, and the shoes completely schematic, Vargas often invests the shoes with great presence and removes contrast and color from the rest of the figure. In Vargas's pinups we see a different version of the emergence narrative. The outline of the figure is diffuse, while the outer borders separating body parts from unpainted paper often do not exist. His approach does not imply a hierarchical ordering between "important" body parts and mere props. In a Petty pinup, the white background is safeguarded and kept especially separate from the figure. Vargas instead animates the background as well, by treating it to imply color and a light source. This often means that the paper or canvas background may acquire the same color as the skin tone, a fact unfortunately lost in later reproductions of these works. Precisely because of Vargas's style, his work is very hard to reproduce. Recent editions usually recontextualize the pinup style by removing the original yellowish background and presenting a much more solid outline on a white background. Vargas also uses a frisket, but he often does so to leave internal parts of the figure as transparent as possible (patches of the hair, for example, or the most rounded part of a limb), not to protect the background.

For Vargas, therefore, the narrative of emergence is distributed in the painting as a diffuse sense of imminent differentiation, as he accentuates the lack of difference between the body and the background. Also, because Vargas started out as a portrait artist for the Ziegfeld Follies, his compositions are often "action" figures. They are depicted in poses that accentuate the lack of background, and they often float or fly across the paper. The extreme diagonal that Vargas favored allows the figure either to be elongated to a vanishing point or implies that she is about to exceed the boundaries of the paper and fly or burst away. Even though these compositions follow in the wake of Petty's success, Vargas's emphasis on lightness, movement, and lack of contrast reeducated the audience rather quickly. By 1945, readers of *True* magazine, where the Petty Girl then reigned, wrote that she was "built like a football player," that she had "draft-horse legs," that "the Petty Girls couldn't walk because their legs are too heavy" (Austin 1997, 110–11). The Petty Girl was perceived as too solid, too earthbound, and too short!

The Varga Girl, on the other hand, evoked emergence, movement, and flight. Even the language of the advertisements announcing her appearance acknowledged this connection. This is how the October 1940 edition of *Esquire* advertised her:

> Every once in a while a new girl is born, fully grown and partially clothed, like Venus fresh from the sea. To the sinuous and faintly perfumed ranks of such women . . . *Esquire* introduces the Varga Girl. . . . Her name joins those which over the centuries have made men stir uneasily in their beds, look critically at their wives, and wander to distant parts—pretending to seek a Golden Fleece, a Holy Grail, a Fountain of Youth, or a Northwest Passage. (Robotham 1995, 14)

The magnificent body that slowly arises from a barely separate background, in this case emerging from the sea, invites the viewer to recognize the tropes of emergence already built into the illustrations. The Varga Girl has an obviously unreal body, looks teasingly toward the viewer, remains alone, and is often almost transparent. This is true even though the whole point of the illustration is to register skin, body contours, and flesh tone. The skin barely emerges from the page; the clothes and shoes are lacy or translucent; blond hair merges with the unpainted background; red hair is the same color as the skin; black hair (it is never just brown) is so shiny that it has transparent patches. Neither Petty nor Vargas took any interest in red backgrounds at this time. Red backgrounds, which solidify the outline of the figure, become the definitive mark of pornographic representation after the war.[18] Instead, during the 1940s, the focus lay on foregrounding: the outline of the body was made from a small tone difference applied to the whiteness of the paper. Body parts or body curves were also created through subtle tone and shadow. The nonexistent material of the "dress" reduced it to an outline, lacking any coverage or even color interference. The whole appeared to emerge from the paper, and in the case of the Varga Girls, to be dynamically poised for flight or movement.

With the association of the pinup girl with patriotic rhetoric and the sublime feeling of flight, the pornographic component of the Petty Girl cartoons and early pinups was written out of the history and meaning of pinup images almost overnight. If, in 1940, "Love at Second Sight" created a sexual plot behind the illustration, by 1942, the poems accompanying the Varga Girl in *Esquire* are glorifying, innocent, or sentimental. Figure 5 gives us a visual example of this changed landscape. The pinup itself is invisible as a pornographic image and looks more like a portrait or film close-up. The emphasis on the face instead of the whole body is uncharacteristic—the insistence on full-figure representation makes for part of the definition of the pinup image. The poem by Phil Stack, "Song for a Lost Spring," accentuates the difference between the Petty Girl's savvy one-liners and this prolonged and opaque monologue. The poem asks readers to imagine an idyllic and romantic springtime, and then to compare it to the panic, flight, and lightning of the present time. Obviously, this is far from the money-grabbing persona of the pinup girl. The idealization of the pinup happens precisely because of its role in the war and its assumed patriotic character, and it is so successful as to establish the pinup in a hegemonic pro-war position.

The difference between the before/pornographic and after/patriotic stages of the pinup is intense. Before the war, the pinup plays up sexual elements in the visual and textual representation of the figure. During the war, visual elements such as a provocative pose or nudity become increasingly annexed to the patriotic effort, often tangentially. Figure 6, published in 1941, shows us a dynamic pose in a private, sexual setting. Appearing two years later, the image represented in figure 7 is almost identical in terms of pose: Vargas indeed often restaged certain poses and styles, and no doubt the same sketch or initial drawing was used for both paintings here. But he replaced the transparent, sexy robe with a transparent mantle, on which this pinup girl carries the signs of the U.S. Air Force. Her connection to the ground is now completely removed. The poem that accompanies her in *Esquire* further

5. *Song for a Lost Spring.* The Varga Girl, *Esquire,* May 1942. The poem by Phil Stack gave the caption and title to Vargas's centerfold.

distances her from any pornographic viewing. She is not a girl now, but a "heavenly body," and she obviously literally stands for an airplane or the Air Force. "Her pose is a sign" of the condition of the American troops in the war—and she looks great, therefore America is winning. And the title declares that "There Will Always Be a Christmas," in the most family-oriented and hopeful way.

The transition of the pinup from a sexually alluring image to an idealized or sublime representation of American values is very important, as is the equation between the girl and flight, the Air Force, and airplanes. As a result of this connection, the girl's sex appeal animates the airplane, and the airplane, in standard patriotic fare, protects the girl. The dynamic between the two entities absolutely depends on the possibility of animation, of understanding the Air Force, for example, as a smiling, charming airborne blonde. The pinup thus acquires allegoric significance: it stands for certain values and certain objects, which it animates and physically embodies. In this sublime merger of the pinup girl and the beautiful airplane, older styles of patriotic representation, such as Petty's later recruitment posters, seem antiquated and limited.

6. The Varga Girl, *Esquire*, September 1941. Compare the body styling of this painting by Alberto Vargas to that of figure 7.

7. *There Will Always Be a Christmas*. The Varga Girl, *Esquire*, December 1943. Notice the similarity between the pose of this figure and that represented in figure 6.

The pinup therefore functions as a versatile cultural product that can negotiate multiple transitions in this difficult period. It animates impersonal machinery. It accentuates the attraction of war machines through sex appeal (the girl-as-airplane). It metonymically replaces the process of war and actual fighting (the bomb and pinup in "Blitz Wolf"). It facilitates patriotic identification with "the boys" as they prepare for war. Finally, it creates a normative representation of the soldier as an innocent, starstruck, heterosexual, nonviolent, small-town boy, whose sexual imagination is limited to imagined relationships with illustrated "all-American girls."

Furthermore, the intense deployment of the pinup by a variety of official agencies and army leadership personnel points to an underlying homophobic reaction to the massive mobilization of young men. The long residence of the troops in urban centers such as New York and San Diego brought them in contact not only with exciting big city life but also with the active gay culture of these places. That the army worried about this urban exposure became evident in the increased attention to screening practices for new recruits, both women and men, designed to determine whether a recruit was homosexual on the basis of intrusive physical tests.[19] Among other necessities, this homophobic reaction also demanded an investment in extreme femininity. How else can we understand everybody's blindness to the pornographic potential of the pinup girls, the Oomph Girls, and the Sweater Girls of the time?[20] The November 10, 1944, issue of *The Family Circle*, for example, features an article titled "Something for the Boys." This article, accompanied by a number of photographs of "starlets" in sexy outfits, encourages women readers to clip the pages and send them off to a "boy" they know in the army. The magazine appears completely directed toward women and seems unabashedly unselfconscious about the starlets' sexual or pornographic potential. The soldiers seem similarly innocent, apparently writing to the magazine to request these photos. The models' agent receives praise for "combining publicity and patriotism" after sending approximately 650,000 photographs of "the girls" to "the boys" for free (but only to servicemen, not civilians). In a motherly tone, the narrator suggests: "If you know someone in service whose morale you think would be better if he had one of these photos, why not send him the cover and these two pages of this issue?" In a section called "The Boys Say Thanks," excerpts from the soldiers' letters appear: "Since receiving your picture this noon, my foot locker has become the most popular spot in the company area. You made the morale of the entire outfit jump 100% in the first 15 minutes." Another letter reads "I hope you don't mind that I named my tank after you" (*Family Circle* 1944,

10–11). Here again we see the intimate link between the pinup girls and the machinery they domesticate and sexualize.

Given all these overt tensions in pinup representation, the success of the euphemistic "morale" seems mind-boggling. "The boys" certainly don't point these pinup photos at incoming bombs to protect themselves! Obviously, the pinup cannot act as a shield against actual bullets or bombs. What does it guard the soldiers from, then? Also, are these boys not satisfied with the mainstream edition of *Esquire*, the military edition they get for free, the army-produced *Yank* with its two pages of "pin-up bonus," and the numerous film magazines that publish pinup photos? Why are they looking for pinups in a magazine called *Family Circle*? The key to these questions comes in another soldier's letter. He writes to his favorite starlet: "I am sure that if a vote was taken, you would be chosen the female who each and every one of us would like to be deserted with here (*Family Circle* 1944, 11). The public insistence that male soldiers need to be surrounded by photographs of sexy young women shows a certain kind of anxiety. Everyone wants to forget that the boys are deserted there with other boys. Or, in the xenophobic version of the same argument, everyone wants to forget that the boys may be surrounded and seduced by women of other nationalities, races, or class backgrounds.[21] The public representation of the soldier, therefore, insists on wholesome, optimistic, heterosexual innocence, even as cultural evidence shows that it is not exactly taken for granted. It seems obvious that the pinup facilitates redirecting any possible aggression or desire toward a picture of normative middle-class American heterosexuality.

The patriotic pinup of the 1940s, with all its powerful hegemonic uses and effects, is placed in the equivalent of cultural brackets soon after the end of the war, and its pornographic possibilities are negated, disavowed, and forgotten. The images, poses, styles, and body types apparently so sublime in the 1940s, were soon deemed too sexual and again became part of a pornographic subculture. In a short essay called "Entomology of the Pin-Up Girl," published after the end of World War II, André Bazin writes of the necessary distance between pinups and pornographic images:

> First, let us not confuse the pin-up girl with the pornographic or erotic imagery that dates from the dark backward and abysm of time. The pin-up girl is a specific erotic phenomenon, both as to form and function. . . . A war time product created for the benefit of the American soldiers swarming to a long exile at the four corners of the world, the pin-up girl soon became an industrial product, subject to well fixed norms and as

stable in quality as peanut butter or chewing gum. Rapidly perfected, like the jeep, among those things specifically stipulated for modern American military sociology, she is a perfectly harmonized product of given racial, geographic, social, and religious influences. (1971, 158)

For Bazin, as for other post–World War II European artists and writers, the mainstream pinup as a self-conscious product is historically specific, forever linked to the worldwide American military presence during the war years. Bazin identifies the pinup as an industrial product associated with American consumer goods (chewing gum, peanut butter) and, again, military industrial equipment (the Jeep). It accompanies soldiers to the "four corners of the world," where it carries ideological Americanness to a global setting. And because of all these particularities, it is not an erotic image the way other pornographic images are: the classic pinup girl is characterized by "childlike and unsophisticated simplicity." In contrast, the postwar pinup is inauthentic, and either too mainstream or too pornographic. Bazin condemns the newer version of the pinup girl as decadent or hypocritical, a silly attempt to represent newer domestic values. "In the United States there are even contests for 'pin-up mothers' and 'pin-up babies,'" he complains (160).

Bazin thus alerts us to the cultural impulse to separate the pinup into two categories after the war: the type of illustration that can function as a wholesome household product ("pin-up moms") and the type of image that will again be relegated to a pornographic category in the new, more explicit and more photographic men's magazines. The increasing insecurity about the pornographic content or potential of the pinup, held at bay during the war because of its sublime configuration as a patriotic icon, resulted in a double removal from the mainstream after the war ended. On the one hand, the patriotic pinups of the 1940s were closed off as historical monuments, and their pornographic possibilities were completely forgotten. On the other hand, newer photographic or artistic pinups were evacuated of the history and iconicity of their predecessors as their pornographic content doomed them to a subcultural position. The proliferation of men's and so-called girlie magazines allowed for an explosion of pinup production, but not on the same terms. By 1951, the same studio that created "Blitz Wolf" featured girls in bathing suits in every possible setting and on any imaginable occasion. In a cartoon called "T.V. of Tomorrow," for example (dir. Tex Avery, 1951), the "tired businessman" can relax with a new television model that has two screens: one for the top part of the model (the acceptable and mainstream smiling face and shoulders) and a second screen where the rest of the girl

8. *Sexy Robot* by Hajime Sorayama, 1978. The new pinup uses the classic vocabulary of poses but seems to have no representational limits. In his *Sexy Robot* and *Gynoid* series, Sorayama further externalizes the pinup's relationship to technology through the use of metal surfaces and overt technological props (cars, motorcycles, weapons, wiring, computer equipment, and other machinery). Copyright 2003 Hajime Sorayama/Artspace/ Uptight.

is visible. Another tired businessman watches a bathing suit–clad girl while the narrator advertises another new TV model: "This advanced model automatically eliminates picture distortion from passing airplanes." The top of the TV set opens up, and an anti-aircraft weapon comes out and starts shooting at the ceiling. An airplane with a very surprised pilot falls through the house. Obviously, the pinup girl is still remembered as a weapon, but her functionality is now dubious.

Part of the difficulty in dealing with complex cultural processes of the past is that the perspective of the present inevitably alters our understanding of what matters and how. In order to avoid making claims from a removed and secure point of view, I have based my reading of the pinup on texts of the period. I focused on a number of negotiations that the pinup facilitates as it allows a space for the projection of cultural anxieties. The pinup is represented during the 1940s as a perfect woman, as a New Woman, as a talismanic entity, and as a weapon. If we understand the intense social and cultural functionality of the pinup, we can reevaluate both the instrumentality of popular images, and the interaction between pornographic and mainstream modes of address.

Furthermore, this approach provides the groundwork for explaining the recurrent theme of techno-pornographic representation (figure 8). Seeing the animating fantasy in the setting and rhetoric of the pinup creates a culturally relevant framework for the kinds of cultural productions often seen as standing "outside" culture. I have tried to explain what makes certain images attractive without reverting to an essentialist framework (nude women are attractive to men). After all, not all nudes are as attractive as all other nudes. At different times, one kind of representation is more resonant than another, and figuring out what makes a difference is absolutely necessary in culturally relevant work. Indeed, this characteristic of soft-core erotic images, that they lose their ability to arouse us, is telling both of the specific requirements we have of pornographic genres and of the necessary modernity and contemporaneity involved in their enjoyment. Because they go out of style, pinups specifically do not depend on the visibility of body parts. Instead, they borrow their sexual energy from a wide range of elusive cultural, technological, and social negotiations. The technological mediation that was my focus in this essay is central in these negotiations. The fluctuating and tricky embodiment pinups are able to perform is exactly what we need in order to render strange new technologies visible.[22]

Notes

I would like to thank Hajime Sorayama and his representative in the United States, Miharu Yamamoto, for their help and generosity. More information about Sorayama's artwork can be found on his official Web site, available at www.sora yama.net.

1 The merger between function (propaganda) and form (the pinup) has a long-lasting effect: later military campaigns often redeploy the idea of the innocent, nostalgic World War II pinup in other mobilizations. In Operation Desert Storm, for example, even though the Air Force did not allow images on airplanes any more, pilots were allowed to design surprisingly explicit pornographic or anti-Arab pinups for their "nose art." Most planes were allowed to fly with those new pinups while in the Middle East, but were repainted before returning to their U.S. bases (Wood 1996, 29–30). This pinup art received very little publicity because it was seen as insensitive and pornographic. For World War II pinups, however, no such limitation exists: their American, smiling wholesomeness still occupies the hegemonic and patriotic place it did in the 1940s.

2 See, for example, imageNETion (www.imagenetion.com), a massive visual library created by Paulo Paulista Goncalves in Brazil. The site currently features more than 19,000 scanned pinup images, ranging from early work by famous illustrators to contemporary pinup photography.

3 There is renewed scholarly interest in the pinup as well, including a recent exhibit, *Alberto Vargas: The Esquire Pinups*, at the Spencer Museum of Art, University of Kansas. For recent scholarship, mostly historical, see Mary 1983, Collins 2000, Dunlop 2001, and Buszek 1999, 2001.

4 The rumor was widely distributed at the time. This photographic image was of Rita Hayworth in a negligee, perched on a bed with satin sheets. It was an intensely popular pinup of the war years, and rival of the well-known image of Betty Grable. It first appeared in *Life* on August 11, 1941, when the magazine proclaimed her "The Goddess of Love of the Twentieth Century." See Stein 1974, 145, and Gabor [1972] 1996, 23, 150.

5 We also should not forget that the calendar with the racing cars often features female models in swimsuits posing with the cars, in the well established link between pinups and machinery.

6 The initial circulation of *Esquire* was an astonishing 100,000 copies, which amounted to the combined circulation of three of the day's best periodicals (*American Mercury, Town and Country*, and *Vanity Fair*) and the high circulation expected for top monthlies such as *Harper's, Atlantic*, and *Fortune* (Austin 1997, 31).

7 Petty also starred in advertisements as a celebrity spokesperson. A Gruen wristwatches ad of 1937 shows a photograph of his hands over one of his bathing suit drawings, with the caption reading, "No Wonder People Envy the Wristwatch George Petty wears. . . ." The wristwatch is a new model called the "custom curved *Gruen Curvex*." The pun between the "curves" of the drawing and the "curved" wristwatch explains why the company specifically chose Petty for this campaign.

8 In a newspaper-sponsored poll, the Princeton class of 1939 chose Petty as its favorite artist, with Rembrandt and Titian in second and third place. *Life* magazine responded to this news with alarm at the students' challenge to serious art, but it also devoted three full pages to a special report on the Petty family.

9 In contrast, more pinups of the 1950s and 1960s reinvest the painter/model relationship with the possibility of a sexual encounter. This returns the iconography to a pre-1940s rationale for the image: the woman is a professional model and therefore has accepted the sexual nature of the relationship on her own terms.

10 For historical information on working conditions for women operators, as well as their labor strikes and the public response to them, see Sangster 1978.

11 It is important to note that in promoting these "girl-less" networks, companies presented a very different profile for the telephone operator. Instead of the beautiful, independent, fashionable, urban young woman, they represented the operator as an old country gossip who listens in on other people's phone calls.

Customers were informed that the automatic process would never be "surly" or "saucy" and would never gossip. Compared to that intrusive and unappealing persona, the impersonal automatic switches were supposed to be a welcome change. Lipartito 1994, 1101.

12 The text continues: "In telephone service, also, a host of capable, loyal daughters of America still find expression for their ambition and ability. These girls are privileged to play an indispensable part in the nation's welfare. They have in their keeping the myriad avenues of telephone communication through which the nation's industry is guided." Lipartito 1994, 1074.

13 The illustration works both ways: it supplies us with the beautiful body and invites us to imagine the sexy voice. On the other hand, any woman's voice on the telephone may evoke the image of this body. The attempt to give a body to the disembodied voice, and to engage a narrative expansion of the image, allows the viewer to be in many places at the same time. One can imagine being on the phone talking to this woman; being with her while she talks to someone else; or looking at her while she cannot see us. Phone sex advertisements placed in contemporary newspapers also make a point of supplying visual components (and a long list of specific preferences in terms of age, race, and body type) for the disembodied voice.

14 The first gatefold appeared in 1939. After increasing tension between Petty and the editors ensued, Alberto Vargas was hired in 1940. His appointment was the focus of a great deal of publicity about the Varga Girl, which first appeared as a gatefold in October 1940. Two months later, a whole calendar was published with Varga Girls. This calendar became a national sensation (Robotham 1995, 14). The saturation of the market with Petty and Vargas pinups was fantastic for the time. *Esquire* published its monthly magazine—which sometimes included three gatefolds by Vargas—one or more annual Vargas calendars, and a monthly "military edition."

15 *Esquire*'s sister publications were also in trouble: *Coronet*, a pocket-sized magazine, was not doing well, while the large-format newsmagazine *Ken* closed after only eighteen months. Austin 1997, 71.

16 Reid Steward Austin was art director of *Playboy* magazine for many years, and he has been an influential pinup art collector and personal friend of Alberto Vargas. He has written authoritative biographies of Vargas and Petty, in which he asked Vargas and Marjorie Petty to elaborate on studio techniques, color selections, and other artistic details. My information about their actual studio practices comes from these personal essays (Austin 1978, 1987, and 1997).

17 The airbrush technique was invented by Charles Burdick around 1893 and was mostly used for touching up photographs until the poster art of the Bauhaus and the commercial art of the 1930s. For a historical and theoretical discussion of the airbrush, see Wakerman 1979.

18 This standard was probably set by the photographic pinups of Marilyn Monroe, first published as a calendar in 1951 and reprinted in the first issue of *Playboy*

(1953). Monroe posed for an ordinary session with photographer Tom Kelley in 1949, for which she was paid $50. She was still an unknown model then, but by the time of publication, she had appeared in *The Asphalt Jungle* (dir. John Huston, 1950) and *All About Eve* (dir. Joseph Mankiewicz, 1950). The red background used for her nude posing was by no means new, but its success through *Playboy* established a favorite mode for full-color photographic pinups. For more information on the photographer, see Stein 1974, 163–68.

19 Historians of gay life in the military consider World War II a central cultural moment in the emergence of gay identities and the culture's awareness of homosexuality. For more historical information, see Bérubé 1990 and Scott and Stanley 1994. My information on screening tests for new recruits comes from the unpublished research of Aaron Belkin, from our conversations in November 1998 and January 1999.

20 Almost every actress of the time was publicized as a specific product, based on an actual or invented physical attribute. This nicknaming practice has a long history in Hollywood, where it was used to identify stars such as the Keystone Girl (Mabel Normand), the Vamp (Theda Bara), the It Girl (Clara Bow), and so on. There was obviously only one of each "girl." Ann Sheridan was the Oopmh Girl (see the film *Navy Blues* [dir. Lloyd Bacon, 1941]). The Sweater Girl was Lana Turner. The nicknames were often strange: Carole Landis, for example, was known as the Ping Girl and was often photographed in profile so that her pointed breasts would deliver the meaning of *ping*.

21 This is the theme of the well-known song from World War I "How 'Ya Gonna Keep 'Em Down on the Farm (now that they've seen Paree)." The song was featured in *For Me and My Gal* (dir. Busby Berkeley, 1942).

22 The airbrush, favorite tool of pinup illustrators, is exceptionally well adapted to these effects. By creating lifelike, photographic-quality illustrations, the airbrush itself bridges the gap between the technological and the organic. The ability to represent detail, complexity, and clarity while at the same time imparting a sense of imminent emergence is what makes the airbrush the favorite tool of technical illustrators and pornographic illustrators alike.

Works Cited

Austin, Reid Steward. 1997. *Petty: The Classic Pin-up Art of George Petty*. New York: Gramercy.

Austin, Reid Steward, with Alberto Vargas. 1978. *Vargas (Authorized Biography)*. New York: Harmony.

———. 1987. *Varga: The Esquire Years*. New York: Marck.

Bazin, André. 1971. "Entomology of the Pin-up Girl." In *What Is Cinema*. Vol. 2. Trans. Hugh Gray. Berkeley: University of California Press. 158–62.

Bérubé, Allan. 1990. *Coming Out under Fire: The History of Gay Men and Women in World War Two*. New York: Free Press.

Buszek, Maria Elena. 1999. "Representing 'Awarishness': Burlesque, Feminist Transgression, and the 19th Century Pin-Up." *TDR: The Journal of Performance Studies* 43, 4: 141–62.

———. 2001. "Of Varga Girls and Riot Grrrls: The Varga Girl and WWII in the Pin-up's Feminist History." In *Essays on the Occasion of the Exhibition "Alberto Vargas: The Esquire Pinups."* Available at *www.ku.edu/~sma/vargas/buszek.htm*

Collins, Max Allan. 2000. *For the Boys: The Racy Pin-ups of World War II.* Portland, Ore.: Collectors Press.

Cott, Nancy F., ed. 1993. *History of Women in the United States: Historical Articles on Women's Lives and Activities. Vol 7, Industrial Wage Work.* Munich: K.G. Saur.

Dunlop, Beth. 2001. *Beach Beauties: Postcards and Photographs, 1890–1940.* New York: Stewart, Tabori and Chang.

Family Circle. 1944. November 10, 10–11.

"Five Hundred 1963 Girl-a-Week and Joke-a-Day Calendars—Good for 2002—Donated to U.S. Special Forces Fighting for Freedom." *PR Web*, November 7, 2001.

Gabor, Mark. [1972] 1996. *The Pin-up: A Modest History.* Cologne: Taschen.

Life. 1941. August 11.

Lipartito, Kenneth. 1994. "When Women Were Switches: Technology, Work, and Gender in the Telephone Industry, 1890–1920." *American Historical Review* 99, 4: 1075–III.

Mary, Bertrand. 1983. *La Pin-up, ou, La fragile indifférence: Essai sur la genèse d'une imagerie délaissée* [The pinup; or, fragile indifference: An essay on the origin of a forgotten imagery]. Paris: Fayard.

Robotham, Tom. 1995. *Varga.* New York: Smithmark.

Sangster, Joan. 1978. "The 1907 Bell Telephone Strike: Organizing Women Workers." *Labour/Le Travail* 3: 109–30.

Scott, Wilbur J., and Sandra Carson Stanley, eds. 1994. *Gays and Lesbians in the Military: Issues, Concerns, and Contrasts.* New York: De Gruyter.

Sorayama, Hajime. 1983. *Sexy Robot.* Tokyo: Genko-sha.

———. 1984. *Pin-up.* Tokyo: Graphic-sha.

Stein, Ralph. 1974. *The Pin-up: From 1852 to Now.* Chicago: Ridge Press/Playboy Press.

Toman, Rolf. 1993. *Airbrush in Japan.* Vol. 1. Singapore: Page One Publishing.

Wakerman, Elyce. 1979. *Air Powered: The Art of the Airbrush.* New York: Random House.

Wood, J. P. 1996. *Aircraft Nose Art: Eighty Years of Aviation Artwork.* New York: Smithmark/Salamander.

Gauging a Revolution: 16 mm Film and the Rise of the Pornographic Feature

ERIC SCHAEFER

✳ The relationship between the entertainment industry and filmed pornography is much like that between the proper moneyed family and the slack-jawed black-sheep cousin locked away in the attic. No one wants to acknowledge that it exists. No one wants to be caught near it. And certainly no one wants to admit it has a history, for fear of being tainted by revelations about its past. So the history of filmed pornography—such as it is—remains fragmentary, frequently unreliable, and as much the stuff of whispers and folklore as of fact. What history has been written is most often told in the histories of other, albeit related, topics, such as obscenity law.

Kenneth Turan and Stephen F. Zito's *Sinema*, published in 1974, offers a fairly standard account of the development of the hard-core feature. It runs as follows: during the 1960s, feature-length soft-core sexploitation films gained a foothold in the marketplace with *Playboy*-inspired imagery of nude women and later of simulated sex. Around 1967, the sexploitation film "had gone about as far as it could go" (Turan and Zito 1974, 77). At about the same time, shorts known as beaver films, which had previously circulated underground and showed full female nudity with a focus on the genitals, began to appear above ground in San Francisco. The split beaver, action beaver, and hard-core loop began to appear shortly afterward.[1] By 1969–70, a series of "how-to" features emerged, sometimes referred to as marriage-manual films or "white-coaters," wearing the mantle of scientific respectability as they ticked through visual rosters of sexual positions. Concurrently, a group

of documentaries hit the screens, purporting to examine the legal and social changes surrounding the emergence of pornography in Denmark and
the United States, while offering hard-core sequences by way of illustration.
Compilation features, presented as histories of the stag film, quickly followed.[2] By mid-1970, the first hard-core narrative feature, *Mona* (dir. Bill
Osco, 1970), appeared. Much of this history is recounted by Linda Williams,
who concludes that in 1972 the "transition from illicit stag films to the legal,
fictional narratives" was signaled by the arrival of *Deep Throat* (dir. Gerard
Damiano, 1972), which "burst into the public consciousness" (1999, 98).

Even though we lack a programmatic history of filmed hard-core pornography, its development, as evidenced above, has been narrativized. The
result has tended toward an overly rigid chronology: filmmakers jumping
across a series of hurdles, offering greater explicitness with each leap on
their way to a predetermined end—nonsimulated representations of sexual
acts on screen.[3] This same account of a steady, teleological march undermined general film history for years and obscured many of the economic
and industrial reasons for the eventual dominance of the narrative form in
theatrical motion pictures. What has become increasingly evident is that the
feature-length hard-core narrative constituted merely an entr'acte between
reels of essentially plotless underground stag movies in the years 1908 to
1967 and the similarly plotless ruttings of porn in the video age (emerging in the mid-1980s and continuing to the present). Although the period
between the early 1970s and the mid-1980s is now widely regarded as the
"golden age" of the hard-core feature, little effort has gone into explaining
how and why the hard-core feature emerged when it did.[4] The many difficulties involved in answering this question—and of constructing a history
of the pornographic film—necessitate an approach that accounts not only
for basic legal and industrial considerations but also for such causal factors
as technology. This history must then be considered within the appropriate
social and political context.

The purpose of this essay is to explore the origins of the hard-core narrative feature in the period from 1967 to 1972, the year *Deep Throat* thrust
it into the center of the cultural stage. By examining articles in trade magazines and newspapers, advertising, product catalogs and brochures, and the
films themselves (notably the overlooked so-called simulation movies), as
well as the discourse surrounding the films and the sexual revolution, we can
arrive at a more nuanced understanding of how and why the pornographic
feature developed and why narrative became, for a time, the dominant paradigm in porn. What I want to suggest is that a set of historically specific

material conditions of production and reception—notably the introduction of 16 mm as a theatrical mode in the adult market—contributed to the rise of the pornographic feature. These conditions proved just as important as the individual legal decisions and the porn auteurs, often cited as major causes in the development of the feature. Indeed, 16 mm films revolutionized the adult film market, bringing hard-core films out of the back room and placing them "on scene" in cities around the United States. The discourse of revolution—sexual and otherwise—was mobilized to differentiate the new 16 mm films from existing adult motion picture product. Moreover, the sexploitation film, which has been characterized as a dead end in the history of filmed pornography, competed directly with 16 mm films, making the former instrumental in the development of the hard-core feature.

This inquiry affords us several important outcomes. First, it fills in some of the gaps in the history of filmed pornography, a history that has generally gone ignored in film studies, despite the cultural and economic impact the form has had on American entertainment since the late 1960s. Whether one is "fer it or agin' it," an accurate understanding of the history of the pornographic feature would seem a prerequisite for continuing critical, social, or legal discussions. Second, recent work has demonstrated the degree of influence sexploitation and pornography had on mainstream film industry practices in the 1960s and 1970s (Wyatt 1999; Lewis 2000). It is thus important that our understanding of the history of sexploitation and pornography approach the level of our understanding of Hollywood during this period. Third, and finally, this history helps us acknowledge the diverse ways in which the 16 mm gauge has been used—in amateur moviemaking, experimental film, education, industry, and pornography.

The Sexploitation Film

Some discussion of the sexploitation market is necessary for contextualizing the arrival of 16 mm pictures and the emergence of hard-core features. In *"Bold! Daring! Shocking! True!,"* I discuss how from the early 1920s to the late 1950s "classical" exploitation films offered U.S. audiences the sights forbidden by the Production Code as well as by many state and local censorship bodies. Usually couched as exposés of contemporary problems, educational tracts, or morality plays, classical exploitation films maintained their position in the market by including moments of spectacle unlike anything seen in mainstream movies: scenes set in nudist camps, shots of striptease dances, and footage of childbirth, victims of venereal disease, and people engaging in a range of vices. The films survived in an often hostile environment by including a "square-up," an introductory educational statement that explained how exposure of the problem in question was necessary to bring about its eradication. But as the Hollywood studio system crumbled in the 1950s, and with it the self-regulatory infrastructure that had been in place since 1922, mainstream productions began to reintegrate most of the topics taboo under the Production Code (Schaefer 1999).

By the late 1950s and early 1960s, a new crop of so-called nudie-cuties appeared—films that contained nudity but did not have an educational imprimatur. Russ Meyer's *The Immoral Mr. Teas* (1959) is generally acknowledged as the first of this new breed of exploitation film. It was quickly followed by a raft of others, such as *The Adventures of Lucky Pierre* (dir. Hershell Gordon Lewis, 1960) and *Mr. Peter's Pets* (dir. Dick Crane, 1962). Most of the nudie-cuties operated as comedies, and the dialogue or narration was often sprinkled with double entendres, but they lacked overtly sexual situations. Although female nudity provided the draw, it always remained discreet. Actresses were shot only from the waist up or from behind.

Nudie-cuties gradually gave way to a greater range of sexploitation films that usually, though by no means always, constituted fictional narratives including spectacle: nudity in the context of sexual situations, and, in time, simulated sexual activity. The range of sexploitation films made during the 1960s included suburban exposés (e.g., *Sin in the Suburbs* [dir. Joe Sarno, 1964]), dramas about big-city decadence (e.g., *To Turn a Trick* [dir. Charles Andrew, 1967]), psychodramas about sexual obsession (e.g., *The Curse of Her Flesh* [dir. Julian Marsh, 1968]), and spoofs of classic tales (e.g., *Dracula the Dirty Old Man* [dir. William Edwards, 1969]) and contemporary genres (e.g., *Thigh Spy* [dir. William Hennigar, 1967]).

Shortages of Hollywood movies and foreign "art" films in the early 1960s had forced many exhibitors to turn to sexploitation. The *Technical Report of the Commission on Obscenity and Pornography* states that by 1969, roughly six hundred drive-in and hardtop theaters, including specialized chains such as the Art Theater Guild and Pussycat, regularly played sexploitation product (Sampson 1971, 37). Louis Sher's Art Theater Guild, for example, began as a string of houses specializing in European art films in 1954. By 1965, Sher had moved into distribution, releasing Andy Warhol titles like *Lonesome Cowboys* (dir. Andy Warhol and Paul Morrissey, 1968) and *Flesh* (dir. Paul Morrissey, 1968), and eventually sexploitation and porn films such as *The Stewardesses* (dir. Alf Silliman Jr., 1969), *Mona*, and *History of the Blue Movie* (dir. Alex DeRenzy, 1970) ("Sherpix" 1972, 21). In 1961, businessman

Vince Miranda bought and renovated a Los Angeles building that contained a theater. After being arrested by the sheriff's department for showing an allegedly obscene movie, Miranda was drawn more deeply into the porn business as he expended time and money fighting the charge. Over time, he purchased more theaters, which ultimately became California's Pussycat Theater chain. By 1981, Miranda operated forty houses (Kaminsky 1981, 14). Meanwhile, dozens of other urban theaters and rural drive-ins—particularly in the South—programmed steady streams of sexploitation movies.

In addition to theaters that regularly played sexploitation films, hundreds of others booked them from time to time during the 1960s. This number grew, especially as breakout pictures such as *I, a Woman* (dir. Mac Ahlberg, 1966), *Vixen* (dir. Russ Meyer, 1968), and *Without a Stitch* (dir. Annelise Meineche, 1970) had long runs in showcase and neighborhood theaters. As *Variety* observed, when Audubon's Danish import *I, a Woman* "freed itself from the exploitation houses, it invaded suburbia and immediately struck paydirt" ("Far Out" 1967, 13). The film broke into respectable venues early in its American run in 1966, when it played the Trans-Lux on Eighty-fifth Street in Manhattan (Corliss 1973, 23). Other sexploitation titles followed—enough that the major film companies and their representatives became concerned that sexploitation pictures were getting bookings in major chains—and in early 1970, Motion Picture Association of America (MPAA) president Jack Valenti launched a campaign to dissuade exhibitors from booking sexploitation films ("Metzger and Leighton" 1970, 4; "Valenti on 'Personal' Campaign" 1970, 4–5; "Valenti: Too Many" 1970; "Valenti's Personal" 1970, 4–5).

An established group of distributors and subdistributors served the hundreds of theaters playing sexploitation product, either regularly or occasionally. American Film Distributing (AFD), Audubon, Boxoffice International, Cambist, Distribpix, Entertainment Ventures, Eve, and Olympic International were just some of the larger companies that carved out a lucrative segment of the motion picture marketplace. In 1968, AFD, Boxoffice International, Distribpix, and Olympic International collectively released thirty-two pictures. In 1969, between 135 and 150 feature-length sexploitation pictures hit the circuit (Sampson 1971, 33). A catalog issued by Distribpix in 1971, which listed product from the previous five years, included one hundred feature-length titles, the vast majority in color (Distribpix Catalogue 1971). In addition, dozens of smaller companies issued a film or two per year.

Sexploitation films were produced and exhibited in 35 mm for $15,000 to $25,000, with "a fair number" coming in at $40,000. While some were cobbled together for as little as $5,000 to $10,000, a few of the more elaborate color productions made in 1969–70 cost more than $100,000 (Sampson 1971, 32–34). Rental terms differed from city to city and state to state. Low-end and mid-range product usually rented for a flat fee, generally depending on the size of the market and past performance. Better features could command percentages (40).

By 1970, the sexploitation industry began to fracture. Traditional sexploitation theaters were becoming either low-end houses, which ran the cheapest material possible, or high-end operations, such as the Pussycat chain, which sought out only the highest-quality product (Kaufman n.d.). But more important to the development of hard-core motion pictures, the industry was also cleaving along the lines of 16 mm and 35 mm production and exhibition.

Eager Beavers and Storefront Theaters

By 1923, 16 mm equipment was standardized and began to be marketed as an "amateur" gauge, in contrast to the 35 mm gauge for "professionals." From that point on, companies such as Kodak and Bell and Howell marketed the 16 mm gauge as a leisure product for middle- and upper–middle-class families (Zimmermann 1995, 17–31). Families not only shot amateur movies and family subjects but also bought and rented short films on a wide range of topics. Outfits such as Castle Films, Official Films, and Blackhawk specialized in newsreels, sports films, and comedies, but other companies produced adult "art studies," available to home collectors via direct mail and through camera stores and other outlets (Schaefer forthcoming). Since at least the mid-1930s, several individuals and companies, including NuArt Productions, Pacific Ciné Productions, and Vanity Productions, produced and sold these nonnarrative shorts, which usually featured one or two women lounging around on a set, in an apartment, or in a landscape. Many shorts included full frontal nudity, as well as the caveat that they were "produced for the exclusive use of artists and art students." The status of 16 mm changed during World War II and in the postwar period as a result of its use in combat and newsreel photography, as well as in the burgeoning educational market. As lower-priced, easier-to-use 8 mm equipment became popular among amateurs and home-movie enthusiasts in the 1950s, 16 mm came to be considered a semiprofessional—but still a nontheatrical—gauge (Zimmermann 1995, 117–18).

Sixteen-millimeter adult films began to move out of the home and into public exhibition at the beginning of 1967, the year the *San Francisco Examiner* advertised the first beaver films. The Roxie, a traditional theater with several hundred seats at Sixteenth Street and Valencia, had been serving up a steady stream of so-called nudies when it offered "Naughty Nymphs and Eager Beavers at Their Busy Best," and proclaimed itself "Home of the Eager Beaver Films." A little over a month later, the Peerless, at Third and Mission, also began advertising "Eager Beaver Films." Those two houses were soon joined by the Gay Paree and other venues. The designation of *eager beaver film* may have described the enthusiasm of the on-screen performers, but, more important, the term served as a signal for those who knew that *beaver* was a euphemism for the female pubic area. The Gay Paree and Peerless used standard ads that indicated when their programs changed. The Roxie was far more imaginative in its advertising, announcing program changes with new titles such as "Beaver Picnic," "Beaucoup Beavers," "Beavers at Sea," "Beavers in Bloom," and "Eager Beavers Demanding Their Rights" in "Beaver Protest."

The beaver films emerged from the tradition of home and arcade films shot on and exhibited with 16 mm equipment and featuring completely nude models. Beyond use of the 16 mm gauge, early art studies and the beavers shared certain attributes. At the basic structural level, each featured a naked female, or females, posing for the camera. The films tended to be between three and ten minutes long and were usually constructed of a series of shots, rather than a single long take. The women who posed for the camera tended to acknowledge its presence and that of the unseen spectator.

But differences between the art studies and the beavers existed as well. The women in the art studies were more quiescent, in keeping with the contemplative qualities of the nude (Nead 1992, 5–33.). By contrast, the women in the beaver films employed more overtly sexual gazes and movements: they licked their lips, ground their pelvises, and humped the beds or couches on which they reclined. As Eithne Johnson suggests, the beaver films "were influenced by the 'moving camera' style of documentary productions [and] of amateur filmmaking," which implied an "intimacy and spontaneity" that conveyed an "apparently spontaneous, seemingly unscripted scene of sexual display." The increased sense of intimacy and spontaneity in the beaver films were part and parcel of the 16 mm gauge and the discourses of "naturalism" attached to it (1999, 312–14).

The shift in where 16 mm adult films were shown—from homes, arcades, and low-profile peep-show venues to theaters—occurred for several reasons. First, in the home market, 16 mm had been displaced by cheaper

8 mm and super-8 products. Those who made 16 mm adult movies were in search of a new market for their wares. Second, students in college film courses were using 16 mm equipment to make adult movies, both to earn extra money and to hone their filmmaking skills. Making 16 mm films with borrowed equipment in a field with no set ground rules was a realistic option for these students; making 35 mm sexploitation films would have proven difficult. Third, and finally, sexploitation films were gradually becoming more explicit. By 1967, full frontal female nudity—usually limited to fairly brief flashes—was a regular feature of sexploitation films. That 16 mm production remained relatively anonymous and inexpensive and that sexploitation films were somewhat more daring (as well as protected by increasingly "liberal" court decisions) seems to have given 16 mm filmmakers and other low-end operators reason to push acceptable theatrical limits and make and show inexpensive beaver films.[5]

Initially, there was little incentive for sexploitation theaters equipped with 35 mm projection and a steady customer base to install 16 mm projectors to show plotless shorts. Indeed, the limited brightness of standard 16 mm projection made 16 mm hardly ideal for hardtops, and even less so for drive-ins. This necessitated the creation of new, smaller venues. Storefront theaters, sometimes called "pocket theaters" or "mini cinemas," began to crop up, many operated by those who made the films. These theaters were considerably different from sexploitation houses not only in the product they showed but also in their layouts and start-up and operating costs.

Much like turn-of-the-century nickelodeons, these theaters were, literally, storefronts. They had no more than two hundred seats, and some had as few as forty. In many cities, operators could evade zoning regulations and fire codes, as well as having to pay license and insurance fees, because they often had too few seats to qualify as theaters ("AFAA: Danger" 1970, 4). This meant that storefront theaters—and their product—could escape initial, potentially negative scrutiny from city officials, thus establishing a foothold before opposition could mount. Moreover, a storefront could open and operate on a significantly lower investment than a standard hardtop or drive-in. Although some operators claimed to have poured as much as $65,000 into storefront conversions (much of it to construct raked floors), a couple of days and a few thousand dollars were really all that was needed to convert a loft or a basement into a mini cinema. Pete Kaufman of Astro-Jemco, a Dallas-based sexploitation distributor, estimated that a 16 mm operation could be started for about $3,000 (Kaufman n.d.). The most important and expensive piece of equipment was the 16 mm projector. Beyond that, in the earliest days, when beaver films did not have synchronized sound, a record or a tape player was necessary to provide music.[6]

Like the start-up costs, operating costs for storefronts were low. In San Francisco, average weekly operating budgets in 1970 totaled roughly $3,500 —$250 for rent, $750 for projectionists, $400 for other employees, $500 for management and miscellaneous expenses, $500–$750 for advertising, and $750 for film. Operating costs were lower for venues with sufficient walk-in trade to make advertising unnecessary or that operated for fewer hours. Storefronts made up for their small number of seats with inflated ticket prices, usually at least $3 or $4, and sometimes $5. "Five bucks, no matter who you are," wrote James Fulton in 1969, "is a lot of bread for a movie. But it is, I still maintain, worth it" (1969, 75). The five-dollar ticket price tended to be higher than what sexploitation theaters charged, which in turn was more than the average admission ($2) at mainstream cinemas. The higher price conveyed a sense of forbiddenness, but it also helped defray the periodic legal bills.

Some storefronts, such as the Venus Adult Theater in Pasadena, California, even imposed membership fees.[7] Others offered discounts of a dollar or two for couples and senior citizens or free admission for women with escorts ("A Reader's Review" 1973, 8). Lengthy hours of operation also helped make up for minimal seating capacity. Most storefronts were open by mid-morning and drew their largest crowds during the business day. Successful storefront theaters in San Francisco were able to pull in as much as $10,000 per week, although researchers at the time claimed that most settled for weekly takes on the order of $4,000 (Sampson 1971, 55).

The success of 16 mm adult films in San Francisco, and the fact that they remained relatively unmolested by law enforcement officials there, led to the proliferation of similar enterprises across the city and then the country. The Commission on Obscenity and Pornography estimated that as of June 1970, there were about fourteen storefronts operating in San Francisco and at least one hundred in Los Angeles. The Los Angeles area sported the Sandbox Adult Theater, the Xanadu Pleasure Dome, Cinematheque 16, the Film Festival in Hollywood, and the Venus Adult Theater in Pasadena. Most of these places were fairly nondescript and avoided provocative posters or pictures that might offend moral watchdogs. Perhaps the "loudest" front was the Film Festival, with its large "Open 24 Hours" sign and promise of "Hollywood's New Super Stags." The Xanadu's large marquee discreetly promised "Adults Only — Fantastic Color Features — Best in Hollywood." The entrance

1. This 1969 newspaper ad for the Center Theatre in Los Angeles aligned the sexually explicit 16 mm beaver film with "experimental underground films." Collection of the author.

to the Cinematheque 16 was little more than an anonymous doorway under an awning ("A Reader's Review" 1973, 8).

New York was somewhat slower to make the move into 16 mm. Regular cleanup efforts by police and politicians created a more cautious atmosphere, but by June 13, 1968, ads for beaver films had begun to appear in the *Village Voice*. Advertising for 16 mm movies began to appear regularly in late 1969, and by early 1970, the beavers were firmly ensconced ("N.Y. Rivals" 1970, 4). The Commission on Obscenity and Pornography estimated that about three dozen 16 mm houses were in operation in New York City by mid-1970 (Sampson 1971, 55). One could see 16 mm films at the Avon on Seventh Avenue or the Circus Cinema on Broadway between Forty-seventh and Forty-eighth Streets. Rex and Chelly Wilson operated the Cameo and the Tivoli, as well as the Eros 1 and 2, which started with beaver shorts and moved into 16 mm features (Verrill 1970e, 3). There were also the storefronts of the New Era chain—considered the lowest of the low. The marquee of the Paree Adult Cinema on Seventh Avenue covered the sign of a billiard parlor, and the theater itself was little more than a space sectioned off from the pool room by two-by-fours and Sheetrock ("Crackdown under Way" 1970, 4). The Mermaid Theater on Forty-second Street offered female beavers on one screen and male "beavers" on a second ("N.Y. Rivals" 1970, 4). Other major cities had at least five or six storefront operations, and even some small towns had one or two. In a 1970 article entitled "How Skin Flicks Hit Bible-Belt Waterloo, Iowa," *Newsweek* described the ninety-six-seat Mini Cinema 16, which had opened on Commercial Street to cater to farmers, traveling salesmen, and students from the University of Northern Iowa (28).

Except for possible legal bills, the largest ongoing expense to operate storefront theaters came from the films themselves. As with the young movie business at the turn of the century, pictures were initially sold outright to storefront exhibitors. When interviewed by John Sampson for the Commission on Obscenity and Pornography, San Francisco exhibitor Les Natali claimed that there was no system of national distribution for 16 mm storefront films (Natali n.d.). He noted that one company, Able Film of Los Angeles, had traveling salesmen who peddled films from city to city. Adult film maven David F. Friedman has recounted how producers would send couriers out to sell prints directly to exhibitors for cash (Friedman 1996). Since sales often took place one on one, 16 mm producers—unlike sexploitation producers—did not have to provide posters, press books, or other advertising materials. Printed lists or one-page fliers, sometimes with a photograph or a crudely drawn picture, announcing a film's availability to the storefront operator were all the promotion that was necessary, further shaving costs. Producers could hope to sell twenty to thirty prints to storefronts in various cities before pirates nabbed films and started duping them. (Because they operated on the borderline of legality, there is no evidence of producers trying to prosecute the pirates.) Natali stated that the average charge for a four hundred–foot color print was $50–$60. This figure is backed up by a sales brochure from Los Angeles-based M&B Enterprises, which offered four hundred–foot reels for $45 and five hundred–foot reels for $50 (Natali n.d.; M&B Enterprises 1970).

Some exhibitors produced their own 16 mm films, and, after they had played in their theaters, they peddled them to other storefronts. Not only did this allow the exhibitors to remain aware of local obscenity prosecutions but it also kept them in touch with what their patrons liked and disliked. For example, most of the two hundred or so movies made by the Mitchell Brothers prior to *Behind the Green Door* (1972) were rarely shown anywhere else but in their own theater, the O'Farrell in San Francisco, and Leo Productions, run by Arlene Elster and Lowell Pickett, produced films for the Sutter Cinema, also in San Francisco (although both the O'Farrell and the Sutter were considered a step above typical storefronts).

The quality of the films that played storefront theaters ran the gamut. Initially, the films were short and silent, but the spread of 16 mm storefronts pushed entrepreneurs to differentiate their theaters not only from sexploitation houses, by showing more graphic content, but also from competing storefronts. In addition to becoming more explicit by showing so-called split beavers and action beavers, by spring 1969, 16 mm theaters introduced a number of variations, including sound-on-film ("talking beavers"), 3–D, multiple screens, lesbian action, and male films.[8] Announcing a "new policy" was also a fairly regular ploy to attract patrons. An ad for San Francisco's Paris Theater in the August 1, 1969, *Examiner* claimed that the theater was no longer showing one-girl-only shorts. "All of our films," stated the ad, "are featurettes with boys and girls, girls and girls, and various combinations" (Paris Theater 1969). Two weeks later, the Pink Kat advertised sixty minutes of "brand new favorites"—shorts—in synch sound, as well as a one-hour feature. It was the move to feature-length narrative films that gave the 16 mm format continued viability (Pink Kat 1969).[9] In 1969, James Fulton described how boredom set in for the beaver film patron after only an hour: "You find yourself getting bored, even though, when you glance up at the screen, the Thing is still there in all its glory. Suddenly you are frightened. Is this it? You ask yourself. Am I getting too old to cut it?" (75).

Sixteen-Millimeter Features and Revolutionary Discourse

Audience boredom may have helped push 16 mm producers to move into features. But the 16 mm producers were compelled into a position of innovation to stay a step ahead of traditional 35 mm sexploitation, which, in turn, had been forced into greater explicitness by the arrival of the beavers and increasingly sexy Hollywood fare. Running out of variations for short films, the 16 mm outfits began to improve their technical qualities and incorporate story lines into their displays of genital explicitness (Rhys 1971, 55–56; "Porn and Popcorn," 1971, n.p.).[10] The initial feature-length 16 mm sex films, often clocking in at barely one hour, were known in the trade as simulation films. These combined the increased genital explicitness of the beaver with the narrative conventions of the established sexploitation movie.

In an interview with Dan Rhys, Joan of MJ Productions and Mar-Jon Distribution explained that as of 1970, the 35 mm sexploitation market and the

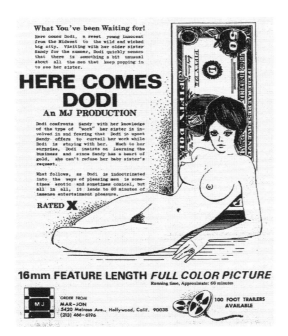

What You've been Waiting for!

Here comes Dodi, a sweet young innocent from the Midwest to the wild and wicked big city. Visiting with her older sister Sandy for the summer, Dodi quickly senses that there is something a bit unusual about all the men that keep popping in to see her sister.

HERE COMES DODI

An MJ PRODUCTION

Dodi confronts Sandy with her knowledge of the type of "work" her sister is involved in and fearing that Dodi is upset Sandy offers to curtail her work while Dodi is staying with her. Much to her surprise, Dodi insists on learning the business and since Sandy has a heart of gold, she can't refuse her baby sister's request.

What follows, as Dodi is indoctrinated into the ways of pleasing men is sometimes erotic and sometimes comical, but all in all, it lends to 60 minutes of immense entertainment pleasure.

RATED **X**

16mm FEATURE LENGTH *FULL COLOR PICTURE*
Running time, Approximate: 60 minutes

ORDER FROM
MAR-JON
5420 Melrose Ave., Hollywood, Calif. 90038
(213) 466-6196

100 FOOT TRAILERS
AVAILABLE

2. Fliers such as this one— for MJ Productions'*Here Comes Dodi* (1970) — alerted storefront theater operators of the availability of new features. Courtesy of Something Weird Video Collection.

16 mm market began to meld. "There is a lack of 35 mm sexploitation product," she explained, "and the majors are producing general release films as hot as the old 35 mm sexploitations were. So now the 35 mm sexploiters have to get hotter, the same as the 16 mm producers have been going for a long time. But they are not producing enough to satisfy the theaters. So the exhibitors are equipping now for 16 mm films so they can have a continuous show every week." Although some exhibitors who had started with beaver loops were reluctant to change because they had a regular clientele, new 16 mm theaters tended to open with features (Rhys 1971, 56).[11]

We can look to Cosmos Films for an example of the convergence between the explicitness of the beavers and the conventions of sexploitation. Ted Kariofilis, owner of the Capri Cinema, a New York sexploitation house, formed Cosmos around 1967 to produce sexploitation movies (Something Weird 1992).[12] The company initially made four 35 mm black-and-white features in New York. These films operated squarely within the sexploitation conventions of the day: a loosely structured narrative was combined with scenes of nudity and/or simulated sex. For instance, *Hot Erotic Dreams* (dir. Mort Shuman, 1968) follows a woman in New York who experiences a series of erotic daydreams and sexual encounters, several centered around a used book shop. Although the cause-and-effect relationships are not particularly strong, a general trajectory emerges as she seeks, and eventually finds, sexual satisfaction. *The Mind Blowers* (Harlan Renvok, 1968), a satire on sex research, concerns Professor Gotterdam, who captures the sexual fantasies of his subjects by recording their brain waves. Havoc ensues when his assistant mixes up the tapes and induces alternate fantasies in the subjects. In these films, men in undershorts "humped" naked women, and women wore ecstatic expressions as men—or women—dipped below the frame to offer them oral pleasure.

In the latter part of 1969, Cosmos financed a series of 16 mm color features shot in California. Like the sexploitation films, these simulation features included a narrative, albeit a rather limited one. For instance, in Cosmos's *The Line Is Busy* (1969), Jack spends his time finding women's phone numbers in men's rooms or on the walls next to pay phones. A call and some smooth talk lead him from one sexual adventure to another. "Unbelievable," he exclaims; "two days, three broads, and it only cost a dime." Jack's escapades are cut short when he visits his doctor who tells him, "You're in the advanced stages of a very rare genital disease. . . . Jack, I'm afraid your sex life is over forever." *The Runaround* (1970) is the story of Fred and Jackie, who suffer from marital problems. Jackie is always in an amorous mood when Fred returns from work, but he complains he is too tired to make love to her. This is because he spends all his time at work having sex with his secretary or other women with whom his office mate Richard hooks him up. At one point, Richard arranges for Fred to meet a "hot number" at a motel room. It turns out to be Jackie, who finally gets what she wants from her dallying husband.

What set Cosmos's 16 mm features apart from 35 mm sexploitation movies—both its own and those made by other companies—and aligned them with the beaver and other 16 mm shorts was the degree of "heat" they included. This included full male nudity without erections and, as in the beaver films, women on beds or couches with their legs spread, offering clear, full views of their vaginas. These "spread women" were caressed by men or women (or by themselves), running hands over thighs and vulvas. After a good deal of this foreplay, the men would mount the women and begin to simulate the movements of intercourse.

Working with Tom Gunning's concept of the "cinema of attractions," I have explained how, in classical exploitation films, narrative was interrupted in varying degrees by moments of spectacle in the form of displays of nudity, sex hygiene footage, drug use, and so on (Schaefer 1999, 76–95). Similar arguments, albeit using somewhat different theoretical models, can be found in Williams's discussion of "narrative and number" in hard-core features of the 1970s and 1980s and in Craig Fischer's analysis of "narrative and description" in Russ Meyer's sexploitation film *Beyond the Valley of the Dolls* (1970) (L. Williams 1999; Fischer 1992).[13] Regardless of the terminology used, in each of these instances, we witness an oscillation between narrative exposition and instances of sexual display. The 16 mm simulation films married the narratives of sexploitation films, loose as they were at times, with the increased explicitness of plotless beavers. Much like the gravitation toward narrative in the early days of cinema, the addition of narrative to the 16 mm film served to stabilize production and enabled producers and exhibitors to differentiate their films more clearly by title from shorts and loops, most of which did not have titles. The introduction of narrative made it easier to attract a broader audience of more than just single men. In 1964, the Supreme Court's decision in the *Jacobellis v. Ohio* case established the principle that material dealing with sex in a manner that advocates ideas, or that has literary, scientific, or artistic value or any other form of social importance, could not be held obscene. Narrative may have served a legitimizing function for pornographic films because it was less of a stretch to argue that feature-length narratives contained social or artistic significance and therefore were not obscene under the *Jacobellis* standard.

The 16 mm adult films rode the crest of a more general enthusiasm for 16 mm as a gauge. As Addison Verrill wrote in *Variety* in 1970, "Up to a year ago, 16 mm was considered a nontheatrical mode of exhibition, primarily geared to college film societies and private film libraries" (1970f, 18). The association of 16 mm film with college students implicitly linked the format with radical change since that cohort was often seen in newspapers and magazines, on television and in the streets, engaging in protests or rejecting the status quo in more symbolic ways—by growing their hair long, for example. Many of Leo Productions' 16 mm films were made by students from San Francisco State University's film department: "For their first film, they were given 600 feet of stock and paid something like $35 (the same fee the actors and actresses got). If the finished product was accepted, they were allowed to make a longer film for more money. If that was good, they moved up to features" (Morthland 1973, 14).

The 16 mm gauge was also the choice of avant-garde and independent film artists. Juan Suárez describes how the oppositional thrust of 1960s underground filmmakers (Kenneth Anger, Jack Smith, and Andy Warhol among them), most of whom made their films with 16 mm, was tied "thematically and ideologically with other waves of dissent in the 1960s, such as youth movements, sexual liberation fronts, civil rights organizations, and other forms of protest and social experimentation often referred to as the 'counterculture'" (1996, 53).[14] Venues such as Cinema 16 and Anthology Film Archives cemented the link between 16 mm, independent means of production and distribution, and, often, a radical aesthetic. In the preface to his 1969 *Guide to Filmmaking*, Edward Pincus alluded to the revolutionary potential of 8 mm and 16 mm production, concluding, "Film to the filmmakers, that they may change the world" (1972, 2). Finally, Patricia Zimmermann has noted that 16 mm's "amateurism" could be "reinvented as an asset and a resource for the filmmaker. It countered big-budget productions with high barriers to entry with low-cost films. It displaced expertise with imagination. It replaced professional equipment with simple cameras" (1995, 132). Indeed, the makers of 16 mm sex films replaced professional equipment with simple cameras. They also countered bigger-budget sexploitation productions, with their (comparatively) higher barriers to entry, with low-cost films. And they displaced expertise, if not with imagination then with greater explicitness. Low cost, fueled by imagination, expanded the possibilities of the film medium. This "expanded cinema," to use the title of Gene Youngblood's popular—and eccentric—book, could, in turn, lead to an "expanded consciousness" and social change (1970, 41). "The more I make love, the more I make revolution" (Peck 1985, 207)—that and similar slogans were common among the counterculture during the late 1960s.

The association between 16 mm film, alternatives to mainstream practice, and freer sexual expression and social change was not lost on many of those who made storefront films or on those who observed the phenomenon. The *New York Times Magazine* labeled "the dirty movie" as "another aspect of hip culture," claiming that many of the young filmmakers working in the Bay Area were using porn "to make a statement" and characterized Alex de Renzy as the "Jean-Luc Godard of the *nouvelle vague* in porn." Arlene Elster, who ran the Sutter Cinema in San Francisco, spoke of the films as part of a move toward greater openness that appealed to the young, and the San Francisco Erotic Film Festival, which she and Lowell Pickett sponsored, was said to be an expression of their idealism (Murray 1971, 22–23).

Advertising continually made reference to the ways in which 16 mm sex films challenged the status quo.[15] Even some of the performers took their roles as sexual revolutionaries seriously, choosing only to do films they felt had plots and some measure of social relevance. One model told the Commission on Obscenity and Pornography that when she worked with "serious" directors, "the feeling I get is a positive, artistic one" (Nawy 1971, 181). Whether as producers, talent, or viewers, individuals associated with 16 mm sex films were encouraged to think of their involvement as a countercultural act. The new, franker 16 mm movies marked the convergence of the revolution in film aesthetics and the sexual revolution.

The number of companies making 16 mm films for the adult market proliferated rapidly.[16] This growth not only signaled the importance of 16 mm film in the adult market in the late 1960s but also demonstrated the comparative ease with which one could move into the field. Since the 16 mm productions went further than sexploitation and, depending on the locality, were theoretically—if not always in actuality—more vulnerable to prosecution, there was little incentive to invest much in production. An hour-long 16 mm feature could be completed for less than $2,500, with most of the budget going to film stock and lab work—in other words, on average, for one-tenth the budget of a fairly basic 35 mm sexploitation feature (Nawy 1971, 180; Rotsler 1973, 151). On the one hand, the lower budgets and amateur aesthetics of the 16 mm films inscribed them with more naturalism or "authenticity" than sexploitation movies. On the other hand, the profits were very professional. By the end of 1970, Bill Osco and Howard Ziehm's Graffitti Productions was expected to gross more than $2 million. The company, which had begun operation a little more than a year before, had started by cranking out some twenty beaver loops per week (Verrill 1970a, 5). But the plotless loops began giving way to features. Harold Nawy, working for the Commission on Obscenity and Pornography, determined that by 1970 features were commanding the market, and even though they required a greater capital outlay, "the returns [were] more substantial than those from stag movies [shorts]" (1971, 178).

As the range of films expanded to include men and women together and as the films shifted from shorts to feature-length narratives, some operations began aggressively seeking out a more varied clientele who viewed attendance at pornographic films as part of their participation in the sexual revolution. The Sutter in San Francisco offered a couples rate, and Arlene Elster voiced pride in the fact that young people and couples made up a good portion of the audience (Murray 1971, 23). The Sutter's ads, with gentle drawings of men and women, lines from Elizabeth Barrett Browning's poetry, and promises of "sensitive and creative exotic entertainment," were clearly designed to attract a wider audience than the ads for beaver movies. The crowd at the Mini Cinema 16 in Waterloo, Iowa, was estimated to be about 40 percent women—no doubt most from the local university ("How Skin

3. A typical advertisement for San Francisco's Sutter Cinema stressed the narrative nature of their presentations as a way of attracting a more diverse audience. Collection of the author.

Flicks Hit" 1970, 28). Osco and Ziehm claimed that "80 percent of their audience are couples, most of them in their 20s and 30s, and not just the 'dirty old men' of popular belief." In an effort to attract more women, the pair "redecorated their theaters 'so they won't be so sleazy' and changed the name of one from 'The Eros' to 'The Beverly Cinema'" ("Porn and Popcorn," 1971, n.p.). "Mary S.," the ticket clerk and manager of the Peekarama, another San Francisco operation, explained that the theater did a good business with couples, perhaps because they had a special area for lovebirds, who were cordoned off from the single men. She found that women were especially fond of movies like *The Runaway Virgin* (dir. Bill Osco, 1970), which had a strong emotional story line coupled with explicit action (R. Williams 1973, 9). In addition to helping to draw a wider audience, the inclusion of narrative gave exhibitors firmer legal ground if they were prosecuted.

From Simulation to Hard-Core Features

David F. Friedman has identified the 16 mm simulation feature, which came to dominate storefront theaters, as the "missing link" between the sexploitation film and the hard-core feature (1998). Indeed, by 1970, the line between simulation and hard core was razor thin. When Marci of MJ Productions was asked to define hard core late in the year, she used as her criterion a single word: "insertion" (Rhys 1971, 57). At the time, MJ Productions did not qualify as hard core under Marci's definition. For instance, an MJ feature from 1970, *Model Hunters*, tells the story of two bickering bisexual roommates, Kim and Emma. Kim, who supports Emma, takes a job doing nude modeling for John, a photographer. Emma's jealousy is aroused when she discovers that Kim has had sex with the shutterbug. Kim makes a second visit to John with Emma in tow. This time Kim has sex with a model, Pam, and with another photographer, Dave. John seduces Emma. When the roommates return home, Emma's jealous streak is revived. Kim says that she will move out if Emma keeps it up. But Emma turns the tables by announcing she is leaving—John has invited her to move in with him. While hardly an elaborate narrative, like most sexploitation films, *Model Hunters* operates as a chain of cause-and-effect relationships that link and justify the scenes of sexual spectacle. And, like the beaver shorts, it features beaver close-ups, simulated oral sex, and simulated intercourse between fully nude participants, as well as male erections. The only thing missing is, to use Marci's criterion, "insertion." Thus the only difference between the 16 mm simulation films and what would become hard-core features was the lack of camera angles or close-ups that validated penetration, be it genital, oral, or anal.[17] Whether Graffitti's *Mona* was the first feature actually to cross that line may be open to debate, but when it debuted in San Francisco in mid-1970, it was certainly the first such film to make a splash. Ads for De Renzy's Screening Room assured patrons that the Sherpix release "surpasses its predecessors in a way that makes them instantly obsolete. The degree of explicitness and freedom exercised in *Mona* is unprecedented. It makes the so-called stag movies passé" (*Mona* ad 1970).

One of, if not the, first hard-core sites in New York was the automated 16 mm Mini-Cinema at Seventh Avenue and Forty-ninth Street, which began presenting a program of "San Francisco hardcore" at the beginning of September 1970. One of those early two-hour slates consisted of five color shorts and the feature *Electro Love* (a.k.a. *Electro Sex*), "the kind of thing that used to be run off at bachelor parties: all action and no 'redeeming' sex-education or documentary commentary on the soundtrack" (Verrill 1970c, 3). While *Electro Love* lacked the serious trappings the white-coaters used for protection in court, reporter Addison Verrill's assessment was somewhat overstated, since the film did have a semblance of a plot. He estimated that at $5 per head and ten shows per day (at least some of which were standing room only), the house could pull in more than $40,000 per week. The lure of a high return on a minimal investment certainly spurred producers and exhibitors to cross the line from simulation features into hard-core features. In New York City, distributor priorities favoring East Side theaters coupled with product shortages contributed to what Verrill called "creeping beaveritis" in the Times Square area. Some thirty-five theaters in the vicinity were playing not only sexploitation features but male and female beaver loops, and at least three sites were playing hard-core loops (1970a, 5). Within two months, six other sites had either opened or converted to a hard-core format (Verrill 1970d, 18).

Because production was not centralized and there were varying degrees of prosecutorial tolerance of sex films, it would be fruitless to attempt to identify a clearly discernible moment when the production of hard-core 16 mm features began to outstrip the production of 16 mm simulation features. Indeed, they coexisted for months, if not for a couple of years. Saul Shiffrin, vice president of Sherpix, stated, "We believe that 'Pornography is Geography,' which means giving people what they want at the proper geographical locations" (Macdonough 1971, 20). This was particularly true in the 16 mm market. Storefront theaters showing 16 mm features quickly became recognized as places to see films that pushed the boundaries as far as they could go—be that simulation or hard core. Like their simulation counterparts, the plots of 16 mm hard-core features were usually loosely tied together by a series of sexual episodes. *Electro Love* is such an example, involving a chunky, jeans-wearing counterculture type who introduces his friend to the three female robots he has created to give him (and each other) sexual pleasure. He and his friend partake, trading off periodically, until they realize the robots cannot be turned off and they "end up literally devouring the gentlemen's credentials" (Verrill 1970c, 3).

While also largely episodic, *Mona* included a greater degree of psychological motivation, as the titular heroine engages in fellatio with her boyfriend and a series of others in order to remain a virgin for her wedding night. Structurally, *Electro Love* and *Mona* were virtually identical to their simulation counterparts, such as *The Line Is Busy*, *Runaround*, and *Model Hunters*. It was only in their use of certain camera angles or the insertion of "meat shots," close-ups that validated penetration or oral-genital contact, that they differed. While this difference may seem obvious now, such distinctions were rarely made in the marketing and exhibition of the films.

The arrival of the 16 mm feature signaled a crisis in the adult film industry. The site where this divisiveness most clearly manifested itself was in the Adult Film Association of America. In November 1968, Sam Chernoff of the Dallas-based Astro Film Company addressed a letter to his fellow sexploitation exhibitors, encouraging them to organize in order to stave off harassment by law enforcement agencies (Chernoff 1968). In January 1969, 110 people representing some three hundred theaters, as well as producers and distributors, met in Kansas City to form an adult film trade association. Chernoff was elected president of the organization, initially called the Adult Motion Picture Association of America, soon changed to the Adult Film Association of America (AFAA). The AFAA's first order of business was to put together a "legal kit," prepared by Los Angeles attorney Stanley Fleishman, for the defense of motion pictures (Byron 1968, 24; "Set Up New Trade" 1969, 1, 95; "Sexploitation Filmmakers" 1969, 8). But within a year, the sexploitation producers and exhibitors who made up the AFAA faced pressure not only from law enforcement but also from the mainstream industry in the form of Jack Valenti and the MPAA. Because of the inroads 35 mm sexploitation had made into major chains, the MPAA started a campaign to dissuade theater owners from showing sexploitation films. In 1970, Valenti began a vendetta against exhibitors of these films, fearing that they would "clog the outlets for quality films," and went so far as to suggest that eventually "no responsible producer will find a theater to exhibit his product" ("Valenti on 'Personal' Campaign" 1970, 4).

At the same time, the AFAA was concerned about the 16 mm operators it referred to as "the heat artists," who went "too far" and were giving the exploitation industry a bad name ("Adult Film Group" 1970, 15). In November 1970, with the blessing of the city council, the New York City police began a crackdown on storefront theaters showing hard core. The Paree and the Capri on Seventh Avenue and the Avon 7 on Eighth Avenue had speakers ripped from walls and prints and projectors confiscated ("Crackdown under Way" 1970, 4; Verrill 1970d, 18). Some speculated that officials were hoping either to frighten exhibitors away from showing hard-core films or to put the adversary hearing rule to the test (Verrill 1970d, 18). If they succeeded in frightening anyone, it was AFAA members. Members feared that prosecution of 16 mm film exhibitors could expand to 35 mm sexploitation. Established producers and distributors also found their hand being forced by the explicitness of 16 mm films; they, along with exhibitors who had long played 35 mm films, feared that the upstart movies were cutting into their business. A few consoled themselves with the belief that, as sexploitation producer/distributor Lee Hessel said, "audiences are tiring of [rutting bodies] and are demanding storylines and character interest along with the straight sex." He noted as a good sign for the sexploitation business that some sites described as hard core had dropped their prices from $5 to $2 ("Cambist's Hessel" 1971, 7). Of course, Hessel seemed to think that the audience with a yen for "story-line and character interest" would find its way back to sexploitation films. He overlooked that simulation features had those elements to varying degrees and that by simply changing camera angles or adding some meat shots, a simulation film could become hard core. Other companies making 35 mm sexploitation, such as Donn Greer's Xerxes, jumped on the 16 mm band-wagon because of better profit ratios (Malone 1971, 54). When 16 mm the-atrical features were shown in public halls, schools, and churches, they had been seen as a threat to exhibition in the mainstream industry (Shyler 196).[18] Now the same pattern was replicated in the adult marketplace. The AFAA ini-tially directed their objection to 16 mm at the storefront theaters themselves, with claims that the small sites were not subject to the regulations affecting most places of public assembly and that some were "fire traps and unsafe for exhibition without required facilities demanded of theaters" ("AFAA: Dan-ger" 1970, 4). Then, at a meeting in New York in October 1970, the organiza-tion debated the status of 16 mm hard-core producers within the organiza-tion. Writing in *Variety*, Addison Verrill noted that the discussion "showed how money worries can quickly make establishment figures out of former 'outlaws' and how principles vital to one's existence can be bent to protect one's bankroll" (Verrill 1970f, 5). He described how 16 mm films could be made quickly and cheaply, putting them ahead of the 35 mm producers in "the sexual 'can you top this' game." Arguments were put forth that 16 mm producers should not be included in the organization because 16 mm was a nontheatrical gauge or because their product was "operating outside the law"—even though that question was still being argued in the courts. Many members of the AFAA found themselves in an untenable position: "While crying total freedom of the screen to protect their business, they would at the same time act as censors themselves and force the 16 mm people out of the game" (Verrill 1970f, 18). By the end of the meeting, the organization had voted to reaffirm its open-admission policy ("Old-Time N.Y." 1970, 5).

But the issue did not disappear, and in fact it was exacerbated as 1970 turned into 1971. With more sexploitation films, such as *Vixen* and *Without a Stitch*, achieving long, profitable runs in major chains, some sexploitation houses found their choice "to be between cheapjack sexploiters that have not been booked by product-short major houses" and 16 mm fare ("Old-Time N.Y." 1970, 5). In the face of the 35 mm sexploitation shortage, and as more 16 mm features became available, including hard-core titles such as *Caught in the Can* (1970), *The Coming Thing* (dir. David Reberg, 1970), *Journal of Love* (dir. Sybil Kidd, 1970), *The Nurses* (dir. Terry Sullivan, 1971), and *The School Girl* (dir. David Reberg, 1971), the choice to go hard-core was becoming an easier one. Joan of Mar-Jon explained that many 35 mm exhibitors were augmenting their situations with 16 mm outfits and that "a lot of 35 mm exhibitors have turned in their 35 mm projectors and converted completely to 16 mm. So, with more and more conversion, the 16 mm feature is a growing market" (Rhys 1971, 56).

The friction between the 35 mm stalwarts and the 16 mm newcomers re-emerged at the third annual AFAA meeting in Los Angeles in January 1971. The "generation gap" between the sexploitation producers and the revolutionary 16 mm filmmakers became obvious to Kevin Thomas, writing for the *Los Angeles Times*:

> On the one hand, there are the old-line sexploitation producers who film in 35 mm and don't go "all the way" but frequently equate sex and nudity with violence and morbidity on the screen and in their ads. On the other hand, is a group of younger filmmakers, working primarily in San Francisco and in 16 mm, who are dedicated to total explicitness and attempt to present it artistically. (Privately, a veteran producer will admit he's only against 16 mm upstarts because they're ruining his business. In San Francisco, a 35 mm production that once might make as much as $20,000 in two months can't even get a booking there.)(1971, n.p.)

Lowell Pickett accused the sexploitation producers of equating sex with violence and of being guilty of fraud. He claimed that the 16 mm producers were delivering "the goods": "We're attracting the under 30s—couples—and your audience is getting old and dying off. Our audiences don't want to see people being punished in a Nazi camp," he said, most likely referring to Olympic International's *Love Camp 7* (dir. R. L. Frost, 1968). By focusing on generational conflict, Pickett mined the discourse of the counterculture to elucidate the differences between 16 mm and 35 mm films. Some producers expressed concern that 16 mm filmmakers engaged in "flagrant abuses of the freedom of expression," but Jay Fineberg of the Pussycat chain reasoned that "we cannot say what we do is all right and in good taste and what the hardcore guy does is not. We're prejudicing even before the courts do!" (qtd. in Thomas 1971, n.p.). Throughout the discussion, the sexploitation old guard pointedly described 16 mm product as the most problematic, not the white-coater or the porn documentaries that contained hard-core scenes but were usually distributed in 35 mm and may have played in their own theaters. It was clear within the industry that by crossing the hard-core line, 16 mm films were driving innovation and change and that to remain viable, the 35 mm sexploitation producers would have to cross the line as well. While some of the major hard-core producers, notably the Mitchell Brothers, came from the ranks of 16 mm production, sexploitation stalwarts, such as Audubon, Distribpix, EVI, and Mitam, were pushed into making the switch to hard core. According to David F. Friedman, 50 percent of the AFAA membership was making hard core by 1974 (1998).

In his assessment of the porn industry for the Commission on Obscenity and Pornography, John Sampson wrote, "By the time this report is published, it is possible that 16 mm theaters will have assumed a more important role in the overall traffic of sexually oriented films" (1971, 57). They became, in fact, important and influential. The limited capital necessary to produce and exhibit 16 mm films meant that entrepreneurs were willing to risk fines or the jail time that showing genital explicitness could bring about in exchange for potentially large returns. Sixteen-millimeter producers and exhibitors also rode the crest of the liberatory rhetoric of the sexual revolution and of changing filmmaking practice as exemplified by experimental filmmakers, college film societies, and other users of 16 mm. Not only were these 16 mm movies more daring than sexploitation and mainstream movies—pushing their direct competition, sexploitation movies, to become more graphic—but those who had produced beaver loops and were just setting out with 16 mm cameras were in turn forced to embrace the narrative elements of sexploitation films. The longer format necessitated material that could link the scenes of sexual spectacle in a logical fashion. Narrative filled the bill in a way that offered flexibility and potential for variation—and hence could draw repeat customers, including the lucrative couples market emerging from sexploitation. Moreover, narrative helped to legitimize hard-core films by permitting exhibitors to mount arguments that hard core did not appeal solely to prurient interest but could have artistic merit or social importance. Despite fears that hard-core features could bring about increased censorship, many of the established sexploitation producers moved into hard-core features just as many 16 mm producers shifted to the professional 35 mm gauge.

The adult film industry has often been characterized as a monolithic, multimillion- (or -billion, depending on the decade) dollar industry that moves with the steady, unified flow of a glacier. But just as we have come to see the mainstream Hollywood filmmaking industry as dynamic and made up of different (and often conflicting) interests, the foregoing account should point to the necessity of reconceptualizing the porn industry. More-over, in the late 1960s and early 1970s, the adult film industry did not exist in a vacuum. Hollywood was being influenced by, and influenced, the pro-ducers and exhibitors of sexploitation films, and they, in turn, were jockey-ing for position with the insurgent manufacturers of 16 mm hard-core films. Finally, the above account should help us recognize that the hard-core fea-ture developed as a reaction to conditions in the adult film marketplace, in addition to more obvious social conditions. The hard-core feature was cer-tainly not a predetermined end.

The hard-core narrative feature thrived until new changes in the adult market reached another critical point in the mid-1980s, when the introduc-tion of video shifted the viewing space from the theater to the home. This new set of conditions and patterns of viewing practice contributed to the decreased emphasis on narrative and to the return to a pre–golden age em-phasis on pure sexual spectacle.

Notes

My thanks to Linda Williams for her comments on this paper. Thanks also to David F. Friedman for talking with me about the AFAA and the period, to the staff at the Lyndon Baines Johnson Library in Austin, Texas, and to Mike Vraney and Lisa Petrucci of Something Weird Video for access to some of the materials used in the preparation of this article. As always, my largest debt is to Eithne Johnson for sharing her tremendous intelligence and insight.

1 Split beavers referred to shots of spread labia. Action beavers usually referred to autoerotic manipulation of the genitals, or manipulation by a partner. The hard-core loop involved male-female sexual intercourse.

2 While the white-coaters and porn documentaries have been seen as important stops on the road to hard-core features, it is becoming increasingly clear that, from an industrial standpoint, they constitute a mere footnote. See my note 9.

3 Both *Sinema* and *Hard Core* are exemplary in their own ways, and my points about their brief takes on the history of the form should not be considered a criticism of their primary purposes: to provide a "snapshot" of the porn industry circa 1974, and a complex exploration of the generic parameters of the hard-core feature from 1972 to the early 1980s, respectively. Turan and Zito include a chapter on 16 mm hard-core features, although they did not account for the generative role that the technology itself played in the development of the hard-core feature. Moreover, they did not discuss the 16 mm simulation feature, an important step in this development, as outlined below. In any case, both the Turan and Zito and Williams books serve as a reminder of just how difficult it is to write historical accounts of pornography.

4 At the World Pornography Conference in Los Angeles in August 1998, the diverse conferees—academics, lawyers, physicians, porn producers and performers, and some fans—all seemed to be in accord on one thing: the time from 1972, when *Deep Throat* was released, to the point when video came to dominate the production and distribution of hard-core in the mid-1980s constituted a classical period. Echoing some of the contemporary discourse about the Hollywood studio system, adult film stars (such as Veronica Hart, Richard Pacheco, and William Margold) were rueful that the days of high pay (comparatively), leisurely shooting schedules, posh premieres, and even a certain celebrity status outside the confines of the porn world were a thing of the past. See also Holliday (1999).

5 Unlike 35 mm films, 16 mm movies could be easily chopped up and used as loops in peep shows and booths.

6 In addition to the storefronts, 16 mm films turned up in bars and nightclubs in Washington, D.C., Los Angeles, and, presumably, other locales ("Storefront Boom" 1971). In 1969, the Famous Iron Horse Cinema Bar, on Eighth Street between Normandie and Western, offered "2 giant screens, 24 movies changes [sic] all the time." An ad asked, "Is there a theater with a plush night club atmosphere where for $2.00 you're served a beer by nudely clad models at your own tables, listen to sexy records, see sound flicks, smoke, visit all you want and see all?" (Famous Iron Horse ad 1969).

7 Membership fees enabled exhibitors to argue, if they were prosecuted, that their venues constituted private clubs, and not public places of amusement.

8 Gay films began to emerge "out of the closet and into the theaters" around 1967 as small-gauge mail-order "physique" films made the transition to theaters such as Los Angeles's Apollo Arts and Park Cinema and New York's Park-Miller. For more information, see Waugh 1996, especially 269–73.

9 White-coaters, such as *Man and Wife* (dir. Matt Cimber, 1969), *He and She* (dir. Matt Cimber, 1970), and *Black Is Beautiful* (1970) are generally cited as milestones in the development of the hard-core feature. This assumption seems to stem from the fact that they included scenes of sexual intercourse and were of feature length, rather than because of any industrial or generic similarity to subsequent features. There was, of course, little affinity between the white-coater, traditional sexploitation, and the hard-core feature as it would develop. White-coaters were most often released in 35 mm and shown in larger venues, many of which were "legitimate" theaters. This enabled the movies to draw curiosity seekers, as well as the regular adult film audience, and they initially racked up sizable grosses. Although many of the films had long runs in some cities, the form itself had a short shelf life, offering nothing on which to create a base of regular customers. This also holds true to a large extent for the so-called porn documentaries such as *Pornography in Denmark: A New Approach* (dir. Alex DeRenzy, 1970).

10 In a 1970 interview with San Francisco porn entrepreneurs the Mitchell Broth-

ers, one of them, Jim, discussed audience responses to the films shown at their theater, the O'Farrell: "Here's something interesting. Like, on this questionnaire we said, 'Would you rather see films in documentary or dramatic form?' Dramatic form, 98 %. Nobody wants to see documentary films." Asked about where they would go when people wearied of big-screen stag movies, his brother Art said, "I think story lines, better film techniques. You know, getting into the people, making it believable," to which Jim added, "character development." Although they were gravitating toward narrative, the Mitchells indicated at the time of the interview that they planned to stick to the production of shorter films ("The Making of a Movie" 1970, 19).

11 Unfortunately, the article identified Marci and Joan, the principals of MJ and Mar-Jon, only by their first names.

12 Kariofilis has been identified through other records.

13 For another take on the "cinema of attractions" in relation to pornography, see Lehman 1995–96.

14 Suárez notes that the term *underground film* was applied to avant-garde filmmakers as early as 1962 (1996, 54–55). But by the late 1960s, the makers and exhibitors of 16 mm sex films had picked it up and exploited it. Advertising the film *Sophie*, the Gay Paree Theater in San Francisco referred to itself and other "sex exploitation" houses as "underground theaters" (*Sophie* ad 1969). Because both avant-garde movies and sexploitation/porn films offered nudity and frank depictions of sex, the term *underground film* was often applied to both types of film without much distinction.

15 For instance, after a show at San Francisco's Peekarama was "charged as being for mature audiences to view," ads claimed that the theater obtained a restraining order "to insure that you are not deprived from seeing what you've asked for time and again. This weeks [*sic*] show is right up your alley. We call it 'Gutsy'" (Peekarama ad 1970). Such an oppositional stance in advertising was not infrequent. In announcing the move to full-length "talking stags" with *The Runaway Virgin* several months later, the theater claimed, "This picture is sure to 'Revolutionize' the Adult Film Industry" (*The Runaway Virgin* ad 1970).

16 Among the outfits operating between 1968 and 1971 were A.I.M. Productions, America Film Productions Co., Athena, Beyond the Pleasure Principle, Cherry Productions, Cinema 7, Clamil, Cosmos Films, Dragon Films, Dun-Mar, Fearless Productions, Fleetan, Graffitti, Impressive Arts Productions, Jahk Productions, Janus II–Academy Productions, Jo-Jo Productions, MJ Productions, John Samuels Films Ltd., Topar Productions, and Xerxes. Distributors of 16 mm films included Able, Canyon Distributing Company, Dekan, Exhibitors Distributing Ltd., Jo-Jo Distributors, Kariofilms, M&B Enterprises, Mar-Jon, Probe Films, and Stacey. Sherpix, which dealt primarily in 35 mm, also did some 16 mm business. Able and Stacey alone released thirty-five and fifty-nine films, respectively, in 1970. This list is derived from material in the Something Weird Video collection, the author's collection, and *The American Film Institute Catalog* (1976).

17 Marci's analysis was confirmed by porn director Clay McCord. According to Mc-
Cord, "The *meat shot* is the only *real* difference, outside of fellatio and cunnilingus, between pornos and the simulated sex film" (Rotsler 1973, 151; emphasis
original). What would come to be known as the money shot—the shot of an
ejaculation, validating male sexual pleasure—was not even at issue in the early
1970s, since in the earliest hard-core features, it had not yet emerged as an un-
varying convention.

18 The "problem" of competition from 16 mm exhibition extended back to at least
the 1930s.

Works Cited

"Adult Film Group Meets in Houston." 1970. *Independent Film Journal*, January 7, 15.

"AFAA: Danger to Let States Set Standards of Obscenity." 1970. *Independent Film Journal*, August 5, 4.

The American Film Institute Catalog of Feature Films, 1961–1970. 1976. Berkeley: University of California Press.

Byron, Stuart. 1968. "Sex Films' Script for Action." *Variety*, December 18, 1, 24.

"Cambist's Hessel Sees Smart Sex Come-on Weathering 16 mm Excess: Story, Characterization Still Count." 1971. *Variety*, January 20, 7.

Chernoff, Sam. 1968. Letter to fellow exhibitors, November. Something Weird Video
collection, Seattle.

Corliss, Richard. 1973. "Radley Metzger: Aristocrat of the Erotic." *Film Comment* 9,
1: 19–29.

"Crackdown under Way on Storefront Theaters." 1970. *Independent Film Journal*, December 9, 4.

Distribpix Catalog. 1971. Something Weird Video collection, Seattle.

Famous Iron Horse Cinema Bar advertisement. 1969. *Los Angeles Free Press*, June 27.

"Far out (Long Island) Sex." 1967. *Variety*, 14 June, 13.

Fischer, Craig. 1992. "*Beyond the Valley of the Dolls* and the Exploitation Genre." *Velvet
Light Trap* 30: 18–33.

Friedman, David F. 1996. Telephone interview with the author. January 24.

———. 1998. Telephone interview with the author. August 5.

Fulton, James. 1969. "Dirty Movies Are Dirtier Than Ever." *Adam Film Quarterly* 8:
74–78.

Holliday, Jim. 1999. "A History of Modern Pornographic Film and Video." In *Porn
101: Eroticism, Pornography, and the First Amendment*, ed. James Elias et al. Amherst, N.Y.: Prometheus. 341–51.

"How Skin Flicks Hit Bible-Belt Waterloo, Iowa." 1970. *Newsweek*, December 21, 28.

Johnson, Eithne. 1999. "The 'Coloscopic' Film and the 'Beaver' Film: Scientific and
Pornographic Scenes of Female Sexual Responsiveness." In *Swinging Single: Representing Sexuality in the 1960s*, ed. by Hilary Radner and Moya Luckett. Minneapolis: University of Minnesota Press. 301–24.

Kaminsky, Ralph. 1981. "Pussycat Chief Credits 'L.A. Times' and Vice Squad for Entering Business." *Film Journal*, March 23, 14.

Kaufman, Pete. N.d. Interview. Commission on Obscenity and Pornography Records, box 19, Pete Kaufman file. Lyndon Baines Johnson Library, Austin.

Lehman, Peter. 1995–96. "Revelations about Pornography." *Film Criticism* 20, 1–2: 3–16.

Lewis, Jon. 2000. *Hollywood v. Hard Core: How the Struggle over Censorship Saved the Modern Film Industry*. New York: New York University Press.

Macdonough, Scott. 1971. "The Story of Sherpix: Soft-Core, Hard-Core, Encore." *Show*, July, 20.

M&B Enterprises Flier. [1970]. Something Weird Video collection, Seattle.

"The Making of a Movie: How the O'Farrell Does It." 1970. *San Francisco Ball*, 17–19.

Malone, Sybil. 1971. "Donn Greer—Where the Action Is." *Adam Film World* 2, 12: 54–55.

"Metzger and Leighton Have Two Words for It: 'Playing Time.'" 1970. *Film Journal*, February 18, 4.

Mona advertisement. 1970. *San Francisco Examiner*, August 6.

Morthland, John. 1973. "Porn Films: An In-Depth Report." *Take One*, March/April, 12–17.

Murray, William. 1971. "The Porn Capital of America," *New York Times Magazine*, January 3, 8–9, 20–25.

Natali, Les. N.d. Interview. Commission on Obscenity and Pornography Records, box 21, Lou Sher file. Lyndon Baines Johnson Library, Austin.

Nawy, Harold. 1971. "The San Francisco Marketplace." In *Technical Report of the Commission on Obscenity and Pornography*. Vol. 4. Washington, D.C.: United States Government Printing Office.

Nead, Lynda. 1992. *The Female Nude: Art, Obscenity, and Sexuality*. New York: Routledge.

"N.Y. Rivals Frisco's Beavers: Female and Male Nudes alongside on Separate Screens at Mermaid." 1970. *Variety*, February 25, 4.

"Old-Time N.Y. Sex Site Showman Begins to Yearn for Censorship." 1970. *Variety*, 2 December, 5.

Paris Theater advertisement. 1969. *San Francisco Examiner*, August 1.

Peck, Abe. 1985. *Uncovering the Sixties: The Life and Times of the Underground Press*. New York: Citadel.

Peekarama advertisement. 1970. *San Francisco Examiner*, February 19.

Pincus, Edward. 1972. *Guide to Filmmaking*. New York: Signet.

Pink Kat advertisement. 1969. *San Francisco Examiner*, August 14.

"Porn and Popcorn." 1971. *Parade*, March 21, n.p.

"A Reader's Review of Erotic Theaters." 1973. *The Sensuous One*, 8.

Rotsler, William. 1973. *Contemporary Erotic Cinema*. New York: Penthouse/Ballantine.

Rhys, Dan. 1971. "'M-J Productions Presents!' ('M' Is Marci and 'J' Is Joan)." *Adam Film World* 2, 11: 54–58.

The Runaway Virgin advertisement. 1970. *San Francisco Examiner*, June 24.

Sampson, John J. 1971. *Technical Report of the Commission on Obscenity and Pornography*. Vol. 3, *The Marketplace: The Industry*. Washington, D.C.: United States Government Printing Office.

"San Francisco Outdoes Copenhagen." 1970. *Variety*, September 16, 3.

Schaefer, Eric. 1999. *"Bold! Daring! Shocking! True!": A History of Exploitation Films, 1919–1959*. Durham, N.C.: Duke University Press.

————. Forthcoming. "Plain Brown Wrapper: Adult Films for the Home Market, 1930–1969." In *In the Absence of Films: Towards a New Historiographic Practice*, ed. Eric Smoodin and Jon Lewis. Durham, N.C.: Duke University Press.

"Set up New Trade Assn. for Adult (Sex) Films." 1969. *Variety*, January 15, 1, 95.

"Sexploitation Filmmakers: Showmen Form Adult Motion Picture Ass'n." 1969. *Boxoffice*, January 20, 8.

"Sherpix: The Unusual Company." 1972. *Independent Film Journal*, April 27, 20–21.

Shyler, Ben. 1964. "The 16 mm Problem." *Boxoffice*, February 17, 3.

Something Weird Video Catalog, Supplement 2. 1992. Seattle: Something Weird Video.

Sophie advertisement. 1969. *San Francisco Examiner*, June 28.

"Storefront Boom in Capital; Sex Policy Boosts Grosses." 1971. *Independent Film Journal*, January 21, 5.

Suárez, Juan A. 1996. *Bike Boys, Drag Queens, and Superstars: Avant-Garde, Mass Culture, and Gay Identities in the 1960s Underground Cinema*. Bloomington: Indiana University Press.

Thomas, Kevin. 1971. "Current Censorship Status in Adult Film Market." *Los Angeles Times Calendar*, February 7, n.p.

Turan, Kenneth, and Stephen F. Zito. 1974. *Sinema: American Pornographic Films and the People Who Make Them*. New York: Praeger.

"Valenti on 'Personal' Campaign to Keep Sex Films out of Respectable Theaters." 1970. *Independent Film Journal*, February 4, 4–5.

"Valenti: Too Many Playdates to 'Frankly Salacious Films.'" 1970, *Independent Film Journal*, January 21, n.p.

"Valenti's Personal Campaign Draws Fire of Independents: Lawsuit Charges Industry Conspiracy against Import." 1970. *Independent Film Journal*, February 18, 4–5.

Verrill, Addison. 1970a. "Bill Osco, Boy King of L.A. Porno, Grossing Over $2,000,000 Presently: 10-City Nucleus: 'Actors' A-Plenty." *Variety*, December 30, 5.

————. 1970b. "B'way: Glory Road No More," *Variety*, September 30, 5.

————. 1970c. "Hard-Core Porno: $40,000 a Week: San Francisco Outdoes Copenhagen." *Variety*, September 16, 3.

————. 1970d. "Raid-&-Rip N.Y.: Hard-Core Pix." *Variety*, November 25, 18.

————. 1970e. "Sexpix Simplified: They Pay." *Variety*, April 1, 3.

————. 1970f. "Skinpix Face 'New Dilemma.'" *Variety*, October 21, 5, 18.

Williams, Linda. 1999. *Hard Core: Power, Pleasure, and the "Frenzy of the Visible."* Exp. ed. Berkeley: University of California Press.

Williams, Rex. 1973. "The Porno Movie Scene." *Sensuous One*, 9.

Waugh, Thomas. 1996. *Hard to Imagine: Gay Male Eroticism in Photography and Film from Their Beginnings to Stonewall.* New York: Columbia University Press.

Wyatt, Justin. 1999. "The Stigma of X: Adult Cinema and the Institution of the MPAA Rating System." In *Controlling Hollywood: Censorship and Regulation in the Studio Era*, ed. Matthew Bernstein. New Brunswick, N.J.: Rutgers University Press.

Youngblood, Gene. 1970. *Expanded Cinema.* New York: Dutton.

Zimmermann, Patricia R. 1995. *Reel Families: A Social History of Amateur Film.* Bloomington: Indiana University Press.

Video Pornography, Visual Pleasure,
and the Return of the Sublime

FRANKLIN MELENDEZ

✳ In postmodern theory, pornographic viewership has emerged as a central category, providing the model for a new, historically specific construction of pleasure: one that is purely visual and given over entirely to the consumption of commodity images.[1] However, precisely because it realizes postmodernity's logic, pornographic viewership also betrays postmodernism's greatest anxiety, or at least a crucial point of ambivalence, namely, the displacement of the real by the simulacral. This ambivalence underlies the work of Fredric Jameson, who construes the visual as "*essentially* pornographic, which is to say that it has its end in rapt, mindless fascination" (Jameson 1992, 1); and it emerges more dramatically (and ambiguously) in the critical work of Jean Baudrillard, which gives the pornographic the character of something resembling a postmodern epistemology. In *Simulations*, for instance, the effacement of the real unfolds as an allegory of looking enthralled by the hypnotic display of repeated bodies: "Like those twin sisters in a dirty picture: the charnel reality of their bodies is erased by the resemblance. How to invest your energies in one, when her beauty is immediately duplicated by the other? The regard can go only from one to the other; all vision is locked into this coming-and-going" (Baudrillard 1983, 144). For Baudrillard, this doubled beauty speaks to an image whose lurid appeal is inextricably linked to reproduction because the very indistinguishability of these bodies offers itself as the locus of visual pleasure.

Although the close association between the visual and the pornographic only functions as tantalizing elucidation, it provides me with a starting point for rethinking pornographic viewership by addressing pornography as a genre whose pleasures are predicated as much on technological reproduction as on the sexual spectacle made visible. Rather than simply affirming Baudrillard's claim, the relationship between the sexually explicit image and its reproduction (or medium) places pressure on the underlying presuppositions of his critique, particularly by questioning the categorical status of "pleasure" and "vision"; for these key concepts must be assessed with respect to production *and* consumption, two inextricably linked processes nevertheless far more distinct than most postmodern criticism would suggest. Thus, in an effort to examine visual pornography not only as an illustration of postmodernism's greatest anxieties but also as the complex intersection of visuality, sexuality, commodity, and technology, I begin by linking the product to the specific mediating technologies whose operation must be seen as constitutive of the image's seductiveness. With this in mind, I turn to video.

In the wake of the vcr revolution, video has replaced film as the primary medium of moving-image pornography. Initially utilized to recycle earlier films, video's lower production costs and broader distribution provided the ideal vehicle for increasingly niche-conscious pornography; today most (if not all) pornographic "films" are produced directly on or for video.[2] This shift, I would argue, has altered the language of moving-image pornography; for if, as Baudrillard suggests, the currency of the product relies as much on its format as on its content, then the medium, its reproductive technologies (TV, VCR, remote control), and its inherent formal structures must inform the genre's construction and transmission of bodily pleasure. Stanley Cavell terms this mutually defining operation between the image and its modes of (re)production the "material basis of the medium"—an insight I find particularly enabling in discussing video pornography, for in scrutinizing particular deployments of information, Cavell begins to gesture toward the function of the image's specific address to viewers (1986, 198). The material specificity of particular technologies destabilizes the conception of pleasure and visuality as transhistorical and homogeneous, prompting a reevaluation of these critical categories not only as *represented* in the genre, but as *experienced* by a viewing subject.

With this revision in mind, I return to Baudrillard, whose allegory illustrates the limitations of reading the interaction of viewer and viewed object as unitary. Baudrillard neatly maps the erotic relationship between consumer and commodity onto a gendered subject/object division: anonymous gazing at doubled, female bodies. If we pause to scrutinize the status of this hopelessly vacillating look, we discover a structure of vision predicated on objects (female bodies) displaying themselves for consumption, a shameless offering-up that enthralls the looker. Yet this very structure, in its emphasis on the object, reduces the viewing subject's engagement to an abstracted, almost subjectless activity: looking. This theoretical (rhetorical) effacement of the viewing subject constitutes a crucial move that vividly captures the degree to which mediating technologies determine our experience of the image. In my essay, I want to scrutinize this theoretical move (and the model of vision it presupposes) in order to assert its structural usefulness while simultaneously acknowledging its limitations, which remain inextricably linked to lingering anxieties about the mass-produced as such.[3] Ultimately, I want to contend that while this model of vision, a type of disembodied gazing, accounts for (re)production as an integral component of pleasure in visual pornography, it fails to address the effects of a genre so deeply invested in moving the viewer's body.[4] For me, the complex relationship between pornography, video technology and visual pleasure necessarily unfolds both in the Baudrillardian/Jamesonian structures of (re)production, as well as in what Jonathan Crary calls the "carnal density of vision" (1998). For precisely at the moment where the visible becomes an extension of the physical body, we can begin to conceptualize how a viewer experiences video pornography as a *mediated* image of undeniable *immediacy*.

My analysis addresses two recent, exceptional examples of pornography, *Naked Highway* (dir. Wash West, 2000) and *Shock* (dir. Michael Ninn, 1996), which in their distinct ways simultaneously reveal and redefine the boundaries of the genre by maximizing the representational possibilities presented by the available technology. I want to stress, however, that these works are exceptional only insofar as they focus *thematically* on the relationship between viewer, technology, and sexual fantasy in their narratives and sexual numbers. Ultimately, I also want to read these works as typical, in that they make visible the structures and mechanisms of video pornography as a genre.[5] In effect, both of these videos offer revelations of their genre/medium, what Cavell calls "acknowledgements" of the material conditions determining the very format of the sexually explicit. Thus, despite being produced for distinct markets (gay and straight, broadly speaking), these videos rely to a remarkable degree on the same formal structures to convey bodily pleasure. By this I mean that the techniques utilized to edit together individual shots and scenes become as vital to the construction of pleasure as the sexual event itself. Although the visibility of the processes of representation stresses the genre's active commodification of "sexual pleasure," I would pause at this point and question if, indeed, this fact of production *exclusively* determines the viewer's visual experience: does it point to the production of a sexuality—operating through/as the visual—which is only an extension of the impersonal functioning of the machine, or can we reimagine the viewer's activity as an encounter with the voluptuousness of the image?

Here, the video's *form* proves most revealing, for the reflexive acknowledgment of video's address to its viewer stresses the importance of an embodied experience that encompasses two types of pleasure: *possessing the image* and *being moved by the image*. One mode of viewing—a disembodied gazing predicated on consumption/visual possession[6]—must be seen as operating in conjunction with corporealized vision, which accounts for the pleasure of pornography's physical effects on the body. In this way, experience comes to complement the facts of production, and pornographic viewership unfolds in the vacillation between two seemingly opposed poles, producing a visual pleasure that emerges as a function of both material production and physical consumption. The relation between these models of vision (disembodied/embodied), then, captures the complexity of an embodied viewer's encounter with historically specific modes of (re)production. If the meeting of the viewer with video technology constitutes a moment when, as Baudrillard would have it, vision is seduced by the indistinguishability of mass-produced images, then it is also a moment when vision's corporeality touches the very modes of (re)production. This touching, the encounter with the image's own tactility, also reveals the very materiality of reproduction, which these videos (and, I would ultimately argue, the genre as a whole) attempt to pass off as the sign of physical pleasure. The moving of the corporealized viewer, then, is enabled by a brush with the limits of a technology whose convulsions come to signify both the throes of sexual pleasure and the impossibility of its representation.

The narrative of *Naked Highway* explores the ways in which pornography and other commodity forms shape (and intrude on) our fantasy life, offering themselves as vehicles, perhaps even substitutes for our erotic investment. The provocative opening number foregrounds this relation between mass production and personal pleasure by impishly acknowledging pornography's inadvertent encoding of the genre's "pleasures" in certain conventions of production: bad acting, dialogue, sets, titles, and so on, as well as, of course, its medium: the ever-present video cassette. The construction of the ensuing sexual number suggests that this encoding also operates *formally*, and here we can identify the surprisingly visible imprint of video (as a mediating technology) in the representation of sexual pleasure. The scene begins when the protagonist, Colorado, receives a mysterious package from the bartender of the local bar, where he has been wallowing in self-pity since his lover departed for Los Angeles in pursuit of a "film career." "You know what kind of movies he's making," the bartender indignantly asserts, "dirty, pornographic movies!" The package reveals an unmarked video tape, which a curious Colorado sticks into the VCR. And true enough, the video is a dirty movie, *Extra Topping*, featuring his estranged lover in the starring role.

By self-consciously playing with the infamous mythology of the porno industry, the narrative incorporates the banal technologies of TV/VCR into the sexual number as integral components. The sequence opens with a medium long shot of the room illuminated by the blue light of the television monitor into which Colorado inserts the video tape. Much like a self-reflexive moment in seventies or eighties film pornography, this scene stresses the material conditions necessary for viewing, not only in terms of technologies but also of a viewing space.[7] The shift from the theater to the living room, I would argue, has altered not only the look and feel of the product but also the viewer's relation to, and experience of, the image. The sexual number's structure—the viewer watches Colorado watching the dirty movie—hints at this redefinition with its two modes of representing sexual action, which convey two distinct visual relations. The first—the viewer watching Colorado watching—renders the action in close-ups of the television screen whose texture is enhanced by double mediation (fig. 1); the second—what Colorado is watching—presents the low-budget porno, *Extra Topping*, without the additional layer of mediation, as if the viewer were occupying Colorado's position. As the number intercuts between these visual relations (close-ups of Colorado watching, close-ups of the TV screen, and close-ups of the action), it foregrounds the two focal points of erotic investment for Colorado and the viewer: the performers' bodies *and* the television screen. These focal points are not only visual but also tactile, since in the intercutting, they are differentiated less by their content (which remains the same) than by their respective textures: the texture of the bodies and the enhanced texture of the television screen (fig. 2). By visually distinguishing these two relations by juxtaposing two distinct textures, the editing begins to question the priority of content over the medium in defining the pleasure of viewing video pornography.

The vacillation between the corporeal and the technological suggested by these shifting textures reveals the eroticization of mediation, a process that is part and parcel of the act of making visible the sexual spectacle to a viewer. The prominence of the reproductive apparatus as a "physical" presence requiring the viewer's contact (the insertion of the video cassette, the operation of the remote control) points to another equally important interface occurring on the visual register: the consumption of video pornography as commodity. The reflexive construction of the scene thus achieves a particular form of address in which pornography presents itself *as pornography* to the viewer. As evident in the close-ups of Colorado watching a video within the video, this address invites and/or produces an erotic investment that is in excess of the performing bodies, but that is also, let us say provisionally, *propped* upon these bodies.[8] The eroticization of the image's commodity texture suggests that the viewer's pleasure intertwines with reproducibility; or, more specifically, that reproducibility operates as one of the dominant signs of pleasure in the genre (fig. 3). The facts of production (film careers gone awry), the necessary technology (TV/VCR), and the act of viewing construct *and* constitute a pleasure irreducible to a single, visible body part.

Naked Highway stages, I would argue, the formal operation of video pornography: the manner in which mechanical reproduction becomes inextricable from the performing bodies in the moment of display. It is in this relation between content and format that we can begin to see how the genre's language of visible pleasure reconfigures the notion of the "sexual." Michael Ninn's remarkable *Shock* provides another ideal example since it is, in many ways, an attempt to broaden the possibilities of high-end, straight pornography produced on the industry's equivalent of a Cecil B. DeMille budget. Structurally and thematically, *Shock* preoccupies itself with the persistent problem of representing and conveying sex through seemingly constricting technological avenues. In an effort to convey sexual ecstasy, *Shock* experiments not only with extravagant content details like costumes and mise-en-scène but more radically with the very workings of the video medium. Like *Naked Highway*, *Shock* figures the performer's bodily pleasure through its editing, shifting between different angles and scenes, creating a rapid succession of images, a frenzied temporality of simultaneities that has become the very organizational principle of video.[9]

Shock opens with an elaborate number involving an anonymous male and a Marilyn Monroe impersonator, neatly illustrating the gendering of commodity—at least in heterosexual porn (Fig. 4). The scene begins with a medium shot of Marilyn masturbating with a fluorescent dildo, a spectacle

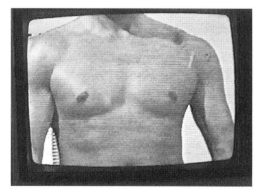

1. Here, the viewer is watching Colorado watching. From *Naked Highway*.

2. This still from *Naked Highway* shows the almost tactile texture of the television screen.

3. While narratively the "object" of Colorado's desire is clear, can we make this distinction formally too? Is the screen as important as the body it makes visible? From *Naked Highway*.

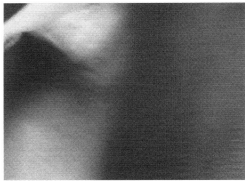

4. The Marilyn impersonator: commodity as total image and consumable body. From *Shock*.

5. The sexual spectacle dissolves into abstracted movement—where is our erotic investment during such moments? From *Shock*.

conveying the female performer's pleasure in the visual contrast between the brightly colored prosthesis and her black-and-white skin.[10] This dissolves into a medium shot of intercourse with the mysterious man called "Johnny," establishing the frantic pace of a sexual number composed of varying angles of genital activity intercut with close-ups of the actress's face, her mouth, another sex scene (with different actors in color), and stills of Marilyn posing. Like the vacillation between spaces in *Naked Highway*, the "truth" of the sexual spectacle seems to rely less on individual shots than on their manic succession—a structural repetition that creates the fiction of immediacy, but is also the visible trace of mediation.

As is implicit thus far, *Shock*'s aesthetic attempts to convey bodily pleasure visually. To a certain degree, this representational problem preoccupies all pornography as a genre invested in capturing and conveying bodily experience. What is interesting about certain moments of *Shock*, such as this scene, is that in the quest for "visible proof," the constructedness of the scene subsumes the display of bodies, so that the imprints of commodification and reproduction become the dominant signs of sexual pleasure; it is the video's glossiness as a product (sets, costumes, strobe light), the performance, the artificial textures, the traces of the representational mechanisms themselves, which emerge as the site of sexual truth in the scene.

We can see the construction of this truth more clearly when we take into account pornography's drive to achieve maximum visibility, its aim to convey pleasure through the exposure of bodies.[11] The syntax of this scene from *Shock* compromises the correlation between the truth of pleasure and the visibility of bodies, as the syntax itself strives for maximum visibility. This becomes evident not only in the frenzied intercutting but in small details, such as the strobes backlighting genital close-ups both highlighted and obscured by the pulsating flashes of light, or the camera work itself, which at times seems to convulse with (perhaps even instead of) the performers, resulting in nothing but abstracted movement (fig. 5). Precisely at these moments of abstraction, a shift occurs in the organization of pornography's truth—a shift that does not negate previous conventions (performing bodies are still there), but that reconfigures them according to new, historically specific methods of (re)production whose language comes to stand for the body in ecstasy.

We must understand this reconfiguration of pleasure in relation to video as a medium, whose operation, as *Naked Highway* suggests, is intimately connected to the technology of television. While television and video are not interchangeable, I would argue that the latter inherits its semantic structures from the former, whose own language is that of time commercialized through segmentation. Jameson characterizes video's syntax, its particular mode of arranging and conveying information, as this distinct temporality: "A ceaseless rotation of elements such that they change place at every moment, with the result that no single element can occupy the position of . . .'primary sign' for any length of time but must be dislodged in turn in the following instant (the filmic terminology of 'frames' and 'shots' does not seem appropriate for this kind of succession)" (1999, 90). Although this movement resonates structurally with montage as we know it in film, I stress Jameson's distinction because video undermines the construction of meaning film achieves through shot juxtaposition. He posits the "ceaseless rotation of elements" as an alternate logic, one that we can trace to the development of television as a commercial vehicle.[12] This editing is video's particular signature, inherited (in part) from its immediate technological predecessor, television; in both cases, the editing functions both as a break between independent units *and* as a suture between them. Unlike in film, the logical sequence between individual units consists only in their arrangement in a sequence; no "unity" in a gestalt sense exists here, since commercials are similar only in form to the programs they interrupt (R. Williams 1975, 77). While this does not foreclose the possibility of narrative unity in television or video (since they have obviously produced many successful examples), it does mean that the syntax of the medium constructs narrative unity in a different way, or, more precisely, that we *experience* its logic differently, as the distinct temporality of commodity consumption.[13]

The very rhythm of *Shock* has more to do with video's function as a commercial rather than a narrative medium.[14] While the two certainly do not remain mutually exclusive, one does have priority over the other, I would argue, in constructing a visual language locating pleasure in the convulsions not of the body, but of the machine.[15] This convulsing, this "truth," is key because it invites a specific mode of looking, one defined by the constant shifting of different, simultaneous angles of vision; it is a looking predicated on the seeming *immediacy* of material things, flashing before the viewer as a series of trembling simultaneities. By encoding visual pleasure in the modes of (re)production, these works may be seen as collapsing sexualized viewing and commodity consumption into one efficient activity that has as its aim the visual possession of objects on display.

Video pornography, thus, lends itself neatly to the arguments of Jameson and Baudrillard, who see the viewer's impending collapse into late capitalism's economy of commodity images as assured by the shameless eroticizing of modes of production. Formally, *Shock* and *Naked Highway*, in their specific ways, evoke Baudrillard's account of simulation, of the displacement of mundane reality by a looking caught up in a "kind of thrill of the real, or of an aesthetics of the hyperreal, a thrill of vertiginous and phony exactitude, a thrill of alienation and of magnification, of distortion in scale, of excessive transparency, *all at the same time*" (1983, 50; emphasis added). Simultaneity is key here, for the structural segmentation of television arrests temporal flow, thereby producing an almost tactile immediacy by creating a sequence of images, each of which occupy an urgent Now (one only has to think of the movement between commercials to see this). This Now and its implicit mode of address — the thing offering itself for visual consumption — can be seen as striving to mold a particular type of viewing subject, one who becomes an extension of the material basis of the medium, a receptor interpolated via his or her own pleasure into the flattened temporality of video. We may thus read the visual aesthetic of *Shock* and *Naked Highway* as working toward the impending collapse of the digital and the tactile into a single experience that seemingly confirms Baudrillard's ultimate prognosis for the postmodern: "It is in effect the medium—the very style of montage, of decoupage, of interpellation, solicitation, summation by the medium—which controls the process of meaning" (1983, 123).

And yet, let us look closer at the implicit structural presuppositions of this conclusion, particularly the merging of consumption and production allowing for the medium to control the "process of meaning." For Baudrillard (and also for Jameson), this collapse occurs *through* the tactile, which displaces the visual as the organizing principle of experience in the aptly named "era of tactile communication":

> We are closer here in effect to the tactile than to the visual universe, *where the distancing is greater and reflection always possible.* At the same time as touch loses its sensorial, sensual value for us (touching is an interaction of the senses rather than a simple contact of an object with the skin), it is possible that it returns as the strategy of a universe of communication—but as the field of tactile and tactical simulation, where the message becomes 'massage,' tentacular solicitation, test. (Baudrillard 1983, 124; emphasis added)

Vision operates in this passage as the privileged arena of reflexivity, a consciousness predicated on the distance between subject and object. Baudrillard figures the loss of this crucial distance in the increasing dominance of the tactile: message becomes massage, meaning becomes sensation. The categorical status of vision here implies a hierarchy of the senses, since it is through touch and its susceptibility, vulnerability to stimuli, that the simulacrum can pass itself off as real, as experience. The Marilyn impersonator comes to mind, presenting an almost archetypal illustration in reproducing an icon whose beauty strategically conflates sexuality and reproducibility (as Warhol suggests). The commodified body of "Marilyn" is the very strategy that transforms "message into massage" since it is her uncanny ability to offer herself as desirable body that destabilizes the distinction between the visual and the tactile—between what we *know* and what we *feel.* The taking of "Marilyn" as an object of desire (if only temporarily), then, marks a moment when the viewer surrenders to the structures of production—let us also recall the image of Colorado brushing the screen (fig. 3). It is this collapse of viewer into object that signals the "precession of the simulacrum": the fate of the subject in the deluge of mass-produced images that become indistinguishable from the "real" sensory experience they ultimately displace.

In discussing the viewing structure created by video, Jameson echoes

Baudrillard's description of the absorption of the subject (the "spectator") into the indistinguishability of the mass-produced:

> The machine on both sides, then: the machine as subject and object alike and indifferently: the machine of the photographic apparatus peering across like a gun barrel at the subject whose body is clamped into its mechanical correlative in some apparatus of registration/reception. The helpless spectators of video time are then as immobilized and mechanically integrated and neutralized as the older photographic subjects, who became for a time, part of the technology of the medium. (Jameson 1999, 73)

Like Baudrillard, Jameson repeatedly turns to the trope of depersonalization, signaled by the loss of reflective distance brought about by the body's susceptibility to the simulated perceptions produced by the machine.[16] Interestingly (if not paradoxically), while this passage articulates depersonalization as the machine's violent effect on the viewing body, Jameson's theatrical (if somewhat paranoid) rhetoric betrays an underlying anxiety concerning not the entrapment, but the *yielding* of the body. I emphasize *yielding* over helplessness because, as Baudrillard more clearly suggests, the body is figured as always to some degree in collusion with the machine; the body provides an *object*, the very materiality of which allows for its immobilization. In these accounts, the body emerges as something of a liability as it all too easily surrenders to the false sensations produced by mechanized spectacle. We are too easily hypnotized by the uncanny, doubled beauty of those twin sisters.[17]

Ultimately, I think the type of viewership informed by these presuppositions must be revised (or at least supplemented) because it only partially accounts for the pleasures of commodity, failing as it does to acknowledge that the seduction by the mass-produced entails not only possessing but also being possessed. I stress revision because I think these models provide a crucial historical/material specificity that must be accounted for in any construction of visual pleasure. However, I find the criticisms' ambiguities about the body and its relation to technologies rather limiting in discussing video pornography as a genre invested in *moving* the viewer's body. As we have seen in these accounts, corporeality is, at best, a negligible participant in the act of looking; in fact, at times, the body is reduced to something of a structural weakness, compromising the viewing subject's "reflective" distance. My analysis of these videos, which seemingly present (re)production as the truth of sexual pleasure, in effect constitutes an attempt to explore the questions raised by this assumption. I wonder if the moving of the viewer's body by the mass-produced must always inevitably mark the collapse into simulation, a depersonalization producing the "machine on both sides"? More importantly, must corporeal surrender (or even corporeal presence) compromise the constitution of the subject? Or is there another way of imagining not only subjectivity but also the body's experience of technology?

To reformulate the relationship between visual pleasure and the reconfiguration of pornography's "truth," we must begin with a fuller account of the viewer's bodily experience. Bodily experience calls into question our understanding of visuality and temporality, which must be regarded not only as products of the machine but also as part of a subject's viewing position. This means that the temporality structuring experience inheres both in the technology *and* in the body as it exists over time. Hence, if the viewer's contact with the mass-produced image entails a surrender, it may only be a momentary one. And thus what is figured in the works of Jameson and Baudrillard as a collapse, may be read as part of an interaction, a negotiation between different pleasures and different modes of viewing not necessarily locked into a static subject/object relationship—which may indeed transcend, or at least destabilize this opposition.

In rethinking this relationship, the differentiation between modes of viewing proves useful, for, as we have seen, the construction of pleasure in these videos invites a particular kind of looking. Cavell's distinction between film and television watching (*viewing* in film versus *monitoring* in television/video) proves particularly helpful because it brings multiple modes of looking into play.[18] Cavell describes monitoring as "preparing our attention to be called upon by certain eventualities"; it is the vacillation between the eventful and the "*uneventful*, the repeated, the repetitive, the utterly familiar" (1986, 209). The segmented language of television, which Jameson links to video and which manifests itself in the editing or visual flow of *Shock* and *Naked Highway*, is precisely a function of monitoring. When seen as such, the visual flow of these particular examples of pornography can be seen as performing multiple (and often opposing) functions: conveying bodily/sexual pleasure *and* revealing the mediatedness of this pleasure, the functioning of the medium itself. However, since monitoring consists of repetition and interruption, the viewer experiences or makes sense of these effects one at a time, in a kind of beat. Conceiving of this beat as the organizing logic not only of my examples but of video as a medium, suggests (as I would ultimately argue) that the pleasure of the video image is not constant, but is structured and experienced like this beat, in the alternation between two modes of viewing.

Through this structure of the beat we can begin to account for what Crary terms "the carnal density of vision" in the visual experience of video pornography. Rosalind Krauss explores this notion of the beat or pulse more fully in her analysis of the surrealists' use of mass-produced objects to systematically explore the relationship between capitalism's detritus, sexuality, and physicality.[19] Krauss focuses on Max Ernst's integration of late-nineteenth-century philosophical toys into his collage novels to address an emerging form of spectatorship predicated on embodied experience. In her analysis of the zoetrope (a reoccurring motif in Ernst), Krauss describes an alternate experience of the mass-produced, one that challenges the inevitability of the viewer's collapse: "The spectator will occupy two places simultaneously. One is imaginary identification or closure with the illusion . . . *as if it were unmediated* . . . the second position is a connection to the optical machine in question, *an insistent reminder of its presence, of its mechanism, of its form of constituting piecemeal the only seemingly unified spectacle*" (1988, 58; emphasis mine). Krauss defines this visual experience as the vacillation between a *surrender* to the optical illusion produced by the machine and an *awareness* of the technology's materiality. Visual pleasure, then, unfolds like a pulse in this interaction between embodied observer and mediated image, which entails two models of visuality (disembodied/embodied) and two types of pleasure. That is, the viewer alternates between the two types of pleasure derived from occupying a particular position in a viewing structure; the act of viewing thus vacillates between the active pleasure of possessing (consuming) the image as object/commodity (the viewer as gazing subject), and the passive pleasure of being moved by the image (the viewer as object). As visual pleasure unfolds in the vacillation between these two poles, the carnal density of vision becomes the defining component in a visual experience neither constant nor unilateral, but fractured and polymorphous.[20]

While a nineteenth-century philosophical toy remains in many respects far removed from the complexities of video and digital technologies, I use it here to suggest that the observer's experience, shaped by the historical development of epistemological structures, changes at a far slower rate than specific gadgets.[21] The television, the VCR, and even the remote control do not operate as zoetropes, but they do share similar material structures. The faster, more complex deployment of information by these more evolved gadgets does not negate their banality, their constructedness, a fact which, I want to argue, the subject incorporates into the process of viewing. The viewer's experience of video's segmented language unfolds, like Krauss's account of the zoetrope, like a rhythm experienced over time. This rhythm or beat is itself organized by the viewer's alternation between the distinct pleasures produced by the modes of viewing enabling the interaction between embodied observer and apparatus.

Baudrillard and Jameson can then be seen as describing one side, or one pole, of this interaction, one that speaks to a looking inextricable from commodity consumption, a type of disembodied gazing that possesses (in the sense of owning, but also ingesting or incorporating) images. This pleasure in (re)production entails a *fixing*: a capturing of objects by transforming them into total images; it is a pleasure in the morbid stillness of the image, a stillness that allows for its consumption. Roland Barthes refers to this process of fixing as "mortification," an apt if somewhat ominous description capturing not only the static image, but the viewer's own seduction by (and momentary surrender to) a visual economy of objects.[22] For the viewer is also fixed by his or her own pleasure, lured by the object offering itself up. For me, *mortifies* all too clearly describes the black-and-white effect of "Marilyn" in *Shock*, whose visual appeal inheres in her very status as icon—a manufacturedness enabling the circulation of her prepackaged sex appeal (fig. 5).[23] This process of objectification strives to condition the viewer by localizing pleasure in representation qua representation, in *reproducibility*. This conditioning can be seen functioning not only in content details but also formally, as the segmented flow of video: a repeating temporality (a Now) that gives the commodity image an urgent immediacy.

And yet, the viewer's surrender to the spectacle (and its economy of objects) is, as Krauss suggests, a momentary "closure with the illusion," one interrupted by the body's *interpretation* of the spectacle presented. This becomes clearer when we regard pornography as a "body genre," a genre, like the horror film and the melodrama, that strives to *move* the spectator—either to tears, terror, sexual arousal, or some mixture of all three. In effect, these genres subject their audiences to these emotions, and pleasure consists in the viewer's passive reception, in being moved despite him- or herself.[24] Perhaps this encounter can be described more accurately in terms of touching rather than viewing, for instead of visual seduction, this mode of looking marks a moment when the viewer (through the body's involuntary reaction) invests the mechanical with a critical corporeality.[25] In the process of moving, the medium ceases to be an objective mode of representation and becomes a subjective, corporealized operation. The body's reaction (achieved by the viewer's passivity) is thus what realizes the "illusion," and yet in so doing, it emphasizes the subject's body over the object, disrupting a gazing predicated on visual distance and the clear distinction between object and subject. The moment of convulsion is one of bodily awareness, one that eclipses the object, if only momentarily.

The viewer's return to the body is acknowledged by the thematization of masturbation in these videos — a testament to the tenacity of corporeality in the viewing experience. In its persistence, the body becomes the dominant term in the specular relation: the privileged site of pleasure the medium attempts to emulate. We see this enacted vividly in a solo scene from *Naked Highway* at a moment when, as the actor reaches climax, the editing strives to mimic his pleasure. A series of still shots of the actor's body parts, edited into a frenzied pace, attempts to achieve this, so that the convulsive movement of the cutting, the rapid presentation of frozen images, is offered as the sign of his pleasure. However, the medium's convulsions betray the seams of the illusion it constructs, for it attempts to pass off these very seams as the truth of the bodily experience it is trying to capture. The scene functions only insofar as the viewer surrenders to the illusion; and hence, the surrender doubles as an acknowledgment of the materiality of the reproductive technology, of its boundaries. As with the zoetrope, the viewer's surrender both eclipses and reveals the machine's presence, "its form of constituting piecemeal [an] only seemingly unified spectacle" (Krauss 1988, 53).

We can read the clever ending of *Shock* as similarly turning on the viewer's awareness of the machine's materiality. The video's closing reveals that the entire narrative has been the elaborate delusion/liberation fantasy of our heroine, Mangrove. While this ending has dubious gender politics, I am intrigued by how the structure of fantasy (seeing oneself performing) is revisited as a visual theme, one that comes to mirror the structure of viewership (and the position of the viewer him- or herself). For example, in one particular number, various girls accompany the male protagonist (a.k.a. Johnny) to a cabaret. Once seated, they proceed to enjoy the "stage act," which is performed by the same actors (Johnny and the anonymous girls). This effect creates a strange doubling of bodies, as the actors simultaneously occupy multiple positions and perform various functions: viewing and being viewed. This scene's emphasis on an almost narcissistic performance (pleasure in seeing oneself) hints at the polymorphous nature of the viewer's pleasure, which derives not from a single position but from a constant movement between positions — from viewing subject to viewed object. We may further complicate this viewing when we take into account the complex field of identification. Is the pleasure here primarily that of a male viewer observing the spectacle of a convulsing female body? Is it a female viewer identifying with the represented pleasure of a female body? Or is it, perhaps more dubiously, a male viewer identifying with the masturbation of a female performer, whose surrender to a technological device mirrors his own? Or is it all those things simultaneously? Freud's notion of the matrix, as it operates structurally in fantasy, proves useful here because it opens the possibility of these relations existing simultaneously, yielding distinct pleasures (although not necessarily with the same intensity).[26]

Rather than absorption by the modes of production, I would propose that the embodied viewer's possibilities of phantasmatic and bodily movement mark a momentary transcendence of the very limits of (re)production. This may provide at least a partial resolution to "one of the paradoxes of erotic and pornographic images" that manage to "deliver the goods of bodily sexual arousal . . . despite the many protestations to the contrary by observers who describe the imagery as repetitive and/or boring" (L. Williams 1995, 14). By offering up their "material basis" as simulations of bodily pleasure, these pornographic videos simultaneously create and deconstruct an optical effect, for the simulacrum is only acknowledged as a sign of pleasure at the instant the body's involuntary reaction eclipses it. Touching, then, perhaps more accurately describes the mode of contact between the viewer and the image, for the viewer's surrender is, in fact, a meeting of two materialities, two embodiments: physical and mechanical. However, this touching unfolds on the visual plane, as the encounter between viewer and technology constitutes a mutual revelation: both image and viewer can be seen as *moving* but also as *moved*. And in that moving, the medium becomes an event, a finite happening, almost as if in the effort to represent the ecstasy of the body the medium is driven beside itself as well. Possession and movement, then, cannot be understood as fixed activities with a clearly defined object in the viewer/technology (subject/object) interface; rather than determining a single component, they represent two poles momentarily occupied by each term, thus constructing a binary opposition while simultaneously traversing the boundaries this binary establishes. This moment of convulsing, of indistinguishability between object and subject presents itself, I would contend, as a move *beyond* binary structures.[27]

For me, this mutual touching of the bodily and the mechanical evokes a certain definition of the sublime as the instant when, in the encounter between embodied viewer and image, the image can move the viewer to experience something beyond its material components—beyond merely words or paint, or even pixels. This moment—a sublimity reconfigured for the digital age—marks a potential point of rupture located not in the internal structures of production but in the moment the mass-produced image meets the thickness of vision. Barthes alludes to something akin to this rupture when he describes the breaking of the deathly pose by the act of photographing:

> Strangely the only thing that I tolerate, that I like, that is familiar to me, when I am photographed, is the sound of the camera. For me, the photographer's organ is not his eye (which terrifies me) but his finger: what is linked to the trigger of the lens, to the metallic shifting of the plates (when the camera still has such things). I love these mechanical sounds in an almost voluptuous way, as if, in the photograph, they were the very things—and the only thing—to which desire clings, their abrupt click breaking through the mortiferous layer of the Pose. (1981, 15)

Although obviously removed from video technology, Barthes's description isolates a point of breakthrough located precisely at the point the subject/object divide blurs. In this passage, Barthes transitions from the thing viewed (a body captured by the camera) to active subject. This shift is enabled by a fixation on the palpability of the machine: its sounds, the shifting of the plates, the triggering, the touch of the photographer's finger, at once mechanical and sensual, foreign and intimate, all unfolding as temporal occurrence. The erotic investment thus transforms the camera's functioning from an objective (removed) form of representation (which captures the helpless body in a glacial Now), to a material presence that interacts with another corporeality at the moment the shutter exposes emulsion to light. This momentary corporealization of representation precisely captures what enables the interface between viewer and image (technology); it is, in effect, what allows the viewer to "make sense" of the visual experience, to interact with something at once immediate and removed. And in this interface, the body, and not the machine, functions as the privileged site; for the body's moving enables the image to traverse the space separating subject and object, viewer and image. In crossing this space, the image becomes, if only briefly, more than an object.

In this way, we can return to the opening of *Naked Highway*, the scene of Colorado viewing (fig. 1), and ask not only what material components are necessary for the interaction to take place (the actual gadgets themselves: remote control, TV, VCR, viewing space, etc.) but also what the affective investment is that enables the closure with the illusion? I would contend that this question (of the necessary erotic investment) is particularly pertinent for these home technologies whose proliferation and diminution in scale alter the viewing experience (Darley 2000, 183–84). I would venture to say that, in fact, this calls for a "greater" investment on the part of the viewer than, say, a large-scale movie theater, for the currency of the spectacle (its ability to be spectacular) is not predicated on its magnitude, but on the viewer's ability to *touch*—to breach the space between him or herself and the image.

Ironically enough, in this culture saturated by images where the viewer readily surrenders to the optical effect, video pornography makes for the site where the viewer is moved beyond the material capacity of the image to move. Perhaps this is why the complex interaction between the materiality of video pornography and the viewer ultimately evokes, for me, Barthes's description of the *punctum*, of the prick received "right here in my eyes" (1981, 43). Experienced at the level of vision's corporeality, the punctum constitutes not only the very immediacy of the image but also that something that accosts the senses and moves viewers, despite themselves, beyond the field of representation.[28]

Naked Highway and *Shock*, in their effort to convey the corporeal visually, inadvertently gesture to this beyond erupting at those moments when their aesthetic reaches that critical point of materiality, mimicking bodily pleasure at the cost of exposing the very limitations of the medium. If nothing else, these moments reveal that the corporeal and the visual are not mutually exclusive (as the sexual and the digital are not either). At least, this is what I see in those instances when the frenzied editing and camera movement take on the aspect of bodily convulsion, when the medium itself becomes the spectacle. Here, I become aware not only of the performing bodies before me but of my own embodied pleasure in viewing, a pleasure that is both my collusion with and struggle against the materiality of the medium. Thus the texture of the video becomes a sign of mediation *and* immediacy as it convulses along with the bodies when the camera shifts between angles, representing nothing but its own movement, rendered visible as tactile abstraction.

The medium as temporal occurrence lies precisely at the heart of Jean-François Lyotard's account of the sublime as an experience between historically situated viewer and image. His sublimity speaks to a pleasure comprised of a mixture of possessing and being possessed, embodiment and disembodiment, a momentary suspension or indeterminacy also moving beyond the pleasurable: "[The sublime] is a pleasure with pain, a pleasure that comes from pain. In the event of an absolutely immense object . . . which like all absolutes can only be considered without reason, the imagination and the ability to present fail to provide appropriate representations. This frustration of expression kindles a pain, a kind of cleavage within the subject between what can be conceived and what can be imagined" (1984, 40). This crisis of representation, this sublime experience, unfolds as a moment, a Now tied to a particular place and time: "Now the sublime is this—not elsewhere, not up there or over there, not earlier or later not once upon a time, but here, now it happens—and it's this painting. Now and here there is this painting where there might have been nothing at all, and that's what is sublime. Letting go and disarming all grasping intelligence, recognizing that this occurrence of painting was not necessary and is barely visible, an openness to *is it happening*?" (37; emphasis added). By stressing the here and now, Lyotard's account encompasses both consumption and production; the image and the fact of its making converge in an experience embedded at a particular time and place. This here and now of the sublime captures the intersection of historically specific modes of production with a particular, subjective bodily experience, and it also begins to articulate (and stress) the affective dimension involved in this exchange.

For me, the closing sequences of *Naked Highway* evoke this excessive pleasure of the here and now. Unfolding as the visible pulse, the sequence begins with the flash of super-8 footage transferred onto video, a degraded, palpable texture conveying the urgency of the sexual act depicted; the video cuts rapidly to a close-up of a kiss (just video), which then cuts to the same shot doubly mediated by the super-8 on video; this cuts to a super-8 close-up of oral sex, which dissolves into a close-up of a super-8 kiss; this cuts to a moving camera that wanders off from the primary object and becomes lost, first in the scenery, and then in its own movement (direct video); finally we return to the close-up of the kiss (fig. 6). Here, the spectacle of the bodies collapses into the very palpability of the media, its sumptuousness: the pixelation of the video, the fluttering of the super-8, the shakiness of the camera, and their collective emulation of bodily pleasure. The occurrence of the medium here, its urgency, its shameless display of its sutures and seams, constitutes the very revelation of its limits, a turning onto itself in a moment of simulated carnal ecstasy. And yet, my surrender despite this display, or maybe because of it, is a mutual transcendence that is not a merging of body and machine, but a brushing of their tactile membranes.

This sublime, as the pleasure of the convulsing machine, is caught up in the viewer's surrender to the very syntax of the medium, to a structural

6. In this scene from *Naked Highway*, the urgency of the sexual act appears to be conveyed by the medium's degraded texture.

repetition revealing the image's constructedness. This brush with the limits of representation is something that the surrealists knew all too well and that informed their experiments with the detritus of the mass-produced, which have "to do less with the beautiful than with the sublime, for convulsive beauty not only stresses the formless and evokes the unrepresentable as with the sublime, but it also mixes delight and dread, attraction and repulsion" (Foster 1997, 50). The momentary mixture of these emotions, their ephemeral indistinguishability, ultimately presents a new way of imagining the interaction between viewer and image, one in which the relationship between the two is far from stable; in fact, it may very well be this instability that is experienced as pleasure, for, as Freud would have it, pleasure is always inextricably linked to unpleasure.

I invoke the sublime because, as it has been noted, video pornography (and pornography in general) presents an interesting paradox: the simultaneous seduction by the foreign and the banal, the enthralling and the repetitious. And yet, what allows a viewer to surrender to a pixilated image on the screen? What allows those pixels to transcend their own material boundaries, to move as well as be moved? Only the transcendence of experience can account for this, and it is this which lies at the heart of the sublime. By this I do not mean to posit pornography as a transcendent genre (as some artists might suggest); rather, I want to acknowledge its uncanny ability to move, to convulse along with the viewer. It is in this ability to render itself almost physical in the meeting with the viewer that video pornography provides a new model for relating to the mass-produced, one in which the body's susceptibility constitutes both a yielding *and* a resistance to the hypnotic seduction of the image.

Notes

1 For a fuller elaboration of this take on postmodernity, see Jameson 1992, in particular the introduction (1–6). Here, Jameson discusses the increasingly central role of the visual in the organization of contemporary culture, where it operates as the sole determinant of "pleasure."

2 For an overview of the impact of video and other new technologies on the U.S. pornography industry, see *U.S. News and World Report*, February 10, 1997, 43–50. The study estimates that hard-core video rentals reached a high of $665 million in 1996, which, combined with purchases, makes up a large part of the more than $8 billion spent on explicit sexual products.

3 In many ways, this appeal to abstracted looking and the implicit claim to a neutrality of vision suggests the operation of an epistemological model that divorces the activity of looking from corporeality (what Jonathan Crary calls the "thickness" of the body) in order to construct an "objective" world that displays itself as categorical truth. For an in-depth study of this "disembodied vision" as a historically produced epistemological structure, see Crary 1998. In particular, see chapter 2, "The Camera Obscura and Its Subject," where Crary begins to distinguish between embodied and disembodied vision, as well as its philosophical and material implications.

4 See L. Williams 1995.

5 Because the question of genre is such a complex issue, I want to clarify my usage of the term. Like Linda Williams, I want to refer to pornography as a genre in the sense of a set of narrative and iconographic conventions shared by a number of films/videos. See for instance chapter 5, "Generic Pleasures," of L. Williams 1999. However, I want to utilize the term in a way that encompasses aesthetic strategies but also incorporates the medium and technology of video (hence stressing the distinction between video and film). In this way, my definition of *genre* is influenced by Cavell's account. For a fuller elaboration, see Cavell 1986, 192–205.

6 I want to clarify why I want to describe this mode of looking as disembodied. First, I want to stress the structure of gazing, in which the world is displayed in/as objects. The aim of this gazing, in a psychoanalytic sense, is mastery, and in a material sense, it is possession. Here, my description would follow Laura Mulvey's account of the male gaze in "Visual Pleasure and Narrative Cinema." The absence of the body is key because it exempts the gazer from being looked back at (or being seen). Thus this visual mastery (active, even sadistic, in the psychoanalytic sense) may be read as predicated on its disembodiment.

7 See, for example, *The Opening of Misty Beethoven* (dir. Radley Metzger, 1975) and its various scenes involving early illicit xxx-theaters.

8 I borrow this term from Laplanche 1985, in his account of the emergence of sexuality in relation to the vital order. In particular, I am interested in this term as describing the emergence of a surplus erotic enjoyment in a given activity.

In his account, Laplanche describes the development of sexuality propped on life-sustaining nourishment as the bodily enjoyment that occurs in excess of the function of these activities. I use the term to resonate with the intermingling of the technological and the sexual; or, more precisely, to describe the presence/operation of different or diverging pleasures along with what seems to be the sole investment in pornography: the sexual spectacle.

9 I will elaborate on this idea more fully when I turn to a more detailed discussion of the video medium.

10 The black-and-white "Marilyn" is one of the more intriguing optical effects of this video. When a shot presents the actress alone, this effect is achieved by black-and-white video, with digitally added dust traces giving an aged film look. When she is shot with a partner, the effect is produced by body paint, costume, and lighting. In both instances, the sexual activity seems to become, at times, subsidiary to the visual spectacle of competing textures (flesh versus plastic) and color schemes (black-and-white versus color).

11 As Linda Williams writes: "This principle has operated in different ways at different stages of the genre's history: to privilege close-ups of body parts over other shots; to over-light easily obscured genitals; to select sexual positions that show the most of bodies and sexual organs" (1999, 49).

12 As Raymond Williams notes, the "new visual rhythms" created by segmentation are meant to naturalize commercial interruptions by incorporating them as parts of a larger, unified structure: "Both commercials and programs are assembled out of the same syntax: the linear succession of logically independent units of nearly equal duration. . . . this mechanically divisible, metrical presentation has none of the percussive or disjunctive properties of radio presentation . . . because of the conventions of the camerawork and the editing that have developed to sustain the shock of basically mechanical procedures" (qtd. in Antin 1986, 159).

13 It is interesting to note that television itself inherited this segmented format from commercial radio. As David Antin notes: "TV inherited the split roles and the two time signatures from radio, as well as the habit of alternating them in regularly recurrent intervals, which creates the arbitrary-appearing, mechanical segmentation of both media's presentations. But television carried this mechanical segmentation to a new extreme and presented it in such a novel way—through a special combination of its own technological and production conventions—that TV time, in spite of structural similarity with radio time, has an entirely different appearance from it, bearing the relationship to it of an electronically driven, digital counter to a spring driven, hand wound alarm clock" (1986, 156). As Antin's description suggests, this temporality has a certain feel, or its structure, to a certain degree, determines the viewer's experience of the medium as a structural segmentation that moves in a flow.

14 Here, perhaps, we can think of the music video as the prime instantiation of this logic. The music video in essence constitutes a fragmented assortment of

images, designed for commercial purposes. However, as it has been recently argued, this does not necessarily eliminate the aesthetic possibilities of this relatively new cultural form (Darley 2000, 102–3).

15 As the early stag film *A Country Stud Horse* (ca. 1920) suggests, the merging of technology and pleasure is not necessarily new. The reel presents a man peering into a mutoscope (a type of hand-cranked viewing machine), which displays a woman's tantalizing striptease. As the man continues peering, he begins to fondle himself while he cranks the machine, a scene that abruptly cuts to a hardcore sexual number. This example of pornography adheres to the principle of maximum visibility, characterized in Linda Williams's analysis by a "frontality" she links to the construction of a specific "truth" of sexual pleasure organized around the quantification of the object—clearly at work in gender divisions: male/viewer versus female/object (1999, 76–80). However, I would stress that the "truth" of commodification, as I have been discussing it, is here subordinate to the spectacle of moving bodies; the technological operates more or less on the lower frequencies.

16 Jameson writes: "Video is unique . . . because it is the only art or medium in which [the] ultimate seam between space and time is the very locus of the form, *and also because its machinery uniquely dominates and depersonalizes subject and object alike, transforming the former into a quasi-material registering apparatus for the machine time of the latter and of the video image or 'total flow'*" (1999, 76; emphasis mine).

17 Not surprisingly, we find this anxiety concerning the body to be related to the old high/low culture divide (Darley 2000, 5). It is certainly not difficult to see why pornography would once again provoke this seemingly obsolete debate. (And we must note that even though pornography enters as a critical category in Jameson and Baudrillard, it is not addressed directly.) It is perhaps a bit more difficult to see why video would provoke this unease, but a fuller answer requires a historical engagement that exceeds the limitations of this brief essay. However, let me at least suggest two possible avenues for further exploration. First, we must read this ambivalence historically, linked to the mass proliferation of the VCR (like the television a few decades earlier); in particular, its infiltration of domestic spaces, which is figured as something of an invasion, the intrusion of an alien presence. As Andrew Darley notes: "Digital visual culture is a spectacle of a peculiar hue: the television, video and home computer are precisely machines that defy social location, the rooms they exist in cut across such categories as urban, suburban and rural" (2000, 183). I wonder if the constant trope of "collapse" is not related to this destabilization of social divisions/structures by emerging technologies.

Second, I think the VCR plays into issues of social isolation, of individuals being compartmentalized by increasingly self-sufficient (technologically realized) imaginary worlds—one should recall criticisms accompanying the rise of the novel in the early nineteenth century. This new medium may be seen as "producing new forms of generalized narcissism, a withdrawal of the individual into an ever more isolated and isolating private world of which we have unlimited access via our screens" (Darley 2000, 66). Implicit in this claim is the specter of onanism—which in the present context we must take quite literally, but also as signifying a cultural trend in which individuals become increasingly locked in a hermetically sealed, technology-based fantasy world. The "real" (and the social) once again falls by the wayside, or its hegemony is challenged by multiple, individualized simulations or hyperrealities. Video pornography, then, comes to realize both of these cultural trends, as it cuts across consumer groups (diverse cultural demographics) and employs particular technologies that openly engage onanistic pleasures.

18 Although initially I would stress that particular media produce/invite different modes of looking, I do so only to contend, after Cavell, that these various modes operate simultaneously: "The intimacy of such a difference prompts me to emphasize that by monitoring and viewing, I mean to be calling attention to aspects of human perception generally, so that film and video will not be expected to capture one of these aspects to the exclusion of the other, but rather to stress one at the expense of the other—as each may be stressing different aspects of art; video of its relation to communication, film of its relation to seduction" (1986, 211).

19 For another in-depth discussion of the surrealists' relation to sexuality and the refuse of capitalism, see Foster 1997, particularly chapter 6, "Outmoded Spaces."

20 I am utilizing *polymorphous* in the psychoanalytic sense here.

21 As Andrew Darley notes in his study, many contemporary cultural forms and media are in fact part of a larger lineage that we can trace back to the decades preceding the advent of cinema. This lineage does not entail a linear history, but as Darley asserts, "revealing something of the nature of the ancestral background involved here can also begin to give us clues and cues to understanding the formal make-up of these latest forms, thereby telling us much about how and why people enjoy them" (2000, 38). For an in-depth discussion, refer to chapters 2 and 3 of *Visual Digital Culture: Surface Play and Spectacle in New Media Genres.*

22 Interestingly enough, Roland Barthes articulates this process as his defensive reaction to being photographed: "I constitute myself in the process of posing, I instantaneously make *another body for myself, I transform myself in advance into an image*. This transformation is an active one: I feel that the photograph creates my body or *mortifies* it, according to its caprice" (1981, 10–11; emphasis added). This image of being captured by the machine resonates with Jameson's own rhetoric, with the prime difference being that Barthes describes it as a momentary, rather than a constant immobilization. Thus the body here comes in contact with the machine, but is not assimilated into its operation, a key difference which has, as we shall see, important implications.

23 Something of the uncanny, in a strictly Freudian sense, may be seen operating here in this pleasure invested in the conversion of the animate into the inanimate, or, perhaps more accurately, in the blurring of the two. Appropriately,

"Marilyn" evokes the mannequin; an illuminating example for it presents "the human figure given over to commodity form—indeed, [it] is the very image of capitalist reification" (Foster 1997, 21). This uncanny appeal of commodity's incarnation is the organizing aesthetic principle of *Shock*, which dwells compulsively on the spectacle of the coupling of organic and inorganic. For instance, the second scene stages an elaborate encounter between an actress who has fallen into an evil criminal's mind and two gargoyles who come to life in his mental landscape. This scene is spectacular less for its explicit sex than for the high production value (the makeup/prostheses of the actors, the sets, etc); in fact, sex, as a physical act, is visible only as the total image effect. This aesthetic is particularly prevalent in scenes involving all female performers, who are often clad in indistinguishable costumes and orchestrated to resemble something of a Busby Berkeley–style hard-core number (the pornographic number coming as close to its musical roots as possible).

24 As Linda Williams writes, the "ecstatic excesses" of these genres "could be said to share a quality of uncontrollable convulsion or spasm—of the body beside itself with sexual pleasure, fear and terror, or overpowering sadness" (1995, 703). For a full discussion of body genres, see L. Williams 1991.

25 This spectatorship evokes Vivian Sobchack's revision of film as more than a visible object because in the process of moving, the viewing subject and the viewed object destabilize the viewer/viewed binary. See Sobchack 1995.

26 For an in-depth discussion of the functioning of the matrix, see Krauss 1988.

27 Vivian Sobchack articulates something quite similar in relation to film: "In the act of vision, the film transcends its existence as merely a visible object reducible to its technology and mechanisms, much as in similar acts of vision, the filmmaker and spectator transcend their existence as merely visible objects reducible to their anatomy and physiology" (1995, 51).

28 It is interesting to note that Barthes quickly qualifies the types of images that have the potential to move him. In elucidating the punctum, he contrasts a subcategory of images, called "unary," characterized by their banality, their flatness. Here, the pornographic image becomes paradigmatic: "Another unary photograph is the pornographic photograph (I am not saying the erotic photograph: the erotic is a pornographic that has been disturbed, fissured). Nothing is more homogenous than a pornographic photograph. It is always a naïve photograph, without intention and without calculation. Like a shop window which shows only one illuminated piece of jewelry, it is completely constituted by the presentation of only one thing: sex: no secondary, untimely object ever manages to half conceal, delay or distract" (1981, 41). It is even more interesting that he utilizes as proof *a contrario* the work of Robert Mapplethorpe. The distinction between the erotic and the pornographic is tenuous at best, for it presupposes a certain homogeneity of the sex act that allows for its ready display. And yet it seems to me that at the very core of this touching (of this punctum) lies the fact that the *something* is not necessarily located in the photograph itself, that is, the some-

thing is not stable; it is rather the parallax of the intersecting "visions" of viewer and viewed object alike.

Works Cited

Antin, David. 1986. "Video: The Distinctive Features of the Medium." In *Video Culture: A Critical Investigation*, ed. John G. Hanhardt. New York: Visual Studies Workshop Press. 147–66.

Barthes, Roland. 1981. *Camera Lucida: Reflections on Photography*. Trans. Richard Howard. New York: Hill and Wang.

Baudrillard, Jean. 1983. *Simulations.* Trans. Paul Foss, Paul Patton, and Philip Beitchman. New York: Semiotext[e].

Cavell, Stanley. 1986. "The Fact of Television." In *Video Culture: A Critical Investigation*, ed. John G. Hanhardt. New York: Visual Studies Workshop Press. 192–205.

Crary, Jonathan. 1998. *Techniques of the Observer: On Vision and Modernity in the Nineteenth Century*. Cambridge, Mass.: MIT Press.

Darley, Andrew. 2000. *Visual Digital Culture: Surface Play and Spectacle in New Media Genres*. London: Routledge.

Foster, Hal. 1997. *Compulsive Beauty.* Cambridge, Mass.: MIT Press.

Jameson, Fredric. 1992. *Signatures of the Visible*. New York: Routledge.

———. 1999. *Postmodernism; or, The Logic of Late Capitalism*. Durham, N.C.: Duke University Press.

Krauss, Rosalind. 1988. "The Im/pulse to See." In *Vision and Visuality: Discussions on Contemporary Culture*, ed. Hal Foster. Seattle: Bay. 51–75.

Laplanche, Jacques. 1985. *Life and Death in Psychoanalysis*. Trans. Jeffrey Mehlman. Baltimore, Md.: John Hopkins University Press.

Lyotard, Jean-Francois. 1984. "The Sublime and the Avant-Garde." *Artforum*, 22 April. 36–43.

Mulvey, Laura. 1986. "Visual Pleasure and Narrative Cinema." In *Narrative, Apparatus, Ideology*. Ed. Philip Rosen. New York: Columbia University Press. 198–209.

Sobchack, Vivian. 1995. "Phenomenology and the Film Experience." In *Viewing Positions: Ways of Seeing Film*, ed. Linda Williams. New Brunswick, N.J.: Rutgers University Press.

Williams, Linda. 1991. "Film Bodies: Gender, Genre, and Excess." *Film Quarterly* 44, 4: 701–15.

———. 1995. "Corporealized Observers: Visual Pornographies and the 'Carnal Density of Vision.'" In *Fugitive Images: From Photography to Video*, ed. Patrice Petro. Bloomington: Indiana University Press. 3–39.

———. 1999. *Hardcore: Power, Pleasure and the "Frenzy of the Visible."* Berkeley: University of California Press.

Williams, Raymond. 1975. *Television: Technology and Cultural Form*. New York: Schocken.

part 5

Pornography and/as Avant-Garde

Andy Warhol's *Blow Job*: Toward the Recognition of a Pornographic Avant-garde

ARA OSTERWEIL

Boredom is not far from bliss: it is bliss seen from the shores of pleasure.
—Roland Barthes, *The Pleasure of the Text*

✳ According to Andy Warhol, the first public screening of his 1963 film *Blow Job* occurred at Ruth Kligman's Washington Square Art Gallery, located at 530 West Broadway in downtown New York, in the fall of 1964 (Warhol and Hackett 1980, 79).[1] At Warhol's request, Kligman had invited some friends to the screening—a decision she later regretted.[2] Although Jonas Mekas's Film Culture Non-Profit Organization sponsored the screening, the event remained unadvertised due to the recent seizures of sexually explicit experimental films and the costly and tedious legal battles that ensued. Only a few months before, in the spring of 1964, Mekas himself had been arrested in New York on obscenity charges for screening Jack Smith's sexually explicit film *Flaming Creatures* (1963) along with Jean Genet's *Chant d'amour* (1950) (James 1992, 11).[3] Presenting *Blow Job* at a respectable art gallery was a practical attempt to elide the censors,[4] but it also signified the tension between "high art" and "pornography" that structured cultural reception during the early sixties.[5]

By 1969, *Blow Job* would land in exhibition spaces more compatible with Warhol's own preference for prurience.[6] At the peak of Warhol's fascination with the "beaver craze" that had moved east from San Francisco,[7] *Blow Job* was finally shown in movie theaters specializing in gay porn, with "the admonition to call the theater to find out its name" (Hoberman 1991, 182). Only five years separate the surreptitious attempt to pass *Blow Job* off as a film worthy of exhibition in an art gallery and the film's "coming out" as pornography, but the landscape of film culture would have changed significantly from 1963 to 1969. Nineteen sixty-three marked Warhol's debut as a filmmaker with titles such as *Kiss*, *Sleep*, *Eat* and *Haircut*, but by 1969, Warhol's career as film director had been over for at least a year.[8]

Despite Warhol's early retirement from the cinema, avant-garde film had reached a level of respectability by 1969.[9] Screenings of experimental works still suffered constant shutdowns and necessary relocations, as well as perennial financial obstacles. Nevertheless, by 1969, Mekas, P. Adams Sitney, and Jerome Hill had already begun the creation of the Anthology Film Archives, a permanent center for the exhibition and study of avant-garde cinema, which would have its grand opening on December 1, 1970.[10]

Experimental film was not the only sphere of cinema caught in transformation. The exhibition of sexually explicit moving images underwent momentous changes in the decade that culminated in Stonewall, radically modifying the conditions of mainstream, art house, and pornographic film spectatorship. Jon Lewis notes that the top twenty box office films for 1969 included four adult titles: the studio film *Midnight Cowboy* (dir. John Schlesinger) (despite its self-imposed X-rating, the film had managed to obtain Oscars for best picture, director, and screenplay), *I Am Curious Yellow* (dir. Vilgot Sjoman) and *Three in the Attic* (dir. Richard Wilson) (both of which were released by non-MPAA members), and *Easy Rider* (dir. Dennis Hopper) (which had been independently financed and produced) (2000, 153).[11] The legalization of hard-core pornography in 1969 opened up new theatrical possibilities for both gay and straight porn, but a small industry of peep-show loops, "for individual screening by Andy Warhol and others," had been operating in Times Square since 1966 (Waugh 1996a, 359).

The primary goal of this article is not to document the shifting parameters of the exhibition of sexually explicit images in the sixties,[12] but to analyze Warhol's *Blow Job* in relation to the multiple historical and aesthetic factors that influence, *without determining*, the film's erotic charge. By introducing this essay via a brief discussion of *Blow Job*'s history of exhibition, I hope to at least afford a glimpse of the complex cultural negotiations that surround the film's emergence and that continue to inflect its contested textual status. By focusing exclusively on *Blow Job*, I do not mean to suggest that the film is unique in its status as avant-garde moving-image pornography. On the contrary, it is important to note that the film emerges from a historical moment ripe with formal transgressions and sexual transgressors; the postwar American avant-garde was replete with films that engaged the viewer both corporeally and cognitively. Jack Smith's notorious *Flaming Creatures* and Barbara Rubin's extraordinary but rarely screened *Christmas on Earth* (like *Blow Job*, both of these were made in 1963) are only two examples of experimental films camped at the borderlands between art and pornography during this period. While I hope that these films, and others like them, will inform the background of the following discussion, I have chosen to focus on *Blow Job* because it seems to best articulate the inadequacies of our present modes of classifying and theorizing the diverse pleasures of pornography.

Although much of the American underground cinema of the 1960s and 1970s was consumed with the body moved to sexual excitation, the "on/scenity" of sexuality in avant-garde film has been neglected by critical discourse. Despite their shared investment in corporeality, pornography and the avant-garde are often positioned at odds. Theoretically, it is difficult to compare two traditions that regularly deploy conflicting modes of address and divergent formal vocabularies. Historically, however, it is necessary to breach the divide that still separates the high from the low, and which has myopically—and inaccurately—segregated the domain of art from the possibility of sexual excitation. As an avant-garde film that specifically addresses what is considered pornographic subject matter, *Blow Job* inaugurated the era of structural film with an explicit gesture toward the sex act.

Warhol's cinema emerged from his lifelong interest in sexuality, from his experience as both as a producer and consumer of sexual images. Although the present discussion shall focus exclusively on Warhol's moving images, celluloid was neither the first nor the last medium in which Warhol created sexually explicit documents. Throughout the fifties, Warhol worked on a series of genital illustrations, or "cock drawings," for a proposed "cock book" (Koestenbaum 2001, 42). Since these were never exhibited during Warhol's lifetime, and are still relatively obscure, the centrality of the cock drawings in Warhol's imagination remains rather overlooked.[13] Nevertheless, these drawings prefigure one of Warhol's later hobbies: taking thousands of Polaroids of the "cock and balls" of any willing visitor to the Factory (Warhol and Hackett 1980, 294). And although critics have remarked more on Warhol's connoisseurship of beaver films in the late sixties than on his interest in earlier forms of sexploitation, it is certain that Warhol was an avid consumer of soft-core porn by the time he began to make movies.[14]

Blow Job may have had its public premiere at a respectable art gallery, but its dialogue with pornography — both implied and explicit — undermines this early attempt to sanctify the film as "legitimate" art. Tom Waugh insists on the significance of this other relation; he writes that "porn, pure and simple, is exactly the contextual framework that is indispensable for understanding [Warhol's] films" (1996a, 64–65). It is undeniable that Warhol's cinema manifests the conditions and possibilities of its specific historical moment vis-à-vis pornography — the liminal period of experimentation after the stag era but prior to the rigid legal and discursive codification of hard-core porn in the early seventies. Nevertheless, his films simultaneously parody the very circumstances that enable their existence. Warhol took advantage of the dissipating limits of sexual representation as the sixties progressed; the culmination of his directing career comes with his 1968 film *Blue Movie*, a.k.a. *Fuck*, in which Viva and Louis Waldon are seen engaging in both oral and vaginal intercourse.[15] In *Blow Job*, however, Warhol addressed the notion of "the limit" itself as the generative mechanism of pleasure, a nuance lost in the intervening years with the insistence on maximum visibility in hard-core porn.

If it can be argued that any such thing as "common knowledge" exists about *Blow Job*, it is that "nothing happens," that the film's sexually frank title (which never appears in the actual film) is the only erotic thing about the entire viewing experience. The film's trajectory, however, only partially justifies this attitude. For the entire length of the film,[16] the frame displays the face and neck of a young man in high-contrast black-and-white as he leans against a stone wall. The young man's face is angular and smooth-skinned; his chin and jaw are rugged and his lips pale. His skin is fair, and he has his hair cut short. He appears to wear a black leather jacket, although we only glimpse the collar and shoulders of his apparel. Although the man's face appears in close-up during the entire film — which lacks both sound and color — his face is lit from above, so that his eyes are transformed into hollow, black cavities when he looks at the camera. On several occasions during the film, the man's face is cast in such deep shadow that only the bridge of his nose and his forehead are truly visible (figure 1).

Throughout the film, the man's facial expressions appear to respond to something off-screen; presumably the action occurs below the frame. As his interest in this ambiguous event waxes and wanes, the muscles in the young man's face rhythmically tense and relax. He throws his head back in surges of boredom and ecstasy barely distinguishable from each other. His eyes wander, dart, close, and wince; his hands periodically intrude into the frame to wipe his mouth or scratch his nose. Several times throughout the film,

1. In *Blow Job*, the face is subpoenaed to provide visual evidence of the corporeal exchange that purportedly occurs below the frame. Spasms associated with sexual pleasure bear a great resemblance to expressions of boredom, irritation, and pain. Courtesy of the Andy Warhol Museum, Pittsburgh, Pennsylvania, a museum of the Carnegie Institute.

the man cradles his head in his palms or runs his fingers through his hair. Occasionally, the man straightens abruptly; at other times, his face droops slightly out of the frame as if his knees are sagging. Although the camera does not budge, Warhol uses his standard cartridge technique throughout the film, punctuating the "action" with the white flicker of the emulsion. Near the end of the film, the man's slight convulsions appear to quicken. His position adjusts slightly, and he lights and smokes a cigarette. Soon after the young man has finished his cigarette, the film ends just as it began — abruptly, without title or credits.

While the presence of these awkward gestures of corporeal adjustment in the final, unedited film attest to the presumed authenticity of the sex act, their inclusion simultaneously threatens to undermine the rapt attention of the pornographic consumer. As Roy Grundmann has observed in his book-length study of the film, "the signification of the sex act itself is constantly threatened to be subsumed under the possibility of heightened nonsexual extremes, such as pain and psychological anguish" (1993, 33). For Grundmann, the absence of the type of affect traditionally associated with pornography is not the problem for spectators of Warhol's film. Grundmann points out that although *Blow Job* lacks the kind of "conspicuously obscene facial expressions" that typify performances in hard-core pornography, these expressions have not always been required components of the pornographic text (34). On the other hand, Warhol's "autopsy" of the sex act engages the ambiguity of the body in motion in ways that disarm the viewer. In *Blow Job*, the expressions signifying boredom, pleasure, and pain are situated in an illegible visual lexicon where meaning has become inaccessible. The arrival of pleasure is indistinguishable from the trace of pain; movement itself has lost its abrogated function as a transparent sign.

The still camera never as much as glimpses the blow job explicitly advertised by the film's title. *If* there is an actual blow job occurring below the frame—which seems entirely questionable—the spectator is given no visible proof of the exchange. One wonders whether anything at all is happening in the unseen space of the film narrative. Although "it does seem to be a real live blow job that we're not seeing" (Koch 1973, 47), nothing indicates that Warhol has not faked the entire display, instructing his actor to masturbate, or merely to act as if he is being brought to sexual climax. What is the status of this off-screen "blow job"? Is it real or imagined? Is the exchange heterosexual or homosexual? Do the man's facial expressions and gestures bear witness to the actual occurrence of fellatio, or is his mute testimony merely another put-on? If the blow job did in fact transpire, has the man actually been brought to orgasm, or "organza," as Warhol liked to say (Koestenbaum 2001, 44)?

These questions remain unanswered in Warhol's film, and they have become the subject of much critical musing. Unlike those of the hard-core pornography that succeeded them,[17] the temporal and visual regimes of Warhol's films are, literally, missing in action. Not only does the blow job proposed by the title occur outside of the frame (if at all), but the moment of sexual climax is signaled belatedly and ambiguously by the presumably post-fellatio smoking of a cigarette (figure 2). Part of the frustration involved in watching *Blow Job* is, obviously, the way the film withholds the vision of fellatio to which the spectator feels entitled. There is both a missed space in the film (the space of the supposed fellatio) and a missed time (by the time the cigarette is lit, "it" is already over). Since we do not actually see the fellatio that the film's title promises (and its action seems to imply), we are left in an unresolved state of apprehension. We wait interminably for the moment of orgasm, only recognizing that it may have occurred when it is already "too

2. By the time the cigarette is lit, the audience realizes that "it" is already over. This post-coital ritual stands in as incomplete proof of the film's authenticity. From *Blow Job*, courtesy of the Andy Warhol Museum, Pittsburgh, Pennsylvania, a museum of the Carnegie Institute.

late."[18] The orgasm happens without our seeing or knowing it; the lighting of the cigarette induces a "minor shock of recognition" or a "small jolt in the mind," communicating to the audience that the moment we have waited for has come and gone without our perception (Koch 1973, 47). *Blow Job* situates the viewer in a realm of missed temporalities and lost opportunities. For the spectator, the "action" passes without him or her having arrived at the "scene." The spectator only learns of the sexual climax belatedly, through the "traces" of the sexual event. Like the detective at the scene of a crime, or like the observer of Eugène Atget's photographs, the spectator of *Blow Job* must reassemble the details of the sexual exchange from clues—facial gestures, murmuring lips, and cigarette smoke—without witnessing the event itself.

Although we do not witness the genital space of fellatio in *Blow Job*, the film is hardly eventless. Film critic J. Hoberman describes *Blow Job* as "the most conceptual work of porn ever made" based on its ability to re-define what counts as pornographic "happening" (1991, 182). Hoberman

3. The intrusion of the subject's hand in the frame signifies the escalating intensity of the hard-core action that remains unseen. The slightest transformation of compositional elements constructs not only a cinematic but a pornographic "event." From *Blow Job*, courtesy of the Andy Warhol Museum, Pittsburgh, Pennsylvaia, a museum of the Carnegie Institute.

continues: "When the subject's hand intrudes to scratch his nose, it's like the introduction of a new character—an event" (182). In a similar vein, Douglas Crimp argues that "what defines 'happening,' what counts as incident, event, even narrative, what we see and notice and think about is very different in a film like *Blow Job* than in other kinds of films we've seen" (1996, 114). *Blow Job* transforms what is most often considered peripheral to the erotic experience into the sexual spectacle itself. Furthermore, by projecting the film at silent speed, Warhol recuperates those details ordinarily traversed rapidly in the pornographic presentation of pleasure.

I do not wish to privilege the film's moments of negation and repudiation at the expense of considering those aspects of *Blow Job* that *assert*, rather than *withhold*, sexual and aesthetic pleasure. Rather than regarding *Blow Job* as having failed porn's quest to offer proof of sexual pleasure, we must consider the possibility of alternative pleasures made available by the film. *Blow Job* does deliver proof of sexual pleasure, only via a code so completely antithetical to conventions of hard-core representation that it has become almost unrecognizable to contemporary audiences. The film resignifies the pornographic image by exploring pleasure's intimate relationship to duration, deferral, boredom, and, ultimately, dissatisfaction. By solely regarding *Blow Job* as *destructive*, or deconstructive, of the expectations of temporal coincidence and visibility in pornography, we fail to recognize that the film was, and is, *productive* of a new kind of erotic plenitude.

This erotic plenitude is, necessarily, subject to definition. One of the primary interests of this essay is to investigate the pleasures of looking at the face as a kind of visual pornography. Long considered to reveal the internal struggles of the subject, the face is often cited, in reflections on film and other visual media, as an instrument of unmediated access to psychological interiority. The relationship between portraiture and porn proves particularly compelling: both traditions are invested in accessing the hidden truth of the subject, albeit through different visual means. Pornography radically redefines the relation of the face to interiority; it interpellates the face not as proof of the soul, but as proof of the pleasures of the body. *Blow Job*, as a pornographic portrait, complicates this relation even further. By analyzing the face in *Blow Job*, determining what is revealed and withheld, I shall attempt to articulate the relations between visual pleasure, pornography, and the portrait.

The crucial difference between *Blow Job* and mainstream gay and straight pornography can be located in what we could call the different "face-work" mobilized by each product. Whereas mainstream pornography has traditionally relied on facial gestures to signal the moment of orgasm, the ecstatic face is treated as merely one register of pleasure in hard-core's mise-en-scène. The face, in other words, is displayed in addition to the throbbing genitals and ejaculating penis as a supplemental marker of authenticity. In the hard-core pornography that comes after *Blow Job*, the facial expression anticipates and then confirms what is ultimately the genitals' job to prove.[19] On the contrary, *Blow Job* supplants genital "proof" with the grimaces of the face; the mise-en-scène of the film consists entirely of the face. In *Blow Job*, face-work is not supplemental to the genital action—it *is* the action.

The Perversion of Narrative According to Freud

Despite the long-standing artistic tradition of showing ecstasy in the face, from Bernini's sculpture of Saint Teresa to close-ups of Jeanne Moreau in *The Lovers* (dir. Louis Malle, 1958), Warhol's insistence on the face borders on perversity. In *Three Essays on the Theory of Sexuality*, Freud defines perversions as "sexual activities which either (*a*) extend, in an anatomical sense, beyond the regions of the body that are designed for sexual union; or (*b*) linger over the intermediate relations to the sexual object which should normally be traversed rapidly on the path towards the final sexual aim (2000, 16). *Blow Job* does not merely extend the visual focus of the film to nongenital regions of the body. In fact, the film entirely substitutes nongenital space for the genital action to which its title refers. The entire film is devoted to the significance of a nongenital part of the body, as if the face contained as many erotic possibilities as the penis. In hard-core pornography, the face of a performer in the throes of sexual ecstasy is important for establishing the action of the sexual number. However, it is presumed that the image of the face will be, as Freud puts it, "traversed rapidly on the path towards the final sexual aim."

Blow Job not only lingers but literally "gets stuck" in the perverse space of nongenital happening. The film is a reflection on the missing "meat shot," or the display of genital penetration. According to Linda Williams, the meat shot constitutes the "quintessential stag film shot: a close-up of penetration that shows that hard-core sexual activity is taking place" (72). The meat shot is the expression of what Freud would call normal, rather than perverse, sexuality: it is proof of the achievement of genital union. While feature-length pornography since the 1970s has incorporated the meat shot as only one (albeit important) step along the way to firmer narrative proof of sexual satisfaction (the "money shot," or ejaculating penis), during the era of the stag, the meat shot signaled the zenith of narrative activity.

Historically, *Blow Job* is situated slightly before the transition from meat to money, from stag films to feature-length hard-core films. Although the money shot was not yet a popular convention in pornography, *Blow Job*'s occlusion of the sight of the penis certainly constitutes a deliberate choice to frustrate the audience. Keeping the genitals off-screen when the title of the film so titillatingly implied the penis's on/scenity was, indeed, a sign of the times, but the cruelty of the prank exceeded historical necessity. Waugh evokes Warhol the "cockteaser," explaining that the director "coined titles that served to lure prospective audiences with a promise, or merely a *tease*" (1996a, 51). Waugh urges viewers to situate Warhol's work historically, to recall an era in which "the promise of gratification was routinely deferred and rarely fulfilled" for gay porno consumers accustomed to snatching pleasure from the perusal of officially noneroic art or exercise instructions (61–62). Nevertheless, close-ups of male genitals—like the kind so conspicuously missing in *Blow Job*—were not entirely absent from the spectrum of gay pornographic production. Although "explicit sexual photos were rare compared to physique nudes and beefcake," Waugh, in his book *Hard to Imagine*, notes that illicit photography did take up the "crotch shot close-up" around the thirties. While these close-up shots never became as popular with underground consumers as the "long symmetrical compositions of the partouze sensibility," they did remain in circulation and would have been available to someone like Warhol without much difficulty (1996b, 324).

In many ways, *Blow Job*'s presentation of the sexual show is closer to the stag tradition than it is to the post-1970s incarnation of the genre with which we are more familiar. Like much of the work produced at the Factory, *Blow Job* mimics the primitivism of stag films: the film is silent, without color, has limited narrative action, and lacks the identification of the star or any of the crew.[20] This should not surprise us; technically, the film does come almost a decade before the on/scene explosion of feature-length hard-core film in the early seventies. Nevertheless, *Blow Job* cannot be read as complying with the conventions of sexual representation in the stag film either. Not only is *Blow Job* twice as long as the longest stag film, but the absence of any evidence of genital penetration aligns *Blow Job* with the surreptitious turn-on of the mail-order physique loops popular with gay audiences from 1950 to 1970. As Waugh so perceptively argues, the bare-bones posing of these primitive physique loops prefigured the "minimal structure, duration and 'meta-genre'" experiments by Warhol.

Freud would deem many of the pleasures available to gay audiences in the early sixties perverse. In his early discussion of fetishism in *Three Essays*, he defines fetishism as those cases in which "the normal sexual object is replaced by another which bears some relation to it, but is entirely unsuited to serve the normal sexual aim" (2000, 19). Since Freud's conception of the normal sexual aim is limited to genital contact, rapt or excessive attention to those parts of the body that surpass his formulation is inevitably deemed perverse. Freud writes, "The situation only becomes pathological when the longing for the fetish passes beyond the point of being merely a necessary condition attached to the sexual object and actually takes the place of the normal aim" (20). He never takes into account the possibility that excessive focus on nongenital parts of the body may develop from historical circumstances, in which access to the genitals is precluded by law, censorship, or social taboos. For Freud, perversion is defined as any type of extension or dilation of sexuality that supplants the genitals as its primary focus.

In this sense, *Blow Job* is not only a perverse film but a film that takes on the subject of perversion as the organizing principle of its narrative and visual structure. We do see something in *Blow Job*, but it is neither what we expect to see, nor what we desire to see. The film fails to deliver the sight of the penis, as well as the site of oral penetration. In the place of genital activity, the film offers a face. Hard-core's dual regime of maximum visibility and temporal coincidence can be aligned with Freud's theory of normative sexuality. Hard-core delivers the genital event as the norm of sexuality, within a time frame that avoids unnecessarily lingering over "irrelevant" spaces of the body. The spectator of *Blow Job*, however, misses not only the sight of sexual climax but the temporal awareness of it as well. We are notified of sexual climax only after the fact. Struggle as we may to reconstruct the moment of orgasm, its precise location in time remains impossible to retrieve. Whereas later hard-core features would provide the audience with the well-timed, well-lit money shot, *Blow Job* only offers the postorgasmic smoking of a cigarette. Whereas hard-core porn shows you dick, *Blow Job* only gives you head.

Problematic as it may now seem, the perverse collisions of avant-garde art and pornography in the sixties had begun to seem inevitable to their observers. For Stephen Koch, the uncomfortable marriage of avant-garde and pornographic modes of address was "an inevitable consequence of Warhol's mind" (1973, 49). Similarly, Hoberman writes, "The trajectory of Warhol's film career leads inexorably toward pornography, which back in the early '60s scarcely enjoyed the sanctioned existence it has today" (1991, 182). Although the "primacy of sexual representation in Warhol's oeuvre" cannot be underestimated (Waugh 1996a, 52), Hoberman's claim requires some unpacking. In what ways does Warhol's work "lead inexorably toward pornography," and how is this "drive" simultaneously resisted by Warhol's actual films?

Blow Job may have the most explicit title of Warhol's early cinema, but the film is not unique in focusing exclusively on a discrete bodily activity. "At the time he made *Blow Job*," Koch writes, "Warhol was involved in a model of desire that might have made him the most interesting pornographer of the century—certainly an ambition he entertained and cherished on a grand scale" (1973, 49). How exactly can we characterize Warhol's "model of desire" in the early films? *Kiss*, *Sleep*, and *Eat*—made the same year as *Blow Job*—all pare down the visual and narrative field to concentrate on a single bodily "event." Indeed, many of the elements of pornography already exist in Warhol's first year of filmmaking: a close-up of couples kissing (*Kiss*), the contemplation of a nude man in bed (*Sleep*), and the focus on "low" activities of the body (*Eat*). "Orality is a constant theme of the silents," writes Paul

Arthur (1989, 150); as is the locus of the bed or couch as a kind of pornographic space.

Arthur has noted that "the appeal to certain bodily sensations" in Warhol's early cinema "becomes almost pornographically direct" (150). Warhol admitted as much during his lifetime. In his discussion of the nude theater craze that hit San Francisco in 1969, the artist wrote, "I'd always wanted to do a movie that was pure fucking, nothing else, the way *Eat* had been just eating and *Sleep* had been just sleeping" (Warhol and Hackett 1980, 294). In this comment, Warhol reveals the pornographic gaze that mobilizes his early films. He confesses his obsessive desire to record "the 'thing' itself" (Williams 1989, 49), to focus on a singular bodily activity without distraction. What appears to be missing from Warhol's autopsy of pornography, however, is the phallus, yet this only holds true if we restrict our discussion of pornography to the Warhol films that involve human characters. Warhol's fixed-shot minimalist epic of the Empire State Building (*Empire*, 1964) amounts to an eight-hour hard-on, supplying more uninterrupted phallus than any but the most tireless spectator could endure.

Despite the "pornographically direct" gaze of Warhol's camera on bodily sensations, an important psychoanalytic difference exists between the structure of Warhol's early films and mainstream pornography. In *Three Essays*, Freud writes: "Perhaps the sexual instinct may itself be no simple thing, but put together from components which have come apart again in the perversions" (2000, 28). In Williams's discussion of sexual numbers in hardcore porn, she notes that "a little something is offered to satisfy a diverse, but not all-inclusive, range of sexual tastes" (1989, 126). Hard-core porn is interested in resolving the often contradictory parts of sexual spectacle into a unified whole. "Although built on the premise that the pleasure of sex is self-evident," Williams observes, "the underlying and motivating anxiety [of hard core] is that sometimes it is not." She concludes, "Out of this contradiction comes the need for a combined solution of narrative and number" (134). Hard-core desperately seeks to keep intact the sexual instinct. The genre's combination of narrative and number, as well as the integration of diverse sexual performances into a unified whole, aligns hard core with Freud's notion of normative sexuality. Warhol's early films, on the other hand, attempt to dissolve the sexual instinct back into its component parts. A list of Warhol's early films reads like a catalogue of perversions; each film devotes itself to an activity that has been severed from its relations to the other component parts of the sexual instinct. In Warhol's films, the integration of narrative and number is virtually nonexistent; the number is the narrative.

When Hoberman writes, "Warhol's film career leads inexorably toward pornography," it is as if he imagines all of Warhol's component parts coming together to re-form the sexual instinct that has come apart.

Portraiture and Porn: The Erotics of Knowledge

Rather than "being preparatory to the normal sexual aim," the pleasure of looking at the face in *Blow Job* "supplants" the genital gaze of hard-core pornography. However, while this diversion may initially strike the (non–face fetishizing) viewer as perverse and frustrating, Warhol's strategy calls attention to the often overlooked erotics of the face. Instead of regarding *Blow Job* as the embodiment of the failure of normative sexuality that Freud describes, I contend that the film presents a different, but equally suggestive, kind of erotic presence. The face that has been substituted for the genitals in Warhol's film is, indeed, endowed. Jonathan Flatley observes that "the promise enacted by the title leads us to read the pleasure of the blow job into the face" (1996, 125). As a result, the slightest grimaces of the face take on both a pornographic and an aesthetic fascination, superimposing the prurient gaze on the artistic one. Wayne Koestenbaum astutely and elegantly points out the ways in which Warhol's work "respects the pornographic impulse to build an archive of hunger's object," recognizing "that each body needs to be documented, for every man possesses an individuating detail—a pattern of hairs on the arm, a slope of the nose, a sufficiency of the lips" (2001, 42). Against our initial frustration at the camera's inflexibility, we catch ourselves enraptured by the idiosyncrasies of the image.

In his essay about *Blow Job*, Douglas Crimp argues for the "sexiness" of the film on the basis of its erotic "face value" (1996, 114). Rather than concentrating on what the frame leaves out—what we do not see—Crimp makes a compelling case for the "sumptuous beauty" of the face that we do see (114). Crimp's close reading of the anonymous performer's face pays detailed attention to the subtle gestures, expressions, and contortions to which we, as observers, are privy. He also suggests that it may be more useful to situate *Blow Job* outside of the pornographic moving-image tradition and inside the tradition of artistic portraiture (118). Crimp's insight concerning the usefulness of portraiture as a model within which to contextualize *Blow Job* is crucial. Nevertheless, Crimp here, perhaps unwittingly, asserts the need for a rigid dichotomy of cultural products, in which porn and art are erected as mutually exclusive categories. (*If* we are to situate *Blow Job* within the tradition of portraiture, Crimp implicitly argues, *then* we must wrest it from the tradition of pornography.)

Koestenbaum compares the face of our fellatee to Maria Falconetti's expressive visage in Carl Theodor Dreyer's 1928 film *The Passion of Joan of Arc*, remarking how both portraits more closely resemble paintings than films (2001, 84). While Koestenbaum should never be accused of minimizing the sexual dimension of Warhol's work—in fact, quite the opposite is true of his seductive biography—it would be easy to imagine a situation in which this type of comparison could result in the sacralization of *Blow Job*, rather than the eroticization of *Joan of Arc*. Unfortunately, critics invested in breaching the divide between high and low often attempt to do so by exalting the "degraded" object to the status of high art, thus "redeeming" it from the trash heap to which it was relegated. To me, the opposite transformation seems more compelling. Rather than sacralizing the pornographic in an attempt to legitimize it, it seems more productive to consider the degree to which even enlightened works of so-called high art partake of a pornographic imagination. Why shouldn't we consider the possibility that the intense suffering inscribed on Falconetti's face in Dreyer's silent masterpiece could turn spectators on?

Blow Job forces us to recognize that a single text may participate in multiple histories, genres, and traditions simultaneously, as it calls forth divergent and often contradictory codes and practices via its presentation. Rather than dividing the history of porn from the history of portraiture, it is more productive to *juxtapose* these two traditions, to compare them as parallel attempts to access the interiority of the subject through visual representation and the power/pleasure dynamic. Portraiture is not without its own libidinal yield; one must only think of Edouard Manet's painting of Olympia to visualize this blurring of generic boundaries.

Tony Rayns, in an essay entitled "Andy's hand-jobs," relates Warhol's work to what he calls an "erotics of detachment," in which the prurient element of portraiture proves central (1997, 83–87). Detachment, however, may not be the most accurate way to characterize the effect of the portrait on its observers. The intertwined histories of painting and photography remain beyond the scope of this essay, but we can observe that close-ups of the face have been instrumental to both the history of cinema and the history of film theory. Written nearly half a century ago, Béla Balázs's formulation of the close-up still remains the most compelling account of the effects that film portraits have on spectators. With the advent of the close-up as a cinematic technique, film was able to show the spectator "the hidden life of little things" (Balázs 1952, 54). For Balázs, close-ups of the human face—especially Maria Falconetti's, his most insistent example—made for indispensable tools with which to access psychological interiority—"dramatic revelations of what is really happening under the surfaces of appearances" (56). By focusing on the human face, and magnifying it to larger-than-life proportions, Balázs believed that cinema close-ups revealed subconscious feelings otherwise inaccessible. For Balázs, the close-up of the human face advanced the quest for human knowledge that has been integral to the discursive inscription of the cinematic apparatus. Balázs theorized that the close-up possessed the ability to divulge the meanings behind the intricate play of facial features, rendering "objective" the "most subjective and individual of human manifestations" (60).

Through the "microphysiognomy" of the face, amplified by the close-up on the cinema screen, Balázs claimed to be able to "see to the bottom of the soul by means of such tiny movements of facial muscles which even the most observant partner would never perceive" (63). For Balázs, unconscious, uncontrollable twitches of the face prove especially important for registering what he calls "passions" (72). He writes, "The most rapid tempo of speech lags behind the *flow and throb* of emotions; but facial expression can always keep up with them, providing a faithful and intelligible expression for them all" (72; emphasis added). Balázs defines the close-up of the human face as a kind of unwilling confession of interiority otherwise inaccessible through language. The close-up is erected as proof of the innermost workings of the subject. According to Balázs, that which is not "utterable" in language can be articulated only through the involuntary convulsions of the body—most notably and significantly, in the twitches of the face. Balázs was most interested in "certain regions of the face which are scarcely or not at all under voluntary control and the expression of which is neither deliberate nor conscious and may often betray emotions that contradict the general expression appearing on the rest of the face" (74). The close-up removes the mask of false expression and reveals the "truth" of the subject. Like pornography, the close-up is animated by a drive for knowledge about the subject. We can even detect in Balázs's writing (particularly in his suggestive use of words such as *flow* and *throb*) the movement toward what Williams calls the "out-of-control confession of pleasure, a hard core 'frenzy of the visible'" that characterizes pornography (1989, 50). Moving-image porn and portraiture share an epistemology of the body, or a will to knowledge. For both traditions, the moment of convulsion signifies the bodily confession of truth.

Recuperating Aura: Specters of Distance,
Allegories of Proximity

The pleasures of watching the face in close-up are akin to the pleasures of watching the body in thrall. For Balázs, the face becomes a type of genital space on which an observer can witness the confession of the truth of subjectivity. Although Balázs claims that his interest in the close-up revolves around what it can tell us about the "soul" of man (interestingly, most of his examples are not of men's faces, but of women's), he employs distinctly corporeal metaphors. In this way, Balázs's project resembles Warhol's. Balázs attempts to read the close-up epistemologically; in his text, the face is transformed into an endless source of knowledge about the subject. By "reading the face" as if it were a text, Balázs aims to "take possession" of the subject's interiority. Warhol's early film experiments challenge precisely the kind of knowing to which Balázs aspires. Like Balázs, Warhol inscribes his challenge on the body of the subject—in this case, the performer. For Warhol, however, the body is presented in order to *refuse* access to the subject's interiority. While Warhol's framing asks the spectator to treat the face as if endowed with genital meaning, the actual lighting of the film prevents the spectator from taking possession of the object through looking. Crimp analyzes this phenomenon in great detail: "Warhol's camera captures this face and the sensation it registers, but simultaneously withholds it from us; and he does this through a simple positioning of the light, as if, by chance, a bare light bulb hung from the ceiling just above and slightly to the left of the scene. We cannot make eye contact" (1996, 115).

Rather than viewing the effects of the obscure lighting as a kind of withholding of voyeuristic pleasure, as Crimp does, I interpret this with a slightly different, Benjaminian emphasis. In his classic essay "The Work of Art in the Age of Mechanical Reproduction," Walter Benjamin defines that elusive quality known as the "aura" as "the unique phenomenon of a distance, however close [the object] may be" (1968, 222). According to Benjamin, the aura of a work of art "withers" in the age of mechanical reproduction because of the "desire of the contemporary masses to bring things 'closer' spatially and humanly" (222–23). He writes, "Every day the urge grows stronger to get hold of an object at very close range by way of its likeness, its reproduction" (223). Benjamin's discussion of aura may prove extraordinarily useful to a discussion of pornography. The history of porn can be described as the history of the attempt to bring the object of sexual pleasure closer "spatially and humanly." In this sense, hard core can be read as the most compelling generic example of the contemporary masses' wish to bring the object of desire—in this case, the body in the throes of sexual ecstasy—closer in order to achieve access to the subject's innermost corporeal secrets.

Perhaps *Blow Job* attempts to restore the aura previously lost in the representation of sexual pleasure. By reinstating the forfeited sense of distance-in-proximity, *Blow Job* gives us something *more*, rather than something *less*, than hard-core porn. Michael O'Pray has written that Warhol "attacked the aura of art" (1989, 10), and while this claim may accurately inform many of his paintings and silk screens, it does not seem to hold true for an analysis of his films. By lighting the face from above, as Crimp has observed, Warhol casts the face of the anonymous man—especially the eyes—in deep shadow. Crimp writes, "If there is any sense of frustration in *Blow Job*, it derives, I think, not from not seeing the sexual act—we really don't expect to—but from not being truly able to see the man's face" (1996, 115).

By withholding the "maximum visibility" of the object on two levels, Warhol reintroduced the aura of sexual pleasure to the image. Not only did Warhol make the image of sexual penetration unavailable to the viewer; he also made the object that stood in as substitute notoriously hard to grasp. Benjamin observed that early photographs constituted the last refuge for the aura potentially emanating from a human face (1968, 226). Perhaps Warhol's strange primitivism is able to recapture some trace of the mood inscribed in early photography, "heightened with the mystique of an ungraspable aura" (Shaviro 1993, 212). By transforming the representation of the sexual act into an elusive, shadowy portrait, Warhol offered his audience the suggestive distance from the object that they had lost through the ubiquity of the mass-media image.

Shot at sound speed but projected at silent speed (Angell 1994, 9), deprived of the human sounds that accompany sexual satisfaction—and are so important to authenticating pleasure in hard-core porn and so conspicuously absent in stag movies—*Blow Job* succeeds in making the representation of the sexual act strange. Slow motion has the effect of distancing the viewer from the object by reducing the field of action to an otherworldly pace in which the continuity of motion is uncannily disturbed. Like early silent films, *Blow Job* transforms movement into drift, continuity into a succession of jolts and spasms, and presence into absence. The tempo of the film empties the body on screen of its vitality; the face is made ghostly by the shadows that surround it and the pulse that fails to animate it. Slow motion allows the viewer to experience distance as a lapse in time, a temporal distinction between the world of the viewer and the world of the image. *Blow*

Job shows the face in close-up—bringing the object into the foreground—but at the same time, the film makes the action, and the face itself, seem far away. We cannot quite make out the face we are presumably staring at, we cannot hear the noises that the face and body emit, and the movements of the face appear in modest slow motion, as if they are happening at a great distance from us.

Labor, Boredom, Bliss

What is the relationship between aura and the erotic, between distance and sexual pleasure? Is the perception of aura pleasurable for an observer of pornography? What sensations do viewers have when they watch *Blow Job*, and how do these sensations differ from those we experience when watching sexual representations more accessible to us?

The most commonly articulated response to watching *Blow Job* is boredom. However, this claim is neither as transparent nor as universal as it appears. What does it mean to be bored by an image, and are *boredom* and *pleasure* mutually exclusive terms? (See Zabet Patterson's essay in this volume for some interesting answers to these questions in relation to cyberporn.) Does *Blow Job* move its audience and, if so, how? Rex Reed relates an anecdote, in which Warhol decided to screen *Blow Job* at Columbia University in 1966, worth quoting at length. He writes,

> The audience sat attentively during the first few minutes of the film, which showed a boy's face. That's all. Just a face. But something was obviously happening down below, out of camera range. The audience got restless. . . . Some of them began to sing "We Shall Never Come." They finally began to yell things at the screen, most of them unprintable. Total chaos finally broke out when one voice (a girl's) screamed: "We came to see a blow job, and we stayed to get screwed!" Tomatoes and eggs were thrown at the screen; Warhol was whisked away to safety through the raging, jeering, angry mob and rushed to a waiting car. (Qtd. in Bockris 1989, 210)

Clearly, this audience had been moved to a frenzy, in which its members literally could not control their outbursts. In her book *Excitable Speech*, Judith Butler writes, "Indeed, it may be that what is unanticipated about the injurious speech act [substitute, injurious film act] is what constitutes its injury, the sense of putting its addressee out of control" (1997, 4). Thirty years after its initial release, Crimp was able to write, "These days, when we see Andy Warhol's *Blow Job*, we have no expectation of really seeing the act of fellatio the film's title announces" (111). In 1966, this was not always the case. Audiences expected to see the act of fellatio and were often enraged when the film denied them this vision. The sense of injury—of "getting screwed"—experienced by historical audiences was inseparable from the anticipation of the sexual display. Although this kind of reaction is not the kind sought after in hard-core porn,[21] on a certain level, the spectators' rage very much evidences their own "convulsive" passion. The audience experienced the lack of any real sexual content in Warhol's film as a kind of impossible distance. Does this mean that the experience was not pleasurable—that the joys of hollering at the screen, ejaculating tomatoes and egg, and literally engulfing the director were nonexistent?

In an interview in 1967, Warhol discussed the effect his earlier films had on audiences: "[They] were made to help the audience get more acquainted with themselves. Usually when you go to the movies, you sit in a fantasy world, but when you see something that disturbs you, you get more involved with the people next to you. . . . You could do more things watching my movies than with other kinds of movies; you could eat and drink and smoke and cough and look away and then look back and they'd still be there" (qtd. in Berg 1989, 58). Warhol's observations about the unusual activity of his films' audiences prove revealing with regard to the status of intersubjectivity in his work. Contrary to the disciplined, motionless audience we incorrectly imagine as viewers of Warhol's cinema—and to which we, as critics, often belong—Warhol and Reed describe an audience very literally moved by the image on-screen. While the type of activities described by Warhol (eating, drinking, smoking, and talking) clearly do not equal the involuntary movements activated by "body genres,"[22] avant-garde films also have the capacity to move their audience in multiple ways.

In his essay about Scott Stark's film NOEMA (1998) (in this volume), Michael Sicinski argues for the centrality of the laboring body in pornography. Whereas Stark's film foregrounds the laboring body within the frame (the porn performer), Warhol's cinema often calls attention to the laboring body in the audience (the film spectator). Although many of Warhol's early films are straightforward (*Eat* is *really* about a man eating, *Sleep* is *really* about a man sleeping), they are not "easy" or unambiguous. By refusing so many of the conventions of mainstream cinema (and, as we have seen, the conventions of other "predictable" genres like pornography), Warhol's films compel spectators to "find their own way," to entertain themselves when bored, to make sense of conflicting modes of address, and to sustain physically demanding exercises in duration. *Blow Job*, in other words, makes us *work*. The action promised by the title is implied but never so much as glimpsed; if spectators leave the theater with the impression of having "watched" a blow job (and certainly not everyone does), then this results from the spectator's own perceptual labor. *Blow Job* moves its observer to produce the image of the fellatio that is not recorded, and that may not even have existed.

Tony Rayns describes the tendency of viewers "to mentally edit or redirect movies, to take from them what's interesting, exciting or sexy and to repress or ignore the rest" (1997, 84). Similarly, David Ehrenstein writes, "The pornographic audience partakes of certain images, ignores others, annexes others. The pornographic film is in a continual state of re-editing" (65). If we are to believe these critics' claims, then the observer of *Blow Job* must be a particularly skilled laborer, not only as an editor but also as a cameraperson. *Blow Job*'s spectator must be capable not only of editing out all that is tedious in the film but also of actually lowering the camera in his or her mind in order to see below the frame. Crimp, however, takes a different view of the situation. Rather than regarding the activity of the spectator as a compulsion to visualize what is not there, he views the experience of watching *Blow Job* as liberating. Rather than describing an experience of frustration or boredom, he limns an unparalleled sense of freedom in which the spectator is "freed to look differently" (1996, 114).

While I appreciate Crimp's thoughtful and compelling reevaluation of *Blow Job*, I am again not certain that boredom and pleasure need to be formulated as mutually exclusive categories. I find it particularly compelling to locate Warhol's work at the site of exchange between these two experiences. Warhol writes, "I've been quoted a lot as saying, 'I like boring things.' Well, I said it and I meant it. But that doesn't mean I'm not bored by them" (Warhol and Hackett 1980, 50). Both pornography and the avant-garde are often accused of being boring; conversely, avid fans of either genre often defend the films by denying these claims. In both cases, the division between boredom and pleasure is perceived as intransigent. Rather than regarding pleasure as something achieved when boredom is bracketed, I would argue that the pleasure of the Warhol text—and possibly of much of pornography and the avant-garde—inseparably derives from the experience of boredom. Stephen Koch writes,

> It is interesting that so many people complain that pornography is boring. *It is boring*, of course; anyone who has ever tried to do more than dabble in it knows how boring it is. Yet it is also passionately interesting. It seems

to me that pornography is dull because it is dull to wait—and pornography requires us to wait. . . . Pornography is a patient art. Those who speak of its immediacy are speaking in very considerable confusion. Those who speak of its excitement are being evasive with half truth. *The experience of not being excited* is just as important. Watching, one sits through a vague dissociated sexual awareness, incessantly examining one's own responses, wondering when the thrill will come, why one doesn't feel it here or there, searching for the well-springs of arousal. . . . *While waiting one invents* (1973, 50–51; emphasis mine).

Boredom is thought to occur when either the body or the mind (or, in the worst case, both) is not sufficiently occupied. Patrice Petro observes that boredom is "typically thought to describe a subjective experience—a time without event, when nothing happens, a seemingly endless flux without beginning or end" (1995, 265). Petro, like Koch, associates boredom with waiting and "the expectation of future orientation of subjectivity devoid of anxiety and alienation" (Petro 1995, 270). Waiting, however, does not imply the bracketing of possibility. Rather, boredom invites speculation and the imagined posturing of desire. Along these lines, the French theorist Michèle Huguet has observed that "the subject experiencing boredom is not suffering from an absence of desire, but from its indetermination, which in turn forces the subject to wander, in search of a point of fixation" (qtd. in Petro 1995, 271). Rather than designating a mode of subjectivity bereft of stimulation, boredom may imply "an anxiety of abundance," an overstimulation of both body and mind that constitutes a typical condition of modernity (Petro 1995, 271). Much has been written about the effect of this kind of sensory abundance on subjectivity, but none of it sufficiently addresses boredom's very tangible effect on the body—its corporeal impressions. Jonathan Crary has argued that the collapse of the camera obscura model of vision inserted the human body—with all of its imperfections and idiosyncrasies—into discourses and practices of vision. He writes: "The body that had been a neutral or invisible term in vision was now the thickness from which knowledge of the observer was obtained" (1999, 150). At no time is Crary's insight about the thickness of the body more apparent than when the subject is overcome by boredom. Boredom renders the thickness of the body and the density of the mind excruciatingly palpable. It is precisely when we find ourselves bored that we are most aware of our own "carnal density"—of the turgidity of our thighs, the heaviness of our eyelids, and the dull but unbearable pulsing of genitals. Like pornography, "boring" experimental films such as *Blow*

Job return us to our bodies, impregnating us with apprehension, imagination, and desire. When we are bored, our minds are saturated with thought: we *feel* ourselves thinking.

In mainstream hard-core pornography, the seemingly endless repetition of predictable outcomes induces boredom; the sense of knowing how each sexual number will end, imbues the spectator with a simultaneous sense of monotony and arousal. For avant-garde spectators, boredom often intervenes when, to borrow from Ivone Margulies, "nothing happens" (1996). Whereas the boredom of pornography seems to derive from its uninterrupted and sustained fullness, the ennui of the avant-garde is often generated by the lack (or perceived absence) of narrative event or conventional character development. Can we compare the boredom of satiety with the monotony of lack? Do these two seemingly antithetical categories interact phenomenologically? While waiting, what does one invent?

It would prove too facile an interpretative gesture to conclude that while waiting, the observer transforms what is "wrong" with the pornographic mise-en-scène of plenitude and supplies what is "missing" from avant-garde minimalism. Although the boredom generated by pornography and the ennui generated by the avant-garde are not the same, they come together in Warhol's film *Blow Job* to produce a sustained simultaneity of sexual fullness and structural lack. Roland Barthes cryptically observed that "boredom is not far from bliss: it is bliss seen from the shores of pleasure" (1975, 26). Boredom, in other words, is the bliss experienced while one is pleasured; it is the simultaneity of experience and perception rendered banal by the gesture of fulfillment. By endlessly deferring the gesture of fulfillment (recognized in later hard core as the money shot), *Blow Job* expands the temporality of bliss ad infinitum, stranding the spectator on the excruciating shores of pleasure, in the extraordinary space of the unfulfilled.

Notes

1. In their book *Midnight Movies*, J. Hoberman and Jonathan Rosenbaum state that this screening actually occurred in the summer of 1964 (1983, 62).
2. According to Warhol's biographer Victor Bockris, Kligman—who had been Jackson Pollock's girlfriend and had been in the car with Pollock when he died— expressed both disgust and confusion in regards to the screening: "I showed the film but I didn't like it. Even the word *blow job* offended me. There were all these strange people I couldn't relate to who were all on speed. And there was a kind of prurience I didn't like"(qtd. in Bockris 1989, 149).

3 The first time the New York City police seized one of Warhol's films occurred in March 1964. His three-minute newsreel entitled *Andy Warhol Films Jack Smith Filming "Normal Love"* was mistaken for one of Smith's own films (Warhol and Hackett 1980, 79).

4 Like many of Warhol's films, *Blow Job* was also casually screened at the Factory in a manner that evokes the atmosphere of a post–Thanksgiving dinner home-movie screening (albeit one attended by speed queens and aspiring socialites). In her rather snide memoirs, Warhol superstar Ultra Violet recalls the time she "jump[ed] at the chance to attend a screening of *Blow Job*," in the fall of 1964 at the Factory (1988, 31). She reminisces: "On a Sunday night the audience assembles in the dimly lit Factory, on and around the battered couch, which is so piled with bodies that it looks like a lifeboat. The images . . . are projected onto a white sheet hung between two silvery pillars" (31). Ultra Violet (née Isabelle Collin Dufresne) describes the experience as "mind-numbing" (32). She writes, "I see faces in the audience moving up and down in sync with the unseen protagonist. Is that what you call audience participation? . . . I begin to long for an explosion to bring an end to this submissive—what can I call it? Treatment" (32). Despite Ultra Violet's insistence on her own lack of response to the film ("I'm not for it or against it. I'm not repelled, not attracted, not indifferent, not captivated" [32]), she later admits that "among the girls [at the Factory] we talk about *Blow Job* for days. It takes us a while to recover" (34). According to Ultra Violet, Ingrid Superstar (reputedly considered the "retarded Superstar"—see Koestenbaum 2001, 120) supposedly even went so far as to demand, "what's avant-garde about two fairies sucking?" (34). Although I don't know how the author could have remembered this bit of dialogue nearly twenty-five years after it was spoken, the question itself reveals how the collision of the vanguard with the pornographic in Warhol's films made even the filmmaker's own cadre of hipsters uncharacteristically uncomfortable.

5 Most contemporary discussions of the segregation between the avant-garde and low forms of mass culture begin with Clement Greenberg's important, albeit polemic, essay from 1939, "Avant-Garde and Kitsch." Although Greenberg's distinction between kitsch and the avant-garde fails to take into account the significant ways in which these traditions intersect, this bifurcation has remained one of the most persistent legacies of aesthetic modernism. Lawrence Levine argues that the aggressive separation between the high and the low was instituted in cultural practice by the end of the nineteenth century. Interestingly, Linda Williams claims that by this same period, the observer of the avant-garde and the consumer of low culture both shared a similar experience of spectatorship. Building on the work of Jonathan Crary, she writes, "The loss of perspective of the camera obscura model of vision plunged both the high-modern and the low-popular observer into a 'newly corporealized' immediacy of sensations" (Williams 1995a, 7; Crary 1999). By the sixties, the distinction between high and low became even more problematic than it had ever been before; Andy Warhol

is only one of the many artists whose work breached the boundaries between the high and the low. See Banes 1993 for a more complete description of avant-garde artists who employed low or popular techniques in the early sixties.

6   Warhol boasts of his love of pornography on several occasions. In *POPism*, he writes, "Personally, I loved porno and I bought lots of it all the time—the really dirty, exciting stuff. All you had to do was figure out what turned you on, and then just buy the dirty magazines and movie prints that are right for you, the way you'd go for the right pills or the right cans of food" (Warhol and Hackett 1980, 294). When interviewer Leticia Kent asked Warhol about *Blue Movie*, which had recently been declared hard-core pornography, Warhol insisted that the "misty color" he used while filming made it "soft," rather than "hard" core. He continued: "I think movies should appeal to prurient interests. . . . Movies should—uh—arouse you. . . . I really do think movies should arouse you, should get you excited about people, should be prurient" (Kent 1970, 204). When Warhol's film *Blow Job* was screened at the Park Cinema in Los Angeles alongside the sexploitation film *Nudist Beach Boy Surfers* in July of 1968, he must have been ecstatic. (See the illustration of the fantastic poster advertising this joint screening on page 69 [no pun intended] in Waugh 1996a.) As Warhol's collaborator Paul Morrissey admitted, "Degenerates are not such a great audience, but they're a step up from the art crowd; we would always rather play a sexploitation theatre than an art house" (qtd. in Waugh 1996a, 67).

7   See interview with Warhol quoted in Wayne Koestenbaum's brilliant biography, simply titled *Andy Warhol*. Characteristically deflecting the interviewer's question about his films being a kind of therapy, Warhol extols the splendors of the split beaver and the influence his films had on the beaver crowd (Koestenbaum 2001, 88).

8   Warhol continued to produce films throughout the seventies; many of the films Paul Morrissey directed under Warhol's name, including *Flesh*, *Trash*, *Heat*, *Flesh for Frankenstein*, and *Blood for Dracula* are still mistakenly attributed to Warhol.

9   Sally Banes argues that avant-garde film "had already become fashionable, co-opted by the mainstream" by 1965, even though the 1963–64 season (with films such as Jack Smith's *Flaming Creatures*, Kenneth Anger's *Scorpio Rising*, and Barbara Rubin's *Christmas on Earth*) had outraged the bourgeoisie, the critics, and the law (1993, 173). With Jonas Mekas standing in as experimental cinema's own minister of propaganda, Warhol film star Baby Jane Holzer christened as 1964's Girl of the Year, and the co-optation of underground themes and techniques by popular films like *Easy Rider* and *Midnight Cowboy*, the avant-garde was gaining momentum as a recognized and acceptable cultural force. Jonas Mekas himself commented on its transformation from "vanguard army" to institution. He writes, "By autumn . . . the magazines and the uptown decided to join the underground and make it part of the Establishment" (qtd. in Banes 1993, 173). By the end of the decade, the "strict censorship laws that had for several generations driven sexual content and other forms of 'obscenity' into hiding were being

gradually dismantled" (Banes 1993, 174), reconfiguring the cultural landscape in ways that had not yet materialized in the early sixties.

10   See Jonas Mekas's "Autobiographical Notes" in the appendix to James 1992.

11   The popularity of John Schlesinger's film *Midnight Cowboy* provides a perfect example of the type of cultural transformation that had occurred by 1969. Warhol himself writes that the film marked a crucial turning point in the history of film, when themes associated with the counterculture moved "right up into the mainstream of society," generating "mass commercial success" by saying and doing "radical things in a conservative format" (Warhol and Hackett 1980, 250). *Midnight Cowboy* had begun filming while Warhol was in the hospital recovering from a near fatal gunshot wound inflicted by Valerie Solanas. Before Warhol had been shot, Schlesinger had asked him to appear in the film, playing an under-ground filmmaker in the big party scene. Many Warhol superstars, including Geraldine Smith, Joe Dallesandro, Ondine, Pat Ast, Taylor Mead, Candy Darling, Jackie Curtis, Geri Miller, and Patti D'Arbanville were invited to participate in the film, but only Paul Morrissey, Viva, and Ultra Violet actually appeared in the final cut. Warhol admits to a certain jealousy about the entire project, and not only because he was in the hospital missing all the fun. Up until 1967, Warhol writes, "the underground was one of the only places people could hear about forbidden subjects and see realistic scenes of modern life" (280). With *Hair's* success on Broadway, and *Midnight Cowboy's* success at the box office, Warhol felt that mainstream society was moving into his territory. He had taken on the subject of the male prostitute as early as 1965, in his film *My Hustler*, and he felt that the "attitude" of the Hollywood version lacked the honesty of his own production. (This is one of the few times that Warhol extols the sincerity of one of his own products.) Hollywood's treatment of the hustler "looked better," but was "much less threatening" (280).

12   For a more complete history of the legal battles over sexually explicit cinemas, see Williams 1989, in addition to the aforementioned titles by Thomas Waugh and Jon Lewis.

13   See Koestenbaum's discussion of these drawings (2001, 41–48).

14   See Waugh 1996a, as well as his chapter "Art and Arousal" in Waugh 1996b. In both of these pieces, Waugh quite convincingly argues for Warhol's familiarity with both gay stag films and physique soft-core porn. Waugh also argues, in his chapter entitled "'(Oh Horror!) Those Filthy Photos': Illicit Photography and Film," that "a distinct gay illicit cinema" emerged as a historical possibility after 1960, noting that "a proliferation of about one hundred all-male stag films is documented" from this decade. These 8 mm porn films would have been avail-able in "dubious magazine shops in large urban areas," such as New York's Times Square neighborhood (1996b, 359–60). One of the films Waugh mentions, and which I have not been able to view, seems particularly interesting for contex-tualizing *Blow Job*, although it is unclear from his description how productive the juxtaposition of the two films would be. Waugh writes that *David 44* "appar-

ently from the early sixties, shows a promising interest in auto-fellatio and demonstrates through some curious syntax of simultaneous jerk-offs that gay porn need not have gone the historic route it would soon take: the formula of linear narratives leading inexorably to orgasmic release" (361). This brief description strikes me because of its suggestion of an alternative route for gay pornography that would not necessarily lead to a film like *Boys in the Sand* (dir. Wakefield Poole, 1971), but could encompass less linear, more autoerotic film experiments (like *Blow Job*?). Perhaps my imagination is overeager here.

15 *Blue Movie* is neither the only Warhol film in which genitals are visible, nor is it the only film to show the sex act: *Haircut* (1963), *Couch* (1964), *Tub Girls* (1967), and *Eating Too Fast* (1966) are also sexually explicit. The police seized *Blue Movie* in August 1969 after it had been screened at the Garrick Theater in New York. The next month, the film was ruled obscene (Koestenbaum 2001, 153, 156).

16 The video that I have watched most recently presents a version of the film slightly over thirty minutes in length. In print, I have seen references to a thirty-five-minute version (Koch 1973, 47) and a forty-one-minute version (Crimp 1996, 111). It is unclear to me whether these discrepancies constitute errors or whether several different versions of the film actually circulate.

17 Linda Williams argues that hard-core pornography involves a regime of temporality, as well as one of visibility. She explains, "Non-sadomasochistic pornography attempts to posit the utopian fantasy of perfect temporal coincidence: a subject and object (or seducer and seduced) who meet one another 'on time!' and 'now!' in shared moments of mutual pleasure that it is the special challenge of the genre to portray" (1995b, 154).

18 Video technology, as well as the existence of a bootleg videotape of the film (both of which were unavailable to the historical spectators of *Blow Job*), has allowed me to play and replay *Blow Job* at my own leisure and to my heart's content. Many times, I have searched for the moment in the film that signals orgasm, in the vain hope of determining the moment of bodily "truth" of the anonymous performer. Yet no matter how many times I replay the video, and how fixed to the screen I am, I have never been able to determine when and if the performer actually ejaculates. Certainly, I am not as familiar with the bodily codes of male orgasm as some, but it seems clear to me that even for the most educated ejaculators, this moment is impossible to ascertain.

19 According to Williams, the "principle of maximum visibility" operates in porn in order to deliver hard-core, authentic "proof" of the body in the throes of sexual pleasure. In hard-core porn, proof is demanded not only of the actual occurrence of genital penetration but of the body's involuntary, ecstatic response to it. The principles of maximum visibility originally included privileging the close-up over other shots, overlighting the genitals, and positioning the performers in order to best display bodies and organs, but they have expanded since the 1970s to include the still ubiquitous convention of the externally ejaculating penis, known within the industry as the "money shot" (1989, 49). She writes, "Hard

core tries *not* to play peekaboo with either its male or female bodies. It obsessively seeks knowledge, through a voyeuristic record of confessional, involuntary paroxysm, of the 'thing' itself" (49). It is interesting to note how many of the principles of maximum visibility are elided in Warhol's work, and how the only one he actually observes in *Blow Job* (the privileging of the close-up) is used in order to withhold, rather than deliver, evidence of penetration.

20 See Williams's discussion of the primitivism of the stag film (1989, 60–72).

21 Carol Clover has designated genres such as horror and pornography "body genres" because they aim to move spectators toward a convulsive response (to jump with fear in horror films, or to convulse in sexual ecstasy in pornos). Building on this, Williams has argued that porn consumers are literally encouraged to participate in the action depicted on the screen. Pornography aspires to propel the body of the spectator to "an almost involuntary mimicry of the emotion or sensation of the body on screen" (1995b, 143). For spectators of hard-core pornography, there is an implicit contract between the text and its audience, which stipulates that the viewer will not only see but also experience explicit sexual pleasure. Richard Dyer 1985 makes a similar point about gay pornography. He writes, "The goal of the pornographic narrative is coming; in filmic terms, the goal is ejaculation, that is, visible coming. If the goal of the pornographic protagonist (the actor or 'character') is to come, the goal of the spectator is to see him come (and, more often than not, probably to come at the same time as him)" (28).

22 According to Williams 1995b, body genres include horror, pornography, and melodrama (see previous note).

Works Cited

Angell, Callie. 1994. *The Films of Andy Warhol: Part 2.* New York: Whitney Museum of American Art.

Arthur, Paul. 1989. "Flesh of Absence: Resighting the Warhol Catechism." In *Andy Warhol: Film Factory*, ed. Michael O'Pray. London: British Film Institute. 146–53.

Balázs, Béla. 1952. *Theory of the Film: Character and Growth of a New Art.* Trans. Edith Bone. London: Dennis Dobson.

Banes, Sally. 1993. *Greenwich Village, 1963: Avant-Garde Performance and the Effervescent Body.* Durham, N.C.: Duke University Press.

Barthes, Roland. 1975. *The Pleasure of the Text.* Trans. Richard Miller. New York: Hill and Wang.

Benjamin, Walter. 1968. "The Work of Art in the Age of Mechanical Reproduction." In *Illuminations.* Ed. Hannah Arendt. Trans. Harry Zohn. New York: Schocken. 217–51.

Berg, Gretchen. [1967] 1989. "Nothing to Lose: An Interview with Andy Warhol." In *Andy Warhol: Film Factory*, ed. Michael O'Pray. London: British Film Institute. 54–61.

Bockris, Victor. 1989. *The Life and Death of Andy Warhol*. New York: Bantam.

Butler, Judith. 1997. *Excitable Speech: A Politics of the Performative*. New York: Routledge.

Crary, Jonathan. 1997. "Modernizing Vision." In *Viewing Positions: Ways of Seeing Film*, ed. Linda Williams. New Brunswick, N.J.: Rutgers University Press. 23–35.

———. 1999. *Techniques of the Observer: On Vision and Modernity in the Nineteenth Century*. Cambridge: MIT Press.

Crimp, Douglas. 1996. "Face Value." In *About Face: Andy Warhol Portraits*, ed. Nicholas Baume. Cambridge: MIT Press. 110–25.

Dyer, Richard. 1985. "Gay Male Porn: Coming to Terms." *Jump Cut* 30: 27–29.

Ehrenstein, David. N.d. "Within the Pleasure Principle; or, Irresponsible Homosexual Propaganda." *Wide Angle* 4, 1: 62–65.

Flatley, Jonathan. 1996. "Warhol Gives Good Face: Publicity and the Politics of Prosopopoeia." In *Pop Out: Queer Warhol*, ed. Jennifer Doyle, Jonathan Flatley, and José Esteban Muñoz. Durham, N.C.: Duke University Press. 101–33.

Freud, Sigmund. [1905] 2000. *Three Essays on the Theory of Sexuality*. Trans. James Strachey. New York: Basic Books.

Greenberg, Clement. 1961 [1939]. "Avant-Garde and Kitsch." In *Art and Culture: Critical Essays*. Boston: Beacon. 3–21.

Grundmann, Roy. 1993. *Andy Warhol's* Blow Job. Philadelphia: Temple University Press.

Hoberman, J. 1991. "Bon Voyeur: Andy Warhol's Silver Screen." In *Vulgar Modernism: Writings on Movies and Other Media*. Philadelphia: Temple University Press. 181–85.

Hoberman, J., and Jonathan Rosenbaum. 1983. *Midnight Movies*. New York: Harper and Row.

James, David E. 1992. *To Free the Cinema: Jonas Mekas and the New York Underground*. Princeton, N.J.: Princeton University Press.

Kent, Leticia. 1970. "Andy Warhol, Movieman: 'It's Hard to Be Your Own Script.'" *Vogue*, March, n.p.

Koch, Stephen. 1973. "*Blow-Job* and Pornography." In *Stargazer: Andy Warhol's World and His Films*. New York: Praeger. 47–51.

Koestenbaum, Wayne. 2001. *Andy Warhol*. New York: Penguin.

Levine, Lawrence. 1988. *Highbrow/Lowbrow: The Emergence of Cultural Hierarchy in America*. Cambridge, Mass.: Harvard University Press.

Lewis, Jon. 2000. *Hollywood v. Hard Core: How the Struggle over Censorship Saved the Modern Film Industry*. New York: New York University Press.

Margulies, Ivone. 1996. *Nothing Happens: Chantal Akerman's Hyperrealist Everday*. Durham, N.C.: Duke University Press.

O'Pray, Michael. 1989. Introduction to *Andy Warhol: Film Factory*, ed. O'Pray. London: British Film Institute. 10–13.

Petro, Patrice. 1995. "After Shock/Between Boredom and History." In *Fugitive Images: Photography to Video*, ed. Petro. Bloomington: Indiana University Press.

Rayns, Tony. 1997. "Andy's Hand-Jobs." In *Who Is Andy Warhol?*, ed. Colin MacCabe, Mark Francis, and Peter Wollen. London: British Film Institute. 83–87.

Shaviro, Steven. 1993. "Warhol's Bodies." In *The Cinematic Body*. Minneapolis: University of Minnesota Press. 201–39.

Violet, Ultra. 1988. *Famous for Fifteen Minutes: My Years with Andy Warhol.* New York: Avon.

Warhol, Andy, and Pat Hackett. 1980. *POPism: The Warhol Sixties.* New York: Harcourt Brace Jovanovich.

Waugh, Thomas. 1996a. "Cockteaser." In *Pop Out: Queer Warhol*, ed. Jennifer Doyle, Jonathan Flatley, and José Esteban Muñoz. Durham, N.C.: Duke University Press. 51–77.

———. 1996b. *Hard to Imagine: Gay Male Eroticism in Photography and Film from Their Beginnings to Stonewall.* New York: Columbia University Press.

Williams, Linda. 1989. *Hard Core: Power, Pleasure, and the "Frenzy of the Visible."* Berkeley: University of California Press.

———. 1995a. "Corporealized Observers: Visual Pornographies and the 'Carnal Density of Vision.'" In *Fugitive Images: Photography to Video*, ed. Patrice Petro. Bloomington: Indiana University Press.

———. 1995b. "Film Bodies: Gender, Genre, and Excess." In *Film Genre Reader 2*, ed. Barry Keith Grant. Austin: University of Texas Press. 140–58.

Unbracketing Motion Study:

Scott Stark's *NOEMA*

MICHAEL SICINSKI

On August 9, 1992, Ken Jacobs presented his Nervous System performance film *XCXHXEXRXRXIXEXSX* (pronounced, and hereafter referred to, as *Cherries* [1980]) at the Flaherty Seminar, as part of a series of screenings programmed by Scott MacDonald that year. The series took "motion study" as its theme, and I make reference to Jacobs's performance and the question-and-answer session that followed because to me, the response to Jacobs's presentation represents a concrete discursive event, in which the political stances surrounding a single issue are displayed in an unusually clear manner.

In *Cherries*, Jacobs's re-presents an old French pornographic film, manipulating it by using his Nervous System, a dual-projector apparatus that introduces frame-by-frame analytic motion into the projection of the piece. Jacobs's performance work recycles film imagery by slowing it down and playing consecutive frames against one another in order to draw the audience's attention to microspectacles of incremental motion. Explicitly harking back to the work of Eadweard Muybridge and Etienne-Jules Marey, Jacobs is interested in cinematic motion as a problematic, a phenomenon to be investigated in order to fully apprehend formal and graphic relationships which subtend the usual movie-going experience, but typically elude perception. However, the conflict at the Flaherty arose chiefly due to Jacobs's use of pornography as source material. Jacobs explained his own interest in *Cherries* as, in part, deriving from formal possibilities of his apparatus, "the potential of the Nervous System to work with rounded objects, curved volumes, up-close" (MacDonald 1998, 158). While Jacobs did address his desire to be "as explicit as possible" in his depiction of sexuality, a segment of the Flaherty crowd found his explanations unsatisfactory. One seminar participant angrily objected to Jacobs's appropriation of pornographic footage for an abstract modernist project: "I'm really disturbed that we've spent at least twenty minutes talking about technique—and ignoring *content*! . . . For me to watch this is like watching a rape. Pornographic imagery has to do with women and power. I don't know if you're interested in that, but for me it was just this male gaze thing for two hours. And that's something *we* have to live with *every day*!" (162). Jacobs disagreed with the seminar attendee, and programmer Richard Herskowitz provided thoughtful remarks attempting to locate common ground between Jacobs's and the seminarian's positions. But Jacobs's continuing attempts to speak formally about his piece, along with his insistence that the piece of vintage porn *was not* violent, simply exacerbated the situation. (Jacobs quoted Lenny Bruce, claiming, "Nobody gets socked in the jaw.") After a few nasty exchanges between Jacobs and the increasingly hostile crowd, critic Laura Marks brought the discussion back around to the issue of motion study, making explicit some of the theoretical positions subtending the response to *Cherries*: "The reason why pornography in particular is interesting as a subject for motion study—which your film is, and which is the theme of Scott MacDonald's curating these past two days—has to do with stopping motion to investigate the body and attain a kind of mastery. Pornography is, among many other things, about a gaze that possesses" (162). While Marks went on to say some generally complimentary things about Jacobs's performance, Jacobs fundamentally rejected Marks's location of motion study within the province of, in his words, "the male gaze, and patriarchy, and power" (162). Within minutes, the discussion degenerated into a shouting match, and Jacobs walked out of the screening room.

Although this essay is *not* about the work of Ken Jacobs, I have chosen to preface my discussion of Scott Stark's film NOEMA (1998) with this anecdote from the reception history of experimental cinema because I believe it provides a snapshot of the theoretical environment to which NOEMA speaks. Stark has characterized NOEMA as a motion study employing sequences from pornographic videotapes, tapes that, as the film's description in the 2000 Canyon Cinema catalog states, "are mined for the unerotic moments between moments." So in one sense, we can understand Stark's film as treading on the same dangerous ground that angered the Flaherty audience. But as I hope my discussion of NOEMA will show, Stark is clearly cognizant of

1. Three performers reposition themselves in *NOEMA*.

the arguments around analytic motion study, pornography, and power, and his film represents a humorous and incisive commentary on the missed connections between analytical cinema and its critical reception. While specifically engaging with the issue of pornography and its appropriation for use in experimental cinema, *NOEMA* actually engages a larger question of representation and its suspension in formalist artworks. How do cinematic abstractions ask their viewers to bracket the filmic referent, and what kinds of readings occur when this bracketing breaks down?

For most of *NOEMA*, Stark excerpts and loops the seconds of genital disengagement from hard-core pornographic videos. Against a soundtrack comprised of looped snippets from Samuel Barber's Adagio for Strings, Stark gives us a series of choreographically orchestrated porn sequences in which the awkward entr'actes of sexual position changes are presented, "naked" in themselves, without the hard-core action that bookends such moments of disconnection in the original tapes. Starting with one repeated scene of repositioning during a ménage à trois, Stark begins integrating other such moments into the first part of his film (figure 1). As we meet new actors and actresses in the course of the work, segments from earlier parts of the film return, resulting in an ongoing experience of the new and the familiar rhythmically colliding. Through their repetition, these sequences become increasingly abstract. Instead of the pornographic utopias one might expect from Stark's source material, we see unclothed bodies navigating around others and frequently getting lost; instead of the throbbing banality of cheap synthesizer porno jazz, Stark offers Barber's self-serious neoclassicism, constantly intercepted as it threatens to take flight.

There is certainly an elegant formal logic at work in Stark's film. NOEMA is basically divided into two roughly equal sections, which introduce and elaborate on a visual idea or motive, not unlike the motivic structure of a musical composition. After the start of the soundtrack and a black-leader prelude, Stark introduces the first musical theme and choreographic idea of NOEMA. This series of two-second shots displays lapses in the idealized sexual stamina that typically gives pornographic video its rhythmic and erotic drive. These moments in themselves seem to point to the fallible physicality of the actors—position shifts in sex often occur when one or more of the participants gets exhausted, when elbows lock up, or when a certain arrangement provokes discomfort. (This is true in any sexual encounter, with the complicating factor that in porn the sexual event is orchestrated for a camera, and so there may well be an imperative to "mix it up.") The issues surrounding the "mastering gaze" of motion study can be productively thought in tandem with the first movement of Stark's film.

The photographic motion studies of Muybridge, and to a lesser extent of Marey, have been considered historical precursors for the cinema, and as such have been a site for frequent inquiry by both filmmakers and theorists interested in undertaking an archaeology of the cinema. The relationships between so-called precinema and the cinematic avant-garde have been well-documented, not least by the filmmakers themselves. Ken Jacobs has said, "Advanced filmmaking leads to Muybridge. . . . Closing in on (to allow the expansion of) ever-smaller pieces of time is my personal ever-promising and ever-inviting Black Hole" (program notes, Pacific Film Archive, September-October 1999). Hollis Frampton, whose *Zorns Lemma* (1970) employs a modular structure for the orchestration of depicted human tasks and natural phenomena, has written on Muybridge and used his motion studies as the inspiration for a series of photographic works (on "vegetable locomotion," charting the "movements" of apples and tomatoes). In his book on avant-garde motion studies, Scott MacDonald has characterized the relationship historically as a filmic and photographic mode, which roughly corresponds with minimalism's examination of primary structures: "The way was smoothed by the fact that during the mid-1960s many painters, sculptors, and musicians were exploring serial organizations of imagery as a means of avoiding conventional, traditionally hierarchical arrangements of material, space, and time" (1993, 10).

But beginning in the 1980s, film theorists, particularly feminist critics, began to question the extent to which Muybridge offered an ontological alternative to "traditionally hierarchical arrangements." Most notably, Linda

Williams's 1981 essay "Film Body: An Implantation of Perversions," reexamined Muybridge's motion studies within a Foucaultian feminist framework. As she made abundantly clear, the Muybridge motion studies are saturated with narrativity where the female body is concerned. While men perform hearty labor (in anticipation, perhaps, of eventual Taylorization), women perform elaborate scenarios, pouring water on each other's naked bodies, or languishing together having a smoke (Williams 1986, 518). Williams concludes that "at a time when the cinema was much more a document of reality than a narrative art, women were already fictionalized, already playing assumed roles, already *not there* as themselves" (520). Williams's work drew on the Foucaultian insight that the body is a discursive production, and that motion studies could serve as a method of inscribing lack on the female body. This work on Muybridge would later become a part of Williams's groundbreaking book *Hard Core*, in which she would identify links between motion study and pornography. Both media evince a desire to see the body reveal its "visible 'truth'" in moments of involuntary spasm, physical abandon, or orgasmic "confession" (1989, 39–50).

One can conclude from this that pornography (as motion study) provokes desire by promising to display the truth of bodies. This is accomplished by positioning those bodies along a trajectory toward climax, at which point they fulfill the narrative thrust of completed action. NOEMA continually frustrates this desire, and yet one could argue that by seizing on the awkward moments of sexual uncoupling, Stark is still employing motion study to proffer truths about the bodies of the actors, thereby exercising visual power over them. Such an argument might claim that the humor of these isolated moments of coitus interruptus as orchestrated by Stark serves to showcase the bodies of pornography displaying far more than they intend, for the pleasure of our ironic gaze. To deliver such a reading, however, is to fail to consider the generic conventions of porn and the way in which Stark reverses the flow of power, affording the actors in *his* film a kind of deidealization. This move allows the viewer to look at the bodies of NOEMA with a stance quite different from ironic detachment or clinical scrutiny. By revealing the subtle gestures of labor within the context of adult entertainment, Stark exposes both the structures and excesses of capitalist sex.

In mainstream pornography, such as that recycled in NOEMA, we tend to be sucked into the sexual scene, our visual desire seduced by the seeming inexhaustibility of sexual plenitude. The pornographic scene, in order to be effective, must idealize its participants (as sexual performers who will achieve orgasm at all costs). Even if they are ordinary-looking, we must understand them to be sexual dynamos whose erotic endeavors are not hampered by the material failings of the human body. If this idealized sexual activity is in place, then a viewer is ostensibly capable of overlooking cheap interiors, blemishes, or, for that matter, momentary genital misalignment. We are able to become sutured into the narrative of the sex act, and by mentally effacing the physical gaps in that narrative arc, we can elevate the scene into something more than it is.[1]

So on the one hand, Stark does employ the techniques of motion study to bring these bodies back down to earth. And yet in doing so, he in fact demonstrates the failure of pornographic production to Taylorize sex, even among professionals. In the first movement of NOEMA, we see an actress scratch her head as she waits for the other two performers to get into position. We see a bored-looking woman rub her eye in the interval before penetration. Even those position changes which appear smooth and ballet-like take on the quality of transitioning between tasks. In this regard, the generic constraints of porn become no different than those governing other segments of the entertainment industry. That is, we as viewers are supposed to forget that the men and women on screen are *at work*. Stark repeats for analysis those brief interstices, captured on tape, which remind us that these performers are working bodies, as we see them managing the discomforts which their jobs produce (rubbing their tired eyes, removing hair from their mouths). Like any of the rest of us, their laboring bodies are subject to the disciplines of the workplace. But, as Stark also demonstrates, this discipline can extend only so far. Taylorism is an asymptotic proposition, because no body can be completely disciplined. NOEMA focuses not on the moments in which porn stars "fail" to be sexy enough; it focuses on the moments in between, when they elude professional discipline and succeed at evincing utterly human responses to the physical demands of their jobs. Moreover, these moments in between are precisely those which no amount of disciplinary control could ever fully expunge from the human sexual scene.

I do not want to be misunderstood as saying that the women and men who perform in the sexually explicit tapes excerpted in NOEMA are victims of the sex industry, somehow in need of rescue. Neither I nor, I would conjecture, Stark could say anything authoritative about these performers and their individual circumstances. What I *am* saying is that, like all laborers, they act under certain constraints, and their position within a segment of the entertainment industry largely governed by genre rules throws the gestures of their labor into particular relief.[2] In this regard, Stark's motion study does not serve to create or uphold the discipline of the working body, but

2. A performer decentered
by a painting, in *NOEMA*.

instead looks for the breakdown of that discipline. Rather than maintaining the narrativizing impulse that Williams finds in Muybridge's work, *NOEMA* locates and presents a counternarrative that interrupts the bounds of genre.

Up to now, I have only discussed one set of relations within *NOEMA*, that between the viewer and the performers. This constitutes the primary theme of the first movement of Stark's film, but the second movement draws our attention to the person behind the video camera. That person, probably male, but not necessarily, conceivably the director, but possibly another employee, also steals seconds in between, to embark on visual explorations that go beyond the industrial imperative to titillate. By employing analytic editing to show us what sorts of unexpected visual pleasures might be held in common by porn industry workers, experimental filmmakers, and their respective audiences, Stark shifts the context of motion study, using it to renew our ability to see the limits of industrial discipline on the side of production, rather than performance.

This second sequence of *NOEMA* focuses on transitions between scenes or bumpers around interrupted sexual activity, which will be made to look continuous in postproduction. In these cutaways, Stark discovers quirky modernism, geometrical compositions, and a propensity to think about the relations between bodies, space, and frame (figure 2). In one shot, the screen becomes an ambiguous blue field, equally legible as sky or latex paint, until the emergence of actors on the right of the frame. In another, a cheap Ramada Inn landscape painting above the bed becomes the upper anchor of a compositional diptych. In still another, we are offered a study in shadow against a beige expanse of dirt or concrete, an image that, minus its harsh video glint, would not look altogether out of place in a Nathaniel Dorsky film. Further into the second sequence, Stark shows us a set of still lives and landscape studies, none of them fully formed, but rather interstitial and momentary. The strange texture of a gold eagle lamp, a glass of bourbon on an end table, and other fleeting handheld images are all the more assertive in their non-narrative aestheticism because we know that, just over the boundary of the frame, explicit sex is occurring, or just finishing up. In fact, these abstract moments seem to be proffered as "money shots." Stark accompanies them on the soundtrack with bursting fireworks—a possible *Deep Throat* reference—as well as the sounds of cheering crowds.

It would be easy to think of this second movement of *NOEMA* as a kitschy mockery of the "arty" pretensions of low-budget camcorder porn "auteurs." If we think about *NOEMA* as simply a campy motion study, then we could well see the film in relation to Lisa Cartwright's critique of Marey. She sees Marey's chronophotography as a key moment in the history of dispassionate disciplinary looking, characterized by "a relationship of cool, objective distance from [its] 'test objects'—even when these objects [are] living beings" (1995, 126). Shifting this clinical coolness into the register of irony, it becomes possible to read *NOEMA* as a haughty confirmation of the avant-garde's superiority over video porn, a belief we as viewers might already hold, yet conveniently triangulate through Stark.

The entire film *is* very funny, but I think that simply snickering at naked bodies in awkward positions is really missing the point. If we instead accept the premise that Stark is cognizant of the political stakes surrounding motion study, we can consider his film as a mobilization of analytic editing against the technologies of genre. In considering the above, it's notable that Stark has not selected the "prestige porn" of Andrew Blake, for instance, but a workmanlike "pornography without names." Like the actors who itch, sigh, get tired, or need to shift their centers of gravity, the videographers can be seen supplementing generic constraints in these two-second flashes, demonstrating a breakdown of the discipline of porn production. I am not claiming that these moments represent radical potential—as I said before, without Stark's editing, they are largely overlooked in favor of the "sexy" footage. But by bringing motion study to bear on pornographic imagery, Stark shows us the ordinary, run-of-the-mill lapses in disciplinary production. The professional sex body possesses an unmasterable physical density, and the professional video voyeur can be momentarily distracted by the non-purposive play of light on glass. (The juxtaposition of the roaring crowds and the fleeting abstractions, for example, is quite funny, but it seems rather sincere at the same time — Stark's way of saying "bravo!" to these satisfying interstitial inventions.)

As I hope is evident from the above discussion, NOEMA is more than just a motion study. It constitutes a metacritical consideration of the implication of motion study within a regime of power and of its use for realigning that power in favor of the bodies under investigation. As seen in the comments above, some critics of motion study have taken issue with the disciplinary control of bodies under study. But what is the status of those bodies? Cartwright criticizes the "cool objectivity" with which Marey graphs, marks, and measures his test subjects. Internal to Marey's motion study, the bodies may appear constrained, but how do those bodies exist outside the context of the study? Are they "free" or "undisciplined"? Are they laborers in some other setting, apart from their position as test subjects? Are these relationships admissible to the scene of the motion study?

Clearly those social relations that obtain outside of the motion study always find their way back into the process. Williams's discussion of Muybridge makes this quite clear. But in the case of NOEMA, Stark has fashioned a motion study not out of "people," but out of images. And those images, as I argue above, are images of laboring bodies, taken from the scene of pornographic production. If we agree that the original pornographic videotapes are, among other things, motion studies, then Stark has made a motion study of a motion study. Whereas Muybridge and Marey attempted to strip away the external world in order to better see incremental relations of bodily movement, NOEMA puts "the real world" back on the table. He brings the background back — so aggressively, in fact, that toward the end, we see nothing *but* background. This accomplishes, pace phenomenology, more than meets the eye. In addition to demonstrating that working bodies, including those behind the camera, are never entirely "docile," NOEMA challenges the possibility of seeing bodies in motion as an abstract category apart from specific social circumstances. This not only raises questions about the ethics of motion study itself but about the rhetoric of abstraction that much contemporary experimental film inherits from phenomenological discourse.

NOEMA takes its title from an analytical category found in the philosophy of Edmund Husserl. In *Ideas*, Husserl distinguishes *noema* — a concrete judgment made by consciousness regarding an object — from *noesis* — a secondary reflection on the status of that original judgment. Pol Vandevelde, in his introduction to Paul Ricoeur's commentary on *Ideas*, writes that the meaning of noema is relatively mutable in Husserl's phenomenology: "The noema can cover at least three different elements: it can be the correlate of an act, as a punctual noematic appearance; it can also be the sense (*Sinn* or *Bedeutung*) and as such be the identical or ideal content; and, the noema can name the object constituted in its unity and be, thus, the intentional object" (Vandevelde in Ricoeur 1996, 18). This requires some explication. In the first case, the noema consists of the totality of sensual content that accompanies any given act of perception. One must note the word *act* in the previous sentence, to underscore the fact that for Husserl, perception is intentional, even if understood as passive intention, the intention to receive. So the noema is both the pure sense data from a perception, as well as the drive toward the object perceived, both as yet unshaped by the specificity of the object's "thingness."[3] From this standpoint, the act contains an abstract correlative making it possible, by marking out a space for its intendedness. As Barry Smith and David W. Smith explain it, the real content of an act is its noesis, its intention is that act's noema, and intentionality as such lie within this "noetic-noematic correlation" (1995, 22). The second and third parts of Vandevelde's definition follow from this division of intentional labor. In the second sense, noema is the ideal meaning of the perception itself, analytically separable from its physical constituents. The third definition would refer to the object as an ideality, an object *as* intended by consciousness. In this case, noesis would be the secondary synthetic process by which we shape the information that consciousness actively receives. That actual perception would constitute a degraded form of the noema, which exists as a perfect intellectual concept. This definition of the noema would mark the limit case of philosophical idealism, the object existing in its truest form only in the mind of a hypothetical perceiver.

The fact that Scott Stark has given the title NOEMA to a film comprised of looped fragments of video pornography might seem incongruous at first. But the film's means have a specific historical relationship to questions of perception, intention, and the problem of idealism versus materialism. But more important, NOEMA confronts an ethical dilemma that has shadowed a certain strain of modernism, particularly in cinema. Husserl's phenomenology is able to separate the experience of sense data from the conceptual recognition of objects, particularly as those objects fill out our preexisting categories of understanding. By distinguishing between these two analytical moments, it becomes possible to see shape, form, and motion as discrete entities in themselves. This in turn becomes a single moment in a dialectical tension, as "content" (understood broadly as any meaning not fully immanent to the sensual presence of an artwork) inevitably impresses itself on consciousness. In actual experience, neither of these categories exists separately, nor does either of them arrive before the other. And so, in order to consider one and not the other, a significant degree of effort (that is, intention) is necessary on the part of the viewer.

Stark's film dramatizes this intention as few other films have before. To watch NOEMA is in part to experience hard-core porn presented in a mode that both (a) asks us to "see through" the bodies of copulating men and women in order to appreciate them as design elements within a whimsical motion study; and (b) forces us to confront the complete inability to see these undulating forms as anything other than naked people engaged in serious fucking. Rather than assuming a priori that the viewer of an experimental film can and must look beyond content into a pre-interpretive realm, Stark posits "formalism" as a chiasmus. The viewer of NOEMA is asked to reflect critically on the ability to bracket the representational status of imagery designed to provoke intense heterosexual arousal.

A similar concern can be seen in Stark's earlier films. For instance, in *Satrapy* (1988), Stark used frame-by-frame photography to make a "flicker" film out of playing cards featuring pictures of naked women. The women in the film fly by, mere glimpses of smiles and flesh. As such, they take on the character of *signifiers* of sexually desirable objects, rather than objects of desire per se. In a sense, the film seems to slyly allude to a stereotypical male fantasy regarding the complete exchangeability of women.[4] In *Satrapy*, this exchange rate attains unfathomable proportions, and as such, the male gaze is effectively blitzed. Nude centerfolds become formal features in a game of cards controlled by the "House." This aspect is underscored by the pulsating mathematization of the film's construction: "Rephotographed pornographic playing cards rhythmically intrude upon a piercing 5-beat score of different-sized black parallel lines, injecting a note of 'negative sound' every third beat against the 5-beat background. As the film progresses, contrapuntal variations of 3, 4, 5 and 7 beat rhythms blend and collide, creating an almost indiscernible complexity, until the lined background ruptures and the sounds and visuals become scattered and disordered" (Stark, 1999). As if peering through filmic "blinds" on the movie screen into a private booth filled with blink-and-you'll-miss-them naked ladies, the viewer of *Satrapy* is assailed by disorienting sheets of visual noise (at times hypnotically lovely, at other points frankly painful), through which our hypothetical "he" must look if "he" is to exact Mulveyan visual pleasure.[5] Like the story by Rabelais, in which a man must eat through a wall of crud in order to reach the delicious food inside, *Satrapy* demands that we work for our jollies, snatching "content" while banging our heads against a vibrating wall of "form."

Stark has made other films which, like NOEMA, could be called motion studies. One of the most elegant is *Acceleration*, a super-8 film from 1993, which consists of reflections in the windows of leaving and arriving commuter trains. Shot from the platform, the film shows us other passengers in waiting, as the flicker of window-metal-window creates a phenakistiscope. Jonathan Crary reminds us that the literal meaning of that word is "deceptive view," and this is apposite considering Stark's means.[6] By triangulating the image of his subjects through the reflections of the speeding train, Stark uses the technological "advance" of cinema to record movement as though it were being generated by an earlier, "inferior" paracinematic device. In this way, *Acceleration* reads like a double motion study, examining the movement of its outward subjects (passengers and trains), as well as the camera's own ability to produce illusions of motion different than those usually generated by the apparatus.

But clearly NOEMA is a motion study of a different order. Stark here shifts the emphasis from filming to editing, using found footage from a particular segment of the entertainment industry with its own rules and structures of representation. Regarding his work and interests, Stark has said that he "likes to emphasize the physicality of film while humorously cross-referencing it to the world outside the theater, attempting to lay bare the paradoxes of modern culture and the magical nature of the perceptual experience" (1999). NOEMA brings these paradoxes of perception to bear on material carrying with it a considerable amount of social and political freight. Most viewers have some opinion of or relation to pornography. Given the social environment into which NOEMA is unleashed, the film can scarcely be completely separated from questions of gender, race, sexual orientation, relations between labor and capital, the political character of cinematic spectatorship, and a host of related issues.

This seems utterly intentional. NOEMA actually seems to instantiate a dual response while explicitly thematizing that response. The film's looping motion study of pornography provokes a divided consciousness on the part of the viewer. On the one hand, he or she is aggressively confronted with undisguised pornography. This content will inevitably touch off a set of associations for the viewer. On the other, the viewer cannot help but observe (and, in my opinion, appreciate) the formal repetitions and conjunctions Stark has constructed through editing. This divided response is then reflected on as a second-order problem. The formal relationships within the piece seem to simultaneously demand and prohibit an abstract mode of looking, which could see NOEMA's "rounded objects" going to town, while temporarily "failing" to see pornography. Stark's motion study produces form that will not conform to formalism.

This second-order viewing challenge brings us back to Husserl. Once we reflect on our perception of Stark's film, we recognize that there are no naked people "there." What we are actually evaluating are patterns of light and shadow on the screen. This is the sort of noematic response that both experimental film and analytic motion study often demand of their viewers. We are asked to see *before* we see "things." We are asked to attempt to allow a first-order perceptual experience to marinate before we rush to conceptual judgment. In Husserl's thought, we can separate this noema from its attendant noesis through phenomenological reduction.[7]

In *Ideas*, Husserl explains phenomenological reduction as the process by which we can analytically distinguish the noema from its real world-meanings (including those we would consider cultural or historical). The aim of this is to achieve "the absolutely faithful description of that which really lies before one in phenomenological purity" (1962, 242). This is in order to disentangle the "intentional object" (noema) from the "real object" (noesis) to gain scientific knowledge of the object's activation of our sensorium. In order to free ourselves from the errors of prejudgment, Husserl states that "we must abide by what is given in pure experience, and place it within its frame of clearness just as it comes into our hands." How to achieve this? "The 'real' object is then to be 'bracketed'" (243).

"Bracketing," set off in quotation marks throughout *Ideas*, becomes Husserl's shorthand for the act of phenomenological reduction and has become a popular idiom for the process of tabling a problematic issue in the text ("bracketing" issues of gender or race, for example) while going on to consider other matters which will be rejoined with the bracketed material, but which could not be worked through with that material at the fore. This aspect of the pragmatics of bracketing begins to address the possible ethical difficulties phenomenological reduction can provoke. In this light, reconsider the Flaherty incident. Ken Jacobs was chastised for expecting his audience to be able to phenomenologically reduce, or bracket, the light patterns' perceptual resolution into people having oral sex alfresco. The transcript of the Jacobs question-and-answer session indicates that Jacobs was actually interested in how the tension between views—the sensual/formal and the intellectual/conceptual—would play itself out in *Cherries*. (It seems equally evident that Jacobs's stance in the argument became more "formalist" as he was backed against the wall.) But whereas Laura Marks claimed that Jacobs's means were fundamentally implicated in power relations that, as she presented them, sounded rather unilateral, Stark suggests that one must understand the social relations of the backdrop before one can assess the meaning of bracketing as an intervention.

For Husserl, this act is necessary if we are to analytically distinguish "between the *passing of a judgment* and the *judgment as passed*" (1962, 252; emphasis original). And yet Husserl seems to admit that this procedure is asymptotic, because it strives toward a preconceptual residue somehow prior to actual "experience" as we understand it.[8] There may well be a ground zero of sensual experience, prior to full nominalization and conceptualization. But the noema is a hypothetical construction, extrapolated from "later" conceptual impressions. This is why the effort of bracketing is necessary in the first place. This level of preconceptual understanding can only be achieved retroactively.

This further complicates the ethical issues surrounding the phenomenological reduction. Husserl's brackets are wide because his phenomenology aims to achieve the noema by putting the "real" world aside. In section 97 of *Ideas*, Husserl gives the example of an apple tree, explaining what its reduction would entail.

> We have now to describe what remains over as phenomenological residuum, when we effect the reduction to "pure immanence," and *what in that case should count as a real (reelles) integral part of the pure experience*, and what should not be so regarded. And we have then to be fully clear about this, that whilst the "perceived tree as such," or, alternately, the full noema which is not affected by the suspending of the reality (*Wirklichkeit*) of the tree itself and the whole real world, does indeed belong to the essence of the perceptual experience in itself, on the other hand this *noema*, with its "tree" in inverted commas, is *as little contained realiter (reell) in the perception as is the tree of the real natural order (Wirklichkeit)*. (1962, 260–61)

Later on, Husserl will further distinguish the real noema from actual experience, even at the sensual level. (Neither the noematic essence, nor the "real tree of the natural order" are actually contained in our perception.) This seems to me to underscore the fact that in attempting the phenomenological reduction, we are positing a synthetic noema that we must reconstruct from the sullied noeses of the real world. But as we also see from the passage above, in order to generate that noema, Husserl's phenomenology requires the "suspending" of the "whole real world." This suspension is intimately tied to the conceptualizing process itself, and so our conceptual categories will necessarily become involved in the reduction, what is reduced, and how the reduction will take place. That is, we posit a "real world" in order to strip it away, leaving a synthetic residuum which is the "other" of that stripped reality.

noema dramatizes this perceptual gambit. That is, the pornographic footage reworked by Stark has already been bracketed by the rules of genre. When we watch the pornographic tapes in their original form, the logic of suture induces us to blot out, or bracket, those very moments that could jeopardize our pleasure. The process of self-selected, retroactive editing of the real world excises the in-between awkwardness, the industrial fatigue, and that most excessive realm of all, the aesthetic. By bringing motion study to bear on video pornography, *noema* brackets those seconds in which the bodily needs and visual desires of porn's producers are no longer contained by the logic of manufactured entertainment. *noema* isolates these elements, bracketing them for Stark's own motion study, but in a larger sense *unbracketing* them, bringing them (as emissaries of the "real world" of production) back from the oblivion of psychic expurgation.

In using motion study as a tool for this analysis of generic fantasy, Stark firmly demonstrates that which Jacobs's audience was incapable of conceding—that analytical motion study can do more with power than crudely exercise it over its subjects. But *noema* goes further, because it allows pornography to speak back to motion study's tendencies toward austere formalism. When we see and hear *noema*, the bodies cannot dissolve into pure form; always on the verge of hard-core sex, they hover near but are pulled back from the brink of abstraction. In this way, Stark has created a work of art undermining its own foundation, which is, of course, one of the most radical formal gestures we can ask an artwork to perform, one certainly worthy of the designation "avant-garde."

Notes

For invaluable help and suggestions on this essay, I would like to thank Linda Williams, Minette Hillyer, Jennifer Wingard, and, especially, Scott Stark. *noema* is available for rental on 16 mm from Canyon Cinema, (415) 626-2255, or films@canyoncinema.com. It may also be purchased on videotape from Stark. He may be contacted through his Web site, www.hi-beam.net/mkr/ss/ss-bio.html

1 The fact that the logic of suture obtains even within the seemingly antinarra-

tive logic of pornography can best be understood by considering how suture can work its magic within the photographic motion study. One of the most analytically and theoretically impressive moments in Marta Braun's book on Marey comes in chapter 6, when she meticulously differentiates Marey's work from that of Muybridge. She reprints some key photographic series from *Animal Locomotion* (1885) and demonstrates that there are substantial gaps in Muybridge's "motion" sequences. However, he organizes the images in sequence, using the power of the grid to *imply* continuous motion where it simply isn't there. Braun writes, "The sequence endows its component parts with movement because we believe any sequence to be inherently orderly, logical, and progressive. . . . The sequence invites us to cooperate in creating the illusion of motion, to dissolve in our imaginations the black borders marking off each individual part and then to *fill in the gaps* between the separate phases of the movement given by each single image. Our faith in the sequence allows us to *suspend our disbelief.* But the fact is that the pictures were arranged" (Braun 1992, 237–38; emphasis mine). There is a significant difference between Braun's example of Muybridge and mine of pornography. In the former, there is a gap; in the latter, a surfeit of things to see. Nevertheless, the logic of the suture entails an evaluation (for my purposes, it does not matter whether it is unconscious or a learned competence, although the psychoanalytic provenance of the concept of suture would assume the former) of a trajectory, a temporal narrative arc. The Muybridge example is merely the flipside of the question of porn's "unsexy" moments. If we are sutured into the scene of activity, we both supply what is missing, and ignore what is distracting, in order to allow the arc to complete itself. (To use a metaphor of the road, Muybridge gives us potholes, mainstream porn gives us speed bumps, but neither slow us down for long.) See Braun 1992, 228–62.

2   As with any genre, the "genericness" of porn is an open question. How often can genre rules be violated before the genre designation no longer holds? How many subgenres can a single genre envelop until the designation is no longer of use? Regarding these questions, I defer to Rick Altman's ongoing examination of film genre. In a recent essay, Altman delivers a definition that is more than adequate for my argument regarding pornography. He writes, "Genre films are the films produced after general identification and consecration of a genre through substantification, during the limited period when shared textual material and structures lead audiences to interpret films not as separate entities but according to generic expectations and against generic norms" (1998, 5–6). Given that "pornographic" films and videos all share at least one property so crucial that plot, characterization, and narrative are frequently considered negligible, that property would seem to constitute a genre requirement.

3   While Husserl's system of phenomenological perception is largely structural and relatively value-neutral, Martin Heidegger will bring the question of intentional perception into the domain of ethics. (The term *ethics* is my designation, not Hei-

degger's.) In his later essays, particularly those collected in the volume *The Question Concerning Technology*, Heidegger contends that by insisting that an object assume a thinglike character before us, we are dominating that object, preventing it from coming into being.

4   Exhibiting his usual elegance, Andrew "Dice" Clay joked that the typical "guy" has a "masturbatory Rolodex" in his imagination, paging through until the ideal female image can be fixed. The rapid-fire nudie cards of *Satrapy* give a similar impression, although they are subjected to a formal procedure that draws attention to their rapid inscription on the surface of the film itself. Given this flicker-film effect, Stark's movie makes an ironic point about pornography and plenitude. Ostensibly, the registration of a naked woman on each of the film's frames would prove extremely sexually satisfying, but instead, it is likely to generate more migraines than erections.

5   Mulvey's model of male scopophilia, of course, presumes maximum visual access. *Satrapy* provides a good example of a film destroying the more sexist forms of film pleasure Mulvey originally objected to. Stark's film is funny, thoughtful, and rigorous, and to me it exemplifies the best possible outcome of Mulvey's hope (in 1975) that film might someday give us "the thrill that comes with leaving the past behind without simply rejecting it, transcending outworn or oppressive forms, and daring to break with normal pleasurable expectations in order to conceive a new language of desire" (1989, 16).

6   Jonathan Crary discusses the phenakistiscope and other nineteenth-century "philosophical toys" in relation to the kind of embodied observer they seem to generate. See Crary 1990, 97–136.

7   In this regard, the results of the phenomenological reduction have much in common with the function of "art" and the aesthetic within Russian formalism. Victor Shklovsky, for example, writes, "And art exists that one may recover the sensation of life; it exists to make one feel things, to make the stone *stony*. The purpose of art is to impart the sensation of things as they are perceived and not as they are known. The technique of art is to make objects 'unfamiliar,' to make forms difficult, to increase the difficulty and length of perception because the process of perception is an aesthetic end in itself and must be prolonged" (1965, 3–24). However, in this passage one can certainly observe one key difference between Shklovsky and phenomenology. Phenomenology, as a form of inquiry, does not content itself with perception "in itself." Rather, it attempts to glean knowledge about the object under scrutiny.

8   He characterizes the distinction in this way: "That as *correlatively* related to the judgment as experienced we have *the* judgment *simpliciter* as noema" (Husserl 1962, 261). So we see that the noema is not really our purest form of experience— all experience is inevitably conceptualized—but is a *correlative* to the judgment as experienced.

Works Cited

Altman, Rick. 1998. "Reusable Packaging: Generic Products and the Recycling Process." In *Refiguring American Film Genres: History and Theory*, ed. Nick Browne. Berkeley: University of California Press. 1–41.

Braun, Marta. 1992. *Picturing Time: The Work of Etienne-Jules Marey (1830–1904)*. Chicago: University of Chicago Press.

Cartwright, Lisa. 1995. *Screening the Body: Tracing Medicine's Visual Culture*. Minneapolis: University of Minnesota Press.

Crary, Jonathan. 1990. *Techniques of the Observer: On Vision and Modernity in the Nineteenth Century*. Cambridge, Mass.: MIT Press.

Heidegger, Martin. 1977. *The Question Concerning Technology and Other Essays*. Trans. William Lovitt. New York: Harper & Row.

Husserl, Edmund. 1962. *Ideas*. Trans. W. R. Boyce Gibson. New York: Collier.

MacDonald, Scott. 1993. *Avant-Garde Film: Motion Studies*. Cambridge: Cambridge University Press.

———, ed. 1998. *A Critical Cinema 3*. Berkeley: University of California Press.

Mulvey, Laura. 1989. *Visual and Other Pleasures*. Bloomington: Indiana University Press.

Ricoeur, Paul. 1996. *A Key to Edmund Husserl's "Ideas I."* Milwaukee, Wis.: Marquette University Press.

Shklovsky, Victor. 1965. "Art as Technique." In *Russian Formalist Criticism*, ed. Lee T. Lemon and Marion J. Reis. Lincoln: University of Nebraska Press. 3–24.

Smith, Barry, and David Woodruff Smith, eds. 1995. *The Cambridge Companion to Husserl*. Cambridge: Cambridge University Press.

Stark, Scott. 1999. Artist's statement. http://www.hi-beam.net/mkr/ss/ss-bio.html.

Williams, Linda. 1986. "Film Body: An Implantation of Perversions." In *Narrative, Apparatus, Ideology: A Film Theory Reader*, ed. Philip Rosen. New York: Columbia University Press.

———. 1989. *Hard Core: Power, Pleasure, and the "Frenzy of the Visible."* Berkeley: University of California Press.

Suggested Reading: An Annotated Bibliography

Attorney General's Commission on Pornography. 1986. *Final Report.* 2 vols. Washington, D.C.: U.S. Department of Justice.

> *Known simply as the Meese Commission, this two-volume, 1,960-page report supervised by then attorney general Edwin Meese is a collection of various documents arguing for the classification and subsequent censorship of various forms of "violent" pornography. A joint effort between conservative moralists and radical, antipornography feminists, this document produced an unlikely alliance that attacked pornography as degrading, offensive, and ultimately dangerous to women.*

Bataille, Georges. 1986. *Erotism: Death and Sensuality.* Trans. Mary Dalwood. San Francisco: City Lights Books.

> *Bataille pursues the theme of eroticism through an examination of taboos, religion, death, sacrifice, mysticism, and transgression, pointing to the fact that desire is often predicated on transgression and that eroticism, in an effort to overcome discontinuity, opens the way to death.*

Benjamin, Jessica. 1988. *The Bonds of Love: Psychoanalysis, Feminism, and the Problem of Domination.* New York: Pantheon.

> *Benjamin traces the presence of the domination-submission binary in the heterosexual economy. In her analysis of the interplay between love and the two-way process of domination, she presents a simultaneous critique and reworking of psychoanalysis through feminism and seeks to understand and explain the psychological persistence of domination despite feminism.*

Bright, Susie. 1997. *Susie Bright's Sexual State of the Union.* New York: Simon and Schuster.

> *In this collection of essays, Susie Bright provides personal observations and commen-*

tary on various topics concerning contemporary sexual politics and sexual issues from
AIDS to abortion to vibrators and further promotes her politics of sexual liberation
and expression.

Butler, Judith. 1989. *Gender Trouble: Feminism and the Subversion of Identity*. New
York: Routledge.

*In her arguably most influential work, Butler disputes the feminist notion of the exis-
tence of one category labeled "women," insisting rather that both gender and identity
are fluid variables performatively constituted through repetitive acts and that gender
itself can be troubled through the interrogation of performative practices and gender
norms, as well as the disruption of the traditional binary through the proliferation of
genders.*

———. 1993. *Bodies that Matter: On the Discursive Limits of "Sex."* New York: Routledge.

*Through readings of Jacques Lacan, Luce Irigaray, Sigmund Freud, and others, But-
ler elaborates on her performative theory of gender expounded in* Gender Trouble.
*Building on the notions that gender is a cultural construct and identity incoherent,
Butler shows how heterosexual norms are predicated on various "others" and how
these hegemonic constructions discursively constitute the materiality of bodies.*

Califia, Pat. 1982. "Feminism and Sadomasochism." *CoEvolution Quarterly* 33
(spring): 33–40.

*Through an account of her ostracism from the lesbian feminist community due to her
"outlaw" practice of sadomasochistic activity, Califia launches an argument against
the moralistic drive behind the feminist movement of the late 1970s in exchange for a
more radical form of feminism that would include sexual minorities and subcultures,
as well as sexual practices considered deviant.*

Carter, Angela. 1978. *The Sadeian Woman and the Ideology of Pornography*. New York:
Pantheon.

*Carter argues that the Marquis de Sade put pornography at the service of women, in-
vesting his female characters with a strength and agency atypical of pornography. She
views Sade's work as a potentially valuable resource for women in terms of analyzing
the relationship between power relations, politics, and sex.*

Case, Sue-Ellen. 1993. "Toward a Butch-Femme Aesthetic." In *The Lesbian and Gay
Studies Reader*, ed. Henry Abelove, Michèle Aina Barale, and David M. Halperin. New
York: Routledge. 294–306.

*In her discussion of lesbian subject formation, Case explores the "dynamic duo" of
the butch-femme couple as a possible lesbian subject position both inside and outside of ideology. She analyzes the historical role of the lesbian in feminist history,
the place of camp in the lesbian butch-femme tradition, and lesbian theater that
plays out this couple and concludes with a recuperation of the space of seduction as
a place where butch-femme roles can evade the notion of the female body in feminist
theory, and all of its Freudian baggage, the roles instead acting as signs in themselves.*

Champagne, John. 1997. "'Stop Reading Films!': Film Studies, Close Analysis, and Gay Pornography." *Cinema Journal* 36, 4: 76–97.

>Champagne argues for supplanting the close reading strategies typical in film studies of gay pornographic films with readings that pay close attention to the historical, social, and cultural conditions and practices involved in the making of gay pornography, as well as the tactical responses of its viewers.

Clover, Carol J. 1992. *Men, Women and Chain Saws: Gender in the Modern Horror Film.* Princeton, N.J.: Princeton University Press.

>In her examination of various subgenres of horror film, Clover argues against a simplistic reading of the horror film as one addressed solely to a sadistic position of identification and locates a shift that occurs between identification with the killer and identification with the "Final Girl," which to her indicates both the presence of a female gaze in a notoriously masculine discourse and a more bisexually located point of identification.

Crary, Jonathan. 1990. *Techniques of the Observer: On Vision and Modernity in the Nineteenth Century.* Cambridge: MIT Press.

>Crary reformulates various assumptions about the construction of vision and visual culture in the nineteenth century, arguing that the rupture that occurred with classical models of vision in the early nineteenth century did not result from a shift in the representational practices of art, but rather from a massive reorganization of knowledge, social practices, and techniques of observation.

De Lauretis, Teresa. 1991. "Film and the Visible." In *How Do I Look? Queer Film and Video*, ed. Bad Object-Choices. Seattle: Bay. 223–64.

>De Lauretis uses the unconventional film She Must Be Seeing Things (dir. Sheila McLaughlin, 1987) to articulate ways in which an autonomous form of lesbian sexuality and desire can be rendered on-screen, potentially producing new ways of seeing and therefore altering the standard mode of filmic representation.

———. 1994. *The Practice of Love: Lesbian Sexuality and Perverse Desire.* Bloomington: Indiana University Press.

>De Lauretis offers an eccentric reading of Freud through Jean Laplanche, Jacques Lacan, and feminist revisions in order to articulate a model of perverse desire that accounts for lesbian subjectivity and sexuality. Her analysis examines how fantasy structures identity and how lesbian subjectivity might be imagined through the reappropriation of the tools of psychoanalysis, a discourse initially incapable of imagining the lesbian.

Deleuze, Gilles. 1989. *Masochism: Coldness and Cruelty.* Trans. Jean McNeil. New York: Zone.

>In a reading of Leopold von Sacher-Masoch's Venus in Furs, Deleuze reconceptualizes the subtleties of masochism, arguing that it is a contract between mother and son intended to write the father out of his dominant role. Deleuze also advises against the tendency to unite masochism with sadism, arguing instead that they are stylistically, philosophically, structurally, and politically incompatible.

Dworkin, Andrea. 1979. *Pornography: Men Possessing Women*. New York: Penguin.

> *In her classic of antipornography feminism, Dworkin views pornography as destructive toward women and advocates a politics of liberation that would lead to its complete censorship. She argues that pornography works to establish the sexual and social subjugation of women to men and that it does not constitute a First Amendment issue since women do not have equal First Amendment rights.*

Dyer, Richard. 1985. "Gay Male Porn: Coming to Terms." *Jump Cut: A Review of Contemporary Media* 30: 27–29.

> *Dyer points out the similarities between gay male porn and its heterosexual counterpart. Gay male porn, Dyer argues, could be more subversive to and even disruptive of masculine norms if it were to invest more focus on the role of the penetrated and less on the visible climax of the penetrator.*

Ehrenreich, Barbara, Elizabeth Hess, and Gloria Jacobs. 1986. *Re-making Love: The Feminization of Sex*. Garden City, N.Y.: Anchor.

> *This book reads the transformative effect of the 1970s sexual revolution on women. It proved transmutative in that, for the first time, women became actual consumers of pornography, rather than merely figuring as objects to be consumed by men, and "the feminization of sex" became an important topic of feminist discussion.*

Elias, James, et al., eds. 1999. *Porn 101: Eroticism, Pornography, and the First Amendment*. Amherst, N.Y.: Prometheus.

> *Based on papers delivered at the World Conference on Pornography in 1998, this book examines a wide range of perspectives on pornography, from those directly involved in its production to the lawyers who have defended it from antipornography activists. Topics in the collection include the relationship between censorship and pornography, female pleasure, pedagogical approaches, child pornography, gay male pornography, and a panel discussion bringing members of the adult entertainment industry into dialogue with academics and lawyers.*

Ellis, Kate, et al. 1986. *Caught Looking: Feminism, Pornography, and Censorship*. New York: Caught Looking.

> *This collage of essays and photographs is the collective work of the Feminist Anticensorship Taskforce (FACT) and focuses on the inherent pleasure women get in looking at pornographic images. This collection served as a breakthrough for anticensorship feminism and constitutes one of the earliest documents in which feminists deploy pornographic images as arousing rather than degrading to women.*

Foucault, Michel. 1978. *The History of Sexuality*. Vol. 1, *An Introduction*. Trans. Robert Hurley. New York: Pantheon.

> *In the first volume of a three-part study on sexuality, Foucault refutes the notion of a repressive hypothesis of sexuality, arguing instead that there has been a proliferation of discourses around sexuality. According to him, our knowledge of sexuality has been produced and organized through this proliferation of discourses, and Foucault examines the relationship between power and this knowledge, sexuality as a social construct, and the regulation and control of sexuality at work in society. This work has proven extremely influential in the further development of queer theory.*

Fung, Richard. 1991. "Looking for My Penis: The Eroticized Asian in Gay Video Porn." In *How Do I Look? Queer Film and Video*, ed. Bad Object-Choices. Seattle: Bay. 145–60.

> *Fung looks at the racialized position of Asian actors in gay male pornography produced in North America and argues that the white cultural preconception of the Asian male as undersexed leads to the representation of him as a passive object.*

Gibson, Pamela Church, and Roma Gibson, eds. 1993. *Dirty Looks: Women, Pornography, Power*. London: British Film Institute Publishing.

> *This anthology contains essays by Laura Kipnis, Grace Lau, Chris Straayer, and Linda Williams, among others, and the topics range from pornography as practice, censorship, extended studies of specific performers, s/m, transsexual ads, and pornographic photography. All of the contributions stand staunchly on the anticensorship side of the pornography debate and as a collection dispute any possibility of a monolithic understanding of pornography.*

Hite, Shere. 1976. *The Hite Report: A Nationwide Study of Female Sexuality*. New York: Macmillan.

> *Based on four years of researching women's views on sex through questionnaires, Hite documents women's views on orgasm, masturbation, intercourse, lesbianism, the sexual revolution, and female sexuality in general. With this document, Hite attempted to dispel many of the myths regarding female sexuality as a counterpart and/or complement to male sexuality.*

Irigaray, Luce. 1985. *This Sex Which is Not One*. Trans. Catherine Porter and Carolyn Burke. Ithaca, N.Y.: Cornell University Press.

> *In this collection of essays, Irigaray elaborates on some of the themes of her previous work, Speculum of the Other Woman. Through interrogations of, among other things, psychoanalysis, Western philosophy, language and linguistic representation, and Marxism, Irigaray critiques the governing phallocentric principles behind the one-sex model and proposes a new female-centered way of thinking and writing.*

Juffer, Jane. 1998. *At Home with Pornography: Women, Sex, and Everyday Life*. New York: New York University Press.

> *Juffer focuses on the domestication of pornography and the role it now plays in women's daily lives. In her readings of lingerie catalogs, erotica, and cyberporn (to name a few), Juffer elaborates on the reconciliation of the pornographic with the quotidian, allowing women to consume it free of transgression in the privacy of their own homes. In her conceptualization of pornography as domesticated, Juffer examines women's relationship to pornography, as well as pornography's relationship to everyday life.*

Kendrick, Walter. 1987. *The Secret Museum: Pornography in Modern Culture*. New York: Viking.

> *This book traces the elusive nature of pornography as a concept, rather than as an object, and observes how things come to be classified as "pornographic" by dominant classes in order to control the less dominant classes. According to Kendrick, conceptions of pornography significantly relate to keeping potentially dangerous knowledge*

out of the hands of "others," and the motivation behind the classification of the so-called pornographic is motored by (the ruling class's) desire rather than logic.

Kipnis, Laura. 1996. *Bound and Gagged: Pornography and the Politics of Fantasy in America.* New York: Grove.

> *Kipnis gives an account of pornography as a form of cultural expression and examines the ways in which pornography has shaped and even critiqued contemporary views on sexuality, class, fantasy, aesthetics, power, desire, and commodification. Through the examination of several subgenres of pornography, Kipnis troubles the familiar debates surrounding pornography, and in doing so, she reevaluates its importance as an essential part of contemporary culture.*

Koedt, Anne. 1971. "The Myth of the Vaginal Orgasm." In *Voices from Women's Liberation,* ed. Leslie Tanner. New York: New American Library. 33–46.

> *Written by one of the founders of the radical feminist movement, this article attacks the hypothesis that a vaginal orgasm signifies female sexual maturity and locates the clitoris as the true source of female orgasm. Koedt argues that the "myth" of the vaginal orgasm not only masks the fact that female sexuality is defined in terms of male sexuality but also that it becomes defined in terms of the act most pleasing to men. Koedt then calls for a redefinition of female sexuality based on the centrality of the clitoris in female pleasure and orgasm.*

Laplanche, Jean. 1976. *Life and Death in Psychoanalysis.* Trans. Jeffrey Mehlman. Baltimore, Md.: John Hopkins University Press.

> *In his literal, critical, and interpretative rereading of Freud's texts, Laplanche radically redefines several key concepts in Freud's work and locates two mutually exclusive concepts, the biological polarities of life and death, at work within the texts engaged in a struggle of domination.*

Lederer, Laura, ed. 1980. *Take Back the Night: Women on Pornography.* New York: Morrow.

> *One of the first feminist anthologies against pornography,* Take Back the Night *was written from the collective standpoint that pornography promotes violence against women. This anthology proved extremely influential not only for the women's movement in general but also for future debates revolving around the issue of pornography and censorship. This position in favor of censorship helped to forge the unholy alliance between antipornography feminists and conservative politicians.*

Lewis, Jon. 2000. *Hollywood v. Hard Core: How the Struggle over Censorship Saved the Modern Film Industry.* New York: New York University Press.

> *Lewis traces the relation between Hollywood and its pornographic other, as well as how Hollywood was able to effectively shut out its hard-core competition through the implementation of a rating system by exiling it from mainstream movie houses. Not only a history of relations between mainstream cinema and its pornographic counterpart, this work also provides a history of policy, procedure, and censorship in Hollywood, as well as an account of the primacy of economic function over the political or social utility of cinema.*

MacKinnon, Catharine A. 1993. *Only Words*. Cambridge: Harvard University Press.
>   *Originally presented as three discrete lectures, MacKinnon's text defines femininity in a passive, subservient position to that of men and argues against protecting pornography under the First Amendment. According to MacKinnon, pornography subordinates women through pictures and words, so that it should be restricted for what it does, rather than go protected as speech.*

Maines, Rachel P. 1999. *The Technology of Orgasm: "Hysteria," the Vibrator, and Women's Sexual Satisfaction*. Baltimore, Md.: Johns Hopkins University Press.
>   *Maines explores the role of hysteria in Western medicine, including its paradigmatic function in defining female sexuality as a disease, its conflation with and careful masking of women's sexual dissatisfaction, and the invention of the vibrator as its supposed cure. In her examination of the development of various mechanical devices, Maines emphasizes the detrimental effects of the androcentric model of sex not only on female sexual satisfaction but also on female sexuality.*

Marcus, Steven. 1974. *The Other Victorians: A Study of Sexuality and Pornography in Mid-Nineteenth-Century England*. New York: New American Library.
>   *Marcus points to pornography's place in Victorian society as a natural counterpart to the Victorian obsession with repressing all things related to sex. The sexual repression during the Victorian era, and its views of sex as a problem, inevitably led to a proliferation of discourses around sex, including a large body of pornographic, often "confessional," texts, which further represented an escapist "pornotopia" to counter the extreme sexual repression of the period.*

Mercer, Kobena. 1986. "Imagining the Black Man's Sex." In *Photography/Politics: Two*. Ed. Patricia Holland, Jo Spence, and Simon Watney. London: Comedia. 61–69.
>   *In this article, Mercer argues that Robert Mapplethorpe's photographs of black male nudes simultaneously aestheticize, eroticize, and objectify black male bodies. The agent of the look and actual subject of the photographs would seem to be the white male photographer, and the racial fetishization occurring in these photographs and the interpellation of a white male subject as spectator problematizes the place of the potentially nonwhite spectator.*

———. 1991. "Skin Head Sex Thing: Racial Difference and the Homoerotic Imaginary." In *How Do I Look? Queer Film and Video*, ed. Bad Object-Choices. Seattle: Bay. 169–222.
>   *This article further explores Robert Mapplethorpe's photographs of black male nudes, as well as the problems of ambivalence and undecidability arising when viewing those photographs as a black gay man. Mercer reevaluates his earlier position on the photographs and recontextualizes them in terms of political controversy surrounding Mapplethorpe's work, as well as vis-à-vis recent contributions to the visual arts by black gay and lesbian artists.*

Merck, Mandy. 1993. *Perversions: Deviant Readings*. New York: Virago.
>   *Merck's collection of essays provides unlikely readings on the paradoxes of sexual representation. Often reading sex against politics, Merck provides both counter- and re-*

readings of various perversions. Particularly useful are her essays on gay male porn and the feminist ethics of lesbian s/M.

Mulvey, Laura. 1975. "Visual Pleasure and Narrative Cinema." *Screen* 16, 3: 6–18. Reprinted in *Visual and Other Pleasures*. Bloomington: Indiana University Press, 1989.

In this article, Mulvey lays the groundwork for a feminist theory of (male) spectatorship. Using the tools of psychoanalysis, she argues that the unconscious of a patriarchal society structures film form and that cinematic spectatorship is predicated on a gendered split between the active/male gaze and the passive/female fetishized object of the gaze.

———. 1981. "Afterthoughts on 'Visual Pleasure and Narrative Cinema' Inspired by 'Duel in the Sun' (King Vidor, 1946)." *Framework* 15–17: 12–15. Reprinted in *Visual and Other Pleasures*. Bloomington: Indiana University Press, 1989.

In this reconsideration of her influential article "Visual Pleasure and Narrative Cinema," Mulvey elaborates on a psychosexual model of cross-gender identification for the female spectator. Through a masculine identification, the female spectator can pursue a fantasy of action, which lies at cross-purposes with the demands of femininity.

O'Toole, Laurence. 1998. *Pornocopia: Porn, Sex, Technology, and Desire.* London: Serpent's Tail.

In a mix of reportage, interviews, and critical and historical analyses, O'Toole examines the changing face of pornography as it becomes integrated into an expanding technology in the forms of video, the Internet, and cable television. According to O'Toole, due to the greater sexualization of mainstream culture and the ubiquity of sexual images, porn has emerged from the shadows into the realm of acceptable entertainment.

Reich, June. 1999. "Genderfuck: The Law of the Dildo." In *Camp: Queer Aesthetics and the Performing Subject: A Reader*, ed. Fabio Cleto. Ann Arbor: University of Michigan Press. 254–65.

Reich takes up Sue-Ellen Case's aesthetic argument of butch-femme relations to argue for placing the coupled butch-femme subject in the realm of the phallic. She then claims that the dildo is more phallic than the penis and that both, along with the butch-femme couple, belong to the domain of camp. She defines genderfuck *as an effect of unstable signifying practices; it is a subversive performance that simultaneously traverses and exceeds the phallic economy, and a theory of genderfuck can deconstruct the psychoanalytic concept of difference without subscribing to heterosexist or anatomical truths.*

Rich, Adrienne. 1980. "Compulsory Heterosexuality and the Lesbian Continuum." In *The Lesbian and Gay Studies Reader*, ed. Henry Abelove, Michèle Aina Barale and David M. Halperin. New York: Routledge. 227–54.

In what has become a foundational text for lesbian studies, Rich provides a feminist critique of the political institution of compulsory heterosexuality and sketches out the metaphorical concept of a lesbian continuum as a political affiliation to reestablish loyalty among women. In a radical move, Rich names all women-identified women as lesbians, and she unhinges lesbianism from a solely sexual definition in order to unite all women on the basis of gender.

Rich, B. Ruby. 1998. *Chick Flicks: Theories and Memories of the Feminist Film Movement.* Durham: Duke University Press.

Rich's collection of essays traces the development of so-called cinefeminism, as well as her direct involvement/participation in it, and it represents an extremely significant contribution to feminist film criticism. Bringing together history, experience, and theory, this anthology spans thirty years of Rich's work in the field. Particularly useful are her essays "Sex and Cinema" and "Antiporn: Soft Issue, Hard World (Not a Love Story)."

Rubin, Gayle. 1984. "Thinking Sex: Notes for a Radical Theory of the Politics of Sexuality." In *Pleasure and Danger: Exploring Female Sexuality*, ed. Carol S. Vance. Boston: Routledge and Kegan Paul. 267–319.

Rubin observes a lacuna in feminism with regards to the discussion of sexual minorities and diverse sexual practices. She advocates a pluralistic notion of sexual ethics as well as a feminist critique of sexual oppression and gender hierarchy. Her radical theory of sex attempts to identify and explain sexual oppression and erotic injustice and to provide a more anthropological way of understanding different sexual cultures.

Schaefer, Eric. 1999. *"Bold! Daring! Shocking! True!" A History of Exploitation Films, 1919–1959.* Durham: Duke University Press.

In the first full-scale historical examination of the genre of exploitation film, Schaefer reveals how this pioneering form of cinema evolved over a forty-year period, shaping public policy and attitude and providing a sustained challenge to Hollywood's hegemony. Schaefer also discusses exploitation's relationship to hard-core pornography, which existed as discrete from exploitation until the 1960s.

Segal, Lynne, and Mary McIntosh, eds. 1992. *Sex Exposed: Sexuality and the Pornography Debate.* London: Virago.

This collection of sixteen essays by British, American, and Australian feminists examines the historical debate surrounding pornography, as well as the complex issues and attitudes present within it, showing how the discussions regarding pornography hold a place of absolute centrality within larger debates of feminist politics and female sexuality in general.

Silverman, Kaja. 1992. *Male Subjectivity at the Margins.* New York: Routledge.

Silverman offers a psychoanalytic reading of masculinities that deviate from the phallic norm, thus occupying a traditionally feminine psychic space. Silverman considers various authors such as Freud, Henry James, Marcel Proust, and Werner Fassbinder in her rethinking of ideology, masochism, authorship, identification, desire, and the gaze, and she articulates a "libidinal politics" of male subjectivity, concluding that the latter is more heterogeneous than earlier models suggest.

Smyth, Cherry. 1990. "The Pleasure Threshold: Looking at Lesbian Pornography on Film." *Feminist Review* 34: 152–59.

Smyth reviews a handful of lesbian pornography videos made in the late 1980s pri-

marily by *Fatale Video* in order to examine how pornography might give or withhold pleasure within a lesbian contextual frame. She concludes that by watching pornography, lesbians defend their rights to express and assert their sexuality.

Sobchack, Vivian. 1990. "Toward a Phenomenology of Cinematic and Electronic Presence: The Scene of the Screen." *Post Script* 10, 1: 50–59.

In this essay, Sobchack's primary aim is to figure certain microperceptual aspects of our engagement with the technologies of cinematic and electronic representation. She sees both as having been objectively constituted and subjectively incorporated and examines the relations between the two. According to Sobchack, the electronic rather than the cinematic dominates the form of our cultural representations, and unlike its cinematic counterpart, it denies the human body its fleshly presence and therefore devalues the physically lived body as well as the concrete materiality of the world.

Soble, Alan. 1986. *Pornography: Marxism, Feminism, and the Future of Sexuality*. New Haven, Conn.: Yale University Press.

Soble applies Marxist themes to his study of pornography, and it is within the terms of Marxist discourse that he mounts a defense of pornography — it emerges as a valuable source of escape for the male viewer in regard to the recompense it affords men in the utopic realm of fantasies. In the wake of feminism, he argues, men have responded to their putative loss of power with recourse to a nostalgic past; through the consumption of pornography, they can relinquish their struggle for power in the real world.

Stoller, Robert J. 1991. *Porn: Myths for the Twentieth Century*. New Haven, Conn.: Yale University Press.

This collection of interviews of workers in the pornography industry comprises what Stoller calls his "ethnographic" study on pornography. In an attempt to bring ethnography and psychoanalysis into dialogue with one another, Stoller interviews the workers from a psychoanalyst's point of view and then makes observations rooted primarily in psychoanalysis.

Straayer, Chris. 1996. *Deviant Eyes, Deviant Bodies: Sexual Re-orientations in Film and Video*. New York: Columbia University Press.

Straayer looks at an array of films and videos in an effort to dismantle and subvert dominant notions of patriarchal desire in cinematic spectatorship and its predication of heterosexuality in favor of more deviant forms of identification. She teases out a link between sexual and visual pleasure and in doing so, she connects alternative notions of sexuality to those of spectatorship in what ultimately amounts to an attack on dichotomous thinking.

Strossen, Nadine. 1995. *Defending Pornography: Free Speech, Sex, and the Fight for Women's Rights*. New York: Scribner.

The then president of the American Civil Liberties Union produces an argument against the censorship of pornography, arguing that this censorship, rather than reducing violence against women, actually endangers women's rights and further endorses the stereotype of the helpless female victim. It is censorship rather than pornography, according to Strossen, that proves most harmful to women and their rights.

Studlar, Gaylyn. 1988. *In The Realm of Pleasure: Von Sternberg, Dietrich, and the Masochistic Aesthetic.* Urbana: University of Illinois Press.

In an explicit challenge to Laura Mulvey's model of spectatorship, Studlar asserts the primacy of masochism over sadism as an explanation for the spectator's relationship to the cinema screen. She proposes that the viewing pleasures of cinema arise from similarities to the spectator's pre-oedipal subjection to the mother and that the spectator submits to the on-screen image, rather than attempts to possess it.

Tisdale, Sallie. 1994. *Talk Dirty to Me: An Intimate Philosophy of Sex.* New York: Doubleday.

Tisdale examines the ubiquity of sexual images in American culture, which stands in direct contradiction to the adolescent and conflicted state of American sexuality. Despite the fact that sexual images permeate American culture, she argues that Americans still find it nearly impossible to talk openly about sex and exist in a state of cultural puberty, simultaneously sex-drenched and sex-phobic.

Turan, Kenneth, and Stephen F. Zito. 1974. *Sinema: American Pornographic Films and the People Who Make Them.* New York: Praeger.

An early account of the American pornographic film industry — complete with interviews with its filmmakers and stars — this book capitalizes on the growing ubiquity of pornography after Deep Throat, *as well as the increasing national obsession with cinematic sex.*

Waugh, Thomas. 1996. *Hard to Imagine: Gay Male Eroticism in Photography and Film from Their Beginnings to Stonewall.* New York: Columbia University Press.

In an important contribution to gay history, Waugh looks at approximately one hundred year's worth of gay photos and films and traces familiar narratives in an attempt to piece together a history of same-sex male desire. He examines how history penetrates the zone of the forbidden, as well as the political, social, and cultural ramifications of this queer piece of history.

Williams, Linda. 1989. *Hard Core: Power, Pleasure, and the "Frenzy of the Visible."* Berkeley: University of California Press.

This book outlines the history of pornography and examines how the genre configures power and desire. Williams traces the changes in pornography's various meanings and functions, analyses the repercussions of the role of the woman and her gradual emergence as a potential consumer, and attempts to define and delimit the specific characteristics of pornography as a genre.

———. 1991. "Film Bodies: Gender, Genre, and Excess." *Film Quarterly* 44, 4: 2–13.

In her examination of pornography, horror, and melodrama, Williams expounds on the term body genre, *initially coined by Carol J. Clover, and explores the possibility of understanding how and why these particular genres are able to physically move the body of the spectator through a formal analysis of their systems and structures.*

———. 1995. "Corporealized Observers: Visual Pornographies and the 'Carnal Density of Vision.'" In *Fugitive Images: From Photography to Video*, ed. Patrice Petro. Bloomington: Indiana University Press. 3–41.

In this article, Williams addresses the proliferation of pornographic images both still and moving that occurs in tandem with the so-called media explosion of the late nineteenth and early twentieth centuries. She notes the pervasion of sensation in nineteenth-century accounts of vision and argues the need for a new model of vision and spectatorship — one not predicated on the disembodied phallic eye of psychoanalysis and one that will take into account the corporeality of the spectator and the central role of bodily sensations to modernist vision.

Pornographic Film and Video:

A Select List of Archives and Commercial Sites

Hard-core films and videos are the neglected orphans of moving-image archives. Very few institutions care (or dare) to preserve this heritage, but some also have items they do not publicize. Your best bet as a scholar-student is to develop a relationship with archivists and then ask about hard-core materials. The following are a few useful archival sources known to the authors of this anthology, as well as a number of commercial sites that offer pornography for purchase. It was prepared with the help of Heather Butler, Despina Kakoudaki, Eric Schaefer, and Tom Waugh.

Archives for Stag Films

The Kinsey Institute for Research in Sex, Gender, and Reproduction
> Morrison Hall 313,
> Indiana University, Bloomington, IN 47405
> Web site: http://www.indiana.edu/~kinsey
> E-mail: kinsey@indiana.edu
> *Indiana University's Kinsey Institute for Research in Sex, Gender, and Reproduction has by far the most important collection of hard-core film and video materials (over 1,700 films). Unfortunately, these works can only be viewed on the premises, and the institute does not lend video copies of its materials.*

Institute for the Advanced Study of Human Sexuality
> 1523 Franklin Street
> San Francisco, CA 94109-4592
> Web site: http://www.iashs.edu

E-mail: iashs@ihot.com

San Francisco's Institute for the Advanced Study of Human Sexuality boasts a large vintage erotic film and video collection, as well as more recent titles. The institute is not open to the public, but scholars or students with research needs may send requests and view some works on the premises. Audiovisual material ranges from 8 mm and 16 mm features to recent videos. Unfortunately, the institute has been slow to catalogue materials.

Commercial Video Distributors of Stag Films in the United States

Movies Unlimited

3015 Darnell Road

Philadelphia, PA 19154

Web site: http://www.moviesunlimited.com

E-mail: cusserv@moviesunlimited.com

Movies Unlimited offers a useful basic collection of both hard-core and soft-core materials under such titles as Stag Reels: 1920s–1930s, Flaming Flappers, Nudie Classics, *and the like. It also offers several collections of homoerotic physique movies, such as anthologies from Bob Mizer's studio Athletic Model Guild, for example,* AMG: Fantasy Factory *and* Third Sex Cinema: Inside the A.M.G.

Something Weird

P.O. Box 33664

Seattle, WA 98133

Phone: (206) 361-3759

Web site: http://picpal.com

Something Weird is best known for its extensive collection of exploitation and sexploitation titles. However, it does carry some stag materials (a multivolume series entitled Grandpa Bucky's Naughty Peeps and Stags*) that contain a treasure trove of works unfortunately anthologized mostly without titles. Another series goes by the title* Grindhouse Follies.

Archives for Pinups

imageNETion

Web site: http://www.imagenetion.com

This Web site, created by Paulo Paulista Goncalves in 1996, includes digital versions of pinups, erotic art, photography, and fantasy illustrations with explicit themes. Even though the site does not give biographical or source information for the images, it constitutes a visual encyclopedia of more than five hundred artists.

Commercial Sources for Contemporary Hard-Core Materials

Alpha Blue Archives

> Web site: http://www.alphabluearchives.com
>
> *Alpha Blue Archives contains vintage adult cinema from the 1960s, 1970s, and 1980s.*

Bijou Video

> Phone: 1-800-932-7111
>
> *This retailer offers the best collection of classic and contemporary gay male porn.*

Bluedoor

> Web site: http://www.bluedoor.com
>
> *This Internet site provides contemporary, popular porn on VHS and DVD.*

Bleu Productions

> Web site: http://www.bleuproductions.com
>
> *Bleu Productions exhibits the best work done in the realm of fetish and bondage. It contains exclusively the work of filmmaker Maria Beatty, whose movies orbit the worlds of bondage fantasies, S/M, and fetish performance, including spanking, tickling, sensual teasing, boot worship, and submission.*

Candida Royalle

> Web site: http://www.royalle.com
>
> *Royalle is the longtime successful producer-director of couples hard core with a "woman's touch."*

Eurotique and Stormy Leather (connected)

> Web site: http://www.eurotique.com
>
> http://www.stormyleather.com
>
> *Both sites specialize in erotic wear and sex toys, and also offer extensive collections of contemporary pornography.*

Good Vibrations

> Phone: 1-800-289-8423
>
> Web site http://www.goodvibes.com
>
> *Good Vibrations offers good sources for some classic films from the 1970s, female-friendly current work, lesbian videos, and sex education.*

Movies Unlimited

> 3015 Darnell Road
>
> Philadelphia, PA 19154
>
> Web site: http://www.moviesunlimited.com
>
> E-mail: cusserv@moviesunlimited.com
>
> *Movies Unlimited also carries a large list of so-called general release titles in addition to their older material.*

New Millennium Video
  6 Tower Office Park
  Woburn, MA 01801
  Web site: http://www.vidxpress.com
  This retailer provides adult video VHS and DVD (and has many classic titles).

S.I.R. Video Productions
  Web site: http://www.sirvideo.com
  S.I.R. Video Productions makes edgy dyke porn and adult-oriented sex education videos. They are an all-woman company based in San Francisco.

Something Weird
  P.O. Box 33664
  Seattle, WA 98133
  Phone: (206) 361-3759
  Web site: http://picpal.com
  Something Weird offers a "blue book" collection of X-rated material from the late 1960s through the 1970s. This includes approximately two dozen double bills of simulation films, hundreds of volumes of beaver films, hundreds of volumes of hard-core loops and peeps, and a raft of hard-core features running into the late 1970s. Be sure to request the hard-core catalogue, which they keep cordoned off from their more well-advertised exploitation and sexploitation titles.

Toys in Babeland
  707 E. Pike Street
  Seattle, WA 98122
  Phone: (206) 328-2914
  Fax: (206) 328-2994
  and
  94 Rivington Street
  New York, NY 10002
  Phone: (212) 375-1701
  Fax: (212) 375-1706
  Web site: http://www.babeland.com
  Like its California counterpart, Good Vibrations, Toys in Babeland is also a woman-owned establishment that focuses on women, provides various sex education workshops, and prides itself on being "sleaze free." The company's Web site provides many links to other sex-related sites.

Contributors

HEATHER BUTLER is a graduate student in the department of Italian studies at the University of California, Berkeley. She works on literature, film, and female rage.

RICH CANTE is an assistant professor of media and cultural studies at the University of North Carolina, Chapel Hill.

JAKE GERLI is a graduate student in the department of film studies at the University of California, Berkeley.

MINETTE HILLYER is a doctoral candidate in film studies at the University of California, Berkeley. Her dissertation investigates the history of film, video, and the concept of home.

NGUYEN TAN HOANG is a graduate student in film studies at the University of California, Berkeley. He received his M.F.A. in studio art from the University of California, Irvine. He hopes to track down Brandon Lee one day to cast him in a "counter porno" video in which Brandon finally gives in to the pleasures of bottomhood.

DESPINA KAKOUDAKI is an assistant professor in the department of comparative literature at Harvard University, where she teaches interdisciplinary courses in literature, film, visual media, and technology. She is completing a book entitled *The Human Machine: A Cultural History of Artificial People.*

FRANKLIN MELENDEZ is a Ph.D. candidate in English at the University of California, Berkeley. He specializes in the modern and contemporary novel and has interests in film studies, new media, art history, and cultural studies. His dissertation focuses on constructions of the male consumer in film and literature from 1979 to the present.

ARA OSTERWEIL is a Ph.D. candidate in film studies at the University of California, Berkeley, where she is currently writing her dissertation, entitled "Flesh Cinema: The Corporeal Avant-Garde, 1962–1972."

ZABET PATTERSON is a graduate student in the department of rhetoric at the University of California, Berkeley.

CONSTANCE PENLEY is a professor of film studies at the University of California, Santa Barbara. Her books include *Nasa/Trek: Popular Science and Sex in America* (1997), and *The Future of an Illusion: Film, Feminism, and Psychoanalysis* (1989).

ANGELO RESTIVO is the author of *The Cinema of Economic Miracles: Visuality and Modernization in the Italian Art Film* (2002). He teaches film studies at East Carolina University.

MARIA ST. JOHN is a Ph.D. candidate in film studies at the University of California, Berkeley. Her dissertation deals with Hollywood's fantasy of the "mammy."

ERIC SCHAEFER is an associate professor of visual and media arts at Emerson College in Boston, and is the author of *"Bold! Daring! Shocking! True!": A History of Exploitation Films, 1919–1959* (1999). He is working on *Massacre of Pleasure: A History of the Sexploitation Film, 1960–1979*.

DEBORAH SHAMOON is a doctoral candidate in the department of East Asian languages and cultures at the University of California, Berkeley. She is writing her dissertation on the teenage girl in Japanese literature and film.

MICHAEL SICINSKI is a doctoral candidate in film studies at the University of California, Berkeley.

THOMAS WAUGH teaches film studies and queer studies at Concordia University, in Montreal. He is the author of *Out/Lines: Gay Underground Graphics from before Stonewall* (2002); *The Fruit Machine: Twenty Years of Writings on Queer Cinema* (2000); and *Hard to Imagine: Gay Male Eroticism in Photography and Film from their Beginnings to Stonewall* (1996).

LINDA WILLIAMS is director of the film studies program at the University of California, Berkeley and a member of the rhetoric department. She is the author of *Hard Core: Power, Pleasure and the "Frenzy of the Visible"* ([1989] 1999). Her most recent book is entitled *Playing the Race Card: Melodramas of Black and White from Uncle Tom to O. J. Simpson* (2001).

Catalina Video, 223, 238, 240

Caught in the Can, 392

Cavell, Stanley, 402–403, 413

Celebrity porn, 7; as work, 59. *See also under names of specific celebrities*

Champagne, John, 159, 481

Chan, Jackie, 232

Chan, Tony, 246

Chandler, from "A Day in the Life of Chandler," 113–115, 117

Chant d'amour, 431

Characters: in ladies' comics, 92; in *Night at the Adonis*, 154–155, 160

Chauncey, George, 133–134

Chen, Jean Russo, 246

Chernoff, Sam, 390

Cherries, 461–462, 473

Chew Manchu, 247

Chiao, Hsiung-Ping, 230, 232

Chicago, public sex in, 149–150

Chin, Frank, 227, 251

Chion, Michel, 159

Choice, 116–119; in *Fortune Nookie*, 238; lesbianism as, 170, 172

Chow Yun Fat, 232

Christmas on Earth, 433

Christopher Street (New York), 147

Cinema, "physique," 137–139

Class politics, in porn, 9, 135–136, 311–313; and "white trash," 310–311 (*see also* "White trash")

Cleaver, Eldridge, 289

Clinton, Bill, 2, 6–7; cigar of, 46; "performance" by, 30–33; testimony of, 31–33. *See also* Clinton-Lewinsky affair; Lewinsky, Monica

Clinton, Hillary, 38

Clinton-Lewinsky affair, 2, 27–47; and ejaculation, 40–41; and French women, 38–39; media coverage of, 27–28; public exposure to, 6–7; sex act in, 46–47; testimony on, 29. See also *Starr Report*

Closure, in porn, 320

Clouse, Robert, 229

Clover, Carol J., 230, 481

Coercion, sexual, 237–238

Colbert, Gino, 273

Comic book porn: boy-love in, 85–86; versus film porn, 77, 87; in United States versus Japan, 77–78; visibility in, 88–89; for women (*see* Ladies' comics)

"Coming out," in lesbian films, 177–178

The Coming Thing, 392

Commission on Obscenity and Pornography, 378–379, 385–386, 393. *See also* Meese Commission

Community, in online porn, 110

Computer monitor, man and, 104–105, 107

Condit, Gary, 2

Cosmos Films, 382–383

Couples, heterosexual: anal play for, 189–192; and feature-length porn, 386–387; porn market for, 60; and *Starr Report*, 42–45

Couples Guide to the Best Erotic Videos, 213

Courtney, Susan, 276

"Crackers," as term, 310

Crane, Dick, 373

Crary, Jonathan, 414, 452, 472, 481

Cray, Ed, 315, 318

Crimp, Douglas, 438, 444, 447, 449–450

Critics: on ladies' comics, 79–80; on porn, 5–6; on Vincent's films, 204–208, 212–215

Crockett, Sam, 241

Crossing the Color Line, 273, 275, 276, 281

The Crow, 223, 245

Cruising for sex (website), 148–151, 154

Culler, Jonathan, 63

Cultural product, pinup as, 361, 365

Elks, and stag films, 136
Ellis, Kate, 482
Elster, Arlene, 381, 385–386
Embarrassment, and teaching porn studies, 14
Emergency Clinic, 133
Empire, 443
Eng, David L., 251
Enter the Dragon, 229, 231, 253, 254
Ernst, Max, 414
Ero manga. See Ladies' comics
Erotica, as term, 274–275
Erotic in Nature, 175, 176, 178
Eroticism, versus porn, 6
The Erotic Muse: American Bawdy Songs, 315
Espiritu, Yen Le, 226
Esquire (magazine); Kruger's article in, 321–322; pinups in, 336, 343, 345–346; stance on war, 353–354. *See also* Petty, George; Vargas, Alberto
Eurotique and Stormy Leather, 494
Everready Hardon (character), 317
Everyday life: and film porn, 145–153, 208–209; and online porn, 112–115; porn as part of, 6
Everyday objects, in pinup art, 345
Excitable Speech, 449
Exhibitionism for the Shy, 189
Expenses, of storefront theaters, 380
Experimental cinema, audience reception to, 462. *See also* Avant-garde film
Exploitation films, 372–375; Blaxploitation, 290; conventions of, 382–383; costs of making, 374–375; impact on mainstream film, 372; *The King* as, 169–172; and lesbians, 169–171; narrative in, 383–384; theaters showing, 377

"Facial," 184
Facial gestures: in *Blow Job*, 435, 439,
444–446, 448–449; pleasure in, 439–440, 447–449; and truth, 447
Fairy Butch, 186
Falconetti, Maria, 445, 446
Falcon Videos, 234
Faludi, Susan, 41
The Family Circle (magazine), 361–362
Fanny Fatale (aka Debbie Sundahl), 178–180
Fanon, Frantz, 277–278, 283
Fantasies: and amateur porn, 114–115; in "boy-love" comics, 86; and gay men, 144; and interracial sex, 283–284, 299; of rape, 97–98; and stereotypes, 286
Fatale Video, 178, 189
Fear: and desire, 277–290; and interracial sex, 299
Feature-length film porn, 386; conventions of, 40–41; emergence of, 144; and 16 mm film, 370–394. *See also* Film porn
Feed Me, 33
Female audience, and ladies' comics, 89–90, 99
Female genitalia, in stag films, 127–128
Female orgasm, depicting, 91
Feminist debates, and porn studies, 1–2, 20
Femme, 169, 171. *See also* Butch
The Femme and the Leather Daddy, 189
Ferguson, Frances, 151, 152
Fetishism: Freud on, 35–36, 441; racial, 278–280, 285
Filipinos, sexuality of, 247–278
Film porn; aesthetics of, 142–163; archives and commercial sites for, 491–494; versus comic book porn, 77, 87; as genre, 313–314; history of, 370–372; versus Hollywood films, 1–2; versus home movie, 66; humor in, 318; as industry, 393–394; and musicals, 162; revenues of, 2; sado-

masochism in, 97; statistics about, 1–2; visibility in, 76. *See also* Video porn; *and under titles of specific films*

Fineberg, Jay, 392

Finley, Karen, 324

Fischer, Craig, 384

Fist of Fury, 228, 230, 239

Fizz (ladies' comic), 89, 94, 98

Flaming Creatures, 431, 433

Flatley, Jonathan, 444

Fleischer, Richard, 289, 290

Fleishman, Stanley, 390

Flesh, 373

Flynt, Larry, 322

Fontaine, Dick, 137–138

Ford, Luke, 212

Fortune Nookie, 225, 236–238, 240, 243–245

Foucault, Michel, 272, 309; annotated bibliography of, 482; on confession, 29; on power and sexuality, 13, 35, 46; on talking about sex, 43

Foxworthy, Jeff, 321

Frampton, Hollis, 464

Freud, Sigmund, 47, 45; on fetishism, 35–36; on narrative, perversion of, 439–444

Friedman, David F., 380, 387

Frost, R. L., 392

Fuck (aka *Blue Movie*), 434

Fujimoto Yukari, 95–98

Fulton, James, 378, 381

Function, of porn, 9

Fung, Richard, 224, 233, 238, 246, 483

The Further Adventures of Super Screw, 317

Gabor, Mark, 344–345

Gagnon, John H., 130–132, 135

Gaines, Jane, 279–280, 285, 293

Game of Death, 239

Garber, Marjorie, 183, 226

Garner, James, 321

Gay American History, 154, 160

Gay culture, 146

Gay men, 149–150; fantasy versus reality for, 144; networking of, 147; and public sex, 149–150

Gay politics, and public sex, 145–148

Gay porn, 142; aesthetics of, 7–8, 142–163; Asian (*See* Asian gay porn); and cultural spaces, 153–163; versus heterosexual porn, 7–8; history of, 200; male bodies in, 235; multiculturalism in, 246; penis size in, 240–241; in porn studies class, 15–18; publicness and, 147–148, 162; space in, 142–145; spatial logistics of, 153; and stag film, 318–319; viewers of, 234, 241–243; voice-overs in, 159. *See also* Lesbian porn

Gays/Justice, 146

Genet, Jean, 431

Genitalia, 86–87; in porn, history of, 440–441; in stag films, 127–128

Genre: kung fu film, 229–230; ladies' comics as, success of, 78; porn as, 201, 415; video porn as, 403

Gerli, Jake, 8

Getting His Goat (aka *On the Beach*), 314–315

Giant Robot (zine), 223

Gibson, Pamela Church, 483

Gibson, Roma, 483

Gingrich, Arnold, 347

Gingrich, Newt, 313

Girls Lean Back Everywhere: The Law on Obscenity and the Assault on Genius, 312

Gledhill, Christine, 63–64, 66

Glory Holes of L.A., 246

Goldstein, Al, 214

Gone with the Wind, 291

Goodtime Publishing, 335

Good Vibrations, 185, 494

Goodyear, 128, 316

heterosexual male in, 168; versus heterosexual porn, 7–8; history of, 200; phone sex in, 180; voice-overs in, 177. *See also* Gay porn

Lesbians: and porn, 192; San Francisco, 2, 185–192

Lesbian sex, 182; dildo in, 183–185; in porn films, 172, 177

Lesbian sexuality, 168

Let Me Tell Ya 'bout White Chicks, 281–284, 286

Levi-Strauss, Claude, 309

Lewinsky, Monica, 6–7; Clinton's gifts to, 29; fantasies of, 36, 43; on love for Clinton, 45; "performance" by, 30–33; testimony of, 32–33, 43–47. *See also* Clinton, Bill; Clinton-Lewinsky affair

Lewis, Hershell Gordon, 373

Lewis, Jon, 432, 484

Lincoln, F. J., 38

The Line is Busy, 383, 389

Ling, Jinqi, 247

The Literary Underground of the Old Regime, 312

Literature, erotic, 81. *See also* Ladies' comics

"Little Egypt," 344

Living Art Situations, 32

Lonesome Cowboys, 373

Los Angeles, porn theaters in, 373–374, 378

"Love at Second Sight", 352–354, 358

Love Camp 7, 392

The Lovers, 439

Lowe, Lisa, 226–227

Lust, interracial, 271–303

Lyotard, Jean-François, 419

MacDonald, Scott, 461, 464

MacKinnon, Catherine, 11–12, 70, 80, 485

Mad Magazine, 318, 319

Madono Yuki, 90, 92, 93

Magazine porn, versus online porn, 120–121

Maines, Rachel P., 485

Mainstream film, impact of exploitation films on, 372

Mainstream media, soft-core porn in, 349

Mainstream porn: audience of, 199; boredom in, 453; desire in, 465–466; facial gestures in, 439

Mainstream practice, porn as, 119–121

Male, heterosexual, in lesbian porn, 168

Male body: and computer monitor, image of, 104–105, 107; in ladies comics, 82, 85, 94–95; in porn and marital arts, 235; in Vincent's films, 211

Male homosociality. *See* Homosociality, and stag films

Malle, Louis, 439

Malti-Douglas, Fedwa, 29, 46

Mandingo, 288–303, 296; narrative of, 294–296

"Mandingo sexual encounter," 287–288

Man in a Polyester Suit, 278

Manovich, Lev, 106, 117

Mapplethorpe, Robert, 3, 6, 278, 280–281, 284

Marchetti, Gina, 246

Marci (MJ Productions), 388

Marcus, Steven, 274, 485

Marey, Etienne-Jules, 461, 468–469

Margulies, Ivone, 453

Marks, Laura, 462, 474

Martial arts films, 232; male bodies in, 235; and musicals, 230

Masculinity, 226–228; and Asian men, 233–235; and stag films, 128–129

Masochism, in ladies' comics, 95–98

Master and slave: in film, 291–293; Hegel's, 294

Political porn, 38

Politics, gay, and public sex, 145–148

Porn: characteristics of, 274–275; versus eroticism, 6; as genre, 50–51, 64–65, 313–315, 319–320; as mainstream practice, 119–121; and sexual harassment, 151; studying (*see* Porn studies, teaching); what qualifies as, 60–71. *See also under specific types of porn*

Porn films. *See* Film porn; *and under specific titles*

Porn 101: Eroticism, Pornography and the First Amendment, 4

Porn star, 235–250; who qualifies as, 54–60. *See also under names of specific stars*

Porn studies, teaching: current versus past, 1; and embarrassment, 14; and feminist debates, 1; first class teaching, 12–13; homophobia in, 17–18

Power: in gay porn, 240; relationships of, in porn, 206; and sexuality, 13, 35, 46

Powers, Ed, 2, 56

Preston, Dane, 225

Presumed Guilty, 287–288

Print erotica, as term, 81

Privacy, sexual, 60

The Private Afternoons of Pamela Mann, 173–174

Private versus public space, in gay porn, 161

Production Code, 372–373

Production costs, of exploitation films, 374–375

Production values, of Vincent's films, 199

Propaganda, pro-war: cartoons as, 339–341; pinup as, 337–338

Prostitutes, in stag films, 136

Proyas, Alex, 223, 245

Public, American: and Clinton-Lewinsky affair, 6–7; and *Starr Report*, 29, 37

Public sex, and gay men, 145–150

Public space, and gay porn, 147–148, 161–162

Queen, Carol, 189–191

Queer methodology, in Vincent's films, 200–201, 208–212

Rabelais, 471–472

Rabkin, Gerald, 130–132

Racial ambiguity, of Brandon Lee, 245

Racial Castration, 251

Racial difference, in porn, 275–276, 281–282

Racial fear, and desire, 277–286

Racial fetishism, 278–280

Racial inequality, and interracial lust, 302–303

Racialized sexuality, 272–277

Racial "packaging," of Brandon Lee, 225–226

Racial stereotypes, in porn, 8; interracial porn; of Asian men, 224; and taboos, 277. *See also* African Americans, portrayal of

Rambo, Steve, 238–239

Rape: fantasies, 97–98; and porn, 11–12

Rather, Dan, 28

Raw Talent, 203

Rayns, Tony, 445, 451

Real Live Nude Girl, 189

"Real" people, versus stereotypes, 285–286

Reality television, viewing of, 115–116

"Rebel Flower," 94–95, 96, 98

Reberg, David, 392

Redezu komikku. See Ladies' comics

Rednour, Shar, 185–192, 225

Reed, Rex, 449

Reich, June, 486

Rembar, Charles, 2
Renvok, Harlan, 383
Resorts, Palm Springs, for gay men,
143–144
Restivo, Angelo, 1, 7
The Resurrection of Eve, 320
Revelations, 14
Revenues, porn film, 2
Rhys, Dan, 381
Rich, Adrienne, 486–487
Rich, B. Ruby, 486–487
Rich, Frank, 2, 5
Ricouer, Paul, 469
Robertson, Pat, 319
The Romance Revolution, 98
Romero, Peter, 247
Roommates, 198, 201–202, 204–208
Rosello, Mireille, 284, 286
Ross, Andrew, 42, 312
Roth v. United States, 60
Royalle, Candida, 2, 14–15, 312, 494
Rubin, Barbara, 433
Rubin, Gayle, 487
The Runaround, 383, 389
The Runaway Virgin, 387
Rutherford, John, 234

Sadomasochism, in porn, 97
Sampson, John, 380, 393
San Francisco: "eager beaver" films in,
431; storefront theaters in, 378
San Francisco Erotic Film Festival, 385
San Francisco lesbians, 2, 185–192
San Francisco Lesbians, 187–189
San Francisco Museum of Conceptual
Art, 33
Sarno, Joe, 172–173
Satrapy, 471–472
Sawyer, Dianne, 37
Saxon, John, 231
Scenes from the Oral Office, 38
Schaefer, Eric, 1, 3, 9, 171, 487, 491
Scheiffer, Bob, 28

Schlesinger, John, 432
Schodt, Frederick, 78
The School Girl, 392
Scorsese, Martin, 162
Scott, Jacob, 240
Screen, viewing porn on, 133. *See also*
Viewing experience
Screw (magazine), 214
The Sculpture, 33
scum Manifesto, 328
Sean Martinez. *See* Lee, Brandon (porn
star)
"Second Party for Two," 90–93
*The Secret Museum: Pornography in
Modern Culture*, 77, 312
Sedgwick, Eve Kosofsky, 128, 132
Segal, Lynne, 487
Semen, significance of swallowing,
254–255
Seven, Bruce, 174
700 Club, 319
Sex: representations of, 3; talking
about, 2–4; truths of, 8 (*see also*
Truth, and porn); utopian, 201–202
Sex acts: in Clinton-Lewinsky affair,
46–47; interrupted, 467–468; porn
studies to demystify, 20; in Vincent's
films, 204–207
Sex "number," in gay porn, 158
Sexploitation films. *See* Exploitation
films
Sexual harassment, and porn, 151
Sexual prowess, and stereotype of
blacks, 287–288, 290
Sexuality, 433; of blacks, 279; of les-
bians, 168; and power, 35; and race,
272–277; talking about, 20; and
technology, 9
"Sexy Robot," 364
Shamoon, Deborah, 7
Shanghai Meat Company, 246
Sher, Louis, 373
Sherpix, 388–389

Library of Congress Cataloging-in-Publication Data
Porn studies / edited by Linda Williams.
p. cm.
Includes bibliographical references (p.) and index.
ISBN 0-8223-3300-7 (cloth : alk. paper) —
ISBN 0-8223-3312-0 (pbk. : alk. paper)
1. Pornography — Social aspects. 2. Erotic films —
History and criticism. I. Williams, Linda
HQ471.P59   2004
363.4'7 — dc22   2003025389

Printed in Great Britain
by Amazon